Secwépemc People, Land, and Laws

Yerí7 re Stsq̓ey̓s-kucw

McGILL-QUEEN'S INDIGENOUS AND NORTHERN STUDIES

(In memory of Bruce G. Trigger)

Sarah Carter and Arthur J. Ray, Editors

1 *When the Whalers Were Up North*
Inuit Memories from the Eastern Arctic
Dorothy Harley Eber

2 *The Challenge of Arctic Shipping*
Science, Environmental Assessment, and Human Values
Edited by David L. VanderZwaag and Cynthia Lamson

3 *Lost Harvests*
Prairie Indian Reserve Farmers and Government Policy
Sarah Carter

4 *Native Liberty, Crown Sovereignty*
The Existing Aboriginal Right of Self-Government in Canada
Bruce Clark

5 *Unravelling the Franklin Mystery*
Inuit Testimony
David C. Woodman

6 *Otter Skins, Boston Ships, and China Goods*
The Maritime Fur Trade of the Northwest Coast, 1785–1841
James R. Gibson

7 *From Wooden Ploughs to Welfare*
The Story of the Western Reserves
Helen Buckley

8 *In Business for Ourselves*
Northern Entrepreneurs
Wanda A. Wuttunee

9 *For an Amerindian Autohistory*
An Essay on the Foundations of a Social Ethic
Georges E. Sioui

10 *Strangers Among Us*
David Woodman

11 *When the North Was Red*
Aboriginal Education in Soviet Siberia
Dennis A. Bartels and Alice L. Bartels

12 *From Talking Chiefs to a Native Corporate Elite*
The Birth of Class and Nationalism among Canadian Inuit
Marybelle Mitchell

13 *Cold Comfort*
My Love Affair with the Arctic
Graham W. Rowley

14 *The True Spirit and Original Intent of Treaty 7*
Treaty 7 Elders and Tribal Council with Walter Hildebrandt, Dorothy First Rider, and Sarah Carter

15 *This Distant and Unsurveyed Country*
A Woman's Winter at Baffin Island, 1857–1858
W. Gillies Ross

16 *Images of Justice*
Dorothy Harley Eber

17 *Capturing Women*
The Manipulation of Cultural Imagery in Canada's Prairie West
Sarah Carter

18 *Social and Environmental Impacts of the James Bay Hydroelectric Project*
Edited by James F. Hornig

19 *Saqiyuq*
Stories from the Lives of Three Inuit Women
Nancy Wachowich in collaboration with Apphia Agalakti Awa, Rhoda Kaukjak Katsak, and Sandra Pikujak Katsak

20 *Justice in Paradise*
Bruce Clark

21 *Aboriginal Rights and Self-Government*
The Canadian and Mexican Experience in North American Perspective
Edited by Curtis Cook and Juan D. Lindau

22 *Harvest of Souls*
The Jesuit Missions and Colonialism in North America, 1632–1650
Carole Blackburn

23 *Bounty and Benevolence*
A History of Saskatchewan Treaties
Arthur J. Ray, Jim Miller, and Frank Tough

24 *The People of Denendeh*
Ethnohistory of the Indians of Canada's Northwest Territories
June Helm

25 *The* Marshall *Decision and Native Rights*
Ken Coates

26 *The Flying Tiger*
Women Shamans and Storytellers of the Amur
Kira Van Deusen

27 *Alone in Silence*
European Women in the Canadian North before 1940
Barbara E. Kelcey

28 *The Arctic Voyages of Martin Frobisher*
An Elizabethan Adventure
Robert McGhee

29 *Northern Experience and the Myths of Canadian Culture*
Renée Hulan

30 *The White Man's Gonna Getcha*
The Colonial Challenge to the Crees in Quebec
Toby Morantz

31 *The Heavens Are Changing*
Nineteenth-Century Protestant Missions and Tsimshian Christianity
Susan Neylan

32 *Arctic Migrants/Arctic Villagers*
The Transformation of Inuit Settlement in the Central Arctic
David Damas

33 *Arctic Justice*
On Trial for Murder – Pond Inlet, 1923
Shelagh D. Grant

34 *The American Empire and the Fourth World*
Anthony J. Hall

35 *Eighteenth-Century Naturalists of Hudson Bay*
Stuart Houston, Tim Ball, and Mary Houston

36 *Uqalurait*
An Oral History of Nunavut
Compiled and edited by John Bennett and Susan Rowley

37 *Living Rhythms*
Lessons in Aboriginal Economic Resilience and Vision
Wanda Wuttunee

38 *The Making of an Explorer*
George Hubert Wilkins and the Canadian Arctic Expedition, 1913–1916
Stuart E. Jenness

39 *Chee Chee*
A Study of Aboriginal Suicide
Alvin Evans

40 *Strange Things Done*
Murder in Yukon History
Ken S. Coates and William R. Morrison

41 *Healing through Art*
Ritualized Space and Cree Identity
Nadia Ferrara

42 *Coyote and Raven Go Canoeing*
Coming Home to the Village
Peter Cole

43 *Something New in the Air*
The Story of First Peoples Television Broadcasting in Canada
Lorna Roth

44 *Listening to Old Woman Speak*
Natives and Alternatives in Canadian Literature
Laura Smyth Groening

45 *Robert and Francis Flaherty*
A Documentary Life, 1883–1922
Robert J. Christopher

46 *Talking in Context*
Language and Identity in Kwakwaka'wakw Society
Anne Marie Goodfellow

47 *Tecumseh's Bones*
Guy St-Denis

48 *Constructing Colonial Discourse*
Captain Cook at Nootka Sound
Noel Elizabeth Currie

49 *The Hollow Tree*
Fighting Addiction with Traditional Healing
Herb Nabigon

50 *The Return of Caribou to Ungava*
A.T. Bergerud, Stuart Luttich, and Lodewijk Camps

51 *Firekeepers of the Twenty-First Century*
First Nations Women Chiefs
Cora J. Voyageur

52 *Isuma*
Inuit Video Art
Michael Robert Evans

53 *Outside Looking In*
Viewing First Nations Peoples in Canadian Dramatic Television Series
Mary Jane Miller

54 *Kiviuq*
An Inuit Hero and His Siberian Cousins
Kira Van Deusen

55 *Native Peoples and Water Rights*
Irrigation, Dams, and the Law in Western Canada
Kenichi Matsui

56 *The Rediscovered Self*
Indigenous Identity and Cultural Justice
Ronald Niezen

57 *As affecting the fate of my absent husband*
Selected Letters of Lady Franklin Concerning the Search for the Lost Franklin Expedition, 1848–1860
Edited by Erika Behrisch Elce

58 *The Language of the Inuit*
Syntax, Semantics, and Society in the Arctic
Louis-Jacques Dorais

59 *Inuit Shamanism and Christianity*
Transitions and Transformations in the Twentieth Century
Frédéric B. Laugrand and Jarich G. Oosten

60 *No Place for Fairness*
Indigenous Land Rights and Policy in the Bear Island Case and Beyond
David T. McNab

61 *Aleut Identities*
Tradition and Modernity in an Indigenous Fishery
Katherine L. Reedy-Maschner

62 *Earth into Property*
Aboriginal History and the Making of Global Capitalism
Anthony J. Hall

63 *Collections and Objections*
Aboriginal Material Culture in Southern Ontario, 1791–1914
Michelle A. Hamilton

64 *These Mysterious People*
Shaping History and Archaeology in a Northwest Coast Community,
Second Edition
Susan Roy

65 *Telling It to the Judge*
Taking Native History to Court
Arthur J. Ray

66 *Aboriginal Music in Contemporary Canada*
Echoes and Exchanges
Edited by Anna Hoefnagels and Beverley Diamond

67 *In Twilight and in Dawn*
A Biography of Diamond Jenness
Barnett Richling

68 *Women's Work, Women's Art*
Nineteenth-Century Northern Athapaskan Clothing
Judy Thompson

69 *Warriors of the Plains*
The Arts of Plains Indian Warfare
Max Carocci

70 *Reclaiming Indigenous Planning*
Edited by Ryan Walker, Ted Jojola, and David Natcher

71 *Setting All the Captives Free*
Capture, Adjustment, and Recollection in Allegheny Country
Ian K. Steele

72 *Before Ontario*
The Archaeology of a Province
Edited by Marit K. Munson and Susan M. Jamieson

73 *Becoming Inummarik*
Men's Lives in an Inuit Community
Peter Collings

74 *Ancient Pathways, Ancestral Knowledge*
Ethnobotany and Ecological Wisdom of Indigenous Peoples of Northwestern North America
Nancy J. Turner

75 *Our Ice Is Vanishing/Sikuvut Nunguliqtuq*
A History of Inuit, Newcomers, and Climate Change
Shelley Wright

76 *Maps and Memes*
Redrawing Culture, Place, and Identity in Indigenous Communities
Gwilym Lucas Eades

77 *Encounters*
An Anthropological History of Southeastern Labrador
John C. Kennedy

78 *Keeping Promises*
The Royal Proclamation of 1763, Aboriginal Rights, and Treaties in Canada
Edited by Terry Fenge and Jim Aldridge

79 *Together We Survive*
Ethnographic Intuitions, Friendships, and Conversations
Edited by John S. Long and Jennifer S.H. Brown

80 *Canada's Residential Schools*
The History, Part 1, Origins to 1939
The Final Report of the Truth and Reconciliation Commission of Canada, Volume 1

81 *Canada's Residential Schools: The History, Part 2, 1939 to 2000*
The Final Report of the Truth and Reconciliation Commission of Canada, Volume 1

82 *Canada's Residential Schools: The Inuit and Northern Experience*
The Final Report of the Truth and Reconciliation Commission of Canada, Volume 2

83 *Canada's Residential Schools: The Métis Experience*
The Final Report of the Truth and Reconciliation Commission of Canada, Volume 3

84 *Canada's Residential Schools: Missing Children and Unmarked Burials*
The Final Report of the Truth and Reconciliation Commission of Canada, Volume 4

85 *Canada's Residential Schools: The Legacy*
The Final Report of the Truth and Reconciliation Commission of Canada, Volume 5

86 *Canada's Residential Schools: Reconciliation*
The Final Report of the Truth and Reconciliation Commission of Canada, Volume 6

87 *Aboriginal Rights Claims and the Making and Remaking of History*
Arthur J. Ray

88 *Abenaki Daring*
The Life and Writings of Noel Annance, 1792–1869
Jean Barman

89 *Trickster Chases the Tale of Education*
Sylvia Moore

90 *Secwépemc People, Land, and Laws*
Yerí7 re Stsq̓ey̓s-kucw
Marianne Ignace and Ronald E. Ignace

Secwépemc People, Land, and Laws

Yerí7 re Stsq̓ey̓s-kucw

MARIANNE IGNACE AND RONALD E. IGNACE

with contributions by Mike K. Rousseau, Nancy J. Turner, Kenneth Favrholdt, and many Secwépemc storytellers, past and present

Foreword by Bonnie Leonard

McGill-Queen's University Press
Montreal & Kingston | London | Chicago

ISBN 978-0-7735-5130-5 (cloth)
ISBN 978-0-2280-2635-8 (paper)
ISBN 978-0-7735-5203-6 (ePDF)

Legal deposit third quarter 2017
Bibliothèque et Archives nationales
du Québec

Printed in Canada on acid-free paper

Reprinted 2018, 2019, 2021
First paperback edition 2025

This book has been published with the help of a grant from the Canadian Federation for the Humanities and Social Sciences, through the Awards to Scholarly Publications Program, using funds provided by the Social Sciences and Humanities Research Council of Canada.

Funded by the Government of Canada | Financé par le gouvernement du Canada | Canada

Canada Council for the Arts | Conseil des arts du Canada

We acknowledge the support of the Canada Council for the Arts.

Nous remercions le Conseil des arts du Canada de son soutien.

McGill-Queen's University Press in Montreal is on land which long served as a site of meeting and exchange amongst Indigenous Peoples, including the Haudenosaunee and Anishinabeg nations. In Kingston it is situated on the territory of the Haudenosaunee and Anishinaabek. We acknowledge and thank the diverse Indigenous Peoples whose footsteps have marked these territories on which peoples of the world now gather.

LIBRARY AND ARCHIVES CANADA CATALOGUING IN PUBLICATION

Title: Secwépemc people, land, and laws = Yerí7 re Stsq̓ey̓s-kucw / Marianne Ignace and Ronald E. Ignace ; with contributions by Mike K. Rousseau, Nancy J. Turner, Kenneth Favrholdt, and many Secwépemc storytellers, past and present ; foreword by Bonnie Leonard.
Other titles: Yerí7 re Stsq̓ey̓s-kucw
Names: Ignace, Marianne, author | Ignace, Ronald Eric, 1946– author
Description: Series statement: McGill-Queen's Indigenous and northern studies ; 90 | Paperback reprint. Originally published in hardcover in 2017. | Includes bibliographical references and index. | Text in English; includes some short bilingual sections where Secwépemc language is presented first and followed by an English translation.
Identifiers: Canadiana 20250148862 | ISBN 9780228026358 (paper)
Subjects: CSH: Secwepemc—British Columbia—History. | CSH: Secwepemc—Land tenure—British Columbia. | CSH: Secwepemc—Legal status, laws, etc.—British Columbia. | CSH: Secwepemc—British Columbia—Social conditions.
Classification: LCC E99.S45 I46 2025 | DDC 971.1004/97943—dc23

Set in 10.5/13 Gentium Plus with Source Sans Pro
Book design & typesetting by Garet Markvoort, zijn digital

McGill-Queen's University Press
Suite 1720, 1010 Sherbrooke St West,
Montreal, QC, H3A 2R7

Authorized safety representative in the EU: Mare Nostrum Group BV, Mauritskade 21D, 1091 GC Amsterdam, The Netherlands, gpsr@mare-nostrum.co.uk

Contents

Note on Copyright and Intellectual Property Rights

The copyright of this book rests with the Shuswap Nation Tribal Council (SNTC), save for portions that were previously published, which the authors gave SNTC permission to use. Likewise, for all photographs, the photographers gave SNTC permission to reproduce them in this volume.

The authors and SNTC declare that the Secwépemc people, as represented by the seventeen Secwépemc communities of the Secwépemc nation, have inherent cultural rights and ownership of all oral histories and cultural information on the Secwépemc contained in this volume, as well as further claiming first rights to any intellectual property arising from the cultural knowledge derived from Secwépemc elders and other Secwépemc cultural specialists.

We also respectfully acknowledge that the oral histories and cultural information of other Indigenous nations that we cite in this book represent, in the same manner, the intellectual property of these respective nations.

Tables and Figures

Tables

Figures

Table 0.1 | The sounds of Secwepemctsín written in the practical alphabet

Vowels	*Description*	*Usage*
a	similar to *a* in *father*	*ah* in Eastern Secwepemctsín
é	similar to *a* in *tan*	*a* in Eastern Secwepemctsín
e *(schwa)*	similar to *a* in *alone* or *e* in *enough*	unstressed *e* is deleted in Eastern Secwepemctsín in the surroundings of syllabic *l*, *m*, and *n* and semi-vowels *w* and *y*
i	similar to *ee* in *feet* or *ea* in *beam*	retracted to *ia* before throat sounds (uvulars and pharyngeals)
o	similar to *o* in *rod* or *augh* in *naught*	
u	similar to *oo* in *noon*	retracted to *o* before throat sounds (uvulars and pharyngeal)

Consonants	*Plain stop*	*Glottalized stop*	*Fricative*	*Plain resonant*	*Glottalized resonant*
Labial	p	p̓		m	m̓
Dental-lateral	t	t̓	ll	n, l	n̓, l̓
Alveolar	ts	ts̓	s		
Palatal				y	y̓
Velar-plain	k	k̓	c	r	r̓ *(rare)*
Velar-rounded	kw	k̓w	cw	w	w̓
Uvular-plain	q	q̓	x		
Uvular-rounded	qw	q̓w	xw		
Pharyngeal-plain				g	g̓ *(rare)*
Pharyngeal-rounded				gw	g̓w
Laryngeal	7		h		

Note: The diacritic ´ is used to indicate syllable stress, which can be born by any syllable containing the vowels *é* (as opposed to the always unstressed schwa *e*) *i*, *a*, or *u*. In destressed syllables, *u* is reduced to *ew*, and *e*, *i*, and *a* are reduced to the unstressed *e*. In addition, a period is used to separate two letters that are also used in combination to represent a phoneme (e.g., *t.s* versus *ts* and *c.w* versus *cw*). And parentheses are used to indicate a variation in the spelling and pronunciation of a word, which often reflects a dialect and speech community difference or in some cases an optional affix.

Spelling and Formatting Conventions Used in This Book

The spelling conventions of the Western dialect of Secwepemctsín, the Shuswap language, used throughout this book follow those of the practical alphabet of the language developed in the early 1980s by linguist Aert Kuipers, Secwépemc speaker May Dixon of Canim Lake, and other Secwépemc-language experts at the time. This orthography is used by Secwépemc teachers and learners throughout the territory. The spelling conventions of Eastern Secwepemctsín follow those set out by Kuipers and Secwépemc speaker Cindy Williams (Belknap) of Enderby, also developed during the 1980s. Since the 1990s, however, Chief Atahm School, at Adams Lake, has developed a different Eastern Secwepemctsín orthography, which for the most part follows Western Secwepemctsín spelling conventions.

We use the spelling "Secwépemc" (with stress mark), although "Secwepemc" can be found in many references. When the word "Secwépemc" combines with lexical suffixes, as in "Secwepemctsín" (Shuswap language) and "Secwepemcúlecw" (Secwépemc territory), the stress shifts to the suffix. We use the Anglicized term "Shuswap" only when quoting from sources.

Table 0.1 shows the symbols used to spell the language according to the practical alphabet. Details about the history and structure of Secwepemctsín are provided in chapter 4, where table 4.4 also provides information about systematic sound changes between Eastern and Western Secwepemctsín.

Rendering Narratives on the Written Page: Stsptekwll and Slexéy̓em

This book presents and discusses a large amount of oral history and narrative materials, some of it from previously published sources and much of it from transcripts of elders' narratives recorded during the past thirty years. Narratives quoted from previously published sources are presented with citations. Only quotations of 100 words or more are set off as blocks of text. Previously unpublished narratives that are transcripts from audio or video recordings of elders produced by Mona Jules, Marianne Ignace, and Ron Ignace are presented in interlinear form with a line each for Secwepemctsín and the English translation. Since this book is intended for a general audience rather than linguists, we have refrained from providing morpheme-by-morpheme glosses and/or additional lines of phonetic transcription. Presenting the narratives in verse form rather than continuous running texts, as we have tested with numerous speakers and learners throughout the years, allows for a better rendition of the poetic style in which they are told. The decisions about line breaks derive from repeated listening and our fluent-speaker judgments of Secwépemc elders' narrative style. In translating Secwepemctsín narratives and dialogues, we relied on the translating skills of Mona Jules and subsequently refined our translations as we continued to edit the texts and, in the process, reviewed them and tried them out with other fluent speakers and with learners of Secwepemctsín. The intent of the translations was to render them in an English style that accurately reflects the Secwepemctsín message but also reflects Secwépemc elders' ways of speaking English.

In addition to the Secwepemctsín narratives with interlinear translation, this book presents a large number of key terms and phrases in the Secwépemc language. Many of these terms and their translations are listed in the book's index. In the text, where relevant, we break compound words down into their building blocks of meaning (morpheme analysis); however, without compromising accuracy and detail, we have kept our linguistic notations nontechnical for lay readers.

Finally, as our list of references shows, next to the vast amount of transcribed oral histories, this book makes use of a large number of previously published and unpublished archival sources on the Secwépemc and on Plateau ethnography and ethnohistory, along with scientific works from various other disciplines that we rely on as authors and co-authors. Both published and archival sources are indicated by author-date citations either in the text or in endnotes.

Yerí7 re sqweqwentsín-kt

An Opening Prayer

In the Secwépemc way, when you start a meeting, begin a new project, or venture into something new, like learning about the culture, history, and laws of the Secwépemc, it is customary to begin with a prayer to the Creator in order to gather your strength and in order to get your mind, body, and spirit attuned to the task ahead and to the land, nature, and the Creator. We open with a prayer composed by Ron Ignace and edited by Cecilia DeRose, Bridget Dan, Clara Camille, and Marianne Ignace.

Tqelt Kúkwpi7,
Yerí7 re skukwstsétsemc te skectsétsemc ten sweméme.
Yerí7 re skukwstéc-kucw te skectéc te Secwepemcúl̓ecw ell xwexwéyt re stem te sten nerí7.
Kukwstéc-kucw te skectéc te stet̓ex7éms ell xwexwéyt te tsúwet.s re Secwépemc, ell te xqweltens-kucw.

Tqelt Kúkwpi7,
Knúcwente-kucw es yegwentém re xqwelténs, es p̓7e7cw te Secwépemc me7 xepqenwén̓s cú7tsem re xqwelténs-kucw.

Tqelt Kúkwpi7,
Yerí7 re sqeqeltsínmentsen es knúcwenc-kucw es ts̓elílcstem re xqwelténs-kucw, ell es xyemstém. Re xqwelténs-kucw yerí7 re txexetén̓s ne7élye ne tmicws.
T̓ucw ts̓ílem!

Creator,
I thank you for giving me my life power.
We thank you for our Secwépemc land and all the things in it.
And we thank you also for our elders, for our Secwépemc ways of doing things, and for our language.

Creator,
Help us strengthen our language so that more of our Secwépemc people will learn our language again.

Creator,
I pray to you to help us stand up for our language and honour it. Our language is our power here on our land. May it always be so!

Acknowledgments

Although we (Marianne Ignace and Ron Ignace), with help from Nancy J. Turner, Mike K. Rousseau, and Kenneth Favrholdt, wrote the English-language part of this book, we acknowledge the voices of past and present Secwépemc people who put on record their stories about our homeland, Secwepemcúlecw. These voices are represented in the book's Secwépemc language pages with English interlinear translation. Our elders, many deceased now, contributed their knowledge in the face of our people's dispossession of our land, culture, language, and political autonomy. Knowing and having experienced that terrible unfolding history for more than a hundred years, they have shared their knowledge of our ancient laws and protocols, as well as the stories that were handed down to them by their own Secwépemc ancestors. We thus want to acknowledge and thank the many, many Secwépemc elders from all communities, past and present, who *kecmentsút* (gave themselves) as they graciously shared their knowledge, stories, and experiences. We honour past elders like Sxwéy̓lecken and George Sisyúlecw who told their stories to James Teit, as well as the additional unnamed storytellers and knowledge keepers who shared their stories and knowledge with Teit, Franz Boas, and George M. Dawson during the late 1800s and early 1900s. We also honour the Secwépemc storytellers who recorded their stories with ethnographers and linguists from the 1960s to early 1980s, notably with Aert Kuipers, Randy Bouchard, Dorothy Kennedy, Gary Palmer, and Nancy J. Turner. They include Charlie Draney, Seymour Pitel, David Johnson, Henry Squinahan, Aimee August, Adeline Willard, Ike Willard, Nellie Thomas, Lina Bell, Mike Paul, Edward ("Stobie") Billy, Cindy Williams (Belknap), Michael Dick, Augusta Evans, May Dixon, Lilly Harry, and Rose Thomas. Although at times, as we researched and wrote this book, we wished that we could ask them questions no one thought of asking them at the time,[1] the stories and information they provided represent a treasured box of knowledge. Their wisdom, humour, and willingness to share what they knew continue to inspire us. During the time (1960s–80s) that these elders recorded their stories, Secwépemc people lived in the "dark ages" of social, economic, and physical depression brought on by a century of dispossession of our homeland, by the cultural genocide of the residential schools, by assimilationist policies, and by unemployment and poverty. Few people in our communities were in a position to listen to, let alone record, the stories of their elders.

Finally, we thank the many elders and community members who shared their knowledge during our own research journeys throughout Secwepemcúl̓ecw from the mid-1980s to the present. Many of them have left us, but we honour them with this book. We were able to record most of them in person throughout our journey. Others passed away before we were able to record their knowledge, but they, too, live on in memories and handed-down stories about them. Ron grew up with some others, but we both got to know them much better through a few cherished recordings they left behind. By community, they include the following:

Skeetchestn: Julienne (Sulyén) Eneas and Edward Eneas, Martina Calhoun, Seymour Pitel, Charlie Draney, Francis Ignace, Greg Ignace, Celina Jules, Nellie Taylor, Katie Humphrey, Sam Camille, Theresa Jules, Annie-May Jules, Cecilia Peters, Hilda Jules, Elsie Hewitt, Garlene (Bernadette) Dodson, Daniel Calhoun, Leona Calhoun, Christine Simon, Amy Slater, Florence Simon, James Peters, and Julie A. Antoine.

Simpcw (North Thompson): Ida William and Josephine Wenlock (whose grandfather George Sisyúlecw had told James Teit in the early 1900s many of the stories they themselves had heard as children), Allan William, Chris Donald and Lizette Donald, Angelique Joseph and Sammy Joseph, Henry Celesta and Celestine Celesta, Louis Matthew and Ida Matthew, Wilfred Matthew, Pete Joseph, Fred Eustache and Helen Eustache, Granny Christine Eustache, Pauline Baptiste, Angus Eustache and Casimir Eustache, Clarence Fortier and Caroline Fortier, and Mona Jules (originally of Skeetchestn).

St̓uxtéws (Bonaparte): Louisa Basil, Irene Basil (originally of Esk̓ét), Clarence William and Edna William, Willard Antoine and Marie Antoine, Billy Porter, Maggie Billy, Emily Morgan and Felix Morgan, Benny Morgan, Louis Morgan, Johnny Pierro Sr, Rose Phillips, Ike Phillips, and Andy Pinchback.

Tk̓emlúps (Kamloops): Clarence Jules and Delores Jules, Leslie Jules, Francis Jules, Annie Parker, Angelina Seymour, Joe Frazier, Ricardo Seymour, Joe Leonard, Daniel Seymour, Nels Mitchell, Louise Thomas, and Tessie Dillabough.

Neskonlith: Ike Willard, Aimee August, Adeline Willard, Mary Thomas, Sarah Deneault, Jimmy Sauls, John Tony, and Minnie Manuel.

Adams Lake: Harvey Jules, Leslie ("Lesím") Narcisse, Joe Michel, Annie Michel, Les Williams, and William Jones Ignace.

Little Shuswap: Bill Arnouse and Mary Arnouse and Clara Charlie.

Whispering Pines/Clinton Band: Alice LeBourdais, Joe LeBourdais, Eugene Lebourdais, and Violet Lebourdais.

Qwiqwíyqwiyt (High Bar): Rose Haller and Celestine Haller.

Canoe Creek (Tswécem̓c) and Dog Creek (Xgét̓tem): Lilly Harry, Rosie Sargent (Seymour), Nancy Camille, Clara Camille, and Mary Palmantier.

Tsq̓éscen (Canim Lake): Antoinette Archie, Elsie Archie, Jacob Archie, May Dixon, and Eliza Archie.

T̓éxelc (Williams Lake): Willie Alphonse and Victorine Alphonse, Jean William, Aggie Anderson, and Clothilde Thomas.

Esk̓ét (Alkali Lake): Bridget Dan, Cecilia DeRose, Laura Harry, and Angela George.

Xats̓úll (Soda Creek): George Keener and Minnie Phillips.

Splatsín (Enderby): Lina Bell, Emelina Felix, Florence Nicholas, Celestine Sears, Raymond Joe, Marie David, Rosalind Williams, and Casimir Felix.

Ts̓k̓wáy̓lacw (Pavilion): Desmond Peters Sr and Edward Billy.

Kinbasket (Shuswap Band): Marge Eugene and Ox Eugene.

Not all of these elders are quoted in detail in this book. But they all gave testimony about Secwépemc people, land, and laws that is consistent with, and underscores, those we quote. *Yerí7 re sxyemstúlemt!* We honour you all!

We also wish to thank the co-authors who have contributed to this book. Mike K. Rousseau has carried out academic and applied archaeological research throughout the Interior Plateau of British Columbia for well over thirty years, and we are grateful that he contributed his wealth of archaeological knowledge to chapter 3, along with a large number of photographs and figures.

Mona Jules, originally of Skeetchestn but married into the Simpcw community, contributed to many of the transcriptions and translations of Secwépemc narratives in this volume. She also contributed her knowledge to chapter 4, on the Secwépemc language, as did Bridget Dan, Cecilia DeRose, and Clara Camille. Of course, this chapter also benefited from the knowledge of all of the elders throughout Secwepemcúl̓ecw listed above who shared their knowledge of our language, Secwepemctsín.

Nancy J. Turner, Distinguished Professor emerita in the School of Environmental Studies at the University of Victoria, British Columbia, carried out some of her early ethnobotanical research with Secwépemc elders in the early 1970s and has worked with us on documenting Secwépemc ethnobotanical and traditional ecological knowledge since the early 1990s. Chapter 5, on Secwépemc resource use and stewardship, has tremendously benefited from her knowledge, insights, and many years of fruitful collaboration.

Kenneth Favrholdt contributed to chapter 6 by sharing his historical geography research on Indigenous and fur trade brigade trails throughout Secwépemc territory. The history of "Indian trails" underscores that many modern roads and highways originated as Secwépemc trails. It also shows, in conjunction with the oral histories of elders, how Secwépemc people from different parts of the nation communicated with one another across a complex network of travel routes and how they travelled beyond Secwépemc territory to other nations of the Northern Plateau and the Columbia River Plateau.

Since 2009 we have benefited from the advice and knowledge of the Skeetchestn elders' Secwépemc language group – Christine Simon, Amy Slater, Daniel Calhoun, Leona Calhoun, James Peters, Julie A. Antoine, Cecilia Peters, Garlene Dodson, Doris Gage, Hilda Jules, and Elsie Hewitt – with whose members we were able to check the meaning of many Secwépemc terms and concepts used throughout this book, as well as to engage in a collaborative project of reclaiming stories in Secwepemctsín.

In addition, we would like to thank Jeanette Jules and Freda Jules, Cecilia DeRose, Bridget Dan, and Clara Camille, and Chief Nathan Matthew for supporting the use of their family genealogies. Rhandi Alphonse made available to us a series of interviews from the late 1990s about Secwépemc fishing. At Kamloops, former Simon Fraser University students Tracy Ned, Judy Banks, Jessica Arnouse, and Lorna Billy helped with the transcriptions of numerous interviews and with other research assistance tasks. We also thank Keith Thor Carlson (University of Saskatchewan), George Nicholas (Simon Fraser University), Susan Russell (Simon Fraser University), and Kenneth Favrholdt for reviewing all or parts of earlier versions of the manuscript and for providing valuable comments. We thank Michael Jackson (University of British Columbia) for engaging in fruitful discussion about the issue of Indigenous stories, history, and Indigenous law. Wendy Wickwire (University of Victoria) provided some very useful and interesting discussion of research matters pertaining to Plateau ethnography and ethnohistory. Historian Dan Marshall kindly shared his insights about the gold rushes and the history of mining in the Interior, and Trefor Smith researched a wealth of historical documents from the late 1800s and early 1900s that provided invaluable data for chapters 12 and 13. We thank Andie Diane Palmer (University of Alberta), who acted as external examiner of Ron Ignace's dissertation, parts of which have been updated and integrated into this book. We also thank Noel Dyck (Simon Fraser University), who was Ron's doctoral thesis senior supervisor, Jo-ann Archibald (University of British Columbia), and Dara Culhane (Simon Fraser University), who were part of his thesis committee and provided valuable feedback on his part of the research.

In 2012, 2013, 2014, and 2015, we had the opportunity to present and discuss the content of several of the chapters of this book at a set of workshops on Secwépemc storytelling and Indigenous law, as well as at workshops in Sec̓wépemc territory and on its boundaries held in Tk̓emlúps (Kamloops), Esk̓ét, Splatsín, Adams Lake, Skeetchestn, St̓uxtéws, and Xats̓úll (Soda Creek). These workshops were organized by the Shuswap Nation Tribal Council and hosted by the respective communities. We thank the elders, knowledge keepers, chiefs, councillors, and community members of communities throughout the Secwépemc nation who provided feedback.

We gratefully acknowledge the financial support we received from the Social Sciences and Humanities Research Council of Canada (SSHRC) throughout the years, beginning with a SSHRC postdoctoral fellowship to Marianne Ignace in 1985, which enabled the beginning of her Secwépemc ethnographic work. During the 1990s three SSHRC Standard Research Grants led by Nancy J. Turner supported our joint research on Secwépemc ethnobotany and ethnoecology, and an SSHRC grant led by the late Hari Sharma of Simon Fraser University allowed us to further explore Secwépemc political history. Between 2006 and 2009, through a project on Secwépemc language discourse and narrative also supported by the SSHRC (Marianne Ignace, principal investigator), we recorded additional stories and oral histories with elders. Importantly, this grant also provided the resources to transcribe a large body of narratives in Secwepemctsín, particularly through the tireless work of Mona Jules. Since 2012 an SSHRC Insight Grant on Secwépemc sense of place has enabled further cross-checking and analysis of place names and narratives of place. Finally, an ongoing SSHRC Partnership Grant (2013–20, Marianne Ignace, director) has included partner organizations of various Secwépemc communities and has enabled some of the cross-checking and editing work since 2013.

The work of the Skeetchestn elders' Secwépemc language group between 2009 and 2016 was supported by several grants from the Aboriginal Language Initiative (Department of Canadian Heritage) and from the BC Languages Initiative, both administered through the British Columbia First Peoples' Culture, Heritage, and Language Council, and we gratefully acknowledge this support.

We thank the chiefs and staff of the Shuswap Nation Tribal Council and Tribal Director Bonnie Leonard for enabling this work and seeing it through to completion. Diane Jules helped with the logistics of this project at an earlier stage of writing. Tina Matthew, Reanna Leonard, Kelly Connor, Devan Swaine, and Sally Hunter procured photos, maps, and illustrations, as well as facilitating copyright access to archival photos, maps, and documents, as did Carryl Armstrong of the Secwepemc Museum and Owen Scott of the Kamloops Museum and Archives. Margaret Gardiner, former resource librarian of the former Simon Fraser University program in Kamloops, provided invaluable assistance with tracking down sources and references. We also thank Joanne Hammond of Pacific Heritage Consulting for drawing the map of Secwépemc territory (fig. 1.1), Robert D. Turner for contributing his map of the Salishan languages of North America (fig. 4.1), and Costa Dedegikas of the Stavros Niarchos Foundation Digital Media Lab at Simon Fraser University for drawing the genealogy and kinship charts (figs 8.10, 9.2, 9.3, and 9.4), as well as the map of Tllí7sa and his brothers' travels (fig. 2.6). We also thank Robert D. (Bob) Turner for allowing us to reproduce his map of the Salishan Languages of North America, originally produced for Czaykowska-Higgins and Kinkade (1998). We are deeply appreciative of our anonymous peer reviewers, who gave us many perceptive suggestions.

Finally, at McGill-Queen's University Press, our heartfelt thanks go out to acquisitions editor Jacqueline Mason, managing editor Ryan Van Huijstee, cover designer Will Brown, and all the staff for their help and support in seeing this book through to completion. We especially hold our hands up in thanks to Robert Lewis, who was not only a patient, thoughtful, and meticulous editor of the English-language text but also ensured consistency and accuracy of the many pages of Secwepemctsín text. François Trahan skilfully created the index, and we thank him for his superb work.

All royalties from the publication of this book will be donated to the Shuswap Nation Tribal Council to support awards for Secwépemc undergraduate and graduate university students conducting research on Secwépemc culture, history, and language.

We humbly state that we make no pretense that this work represents all there is to know about Secwépemc people, lands, and laws. Others may have perceptions, representations, and narratives different from ours. We encourage their knowledge to come forward.

Yerí7 re skukwstép-kucw. We thank you all.

Foreword

BONNIE LEONARD

In early 2004 the Shuswap Nation Tribal Council (SNTC) chiefs committed themselves to the creation of an Aboriginal Rights and Title Department. The chiefs envisioned that the department staff would assist the nation with asserting Secwépemc title and rights through the collection, cataloguing, and researching of all materials supporting the legal test required by Canadian courts to prove the same. The materials included oral recordings, both historical and new photos, land use history, and archival materials, such as Hudson's Bay Company journals and other early explorer journals, as well as maps and countless other documents that served to support the Secwépemc people's use and occupancy of the traditional territory. The research work also focused on current land use and resource use by the Secwépemc and the documentation of the same for future reference.

After several years of research and sharing information, including hosting numerous workshops and conferences on the topic, SNTC realized that the scattered sources of knowledge would best be shared by drawing key teachings into one source, easily accessible by the youth, elders, community members, and general public. Our council chiefs decided that the starting point for this work would be a book that outlined the shared wisdom of the elders and combined it with other more scientific aspects of learning, such as archaeology and ethnology.

In 2007 Marianne Ignace was asked by SNTC to spearhead the writing of the book. The book project was never intended to be a comprehensive rights and title resource but is meant to serve as a tool that can be utilized by many to gain insights about and understandings of the values and cultural importance of the Secwépemc people's connection to the land and to their oral histories. In fact, it could be said that this book is a testament to the government's failure to achieve the aims of its assimilation policies, which stretch from the time when British Columbia became a colony in 1858 through to the province's entry into Confederation in 1871 and which continue to be supported by the laws of the twenty-first century. As shown by the Secwépemc elders whose voices are put forth in this book, our people have never lost our language, nor have we forgotten the memories that were handed down from our ancestors, nor have policies and laws been able to silence our experiences, teachings, and memories, which speak to our Secwépemc laws and to our traditional knowledge and wisdom.

I met Marianne Ignace in early 2000 while I was chief in my community of the Tk̓emlúps Indian Band. Marianne was an instructor at Simon Fraser University, fluent in Secwepemctsín and married to Ron Ignace, the chief of our neighbouring band, Skeetchestn. Marianne was well known in our community and had worked hard to create the relationships of trust and respect that she had with the elders in our communities. She was, and still is, a person I look up to when exploring Secwépemc history.

Chief Ron Ignace – who earned his own doctoral degree in 2008 – and I were like-minded when it came to protecting the lands and our people from exploitation. We worked together to gain advantages for our people in commercial developments that seemed to be plowing through our traditional territories. We understood the importance of protecting places and sites that were sacred to our ancestors. However, we also faced the sobering reality that we simply did not have enough monetary resources to stop big industry from taking up our lands. We relied upon the words of our ancestors in the Shuswap nation's "Memorial to Sir Wilfrid Laurier" (Chiefs of the Shuswap, Okanagan, and Couteau Tribes 1910) to guide our actions and our judgment. Given these pressures, we had to compromise in our joint efforts to gain advantages for our peoples, without allowing the extinguishment of our underlying Aboriginal title (Six Mile Agreement) and without surrendering the most important places and spaces, those connected to the stories our elders had told us. This task was, and continues to be, a daunting one.

When I came to work at SNTC as the director of Aboriginal Rights and Title in 2004, I was enthusiastic and ambitious. I had spent years at university, graduating with a bachelor of laws degree from the University of Victoria in 1996, where I focused on Aboriginal rights and title in my course specializations. I had some political experience from my three years as chief of the Tk̓emlúps Indian Band. My heart remained filled with raw emotions – the kind that come from learning about injustice, experiencing stonewalling by government, and knowing the pure joy of learning from the elders in our communities. I knew, and had experienced with my senses, that the songs, the stories, and the very language of our peoples were not gone and lost, as we had been repeatedly told by the colonial government. It was not true, and as I worked for SNTC, I was fortunate enough to understand that our Secwépemc culture will never be lost, as our young people continue to come forward and open their hearts to the cultural teachings, like those offered by Marianne and Ron.

The work presented in this volume, conducted mainly by Marianne and Ron, is complemented by various authors who have lent their expertise in the areas of ethnobotany (Nancy J. Turner), archaeology (Mike K. Rousseau), and history (Kenneth Favrholdt). An initial review of an earlier version of the manuscript was conducted by Keith Carlson (University of Saskatchewan) and by George Nicholas (Simon Fraser University).

SNTC thanks Marianne and Ron for their perseverance in working to complete this momentous task while maintaining their livelihood, caring for family, and participating in community events. SNTC also joins Marianne and Ron in dedicating this book to the elders who have shared their wisdom and allowed us to continue to protect our rights and title by publishing this work to be shared with generations to come.

Bonnie Leonard
Tribal Director
Shuswap Nation Tribal Council

Secwépemc People, Land, and Laws

Yerí7 re Stsq̓ey̓s-kucw

1 Yerí7 me7 re Scneséps-kucw

Introduction

Ron's Story

In the Secwépemc language, we have a word, *tslexemwílc*, that encapsulates how we come to know as individuals, and how, individually but in the end collectively, we are shaped by the knowledge and deeds of those before us. *Tslexemwílc* describes the time when a young child gets to the age where he or she can remember. Many of our elders have used the English translation "when I came to my senses" to index the age of their earliest coherent memories and the mental images and fragments of stories connected with them. My uncle Daniel Calhoun indeed takes this one step further: he thinks of this as "*le tslexemwíwelcstnes re tmicw*" ("when I came to my senses [came to know] about the land"). The "land," what we call *tmicw*, is not about real estate or private property. It is about Secwépemc land in all its dimensions: it is the land our ancestors experienced and marked out for us, and it comprises the living creatures on our land in their relation to humans, as well as the way that this land spoke back to countless generations of our ancestors who passed down their remembrances and the way that it continues to speak back to us.

My connection to the stories of our past that we weave together in this book thus goes back to the time when I "came to my senses" at the age of five or six – about 1950. Living in a large four-generation household on the Skeetchestn Reserve in the heart of Secwépemc territory, I was the oldest among a growing number of cousins and was surrounded by my mother, Lizzy Ignace, several aunts and uncles, and my grandparents, Melani Paul Ignace and Francis Ignace. However, those who took the main role in raising me and indeed adopting me as their own were my great-grandparents Edward Eneas and Julienne (Sulyén) Eneas. Edward was born in 1878 in a *c7ístkteṅ* (underground pithouse) near Walhachin on the Thompson River, the same year that Sulyén was born, and he was our community's appointed hereditary chief during the 1940s, before the Indian Act replaced our hereditary system in 1951. Sulyén's own mother, Melmenétkwe, had been born around 1840 and was raised in an underground home, reaching adulthood before the missionaries set foot on our land and before the first white settlers arrived to settle in our part of the homeland. From what I am told, she survived a raid by the Pesxíxnemc (Tsilhqot'in) at the mouth of Deadman's Creek in her youth, and she then trained in the mountains for several years to become a *ṫkwilc* (shaman). Despite being baptized by the Catholic priests as a young adult, she continued to practise her calling throughout her life, Sulyén following in her footsteps. Sulyén's and Edward's own grandparents were born somewhere between 1790 and the early 1800s and were young adults when the *seme7úẇi* ("real whites"), as our ancestors called the first European traders, came into our country.

My father's paternal great-grandfather was Chief Sisyésq̓t, baptized Hyacinth in 1867, who was the appointed hereditary chief at Skeetchestn between the 1850s and his death in 1894. As my uncle Leslie Jules remembered being told, Sisyésq̓t had been trained as a war chief, a leader of warfare expeditions, and was then appointed political chief of the community at a crucial time during the 1858 gold rush, when droves of gold seekers invaded our homeland. He was one of the Secwépemc chiefs who had fought in the Fraser Canyon War of 1858 alongside the Nlaka'pamux, Stéṫemc (St'at'imc, Fraser River Lillooet),[1] and Tṡwéṅemc (Syilx, Okanagan)[2] warriors against the miners, and he must have been present when the Nlaka'pamux and their Secwépemc, St'at'imc, and Syilx allies made a peace treaty with the miners. Sisyésq̓t was my community's chief throughout the trying times when, on the heels of the 1858 gold seekers, settlers dispossessed us of the valuable lands in our valleys, enabled by the colonial and then provincial land ordinances of the 1860s and 1870s, which specifically prohibited our people from pre-empting, let alone buying, land but awarded up to 320 acres to settlers who staked out a claim and built a fence and a shack on such land. In the early 1860s, Sisyésq̓t opposed settlers taking our land by setting fire to the grasslands in the vicinity of the mouth of Deadman's Creek while the settlers tried to drive their cattle into the area. This earned him the name Sq̓wexúlecw ("smoke coming out of the ground") among our people.

When, after British Columbia joined Confederation in 1871, the federal and provincial governments stalled on setting aside lands for our peoples, let alone agree to treaties, Sisyésq̓t, along with Chief Louis of the neighbouring Tk̓emlúps (Kamloops) community, plotted to join Chief Joseph of the Nez Perce to push back the intruders. Eventually, as the Joint Reserve Commission dealt with him and his peers in 1878, he managed to negotiate a 20,000-acre reserve on Deadman's Creek for our people. Before he passed on in 1894, he designated his niece's husband, Peṫmítṡe7 (Joe Tomá), who was old Cecile Melmenétkwe's brother, to succeed him. Joe Tomá, from then until his death in 1918, was chief of my community during the momentous days of the Indian Rights Movement in the first two decades of the twentieth century, which led to our peoples' memorials and declarations of our unextinguished title and rights to our homelands – declarations that to this day provide what I have called our "Magna Carta," which detail our history, lives, and rights, as well as our grievances with the settler governments.

From what I am told, old Sulyén picked me out to be hers when I was an infant. She "claimed me," as our elders call it, and took adopting me very seriously and literally: when my parents took me to the Kamloops Indian Reserve to keep me there, she got in a taxi – and she was not one to routinely and lightly get in a taxi! – and rode the 60 kilometres to Kamloops to reclaim me. She spoke only Secwepemctsín and did not tolerate us speaking English to her, which made me lucky and privileged to thus acquire my language at an early age.

Although I remember few details of stories from my childhood, I grew up with a deeply ingrained sense that we, the Secwépemc, are a people, that we have rights to our lands and to our own governance of our lands that we never surrendered, and that my ancestors fought for our lands and for our rights.

I vaguely remember seeing my great-grandfather's blacksmith shop filled with tools for repairing and making wooden and metal instruments and tools such as fishhooks, harpoons, and irons for branding herds of cows and horses. My great-grandfather, Edward Eneas, could build his own saddles, headstalls, packsaddles, and harnesses for his teams of horses. He could repair his wagons and sleds, which were used in the winter for hauling wood, hay supplies, and passengers.

When I was a child, our elders stated that while the rest of the world was starving during the Great Depression, they had plants like roots, bulbs, and berries from the mountains; as well as fruits and vegetables; salmon and trout, both dried and salted; dried and fresh meat from their own cattle, deer, and moose; wild birds and chickens; and eggs. From the time I was a young boy, I accompanied my great-grandfather on hunting trips into the mountains, hanging onto him behind his saddle. Throughout the summer and early fall, we harpooned and speared salmon in Deadman's Creek and in the Thompson River. Our root cellars were filled with fruits and vegetables from large gardens, and our rooftops and drying racks were heavy with drying fruits and berries.

I remember seeing my grandmothers and their relatives gardening and canning fruits and vegetables, as well as working with my aunts tanning hides from the community hunting trips, which they made into coats, gloves, and shoes for family wear and for sale. They were also very adept at using Singer sewing machines to make quilted blankets from Salvation Army clothes. These blankets were used among our families, and they were even sold or traded for coffee, sugar, or flour. Often, our clothes were made from bleached cotton flour sacks.

I can still hear one of our old elders, Seymour Pitel, saying, "I have cattle in the bank and money on the range."

I also recall a time when my great-grandmother, being a *t̓kwilc*, took me into her *sq̓ilye* (sweat lodge) and prayed for me. I was about six years old, and this was apparently the only time a young boy could be in a sweat with a female. The *sq̓ilye* is a direct gift to our people from Old One, the Creator. He had given instructions to Scwelús, the spirit of the *sq̓ilye*, and to the spirits of the *qwéltsen* (fir boughs), the *yeqwll* (fire), and the *séwllkwe* (water) to answer the prayers of our people. This blessing was in keeping with my great-grandmother's earlier blessings, during which she had buried my umbilical cord on our land so that I would not and could not be separated from our homeland. My great-grandmother and my grandmother also doctored me with powers derived from the *skem̓cís* (grizzly bear) and from the tiny *tsecwyán̓st* (woodworm) to ensure that I would persevere and be tenacious. My great-grandmother also gave me one of her ancestors' names – Stsmél̓qen ("arrow head") – which is in keeping with our spiritual beliefs that through their names we honour and bring back the spirit of our ancestors and maintain our connection with them. If we did not do so, we would be turning our backs on our ancestors and severing our ties with them. Her final instructions to me were to leave the reserve in order to find out "what the *séme7* (white people) are up to" and then to come home and help my people.

After I ran away from the Kamloops Indian Residential School a few months before completing grade 8, and after several years that I spent on skid row in Vancouver, I took upgrading courses, which eventually got me into the University of British Columbia, where I completed a bachelor's and then a master's degree. It was during my research for my master's thesis on the McKenna-McBride Commission (the grossly unjust 1913–16 Royal Commission on Indian Affairs for the Province of British Columbia) that I came upon archival documentation of the government's oppression of our land rights and the pre-emptions and cut-offs of many of our reserve lands, as well as our own people's resistance to these measures, most eloquently expressed in the Shuswap nation's "Memorial to Sir Wilfrid Laurier" (Chiefs of the Shuswap, Okanagan, and Couteau Tribes 1910). At the time, although I had a gut-level sense of my ancestors' stories of the past, it was the written documents that consumed me, and I could not yet make the connection, in research, to the stories of our elders about these times.

Soon after completing my master's degree, I was called by elders in Skeetchestn to become chief of our band, at a time when our community was in a deep deficit after years of financial mismanagement and when five young children had just died in a devastating housefire. While pulling my community together, I travelled to communities throughout the Secwépemc nation, together with a few other like-minded peers, trying to reorganize our nation and to create a renewed sense of nationhood among our people – a consciousness that had been all but lost during years of the government tearing us apart by dividing us into different Indian agencies and by nucleating our communities through Indian Act administration. I also became chairman of the Shuswap Nation Tribal Council and president of our Cultural Society – entering the political fray to seek recognition of our rights and unceded title to land vis-à-vis the Canadian state, while creating unity within our nation.

As some of our bands and portions of our nation entered into the British Columbia Treaty Process, different questions about our status as a nation of people arose: How did we come into being as Secwépemc? What forces united us as a people in the past, and how can we remind ourselves of our nationhood, of being one people, rather than an aggregate of nucleated "First Nations" (bands)? How did our ancestors perceive what we call the Shuswap/Secwépemc nation, and what happened during their lives to maintain a sense of being Secwépemc?

Given the 150-year history of colonial and then Canadian provincial and federal denial of our existence as a people with our own laws and a territory, I see our past guiding our existence in the future. Thus, in the 1990s, I began listening to the elders I knew, most of whom are now deceased, as well as relistening to, and rereading the words of, those before them. I am grateful for the knowledge imparted by those precious few we have among us who were raised speaking our language and raised, like myself, by the generation who had firsthand knowledge of our ancestors' struggles for us as a people over our lands and rights connected to our laws of the past.

Marianne's Story

In October 1985, in the season that I have since learned to call *llwélsten* (mid-fall), when I was a near-newcomer to Secwépemc life and communities, I took a trip by rail car with three Secwépemc elders, travelling the Canadian National Railway (CN) line that straddles the North Thompson River from Blue River to Clearwater. We were there to survey the impacts that CN's proposed double-tracking of the rail line between Jasper in Alberta and Chilliwack in British Columbia would have on the Símpcwemc, who live in the part of Secwepemcúl̓ecw that contains the mid and upper North Thompson River and the adjacent mountain ranges and watersheds. At a time when Aboriginal rights and title issues were just beginning to make their imprint on the Canadian legal system, CN's corporate solution to trespassing on salmon fishing and spawning grounds by dumping rip-rap into the river to build up a new track was what was then called a "no net loss policy." Its principles went something like this: "We can take away a salmon spawning ground here without causing a problem because we can replace it with a new one in another location." If an Aboriginal salmon fishing ground was in the way of the proposed double track, it could be replaced by another one in a different location. Even Aboriginal graveyards were considered moveable and replaceable on those terms. At some point in the negotiation between CN and the Aboriginal occupants along the river, who insisted on their rights and title as Aboriginal peoples but were also defending their way of life and the existence of living resources, the leaders of the three nations opposing CN's twin-tracking were reminded by CN rail, a Canadian Crown corporation, that its chief executive officer was "one door down from God." CN's corporate economic interests were couched in terms of national economic and energy policies of the early 1980s and were argued as being in the interest of Canadian society. As such, however, they were at the exclusion of Secwépemc rights, which had broadly been affirmed as "existing" in section 35 of the Canadian Constitution in 1982. In practical terms, the calculation of physical impacts on salmon, fishing grounds, and tangible heritage sites that could ostensibly be mitigated by moving them emphasized material impacts without understanding intangible cultural and spiritual impacts. It also denied the impacts on a way of life that had been curtailed, constrained, and outlawed for more than a hundred years – a way of life that had come into existence some 10,000 years ago and had thrived over the course of time until some 150 years ago. Last but not least, it denied the unceded rights of the Indigenous groups to the ownership of, and decision-making rights over, these places.

Travelling the railway tracks along the river, our team included a Canadian National Railway engineer, an archaeologist, a fisheries biologist, three elders of the Simpcw (North Thompson) First Nation – Lizette Donald, Ida William, and Angelique Joseph, all deceased now – and myself, a young mother travelling with a three month old but in my formal capacity a postdoctoral fellow at the University of British Columbia who had just started anthropological research with the Simpcw. The elders and myself, taking turns cradling the baby, sat in the rear of the three-row road-rail vehicle, and the others sat in front. As we passed along what had been identified as "points of interest," the scientist jumped in and out of the vehicle, taking samples and measurements. The engineer followed, charts and maps in hand, taking note of the scientist's measurements, commenting, and adding measurements. Since physically examining tangible heritage sites was his job, the archaeologist joined in, not one to be easily swayed by measurements alone. I was confined to the back row with my elders and my infant. While we travelled through the crisp, golden fall landscape of the mid to upper North Thompson River, past places such as Thunder River, Albreda, Blue River, Finn Creek, and Little Hells Gate, the elders' remembrances of place names and long ago living in this landscape unfolded and coalesced. One of them pointed to a place not far from the railway line where she remembered picking berries with members of her extended family, and the other two joined in with their memories. While the elders bounced my infant daughter on their laps, telling her "*étsxeme, étsxeme*!" ("practice for strength!"), more memories emerged as they recalled the names of places like Cteqtíq̓kwe ("milky or clay-coloured creek," "muddy water," Blue River), Pesqlélten ("has salmon," Finn Creek), Sexqeltqín ("round top up high," Wire Cache). Their stories and the place names they remembered told of places where they had camped, enjoyed the landscape, picked berries, and accompanied their husbands, uncles, aunts, and grandparents to fish for salmon and to hunt for deer, caribou, and moose. Their stories also spoke to the good times they had shared with family members teasing, laughing, remembering, and eating the fruits of the land. Joyful memories also connected to sad memories of the people in those stories who had passed on and to the three elders missing those people's faces, voices, and stories. The stories that anchored experience and memories of places and people to the land, in turn, were interwoven with remembering the taste of sweet huckleberries and blueberries, as well as the recipes for jams they had made from them.

While I took cursory notes of the stories the three elders told, the engineer, biologist, and archaeologist jumped in and out of the car, continuing their measurements, taking samples, and poring over maps and statistical charts. The elders continued their storytelling, and it struck me how the conversation of anecdotes and jam recipes must have appeared as the very antithesis of the scientific and engineering "fact finding" expedition of the technical team.

We progressed to an area along the tracks near Wabron, north of Vavenby, where the CN engineer wanted to point out the only visible evidence of Aboriginal occupation he knew of anywhere along this whole stretch of the river we had travelled. He had previously noticed the well-delineated depression of a small Interior Plateau pithouse some 6 metres in diameter right by the tracks. He was excited about his find, pointing, gesturing, and motioning to the elders to join him by the depression in order to view his exciting discovery. To his disappointment, they did not share his excitement. Ida William remarked dryly, "Oh yeah" – implying, "so what?" – and added teasingly, "Maybe a Sasquatch did that." Unlike the stories Ida had shared with Angelique and Lizette, the pithouse depression did not connect to her lived experience. The scientist and engineer were visibly disappointed that their physical "evidence" of Aboriginal occupation did not mean anything to these elders. The point that they missed, of course, was that the evidence these elders had engaged with throughout the trip derived from lived experience connected to the land by memories and brought to life in their stories. However, within an imbalance of power that valued tangible signs of occupation over oral histories of lived and handed-down experience that left no material signs on the land, the elders' kind of evidence was misunderstood and underrated, its validity denied

After the above encounter on the CN rail line, as I continued my research throughout the next three decades, extending it beyond the Símpcwemc to include many other Secwépemc communities, I was privileged to record the stories of places and people throughout this big and beautiful land that is Secwepemcúlecw. With my husband, Ron Ignace of Skeetchestn, joining in this research since the early 1990s after he had lived these experiences for more than forty years, we connected more and more of the dots that represent the ancient emergence of the Secwépemc as a nation, its stories expressing not only moral teachings and historical connections but also the foundations of Secwépemc culture and customary law as they emerged out of lived experience throughout thousands of years.

Merging Voices

As we merge our voices of what we learned from past generations and elders, coupled with our own experiences on the land, this book explores how Secwépemc history has unfolded over the past 10,000 years. Beyond providing facts and details of Secwépemc history and culture, it sheds light on how the telling of Secwépemc oral history works and on how narrative connects human experience to land, ancestors, and the Indigenous laws of living on this land. At times, as told by our elders, this history's lens is on the very long ago deeds of our Secwépemc ancestors, which were etched into the land and were retold and reflected upon by many generations of past people. Deeply affected by the influx and presence of settler society for more than 200 years, the narratives of present and past elders reflect their voices of resistance to dispossession and colonization. This project has taken us, individually and together, to every Secwépemc community throughout the nation in the past thirty years, and we consider our research to be a work in progress.

In early 2007 we were asked by the Shuswap Nation Tribal Council's Land Title Research Department to prepare a presentation for an Aboriginal law conference hosted by the council. Different from various presentations that dealt with case studies, legal and political questions of Aboriginal title, or litigation and negotiation, this presentation was to be a summary of Secwépemc cultural and social history as well as traditional social institutions based on information from written ethnographic and ethnohistoric sources and from our own research. Much of the information we presented about Secwépemc land tenure, resource management regimes, and social and political institutions drew on oral histories and stories that we had recorded with elders since 1984 and that existed in archived recordings. The resulting visual presentation provided a unique opportunity to present a wealth of information from our collaborative community-based research on Secwépemc culture, language, and history to an audience of Secwépemc elders, chiefs, and councillors, community researchers and members-at-large, as well as lawyers and legal advisors. Our presentation provided a visual and textual overview of what past and present Secwépemc had to say about the coming-into-being of Secwepemcúlecw, our homeland. It presented past and present elders' memories about the land and the way that Secwépemc people for thousands of years made use of its resources; it showed the emergence of the Secwépemc as a nation, including the protocols and laws of access to land and resources, of political and social organization, of the fabric of kinship, and of our spiritual connections with the land, its creatures, and its features. It also showed how in the face of colonization during the past 150 years, our people had continued to transmit knowledge, stories, and practices that connect us to our ancestors and to Secwepemcúl̓ecw.

This presentation provided the initial concept for this book, and we were subsequently invited by the Shuswap Nation Tribal Council to expand the presentation into a book about Secwépemc history, people, land, and laws that presents and analyzes the voices of our ancestors and elders, contextualized with information that European visitors and settlers wrote down about us, in order to show the wealth of knowledge that present and past Secwépemc had about Secwépemc history and culture, told in their own voices. Moreover, this book documents the common trends and concepts that Secwépemc people across our seventeen spread-apart communities share about the past and their existence on the land. Encouraged by elders and community members who have read and commented on this book or portions of it, we use the "we" voice, speaking of Secwépemc experience we have learned about and are part of, just as that experience has become part of us, to describe Secwépemc stories, knowledge, and laws, elders' voices and deeds, and our comments on stories, processes, and events.

The objective of this book is to provide a detailed account of the emergence and existence of the Secwépemc as a nation throughout the past 10,000 years, as narrated through the voices of past and present elders and knowledge keepers, at times in the context of observations made by guests and outsiders who came among Secwépemc people. For an audience of contemporary Secwépemc and non-Secwépemc, we describe the practices, laws, and protocols of how Secwépemc people in the past lived on the land, whose ecology and geography they intimately knew. We show how they harvested and managed the resources this land provided, and we explain the system of land tenure, trespass, and access to resources within the boundaries of the nation and with other nations as these emerged and changed over time. Our work also explains the laws and protocols of leadership in and between communities, how people interacted on the basis of kinship relations, and how they managed conflict. Throughout the book, we weave together the memories and stories of elders about events, people, the way things were done, and the laws behind them. In short, this book explains what in Secwepemctsín we call *yerí7 re stsq̓ey̓s-kucw* ("our laws"), which were first written on the land in pictographs, rock formations, and place names thousands of years ago and which guided Secwépemc people's social and political interaction and their spiritual relationships with all living things (see fig. 1, colour section).

The ancient history of Secwepemcúl̓ecw gave us the *stsq̓ey̓* (laws) that defined us as Secwépemc and gave us what we call "equipment for living" as a people. What is traditionally marked on the land through our own history and existence on the land is mirrored in our ways of dealing with things by giving counsel to one another when issues arise that need to be resolved. Our laws thus require the present-day *tk̓wenm7íple7ten* (advisors) to implement the ways that were set forth by our ancestors. These were literally "written in stone" by way of the activities of *t̓ult* (freeze into stone or turn matter into energy) that these ancestors carried out. Despite the destruction wrought upon our land and its markings by the newcomers, many of these landmarks exist to this day. However, the premises of these activities on the land are by no means "frozen" since our own ancestors continually did the work to interpret them and reinterpret them. Their long ago activities and how they related past activities to new issues provide us with good food for thought for the future (see R. Ignace 2008, 4–5).

Through past and present Secwépemc elders' stories – both *stsptekwll* (oral traditions), which are ancient, handed-down narratives, or "stories," from the past, and *slexéy̓em* (oral histories), which are personally experienced or handed-down memories of lived experience – we thus present the coming-into-being of Secwepemcúlecw as a process of history, not as a once-and-for-all accomplished, immutable event. The Secwépemc as a nation with a homeland did not suddenly come into existence when certain distinct first ancestors appeared on the land. Instead, Secwépemc identity and territory emerged during the past several thousand years as languages shifted, environments changed, and the boundaries of our territory took shape but also kept changing. Throughout this time, there emerged a historical consciousness of nationhood among the Secwépemc. The memorials, petitions, and testimonials of the Secwépemc and surrounding Interior chiefs from the late nineteenth and early twentieth centuries speak to this concept of nationhood and show that we are a nation with distinct laws and cultural protocols, a common language, and a collective territory. Besides detailing the emergence of the Secwépemc as a nation, we present the traditional laws of conduct of the Secwépemc as these emerged out of human action and experience during the history of the past several thousand years. Throughout this process, and in more recent times, our Secwépemc ancestors and elders themselves interpreted and reflected on our history. The history of the Secwépemc and Secwepemcúlecw, as we show, is also the history of taking conscious possession of the land by developing laws of collective ownership and access and by considering the lives and words of ancestors to be *deeds* of collective ownership.

Oral Histories and the Courts

In December 1997 the Supreme Court of Canada made its benchmark decision in *Delgamuukw v. British Columbia* regarding the unique and legitimate role that Aboriginal oral traditions should play in establishing legal evidence of Aboriginal rights and title to land. In his decision, Chief Justice Antonio Lamer noted that courts must "come to terms with the oral histories of aboriginal societies," adding that "the laws of evidence must be adapted in order that this type of evidence can be accommodated and placed on an equal footing with the types of historical evidence that the courts are familiar with, which largely consists of historical documents" (*Delgamuukw v. British Columbia* 1997, para. 87).

Alongside other Indigenous peoples,[3] we celebrated the Supreme Court's validation of our oral histories as something that the courts had previously denied but that had been self-evident to us for a long time, namely the ability to rely on our own understandings of the past in order to represent our historical claims in court. However, with the court system being adversarial, the Supreme Court's decision has by no means translated into an immediate acceptance of our oral histories as proof of our title or our ownership of our lands by the "other side" representing the provincial and/or federal Crown or by judges themselves. Indeed, in Aboriginal rights and title cases argued since *Delgamuukw*, the Crown's expert witnesses have concentrated on discrediting Aboriginal oral histories as unreliable, invalid, and not *on a par* with Western written histories.[4] Canadian Indigenous peoples presenting their elders' memories in court to claim rights and title to their lands have had to do so in "an environment of structural violence whereby Native histories are silenced by the arms of the state" (Preston 2005, 55) and whereby Aboriginal elders as "lay witnesses" rather than as experts are exposed to humiliation in Crown cross-examination. Nlaka'pamux legal scholar Ardyth Walkem (2005, 18; see also Walkem 2009) has reminded us that even though the *Delgamuukw* decision determined that courts should treat Indigenous oral traditions as on the same footing with Western history, legal decisions in the years that followed *Delgamuukw* continued to employ a "methodology of suspicion, premised on the belief that Indigenous oral traditions are less than reliable or accurate." Moreover, she notes that by treating Indigenous oral traditions as merely one kind of "evidence" and by using them to add an "Aboriginal perspective" to what continued to be privileged Western sources of evidence and Western legal arguments, the courts, following *Delgamuukw*, did not treat oral histories as signifying and expressing Indigenous *laws* as understood by Indigenous peoples themselves now and in the past. As we further explain below, it is within a framework of expressing Indigenous legal traditions that we consider our oral histories.

Within the adversarial modes of legal argument and evidence deeply steeped in Western ontology and epistemology, we thus continued to be concerned that judges intuitively continued to side with Western historiography ostensibly rooted in "scientific methodology," "scholarly documentation," and "written records." It did not help that the *Report of the Royal Commission on Aboriginal Peoples* (Canada, Royal Commission on Aboriginal Peoples 1996a, 32–7) characterized Western historiography in contrast to the "non-linear" and "non-objective" nature of Aboriginal oral history, making them appear more incommensurable than we suggest they are.

Since *Delgamuukw*, the present chief justice of the Supreme Court of Canada, Beverley McLachlin, has further elaborated on Aboriginal oral history evidence in the court, setting out a test for the inclusion of oral narratives that can address their "inherent evidentiary difficulties" as "hearsay evidence" within the parameters of what Canadian courts consider valid evidence:

> Since claimants must demonstrate features of pre-contact society in the absence of written records, oral histories may offer otherwise unavailable evidence of ancestral practices and aboriginal perspectives. Oral histories are admissible as evidence where they are both useful and reasonably reliable, subject always to the exclusionary discretion of the trial judge. In determining the usefulness and reliability of oral histories, judges must resist facile assumptions based on Eurocentric traditions of gathering and passing on historical facts. (*Mitchell v. MNR* 2001, para. 27)

Having noted in an earlier decision (*R. v. Marshall* 1999, para. 49) that the "honour of the Crown is always at stake in its dealing with Indian people," Chief Justice McLachlin aimed at reconciling the Canadian courts' general principles governing evidence with the historical, cultural, legal, and evidentiary situatedness of Aboriginal oral narratives about the past. She invoked the principle of the "persuasiveness of evidence" that demonstrates "validity on a balance of probabilities" (*Mitchell v. MNR* 2001, para. 32). In addition to offering otherwise not available evidence, oral histories also uniquely may provide an Aboriginal perspective on the right claimed.

In the 2007 case *Tsilhqot'in Nation v. British Columbia* – where the Tsilhqot'in nation, our northwestern neighbour, claimed Aboriginal title to its homeland – BC Supreme Court Justice David Vickers "operationalized" the court's consideration of Aboriginal oral history as evidence. Justice Vickers asked the Tsilhqot'in to contextualize their legal traditions through their legal counsel and to tell the court how they assess the reliability of oral histories and traditions, how they are transmitted and preserved, who has authority to tell them, and what the community's own practice is with regard to safeguarding the integrity of its oral history, stories, legends, and traditions (B.G. Miller 2011, 37; Newman 2005, 434–5). In *Tsilhqot'in*, Justice Vickers thus created a process for reconciling the Canadian justice systems and the Tsilhqot'in's procedures for maintaining validity, reliability, and Indigenous authority over directly experienced and reported narratives about their past. In the 2014

Supreme Court of Canada decision in *Tsilhqot'in*, which acknowledged the Tsilhqot'in's Aboriginal title and jurisdiction to 1,900 square kilometres of their territory (about 5 per cent of their core lands), the Supreme Court of Canada upheld Justice Vickers's procedure.

In his thoughtful and detailed work *Oral Histories on Trial*, anthropologist Bruce G. Miller (2011, xiii) has perceptively made the case that the courts – in representing an adversarial process – "are far from the best venue to work through the complex issues associated with oral materials." Miller (ibid., 143) suggests that "the possibility of the entry of Aboriginal modes of expressive culture into legal settings through the use of oral narratives introduces an exciting effort at exchange and reciprocity."

Like Miller, John Borrows – whose work we refer to below – and others on both the Indigenous and non-Indigenous sides of the fence, we assert that Indigenous oral histories and Western historiographies are not incommensurable but can be reconciled. Each can strengthen the other's narrative as long as Indigenous oral histories are on an equal footing and do not stand in the shadow of Western ways of telling history.

Deploying Stories as "Drawing out Law"

As we have seen, oral histories were, at least to some degree, validated by the courts following the 1997 Supreme Court of Canada *Delgamuukw* decision, a process that culminated in the 2014 *Tsilhqot'in* decision. Beyond their role in providing evidence of title and rights pertaining to specific oral histories of specific Aboriginal peoples, Indigenous legal historians and other scholars pointed out the important connections between Indigenous stories, history, and traditional laws (see Borrows 2001, 2010a, 2010b). Val Napoleon (2007, 4) defined law, as well as Indigenous legal traditions, as the "intellectual process of deliberating and reasoning to apply rules according to the context."

Secwépemc elders themselves point to the concept of *stsq̓ey̓* as denoting Secwépemc "laws" as marked on the land and connected to stories of the past, as well as denoting Secwépemc "writings" and thus "rights." Throughout the chapters of this book, we detail how the collective memories attached to ancient events that shaped the access to resources within and among nations, rules of trespass, and the appropriate conduct of groups and individuals are "written on the land" as *deeds* in pictographs and rock formations where the energy of ancient transformers was transformed into matter in the landscape, a process referred to as *t̓ult*.

Oral histories of past events in connection to the land not only give the underlying legal and moral charter for conduct but also give conscious narrative evidence of past events. These oral histories, in turn, as connected to the land itself and its visible landmarks, provide the underpinnings of Secwépemc rights derived from ancestors' actions and the underpinnings of the subsequent legal and moral codes that these actions brought about. We have a second concept, *tk̓wenm7íple7*, that is also sometimes translated as "law" by Secwépemc elders. However, unlike the component of law that is "written on the land" and tied to ancient history, *tk̓wenm7íple7* lays out the fluid, mobile, and forward-looking way that we can enact new laws and determine what is best for us as a people. Whereas *stsq̓ey̓* reminds us of the deeds and powers of our ancestors, *tk̓wenm7íple7* gives us a way forward to think of law, give advice to one another, and set things right for future generations based on current issues. *Stsq̓ey̓* gives us the foundation, and *tk̓wenm7íple7* is the life we must continue to breathe into our laws as we reflect on them, apply them to new contexts, and remind one another of how we do things right.

A second objective of this book, therefore, is to show how Secwépemc people of the ancient and more recent past deployed stories, in the words of legal historian John Borrows (2001, 8), in "knitting historic memories more tightly in their minds" in ways that explain the past and connect what goes on now with past events and tellings, thus laying out the Secwépemc laws of conduct on the land. Indeed, in a subsequent publication based on lived Anishinabe experience, Borrows (2010b) uses the term "drawing out law" to refer to the distilling of Indigenous legal concepts out of Anishinabe words, stories, and concepts. In this book, we show that the traditional laws about Secwépemc land and the interactions of Secwépemc people on the land should be understood as "living traditions" that are meant to guide the way for the present and future Secwépemc as a people and for Secwépemc institutions of the future. This book is thus intended to help present and future generations understand how to breathe new life into Secwépemc history as told through stories, how to understand the laws that derive from them, and how to put this knowledge to work guiding the way communities and people within the nation interact, work together, and support one another. We see oral narratives about the past as integrally connected to the present and the future of the Secwépemc as a people. In having continuing relevance, our stories have a "social life," in the words of anthropologist Julie Cruikshank (1998, 2005), and they continue to have *sweméc* (life force) and *seméc* (spirit power) as they exist now on the printed page and hopefully as they will be expressed in the words of future oral storytellers.

We the Secwépemc

At this point, a brief overview of Secwépemc history and culture is useful. "Secwépemc" means "the spread-out people," consisting of the nominal prefix or noun-maker particle *s*, followed by the root *cwep* for "to be spread out" and the lexical suffix *-emc* for "people of" an area or place. Our name describes us as a people who have, for 10,000 years or so, had our homeland in the south-central Interior of what in the late 1850s became the Colony of

British Columbia and in 1871 a province of Canada. Anthropologists classify us as the northernmost of the peoples or nations of the Northern Plateau, which contains the Fraser watershed, with the Southern Plateau comprising the peoples of the Columbia watershed, most of them – save for the eastern and southern groups among the Secwépemc – living south of the 49th parallel in what is now the United States.

We cannot pinpoint exactly when and how our ancestors came here and began to spread out on the land and to develop both a distinct way of living and the laws that guided their behaviour. As we show in chapters 2 and 3, archaeological sources and oral histories point to this having happened some 10,000 years ago, with the earliest physical "evidence" – in so far as archaeological finds and ancestral remains document this – reaching back to at least 8,300 years ago. Some 4,500 to 5,000 years ago, downriver people brought the Salish language into our land, which was eventually dispersed into the separate languages of the diverse Plateau nations in the three millennia that followed. By about 4,500 years ago, Interior Plateau culture as it continued to exist into the recent past – and despite the assaults on it by the colonizers, into the present – came into existence. It included a seasonal round of resource harvesting based on hunting of small game and ungulates (deer, caribou, elk, mountain goat, and sheep), intensive fishing for salmon and a large variety of lake and river fish, root harvesting, and the use of a large variety of berries, greens, seeds, mushrooms, lichen, cambium, and other plants at varying elevations within a known landscape and within a predictable but at times shifting seasonal round. Our ancestors lived in underground pithouses in winter (November to March) and supported themselves with provisions stored not only in cache pits near villages but also along predictable travelling and resource-gathering routes away from villages. Throughout the food-gathering season (April to October), they lived in a variety of long- and short-term shelters. Through networks of kin on both sides of the family, individuals were born into particular communities but maintained ties both with other communities from which ancestors came and with those they married into. Thus, beyond their primary collective access to resources in Secwépemc territory, people developed and maintained ties with neighbouring nations that allowed them to access their resources, thus establishing a resource-sharing system. There was no paramount leadership in the Secwépemc nation; instead, chiefship – partially hereditary – existed at the community level, with certain chiefs acting as spokespeople for other groups. At least in the centuries that preceded Europeans arriving in our territory, there were numerous instances of warfare and raiding, and the boundaries of the nation shifted and adapted.[5] When horses arrived on the Northern Plateau in the 1750s and afterward by way of Indigenous trade, our ancestors adapted travel routes and means of transportation to horse transportation, and travel by horse, horse breeding, riding, and all aspects of horsemanship

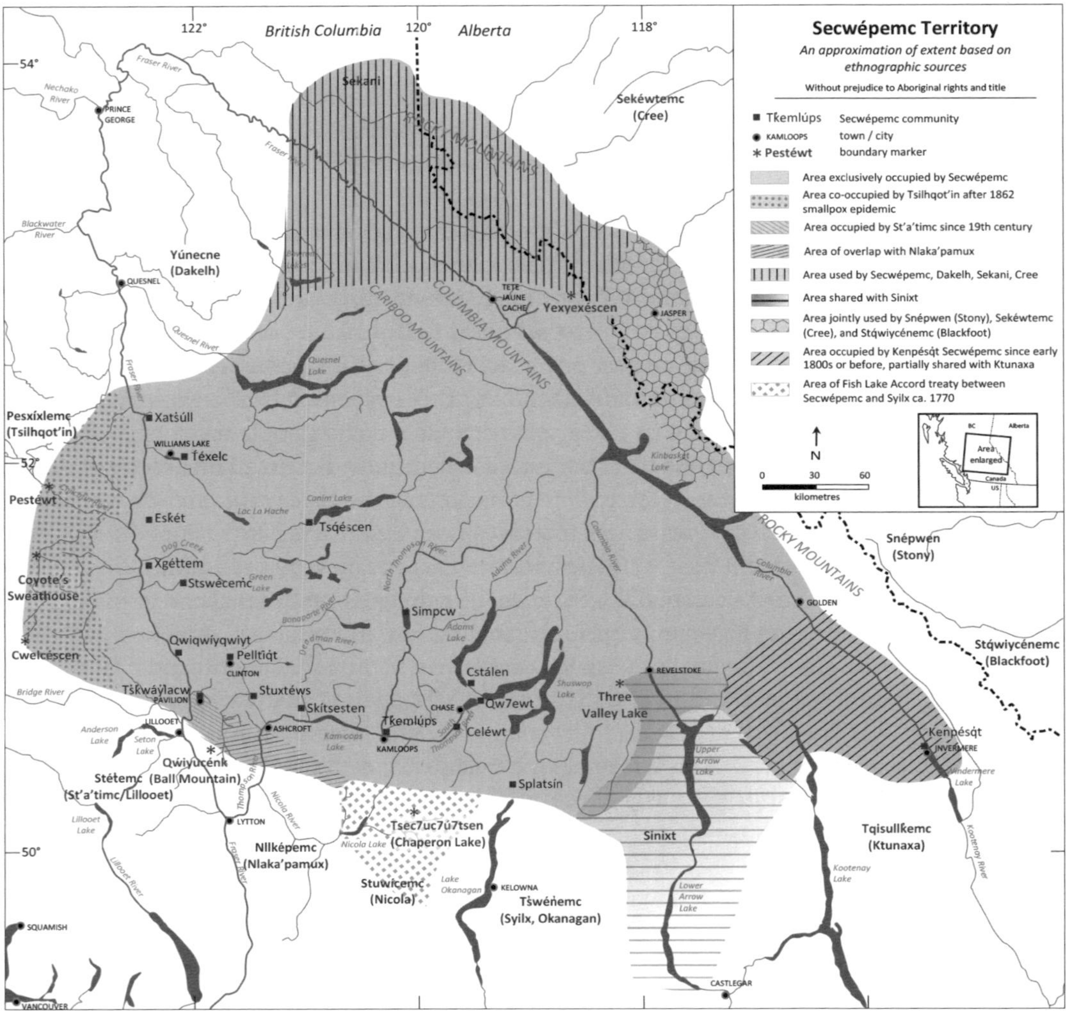

soon became integral aspects that elders whose memories reach back into the 1800s identify with Secwépemc culture. Europeans arrived in our lands relatively late. Although reports of *séme7* (white people/Europeans) farther south already existed, Alexander Mackenzie was the first European to encounter Secwépemc at the northern boundary of our lands in 1793, with more pervasive contact along the Fraser River happening during Simon Fraser's journey in 1808. When David Stuart and Alexander Ross travelled to Kamloops in 1811–12, they established a presence among the Southern and Eastern Secwépemc, travelling on Secwépemc-established trails through our country and setting up a Pacific Fur Company post there, which subsequently became a Hudson's Bay Company post during a fifty-year trade period that lasted into the 1870s.

The gold rush on the Fraser and Thompson Rivers in the late 1850s not only brought about the establishment of the Colony of British Columbia's mainland but also precipitated a small pox epidemic in 1862–63 that killed two-thirds of the Secwépemc population. These devastating events saw settlers trampling over our lands, supported by land ordinances from 1866 to 1870 and onward that disallowed us to be granted or to own fee simple title to the lands we had occupied for thousands of years, instead giving our land away to settlers. After reducing, rescinding, and denying reserves initially set out in the early 1860s, British Columbia joined Confederation, leading the federal government to enact the Indian Act on our lands, which established small reserves comprising 1 per cent of Secwépemc territory and dismantled the ways that we ran our affairs, over the objections of our elders and ancestors.

The narratives of all these events as experienced by Secwépemc people and from our perspective are what we present in the chapters that follow.

Secwépemc Storytellers and Those Who Recorded Their Stories

Some of the elders who told stories and shared their knowledge throughout the research projects that eventually led to this book were born before 1900, and others were born in the first two decades of the twentieth century. The oldest among them had *tslexemwílc* (come to their senses) soon after the turn of the twentieth century and before the Spanish flu pandemic of 1918–19, which took a devastating toll on Secwépemc communities. Many of them were raised by their own grandparents, who were born in the 1830s and 1840s, and therefore these elders learned stories and possessed memories that go back to the first part of the nineteenth century, only one or two generations removed from the first coming of Europeans and the time of the fur trade.

In addition to the memories of elders whom our own research projects have put on record since the 1980s, this work draws on the important earlier research with Secwépemc people by James Teit, George M. Dawson, Franz Boas, and others, as well as on a large amount of ethnohistorical sources from the fur trade area, missionaries, and government agents who dealt with the Secwépemc throughout the latter part of the nineteenth and into the early twentieth century. Of particular importance is James Teit's extensive ethnographic work on the peoples of the Interior Plateau, which exists in a series of books on the Lillooet (1906), Thompson (Nlaka'pamux) (1898, 1900, 1912b), Secwépemc (1909), and Okanagan (1930a), along with many articles and additional books that provide stories, information about rock painting and tattoos, and other topics. Further valuable information derives from his fieldnotes (1898–1910, 1915–21). Teit (1864–1922) had immigrated from the Shetland Islands to the Spences Bridge area in the 1880s and had married a Nlaka'pamux woman named Susanna Lucy Antko (died 1899). He began his ethnographic work at the request of Franz Boas, sponsored by the Jesup

1.2 | Ethnographer James Teit, photographed by Edward Sapir, 1915.

North Pacific Expedition in the 1890s, when he assisted in archaeological and anthropometric work as per Boas's objectives (see chapter 3).[6] Teit's contributions to Secwépemc ethnography – the description of the lifeways, social organization, stories, beliefs, and material culture of the Secwépemc – began in the summer of 1897 and intensified in 1903–04, when he spent the summer and fall with the Secwépemc along the Fraser River, returning via Bonaparte, although he had previously accompanied Boas on his ethnographic excursions in the late 1880s. In 1903 he also visited the Canim Lake and North Thompson Secwépemc, and in 1904 he visited Secwépemc communities at Splatsín, Shuswap Lake, Kamloops, and Skeetchestn, noting, "thus I visited all the bands of the Shuswap, excepting the isolated ones of Upper North Thompson River at Jasper House, the Kinbaskets on Columbia River, and the Arrow Lake band" (Teit 1909, 447). Next, he travelled to "Sisiu'lax" (Sisyúlecw) on the North Thompson. Teit (ibid.) acknowledged that during his 1900 field season on the Fraser River, the bulk of his information was provided by "a very intelligent old man called Sixwi'lexken [Sxwéy̓lecken][7] who was born near Big Bar, and in early days had travelled all over the country inhabited by the tribe [the Secwepemc]. He was particularly well posted on the history, traditions, and customs of his people, and took great interest in relating everything he knew." In his correspondence with Boas, Teit (1907) further mentions that Sexwéyl̓cken was "over 70 years old" and that he also provided nearly all of the Secwépemc stories for the 1909 volume, except for those from the North Thompson provided by Sisyúlecw. Sxwéy̓lecken would thus have *tslexemwílc* by or before the early 1840s, as did Sisyúlecw.

Teit maintained life-long residence among, and collaboration and friendship with, the Indigenous peoples of the Interior. His extensive knowledge, his fluency in the local Interior Salish languages, and the trust he had from the Indigenous people led to his employment by Boas, then affiliated with the American Museum of Natural History in New York, and in the 1910s by Edward Sapir of the National Museum in Ottawa. Teit was tasked with recording information about the cultures of the Interior Plateau people and later the Kaska and Tahltan peoples in northern British Columbia. However, his collaboration with the Interior Plateau peoples in carrying out "salvage" ethnographic work of excellent quality and detail was not his only contribution. As a knowledgeable and literate man who had the trust of chiefs and local First Nations leaders throughout the Plateau, he increasingly functioned as organizer and as letter and petition writer, as well as carrying out many other tasks throughout the Interior peoples' struggle for the recognition of their unextinguished Aboriginal rights to land and jurisdiction over their lands. It was Teit who, as scribe rather than author, committed to paper the "Memorial to Sir Wilfrid Laurier" (Chiefs of the Shuswap, Okanagan, and Couteau Tribes 1910), the "Memorial to the Hon. Frank Oliver, Minister of the Interior" (Chiefs of the Shuswap, Couteau, and Thompson Tribes et al. 1911), and numerous other declarations, petitions, and statements. His untimely death in 1922 was a tremendous loss to the Indian Rights Movement of the time.

Even before he hired Teit, Franz Boas, then at the very beginning of his career, spent about a week in the Kamloops area in 1889 and recorded Secwépemc *stsptekwll* (legends) "with the help of an old French Indian half-blood," who may have been his interpreter. The oral traditions he recorded, probably through the medium of the Chinook Jargon, included Coyote stories and a detailed version of the epic story of Tllí7sa and his brothers, published in German in 1895 and eventually translated into English (Bouchard and Kennedy 2002). His field research also resulted in short ethnographic and linguistic sketches on the "Shushwap" (Boas 1890, 80–95, 131–3) and a listing of kinship terms (ibid., 138–9).

In 1877, 1888, 1889, and 1890, geologist George M. Dawson travelled through Secwépemc territory as he was carrying out work for the Geological Survey of Canada. Interested in Indigenous customs and place names, he wrote down notes on the Secwépemc and neighbouring Interior Salish peoples and compiled a list of more than 200 Indigenous place names (Dawson 1891), although his ethnographic work was very much a colonial project to make settler space (Grek-Martin 2009).

Anthropologist Verne Ray carried out brief primary research in the Northern Secwépemc area in the 1930s, although most of his book *Cultural Relations in the Plateau of Western America* (1939) is based on synthesizing the work of Teit and others into an account of Plateau cultural "traits." During the 1960s, graduate students Catherine Brow (1967) and James Brow (1972) conducted some interviews with elders of the Northern Secwépemc communities, and between the late 1960s and the 1980s, Randy Bouchard and Dorothy Kennedy recorded the stories and memories of several Secwépemc elders, including Ike Willard, Aimee August, Charlie Draney, and Nellie Thomas, all long deceased, and also recorded ethnographic information on a variety of topics with additional elders in the Chase, Enderby, Salmon Arm, and Esk̓ét (Alkali Lake) area as part of assessments to determine cultural heritage impacts before highway construction and other projects. By drawing on some of their original recordings, we were able to add information about Secwépemc laws and protocols of boundary maintenance and other kinds of information. During the same time, Nancy J. Turner and Gary Palmer recorded ethnobotanical information, specifically with Jacob Archie in Canim Lake and with Ike Willard, Aimee August, and Adeline Willard in Neskonlith, and this work has informed the continuing ethnobotanical work by Turner, Marianne Ignace, and others with Secwépemc elders since the 1990s (see M. Ignace, Turner, and Peacock 2017).

Between the late 1960s and the late 1980s, the late Dutch linguist Aert Kuipers (1919–2012) recorded narratives from several Secwépemc elders, including David Johnson and Henry Squinihan of Esk̓ét, Charlie Draney and Seymour Pitel of Skeetchestn, Lilly Harry and Mary Palmantier of Dog Creek, Rosie Seymour, Michael Dick, and Edward ("Stobie") Billy of Canoe Creek, May Dixon of Canim Lake, Aimee August of Neskonlith, Lina Bell, Rose Thomas, and Cindy Williams (Belknap) of Splatsín, Mike Paul of Athalmer (Kinbasket), and Augusta Evans of Soda Creek (Kuipers 1974, 1989).[8] Although Kuipers used these stories for his linguistic analyses of the language rather than to throw light on Secwépemc history and culture, the *stsptekwll* and *slexéy̓em* narratives recorded with these elders provide a wealth of information about Secwépemc travels on the land, hunting, fishing, and the seasonal round during the first decades of the twentieth century, and they give us details of plot and linguistic expression in Secwepemctsín not included in Teit's English *stsptekwll*. They also attest to the unique and fascinating ways that the past generation of Secwépemc-language speakers put to work the categories of the language to give meaning to their connection to land and to their sense of relations with one another.

Another more recent source of Secwépemc narratives is Andie Diane Palmer's (2005) synthesis of narratives about place that chart out "maps of experience" made with the late Angela George and other elders at Esk̓ét in the late 1980s and early 1990s, although recorded mainly in English.

The narratives we ourselves recorded between 1985 and 2014 with elders comprise both the *stsptekwll* and *slexéy̓em* genres. They include Coyote stories that Marianne Ignace recorded in the mid to late 1980s with Chris Donald and Ida William of Chu Chua (Simpcw), George Sisyúlecw's granddaughter. They also include fragments of the Tllí7sa transformer epic recorded with Louisa Basil and Rose Phillips of Sṫuxtéws (Bonaparte) and numerous *stsptekwll* connected to places and place names recorded with Chris Donald of Simpcw, Nellie Taylor of Skeetchestn, and Celina Jules. They also include many hours of *slexéy̓em* recordings, mainly in Secwepemctsín, made by Ron Ignace in 1997–99 with Theresa Jules, Sarah Deneault, Clothilde Thomas, Laura Harry, Sam Camille, Antoinette Archie and Elsie Archie, and Cecilia DeRose. In addition, they include narratives by Neskonlith elder Dr Mary Thomas as she travelled with Christine Simon and Nellie Taylor of Skeetchestn, presented here with their permission. They also include additional recently recorded narratives of Skeetchestn elders.

Secwépemc Stories, History, and Converging Lines of Evidence about the Past

Those who have written about validating Indigenous oral histories in Aboriginal title and rights litigation have suggested the importance of recognizing them "on their own terms," while noting the "cultural context" of the narratives and the many layers in which Indigenous stories convey meaning and invite the listener to connect them to the present. The problem is that our oral histories cannot "stand alone," removed from the way they are told (especially in the Secwépemc language), from the background of experience on the land, and from the protocols and *stsq̓ey̓* (laws) that guided how Secwépemc people of the past interacted, behaved toward one another, and told one another what they knew. The meaning of Secwépemc stories about the past is almost never self-evident. More than giving us "facts" of "events," they operate on multiple levels. Their moral and social messages require careful explanation, and their messages may well vary with context, with the storyteller, and with the audience. Last but not least, they require knowledge of the Secwépemc language and the ways that past Secwépemc people communicated knowledge. Secwépemc storytellers of the past invited their audience, and subsequent listeners or readers, to think about the messages of stories, to find the facts in stories, to see the connection of stories with our environment and our sentient landscape, with all living things, and with our social and political relations, and to tease out the traditional laws that stories convey. Stories are about relationships.

In the past, a fundamental aspect of how the Secwépemc and other Indigenous peoples validated knowledge was the process of ongoing communication within and between communities, where people trained in various ways to obtain knowledge, tried out what they learned, and shared information about recent and long ago events and people. In this way, they shared environmental knowledge and technical knowhow; they reminded each other of places and shared genealogical knowledge. In the words of the late Nellie Taylor (personal communication, 1994, quoted in R. Ignace 2008, 28), this practice constituted a significant and important way not only of transmitting new information but also of verifying past information and correcting or refuting information:

> Long time ago, Secwépemc people looked after the land, and all the animals and plants, everything in it. That's why they always had plenty to fish. They had deer to hunt and plants to gather for food and medicine. But they had to practice for it, and learn about everything on the land first for a long time. Then they knew how to look after it. It was also important for the elders to share each other's knowledge. That was how they learned and built up their understanding. What knowledge they shared had to be exact.

Storytellers thus granted each other authority over reliably and accurately transmitted information. As in the past, storytellers of the present acknowledge, in their own narratives, who it is that has provided them with the information and who their teacher storytellers are. In trying to find a metaphor within Western academia for this Indigenous way of acknowledging the sources of oral histories, and thus authorizing them, Wendy Wickwire (1994) has applied the term "oral footnoting" to this practice. In many of the oral histories and stories that follow, elders acknowledge from whom they learned the information they share (see also K.T. Carlson 2007, 56; and B.G. Miller 2011, 74). During our 2012 community-sharing sessions of this manuscript, Splatsín elder and knowledge keeper Rosalind Williams also reminded us all of acknowledging and naming the particular elder(s) who knew a certain story, thus reinforcing this concept for present and future generations among the audience.

Despite the concerns we raised above about oral histories and traditions being treated as merely one source of evidence and reflecting merely an "Aboriginal perspective" on events sometimes recorded in European visitors' and colonizers' written documents, it should be pointed out that connecting oral histories and traditions to various kinds of information produced by Western science can help us to throw light on the past. Indigenous oral histories and the cultural laws they entail can inform our reading and interpretation of events described by European visitors. This notion is not to diminish their significance as entailing and signifying traditional law, but it helps us to put into perspective and contextualize what is told in stories, thus deepening our understanding of what happened and how it was interpreted. Some years ago, arguing from a European/Western perspective, Jan Vansina (1985, 199) suggested that wherever possible, oral traditions should be cross-checked with other types of information to increase their reliability, but he concluded that "wherever oral traditions are extant they remain an indispensable source for reconstruction. They correct other perspectives just as much as other perspectives correct them."

In what follows, we use this approach by drawing on differing data, including those from the fields of archaeology, linguistics, geology, and paleoecology, to cross-check and *triangulate* evidence that derives from oral history sources. Anthropologist Renato Rosaldo (1980a, 1980b) has introduced the concept of finding "converging lines of evidence" between multiple oral and written accounts of events. These lines can be applied to test the patchwork of personally, socially, and politically situated individual oral history narratives in order to triangulate the occurrence of historical events, the movements of people, and temporary changes in cultural practices. In addition, Rosaldo shows, "converging lines of evidence" can come from external written historical sources, which allow the researcher to date events in terms of a chronological order. Anishinabe scholar John Borrows (2001, 22) likewise suggests this approach of corroboration and triangulation:

> To judge oral tradition as proof of past events I looked for a certain degree of consistency within the accounts and stories I received. I talked to people from different families on the reserve … I spoke to people of different generations (elders, older cousins), and of different but closely associated communities … I also compared these oral accounts with written materials that dealt with the same events. This was a way of scrutinizing both the oral and written sources: to show where one or the other may have gaps, errors or other deficiencies as proof of past events. In such comparisons it is not always the case that oral sources are corrected by written sources, at times oral tradition may prompt significant revisions to the written record which have falsely misconstrued a past occurrence. In order to test the traditions I received for this kind of proof, I searched family histories, published scholarly works, graduate theses, missionary journals, Indian agency correspondence, surveyors notes, band council minutes, newspaper articles, individuals' private papers, "explorers" travel maps and books, and government census material.

As both Borrows and before him and in a different context Rosaldo have noted, such multiple cross-checking, cross-corroboration, and triangulation ensures greater external validity and reliability of the historical information disseminated in these accounts. But beyond that, in the process of his research on Anishinabe treaty making, Borrows (ibid.) also uncovered the "historical meaning that our people applied to the process of treaty making." In short, this form of research allowed him not only to find the Anishinabe account of treaty making but also to uncover the way that Anishinabeg narrate and think about history and the *meanings* that past events hold for present Anishinabeg as they construe their historical, cultural, and political connection to these events (for further approaches, see B.G. Miller 2011).

Applying these ideas to our research of Secwépemc history, we get fruitful insights into the Secwépemc past by looking for "converging lines of evidence" among different Secwépemc elders' oral histories or narratives about the past as we triangulate them with historical accounts produced by Europeans and with ethnographers' descriptions of cultural practices. Beyond comparing and verifying, we explain cultural and historical events and processes through a Secwépemc lense – that is, a Secwépemc way of making sense and interpreting the interconnected social and natural world. What Keith Carlson (2005, 5) has called an "indigenous hermeneutics" derives from 10,000 years of collective experience in a particular land, with ways of doing things and ways of perceiving and articulating interactions among people, animals, plants, and the powers of the land.[9]

Last but not least, we can learn about the conventions of *how* Secwépemc *stet̓ex7ém* (ancestors or elders) spoke about past events. In addition, this approach shows the ways that Secwépemc people of the ancient and recent past interwove the laws of Secwépemc society, as derived from their connection to Secwepemcúl̓ecw, the homeland, with the telling and questioning of events that happened, thus showing how historical consciousness took shape and was transmitted at different periods throughout Secwépemc history all the way into the twentieth century.

This book is organized into fourteen chapters, which roughly present a chronological sequence of the history of the Secwépemc and Secwepemcúl̓ecw throughout the past 10,000 years, ending with the 1920s. Although much has been made about the Aboriginal "cyclical" versus a Western "linear" version of history and narrating the past (Canada, Royal Commission on Aboriginal Peoples 1996a, 32–7), we want to highlight here that Secwépemc historiography – and probably other Indigenous historiographies – involves distinct elements of the ordering of events in time and thus of chronology. In addition, Secwépemc historiography as we practise it here, involves what anthropologist Bruce G. Miller (Miller 2011, 147), in reflecting on the historiography of Sto:lo oral historian Sonny McHalsie, has called "comprehension and thinking through of both oral and written materials." Throughout our chapters, we engage in deep thinking and reflection about the past and the mutual actions of people, plants, animals, and forces on the land, all imbued with agency and animacy and all interconnected in time and space. Secwépemc historiography – as conscious and customary ways of narrating past events and processes – involves telling handed-down events and then building on the knowledge, accomplishments, and legacies, or "deeds," of previous generations through continuous reflection and learning of context and detail. Nowhere is this more evident than in the Tllí7sa stories of the late nineteenth and early twentieth centuries, which brought a previous epic nation builder back to action (see chapters 3 and 13)!

Our journey into the Secwépemc past begins with chapter 2, which details our own perspective on ancient Secwépemc history according to oral traditions, triangulated with information from paleoecology, geology, archaeology, and linguistics. Taken together, these diverse narratives, which begin at the end of the last ice age and take us to some 2,000 years before the present, provide a rich and fascinating account of how the ancestors of the present Secwépemc peopled the land, took possession of the land, and established its laws and boundaries.

Chapter 3, written by Mike K. Rousseau and Marianne Ignace, represents the archaeological perspective on and evidence of the peopling and ancient history of Secwépemc lands before the arrival of Europeans throughout different cultural phases spanning the time from 10,000 years ago to the arrival of Europeans just over 200 years ago. Chapter 3 also includes an analysis of what may have been the fluctuating population size of the Secwépemc over time.

Chapter 4 deals with Secwepemctsín, the Secwépemc language. We discuss its history and connection to neighbouring Salish languages, its dialects, and its orthographies. This chapter also shows how the vocabulary and grammar of Secwepemctsín reflect the knowledge and worldview developed by the ancestors of the present Secwépemc over the course of thousands of years.

Chapter 5, written with Nancy J. Turner, shows how Secwépemc people harvested and figured out ways to maintain and increase the plants and animals in Secwepemcúlecw throughout a seasonal round that involved strategic movement between different ecological zones. It also shows the methods and practical regimes, sustained by an ethic of respect and spiritual connections among all living beings and the land itself, that the Secwépemc used to manage and increase the resources of the land, thereby enacting stewardship of Secwepemcúlecw.

Chapter 6, supported by the research of Kenneth Favrholdt, shows how our ancestors traded goods and products using various modes of transportation throughout and beyond Secwepemcúlecw. They developed travel routes that subsequently became wagon roads and the current highways and roads of the Interior Plateau. In this chapter, we also show how, in addition to foods and utilitarian implements, prestige goods such as shells and copper, including native copper, were socially and spiritually valued goods.

Chapter 7 is about Secwépemc sense of place. We discuss the ways that the Secwépemc language encodes topographic perceptions and knowledge in a variety of ways that complement one another. Terms for landforms map out the terrain and connect to specific biogeoclimatic zones and ecologies. Place naming references not only resources and the nature of geographic features but also human experience on the land in ways that combine perception, knowledge, and emotion. Finally, the use of directionals adds what we call an oral geographic positioning system that allows Secwépemc speakers to visualize, imagine, and communicate human and animal movement in the landscape.

Chapter 8 discusses the extent of Secwepemcúl̓ecw, or the "boundaries" of the Secwépemc nation as they existed from the 1600s to 1800s, and how these changed over time not only through intermarriage, raiding, and warfare but also through conscious Indigenous treaty making. Our discussion of the accounts by the first Europeans who visited, described, and mapped Secwepemcúl̓ecw and the territories of neighbouring nations compares these accounts with the descriptions of resource-producing lands, or "hunting grounds," that Secwépemc people provided to George M. Dawson, Franz Boas, and James Teit. We compare these two sources, in turn, with the descriptions of boundaries and land occupancy of recent Secwépemc elders. In addition, chapter 7 describes the system of collective ownership and the laws and protocols of access to Secwépemc lands and its living resources.

Chapter 9 deals with the Secwépemc ways of recognizing and reckoning kinship, the ways of *k̓wseltktenéws* (being kin to one another), including the complex set of terms for relatives in Secwepemctsín, and the protocols of behaviour these ways entail. At their core are not only the social relations and laws of reciprocal obligations between blood kin on both sides of the family and between people related by marriage, or in-laws, but also a system of resource use and access among Secwépemc that existed among and between the Indigenous nations[10] throughout the Interior Plateau during the 1800s and 1900s and in the preceding centuries. The social protocols and laws of kinship relations, marriage, naming, and adoption ensured that every member of Secwépemc society was part of a social network, was identified with one or more extended families, and maintained relations of reciprocity with members of other families. Moreover, the laws of land tenure and access were uniquely adapted to resource harvesting, given the cyclical nature of game, fish, and plant resources.

Chapter 10 explains the Secwépemc system and concept of political organization from the eighteenth to early twentieth century, including ways that succession to chiefship was determined and enacted, how authority and leadership in the community functioned, and how political authority manifested itself. Especially during the late nineteenth and early twentieth centuries, Indigenous political authority at times functioned within the constraints of the Indian agency system forced upon the Secwépemc and at times continued to function autonomously despite the coercive tutelage of the Indian agents and in a symbiotic relationship with the Durieu system of social and religious order introduced by Catholic Oblate missionaries.

Chapter 11 provides information about the ways that the Secwépemc interacted with powers in nature and with the Creator, and it expands on information presented in earlier chapters that shows how spiritual beliefs and attitudes penetrated all aspects of social life and fostered sustainable harvesting of resources. Beyond elaborating on the spiritual foundations of knowing and using the land as they are discussed in earlier chapters, this chapter examines how, with the coming of missionaries in the mid-nineteenth century, the Secwépemc adapted and integrated Catholic beliefs and practices into prior existing spiritual beliefs and practices, making them work together, although by the early twentieth century our ancestors were increasingly pressured to accept and adopt Catholicism, all the while hiding Secwépemc spirituality in the church.

In chapter 12, we further examine the period of devastating change between the early 1800s and early 1900s as oppression and colonization were wrought upon the Secwépemc by the settler society. Throughout this chapter, we give voice to the ways that Secwépemc people experienced and perceived the coming of the first *seme7úẃi* ("real whites"), the first traders in the late 1700s and early to mid-1800s, and to the ways that Secwépemc people asserted and maintained control over resources and lands. Soon after tens of thousands of newcomers had poured onto the land during a series of gold rushes in the Fraser Canyon and on the Thompson, Cariboo, and upper Columbia Rivers, a devastating smallpox epidemic killed between one-third and two-thirds of the Secwépemc population, and the newly formed colony established and then rescinded reserves in the Interior, eventually setting aside, without treaties, small tracts of land set up by the federal government in concert with the newly established province. As gold seekers stayed to become settlers, they were allowed to pre-empt all arable lands in the valley bottoms at the exclusion of Indigenous inhabitants, whose ancestors had lived there for thousands of years and who experienced this process as it unfolded.

Chapter 13 deals with the time of protest against our ancestors' dispossession of their land and political autonomy. Seeking redress during the first two decades of the twentieth century, the Secwépemc and neighbouring Indigenous peoples took the Canadian government to task in the struggle for recognition of rights to lands and self-governance. At the core of the Indian Rights Movement is the "Memorial to Sir Wilfrid Laurier" (Chiefs of the Shuswap, Okanagan, and Couteau Tribes 1910), where the chiefs of the Secwépemc, Nlaka'pamux, and Okanagan nations articulated their memories of the history of the fur trade and subsequent dispossession. This resulted in the oppressive status quo of the early twentieth century, during which, as the chiefs expressed it, the Aboriginal nations of the Interior and the rest of British Columbia became dispossessed of their homelands, or "ranches." Moreover, the ancestors of these nations were dispossessed of their rights and became wards of a government that steadfastly refused to acknowledge these peoples' rights to land and self-governance. In the memorial, besides telling their side of colonial history and laying out their grievances against the government, whose agents represented "guests" who had come into their "houses" and then refused to reciprocate, the Interior chiefs invoked the laws and practices handed down by their ancestors as they laid out their vision of Indigenous nationhood and the nature and scope of title and rights to land. As it turned out, in a sweeping pre-emptive action, during the 1920s the federal government would not only dismiss their grievances but eventually criminalize First Nations' legal pursuit of the land question by amending the Indian Act.

During the time of the Indian Rights Movement in the late nineteenth and early twentieth centuries, Secwépemc chiefs and storytellers also reflected on these political injustices and on their dispossession of their lands, telling each other stories and satires that had Coyote, Tllí7sa, and other characters getting back at the king of England by capturing his daughter and getting the land back. The latter part of chapter 13 presents and reflects on these little-known stories.

Finally, in chapter 14, we reflect on the meanings and implications that the words and deeds of past Secwépemc ancestors, elders, and chiefs have for our nation in the present and the future. In a chronological sense, our book ends in the 1930s with the voices and memories of the elders and ancestors who experienced that era and who were familiar with the trail of stories from previous decades, centuries, and millennia but who also experienced the cultural genocide of residential schools and the criminalization of their own parents' and grandparents' efforts to address our dispossession of our own lands and laws. Because this trail has become overgrown and overwhelmed by the narrative and physical trails of settler society, we uncover it. Celebrating a cyclical – or, even better, a spiral – sense of Secwépemc history, we invite the reader to reflect on and learn from the lessons of our ancestors, which give us food for thought about action in the present and the future, including the possibility of again *tš̓elícstem re stsq̓ey̓s-kucw* ("standing our laws up"), thus reasserting them.

2 Le Q̓7es te Tellqel̓múcw

The Time of the Ancient Transformers

> At the beginning, the earth was very small, but it gradually became larger, emerging more and more from the waters … The people who inhabited the earth during this period partook of the characteristics of both men and animals. They were called *stsptékwle*. Some were cannibals.[1] At that period many kinds of animals, birds and fishes did not exist, nor many kinds of trees, plants, and berries. The earth was much troubled with great winds, fires and floods. In those days the Old-One … sent Coyote to travel over the world and put it to rights. He was gifted with magical power beyond that of all the other mythological beings, and had great knowledge and cunning; yet often he proved himself to be selfish, lazy and vain, doing many foolish and bad tricks. In fact, he was fond of amusing himself and playing tricks on other people. Nevertheless he did a great deal of work, which benefited the people, and did away with many evil beings. Although Coyote was a long time on earth and travelled all over it, yet he left much of his work undone. Probably his greatest work was the introducing of salmon into the rivers, and the making of fishing-places … The Old-One was the chief of the ancient world, and finished the work of Coyote and other transformers, leaving the earth in the way we see it at present. (Secwépemc elders' handed-down knowledge, ca. 1900–04, quoted in Teit 1909, 595–6)

The dawn of Secwépemc history is connected to events precipitated by climate change more than 10,000 years ago, which in turn shaped the land that became Secwepemcúl̓ecw. In this chapter, we present a composite picture of ancient past events between 11,000 and 3,500 years ago, based on converging lines of evidence from earth science, paleoecology, and linguistics, triangulated with Secwépemc oral histories and with archaeological information, including the information presented in the previous chapter. Taken together, these accounts complement each other and throw light on how the ancestors of the present Secwépemc took possession of the land, made it habitable for humans, and in the process developed what the Secwépemc call *yerí7 re stsq̓ey̓s-kucw* ("our laws").

Paleoecological and paleoclimatological studies of the Southern Interior have shown various periods of profound environmental changes that have occurred in the past 12,000 years,[2] thus reminding us that climate change, although in the past not caused by humans, is nothing new to the environment of the Secwépemc. Generations of Secwépemc ancestors were faced with rapidly changing climates and environments thousands of years ago and successfully adapted to these changes.

PALEOECOLOGY AND PALEOCLIMATOLOGY: WHAT NATURAL SCIENCE TELLS US ABOUT ANCIENT ENVIRONMENTS

The term "paleo" means "the ancient past." Thus paleoecologists study environmental conditions and relationships in the ancient past. Paleoclimatologists study what the weather was like a long time ago. Paleobotany is the study of ancient plant organisms. Paleobotanical research is carried out with a variety of methods, including the study of ancient pollen; the study of tree rings, or dendochronology, which gives us clues not only about the age of trees but also about the climate and growing conditions during a tree's lifetime; and the study of organic sediments on lake bottoms, or paleoliminology, which has analyzed chironomids, small biological water organisms whose remains have survived in lake sediments. The traces left by glaciers as they formed and, with changing climate, melted or increased can give us further clues about ancient weather patterns and environment. In the Interior of British Columbia, paleoecologists, most notably Rolf Mathewes (1985) and Richard Hebda (1982, 1995) and their students (e.g.. Mathewes and Pellatt 2000) have studied samples from several sites, including Pemberton Hill Lake in the Interior Douglas fir zone near Kamloops; pollen diagrams for the southern Fraser River drainage have been studied by Mathewes and Miriam King (1989); and additional sites have been studied by Ian Walker and Marlow Pellatt (2001, 2008).

The Wisconsin Glaciation in the Interior of British Columbia

Between 17,000 and 14,000 years ago, the massive Cordilleran Ice Sheet of the Wisconsin glaciation covered all of the Interior of British Columbia to south of the 49th parallel. At its peak, some 15,000 years ago, the Cordilleran ice sheet was about 1.5 kilometres thick, covering all the valleys and plateaus of the Interior. Only the highest peaks of mountain ranges were above the ice sheets, although it appears that the upper Columbia River drainage system had a less cohesive ice sheet.

In recent years, scientists have reassessed how thick and contiguous the ice sheet actually was throughout northwestern North America. Thus, as Hebda (2007) has pointed out, various *glacial refugia* (hideouts from the ice age) existed at the time of the ice maximum, mainly on the West Coast and in some high alpine areas of northern British Columbia. Interestingly, Catherine Carlson and Kenneth Klein (1996) have discovered evidence of fossilized kokanee salmon – a land-locked form of sockeye salmon – on the shores of Kamloops Lake, which they note were reliably carbon-dated as between 18,000 and 15,500 years old. They suggest that areas of the Interior in the heartland of Secwépemc territory may have formed glacial refugia, not necessarily as ice-free land masses but as bodies of glacial water. As Carlson (personal communication, 2009) maintains, "it appears as if there was more water and less ice during the late glacial maximum in the Southern Interior than supposed by [an earlier speculative model]."

Throughout this time, however, human habitation likely did not exist in the Interior. A warming trend began some 14,000 years ago, and glaciers melted rapidly throughout the Interior. It took 4,000 years or less for the ice to melt, and through that process the landscape that we now know developed. Deglaciation apparently was well underway as early as 13,000 years ago in the upper Columbia drainage system, where a Chinook wind-like air flow produced a steppe tundra of sage, grass, and scattered pine (*Pinus*), true fir (*Abies*), and spruce (*Picea*) forests around that time. As reckoned by archaeologist Wayne Choquette (1996), an environment where humans may have lived existed by some 12,000 years ago in the area now associated with the eastern part of Secwépemc territory, including the Arrow Lakes and areas of the upper Columbia River Valley.

Climate and Vegetation at the End of the Last Ice Age

In the mid-Fraser and Thompson River regions, the Cordilleran ice sheet had largely collapsed by 11,500 years ago, the first ice-free areas being the higher plateaus. The climate period that brought about and then followed the melting of the ice sheet lasted until about 8,200 to 7,800 years ago and was marked by hot, dry summers with frequent fires. Mathewes and Pellatt (2000) and others have referred to it as the xerothermic or "early Holocene xerothermic interval." The study of micro-organisms in lake sediment from this time shows that peak summer temperatures were about 3 degrees Celsius warmer than at present, although winters were likely slightly cooler than at present. A "strong Pacific high" prevailed during the summer months. This period peaked around 9,000 to 8,000 years ago. In other words, the xerothermic period matches, at least in a broad sense, the time of heat, that of "great winds and fires" mentioned in Secwépemc *stsptekwll* (ancient stories), when Old One sent Sk̓elép (Coyote) onto the land, cited at the beginning of this chapter.

During the early xerothermic interval, the upland areas featured scattered stands of pine, alder, and poplar, as well as, with warming temperatures, stands of Douglas fir. The mid-elevation and valley bottom areas were characterized by grasslands and sagebrush. These may have supported large game species like moose, mountain sheep, and a now extinct bison (*Bison occidentalis*) (see also chapter 2).

By 7,000 years ago, the warm dry weather had begun to change to a climate that was still warm but wetter and that lasted until about 4,500 to 4,000 years ago, called the mesothermic period. During this period, the dry grasslands with abundant sage and scattered trees that had become established during the xerothermic period gave way to moister grasslands with expanding forests of Douglas fir and ponderosa pine, as well as red cedar and hemlock.

Another major change occurred after about 4,000 years ago, when the climate got colder but stayed relatively moist and when forests of Engelmann spruce and subalpine fir established themselves at higher elevations. The landscape that emerged at that time, which in Secwepemctsín is called *t7íweltk* (the high, forested plateau; also the area that is high upriver),[3] became a key element in the seasonal round of the ancestors of the Secwépemc.

From geological studies of the Southern Interior, we know that between 13,000 and 10,000 years ago, as the ice had melted in the higher plateaus, there existed a network of ribbon lakes throughout the river basins, held in place by ice dams.[4] At that time, the glacial lake system covering the Thompson River, Deadman's Creek, and Shuswap Lake basins drained into the Columbia River system rather than the Fraser River system, thus draining eastward. The South Thompson drainage east of what is now Kamloops became ice-free first, and a large ice dam just south of what is now the town of Spences Bridge held in place the lake that covered much of the Thompson River system. This lake, Glacial Lake Thompson, at its peak was 200 metres above the current level of the Thompson River and Kamloops Lake. As the water dug its trench through the sediment east of Kamloops and thus lowered the water levels, a second stage of the glacial lake formed, known as Glacial Lake Deadman, named after the Deadman's Creek Valley, home of the Skeetchestn community. This lake stretched from east of Kamloops, including the current Kamloops Lake basin, down through the Thompson River Valley to Spences Bridge. Its water level was some 80 metres above the valley bottom, and thus, although lower than the previous Glacial Lake Thompson stage, it carried much more water than the current Kamloops Lake.

About 9,750 years ago, in a single cataclysmic event, the ice dam near Spences Bridge gave way, draining some 20 cubic kilometres of water down into the Fraser River in a short span of a few days, thus reversing the flow of

2.1 | Landscape in Secwepemcúlecw near the mouth of Deadman's Creek that shows the marks of the sudden drainage of Glacial Lake Thompson, 2015. This drainage followed the breakage of an ice dam near Spences Bridge about 10,000 years ago, which reversed the flow of the Thompson River system from the Columbia River to the Fraser River.

the Thompson River system. The rupture of the ice dam caused the Thompson River system to drain southwest into the Fraser River system. After the reversal of the drainage, and after the flow of the Fraser and Thompson River systems had stabilized, salmon runs established themselves in the Thompson River system.

Even after 10,000 years, the marks of Glacial Lake Thompson and Glacial Lake Deadman are still visible throughout the area. Where the landscape has not been disturbed by urban sprawl, mines, or the plough, the strand (or beach) lines of the successive stages of the glacial lakes are clearly visible on the hills that frame the Thompson River and Deadman's Creek Valleys, nowadays often criss-crossed by cattle trails, dirt roads, and right-of-ways. The scars of the sudden drainage of Lake Deadman are also visible on hillsides throughout the Thompson River Valley. Together, they provide Secwépemc people with an ongoing reminder of, and continuing connection with, that time so long ago. The Secwépemc and Nlaka'pamux peoples of the late nineteenth century knew that these marks on the hillsides were connected to what they called "Coyote's time" and moreover that they were connected to an ancient "flood." Indeed, "the water-marks of this flood may be seen on some parts of the mountains," as recorded around 1900 by ethnographer James Teit (1917c, 13).

There is also a Secwépemc story about how the salmon came into the Thompson River system, which casts the geological events of more than 9,000 years ago in a narrative of emerging relationships between humans and animals, as well as between people of neighbouring nations, adding political, social, and moral dimensions to the geological and ecological knowledge.

Re Sk̓elép ell re Sqlélten | Story of Coyote and Salmon
told by Ronald E. Ignace, 1997, and transcribed by Marianne Ignace and Ronald E. Ignace, 2008

Le q̓7éses ta7 k st̓éxelcs re swewll.
Long time ago, the fish [salmon] did not run up the river.

M-yews re stitéyt.s re Sk̓elép̓ méte k̓wséltktens.
And Coyote and his relatives were hungry.

M-tsútes-ekwe, "Kénmes-enke ks ta7es re st̓éxelcs re swewll?"
He said, "Why is it that the salmon don't run up this way?"

M-néses te setétkwe es xpqenwén̓s k skénems.
He went to the river to find out what had happened.

M-cllgwelcétkwus-ekwe, ell re m-nék̓entsútes, wel re m-xenwéllenes es kwewt.s.
He jumped into the water, and changed his shape, so that he could drift down the river.

Xetéqs m-nek̓entsútes te scenc, k̓émell m-gets̓úcwes.
First, he changed himself into a rock, but he sank.

M-yews re snek̓entsút.s te ptsekll, k̓émell m-súk̓wtes te snewt.
Then he changed himself into a leaf, but he got blown away by the wind.

M-yews ri7 re snek̓entsút.s te sexts̓éy, ell m-kwéwtes!
Then he finally changed himself into a stick, and he was able to drift in the water!

K̓wíncwes-enke tek sitq̓t re skwewt.s wel re m-xléqes-enke nek swétes-enke tek pellsts̓elemín̓s.
I don't know how many days he drifted downstream until he got stuck in somebody's fish weir [across the river].

Nerí7 re sxléqs-ekwe.
There, they say he got stuck.

Stén-ekwe nerí7 wel re m-kitsc ye7éne te tek̓séle te tekt̓kwílc es q̓elnéy̓ens re stṡelemíńs.
He was there until these two Indian doctors arrived to check their weir.

M-wikt.ses-ekwe ye7éne te sextṡéy, m-tsútes, "Me7 kwéntem ye7éne, le7 te stektsúsem."
They saw the stick and said, "We'll take this as firewood."

M-kwénses-ekwe, m-tsq̓wmnúsenses, m-pelq̓ílcwes te s7elkst.s.
They took it and threw it in the fire. Then they returned to work.

M-nek̓entsútes-ekwe re sk̓elép te k̓woyí7se te tuwíwt.
Coyote changed himself into a little baby boy.

M-tṡ7úmes, m-qnímentmes te nuxwnúxwenxw.
He cried and was heard by the women.

M-tskwentémes te t7ikw es ta7es es q̓wlleps.
They took him from the fire so he wouldn't get scorched.

M-tsútes, "Telhénes-enke k st7ékwes ye7éne te sk̓wimémn̓elt?"
They said, "Where did that child come from?"

Mesésq̓t-ekwe nerí7 re sw7ecs re sk̓elép es xpqenwéńs stéṁi k tsúwet.s ye7éne te tekt̓kwílc.
For four days Coyote stayed there so that he could find out what the Indian doctor women were up to.

Le sítestes m-stsílcmenses re nuxwnúxwenxw, m-k̓úlenses es tsqwménks, tkenrí7 yem wel k̓wseltktenéwsmenses.
At night he lay down with the women, he made them pregnant, and that is how he made them into relatives.

Le cwéńwen-uy̓es ne mesésqt, m-qílltes-ekwe.
Early in the morning on the fourth day, he woke up.

M-néses te setétkwe, m-wíq̓enses re nuxwnúxwenxw re stṡelemíńs.
He went to the river and wrecked the women's weir.

M-q̓ewcít.ses te txexetéńs, es ta7es-ekwe cú7tsem es tknémens re sqlélten es ctext̓éxelcs.
He broke their power so they couldn't keep the salmon from going upstream.

Pyin te sitq̓t e qwelmíntmes es kwemtúses es ct̓éxelcs re sqelqlélten, es ta7es k stem cú7tsem es tustém,
Today, if we want the salmon to always come upriver,

yéwske ri7 k sxwtśilc-kt es yecwmenstwécw-kt ell es knucwentwécw-kt.
we should strive to look after one another and help one another out.

Pyin te sitq̓t yeri̓7 re txexetéń-kt.
Today, that's our power.

E ta7es es xenwéllen-kt es xílem-kt, me7 qwenqwentwílc-kt ell me7 k̓wiyúsem-kt.
If we can't do that, we'll become poor and we will suffer.

The Nlaka'pamux have a similar story about the weir strung across the Thompson River guarded by the *ṫkwilc* (Indian doctor) women in this location, which Coyote broke. It is said that after Coyote led the salmon up the Thompson River, "he continued his journey, and led the salmon to the head waters of the North Thompson River, then, returning to Kamloops Lake, he conducted them up the South Thompson to Shuswap Lake. From the latter place he went south through the Spallumcheen and Okanagan to take the salmon up Columbia River" (Teit 1912a, 301). The passage Coyote must have chosen would have taken him from Shuswap Lake to Mara Lake, along the Shuswap River, and then into the Okanagan Lake system. The Syilx (Okanagan) have a story about Coyote breaking a fish weir on the lower Okanagan River and then guiding the salmon upriver into the Columbia system while clearing obstructions in the river and creating fishing places (see ibid.). The story also gives an explanation of why there are no salmon in the Similkameen River. The Splatsín Secwépemc people, whose territory encompasses both the Fraser and Columbia watersheds, identify Coyote's final canoe resting place, Upside-Down Canoe, on a flat close to Falkland, which is near the current headwaters of the Salmon River, itself at the very end of the Fraser-Thompson watershed. In various locations along the Fraser, main Thompson, North Thompson, and South Thompson Rivers are additional "tracks" and rock formations that explain about further incidents and encounters while Coyote conducted the salmon.

The narratives speak to a historical consciousness about ancient events that formed the drainages of the Fraser, Thompson, and Columbia River systems, as well as about the arrival of salmon after large blockages were removed. The *stsptekwll*, however, different from explanations within the framework of natural sciences, frame the agency of these postglacial events as interactions between Sk̓elép and other sentient beings on the land, connected to place names and an ancient memory of place. Furthermore, the *stsptekwll*, beyond explaining natural events and geographic features, cast events in the framework of social relationships, thus providing us with lessons about the historical and continuing interconnection of the Secwépemc and the Nlaka'pamux as connected through intermarriage and kinship. It also gives us lessons about the relationship between humans and salmon, mediated by Sk̓elép's actions.

What Archaeology Tells Us

The archaeological evidence of early human presence in the south-central Interior of British Columbia, as explained in more detail in chapter 3, is sparse. It begins with Gore Creek Man, the headless skeleton of a young man that was found in an embankment about 20 kilometres east of Kamloops in the 1960s, presumably killed in a flash flood and dated at 8,340 years old.[5] After being stored in the Royal British Columbia Museum in Victoria for two decades, Gore Creek Man was repatriated to Secwepemcúlecw in the late 1980s at the initiative of the Secwepemc Cultural Education Society and the Royal British Columbia Museum. Nonetheless, Gore Creek Man served the interests of science: stable carbon isotope analysis, a method developed by Brian Chisholm and D. Erle Nelson (1983), showed that he ate very little marine protein and probably lived on a diet of meat rather than salmon.

As Mike K. Rousseau further explains in chapter 3, archaeologists regard the period between about 7,500 and 6,000 years ago as being characterized by the Early Nesikep Tradition, followed by the Lehman Phase between 6,000 and 4,500 years ago, the latter being identified by different tools and artifacts, as well as by a beginning reliance on salmon. Archaeologists associate the Lehman Phase archaeological sites with upland hunting, valley bottom dwelling, and some use of salmon. A subsequent phase noted by archaeologists is the Lochnore Phase between about 5,000 and 3,500 years ago, which featured a river-oriented adaptive pattern that, as Rousseau, Arnoud Stryd, and others have suggested, developed out of the melding of a pre-existing Interior culture with immigrating groups of Salish-speaking peoples from the coast at some point between 5,550 and 5,000 years ago (Lawhead and Stryd 1985; Rousseau 2004; Stryd and Roussseau 1996; see also chapter 3). This migration coincided with the onset of cooler and wetter climatic conditions. The Lochnore Phase, in turn, overlapped with the later Lehman Phase for at least 500 years – some say 1,000 years – with the new tradition introduced from the coast and the pre-existing way of life being practised side by side and eventually coming together.

Recent DNA analysis by Jerome Cybulski and colleagues (2007; see also Malhi et al. 2010)[6] of 5,000-year-old human remains from the China Lake and Big Bar Lake areas near Clinton supports the idea of a migration into the Interior by coastal people. Whereas the China Lake individuals (two related males) tested as belonging to a DNA sequence commonly found in Asia but not previously found in North American Indigenous populations, the Big Bar Lake individual (an elderly female) tested as belonging to a DNA sequence found among contemporary Nuu-cha-nuulth people on the BC coast. The China Lake males consumed about 37 to 38 per cent (+/- 10 per cent) of marine protein (salmon), whereas the Big Bar Lake female consumed about 24 to 36 per cent marine protein. Salmon thus made up a significant part of their diet, although two-thirds or more of their protein came from land animal sources. The authors of the study conclude that as early as 5,000 years ago, "a genetically diverse population inhabited the [mid-Fraser] region" (Cybulski et al. 2007, 71). As Rousseau shows in chapter 3, around 4,500 years ago the overlapping cultural phases of the Lehmann and Lochnore Phases gave way to the Plateau Pithouse Tradition, associated with the *c7ístkteń* (underground pithouse), extensive reliance on root vegetables processed in underground pit-cooking ovens, hunting for ungulates and other animals in the high plateaus and subalpine areas of the higher mountains, and importantly, intensive salmon production. Stable isotope analysis of human remains from various phases of the Plateau Pithouse Tradition, or less than 4,500 years old, has shown that the more recent ancestors of the Secwépemc relied on salmon for 40 to 60 per cent of the protein in their diets (Lovell et al. 1986).

Reconstructing the Past through Historical Linguistics

Information from historical linguistics provides some interesting points of convergence with the above archaeological and paleoecological information. Despite earlier stipulation by Franz Boas, Charles Hill-Tout, Alfred Kroeber, and others that the Salish language family had Interior origins (see Kinkade et al. 1998, 68), beginning in the early 1960s, linguists Wayne Suttles and William Elmendorf (1963) made convincing arguments for a coastal origin of the Salish language family (see also Suttles 1987b). More recently, linguist M. Dale Kinkade (1991) researched and reconstructed words for plants and animals in Interior and Coast Salish languages, showing that words for several plant and shellfish species that occur only on the coast can be reconstructed only for Proto-Salish and did not occur in Proto–Interior Salish. Kinkade (1990, 204) therefore suggested that the homeland, or *point of dispersal*, for Salishan languages was the lower Fraser River south to the Skagit River:

> The homeland thus delimited for the Proto-Salish would extend from the Fraser River southward at least to the Skagit River, and possibly as far south as the Stillaguamish or Skykomish River. Expansion to the south would probably have been rapid in any case, since the country is relatively open and accessible. From west to east, their territory would have extended from the Strait of Georgia and Admiralty Inlet to the Cascade Mountains. A tongue of the family probably extended up the Fraser River through the Fraser Canyon; this is the most likely route of expansion into the interior (via the Thompson River), although Indians certainly knew a number of routes through the Cascades further south.

Morris Swadesh (1950), using a method called glottochronology,[7] dated the time depth of linguistic divergence between Coast and Interior Salish at fifty-five centuries, or about 5,500 years ago, with internal divergence among Interior Salish languages dated at forty-five centuries, or about 4,500 years ago.[8] Adding measurements of the geographic distance between each of the Interior Salish languages, William Elmendorf (1965) estimated that Coast Salish and Interior Salish diverged between about 6,900 and 5,500 years ago and suggested that the northern (Lillooet, Shuswap, Thompson) branch of the Interior Salish language subfamily, in turn, split from the southern branch (Okanagan, Columbian, Flathead, Kalispel, Coeur d'Alene) between 4,500 and 3,500 years ago, resulting in a further east-south migration of Salish-speaking peoples into the Columbia Plateau, where they mixed with people who already lived there, perhaps the ancestors of Sahaptin-speaking peoples.

The last split in the Northern Interior branch was between Nlaka'pamuxcin (Thompson) and Secwepemctsín (Shuswap), occurring some 2,000 years ago. Remarkably, this points to Secwepemctsín/Nlaka'pamuxcin, representing the last node of language divergence within the Northern Interior Salish subfamily, as being older than the English language by several hundred years.

Elmendorf briefly compared his linguistic data with the sparse archaeological information that existed in the early 1960s but did not examine Interior Salish oral histories. However, he did suggest that the "point of dispersal" – the heartland or cradle – of Interior Salish languages was in the Thompson Lake (Glacial Lake Thompson) area. As shown below, this is exactly the area where the ancient stories of coastal "transformers" or immigrants encountering Interior "transformers" are situated, the former representing groups of people who brought the Coast Salish language into the Interior and mixed it with a language that was already spoken by the earlier ancestors of the Secwépemc, who had already lived here for 3,000 years or more.

Secwepemctsín, then, appears to have been created out of Coast Salish, introduced by immigrants from the coast, melding with the language(s) of the previous ancestors of the Interior Plateau people, the "Coyote people," who already lived here at the time of the Salish immigrations. What their language was, we may never know. Between around 5,000 and 4,500 years ago, during a period of 1,000 to 500 years, the "Coyote people's" language merged with the Salish language of the newcomers, becoming what linguists call Proto–Interior Salish. The Interior Salish languages may well still have residue from what was spoken before,[9] although by the late nineteenth century, the Secwépemc ancestors had developed different accounts of the origins and dispersal of the Interior Salish languages.[10]

Interior Salish Voices of Beginnings

It is also productive to compare the oral histories told by Interior Salish peoples to the information that the scientific record provides. James Teit wrote down fragments of information that Secwépemc, Nlaka'pamux, and St'at'imc elders told him around the turn of the century. In the information provided to Teit by his consultants from all Interior nations – the Nlaka'pamux, St'at'imc, Secwépemc, and Syilx – Coyote or Old Coyote is consistently mentioned as the most ancient of "transformers."[11] Throughout these stories, Coyote is often associated with glaciers and mountaintops: Coyote's house is said to be in a glacier; according to others, it is in the "upper world." The latter is described as a "prairie occupying the top of a plateau with steep sides" (Teit 1898, 23; 1900, 341). As the excerpt from Teit's monograph on the Secwépemc at the beginning of this chapter shows, the Interior peoples said that Coyote's work took place at a time of "great winds, heat and fires," very much like the xerothermic period described by paleoecologists.

Nlaka'pamux elders of the late nineteenth century also told Teit that "in the beginning there were no lakes and rivers." These were said to have originated after a "deluge, which also carried fish into the ponds." As the narrative goes, only Coyote and three men escaped the deluge (Teit 1898, 20), being left high and dry, and they had to take trees for wives.

Teit (1898, 20) described the country inhabited by the "Coyote people" as "the country along the Thompson River east of Lytton." In a footnote he added, "The country referred to includes all the present territory of the Nkamtcinemux[12] and down the Thompson near Lytton, the Nicola, Similkameen, Okanagon and southern Shuswap regions" (ibid., 20n34). According to the information Teit obtained from local people, this country is also associated with coyote (*Canis latrans*) habitat. Teit (ibid., 103n36) was also told that Coyote principally talked in the Secwépemc language and in a peculiar tone of voice: "It is not known whether the Coyote talked in Shuswap just for sake of imitation, or whether that was his natural language." Indeed, among the Nlaka'pamux, Coyote's association with Secwepemctsín, the Shuswap language, appears to have been transmitted through time, having persisted among Nlaka'pamux storytellers of the late nineteenth and early twentieth centuries. As Teit (1917c, 12) found out, "Old Coyote (he is called 'Uncle Coyote' by some) was the ancestor of all Indians. He had many wives. From some are descended the Thompson, from others the Okanagan, from still others the Shuswap ... At one time they all spoke the same language. It was like Shuswap."

In his discussion of "foreign speech" as one variation of "character speech" in Nlaka'pamux narrative, linguist Steve Egesdal further comments on Coyote speaking Secwepemctsín in Nlaka'pamux stories. He notes that linguistically, Secwepemctsín (Shuswap) "retains certain Proto-Salish segments," meaning that it represents a more ancient form of Interior Salish and thus lends itself to providing "authenticity" to stories as ancient: "The mythic language, then, was 'like Shuswap,' and to have Coyote speak Shuswap probably lent a tone of authenticity to the performance of the traditional narrative" (Egesdal 1992, 57). An explanation that is just as plausible, however, is that the Nlaka'pamux Coyote stories, which closely resemble the Secwépemc Coyote stories, perhaps go back to a time when Nlaka'pamuxcin had not diverged as a separate language; the "Secwépemc" language in these stories represents the language that the common ancestors of the Nlaka'pamux and Secwépemc would have spoken more than 2,000 years ago.

Also of interest is the fact that the Upper Nlaka'pamux in the area between Lytton and Ashcroft used the endearment term *sisi sk̓elép* ("Uncle Coyote") to refer to Coyote, who is otherwise called *nk'yep* in their language. Both *sisi* (*síse7*, or "mother's brother," in current Secwepemctsín) and *sk̓elép* are Secwépemc words and do not occur in Nlaka'pamuxcin.

Stsptékwle | Travelling Transformers

At a time in the ancient past when, according to the stories, Coyote was still doing his work, other "transformers" appeared in the country. Some of them were foreigners from the coast, and others were from the core of Secwépemc country and travelled outward. If we understand them as not merely "mythical" but also historical accounts, they give us further clues about events and processes from a time around 5,000 years ago.

The first of the foreign transformers to enter the Interior, according to Nlaka'pamux traditions, were the Qoa'qLqaL (Qwiqwt'qwet' in Secwépemc orthography, from the root *qwit̓* for "smile"), a group of four "brothers" who came up into Nlaka'pamux country through the Fraser Canyon – that is, from Coast Salish country. Throughout their travels up the Fraser and then the Thompson Rivers through Nlaka'pamux country, the brothers had encounters with powerful beings whom they defeated. As the stories go, at various points along the way, they also came across Coyote:

> When the Qoa'qLqaL reached Nkamtci'n [the mouth of the Nicola River], they turned up the Nicola River and traveled until they came to a place near Kwenca'rtEn [32 kilometres up from Spences Bridge]. Here they met Coyote, who was sitting on a stone watching them as they approached. They tried to transform him, but were able only to change his tracks into stone. Therefore the marks of the coyote's feet may be seen on this stone at the present day. Coyote sat with his chin resting on his hand, and stared at them while they were trying to metamorphose him. When they had failed, he cried out to them, "you are making the world right: so am I. Why try to punish me when I have done you no harm? This is my country. Why do you come here and interfere with my work? If I wished, I could turn you into stone; but as you have likely been sent into the world, like myself, to do good, I will allow you to pass, but you must leave this country as quickly as you can. We should be friends, but must not interfere with each other's work." (Teit 1912a, 316)

Along the Thompson River, the Qoa'qLqaL have further encounters with Coyote at his *c7ístkteṅs* (underground house). At a place farther up the Nicola

River "near Jesus Garcia's Ranch,"[13] the Qoa'qLqaL subsequently present Coyote, who is by himself and has to use a tree's knothole for a wife, with real wives, thus helping him out and improving his lot. It was after the "flood" that Coyote had been left without women, "high and dry" in the mountains (Teit 1898, 20).

A number of other episodes in the Qoa'qLqaL epic involve the Qoa'qLqaL brothers killing "cannibals" – evil-minded powerful beings who killed and devoured people at certain localities. In addition, as they travel up the Fraser River into Interior country, they teach the local people how to fish for salmon:

> The brothers, on the way up the Fraser, came to Yale, where, on the opposite side of the river, they saw a man trying to catch salmon with a sharpened pole. He had a wife and two children. They went to him, and found that he pulled the pole out of the water after it had rubbed against a salmon, and, drawing his finger over it, he scraped off the fish-slime which was on it. This he ate, and he gave some to his family. They told him this was bad, and showed him how to make a dip-net and catch salmon, also the methods of cooking and drying fish. (Teit 1912a, 318)

The Qoa'qLqaL also teach the people in the Interior about childbirth: rather than cutting the belly of women open to get out a child, and thus killing the woman, they show them how to extract children from the womb through the vagina with various kinds of string and twine.

Following their adventures on the Fraser and Thompson Rivers, the Qoa'qLqaL are said to have travelled up the Bonaparte Valley above Cache Creek and then turned back downriver to the Similkameen and Nicola Valleys, where "they again met Coyote who objected to their invasion of the country, [and] threatened to destroy them" (Teit 1912a, 317). They return to the Bonaparte and Hat Creek Valleys, where they have a power contest at Hat Creek, following encounters at Nṗétkwe7ten (Pavilion Lake). Finally, the brothers are frozen into stone near Pavilion Mountain after an encounter with a young girl on her *étsxem* (spirit guardian quest). All of these latter occurrences also turn up in the Secwépemc version of the Tllí7sa story (see below). In another version, the Qoa'qLqaL decide to leave the Interior and pass across the Cascade Mountains back to the lower Fraser River. Interestingly, besides these "foreigners" coming up the Fraser River into the Interior, there were also "transformers" who travelled from the Interior down the Fraser River to Coast Salish country below Hope and to Chehalis, causing landmarks to be shaped by transforming people along the way (see Teit 1912b, 1917b).

Another transformer epic shared among Secwépemc and Nlaka'pamux peoples is the story of Kokwela (Qweq̓wíle, or Hogfennel). This one involves a young girl in Secwépemc country, who, according to information provided to geologist George M. Dawson (1891, 31), lived at a place called

"Kwikooi" – apparently Tskwikúy̓, the mouth of Scotch Creek, also listed as the start of the Tllí7sa epic discussed below. Feeling too proud to marry anyone, the girl

> refused all offers of marriage, telling her numerous suitors that none of them were good enough for her. Thus she remained unmarried, whilst all the young girls of her own age soon found husbands. Afterwards, when she became anxious to get married, no one would have her, the young men treating her in the same way that she had treated them. Therefore she married the root Kokwe'la (Qweq̓wíle) and soon afterwards was delivered of a son. The boy, who did not know who his father was, soon grew up, and used to play with the other boys of the place. One day he treated some of his playmates roughly, and in consequence they grew angry with him, calling him names, and styling him "bastard," saying that he was the offspring of the Kokwe'la [Q̓wle7íl̓t]. The boy felt ashamed at this treatment. (Teit 1898, 21)

Upon Q̓wle7íl̓t questioning his mother about his father, she admits that he is indeed the son of Qweq̓wíle. Ashamed, the boy undergoes his *étsxem* in the mountains and develops great powers. After he returns home, "he began to travel over the country, transforming bad people, and others who offended him, and curtailing the powers of those who did injury to their neighbours" (Teit 1898, 46).

Qweq̓wíle root, or *Lomatium macrocarpum*, known variously by the English common names large-fruited desert parsley, biscuitroot, hogfennel, or "Indian carrot," was one of the important staple roots of the Secwépemc and other Interior peoples. The associations of the story with sexual intercourse, fertility, and reproduction are not accidental: the root looks distinctly phallic. In addition, Skeetchestn elder Nellie Taylor described its use as a "prenatal vitamin" to ensure a healthy baby, and Secwépemc and other Interior Salish peoples also used it as a women's fertility medicine. Thus the Qweq̓wíle story includes many layers of social, spiritual, geographic, ecological, and ethnobotanical information.

Qweq̓wíle's journeys take him from his home east of the confluence of the North and South Thompson Rivers and down the Thompson to below the confluence with the Fraser, where he meets the Qoa'qLqaL coming upriver. Power contests show that Qweq̓wíle's power exceeds the powers of the Qoa'qLqaL, but they peacefully "lay side by side," as is evidenced by adjacent rock imprints of the Qoa'qLqaL and Qweq̓wíle just south of Kumcheen at the confluence of the Fraser and Thompson Rivers. They subsequently part ways: the Qoa'qLqaL travel up the Thompson, while Qweq̓wíle travels south down the Fraser to NLaqLaqeten (Nt'aq't'aq'ten, "the crossing") near Kanaka Bar, a place said to mark the boundary of Nlaka'pamux and Uta'mqt (Wutémtk,

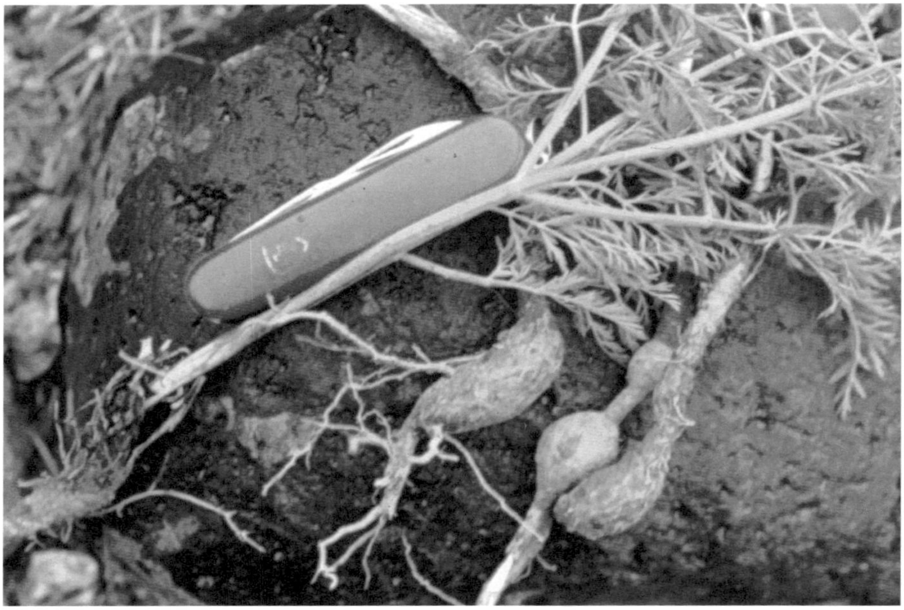

2.2 | *Qweq̓wíle* (biscuitroot, *Lomatium macrocarpum*), ca. 1985.

here meaning Sto:lo territory, although the term is also applied to the lower Thompson territory). As Teit (1898, 109) was told, "below this place, in the Uta'mqt (Wutémtk) country, no kokwela grows; but above this place it grows, and gets more and more plentiful eastward towards the Shuswap country." A contemporary map that plots the distribution of *Lomatium macrocarpum* in British Columbia corroborates Qweq̓wíle's findings; with a few exceptions of sparse occurrences, its habitat closely fits the perimeter of his travels.

After reaching this point at the boundary with Wutémtk (Sto:lo) country, Qweq̓wíle turns around and travels back up the Fraser River to its headwaters, returning full circle by way of "North Thompson or Columbia River" (Teit 1898, 46).[14] In other words, Qweq̓wíle's travels circumscribe the boundaries of what became Interior Salish territory, with Secwépemc territory at its core.

The final group of transformers, connected in genealogy to Sk̓elép, the Qoa'qLqaL, and Qweq̓wíle are Tllí7sa and his brothers. Tllí7sa (from *tellítše7* for "shapeshifter") was the eldest of three or four brothers (most likely three brothers and a nephew) who lived with their aunt (most likely their mother's sister) or perhaps grandmother east of Tk̓emlúps (Kamloops).[15] With the brothers also lived a young boy named Kwelaa'llst (Q̓welálst, "biscuitroot rock"), who was named by one of Teit's (1909, 644) sources as the son of Qweq̓wíle, which appears to tell us that the Tllí7sa story either takes place *after* Qweq̓wíle's travels or involves the same set of events.[16] In George M. Dawson's (1891) account, Q̓wele7ílt – who is Qweq̓wíle's offspring (see above) – starts on his journey from "Kwi-kooi" (Tskwik̓úy̓), at the mouth of Scotch Creek on the north shore of Shuswap Lake. After finding out that the biscuitroot is his father, he joins Tllí7sa and his brothers after they meet up "not far below Kamloops Lake." When they first met Q̓wle7il̓t, the brothers had tried four times to kill him by throwing a boulder on him, but they had failed to hurt him on account of Q̓wle7il̓t's powers. Subsequently, they had made a pact and decided to travel together.

In a story he told to ethnographers Randy Bouchard and Dorothy Kennedy (1979) in the 1970s, the late Secwépemc elder Ike Willard placed the origin of Tllí7sa and his brothers on the South Thompson River "east of Kamloops." Tllí7sa and his brothers' epic journey as narrated by Franz Boas's (1895b, 2002) unknown consultant begins near the mouth of Scotch Creek at Tskwik̓úy̓ ("logs lying down"), on the north shore of the western arm of Shuswap Lake, the same location where Dawson places the beginning of the Q̓wele7il̓t/Tllí7sa epic (see fig. 2, colour section). From Tskwik̓úy̓, the brothers go down Secwepemcétkwe (South Thompson River) to its confluence with Simpcwétkwe (North Thompson River) at Tk̓emlúl̓pe (see fig. 3, colour section). They ascend Simpcwétkwe to just north of Little Fort, return to the confluence and go downstream along Kamloops Lake and its outflow at Sk̓emqín, continue up the Skeetchestn (Deadman's Creek) Valley, and from there travel to what is now Cache Creek and Hat Creek and then north to the Painted Chasm near Clinton. Upon turning back, they travel up Hat Creek, across Marble Canyon to Pavilion Lake, and across Pavilion Mountain to High Bar Canyon on the Fraser River (see figs 4 and 5, colour section).

The following is a summary of their travels, based on a triangulation of Teit's, Boas's, Dawson's, Ike Willard's, and Louisa Basil's accounts and discussed and checked with Skeetchestn elders.

The four boys live with their "mother" (most likely a maternal aunt) at Tskwik̓úy̓ by the mouth of Scotch Creek on Shuswap Lake. The female elder, who has special powers and is a *t̓kwilc* (medicine person), warns them about the Ts̓ecélemc (people eaters, or cannibal powers, on the land) and gives them advice on how to vanquish them. She douses them with medicine, and as a result, the oldest youth attains the power to shapeshift between a dog and a human being, thus becoming Tllí7sa.[17] But she forgets to tell them about a pubescent girl, Chipmunk, who has the power to harm them while she herself is training for power as she becomes a young woman.

At the beginning of their journey, having walked from Shuswap Lake along the South Thompson River, they arrive at a bend in the river called Tkemk̓emém̓qs. Above it is a cliff now known as Hoffman's Bluff but called Sq̓ásca ("hit rock") in Secwepemctsín, which features a cave with a long crack in the rock wall as an opening. Here, Tllí7sa vanquishes a powerful, people-killing groundhog that lives in a still-visible crack in the bluff and turns the animal into the groundhog that is harmless to people and serves

2.3 | Sq̓ásca (Hoffman's Bluff), 2015. Here Tllí7sa vanquished supernatural marmots who lived in the cleft cave. In 2014–15 the plan to widen Highway 1 in this location threatened to blast the cave, but in the end it was preserved.

them as food. Near Monte Creek at a place still known as Pellts̓egtín ("has rattlesnakes"), they transform a woman who kills men with rattlesnakes coming out of her bodily orifices into a woman who is a sexual partner rather than an adversary of men, and they impregnate her.[18] This outcome is commemorated in a prominent round cliff on the north shore of the South

Thompson River called Tsqwmémenk ("pregnant belly") (Sarah Deneault, personal communication, 2011; see also Dawson 1891, 37).[19] Just east of Tk̓emlúps on the South Thompson, at a place called Geyús ("angry face") near the Kamloops suburb of Barnhardtvale, Tllí7sa, being unarmed, obtains arrow stones from four grizzly bear sisters who are the owners of all arrow stone, which the brothers subsequently make into knives.[20] Farther along, "above Kamloops," they change a grizzly bear living with Coyote from a "cannibal" into a "mere animal." On a foray up the North Thompson, as told by the Símpcwemc (North Thompson Secwépemc) (Teit 1909, 651), the brothers travel past Tseqwtseqwélqw and arrive at a place called Xwexwtéṫi ("mountain-goat place"),[21] where two pubescent goat girls in training, their bodies painted red, are bathing in the river below. Tllí7sa transforms them into two red rocks by "drawing away their breath by drawing in his own" (Teit 1909, 651n1).

In a cave above what is now Cherry Creek, 20 kilometres west of Kamloops, Tllí7sa, the most powerful of the brothers, defeats a mean, powerful rabbit who has razor-sharp hind legs, which it uses to kill intruders.[22] They travel on to Sk̓emqín at the outlet of Kamloops Lake, where Tllí7sa defeats a powerful elk who blocks the river. Tllí7sa lets himself be swallowed by the elk's anus and then squeezes the elk's heart, causing the animal to stumble. He then cooks the heart while still inside the elk. Eventually, he alerts his brothers that he is inside the elk, and they cut him out carefully after they find it dead. The brothers then travel up the Deadman's Creek Valley to Pesmémenc ("has-tobacco place"),[23] where the poisonous tobacco tree grew:

> It was a large, very leafy tree, and all around it lay the bones of its victims; for any one who touched the leaves, or rested in its shade, invariably died. Tllí7sa said, "I will smoke tobacco." His brothers tried to dissuade him, but he insisted, and, going up to the tree, he cut it down with his arrow-flaker. Taking the leaves, he smoked them himself, and gave his brothers the stalks to smoke. Then he said, "tobacco will never again kill people. It will be a good plant, and people shall gather and smoke it without harm." (Teit 1909, 646)

As they travel farther west, near the mouth of the Bonaparte River at what is now Cache Creek, at a rock face called Sxwexwṫéqs ("mountain-goat nose"), they encounter a big mountain goat and its dog and kill them,[24] causing the goat to henceforth give its flesh and horns to people and causing the dog to become a companion of humans. Walking north along the ridge above Bonaparte Valley, they observe a person with a small backpack walking below the ridge. Not recognizing him as their young nephew Q̓welálst, who was sent after them by their aunt to warn them of the pubescent girl they would encounter, they roll large boulders down the ridge at him four times but fail to harm him.[25] After they recognize one another, Q̓welálst shares his

2.4 | Sqlewúl̓ecw (the Chasm), near Clinton, 2012. Here Tllí7sa vanquished a supernatural beaver.

provisions of roots and berries with them, which he cooks in a small basket but which magically increase each time someone takes a bit, thus feeding them all. Q̓welálst then takes the name Tq̓wemnélst ("the one they threw rocks on"). However, even though he then joins them, he forgets to tell them about the girl.

The brothers carry on up the Bonaparte River Valley, reaching "Skelawa'ulux" (Sqlewúl̓ecw, "beaver country") and the Painted Chasm north of Clinton, a deep hollow surrounded by cliffs. Here, Tllí7sa's brothers make the hollows and shapes at the base of the cliffs while they search for a big powerful beaver who dragged Tllí7sa into the water and into its lodge after he harpooned it. Tllí7sa kills the beaver and turns it into *sqlew7úw̓i*, the ordinary beaver, which gives itself to people with its skin and its meat. By a creek not far from there and near the "59 mile" post on the Cariboo Wagon Road, at a place called Ncencécen̓ctem (Nxa'nExtem, "stony hollow"), they defeat another powerful marmot who has a house in the rock and, similar to the episode above at Tkemk̓emém̓qs, transform it into the common marmot, valued for its flesh and skin.

They then return back down the Bonaparte River and ascend Hat Creek past Petpút̓emten ("place where one comes out into the open"), about 5 kilometres above the confluence of Hat Creek and Bonaparte River, where they have a power contest on a smooth rock face above the creek. The late Rose Phillips of Sṫuxtéws remembered being told about the travels of Tllí7sa and his brothers through this area; she referred to the place where they had competed to determine who could leave the deepest impressions in the rock with their heads as Cwíẇesqen ("long, tall heads"). The latter was a steep rock cliff along the much-travelled Aboriginal trail connecting Hat Creek with Lillooet that subsequently became the Lillooet wagon road. It showed the human face impressions in the rock face. When the current Highway 99 was built on the previous Aboriginal road, or wagon road, the rock face was destroyed with dynamite, and the physical mark of the brothers' power and travels disappeared.

Along the steep rock walls of Tsmeltáṁ (Marble Canyon), they meet a powerful people-eating golden eagle who lives on the steep cliffs; it is in the habit of killing people by swooping down on them, picking them up, and smashing them against the steep rock face. Seizing some white clay and red iron oxyde from the steep cliffs, Tllí7sa lets the eagle smash him against the steep rocks, making it look as though his brains and blood are oozing from the cliff by spitting out red ochre and lime, which he has hidden in his cheek, and by bracing himself with his arrow-flaker. As the eagle places him in its nest, Tllí7sa kills it, removing its tail feathers, and then commands the young eagles to fly him down, telling them that future people will use eagle feathers to "ornament the heads, clothes and weapons of men" (Teit 1909, 649).

As Tllí7sa and his brothers continue on their journey, they come to Pavilion Lake. Here lives a powerful *splont* (skunk) who is in the habit of killing people. Killing the skunk by emptying its scent bag into the lake, the brothers cause the deep blue colour of Pavilion Lake, thus named Nṗétkwe7ten ("farting lake").

In the words of Louisa Basil of Sṫuxtéws,

Tsuns re qelmúcw "Nṗétkwe7ten."
The Indians call it "Farting Lake."

Neri7 m-ṗúmes re splont ell lu7 ctené7e nu7 re stseqs re tsitcws re splont nu7.
That's where the skunk farted, and that's where his house was.

Nu7 ṗúmes wel q̇wempép re sṗu7s.
And there he farted until his fart was exhausted.

Yerí7 re m-sṗums ṫri7 wel re m-q̇wempép re sṗu7s.
And he farted on until his fart was exhausted.

Ta7 ṫri7 k sxweyt.s nu7 k w7ec.
Those people that were there didn't die.

Lucky es ta7es k sxwayt.s re qelmúcw.
It was lucky that the people didn't die.

W7ec-ske pyin k sṫiqwst.ses re qelmúcw.
If that had happened, it would still be killing people today.

Nobody can see *splont* now.

Nexéll-ske k sṗentém me7 qwtséqes.
They would be afraid to be farted on [sprayed] and die.

Continuing on, Tllí7sa and his brothers encounter Tsqelcwxenéllts̓e ("one who devours men with her teeth") on the opposite side of Pavilion Creek. She is a woman who kills men with her *vagina dentata* ("toothed vagina"). Tllí7sa has "connection" with her, placing his arrow-flaker across the inside of her vagina, and then invites his brothers to join in. "Henceforth, you shall be an ordinary woman, and hereafter men will have connection, and women's vaginae will not bite or kill them" (Teit 1909, 650). After another encounter with a supernatural people-eating rabbit at Kweléwt near the mouth of Pavilion Creek, they ascend north along the ridge high above the Fraser River to High Bar Canyon, where they see the pubescent girl, Chipmunk, who is on her spirit guardian quest on the opposite side of the river. She is dancing, and they stop to watch her, trying to transform her into stone, a process referred to as *ṫult*, but are unable to do so. In the end, the three brothers become transformed into stone on the east bank of the canyon, with Tllí7sa standing behind his brothers, as does Chipmunk on the west bank. The rock columns that represent the brothers are called Sṫulemí7 ("frozen into stone forever"), whereas the column that represents Chipmunk – apparently with "red paint" on her face and a stripe down her back – is called Ṫul-lltiṁt ("dressed up frozen into stone"). The nephew, who was behind them, could not be frozen and survived to tell about it.

Louisa Basil remembered the end of their story as follows:

Way far in the start, way far, right through, three guys.

Long ago, long, long ago, there were three guys altogether.

That's the one make the rocks [Cwíẇesqen] *(see above)*.

The first ones to go all over, I guess.

One neḱu7 ṫucw llépens re kí7ces.
One of them forget about their mother.

2.5 | Storyteller Louisa Basil of Sṫuxtéws (Bonaparte), 1986. Louisa, whose husband's paternal grandfather was Chief Basil Dick (Basil David), remembered parts of the Tllí7sa epic that took place near Cache Creek, Hat Creek, the Chasm, Marble Canyon, and the end of the journey at High Bar Canyon.

Ta7 k slexéy̓ectem te cécu7tem.
He wasn't told about the young maiden.

Núne mé7e ri7 ne Qwiqwíyqwiyt, ṫri7 ́ṫhé7en.
Over at a place called Blue All Over somewhere.

Sts7emét.stem ucw Qwiqwíyqwiyt.
It's called Blue All Over.

Stém̓i cwem ri7 re skewst.s ne séme7, ṫkllúne ne Kíkste7 le tmicws, tselxemstéc?
What do they call that again in English, over there [invisible] in Kíkste7's[26] country, do you know?

Ctenú7-enke mé7e ri7 k w7écwes yerí7 re núnxwenxw étsxemes.
It was apparently over there on the other side of the river where a girl was training for power.

Ell ye7éne … ye7éne tkellés te tutuwíwt, cten7élye w7écwes, yerí7 re slléqelcs.
And these … three young men, they sat down on this side of the river.

Yerí7 ri7 the last one re slexéy̓ems, ptékwllentem.
That's the last one they tell, the last story they tell about them.

Yerí7 re spíqwens re núnxwenxw te w7ec.
They were watching the young woman.

Yerí7 re stsyems, Yerí7 re sqwetséts.s es t̓úlentem ts̓ilem yem.
They sat there, then they started to be like frozen into stone, you know.

Yerí7 re s … Ell well ye7éne tseq̓wgwúg̓wi, xéxe7enke yem.
And then … The youngest one of the boys must have been powerful.

Yerí7 re stqwlútmens ell yeríne7.
He told about the others.

Yerí7 re m-sk̓ult.s re núnxwenxw te scenc.
And the young woman was turned into stone.

Yerí7 ell well newí7s m-k̓ult te scenc.
And they were also turned to stone.

Re m-tsyem-ekwe ri7 tek tkellélem.
They say that there they sat, all three of them.

Re núnxwenxw w7ec re nek̓westsútes te ts̓eléwt.
The girl is standing by herself.

W7ec-enke k t̓éyes yem ri7.
She was apparently Indian-dancing.

Yerí7 wel xwexwéyt pyin w7ec re t̓éyet.
That's why we all Indian-dance nowadays.[27]

Louisa Basil's version places this episode on the Fraser River at or near Qwiqwíyqwiyt ("blue all over"), also known as "Bob's Village," situated on the east side of the Fraser River about 14 kilometres below Big Bar Creek. The area, still known as Qwiqwíyqwiyt by High Bar elder Rose Haller, is nowadays known as High Bar Canyon. As we see, according to Louisa Basil's account, Q̓welálst survived to tell about it, with only the three brothers being turned into stone, as is reflected in the three stone pillars at the site. Qwiqwíyqwiyt

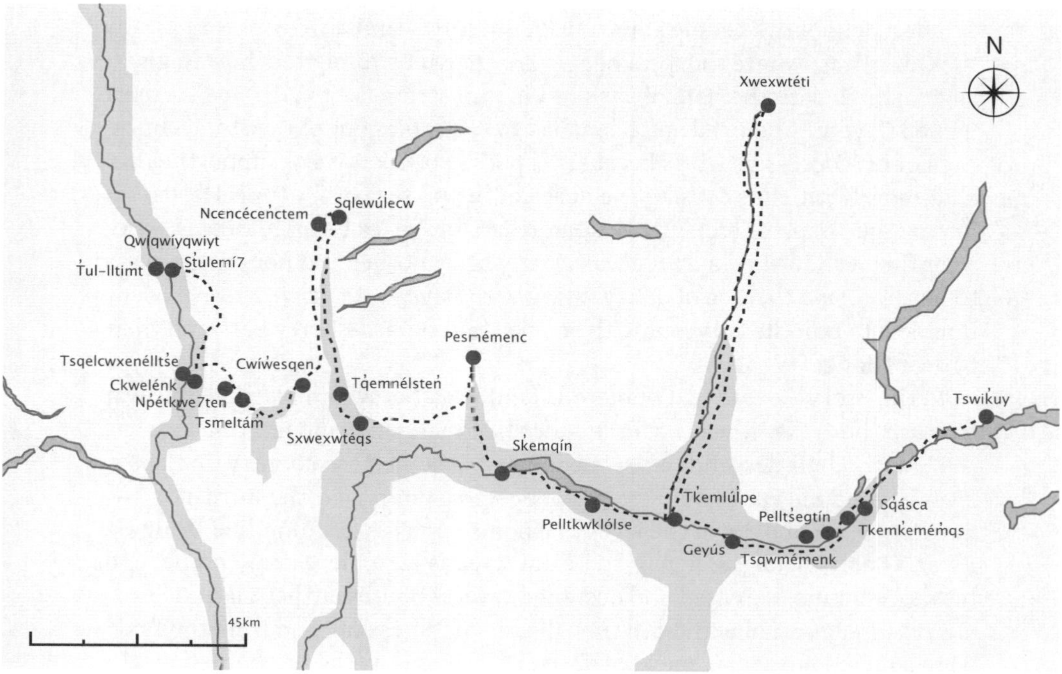

2.6 | Tllí7sa and his brothers' travels.

is also regarded as a boundary marker between the Secwépemc and St'at'imc (Dawson 1891, 5). Among the "transformers," Tllí7sa and his brothers are thus the group that can be characterized as being most closely associated with the boundaries and places of the Secwépemc.

A further group of coastal transformers, the A'tse'mEl', appear in Lillooet (St'at'imc) stories. They represent a group of Coast Salish people, some of whom came up through the Squamish area, whereas others among them came into the Interior by way of Harrison Lake. They were four brothers, accompanied by their sister and another transformer called Qaix (Mink) (Teit 1912b). They travelled from the Fraser River near Chehalis up Harrison River to Harrison Lake, entered the Lower Lillooet River, and continued halfway up Lillooet Lake. They taught the people who already lived there how to weave nets from *spéts̓en* (Indian hemp) and how to catch salmon with dip-nets, cut it up, boil it with hot rocks in baskets, and save the salmon bones, which they returned to the water in order to ensure the return of the salmon. Like the Qoa'qLqaL, they also showed the local Interior people how to give birth without the man having to cut the baby out of his wife and thus kill her. It is said that after leaving their skills behind, these transformers returned to Squamish country.

The origin of the people at Cácl̓ep (Fountain) is similar to the story of the Qoa'qLqaL, where the local people are shown by foreigners how to give vaginal birth with the help of various kinds of string (Teit 1912b, 368). A man named Coyote, who lived at Cácl̓ep, had to cut babies out of the stomachs of each of his successive wives because he had no other ways of supporting his children's birth, thus causing the death of the mother every time. He was visited by the "Nspatse'tceit" (Nlaka'pamuxcin for "black bear children"), who, after they vanquished a dangerous grizzly bear mother and her cubs, are said to have become the Qoa'qLqaL. Visiting with Coyote at Cácl̓ep, they showed him how to pull the baby out with strings, first of bird-cherry bark and then of deer thong.

In this story, Coyote had numerous family, half of whom married Shuswap from up the Fraser River, with the other half marrying Lillooet from across the Fraser. Their descendants settled in and occupied the country up the river beyond Kala'ut (Kweléwt) (see above) to a point near the mouth of Pavilion Creek and down the river to a point opposite the mouth of Bridge River. There, one of them, named Keaxu's, made an underground house, and his descendants increased and occupied several houses at that place. They always intermarried with both the Lillooet and Shuswap, and from the first were a mixed people, as they are at the present day, being neither Lillooet nor Shuswap but part of both and speaking both languages. Their ancestor, Coyote, is supposed to have been a Shuswap or at least to have spoken that language. They are nicknamed "Coyote people" by other Lillooet and used to impersonate their ancestors at dances. The Fountain people are called X'a'xalEpamux (Cácl̓epemc) or the more ancient name Laxo'xoamux.[28]

In short, the above story connects the Upper St'at'imc (Fraser River Lillooet), who in turn had been visited by the Coastal A'tse'mEl', to the Secwépemc and Nlaka'pamux. This story starts at Peténi Valley (Botanie Valley) near Lytton and moves on past Spences Bridge, and then some distance past Spences Bridge, the brothers first begin to encounter "Coyote" and his family, or the "Coyote people," thus joining Secwepemcúl̓ecw.

In conclusion, as we consider ancient *stsptekwll* (oral traditions) in light of scientific investigations into the history of climate, ecology, human occupation, and the spread of Indigenous languages throughout the Interior of British Columbia, we see interesting converging lines of evidence between scientific data and the information contained in *stsptekwll*. Paleoecological information shows that throughout the past 11,000 years, as the area now defined as Secwepemcúl̓ecw became inhabitable, environments and weather conditions were by no means stable but underwent drastic and sometimes sudden changes. The archaeological record throws light on how the ancestors of the Secwépemc adapted to these changing conditions and eventually developed the way of life still lived and known in some respects by contemporary Secwépemc, who learned it from their own elders born in the 1800s.

Parallel to the journeys of foreign transformers from the coast who encountered Interior transformers, linguistic research about the origin and dispersal of languages within the Salish language family strongly suggests that Salish was brought into the Interior by immigrants from the coast, perhaps about 5,000 years ago, a process that led to a new language, Proto–Interior Salish, out of which developed the seven Interior Salish languages of today as Interior Salish speakers further dispersed in a southeast direction from the original point of contact with ancient Coast Salish in the Thompson River area. As the oral traditions put it, the coastal immigrants travelled up the Fraser, along Harrison and Anderson Lakes, and through the Squamish area into the Interior, thus interacting with the "Coyote people" who had already lived there for several thousand years. As archaeologists have shown, there was a period of at least 500 years when Interior and coastal technologies and toolkits existed side by side, eventually merging into the Plateau Pithouse Tradition, with increasingly effective resource-gathering technologies, including large-scale salmon harvesting. In striking parallels and in many converging lines of evidence, ancient *stsptekwll* and paleoecological, genetic, archaeological, and linguistic data all speak to a fascinating and varied ancient history that marked the coming-into-being of the Secwépemc as a people and of Secwepemcúl̓ecw with its resources, places, and landmarks that continue to remind us of that ancient past.

Yerí7 re Stsq̓ey̓s-kucw | Ancient Stories as Deeds to the Land and as Ancient Law

The historical dimension associated with Secwépemc stories is but one small aspect of our *stsptekwll* (ancient stories). Our Secwépemc *stsptékwle* or *tellqel̓múcw* (ancestors)[29] left us a legacy of experience and knowledge handed down through countless generations that, if we connect the dots meticulously, provides the moral and spiritual foundation of our society and the *stsq̓ey̓* (laws) that show us how to act toward one another and with respect for all the living beings on the land that give us life.

Secwépemc *stsptekwll* – here alternately termed "ancient stories" or "oral traditions" – have for countless generations given Secwépemc and other Interior peoples "equipment for living"; they show by example how to behave and how not to behave, as well as illustrating the social, moral, and natural consequences of past ancestors' actions. They remind the present generation of the names and history of places throughout Secwépemc territory, which are in turn connected to rock paintings and to rock formations where past people were "frozen" into stone. The past actions depicted in the *stsptekwll*, manifest in the connection between stories, place names, and features in the landscape, anchor experience to the land as collective memories and represent Secwépemc *deeds* to the land by documenting how the ancestors of the Secwépemc obtained recognized ownership of the land. Moreover, they connect the Secwépemc as a people to essential social norms and values, providing social, moral, and political lessons for the present and the future. They provide the charter for the social institutions of the Secwépemc nation. In that sense, they represent Secwépemc law.

Secwépemc elders of the past summed up the ancient narratives about the adventures of Sk̓elép (Coyote), about outsiders coming in and insiders travelling out and thereby creating the landmarks and boundaries of Secwepemcúl̓ecw, and about taming the creatures within, creating cultural innovation, and establishing *stsq̓ey̓s-kucw* (rules of conduct).

As Ron Ignace (2008, 90) remembers,

> I heard my elders talk about the word *stsq̓ey̓* in my youth. As I understand it, "*re7 stsq̓ey̓-emp*" means "your (plural) rights." I heard the way they phrased sentences, talking about *stsq̓ey̓* in relation to our rights – "*stsq̓ey̓ ne7élye te sw7ec*" – "the right you have to be here (in a place)"; "*re stsq̓ey̓ yerí7 re swestéc*" – "your right to own that"; "*stsq̓eyúl̓ecw re Secwepemcúl̓ecw* – "the land is marked where your rights are, where your boundaries are." I heard these phrases when I was young. As my elders said, and I paraphrase, "The trouble is that most younger people today don't understand, let alone speak our language, so they do not know the origins and meaning of this word."
>
> When paper came along, your rights were put on paper, so nowadays people think the word *stsq̓ey̓* just means "paper." That's how, in Secwépemc dictionaries, you find the meanings of *stsq̓ey̓* as "paper." Our ancestors knew that marking things commemorates events as what is handed down, as the law. Then they saw white people being fixated on papers as guaranteeing their rights – as papers that showed someone's [fee simple] right to land; as the rights guaranteed by written-down legal codes. *Yerí7 re stsq̓ey̓s-kucw*, "our markings/writings/what is stated/what are our rights," took on a new, adapted meaning, however still reflective of old ways: It encompasses what is marked, what is written, and thus what is the collective *right* of our people, hence it signifies Secwépemc *law*. (Emphasis in original)

Thus, in the connection between ancient stories that inscribe the law on the land and the Secwépemc people's rights as an Aboriginal people, the notion of *stsq̓ey̓* plays a crucial role. Past Secwépemc elders and ancestors called rock paintings or pictographs *stsq̓ey̓*, saying, "*yerí7 re stsq̓ey̓s*" ("it is written or marked") and "*yerí7 re stsq̓iy̓ém̓s le q̓7es te k̓wséltktens*" ("this is the writing/how it was marked by our long ago relatives"). In situating Secwépemc laws on the land, *sq̓eyúlecw* means to "mark the land" in the way that the Secwépemc ancestors marked the landscape through their actions, gave names to places, and thus claimed the land as Secwepemcúlecw, fixing its boundaries. In a modern sense, *tsq̓eyúlecw* can therfore be defined as the ways that, through stories and landmarks, the confines and boundaries of the Secwépemc homeland are demarcated and remembered. More than mere remembrance, however, *tsq̓eyúlecw* refers to the ways that the Secwépemc people of the past and into the present expressed their collective *rights* to land by way of the deeds and markings of previous ancestors. As Indigenous legal *deeds* or rights to ownership of Secwepemcúlecw, these markings are manifest in the place names, rock formations, and rock paintings as inscriptions that commemorate past events and, most of all, in the stories that bear testimony to these events. Thus the notion of *yerí7 re stsq̓ey̓s-kucw* entails a historical sequence and multiple dimensions of how Secwépemc people took possession of Secwepemcúlecw and established the laws that governed life in Secwepemcúlecw and with outsiders: the ancient markings in rock formations that attest to events that happened there are referred to as *yerí7 re stsq̓ey̓s* ("it is written"), having been laid down by Sk̓elép, Qweq̓wíle or Q̓wle7íl̓t, Tllí7sa, and others as they "fixed the land" and left their marks of this undertaking for future generations.

Louisa Basil referred to the legacy of the ancient pictographs and rock formations as "*yerí7 re stsq̓éy̓ctels le q̓7es te qelmúcw*" ("this is what the people long time ago marked/wrote for us"), saying at the same time, "*yerí7 re stsq̓ey̓s*" ("that [means] it's our law"). In short, Secwépemc elders taught us that the ancient markings on the land, supported by the stories connected to them, symbolize Secwépemc "law" as Skelép and the transformers laid it out on the land. The fundamental laws of the Secwépemc immanent in the *stsptekwll* include what we can term the law of sovereignty of each nation – or "supreme authority," as the Interior chiefs called it in their "Memorial to Sir Wilfrid Laurier" (Chiefs of the Shuswap, Okanagan, and Couteau Tribes 1910) – which mandated respect for boundaries between nations.

The *stsptekwll* of Sk̓elép and the deeds of the transformers can be interpreted as laying down three fundamental laws for the Secwépemc: the Secwépemc law of sovereignty within Secwepemcúlecw, the law that defines rights of access and rights to resources, and the law that acts as an impetus to make treaties among nations. These were enacted by Sk̓elép when he warned the Wutémtkemc ("downriver people") transformers, or Qoa'qLqaL, that they had come into his country and not to interfere with his work, although he allowed them to trespass and offered them friendship, reminding them that he could *t̓úlem*, or transform them into stone (see p. 43). The Qoa'qLqaL, in turn, were only able to transform his tracks into stone, thus marking this encounter on the land (Teit 1912a, 316).

In the landscape, at least in the undisturbed places visible to this day, we can see and read the signs of the Secwépemc ancestors taking possession of this land, vanquishing the "cannibals," or people eaters, that existed, and making Secwepemcúl̓ecw accessible to the generations after them. We have seen above how the places that are named in the transformer stories of Tllí7sa, Q̓wle7il̓t, and others gave names to the land, took possession of the land for future generations of Secwépemc, and created the laws that should govern future generations.

Re Tsúwet.s re Sk̓elép | Moral Lessons of the Trickster

As we have seen, besides the transformers, it was Sk̓elép – also called Senxwéxwlecw by the Símpcwemc on the North Thompson River and by the Eastern Secwépemc – who initially marked the land and gave laws through his actions. Sk̓elép stories, as we have noted above, are historically situated in the very ancient past; however, as living *trickster* stories, their attraction to present generations is their timelessness. In our ancestors' minds, they connected the past to the present and future. It was Senk̓éwelc (Old One), the Creator, whose stories were all but forgotten even by 1900 (Teit 1909, 623), who had sent Sk̓elép to finish his work. Old One himself had presented people with a few gifts that separated humans from animals, among them being the *sq̓ílye* (sweat lodge), which represents the Secwépemc ancient institution that bestowed humanity, separating humans from animals and all other creatures. After his deeds in Secwepemcúl̓ecw, Sk̓elép then disappeared toward the East, although people waited for his return. More than once, as the first white explorers came into Secwépemc territory, they at least contemplated the thought that he had arrived again.

Sk̓elép stories link the past with the present, continuing to engage our emotions, notions of contradictions, and ambiguities of life through multiple layers of reality and experience. Last but not least, the stories play with the transcending of social and moral boundaries, like life and death, sex and incest, male and female, good and bad, and many other opposites. Sk̓elép shows us the consequences of behaviour that makes a person a nuisance to our community, what we call *yéwyut*, which is someone who defies the norms of acceptable social behaviour by choosing to act against them, someone who knows boundaries yet is ignorant in the sense of not recognizing them. We find a similar concept in Canadian common law: "The two types of nuisance are private nuisance and public nuisance. A private nuisance is a civil wrong; it is the unreasonable, unwarranted, or unlawful use of one's property in a manner that substantially interferes with the enjoyment or use of another individual's property, without an actual trespass or physical invasion to the land. A public nuisance is a criminal wrong; it is an act or omission that obstructs, damages, or inconveniences the rights of the community."[30]

Teit's (1909) book on the Shuswap provides, in his own summarized English words, two cycles of Coyote stories. One, as he notes, was recorded from Sxwéy̓lecken (see chapter 1) of Dog Creek and Big Bar. The second set of Coyote stories was recorded from Sisyúlecw of the North Thompson Secwépemc (Símpcwemc). His English baptismal name was George Louis. He was the father of Mathilde Fortier, Ida William's mother's father. In addition to the above, our memory of Sk̓elép stories survives in what appear as isolated episodes or fragments that linguist Aert Kuipers recorded from David Johnson of Esk̓ét, Lilly Harry of Xgét̓tem (Dog Creek), and Mike Paul of Athalmer (Kinbasket). Bouchard and Kennedy (1979) recorded several episodes from Ike Willard in the early 1970s. In the mid-1980s, Marianne Ignace and Mona Jules recorded from Ida William in Secwepemctsín the same cycle of Sk̓elép stories that Sisyúlecw had told to Teit some eighty years earlier. Although short and reflecting a compact narrative style, Ida William's stories include all of the main episodes of the Sk̓elép cycle that her grandfather told to Teit. One additional story of Coyote and a fox was told by Chris Donald, another Simpcw elder. The episodes of Sk̓elép stories shared between the Símpcwemc (North Thompson), Tk̓emlúpsemc (Kamloops/Skeetchestn people), Sxqéltkemc (Chase people), and Xgét̓temc (Dog Creek people) match closely. These stories involve the following:[31]

Sk̓elép and his son, Kellélst ("three stones"). Coyote lusts for his son's two wives, dupes him into ascending into the Upper World, and then takes his wives, only to have Kellélst eventually return.

Sk̓elép and his cousin, Xgwélemc (Fox). Their story is about the hazards of vanity and envy.

Sk̓elép and his hosts. Their story is about the hazards of trying to copy other people's powers (see pp. 63–72)

Sk̓elép and the children of the four species of grouse: fool-hen/willow grouse, spruce grouse, sharp-tailed grouse, and blue grouse. Coyote glues the grouse children's eyes shut with pitch, but their mothers, each startled into flight according to the natural characteristics of her species, cause Coyote to fall off the cliffs where he walks as he leaves. This story also plays on the physical characteristics, behaviour, and habitat of the four species of grouse.

Sk̓elép guides the Salmon up the Thompson River (see pp. 36–8), followed by Sk̓elép and the Salmon in a bungled host story that deals with disrespect for a living resource and with the consequences of offending a living resource (see pp. 203–4).

Sk̓elép "juggles his eyes." Like the previous story, this one also tells of ecological relations and the characteristics of biological species, including trees, and it imparts knowledge about biogeoclimatic zones and their tree indicator species, as well as about species of grouse in connection to various plants (see pp. 149–52).

Sk̓elép and the girls. In the Nlaka'pamux and Syilx version, this story provides the reason why there are no salmon in the Similkameen River, due to a misunderstanding between Sk̓elép and some young girls he encounters by the river. He addresses them in Nlaka'pamuxcin, asking whether they want some of his penis. As they are across the river, and know only Syilxcen, the Okanagan language, they misunderstand him to mean sheep or ram, and they decline.

Sk̓elép and Grizzly Bear. In a contest between Grizzly Bear and Coyote, the latter excels with his superior ecological knowledge of bird species and determines the number of months in a year and the alternation of day and night. This *stsptekwll* also masterfully addresses the power of negotiation. In another episode, Coyote embarrasses Grizzly Bear by making her fall into her excrement and by taking her stored provisions on the pretext that summer has arrived in mid-winter.

Further stories and episodes in some of the above stories involve Coyote tricking other creatures to get food, sex, or both.

With their moral messages, irreverent humour, and questioning of social order, Coyote stories were adapted by our ancestors to deal with concerns in a changing world. In the late nineteenth and early twentieth centuries, Teit was tasked with recording "myths" rather than contemporary memories of Interior Salish peoples. However, some stories that he recorded in the 1910s, likely during his work in the political movement among Interior Aboriginal leaders, show how Interior peoples (including the leadership) adapted Coyote stories to provide commentary on changing times and to express political satire:

> Coyote once met Old One or Great Chief. Old One said, "You have used your excrements as a counselor for a very long time. However, this method is very inconvenient. Each time you desire advice, you have to defecate. Also there is danger of your excrements getting cold. I will give you a paper. Carry it with you. When you need advice, consult it." Coyote carried it in his hands for several days, but he did not like to carry anything in his hands. One day when he was defecating, or otherwise engaged, he laid it down and forgot about it. Several days later he wanted advice about something and found he did not have the paper. He went back a long way and searched for it, but could not find it. Perhaps the wind had blown it into some hidden place. Coyote had to resort to consulting his excrements again for advice.
>
> This is how Coyote lost the paper. If Coyote had not lost it, the Indians would now know writing, and the whites would not have had the opportunity to obtain written language. It was because of the foolishness of Coyote. (Teit 1937, 173)

We can, on one level, treat this story as a comment about orality versus literacy or about how our ancestors experienced the reliance on the written word by part of settler society in the late 1900s, but even more perceived it as representing the political power of settler society to make written laws that disavowed Secwépemc ownership of lands and decision making. Okanagan storyteller Harry Robinson (2005) tells a story of Coyote travelling to England to meet the king, thus transposing Coyote's satirical deeds into the concerns of Aboriginal rights and the Indian Rights Movement of the early twentieth century.

However, we think there is more to the message of Sk̓elép's loss of the printed page and subsequent reliance on excrement. In reverting to being a scatologist, he also resumes his practical scatological studies, using the excrement left behind by animals to figure out their identity, diet, health or disease, path of coming and going, or pace of travel. The loss of paper thus has Sk̓elép re-engaging with his senses, as opposed to relying on "advice" from the printed page, whose authority is removed from firsthand experience.[32]

Each story of Coyote and other animals teaches us lessons about important values in our society, such as respect for one another and accountability to one another, which we call reciprocal accountability; reciprocal relations among relatives; knowledge of our land and the environment; ecological relations among species; and respect for our natural resources. Most importantly, these stories give us the moral foundation of our society, connected to ancient law, thus giving us direction for our future as peoples, communities, and a nation. As the story about Coyote and his hosts reminds us, we must not try to copy our ways from others but must be true to our own way of doing things.

Tsxlítentem re Sk̓elép / Coyote and His Hosts

Told by Ronald E. Ignace and transcribed and translated by Marianne Ignace and Ronald E. Ignace

W7ec-ekwe re cwesétes re Sk̓elép, ne7élye ne tmicw-kt.
Coyote was travelling here in our land, it is said.

T̓7ek-ekwe, m-yews-ekwe re st7éyens re Skem̓cís.
As he was walking along, they say, he met Grizzly Bear.

Skllíken̓stemt,[33] *yerí7 re skwest.s.*
Back-Fat-Man was his [Grizzly Bear's] name.

M-ts7écwes re Skem̓cís, es wikt.s ye7éne xéxe7 te sqélemcw, xexé7 yem re Sk̓elép.
Grizzly Bear was happy to see this smart man, this powerful Coyote.

M-yews re tsxlítens es ullcws ne tsitcws es metés.
So he invited Coyote to his house to feed him.

M-tsuns re Sk̓elép, "Ye7éne me7 wiktc ri7, ne7éne ren tsútswet."
And he told Coyote, "This, what you will see, is my way."

"Ta7 ews ri7 k stét̓ipentsemc, me7 xéne-k e xwtsi̓lcucw te7 stét̓ipentsemc!"
"Don't copy me, you will get hurt by copying me, when you try it out!"

M-yews re spúsens ne7éne re ck̓míkeṅs re sem7é7ems yem re skeṁcís.
And then Grizzly rubbed his wife's back.

M-ník̓mes nerí7 te spellélleľtcw, oh! Le7 te tsiqw te ts̓i7, le7 te skllíken yem.
And he cut off a thick slice of it, oh! It was nice red meat, nice back fat.

M-yews re sq̓welsentés ne7éne ne syéqwlltems, m-metcít.s ri7 re Sk̓elép.
Then he roasted this in his fire, and he fed this to Coyote.

M-pespúsenses re ck̓míkeṅs cú7tsem, yerí7 re Skeṁcís re sem7é7ms re ck̓míkeṅs.
Then he rubbed her back again, his wife's back.

M-yews yerí7 re sta7es ts̓ílems ks kénems nerí7.
And it was as good as ever.

Oh! M-yews re sptínesems yem re Sk̓elép,
Oh! And then Coyote thought,

"Ah! Xexéx7e-ken yerí7! Xwent ri7 ken sxíxlem!"
"Ah! I am smarter! I can do that too!"

M-yews ri7 re tsxlítens re Sklllikeṅstemt es tsnest.s ne newí7s re tsitcws es metés.
And then he invited Sklllikeṅstemt to come to his house so he could feed him.

Ṫri7 m-yéqwllmes. Xyum re syéqwlltems.
He made fire. He made a big fire.

M-tsut es q̓welsentés yem re ck̓míkeṅs es metés re Skeṁcís.
He wanted to roast his back to feed Grizzly.

K̓émell tsukw ṫucw m-c7etscíkeṅem!
But instead, he scorched his back!

Oh! K̓ist re stcwelṡ yem. M-welépes ye7éne re ṫémens.
Oh! What a bad smell. He scorched his fur.

Téke, wel ta7ks le7s re sts̓exténs pyin re ṫémen ne ck̓míkeṅs re Sk̓elép.

That's why the fur on Coyote's back does not look nice.

Oh, m-tsúntmes te Skem̓cís, "Téke, xentéke mé7e."
And he was told by Grizzly, "See, I told you."

M-tsúntsen, "Ta7ews ks tét̓ipentsemc, me7 xéne-k, téke, xenstsút-k."
I told you, "Don't copy me, or you will get hurt, you will hurt yourself."

M-yews ri7 re scwesét.s cú7tsem re Skelép.
And then Coyote travelled again.

M-tskítsenses re sqélemcw, ne7éne te sqlélten te sqélemcw.
And he met a man, a salmon person.

Styú7qenstim̓t ri7 re skwest.s.
His name was Fish-Oil-Man.

Oh, m-téytes, m-tsútes, "Tsxwénte, tsxwénte, yerí7 re stsécwmíntsen."
And being hungry, he was told, "Come here, come here, I welcome you."

"Tsxwénte, me7 metsín!"
"Come here, I'll feed you!"

M-kwens re Styú7qenstim̓t ye7éne re tseck̓púpcws.
Fish-Oil-Man took his bowl.

Nerí7 ne tqeltks ne7éne re syeqwlltems m-tentés yem.
And he put it on top of his fire.

M-tntéses re kelcs nerí7 yem, re stextétxmens, oh!
And he put his hands, his fins, on top of it, oh!

M-tsímtes ye7éne re styu7qíns yem re sqlélten, m-ct7ék̓es re tseck̓púpcw.
The salmon's oil was melting, and it filled the bowl.

M-yews re tsut.s es kectés re Sk̓elép. "Tsxwénte, íllente ye7éne!"
And he wanted to give this to Coyote. "Come here, eat this!"

Oh, xetéqs re stsk̓émsens re Sk̓elép, k̓ém̓ell m- tsúntem, "Í̓llente! Le7 yerí7!"
Oh, at first Coyote didn't want it, but he was told again, "Eat it! It's good!"

M-xwts̓ilcmens es íllens, m-yews re s7íllens. Oh! Le7 yerí7!
He started to eat it, and he ate it. Oh! It was good!

Oh, m-tsúntem re Sk̓elép, "Me7 wiktc ne7éne ri7 ren tsútswet."
Coyote was told [by Fish-Oil-Man], "You see, this here is my power."

"Ta7 ews ks tét̓ipentsemc. Me7 xenstsút t̓ri7 e xílmucw!"
"Don't copy me. You will hurt yourself if you do this!"

K̓émell re Sk̓elép m-ptínesem, "Me7 tsútsenmecten ri7 xexéx7e-ken yerí7!"
But Coyote thought, "I will show him that I am more powerful!"

M-yews re stsxlítens yem re Styú7qenstim̓t es tsnes ne tsitcws yem es metés.
He then invited Fish-Oil-Man to come to his house to feed him.

Oh! M-yéqwlltem, xyum re syéqwlltems re Sk̓elép.
He made fire. Coyote made a big fire.

M-tntés re xyum te tseck̓púpcw ne tqeltks re t7ikw.
He put a big bowl on top of the fire.

M-yews re stntés neri7 re kelcs, es tsímens re styu7qín.
And then he put his hands on there, to melt some fat.

Oh, t̓ucw re m-welpékstes.
And all he did was burn his hands.

Telrí7 yem wel re Sk̓elép pyin m-tsqesq̓úscn̓es ell re-m-qwiq̓wícen̓es pyin e m-wíktcwes.
That's why Coyote now has burnt and black paws, as you can see nowadays.

M-yews re sleq̓wépems re Sk̓elép, "Képkept yem re sxenstsútst!"
And Coyote hollered, "I'm sore, I hurt myself!"

M-yews re stsúntem, "Téke mé7e, kénem mé7e re stét̓ipentsemc?"
And he was told, "See, I told you, why did you copy me?"

"Téke, wel re7 m-xenstsút, m-xéne-k!"
"See, you hurt yourself, you're hurt!"

Huu yem, qwetséts re Sk̓elép ne7éne m-t7éyentmes te Sqlew̓stímt,
And Coyote left, and then he met Beaver-Man,

ye7éne te sqlew̓ te xexé7 te sqélemcw.
this wise man who is a beaver.

Oh, m-ts7écwes re Sqlew̓stímt es wíkt.s.
And Beaver was happy to see him.

M-tsúnses, "Tsxwénte, ts7úllcwce nen tsitstcw, me7 metsín, yerí7 re sxyemstsín."
He told him, "Come here, come into my house, I'll feed you, I will honour you."

M-yews re s7ullcws ne7éne re Sk̓elép.
And Sk̓elép entered there.

M-kwénses re st7iq̓welq̓wtens yem re Sqlew̓stímt,
And Beaver took the scraper,

m-yews re snest.s ne7éne ne tsrep, ne s7eytsqwllp te tsrep,
and he went to that tree, the ponderosa pine,

m-yews re sk̓úlems te st7iq̓welq̓w.
and he made some cambium.

Cw7it re m-tsclems ne tseck̓úpcw, wel re m-tskwénses.
There was lots that he got in his bowl.

M-yews re skectés re Sk̓elép es íllens.
And he gave it to Coyote to eat.

Oh! Tsk̓ems ne sxetéqs re Sk̓elép, "Ta7 ri7 k sxwexwistéten es í7llen re sextsétṡi!"
At first Coyote, refusing it, said, "I don't like to eat sticks!"

"Ta7 ri7 k sextṡéys, le7 ri7 te stsillen, íllente!" tsúntem te sqlew̓.
"It's not sticks, it's good food, eat it!" is what Beaver said to him.

Oh, m-íllenses, wenécwem yé-enke k sle7s! Oh, q̓wempstéses re Sk̓elép.
Oh, and he ate it, and it was really good! Coyote ate it all up.

M-tsuns, "Le7 ri7 re m-smetsétsemc! Me7 metsín ell es xyemstsín!"
He told him, "It's good that you fed me. I'll feed you, too, to honour you!"

M-yews ri7 re skítsentmes ye7éne te tsk̓éwelc te sqélemcw, Sqlew̓stímt
And this is how that old fellow, Beaver, arrived at his place.

M-kwéctses te ct7íq̓welq̓wtens, m-néses ne7éne. M-t7iq̓welq̓wctmes.
He [Coyote] took his sap-scraper, and he went on. He went sap-scraping for him.

Ta7 ks ḱúlems cwem te st7íq̓welq̓w.
But he didn't make any cambium.

Ḱémell tskwens, t7íq̓welq̓wens re ṕeléńs re mulc.
All he got was the [outer bark] of cotton wood.

M-tsútes es metés ye7éne re sqleẃ!
That's what he wanted to feed Beaver!

M-tspíqwenses ye7éne re sqleẃ, "Stéḿi k stsútsentsemc es metsétsemc?"
Beaver looked at this stuff and asked, "What are you trying to feed me?"

"Ta7 ri7 wes k sts7íllenstnes!"
"I can't eat that stuff!"

Ah! Tsúntsen, "Ta7ews k stét̓ipentsemc, ta7 ri7 k stselxemstéc stéḿi ke7 sw7ec!"
Ah! I told you, "Don't copy me, you don't know what you are doing!"

M-qwetsétses re Sqleẃstímt. M-llwélenses re Sḱelép.
Beaver-Man took off. He left Coyote behind.

M-t̓7ek-ekwe cuẏtsem re Sḱelép.
Then Coyote went along his way once again.

M-yews yeŕi7 re s7istks.
And then it became wintertime.

M-t7éyentmes te Tślostíḿt.
He was met by Kingfisher-Man.

Tśłos-ekwe ye7éne te tsḱéwelc te sqélemcw.
This old man was Kingfisher, they say.

Oh, ts7ecw re Tśłostiḿt es t7éyens ye7éne te xexé7 te sqélemcw.
Oh, Kingfisher-Man was glad to meet this powerful man.

M-tsuns, "Tsxwénte, me7 metsín, me7 xyemstsín! Ts7úllcwe nen c7í7stkteń!"
He told him, "Come here, I'll feed you, I'll honour you! Come into my underground house!"

Re Tśłostíḿt, m-mútes ne c7ístkteńs ne q̓wemtsíns re tswec.
Kingfisher-Man lived in his underground house on the shore of the creek.

M-yews nerí7 re s7ullcws re Sk̓elép.
And Coyote went inside there.

M-tsúntmes te Ts̓lostím̓t, "Ne7élye, me7 wiktc ri7, ye7éne ren tsútswet."
He was told by Kingfisher-Man, "This, what you will see, is my way."

"Ta7ews tét̓i7pentsemc, me7 xéne-k, me7 xenstsút-k!"
"Don't copy me, you'll get hurt, you'll hurt yourself!"

Tq̓mútes ne7éne ne txelcenténs, ne tqeltks re c7ístkten̓s, núne re tq̓mútes.
He climbed to the top of his ladder, on top of his underground home, that's where he climbed.

M-ústes ne séwllkwe, oh, m-k̓wnémes te ts̓olleníw̓t. Mmm, le7 re sts̓exténs.
He dove into the water, oh, and he brought back a rainbow trout. Mmm, it looked nice.

W7ec re welík̓tes ne segwsés yem ye7éne swewll te m-kwenwén̓ses.
It glistened in the sun, this fish that he took.

M-q̓welsentéses, m-metéses re Sk̓elép.
He roasted it and fed it to Coyote.

M-yews re stsuns cú7tsem, "Téke, ye7éne ri7 ren tsútswet, ta7ews k stét̓i7pentsemc."
And he told him again, "Look, this is my way, don't copy me."

"Me7 xéne-k yem e xwts̓ílcucw t̓ucw te7s xílem."
"You'll get hurt if you do that."

K̓émell re Sk̓elép, m-ptínesem, "Ah! Xexéx7e-ken, me7 wikt.s ri7!"
But Coyote, he thought, "Ah! I'm smarter, he'll see!"

M-yews re sxlítens re Ts̓lostím̓t es tsrxes ne tsitcws es metés yem.
And he invited Kingfisher-Man to come to his house, so he could feed him.

Oh, m-kítscwes re Ts̓lostím̓t ne tsitcws re Sk̓elép, ne ck̓elpéllcws.
And Kingfisher-Man arrived at Coyote's house, at his coyote den.

Cpupéw̓tsnmes. "Ts7úllcwe!" m-tsúntmes.
He knocked on the door. "Come in!" he was told.

M-yews re sts7ullcws nerí7. Ts7ullcw-ekwe nerí7 es metéms te Sk̓elép.

And he entered. They say that Kingfisher-Man entered to be fed by Coyote.

M-tsúntem te Sk̓elép, "Me7 metsín!"
He was told by Coyote, "I'll feed you!"

Téke, re Sk̓elép m-tq̓emtqín̓em, m-teq̓mútes ne stxelqín̓s re tsitcw.
And Coyote climbed up to the roof of his house.

M-ústes ne tswec. M-ústes ne tspetúkws re scúyent.
And he dove into the creek. He dove through a hole in the ice.

Re Tsl̓ostím̓t, m-tsk̓elém, m-tsk̓elmíns yem es meméms te Sk̓elép.
Kingfisher-Man, he waited, he waited for Coyote to feed him.

Oh, m-estk̓ey wel re m-tsut, "Héqen me7 tcúcsmen."
He waited, until he said, "Maybe I'll go look for him."

M-néses t̓kllu7 es tcúsmens re Sk̓elép, m-kénmes-enke yem re Sk̓elép.
And he went to look for Coyote, to see what had happened to Coyote.

M-tcúsmens. Oh, stp̓en̓llexwes ne7éne te Sk̓elép re tsitcws, re sk̓lepéllcws yem.
He went looking for him. Oh, he stepped out of Coyote's house, out of his coyote den.

M-tcúsmens re úq̓wis.
He went looking for his brother.

Oh! Wikt.s ne7éne tsxleq. Tsxleq-enke ne7éne ne tspetúkw te scuyent.
Oh! He saw that he was stuck. He was apparently stuck in the ice-hole.

M-xqwetsqpétkus!
He had drowned!

Re Tsl̓ostim̓t m-néses neri7, m-tsúnses,
Kingfisher-Man went there, he told him,

"Tsútsen ye7éne, 'Ta7ews ks t̓ét̓i7pentsemc, me7 xenstsút-k!' Téke, pyin me7 xqwetsqpétkwe-k!"
"I told you, 'Don't copy me, you'll get hurt!' See, now you are going to drown!"

Xetéqs yerí7 re spetínesmens re Tsl̓ostím̓t es melcúpsens ne tspetúkw te scúyent.
At first Kingfisher-Man thought he'd kick him into the ice-hole.

K̓émell ta7 k sxillt.s yem. M-tskúmst.ses re Sk̓elép.
But he didn't. He pulled Coyote out.

Yerí7 re skectés cú7tsem te swumécs.
And he gave him back his life.

"Téke yem, me7 kectsín cú7tsem te7 swuméc. M-tsúntsen, 'Ta7ews k stét̓i7pentsemc.'"
"See, I'll give you back your life. I told you, 'Don't copy me.'"

"Téke, wel xqwetsqpétk-ucw, k̓émell me7 kectsín cú7tsem te7 swuméc."
"See, you drowned in the ice-hole, but I'm giving you your life back."

"Ta7ews ks t̓éypenc k swet re tsúwet.s."
"Don't copy other people's ways "

"Tsukw re newí7 re7 tsúwet yewske ri7 re swestéc."
"It's your own ways that you must hang on to."

"E ta7wes t̓ri7 ke7 sxílem, me7 xéne-k, me7 xenstsút-k."
"If you don't do it that way, you'll get hurt, you will hurt yourself."

Téke, pyin re qelmúcw w7ec re t̓éy̓penst.ses re semséme7.
See, nowadays our [Aboriginal] people are copying the white people.

T̓ri7 re m-xéne-kt, m-xenstsút-kt, m-xenstwécw-kt yem.
That way, we have got hurt, we have hurt ourselves, and we have hurt one another even.

Llépentem re xqweltén-kt, llépentem re stsptekwll-kt,
We have forgotten our language, we have forgotten our stories,

t̓ri7 xwexwéyt te stem re tk̓wenm7íp.e-kt.
all the ways of governing ourselves.

Téke, wel qwenqwént-kt pyin.
See, we have become pitiful.

M-kwéctels te tmicws re semséme7.
The white people have taken our land from us.

Ye-ekwe ri7 k spelq̓ílcmentem ye7éne le q̓7es te qelmúcw re tsúwet.s,
That's why we must return to our own ancestors' ways,

es cúỷtsem es letwílc-kt es cwetwílc-kt.
so that we can heal ourselves and once again become numerous.

Ne7élye es xenwéṅtem es ḱúlentem re semséme7 es súcwentels ne tmicw-kt.
And so that we can get the white people to recognize our existence on our land.

In this chapter, we have connected the emergence of the Secwépemc as a people to the environmental history of the Interior by drawing on evidence from the travels of "transformers" who tamed the land and made it inhabitable for future generations. We have also considered the implications that the transformer travels and deeds have for the Indigenous laws and protocols of past, present, and future generations of Secwépemc, lest we forget the stories that encode them. The next chapter considers the 10,000-year history of the Secwépemc in Secwepemcúl̓ecw from the point of view of an archaeologist. Although written autonomously and independently of chapter 2, we see converging lines of evidence between what our analysis of oral histories shows and what archaeological research tells us.

3 Re Tsúwet.s le Q̓7es te Stet̓ex7éms-kucw

What Archaeology Tells Us about the Initial Peopling and Life of Secwepemcúl̓ecw

MIKE K. ROUSSEAU AND MARIANNE IGNACE

In chapter 2, we presented what has been called an "internalist archaeology" (Yellowhorn 2006) perspective about the ancient Secwépemc past, focusing on *stsptekwll* as expressing the Indigenous voice about historical events that can be contextualized and triangulated with ethnographic data, traditional knowledge from elders, and data from Western sciences like historical linguistics, archaeology, paleoecology, and geology. We also showed how in their multiple layers, *stsptekwll* account for past and continuing cultural value systems and practices, for ecological knowledge and relations, and for Secwépemc *stsq̓ey̓* (laws).

This chapter takes a more detailed look at what archaeological information tells us about Secwépemc history, thus providing a different kind of narrative about the past. Archaeology is the study of past human activity based on material evidence that can be recovered. By employing a wide range of scientific analyses, archaeologists are able to reconstruct past lives in sometimes amazing detail, enabling us to learn about past living arrangements and settlement patterns, modes of resource harvesting, tool manufacture and use, nutrition and dietary patterns, and genetic profiles of groups and genetic relations between groups. By observing patterns in the geographic distribution of artifact styles, and then situating those patterns in time through a variety of dating methods, archaeologists are able to develop historical sequences of human occupation and patterns of human activity.

However, archaeology does not come without baggage. Over the past century or more, Indigenous peoples in North America and elsewhere have had a troubled relationship with archaeology, as it has comprised grave robbery and made Indigenous peoples' appropriated cultural property the object of a collecting enterprise in the creation of Western empire. It resulted in Indigenous peoples' dispossession of the sacred and secular tangible legacies of their past at the same time that dispossession of lands and of cultural and political autonomy unfolded (see Deloria 1995). Like anthropology, throughout much of the twentieth century, the archaeological enterprise separated Indigenous peoples from their pasts and long ago ancestors and made "aboriginal historical identity contingent on a European [intellectual and physical] presence" (Yellowhorn 2006, 198) in the process of colonization and oppression.[1] The history of archaeology on Secwépemc lands is part of the way Western powers asserted their colonial hegemony. However, recent years have seen a shift in attitude and participation among Secwépemc people through a combination of the assertion of heritage stewardship by First Nations communities, legal cases, and the training of Aboriginal people in archaeological methods and interpretation both facilitated by their communities and pursued individually.

Archaeology in Secwepemcúl̓ecw: From the Collecting Efforts of the Jesup North Pacific Expedition to Indigenous Archaeology

The beginnings of archaeology in Secwépemc territory are tied to the Jesup North Pacific Expedition. In 1897, not long after he engaged James Teit to carry out research in Secwépemc communities, Franz Boas hired a young man, twenty-five-year-old Harlan Smith, to conduct archaeological work for the expedition. Its goal was to gather detailed information about the livelihood, social organization, mythologies, material cultures, physical anthropology, and languages of the peoples of northwestern North America and northeast Asia in order to determine origins, migration routes, and historical relationships. Part of the work was thus to recover cultural artifacts and human remains, to gather "anthropometric" data through measurements of height, skull size and shape, and so on, and to conduct photography as ethnographic illustration.[2] Harlan Smith arrived at Lytton in 1897, accompanied by Boas, and met up with Teit. He subsequently travelled to Tk̓emlúps (Kamloops), where, as arranged by Teit, the Oblate missionary Father Jean-Marie-Raphaël Le Jeune was his conduit to Chief Louis and to the Secwépemc community. Smith (1897) reported, "Indians here object to my taking bones away – They are friendly & will allow me to dig graves & take all but the bones. I have seen [Indian] Agent and Indians are on the fence. We hope they will change their minds & allow bones to go to N.Y. for study not for Joke as they fear." After Father Le Jeune at a big council meeting supported Smith's request to take "a few bones" in order to "teach" people in New York about the Secwépemc, and after Smith showed the council photographs of the Northwest Coast Hall of the American Museum of Natural History, which displayed the "wonderful works of the Indians" (Smith 1898, 101–2), he was allowed to work at a burial mound and at village sites on the Kamloops Indian Reserve, resulting in a substantial collection of human remains and artifacts, which he sent to the museum. Smith returned in the spring of 1898 and 1899 and collected further materials and human remains that had been exposed by the wind at the same sites. He also took a good number of photographs of people and dwellings.

3.1 | Chief Louis of Tk̓emlúps (Kamloops), photographed by Harlan I. Smith, 1897.

In getting Chief Louis's consent for anthropometric work – which involved being cast in plaster, measured, and photographed – Boas admitted using a ruse, telling the chief that Queen Victoria had requested a photograph and bust of him, in recognition of his being a great chief. Of course, for Chief Louis and other Interior chiefs, the relationship with the Crown symbolized unextinguished title and land rights, as the chiefs would state in their memorials and petitions a few years later (see chapter 13). At a lecture to the British Association for the Advancement of Science in early 1897 Boas noted,

> I am afraid that, in trying to coax him to submit to the operation, I gave him a rather wrong impression in regard to the character of our work … I told him that the Queen desired to see the great chief of the Shuswap, and since she was too old to visit him, I had been requested to take his portrait and bring it to her, and that at the same time she had asked me to present him with his own bust, which he was to place in his house, so that his people might understand how important a man he was. This argument removed all his objections, and, after he had consented, there was of course no difficulty in getting just as many men of his tribe as I pleased.[3]

Different from what he was promised, Chief Louis's anthropometric photographs were subsequently shown as anonymous "types" of Secwépemc males, although a 1997 exhibit at the American Museum of Natural History restored his name.[4] We here restore his purpose and the purpose of the chiefs who sat for portraits at the same time: clearly, they consciously did so in the context of their struggle for Secwépemc rights and title.

Smith's work left an ambivalent legacy. As Catherine Carlson (2005, 166) notes, "despite Smith's careful negotiations, he took several risks in removing skeletons without permission, or removing more than he had been authorized to." The human remains taken by Smith, let alone the grave goods he deposited at the American Museum of Natural History, have not yet been repatriated, and knowledge of the nature of his work has contributed to the perception among Secwépemc individuals and communities that they have been subjected to such archaeological endeavours for the sake of colonizers' collections. Nonetheless, Smith's publication on the "Archaeology of the Thompson River Region" (1900) has left a legacy that has allowed current generations a glimpse at the kinds of artifacts and materials used by their ancestors for burials and grave goods, including lithics and utilitarian objects, as well as objects of spiritual value, such as nephrite, copper, and copper clay. Smith's work continues to be used as a valuable source by contemporary researchers and as a source for ethnographic and archaeological reports that document Secwépemc land use and occupancy. It is time for reconciliation and healing by repatriating the human remains that were collected at that time, let alone the grave goods that were taken from these long ago deceased people, and by repossessing these legacies, although this endeavour will not be easy.[5]

Following Smith's work, no significant archaeological research was carried out until the 1960s, when, at the request of the Adams Lake and Neskonlith Bands, David Sanger (1968a) conducted a salvage excavation at a burial mound near Chase as it was being looted by souvenir seekers. Academic archaeological work involving excavation and analysis intensified throughout the 1970s and 1980s (Pokotylo, Binkley, and Curtin 1987; Pokotylo and Froese 1983; Sanger 1970; Stryd 1972), and these projects provided increasing detail and refinement of the long history of occupation of the Interior Plateau as a whole, as well as particular places within Secwepemcúl̓ecw. With new dating methods becoming available, such as carbon-14 analysis, it was shown that the Interior Plateau was occupied many thousands of years earlier than Smith and Boas had suspected. Archaeological researchers established and refined a chronology of cultural periods, phases, and horizons, establishing a narrative that informs the second part of this chapter (Richards and Rousseau 1987; Rousseau 2004; Rousseau and Richards 1985; Sanger 1967; Stryd and Rousseau 1996). Knowledge from the extensive excavations at Keatley Creek (Hayden 1997, 2000a, 2000b) and at Bridge River (A.M. Prentiss and Kuijt 2012; W. Prentiss and Kuijt 2004) led to the formulation of theoretical ideas about complex hunter-gatherers and social stratification on the Interior Plateau. Additionally, by the 1980s, a good deal of the focus of archaeology shifted away from academic research to archaeological impact assessments in light of resource extraction (e.g., logging and mining) and land development permits, with court decisions having determined the Crown's obligations regarding potential Aboriginal title and rights, as well as the duty to consult First Nations in whose traditional territories such developments occurred.[6] First Nations communities and their organizations increasingly articulated their concerns about cultural heritage resources as part of the wider issue of Aboriginal title and rights in light of the ongoing destruction of traditional lands and resources, as well as in relation to the enactment of Indigenous heritage stewardship.[7]

Together, these factors have contributed to the growth of what George Nicholas (2008; Nicholas, Jules Bonneau, and Westfall 2017) calls "Indigenous archaeology":

> Over the last twenty years substantial change has occurred in archaeology, resulting in a broadening of the discipline to include greater input from, and recognition of, Aboriginal interests and values. As a result of critiques both from outside and from within the discipline, a new flavor of archaeology has emerged that goes far in addressing some of the issues raised by Indigenous peoples. "Indigenous archaeology" brings together elements of Aboriginal and Western ways of knowing the past, but also addresses concerns about the process of archaeology and its products, benefits, and goals. (Nicholas n.d., 8)

Nicholas notes the importance and "transformative practice" of archaeology training programs with, for, and by Aboriginal peoples and communities in the articulation and unfolding of Indigenous archaeology. Notably, the archaeology program and field school that was operated in partnership between Simon Fraser University and the Secwepemc Cultural Education Society of the Kamloops Indian Band, which he led for twenty years,[8] greatly contributed to decolonizing archaeology and to providing training and credentials in archaeology to dozens of Secwépemc people and Aboriginal peoples from surrounding groups. As Nicholas (2008, 1660) states, "What has slowly emerged is an archaeology that is more representative of – and relevant to – Indigenous peoples. This has been achieved not just through theoretical discourse amongst archaeologists, but primarily by the increased participation of First Nations individuals and communities in archaeological projects and other aspects of cultural heritage management services to the communities."

In sum, our understanding of the ancestral Secwépemc has expanded substantially in the past forty years. This has been the result of the large number and wide variety of archaeology projects that have taken place on the Interior Plateau and specifically in Secwepemcúlecw, many of which are the result of initiatives in cultural resource management led or co-led by First Nations communities or initiated by First Nations themselves. Results of academic and applied investigations, as detailed in what follows, have provided much insight into the lives of the ancestors of the Secwépemc people who are now conducting and co-conducting archaeological research. Although such investigations began without the active participation of the Secwépemc community and continued in that fashion well into the 1970s – despite involving the committed interest among Secwépemc leaders to protect the physical and spiritual integrity of burial sites (see E. Rousseau and M.K. Rousseau 1978; and Sanger 1968a) – they have since involved the active lead and participation of trained Secwépemc community members and bands' cultural resource departments, although much more capacity building needs to be done.

What follows is a detailed account of the initial peopling and human occupancy of what became Secwepemcúl̓ecw over the past 10,000 years expressed as an archaeologist's narrative. It maintains the autonomy of Mike K. Rousseau's archaeological analysis, but through joint reading, rereading, and editing of how things are explained, we became comfortable with each other's language, respecting each other's kinds and sources of knowledge. The narrative of this chapter is based on data obtained by archaeological methods, but within the scope of this book, we see this account as being in dialogue with the overall objective of providing a Secwépemc perspective on Secwépemc history and the unfolding of Secwépemc occupation and land use, on cultural practices and the belief systems that sustain them, and on the articulation of Secwépemc laws on the land.

Emergent Secwépemc Lifeways and Their Interpretation

The many beautiful and diverse river systems and their adjacent upland regions comprising Secwépemc traditional territory on the Canadian Plateau contain thousands of archaeological sites spanning the past 12,000 years or so (see figs 6 and 7, colour section). Its considerable ecological and geographic diversity is due to dynamic forces of glaciation and deglaciation, numerous lakes and rivers of all sizes, seasonal prevailing winds, mountain ranges and rain shadows, and a striking ability to support a very wide variety and abundance of plants and animals in all environmental niches and altitudes. This great abundance and variety of natural resources permitted the Indigenous people who began living in this land likely some 10,000 years ago to survive and thrive through many millennia, eventually developing a series of unique cultural patterns over the past 4,500 years, defined by contemporary archaeologists as associated with "complex hunter-gatherers" (W. Prentiss and Kujit 2004).

The account presented here is based mostly on Mike K. Rousseau's experiences working as an archaeologist on the Canadian Plateau over the past forty years, as well as on close consideration of data shared and provided by many other archaeologists, First Nations communities, universities, museums, the BC Archaeology Branch, and the general public. Several summary books and articles on Canadian Plateau prehistory have been written over the past twenty years, and the reader is referred to these sources for greater detail, supporting data, and references to published articles and reports (R.L. Carlson and Magne 2008; A.M. Prentiss and Kuijt 2012; W. Prentiss and Kuijt 2004; Richards and Rousseau 1987; Rousseau 1993, 2004, 2008; Stryd and Rousseau 1996).

A good number of detailed studies involving intensive surveys and excavations have been undertaken over the past fifty years in the Shuswap, South Thompson, Thompson, and mid-Fraser River drainages and adjacent highlands, and these studies have provided a good amount of information about the past 6,500 years or so of human occupation. By contrast, the North Thompson River, Cariboo, and southwest Chilcotin regions are much less known archaeologically, but there have been a few detailed studies in these regions that add to our current knowledge and understanding of the sequence of human occupational history presented below (for a summary, see Pokotylo and Mitchell 1998; see also Cybulski et al. 2007; and I.R. Wilson, Twohig, and Dahlstrom 1998).

Early Environments and First Peoples

To reiterate from chapter 2, by about 13,000 years ago, most glacial ice had melted in south-central British Columbia, although some valley bottoms contained residual decaying ice, and large glacial lakes formed by impounded meltwater existed from deglaciation up to around 10,500 years ago. These lakes were very cold and devoid of any significant aquatic life. The landscape at that time was rocky, bleak, and raw, with strong, bitterly cold winds blowing relentlessly over vast, treeless, rocky wastelands supporting only sparse grasses and shrubs. Eventually, by 12,000 years ago, grasslands and plant and tree communities had expanded and diversified, attracting and maintaining sparse populations of small animals and birds, as well as solitary and herding migratory herbivores such as bison, antelope, elk, sheep, moose, and deer. These large animals provided basic sustenance for humans and other predatory animals. Upland "plateau" areas were dotted with thousands of small, shallow meltwater lakes that warmed in summer, sustaining aquatic plants, migratory birds, and small animals.

About 11,000 to 10,500 years ago, the climate started to become somewhat warmer and drier, with large expansive grasslands and forests beginning to support an array of edible plants and animals. By this time, most large glacial lakes formerly occupying several main valley bottoms had drained, and rapid extensive river downcutting had begun, carving hundreds of valleys and forming major extensive river terraces along their sides. Upland lakes were still common, but many of them drained and shrank with increasing warmth. By 10,500 years ago, a favourable and moderately diverse environmental stage was set for commencement of sustained human occupation everywhere in south-central British Columbia.

Although scientists have much to learn about the time, routes, and circumstances of the Indigenous population of the North American continent, it appears that several immigration episodes involving small numbers of eastward-moving culturally diverse people from Asia had entered the Pacific Northwest by around 13,500 years ago, when glacial ice began to melt. Some came in boats along the south coast of the Bering Land Bridge, which connected North America and Russia, and then southward along the coast of the Alaska Panhandle and west coast of British Columbia. Others migrated eastward on foot across Beringia and then southward through the "ice-free corridor" east of the Rocky Mountains in pursuit of more abundant game, edible plants, and warmer climate (Dixon 1999; Matson and Coupland 1995). These First Peoples must have been extremely hardy, but lifespans must have been short, and mortality rates would have been high from having to cope with sparse resources and extreme environmental conditions, although the very arrival and survival of these First Peoples attests to their successful adaptation to changing environments and to their effective resource-gathering skills.

Despite the current lack of excavated and solidly dated archaeological evidence for any occupations dating before 8,500 years ago on the Canadian Plateau, there is general consensus among many archaeologists that initial human occupation likely began sometime around 11,500 to 11,000 years ago, when some plants and animals were reasonably well established. The following description of the First Peoples' lifeways is based partly on data extrapolated from archaeology conducted in adjacent regions and partly on some speculation and conjecture on the part of Mike K. Rousseau.

In south-central British Columbia, the earliest peoples to enter the area were primarily big-game hunters who targeted large mammals, but smaller animals such as rabbits, birds, and rodents were also taken during their travels as opportunity presented. When possible, this predominantly meat diet was supplemented by gathering patchy and sparsely distributed edible shrubby plants, and occasionally low numbers of fish may have been taken where possible along shallow streams or lakeshores. Small, highly mobile extended-family groups of up to twenty people were the basic social unit, with only one or two such groups occupying any given major valley system. Their small short-term camps were established in valley side, mid-altitude, and upland settings beside streams, ponds, marshes, lakes, or large rock shelters. These early peoples typically left faint trace evidence of their presence. With a low population density and living in small family groups, they stayed only very briefly at most residential camps, wasted very little, and carried much

3.2 | An exceptionally large rock shelter in the upper mid-Fraser River region, 1990. Although relatively rare, large rock shelters like this one were frequented 11,000 to 7,000 years ago. Some contain significant quantities of intact cultural deposits, but only a few small rock shelters in Secwépemc territory have been excavated. Pictographs are commonly found on rock shelter ceilings (inset).

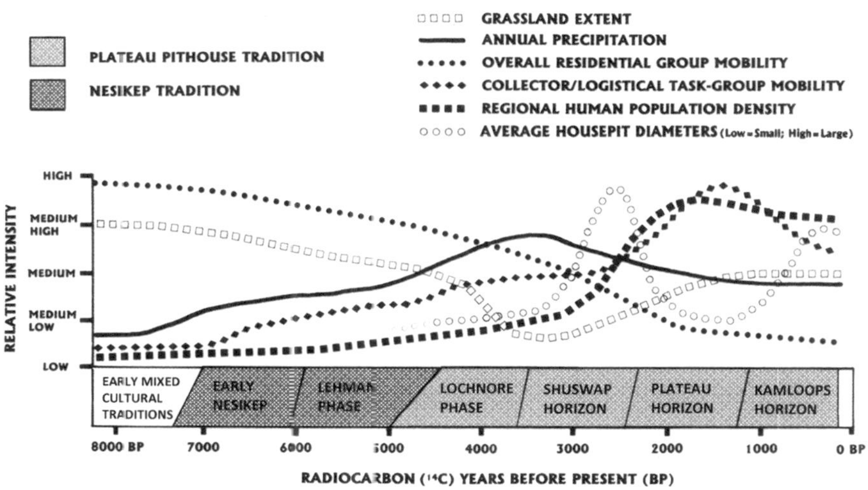

3.3 | Relative intensity and magnitude of climatic events and conditions, environments, general human subsistence behaviours, average pithouse sizes, and regional population densities over the past 8,000 years on the Interior Plateau.

of what they needed to survive while participating in a very demanding and highly mobile way of life.

Basic toolkits likely included thrusting spears and atlatls (large dart- and spear-throwing devices), large cores (cobbles and pebbles from which flakes are struck), simple chipped-stone (lithic) tools made from "flakes" struck from cores, discarded "waste flakes" not used for any purpose, chopper-like tools made from large elliptical cobbles, and simple perishable implements, handles, and projectile tips made from wood, bone, and antler. Various forms of large chipped-stone "bifaces," made from large thin flakes by chipping their outline on both faces/sides of the flake, were also part of the toolkit.

Evidence for Early Cultural Traditions in Secwépemc Territory

Evidence for people belonging to early cultural traditions is currently restricted to museum and private collections, conisting of an assortment of very distinctive formed bifaces (spear points and/or knives formed by removing small flakes from both sides of a large flake) that functioned as spear and atlatl-dart projectile points and as knives. These bifaces are stylistically and technically similar to those found and well documented in adjacent culture areas dated to between 11,500 and 8,000 years ago, and many functioned as both thrusting spear tips and knives used to process salmon and meat, but they were also used in a wide array of everyday tasks where cutting organic materials was required.

South-central British Columbia is adjacent to, and contiguous with, markedly different culture areas with their own unique culture histories, as reported by archaeologists. Because following the glacial melting there were no major geographic barriers or impediments to human travel, Secwépemc territory was easily accessible through many major and minor valley systems that linked directly with northern British Columbia, with the Kutenai region and Northern Plains to the east, with the Columbia Plateau to the south in Washington State, and with the Northwest Coast of British Columbia via the Fraser and Chilcotin River Valleys. Since the Canadian Plateau is completely surrounded by these areas, early groups of people participating in different cultural systems surely ventured and lingered there. There are currently four distinct early cultural traditions that have been identified and defined for the Pacific Northwest (R.L. Carlson and Magne 2008). There is artifactual evidence for all of them being represented in Secwépemc territory, although sites containing occupations solidly dated to before 8,500 years ago have never been subjected to any detailed excavations.

Large chipped-stone bifaces attributable to the Western Post-Clovis Tradition have been found and excavated in many areas of the Pacific Northwest dated to between 11,000 and 9,500 years ago but not yet in south-central British Columbia. However, three large triangular bifaces noted in collections

3.4 | Large bifacially flaked spearpoints/knives from the Shuswap Lake and Kamloops areas: (a–d) large points that are formally consistent with triangular bifaces of the Western Post-Clovis Tradition found elsewhere in the Pacific Northwest and dated to between 11,000 and 9,500 years ago; (e–j) large stemmed bifaces in museum and private collections that are similar to those found in sites belonging to the Early Intermontane Stemmed-Point Tradition, which dates to between 11,000 or 10,500 and 9,000 years ago; (k–p) bifaces from museums and collections that have striking formal and technological similarities with Plano Tradition bifaces of the Northern Plains east of the Rocky Mountains, where they are found in occupations dated to between 9,500 and 8,000 years ago.

from the Shuswap Lake region donated to the Kamloops Museum exhibit some classic "Clovis point–like" formal design and technological characteristics (see fig. 3.4, items a, c, and d). A fourth smaller biface with similar attributes was recovered immediately above glacial gravels during hand-excavation of a sand pit on Quaaout Indian Reserve No. 1 east of Chase (Rousseau 2008) (see fig. 3.4, item b).

The Early Intermontane Stemmed-Point Tradition (11,000 or 10,500 to 9,000 years ago) is represented in several private and museum collections that contain large, well-made, lanceolate stemmed bifaces (see fig. 3.4, items e to j), which show similarities with early stemmed points found elsewhere in the Pacific Northwest. Some forms are very similar to classic Windust bifaces of the Lower Snake River Region in Washington State dated to between 10,000 and 9,500 years ago (Ames 1988; K.T. Carlson 1996; L.G. Davis and Schweger 2004). There is still unresolved debate between early period researchers as to whether the Early Intermontane Stemmed-Point Tradition was introduced a bit earlier than the Western Post-Clovis Tradition in the Pacific Northwest. I presently believe that it appeared sometime between 10,500 and 9,500 years ago, but future data may prove me wrong.

The Plano Tradition (9,500 to 8,000 years ago) people of the Northern Plains produced several kinds of well-made, very large, formally distinctive bifaces. It is a certainty that highly mobile hunters of the Plains to the east occasionally ventured into the Canadian Plateau via the North Thompson River Valley and via several passes through the Rocky and Monashee Mountains, as they continued to do in recent millennia and centuries (see chapter 6). Several museums and personal collections in southern British Columbia contain small numbers of well-made bifaces (see fig. 3.4, items k to p) with technological and formal similarity to those defined for this tradition on the Northern Plains dated to between 10,000 and 9,000 years ago.

Early occupations belonging to the Old Cordilleran Tradition, also called the Early Pebble Tool Tradition (9,000 to 6,000 years ago), have been identified and investigated in detail at many early archaeological sites in the Pacific Northwest. Although sites of this tradition have been provisionally identified on the Canadian Plateau, none have been studied in any detail. Items commonly made and used during this tradition include cobble/pebble choppers and large cores, edge-ground cobbles, medium-size and large simple, unmodified flake tools, lithic core-reduction waste flakes, and large leaf-shaped, lozenge-shaped, and elongate tear-shaped bifacial knives. Examples of the latter exist in some museum collections, and several specimens were found in the Dutch Lake locality in the North Thompson River Valley near Clearwater.

At present, the earliest direct excavated, dated, and confirmed evidence for human occupation is the postcranial (headless) skeletal remains of a human male found along Gore Creek in the South Thompson River Valley near Pritchard, mentioned in chapter 2. These ancestral remains are known to archaeologists as Gore Creek Man, and it appears this individual met an accidental death in a small ancient mudslide and eventually became exposed in the creek gully sometime in the mid-1900s. His remains were excavated and removed, but no associated artifacts were found. The skeleton was recovered beneath an unbroken layer of volcanic ash (tephra) that blanketed much of south-central British Columbia following the violent eruption of Mount

3.5 | Archaeological deposits in relation to Mazama tephra (6,700 years ago) and Mount St Helens "Y" tephra (3,200 years ago): (a) recovery location of Gore Creek Man, near Pritchard in the South Thompson River Valley, and two major volcanic ash/tephra deposits exposed in profile; (b) Scheidam Creek gully, near Kamloops, showing depths of volcanic ash/tephra deposits of (1) Mount St Helens "Y" and (2) Mount Mazama, with early cultural deposits present below the Mazama layer; (c) a typical section of eroding riverbank on the South Thompson River showing exposed cultural deposits and Mount St Helens "Y" volcanic ash/tephra between them.

Mazama in Oregon around 6,800 years ago. As previously noted, radiocarbon dating of a small portion of the skeleton itself provided an age of 8,340 years old, and isotope analysis indicated that he relied primarily on meat-derived protein. Salmon comprised only a small proportion (10 per cent) of this person's protein diet, indicating that sea-run salmon had not yet been realized as a major reliable food resource and/or that no technological system at that time provided an effective way to harvest them in any significant numbers.

From deglaciation to about 7,500 years ago, the admittedly scant archaeological evidence suggests that small groups of highly mobile people belonging to these early "peripheral" cultures – Pre-Clovis, Plano, Intermontane, and Old Cordilleran – ventured into what is now Secwépemc territory and decided to permanently reside there. There can be little doubt that these groups frequently encountered and interacted with each other during their many travels, resulting in the exchange of technologies, languages, and genetics. It is presently hard to know which of these early cultures had the most presence and/or influence at that time. An eventual melding of people participating in these early technological and cultural traditions resulted in the emergence of a unique cultural system that began sometime between 8,000 and 7,500 years ago, and it was fully developed and widespread over the majority of the Canadian Plateau by at least 7,000 years ago (see fig. 3.3).

Emergence and Persistence of the Nesikep Tradition (7,500 to 4,500 Years Ago)

After about 7,500 years ago, the Southern Interior of British Columbia continued to experience a relatively warm and dry climate, but there was a slow and steady trend toward decreasing annual temperatures and increasing annual precipitation that persisted until about 4,000 years ago. Expansive grasslands consisting of bunchgrass, blue wheat ryegrass, sagebrush, and prickly pear cactus covered many regions, as did a variety of edible root plants and berries at various altitudes. Small shallow lakes in upland areas once again formed in previously dry catchment basins, creating prime habitat for deer, elk, moose, and possibly antelope. By that time, salmon and other fish were well established in the Thompson, Fraser, and Columbia River systems, and a variety of smaller animals and game birds were abundant in all environmental contexts and at all altitudes, providing reliable sources of protein for highly mobile people of the Nesikep Tradition, who were very adept hunters and gatherers as well as part-time fishers.

The Nesikep Tradition was initially defined by David Sanger (1969, 1970), but its temporal duration has since been shortened, and its definitive characteristics have been redefined (Rousseau 2004, 2008; Stryd and Rousseau 1996). The Nesikep Tradition was a unique cultural system developed through the interaction of people who had already established themselves on the Interior Plateau, including in what became Secwépemc territory, with several very early Pacific Northwest cultural groups. It seems to have initially emerged and spread from either or both of the drainage regions of the mid-Fraser and Thompson Rivers, but a current lack of data does not allow this to be confidently inferred. For now, the Nesikep Tradition has been divided into the initial Early Nesikep Tradition (7,500 to 6,000 years ago) and the later Lehman Phase (6,000 to 4,500 years ago). Exact start and end dates for these cultural patterns may be revised based on future data.

Early Nesikep Tradition (7,500 to 6,000 Years Ago)

Early Nesikep people's residential base camps were typically small, were occupied for relatively short periods (e.g., from days to several weeks), and were often established along valley sides at or near river-creek confluences in sandy areas protected from winds. Many sites have excellent vantage over the surrounding area and are near extinct or extant sources of drinking water close to game-rich localities and near salmon-fishing locations at tributaries. Field camps were small, numerous, and short-term, and they were found in all ecological niches and altitudes but were especially common on raised terraces beside upland lakes and streams (see figs 6 and 7, colour section). As the triangulation of archaeological, linguistic, and oral history data presented in chapter 2 suggests, it is very likely that these people spoke a non-Salish language that evolved from a mix of early languages.

Regional human population densities during the Early Nesikep appear to have been relatively low, as most residential and food-processing sites of this age are small, as well as less common than those associated with later periods. No Early Nesikep dwelling depressions or floors have been identified in excavated sites, but during the more adverse winter months, small "brush huts" or lean-to-like shelters were probably constructed and occupied for short periods. Since they were not built over intentionally dug depressions, and their occupants usually left scant evidence behind, these dwellings are visually difficult to recognize in the field. During detailed excavations, they could easily be mistakenly identified as being just typical outdoor activity areas. Large rock shelters may also have been commonly occupied (see fig. 3.2).

Excavated Early Nesikep lithic tool assemblages often include distinctive, well-made, medium-size and large lanceolate, corner-notched, barbed, and shouldered formed bifaces that served as both spear points and knives (see fig. 3.6, items a to h; and fig. 3.8); a high incidence of well-formed unifaces, notably tabular oval, circular, and horse-shoe-shaped scrapers (see fig. 3.7, items m to y); microblade technology (see fig. 3.7, items a to l); a variety of thin unformed unifaces and utilized flakes; antler wedges; ground rodent incisors; bone points and needles; and red ochre.

Most complete Early Nesikep bifaces are well made, relatively thin, and lanceolate in outline, they have straight or recurved lateral margins and thin lenticular cross-sections, and some have micro-serrated lateral edges. These bifaces display traits that are strikingly similar to those noted on early Plano Tradition biface forms of the Northern Plains. It may be that some technological aspects of the biface technology of the Early Nesikep Tradition were derived directly or indirectly from people participating in the Plano Tradition prior to 8,000 years ago. Early Nesikep bifaces have been located as "isolated finds" in almost every environmental niche and geological context and at almost all altitudes. Their distribution indicates high human mobility and frequent loss of spear or atlatl-dart projectile points during hunts. They were also regularly employed as knives to process meat and/or fish.

Early Nesikep people were avid users of microblades, which are small, thin, elongate blade flakes that were pressed from small specially prepared wedge-shaped cores (see fig. 3.7, items h to l). Microblade technology was in use on the Canadian Plateau by at least 8,500 years ago, and it may have been initially introduced as early as 9,000 or 10,000 years ago from coast regions

3.6 | Common biface forms of the Nesikep Tradition (7,500 to 4,500 years ago): (a–h) bifaces of the Early Nesikep Tradition (7,500 to 6,000 years ago) used as projectile points and knives; (i–t) complete and fragmented bifaces of the Lehman Phase (6,000 to 4,500 years ago) used mostly as knives, with narrow, deep, obliquely set notches being common on many specimens; (s) item reworked into an end scraper.

to the southwest and west (Kuzmin, Keates, and Shen 2007). Evidence for microblade production and use spans several thousand years, but it is absent from all occupations after 3,500 years ago. Microblades were commonly used by highly mobile groups in situations where extensive cutting and

3.7 | Microblade technology from occupations dated to between 7,000 and 3,500 years ago: (a–g) microblade cores; (h–l) microblades; (m–y) examples of typical tabular formed unifacial scraping tools commonly found in occupations dated to between 7,000 and 3,500 years ago. Microblade technology appeared on the Interior Plateau around 8,500 years ago and persisted until 3,500 years ago. Some scraping tools were used to scrape hides, and some were used to remove kidneys from salmon and other large fish.

processing of meat or fish were required, where there was a need to conserve good-quality stone and maximize its functional potential, and where sources of good-quality flakable stone were not locally available.

Excavated Early Nesikep animal bone assemblages are dominated by deer remains with lesser proportions of elk, salmon, steelhead, bird, and freshwater mussel (R.L. Carlson and Dalla Bona 1996; Rousseau 2004). Presumably, a variety of plant resources were consumed when seasonally available. Current data indicate that Early Nesikep people engaged in a subsistence and settlement strategy that consisted of basic hunting and moderate foraging, where animals and plants were taken either as they were encountered during times of mobility or within relatively short distances from residential base camps. Salmon and other fish were taken in small numbers when seasonally available. At this time, there is no direct evidence to suggest that salmon was a significant source of protein.

The violent eruption of Mount Mazama in Oregon around 6,700 years ago was a major catastrophic event that had immediate negative effects on humans, animals, and plants throughout the Canadian Plateau. Contemporary post-eruption studies show that plants, animals, and fish are immediately and severely negatively affected by ash fall (tephra), but subsequent periods of environmental recovery are relatively short. During the ash fall, Early Nesikep people and other large mammals would have experienced difficulty breathing, eye and nasal irritation, and intestinal inflammation. Many would have succumbed to starvation and/or ash-related respiratory complications. Salmon populations would have been impacted if the blast occurred during spawning runs or the early emergence of salmon fry. No doubt, the Mazama ashfall claimed many victims, but those who could leave the affected regions managed to survive in neighbouring areas, probably returning to their homelands months later when environmental conditions stabilized and began to improve.

A great deal remains to be learned about the Early Nesikep Tradition, and we desperately need radiocarbon dates and much more empirical data from several well-excavated components to determine its approximate start and end dates. Despite this presently poor understanding, it is clear that Early Nesikep people participated in a unique, highly mobile reliance on hunting, gathering, and fishing resources and on a settlement strategy that persisted for at least a millennium and possibly longer.

Lehman Phase (6,000 to 4,500 Years Ago)

Between 6,000 and 4,500 years ago, the climate on the Canadian Plateau was warmer and drier than today, with a slow general trend toward cooler and wetter conditions over that period (see fig. 3.3). Scant vegetation cover and strong winds resulted in deposition of thick layers of airborne silts on many valley bottoms and sides, particularly on the bottoms and sides of the South Thompson and Thompson River Valleys (see fig. 5, colour section). The rate of wind-blown sediment deposition appears to have been greatest from about

6,000 to 4,000 years ago, rapidly burying many occupation sites that were created during this time and preserving most or all bone and antler deposited at them. Other sites were deflated by dry winds, sometimes resulting in mixing of artifacts from different occupations on the same exposed ground surface, allowing for the rapid deterioration of organic materials and for the co-mingling of items that may originally have been separated by several hundred or even thousands of years.

Vast dry-adapted desert and grassland plant communities dominated major valley bottoms and expanded rapidly into the mid- and high-altitude areas of the Plateau. These habitats supported big herds of large grazing herbivores (notably elk and deer) and populations of smaller animals, providing ample sources of protein for small, highly mobile groups of adept hunters. Many small and shallow upland lakes that had expanded during the Early Nesikep Tradition shrank or dried completely, and larger lakes had lowered shoreline levels. Winters were short and mild, and during typical extremely hot summers, water volumes in many major river systems, such as in the Shuswap, Thompson, North Thompson, and South Thompson Valleys, were significantly reduced, and this may have negatively affected Thompson River salmon runs and populations during this time. However, these slower and warmer rivers supported an abundance of several species of freshwater mussels, which people regularly gathered and processed in large numbers.

People who lived during this time, termed Lehman Phase people, were direct descendants of Early Nesikep Tradition Interior Plateau residents, and as chapter 2 showed, they spoke the same non-Salish language fused during or before the Early Nesikep Tradition. This ethnic continuity is indicated by very clear similarities in several specific and unique behavioural and technological traits reflected in the general nature of basic lithic tool types, by the similarity in size and form of large bifacial projectile points and knives (see figs 3.6 and 3.8), and by the use of microblades at some sites. They also practised the same patterns of basic hunter-gatherer resource harvesting and settlement that characterized the Early Nesikep people, but they also included some seasonal salmon fishing. The transition from the Early Nesikep Tradition to the Lehman Phase appears to have been a gradual and relatively seamless process, but a few subtle differences do exist.

During the Lehman Phase, composite, notched, multipurpose knives (see fig. 3.6, items i to t) were common, whereas microblade manufacture and use declined. When compared with the Early Nesikep Tradition, Lehman Phase occupations often contain a slightly greater proportion of colourful, high-quality, easy-to-flake lithic materials obtained from a variety of quarry sources located within and beyond Secwépemc territory, indicating that these people travelled and traded within a large radius and would have had knowledge of resources within that radius. High-quality, flakeable lithic materials such as vitreous and fine-grained basalt and various silicate rocks from isolated upland quarry sources were in common use during the Lehman Phase. Many sites contain unmodified and unused medium-size and large flakes in high densities, indicating lithic raw materials were naturally abundant in many areas. Major sources of basalt and other silicates were known in the Arrowstone Creek, Cache Creek, Hat Creek, and Maiden Creek drainages (Rousseau 2015).

The low site density and small size of most Lehman Phase sites imply relatively low regional populations, but there are more known Lehman Phase occupations compared with the Early Nesikep Tradition, indicating slow and steady population growth during the Late Nesikep Tradition (see fig. 3.3). It also appears that during this time, relatively mobile extended-family groups consisting of twenty to thirty individuals were common, but regional populations rarely exceeded a few hundred people.

Most occupations represented at Lehman Phase sites are small, deeply buried, relatively short-term, and contain medium to high densities of lithic artifacts and waste flakes, bone, and freshwater mussel shell. Field camp and residential sites lie on terraces in protected settings along the sides of main river valleys, beside confluences of major creek and river valleys, and on extinct river channel terraces well above present river base levels. Many occupations belonging to the Lehman Phase have been exposed along terrace edges in the mid-Fraser and Thompson River regions. Mid-altitude and upland Lehman Phase sites are fairly common beside small lakes and streams, being the remains of short-term seasonal (May to September) field camps occupied by small groups of people. No dwelling structures have been identified or excavated, but again these people probably made shelters that they occupied during the cold season, much like their Early Nesikep ancestors.

Excavated Lehman Phase faunal (animal bone) assemblages show that a wide variety of animals were consumed, with an emphasis on hunting between about 6,000 and 5,000 years ago, elk and deer being preferentially targeted. After 5,000 years ago, typical diets shifted to include greater use of salmon, but there is currently no direct evidence for intensive salmon consumption or for attempts to dry and store it. Freshwater river mussels were collected and consumed along the Thompson and South Thompson River systems, where dense concentrations of hundreds of mussel shell "middens" are eroding out of riverbanks and railway cuts in many locations.

Plant resources were no doubt exploited regularly during seasonal resource-harvesting routines near base camps or while travelling to new camp locations. Mid-elevation and upland areas were frequented in spring to exploit spawning non-anadromous fish such as rainbow (or Kamloops) trout and suckers. Microblades are well suited to cleaning small fish, and their presence in many upland stream and lake contexts may be linked primarily to this activity.

The Transition from the Lehman Phase to the Lochnore Phase (5,000 to 4,500 Years Ago)

There can be little doubt that people at the end of the Lehman Phase (5,000 to 4,500 years ago) had direct and indirect contact with people and cultural systems of the south and central coast, as well as the Columbia Plateau in the south. When it comes to explaining causes for the transition from the Lehman Phase to the Lochnore Phase, I am a firm supporter of the "Coast Salish incursion model," which was initially proposed by Stephen Lawhead and Arnoud Stryd (1985). It offers that sometime around 5,000 years ago (or shortly afterward), small moderately mobile Coast Salish groups residing in the lower Fraser River and Fraser Canyon regions (and perhaps from the lower Columbia River region) travelled upstream and inland along major drainages during the warmer months of the year when salmon were plentiful in the Fraser and Thompson River drainage systems. Relying on simple but highly effective portable fishing technologies developed several centuries previously on the West Coast, these seasonally migratory Salish groups fished salmon in the lower mid-Fraser and lower Thompson River drainages from late spring to early fall. When cooler fall weather set in, these Salish groups returned to their permanent winter villages in the lower Fraser River region.[9]

By 4,700 years ago, these small groups of Coast Salish–speaking, fishing-dependent, riverine-adapted people began regularly spending winters in the mid-Fraser and Thompson River Valleys, establishing permanent residency. This was made possible by construction of small shallow pithouses, which were already in common use in the lower Fraser River region starting around 5,000 years ago (Hanson 1973) (see figs 3.9, 3.10, and 3.11). Over several generations, these pioneering Salish "immigrants" established a widespread permanent presence along major salmon-bearing rivers on the Canadian Plateau. Episodes of direct physical interaction between these riverine-adapted people and long-time resident hunting-gathering Lehman Phase people between about 5,000 and 4,500 years ago resulted in a lengthy period of mutual acculturation (melding of cultures). This process involved exchanges of genes, technological traits, knowledge about effective and successful resource-harvesting practices, and the beginnings of a language that was similar to, but distinct from, the Coast Salish dialect. We saw in chapter 2 how data from historical linguistics as well as Secwépemc and Nlaka'pamux oral histories support this view. In archaeological terms, we speak of this period of Coast Salish immigration and cultural contact as the Lochnore Phase.

Archaeological data suggest that during that 500 years (or so) of coexistence and cultural merging, both groups targeted different primary protein sources, salmon being consumed by migratory early Lochnore Phase people and terrestrial game by the late Lehman Phase people, so intergroup

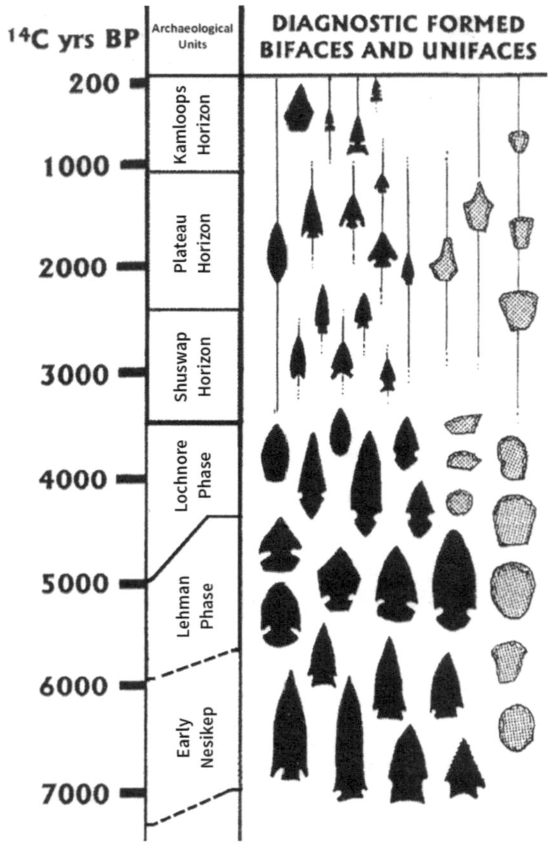

3.8 | Common forms of temporally diagnostic bifaces and unifaces (spears, knives, and scrapers) found in sites dated to the past 7,000 years in Secwépemc territory on the Interior Plateau.

competition or physical conflicts pertaining to matters of resource harvesting may have been relatively rare. The melding and mutual acculturation of these two "parent" groups was a relatively slow transitional process lasting several hundred years, and by 4,500 years ago, it appears that the basic Lochnore Phase cultural pattern proved to be the more dominant successful strategy for coping with the onset of wetter and cooler environmental conditions at about that time. The eventual result was a more "homogenous" basic Lochnore Phase cultural pattern that prevailed from 4,500 to 3,500 years ago. By 4,500 years ago, the merger of these two culture groups appears to have been relatively complete, marking the beginning of the Plateau Pithouse Tradition.

Emergence and Persistence of the Plateau Pithouse Tradition (4,500 to 200 Years Ago)

The Plateau Pithouse Tradition of the Late Prehistoric Period spans at least five millennia, beginning with the Lochnore Phase discussed above (5,000

3.9 | The structure and decay of pithouse dwellings: (a) exterior view of a reconstructed pithouse with notched ladder at Scotch Creek, Shuswap Lake; (b) inside a large reconstructed pithouse on Kamloops Indian Reserve 1; (c) a partially collapsed reconstructed pithouse near Salmon Arm; (d) a typical housepit depression as we find them today.

to 3,500 years ago) and followed by the Shuswap (3,500 to 2,400 years ago), Plateau (2,400 to 1,200 years ago), and Kamloops (1,200 to 200 year ago) Horizons (see figs 3.3 and 3.8) (Richards and Rousseau 1987; Rousseau 2004; Stryd and Rousseau 1996). This lengthy cultural tradition is characterized by the appearance of small seasonal (winter) pithouses sometime around 4,500 years ago and their common persistence to the mid-1800s and in some instances to the early 1900s; a general continuity in fishing, hunting, and gathering strategies and economies; use of sophisticated and well-organized resource-harvesting technologies; increased semi-sedentism and inter-regional cultural diversity; and development of several adaptive behaviours, technological innovations, and resource-harvesting and settlement patterns specifically unique to the Canadian Plateau.

Between about 5,000 and 3,000 years ago, the climate was cooler and wetter than at present, resulting in an expansion and lowering of treelines and a shrinking and lowering of grasslands. Shortly after 5,000 years ago, colder winters and deeper snowfalls eventually forced mobile groups belonging to the late Lehman Phase and early Lochnore Phase to reduce their winter mobility and construct small semi-permanent dwellings on the sides and bottoms of major valleys near rivers where treelines and grasslands met. There, food resources were more abundant, varied, and accessible, and snow cover was least.

3.10 | Pithouse village sites: (a) a small pithouse village site in the south Cariboo region; (b) a large village near Williams Lake; (c) a large village near Dog Creek in the upper mid-Fraser River region.

Prominent characteristics shared by the four successive cultures of the Plateau Pithouse Tradition included seasonal (winter) use of semi-subterranean pithouses or semi-permanent villages for four and a half millennia; seasonally scheduled resource harvesting; a hunting and plant-harvesting mode with additional emphasis on salmon fishing; and use of food storage technology such as salmon- and meat-drying racks, cache pits, and scaffolds. The Plateau Pithouse Tradition was a widespread, dynamic, interactive, and evolving cultural continuum of Interior Salish–speaking people,

3.11 | Archaeological excavations: (a) postexcavation view of a buried, small, shallow housepit of the Lochnore Phase occupied 4,400 years ago near Monte Creek on the South Thompson River; (b) excavations underway at a 3,200-year-old hide-processing site near Williams Lake; (c) post-excavation view of a small, shallow mat lodge depression of the Plateau Horizon on Adams Lake; (d) postexcavation view of the eastern half of a large housepit of the Kamloops Horizon on Adams Lake; (e) excavation of a large central hearth on the floor of a 900-year-old pithouse on the Shuswap River east of Enderby; (f) postexcavation view of a small 3,300-year-old pithouse dwelling and adjacent peripheral activity area near Williams Lake.

with each major archaeological phase or horizon representing long periods of relative adaptive stability that can be separated by short periods of rapid and significant culture change.

Lochnore Phase (5,000 to 3,500 Years Ago)

Between 5,000 and 4,000 years ago there was a gradual change from moderately warm and dry conditions to cooler and wetter conditions. This trend continued between 3,500 and 2,500 years ago, producing significantly cooler and wetter conditions during that interval (see fig. 3.3) (Walker and Pellatt 2008). Details about specific effects that this climatic change had on various aspects of local environments, ecosystems, and cultural patterns during this time are not yet entirely clear, but they no doubt played an important part during the merger of early Lochnore and late Lehman Phase peoples.

Residential and field camps are often small to medium-size and fairly deeply buried, and they suggest relatively short-term occupation episodes with medium- to high-density scatters of lithics, bone, fire-altered rock, and freshwater mussel shell. Many sites lie on edges of flat upper river terraces along sides of main river valley bottoms, especially at or near junctures of major tributary creek valleys. Some larger residential sites indicate repeated occupations. Field camps have also been identified in mid-altitude valley contexts beside small lakes and streams and appear to have been occupied by groups of ten to twenty people for short periods.

The earliest investigated pithouses on the Canadian Plateau are located in the South Thompson River region (see fig. 3.11, image a), and their occupation dates from 4,400 to 4,200 years ago (I.R. Wilson et al. 1992). Excavations revealed that Lochnore Phase pithouses were small, shallow, round, or oval in plan and had structurally lighter and more hastily constructed roofs compared with those of larger, later pithouses of the Shuswap Horizon. During the colder months, small numbers of these dwellings would be constructed by moderately mobile groups consisting of one or two extended families. Some house depressions may have been used several times. It is not known when mat lodges, discussed and presented in the late-1800 to early-1900 ethnographic literature (Teit 1900, 1906, 1909, 1930a; see also Teit 1900, plate 16), were first used or whether they were a pre-Lochnore or Lochnore Phase innovation.

Distinctive lithic artifacts and technological traits of the Lochnore Phase include large and medium-size, lanceolate, willow-leaf-shaped, formed bifacial points/knives with wide, shallow to moderately deep opposing side notches, heavy basal edge grinding, and pointed or convex bases; leaf-shaped and bipointed bifaces without notches; leaf-shaped bifaces with straight or slightly convex basal margins; oval bifaces (see fig. 3.12); small and medium-size, round and oval, formed unifacial scrapers on thick flakes; concave-edge end scrapers and/or side scrapers (see fig. 3.7); edge-battered, ground, and abraded cobbles; unifacial pebble tools/choppers; notched flat pebbles (net sinkers) and chipped-stone fish gorges (see fig. 3.13); and common use of basalts to make stone tools, with minor use of colourful high-quality silicates and sometimes very small amounts of obsidian. During the initial half of this phase, some foliate bifaces had serrated lateral blade margins. Unnotched foliate forms were more common during the latter half of the Lochnore Phase.

Microblade technology (see fig. 3.7) is not found in all occupations, but at some sites blades can number in the hundreds or thousands. Around the end

3.12 | Examples of complete and fragmented biface types of the Lochnore Phase (5,000 to 4,500 years ago). Note denticulated lateral blade margins and the variety of side-notching patterns. These bifaces were used both as knives and as projectile points.

3.13 | Large stone tools in common use at large field camps and winter villages during the Plateau Pithouse Tradition (5,000 to 200 years ago): (a–e) pestles, mauls, and hammer stones; (f) large anvil with evidence of intensive battering and pitting; (g) large multipurpose hammer/pounder and anvil stone; (h–j) notched fishnet or fishing-line sinkers made from flat discoidal cobbles; (k-l) groundstone adze blades; (m) sandstone arrow shaft smoother; (n–p) large bifacial knives used to process meat and fish; (q) quartzite cobble-spall knife; (r) tabular mica schist knife.

of this phase (4,000 to 3,500 years ago), use of microblades declined significantly. This change is not surprising, since microblade technology was most practical for high-mobility hunting and foraging people, and by this time most regional groups were less residentially mobile and were organizing their animal and plant resource harvesting around a spring to fall resource-production schedule, while living in pithouses during the winter months and relying on stored provisions of dried meat, salmon, roots, and berries. It appears that this lifestyle also entailed stockpiling tool stone (mainly glassy basalt or dacite) at or near winter villages for making tools, as opposed to manufacturing microblades at camps.

Common bone and antler items include bone splinters used for fish-hook barbs, antler tine flakers, antler wedges, unilaterally barbed antler points, worked rodent incisors, animal tooth and claw pendants, and occasional marine shell beads. Lochnore Phase peoples engaged in a generalized resource-harvesting pattern of broad-spectrum foraging of animals and plants encountered on a daily basis. Included in sites that have been studied are remains of deer, elk, beaver, migratory birds, salmon, turtles, and fresh-water mussels. There is no direct evidence for intensive consumption of salmon during this phase, but it was likely fairly considerable since bone and antler artifacts clearly indicate a very capable fishing technology. Small quantities of dried salmon and edible plants were sometimes stored by larger families in the late summer or fall for later winter consumption. No subterranean food storage pits dating to this phase have been identified, but their absence may be attributable to the fact that very few sites of this age have been investigated in detail, as well as to the decomposition of plant and animal remains during the lengthy timespan in question. Perhaps above-ground wooden storage scaffolds similar to those used by Plains groups to the east were used during this time.

Shuswap Horizon (3,500 to 2,400 Years Ago)

The reasonably well-known Shuswap Horizon culture corresponds to a major cooling neoglacial event that began around 3,500 years ago and climaxed around 3,300 years ago. Between 3,000 and 2,500 years ago, cool and moist conditions gradually changed to warm and dry conditions similar to those experienced today (see fig. 3.3). At this time, increased precipitation enhanced rearing and spawning habitat for anadromous salmonids, and there was an increase in salmon harvesting and consumption along major rivers. Forests and plant communities expanded, and treelines lowered to include valley sides and bottoms. Grasslands were at their absolute minimum, forcing many large grazing and browsing animals like deer, elk, and moose to subsist on valley sides and bottoms. Terrestrial animal populations expanded and proliferated. Excavated animal and fish remains from Shuswap Horizon occupations provide ample evidence that it was a time of food resource variety and plenty. The Shuswap Lakes area presently has biological characteristics that are very similar to those experienced during the Shuswap Horizon, although during the Shuswap Horizon this general "wet forest" environment type extended throughout many valley bottoms on the Canadian Plateau. It was a time of food and textile resource abundance and variety.

The very successful Shuswap Horizon cultural system, which evolved directly from the late Lochnore Phase way of life and likely developed and emerged in the Shuswap Lakes and South Thompson River regions sometime around 3,500 years ago, is also well represented in the mid-Fraser region. Shuswap Horizon people were direct descendants of well-established resident Interior Salish–speaking groups of the late Lochnore Phase. At the beginning of the Shuswap Horizon, there was a rapid change from what archaeologists would characterize as the moderately mobile, seasonally sedentary foraging and occasional collecting that we can identify for the Lochnore Phase to a resource-harvesting strategy that, as evidence suggests, focused on storage of dried plant and animal foods and was characterized by regular occupation of pithouses for most of the colder months. During this time, valley bottoms were resource-rich, permitting a resource-harvesting pattern that emphasized around-the-seasons procurement of small game and fish, along with procurement of targeted large-scale resources like riverine salmon runs, trout runs in upland lakes, and large-scale fall hunts for ungulates (elk and deer). Small, moderately mobile bands established winter residential base camps on valley bottoms, where food and material resources were most abundant and varied. There is currently no direct evidence of root-roasting pits, digging stick handles, carbonized floral remains, or any upland or valley bottom intensive plant exploitation. Nevertheless, it is highly probable that a broad range of plant resources were available and routinely collected.

Shuswap Horizon regional populations increased slightly relative to the preceding Lochnore Phase, with about two to five sites containing from three to ten pithouses in most major valley systems. Population growth seems to have been relatively slow and steady at the beginning of the Shuswap Horizon, but there was a marked increase from 3,000 to 2,400 years ago that continued into the Plateau Horizon (see fig. 3.3).

Residential group mobility steadily decreased throughout the Shuswap Horizon. This trend grew with lessening precipitation, a rise in seasonal temperatures, and the growing frequency of small groups being dispatched from main villages to undertake resource-harvesting activities. For the Shuswap Horizon, dried salmon storage in small outdoor subterranean pits has yet to be confirmed, but storage and refuse pits in excavated pithouse floors have yielded abundant salmon bones. Intensive salmon drying and storage may not have been considered necessary during most of the Shuswap Horizon since a wide variety of other hunted animal protein was readily available year-round.

Most currently known Shuswap Horizon pithouse sites lie on main valley bottoms or their tributaries beside or near rivers, streams, and large lakes. These villages are relatively small when compared with those of later horizons (see fig. 3.16). Pithouses are quite large, averaging 11 metres in diameter and ranging from 7.5 to 16 metres in diameter, and some foundations were dug

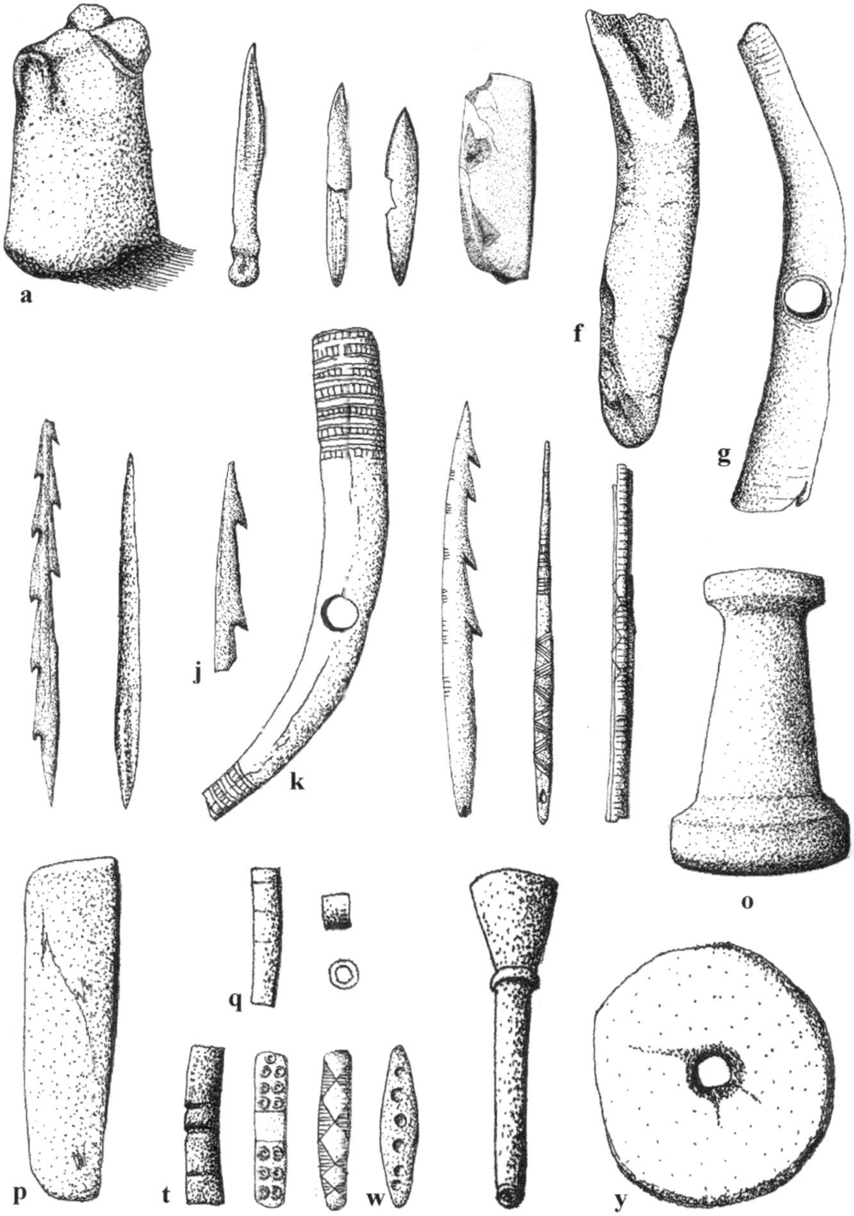

3.14 | Artifacts occasionally found in sites of the Plateau Pithouse Tradition (5,000 to 200 years ago). Shuswap Horizon artifacts from pithouse village EeRb 10 in Kamloops: (a) hand maul with a bear head effigy; (b) blanket/clothing pin; (c-d) fish gorges; (e) nephrite (jade) adze blade/celt; (f) antler wedge or digging tool. Plateau Horizon artifacts: (g) digging stick handle; (h) bilaterally barbed antler point; (i) leister barb; (j) unilaterally barbed antler point. Kamloops Horizon artifacts from sites along the South Thompson River: (k) antler digging stick handle; (l) unilaterally barbed antler point/harpoon; (m) incised basket needle; (n) incised drinking tube; (o) hand maul (hammer); (p) nephrite (jade) adze blade/celt; (q–s) dentalium shell beads; (t–w) lahal gaming pieces; (x) steatite (soapstone) smoking pipe; (y) spindle whorl.

3.15 | Common bifacial projectile point form types and large leaf-shaped knives of the Shuswap Horizon (3,500 to 2,400 years ago).

quite deep, up to 2 metres. Housepit floor plans vary, with round, oval, and subrectangular forms being common. Most housepit depressions lack obvious peripheral heaped rims along the outer edge of the house floor. Big houses intended for occupation by extended-family groups were most practical for these moderately mobile groups since they required less time and energy to construct, maintain, and heat compared with numerous smaller houses best suited for smaller, perhaps nuclear, families or individuals.

Shuswap Horizon formed bifaces include a variety of stemmed, basally indented, shouldered, and corner-removed projectile points and leaf-shaped knives (see fig. 3.15). Many early Shuswap Horizon projectile point forms are strikingly similar to those found during the Middle Period on the Northern Plains. This suggests that some sort of direct or indirect interaction occurred with Plains groups to the east between about 3,500 and 2,800 years ago. Early housepit sites near Banff in the Rocky Mountains dating to the same time attest that Shuswap Horizon people occasionally visited and wintered along the western fringe of the Rockies and Alberta Plains (Shuswap Indian Band 2008). This evidence suggests that they regularly interacted with highly mobile hunting groups living on the western fringe of the Northern Plains and Rocky Mountains, resulting in some shared aspects of hunting weaponry systems, including adoption of a variety of Plains-like projectile point forms. Contracting stemmed points are more common in assemblages dated to after about 2,800 years ago, attesting to adoption and common use of stemmed point styles and other biface forms found on both the Columbia Plateau and south coast at that time. Medium-size and large foliate, tear-shape, and oval knives are also present in low to moderate numbers in assemblages, and in many respects these items are formally similar to some of the larger bifaces made and used during the preceding Lochnore Phase.

Other important lithic technological traits include initial production and use of key-shaped formed unifaces used to work wood (see fig. 3.20, items c to g); a variety of small and medium-size unifacial scrapers; unifacial gravers, perforators, piercers (see fig. 3.20, items h to m), and large split cobble scrapers; and an abundance of utilized and unifacial flake tools. Generally, lithic toolkits are simple in composition and exhibit fair to moderate levels of lithic technological proficiency, as well as primary use of locally obtained, fair- to good-quality flakable stone. There was also a well-developed bone and antler technology (see fig. 3.14). The deceased were buried in pits within pithouse floors.

Sometime around 3,200 years ago, Mount St Helens in present-day Washington State erupted, depositing yet another large blanket of volcanic ash over much of the southern Canadian Plateau (see fig. 3.5). Effects of this eruption on Shuswap Horizon people were likely similar to those experienced by people who lived during the eruption of Mount Mazama 6,700 years ago, but because of wetter conditions and more vegetation, adverse effects on regional environments and human lifeways may not have been as severe or widespread. The Shuswap Horizon ended about 2,400 years ago when a warmer and drier climate similar to that of today was established.

Plateau Horizon (2,400 to 1,200 Years Ago)

Shortly after 2,500 years ago, a climate and environments similar to those of today were established, and there were obvious changes in several key

3.16 | A rare 1928 aerial photograph of Kamloops Indian Reserve 1 at the confluence of the North and South Thompson Rivers, showing the location of the small Shuswap Horizon pithouse village EeRb 10 and the much larger Plateau Horizon pithouse village EeRb 3, which once contained over 150 pithouses and hundreds of associated cache pits and earth ovens. During the peak of the Plateau Horizon, site EeRb 3 was probably the largest village site on the Plateau. These sites no longer exist.

aspects of Secwépemc material culture. We refer to this time as the end of the Shuswap Horizon, marked by lifeways that led to the commencement of the Plateau Horizon around 2,400 years ago. The Plateau Horizon was a developmental zenith of Canadian Plateau Interior Salish cultures and was a period of rapid human population growth, with regional populations peaking around 2,000 years ago and declining steadily thereafter until about 1,200 years ago (see fig. 3.3). Sites and occupations belonging to this horizon are abundant and are found in all environmental settings and at all altitudes, suggesting that a wide range of economic activities was conducted by the ancestors of the Secwépemc in lands that were associated with Secwepemcúlecw for many hundreds of years before the arrival of Europeans.

Although the sizes of Plateau Horizon pithouse villages vary, most are much larger than those of the previous Shuswap Horizon, with many village sites having between 10 and 150 housepits (see fig. 3.16). Larger pithouse villages indicate continuous reoccupation over many generations and are situated in resource-rich valley bottom or valley side areas at or near major salmon fisheries, where important plant resources were prolific. In Secwépemc territory, typical Plateau Horizon housepits range from 4 to 8 metres in diameter and are between 1 to 2 metres deep. They are mostly circular to oval in plan and lack raised earth rims on their perimeter. Widespread use of smaller winter houses during the Plateau Horizon was likely due to increased residential sedentism and/or perhaps a common desire to live in more private, nuclear, family-size dwellings. Small houses provide greater privacy, are relatively easy to construct and maintain, and require much less fuel to heat than the large houses used during the preceding Shuswap Horizon. Mat lodges were used at field and residential camps during the cooler and warmer times of the year, but again they are difficult to visually identify due to the lack of any depression or rim.

When compared with earlier and later horizons, the archaeological record suggests that regional populations reached a temporary peak during the Plateau Horizon (see fig. 3.3). This occurrence is substantiated by many large winter village sites, extensive and intensive use of upland resources, the impressive abundance of observed Plateau Horizon sites, and very high numbers of "isolated" corner-notched projectile points (see fig. 3.17) found almost everywhere in the Fraser and Thompson River drainage areas. Populations were most dense between about 2,000 and 1,600 years ago.

It was during the start of the Plateau Horizon, around 2,400 years ago, that intensive balsamroot (see fig. 5.14; see also chapter 5) harvesting and processing with earth ovens (see fig. 3.19) became a common practice. Feeding and maintaining the increased regional populations imposed considerable resource-harvesting stress on valley floors and sides, thus leading to intensification of readily available root plants, which required applying knowledge about chemical conversion of inedible to edible carbohydrates by pit-cooking them (see chapter 5). Digging stick handles with incisions indicating the trenches dug by their owners (Teit 1900, 1909) (see fig. 3.14, item k) start to appear in currently known archaeological sites around the same time. Resource stresses were also partially alleviated by well-organized extensive exchange (trade) networks that moved large quantities of preserved food, textiles, medicine, stone, people, and other commodities for many hundreds of years throughout the Canadian Plateau. These networks created an intensive and far-reaching social and economic "interaction sphere" that continued to operate at the time of Euro-Canadian contact and beyond.

A high level of proficiency in lithic tool production and a high level of use of sophisticated tool production techniques were prominent features of Plateau Horizon culture (see fig. 8, colour section; and figs 3.14 and 3.17). In some larger villages, there may have been technical specialists who regularly produced well-made bifacial points and knives that were exchanged with community members for other necessities. Most bifaces are well made, as are an array of formed unifaces, including convex-edged, chipped-stone "hide" end scrapers, side scrapers, gravers, piercers, haftable drill bits, and key-shaped wood-working tool bits (see fig. 3.20). The latter were more common during this horizon than in the preceding Shuswap Horizon. Many Plateau Horizon

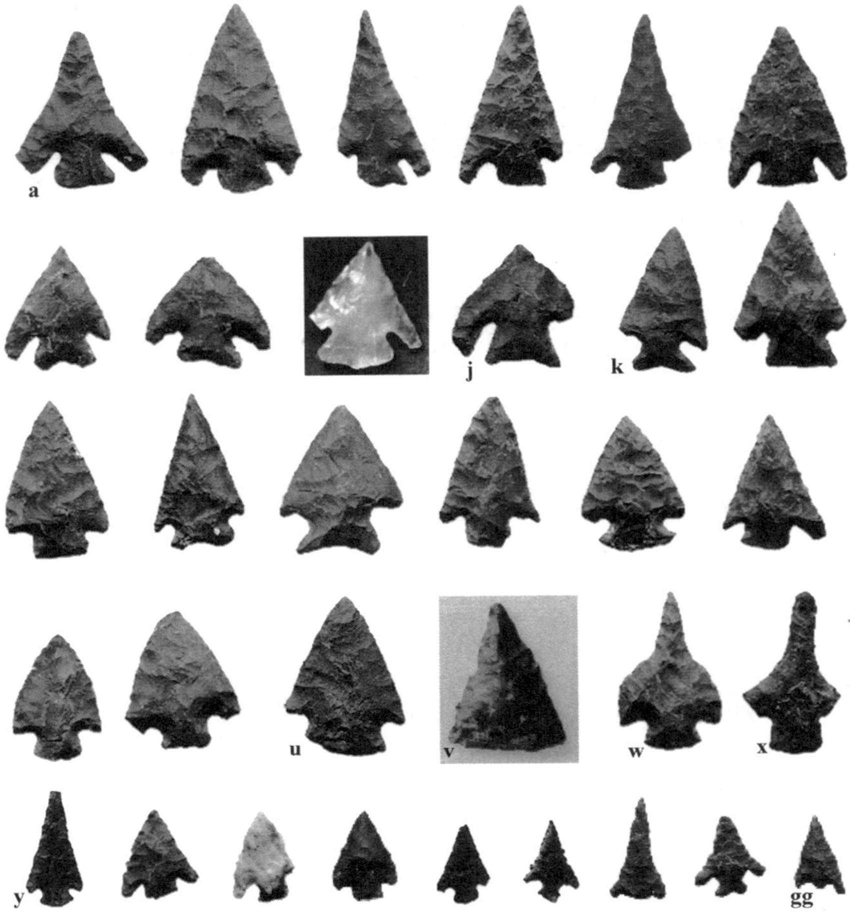

3.17 | Examples of Plateau Horizon projectile points from occupations dated to between 2,400 and 1,200 years ago: (a–j) basally notched atlatl dart points, which tend to appear earlier; (k–u) more typical corner-notched forms, which tend to appear later; (v) unnotched triangular point preforms, which are found in low numbers; (w-x) perforator/piercer/drill bits made from recycled corner-notched projectile points; (y–gg) small basally notched and corner-notched arrow points found in occupations dated to between 1,600 and 1,200 years ago, which indicate that bow and arrow technology was introduced to the Plateau around 1,600 years ago.

chipped-stone assemblages contain much higher proportions of good-quality lithic raw materials compared with previous Shuswap Horizon and later Kamloops Horizon occupations.

Plateau Horizon projectile points are typically triangular in overall outline, are prominently barbed with either corner or basal notches, and have convex and straight basal margins (see fig. 3.17). Unnotched triangular bifaces (see fig.

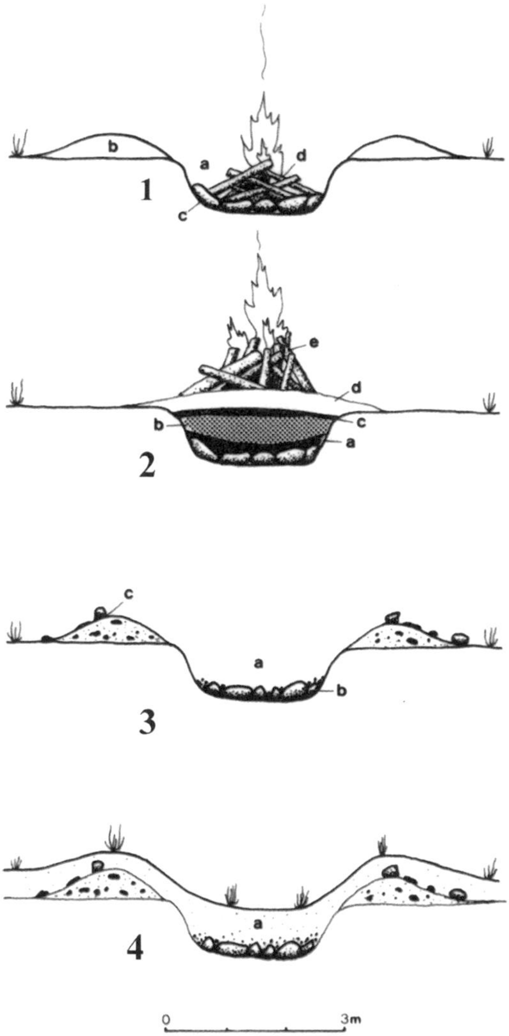

3.18 | The life of a food-roasting pit (idealized cross-section), based on James Teit's (1900, 1909) ethnographic account. A basin-shaped pit (1a) is excavated, and the earth (1b) is piled on the periphery. The bottom is lined with flat rocks (1c), which are heated with fire (1d). The fire is removed, and the rocks are covered with a layer of damp earth, branches, and pine needles (2a). Edible roots (2b) are put in, and another layer of branches (2c) is placed over the roots. A layer of earth (2d) covers the pit contents, and a fire (2e) is built on top. After the roots are cooked, the pit contents are removed (3a), leaving fire-altered rock and charcoal (3b) in the bottom of the pit and a mixture of earth, charcoal, and fire-altered rock (3c) around the outside, forming a rim. After abandonment, wind-blown silts (4a) cap the pit, and that is how these pits appear today.

3.17, item v) are sometimes also found in low numbers, being unfinished point preforms or knife blades. Basally notched forms (see fig. 3.17, items a to j) are most common from 2,400 to 2,000 years ago, and corner-notched forms (see fig. 3.17, items k to u) are most common from 2,000 to 1,200 years ago. Rare leaf-shaped and stemmed points are also present, and most of them probably functioned as knives or were scavenged from sites predating 2,400 years ago. A progressive reduction in overall general projectile point size (see fig. 3.17, items y to gg) is evident during the latter half of this horizon, particularly after 1,600 years ago, which is when bow and arrow technology was introduced to the Pacific Northwest from the Northern Plains and rapidly became the favoured and dominant hunting weaponry system. Bow technology is hallmarked by the appearance of these small triangular, corner-notched point forms. The atlatl was used concurrently with the bow and arrow for several hundred years but was phased out of common use shortly after 1,200 years ago.

Common use of bow and arrow technology started around 1,600 years ago and was a significant technical and cultural milestone for Secwépemc people. It was a hunting technology that dramatically enhanced hunting efficiency, thereby allowing a number of important behavioural and cultural changes. Simply put, preferential use of bow and arrow technology substantially enhanced the ability to hunt, and its regular and perfected use resulted in significant lessening of time needed for hunting, allowing more time to devote to different resource-harvesting pursuits, family, personal interests, art, ceremonialism, and other forms of complex social behaviour.

There was also a well-developed bone and antler technology in common use during the Plateau Horizon (see fig. 8, colour section). Typical items made from antler include digging stick handles, wedges, pressure flakers, billet flakers, elongate barbed harpoon points, toggling harpoon valves, and a variety of simple unipoints and bipoints that served many functions. Common bone items include a wide variety of simple pointed bone slivers, gaming pieces, small bipointed fish gorges, awls, piercers, needles, pressure flakers, and drinking tubes (straws). Dentalium shell beads and other marine shells traded inland from the coast were used for personal adornment and clothing.

It was during the beginning of this horizon that efficient large-scale harvesting, drying, and storage of salmon for later consumption became common (see fig. 3.19). This practice allowed food shortages to be offset during leaner winter months. It involved drying salmon sides in large volumes and storing them in small, subterranean, vertical-walled, bark-lined pits that measured from 1 to 2 metres in diameter and were 0.75 to 1.5 metres deep. In some localities where salmon were taken in great numbers, large storage pits up to 3 metres in diameter and 3 metres deep are sometimes present. Such storage pits are common within larger winter village confines and/or are clustered in large groups nearby.

Plateau Horizon mortuary practices are poorly known, but some excavated and incidentally encountered data are available. Cremation was a common mode of treatment either before or during interment. It was particularly practical in large pithouse village communities where mortality was frequent. It was also during this horizon that medium-size stocky dogs appear in the archaeological record. Pack dogs were very valuable since they were willing to transport heavy loads of dried fish, plants, and other materials involved in organized exchange (trade) systems (Crellin 1994; Crellin and Heffner 2000).

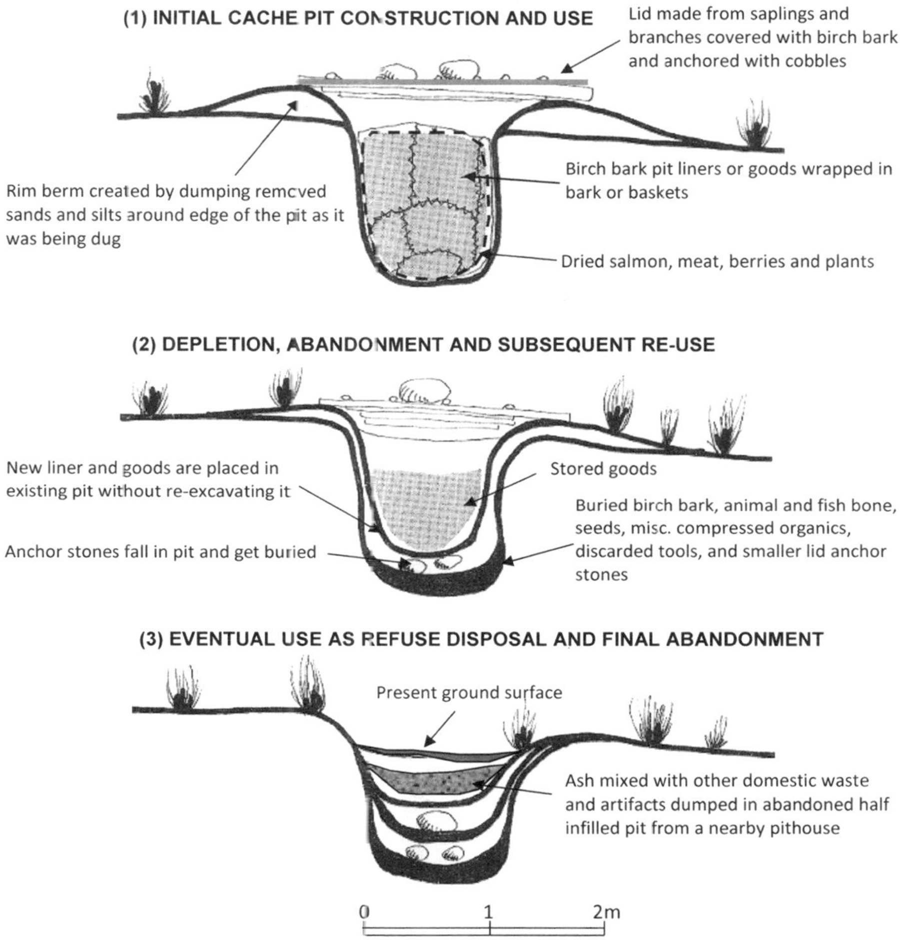

3.19 | Typical use history of a food cache pit (vertical cross-section), commonly used at winter villages during the Plateau Pithouse Tradition (3,500 to 200 years ago).

In sum, from the frequency, distribution, and attributes of Plateau Horizon sites, we can infer that the Plateau Horizon saw a fairly steady and rapid population growth that climaxed around 2,000 years ago. Intensive seasonal mid- and high-altitude resource procurement was common. There was low residential group mobility during winter months but high task group mobility for the remainder of the year. Plateau Horizon people practised what archaeologists call a highly organized "collector" resource-harvesting and settlement pattern that was more logistically complex than the preceding Shuswap Horizon and, to some degree, more complex than the later Kamloops Horizon

3.20 | Hafted stone tools. (a) Replica of a Nesikep Tradition "composite knife," whose blade (top) is a typical Lehman Phase obliquely notched biface, with a tabular scraper hafted into the bottom. They were ideal "multipurpose" knives and very well suited for cleaning and dressing salmon and processing meat. (b) Replica of a key-shaped formed uniface (outlined) set in a wooden handle, wrapped with leather, fixed with pine pitch, and put to use. They were very competent woodworking tools, allowing bark to be easily stripped and green wood to be carved with ease. (c–g) Examples of key-shaped formed unifaces used as woodworking tools. Most were also used hafted and made from high-quality, hard, durable, colourful silicate (agate-like) stones to ensure long use life. They start appearing in sites around 3,000 years ago with the latter part of the Shuswap Horizon, were commonly used for the next two millennia, and are very rarely found at sites dated to after 1,000 years ago. They were used to carve atlatls, spears, atlatl dart shafts, hafts, and other wooden items involving the debarking and carving of green branches. (h–n) Examples of incising, graving, and piercing tools. (o–p) Chisel bits used to work wood, antler, and bone.

(see fig. 3.3). The Plateau Horizon represents a great resource florescence among Canadian Plateau hunter-gatherer-fisher cultures, and importantly, it coincided with a similar peak in cultural development during the Marpole Phase on the south coast (Burley 1980; Matson and Coupland 1995).

Kamloops Horizon (1,200 to 200 Years Ago)

There is more information gathered from archaeological sites pertaining to the Kamloops Horizon than there is for the preceding Plateau Horizon. Although it appears that regional populations were lower than during the preceding Plateau Horizon, there is ample evidence of human occupation and presence throughout many contiguous regions of the area that by then had linguistically and culturally become Secwepemcúlecw (see chapter 2). Several large established Kamloops Horizon village sites contain occupations belonging to the previous Plateau and Shuswap Horizons. Some important aspects of resource harvesting and settlement remained constant or similar during the Plateau and Kamloops Horizons, including a highly organized resource-harvesting and settlement strategy; occupation of winter pithouse villages; use of upland base camps in locations proximal to major food resources; continued extensive use of mid-altitude and upland plants; a heavy reliance on salmon supplemented by ungulates (deer, elk, mountain sheep, mountain goat) and small animals; active participation in well-developed interregional exchange networks; and continuation of a unique Plateau art tradition represented in bone, antler, and occasionally marine shell (dentalium and pectin) (see fig. 3.14; and fig. 8, colour section).

With respect to resource-harvesting and settlement strategies, it appears that there was a change in harvesting and processing strategy between the late Plateau Horizon and Kamloops Horizon (see fig. 3.3). The latter saw a decline in the number and amount of root-processing oven sites in uplands, but they may have subsequently increased again during the Kamloops Horizon, although the size of roasting pits remained smaller (Lepofsky and Peacock 2004). If use of upland plant and animal resources declined somewhat during the Kamloops Horizon, this change could be attributed to the adoption of bow and arrow technology, as it enabled people to refocus their attention on previously unattainable fast-fleeing protein resources (deer, birds, hare, and other small animals) available on valley bottoms near permanent villages. These protein resources would have lessened the need to maintain continued intensive reliance on upland resources in order to supplement dietary needs and offset food shortages. However, ethnographic information about seasonal round and upland use during the end of the Kamloops Horizon and the 1800s (Teit 1900, 1909; Dawson 1891), along with oral histories about the seasonal round and upland use of plant foods, ungulates, and lake fish in the early to mid-twentieth century (see chapter 5), attest to detailed knowledge and use of upland resources throughout the 1800s and 1900s (see also Alexander 1992, 1996, 1997, 2000).

Significant culture traits unique to the Kamloops Horizon include the use of medium-size and large housepits with a variety of floor plans and depths; the appearance and persistence of Kamloops side-notched arrow points (see fig. 3.21) and the complete absence of small corner-notched point forms after 1,000 years ago; significant elaboration in mobile art and the decoration of utilitarian items (see fig. 3.14; and fig. 8, colour section); a marked decline in frequency and intensity of exploitation of upland plant resources; and a widespread reduction in population densities, particularly after 1,000 years ago.

Housepit diameters range from 6 to 20 metres and are either oval, circular, rectangular, or square in plan. Most have prominent or fairly well-defined

3.21 | Projectile points and knives of the Kamloops Horizon (1,200 to 200 years ago). (a–t) Small arrow points known to archaeologists as "Kamloops side-notched," which are the predominant projectile point style of the Kamloops Horizon. Their appearance around 1,200 years ago is coincident with commencement of the Kamloops Horizon way of life. (u–y) "Kamloops multinotched points" with serrated edges on one or more lateral margins. They appear in occupations dated to from 400 to 200 years ago and may be related to interpersonal conflict. (z–cc) Larger versions of "Kamloops multinotched points" (bottom row) are occasionally found in occupations dated to between 600 and 200 years ago. (dd–ff) Large "pentagonal knives" in common use during the Kamloops Horizon.

raised earth rims surrounding the foundation. Side entrances are sometimes evident. Many have bowl-shaped, saucer-shaped, or basin-shaped interiors and vary from 0.1 to 1.5 metres deep. Use of medium-size and large pithouses may reflect extended-family groups once again commonly constructing and occupying single large residences. Variation in house sizes during the Kamloops Horizon probably simply reflects the relative number of people in a close-knit family or economic group, intended duration of occupation, and availability of suitable construction materials. Ethnohistoric and archaeological evidence from the early 1800s also shows the use of large pithouses for social gatherings and ceremonies (C. Carlson 2006; A. McDonald 2001; see also chapter 11). In warmer months, mat lodge dwellings ranging from 4 to 7 metres in diameter were erected in upland locations near important seasonal food resources and water. These temporary dwellings were commonly used during the Kamloops Horizon, but identification of their floors is difficult since in most cases little or no intentional modification of the ground was involved in their construction.

Biface technology during the Kamloops Horizon was well developed and well represented, but generally bifaces reflect only mediocre to fair technical ability compared with those made by preceding Plateau Horizon technicians. Projectile points are typically small, triangular, side-notched forms known as Kamloops side-notched arrow points with small laterally initiated opposing U-shaped notches of varying widths and depths (see fig. 3.21). Larger points of identical style are also occasionally found in occupations dating to 600 years ago. Multinotched variants with two or more deep, narrow, U-shaped notches along one lateral blade margin (see fig. 3.21, items u to y) and occasional large side-notched specimens appear 400 years ago. It may be that the latter were designed and primarily intended for use in situations involving serious interpersonal conflicts since extra notches and micro-serrated edges promote greater damage to flesh during arrow penetration and subsequent attempted forceful removal. The written ethnographic record (Teit 1906, 1909, 1930a) and Secwépemc oral histories (see chapter 7) refer to intergroup conflicts and tensions for three centuries prior to the arrival of Euro-Canadian settlers.

Medium-size and large bifacially flaked, unnotched, leaf-shaped, ovate, triangular, tear-shaped, stemmed, and foliate bifacial knife blades also appear in Kamloops Horizon components. Many functioned as knives, and they were used primarily to dress salmon and cut meat. Of interest are Kamloops Horizon pentagonal bifaces/knives (see fig. 3.21, items dd to ff), which are formally recognized as fairly reliable identification markers for Kamloops Horizon occupations. Initially, during early stages of use, these distinctive bifaces were much larger and broader, but they were hafted and consistently resharpened by small flake removals during their use, eventually arriving at the overall "pentagonal shape" before they were discarded.

A variety of formed chipped-stone tools are common, including well-made formed scrapers, gravers, and perforators. Key-shaped formed unifaces (see fig. 3.20, items c to g) have been found in early Kamloops Horizon occupations, but their use was discontinued around 1,000 years ago. Small thumbnail-shaped scrapers are also common in some sites. As was the case for the earlier Plateau Horizon, the primary tool stone was glassy basalt (dacite), but a variety of good-quality, colourful, "exotic" stone types were also regularly employed to produce stone tools.

Kamloops Horizon human burial practices varied widely, particularly during the last 500 years of the period. The dominant pattern was interment in unmarked shallow pits. Others include wooden cists marked with cobble cairns, multiple "tomb" burials along sandy ridges, talus slope burials, and graves with fires built over them. A perceived marked reduction in human populations throughout the Plateau between 1,200 and 1,000 years ago could also be due to a highly contagious, fatal biological pathogen that may have caused a widespread epidemic, although the existence and effects of any prehistoric epidemics remain to be identified in the archaeological record or in oral histories on the Canadian Plateau.

Although artifacts like barbed harpoon points and stone net and line sinkers (see figs 3.13 and 3.14) from excavated Kamloops Horizon assemblages lack clear evidence of any significant major changes or improvements in fishing technology compared with the Plateau Horizon, archaeological evidence so far from fishing weirs shows the existence of large-scale fishing weir technology during the late Plateau Horizon and especially the Kamloops Horizon, requiring large-scale organized labour for their production and maintenance (see fig. 5.3) (Nicholas 2002; Nicholas, Jules Bonneau, and Westfall 2017).

THE PREHISTORIC SECWÉPEMC POPULATION

by Marianne Ignace

It is difficult to arrive at reliable and accurate estimates of the Secwépemc population throughout different periods of time during the past several thousand years. The above discussion of the Plateau and Kamloops Horizons suggests a relatively high population density – and perhaps high population levels – during the time between 2,500 and around 1,000 years ago, followed by lower population density during the last several centuries before contact, although by the time of contact, the Secwépemc population was on the rise.

With an increased archaeological data base of prehistoric settlement patterns, an improved understanding of Aboriginal resource use, and a better understanding of the impact of imported diseases, estimates of Indigenous precontact population levels throughout North America have been revised upward since James Mooney's (1928) and Alfred Kroeber's (1939) estimates that the total precontact Indigenous population north of the 49th parallel comprised a mere 221,000 people. Current estimates of the Indigenous population of what is now Canada suggest a precontact population of at least 500,000 (see Canada, Royal Commission on Aboriginal Peoples 1996a, 13; and

Dickason and McNab 2009, 63). Meriwether Lewis and William Clark (2003), who visited the Plateau just south of the 49th parallel in the early 1800s, noted a very early contact count of 40,560 people for the Columbia Plateau in 1805, although Robert Boyd (1999a) estimates that at that time, there had already been a population loss of some 40 per cent due to epidemic diseases contracted from other Indigenous peoples to the east and southeast infected by Europeans who had come among them. Boyd suggests a pre-1774 population of 68,000 for the Southern (Columbia) Plateau. If one assumes a similar 40 per cent population loss due to the 1780 smallpox epidemic and other diseases introduced before 1850, the Secwépemc population of the 1770s would have been in the range of 12,000, although introduced diseases early on had a bigger impact on the population of the Columbia Plateau than the Northern Plateau during the period between the 1770s and 1850.

In his ethnography, James Teit (1909, 464–6) provided estimates of the Secwépemc population in each of the divisions and Indigenous bands for the year 1850, as given by his informants in the early 1900s. In total, his 1850 population estimates for the seven geographic areas, or "divisions" (see chapter 7), add up to 7,200 people for all of Secwepemcúĺecw. By comparing these population data for 1850 with the census data of the federal Department of Indian Affairs for 1903 and 1906, which show 2,185 and 2,236 respectively, Teit (ibid., 463) concluded that the Secwépemc population at the turn of the twentieth century was "less than one-third of what it was fifty years ago" in 1850.[10] There had been enormous population losses as a result of epidemics in the 1780s, even before the Secwépemc came into indirect and then direct contact with Europeans, and such losses escalated during the second half of the nineteenth century. A large proportion of the two-thirds population loss among the Secwépemc between 1850 and 1903 was likely due to the 1862–63 smallpox epidemic, which took a devastating toll on the Indigenous populations throughout western North America (Boyd 1994, 1999a; Hunn and Selam 1990). Further diseases like measles, influenza, tuberculosis, diphtheria, and whooping cough took further tolls on the Secwépemc during the nineteenth and early twentieth centuries (see chapter 13). As in other parts of the world, such epidemics took a particularly heavy toll on Indigenous "virgin populations" not previously exposed to European diseases and thus lacking immunity against them. Since all population data prior to 1850 are based on estimates and inferences, the prehistoric and early historic population numbers of the Interior Plateau are tentative at best.

Many researchers, notably archaeologists and ethnohistorians, have linked the precontact population density on the Plateau to the local abundance of salmon, although taking into account that the salmon available to upstream peoples like the Secwépemc and Syilx – and to a lesser degree the St'at'imc

/*continued*

and Nlaka'pamux – were leaner than those available to downstream peoples (see Kew 1992). High population density based on fairly sedentary villages – as opposed to lower population density among more mobile and dispersed populations – has been noted for precontact villages such as Keatley Creek and for the Fraser Canyon Secwépemc division.[11] Brian Hayden (2000a, 2000b), who has carried out intensive archaeological work at Keatley Creek, figures that before its "collapse," it had a population of 1,000 to 1,500 during its "golden age" some 1,000 years ago. Hayden calculates that the Keatley Creek area had a population density of 0.772 persons per square mile during this time. Another large aggregate pithouse village with more than 50 depressions and more than 100 cache pits existed in the Kelly Creek Valley near Clinton. Judging by the size of fir trees in pithouse depressions at Kelly Creek, measured at 70–100 centimetres in diameter by James Teit (1909, 459), this village was abandoned or depopulated at least 200 years before that time. A large pithouse village with nearly 50 housepit depressions was on the North Thompson River south of Clearwater.[12] European visitors to the area during the time of the 1862–63 smallpox epidemic found it abandoned, with bodies lying about. Finally, a large village existed at Tk̓emlúps (Kamloops) near the confluence of the North and South Thompson Rivers. This village (see fig. 3.16) featured more than 150 pithouses with many additional features, including cache pits and earth ovens. During the Plateau Horizon, this village may have been the largest village on the Canadian Plateau. Alexander Ross and David Stuart of the Pacific Fur Company reported finding more than 2,000 people encamped at "Cumcloups" (Tk̓emlúps), at the confluence of the North and South Thompson Rivers, when they visited the area in May 1812 (Ross 1849). Just over a decade later, Hudson's Bay Company chief trader Archibald McDonald was invited into a pithouse to join a feast attended by well over 300 people (Cole 1981). In 1808 Simon Fraser encountered 400 people at Kumcheen (Lytton) and was then taken across the river to another encampment, where 1,200 people met him (Fraser 1960).

Ethnohistorian Henry Dobyns (1966), who had carried out epidemiological and demographic studies of Caribbean and Central American Indigenous groups following contact, suggested much higher population levels for all of precontact "hemispheric" populations of North, Central, and South America. According to Dobyns's "formula," a reliable estimate of precontact Indigenous population levels in the Americas can be arrived at by multiplying the postcontact "nadir," or low point, of an Indigenous population by twenty. Based on the Secwépemc nadir population of just over 2,000 in the early 1900s (Teit 1909, 466), this formula yields a precontact population of 40,000 prior to the decline brought on by disease before and after contact. Dobyns's formula has been questioned as too sweeping and not based on detailed and precise data for specific local groups, especially in North America. Moreover, it does not account for the diverse carrying capacities of local ecologies, the spread and impact of diseases among specific populations, and the specific histories of contact. Although with existing data it is impossible to account for a Secwépemc population in the late 1700s as high as 40,000, the statements by "old Indians" in Teit's (1900, 175) time that formerly the Indigenous population was like "ants about an ant-hill" points toward Dobyns's formula.

Anthropologist Gary Palmer (1975a) provided an estimate of Secwépemc population levels from precontact to early contact based on the Secwépemc territory's *carrying capacity* of humans and on their use of important resources within its confines, as James Teit (1909) had mapped out in his book on the Shuswap.[13] The carrying capacity of humans, animals, and plants in an environment is the population size of the species that the environment can sustain in the long term, given the resources (food, habitat, water, and other necessities) available in that environment. Using estimates of sockeye salmon runs in the rivers and tributaries within Secwepemcúĺecw as well as deer and elk populations as sustained by grassland forage in the area, Palmer divided the annual caloric yield that these two resources provided by the human calorie needs they could sustain. He arrived at a carrying capacity of between 5,280 and 9,120 persons for Secwepemcúĺecw, which, as he points out, was nearly reached in 1850, based on Teit's count of 7,200 persons. It must be pointed out, however, that prehistorically the Secwépemc relied as much or more on Chinook salmon as on sockeye, in addition to coho, steelhead, trout, and other kinds of fish. In addition, beyond deer and elk, other ungulates like caribou, mountain goat, and mountain sheep, along with a variety of small mammals, were significant parts of the diet, as is evidenced by faunal remains in Secwépemc archaeological sites discussed in chapter 3. Finally, as chapter 5 explains, staple root plants and other plant foods accounted for a significant part of the Secwépemc diet. Although they may have accounted for a smaller part of the diet than in the Columbia Plateau, where they comprised up to 50 per cent of the caloric intake, plant foods, especially staple root plants, which were intricately managed and proliferated (see chapter 5), would easily have accounted for about one-third of the precontact diet, thus further increasing the carrying capacity of Secwepemcúĺecw. Together, these additional animal and plant resources could perhaps have doubled the carrying capacity of the Secwépemc homeland.

We must also remember that throughout the thousands of years that the ancestors of the Secwépemc lived on the Interior Plateau, the carrying capacity of the land was by no means static. In chapters 2 and 3, we saw how climate change and geological events produced ecological change, which in turn affected the availability of resources for humans. Moreover, due to the diversity of terrain and biogeoclimatic zones throughout Secwepemcúĺecw, population densities varied not only over time but also among regions. As chapters 2 and 3 show, climatic and ecological changes at key points in time during the past 8,000 years would have caused fluctuations and changes in population rather than steady and continuous increases throughout time.

In sum, the human occupation of what became Secwépemc territory on the Canadian Plateau during the past 10,000 or more years has involved a very remarkable series of social, economic, technological, and behavioural achievements and transitions in ever-changing environments. This population moved from very early hunting of big and small game, supplemented by plant gathering, to moderately mobile opportunistic foraging and then to a highly organized culture characterized by intimate knowledge of numerous resources and their seasonal availability across multiple environments, as well as by innovation and adoption of sophisticated technologies to harvest and store these resources. Even with the "Coast Salish incursion" about 5,000 years ago, the archaeological data suggest a clear developmental sequence that links the ancestors of contemporary Secwépemc – whom we can genealogically trace back to the middle of the Kamloops Horizon (see chapters 8 and 9) – with their previous ancestors during the Plateau and Shuswap Horizons, before that during the Lochnore and Lehman Phases, and ultimately during the Early Nesikep Tradition. Although, as we saw in chapter 2, DNA studies also suggest a genetically diverse population in the south-central Interior by 5,000 years ago (see Malhi et al. 2010), much is to be learned about the genetic profile of the ancestors of the Secwépemc, and much more hopefully will be learned about the Interior Plateau past from archaeological enquiry, as innovative techniques and methods develop. As for the context of Indigenous archaeology and Secwépemc archaeology as building bridges between Indigenous knowledge and what Western science can provide, in cross-fertilizing these types of knowledge, we find that in Secwépemc communities the respect for good archaeology has grown, and likewise the respect for the truths and wisdom contained in Secwépemc *stsptekwll* has grown both among scholars and among Secwépemc people who were deprived of these stories in their own pasts and in their own upbringing.

In chapter 4, we shift our focus to the Secwépemc language. Aside from further discussing its historical connection to neighbouring Salish languages, we show how Secwepemctsín provides a window on past collective experience and on ways of organizing that experience in a lived and living environment. We present Secwepemctsín as a unique way of organizing experience and thought connected to historically and culturally situated protocols. These protocols, in turn, are connected to, and mutually recognized by and alongside, those of other Salish communities.

4 Secwepemctsín
The Shuswap Language

This chapter examines the crucial role that Secwepemctsín, the Shuswap language, plays in the telling of stories and in the sharing of knowledge about the past.[1] Such shared knowledge in turn is connected to individual and collective experiences on the land and to the ways that the language embeds, expresses, and organizes social and cultural experience. It is through the knowledge and wisdom contained in Secwepemctsín that the ancestors speak back to us. In various ways, our language has shaped our people's thought and cognition. The Assembly of First Nations (1992, 14) has expressed the role and function of language in the transmission of culture as follows: "Language is the principal instrument by which culture is transmitted from one generation to another, by which members of a culture communicate meaning and make sense of their shared experience. Because language defines the world and experience in cultural terms, it literally shapes our way of perceiving – our world view." As we are facing an unprecedented global decline of Indigenous languages, their speakers, along with linguists and language advocates, have eloquently expressed the fundamental value of particular Indigenous languages as connected to the personal, social, and spiritual identity of their speakers.[2] Among the diversity of languages, "each contains a way of perceiving, categorizing and making meaning in the world, an invaluable guidebook developed and honed by our ancestors" (Boroditsky 2011, 65). Recent research in linguistics and cognitive psychology has taken us on new paths of learning about the way that languages not only refract cultural experience but also shape how we think.[3]

In this chapter, we expand on our brief discussion in chapter 2 of how Salish became the language of the Indigenous homeland of the Secwépemc some 5,000 years ago. We begin by providing further information about how our language is related historically to the other twenty-two languages in the Salish language family, a fact not only acknowledged by linguistic research but also evident in the affinities and similarities in vocabulary and structure that speakers of Secwepemctsín and other Salish languages perceived in the past and still perceive. Next, we explain the sound system of the language, and we show how Secwepemctsín, although it existed as an orally transmitted language for hundreds of generations, has been written with the help of

4.1 | Salishan Languages of North America. Territorial boundaries are approximate and without prejudice to Aboriginal groups’ territorial claims. In some instances, speech communities and linguists may use slightly different spellings for the names of these languages.

a practical alphabet for the past forty years or so. However, even before that, in the late 1800s to early 1900s, thousands of Secwépemc learned to write the language using the Chinook shorthand writing system. We also discuss some ways that Secwépemc words and grammar (the way that small chunks of meaning are organized into sentences) represent a unique and interesting system of organizing thought and experience, itself an expression of the Secwépemc and Salish past.

Table 4.1 | Words for "Coyote" in Secwepemctsín and neighbouring Interior Salish languages

Language	*Word*
Secwepemctsín	*sk̓(e)lép/sek̓lép*
Nlaka'pamuxcin	*snk'yap*
St'at'imcets	*nk'yáp*
Nsyilxcn/Okanagan	*snk'lip*
Kalispel	*sencelép*

Secwepemctsín and the Salish Language Family

Contemporary Secwépemc elders and those of many generations before them knew and acknowledged that Secwepemctsín (the root *cwep* for "spread out" plus the lexical suffixes *-emc* for "people" and *-tsin* for "mouth, talk") is related to the languages of the neighbouring peoples – the Nlaka'pamux, St'at'imc (Lillooet), and Syilx (Okanagan) – and also to the languages of several Indigenous nations in what is now Montana, Idaho, and eastern Washington. Included among the latter are the Kalispel (Flathead), Nxaʔamxcín (Columbian), and Coeur d'Alene languages. In addition, for countless generations, Secwépemc people have known and acknowledged that, more remotely, Secwepemctsín is related to numerous languages spoken on the lower Fraser River and at its mouth, on southern and eastern Vancouver Island, and on the coast north of the mouth of the Fraser. Indeed, speakers of Secwepemctsín notice that words like *tmicw* (land, world, earth, or country) correspond to very similar words in nearly all of these neighbouring or coastal languages. More words are similar or even identical among the languages of the Interior than between the Interior and coastal languages. For example, the word for "coyote" (as both the animal and ancient trickster-transformer) shows similarity between different Interior languages.

If we compare the words for "coyote" in other neighbouring languages like Ktunaxa, where it is *skinku¢*, Tsilhqot'in, where it is *chelʔig*, or Carrier (Dakelh), where it is *chuntulhi*, we see immediately that there is no similarity with the Secwépemc word *skel̓ép* or with any words for "coyote" in any of the neighbouring or nearby languages listed in table 4.1.[4]

The sound changes between the different languages listed in table 4.1 are not random; rather, linguists figure that they developed systematically as languages split off from one another or split apart from a common ancestor language. Thus, in certain sound combinations, the sound *l* in Secwepemctsín became *y* in Nlaka'pamuxcin, as can be seen in the respective words for "coyote." Speakers also recognize this changeover from *l* to *y* between Secwepemctsín and Nlaka'pamuxcin in the respective words for "good," which is *le7* in Secwepemctsín and *ye7* in Nlaka'pamuxcin. A mid- to low vowel, written *é* or *á* in Secwepemctsín, Nlaka'pamuxcin, and St'at'imcets, systematically changes to *í* in Nsyilxcn (Okanagan). Hence, *skelép*, *nk'yáp*, and *snk'yap* change to *snk'líp* in Nsyilxcn (Okanagan).

Beginning with ethnologists William Fraser Tolmie and Horatio Hale, European scholars realized as early as the 1840s that there was a connection or relationship among many of the different "dialects" (languages) of the Interior Plateau and the coast surrounding the mouth of the Fraser River and continuing south. By the late 1800s, Franz Boas and John W. Powell had grouped twenty-three languages in this area into what came to be called the Salish(an) language family. The term "Salish" derives from the word "Seliš," which, in the language of the Flathead people of northern Montana, is their name for themselves as a people and for their homeland, the Bitterroot Valley. The term "Salish" or "Salishan" was then extended to refer to the whole group of twenty-three languages that came to be known as related because of shared similarities in vocabulary, sound system, and structure.

During the nineteenth century, linguists showed how languages that can be grouped into a *language family* on the basis of such similarities are also *historically* related: they go back to a common ancestor language called a *proto-language*, now extinct, but out of which have developed the various languages of the family over time. For the Salish language family, this ancestral language, no longer spoken, is Proto-Salish. Obviously, its words are reconstructed according to the systematic ways that sounds changed between languages over time.

In chapter 2, we pointed out that earlier anthropologists and linguists believed that the Salish language family originated in the Interior. However, since the 1960s, linguists have determined a coastal origin for Salish, with an original homeland south of the mouth of the Fraser River (Elmendorf 1965; Kinkade 1991; Kinkade et al. 1998; Suttles 1987b; Suttles and Elmendorf 1963). Given that glottochronological reconstructions into the remote past of more than 6,000 years ago are futile, it is difficult to triangulate the emergence of Proto-Salish with archaeological timelines. The oldest archaeological sites near the mouth of the Fraser River are the Glenrose Cannery site, whose earliest deposits are just over 8,000 years old, and the Milliken site near Yale in the Fraser Canyon, whose occupation dates back 9,000 years. However, archaeologists agree that following the retreat of the Sumas Glacier, the area from the Lower Mainland to the Fraser Canyon was inhabitable by 11,000 to 10,500 years ago (see R.L. Carlson and Dalla Bona 1996).

ItNuxalkmc (Bella Coola), spoken in the Bella Coola Valley and along Bentinck Arm near the central coast of British Columbia, is believed to be one of the earliest languages to split from the Salish ancestor language(s), probably some 6,000 to 5,500 years ago.[5] In some cases, words sound remarkably

Table 4.2 | The Salish language family

I	1	Nuxalk (ItNuxalkmc, Bella Coola)
II	Coast Salish	
	Central Coast Salish (Central Salish)	
	2	Comox (inc. Comox or Q'ómox̣ʷs and Sliammon ʔayʔaǰúθəm)
	3	Halkomelem (inc. Island Hul'q'umi'num', Downriver hən̓q̓əmin̓əm̓, Upriver or Sto:lo Halq'əméyləm)
	4	Lushootseed (Puget Salish, Skagit-Nisqually, Dxʷləšúcid)
	5	Nooksack (Łə́čələsəm)*
	6	Pentlatch (Pənƛ̓áč)*
	7	Sháshíshálh (Sechelt, Seshelt, Shashishalhem, šášíšáɬəm)
	8	Sḵwxwú7mesh snichim (Squamish)
	Straits Salish (Straits)	
	9	Klallam (Clallam, Nəxʷsƛ̓áy̓emúcən)*
	10	Northern Straits (Straits, SENĆOŦEN, and other dialects without first-language speakers)
	11	Twana (Skokomish, Sqʷuqʷúʔbəšq)*
III	Tsamosan*	
	12	Cowlitz (Sƛ̓púlmš)
	13	Upper Chehalis (Q̓ʷay̓áyiɬq̓)
	14	Lower Chehalis (łəw̓áľməš)
	15	Quinault (Kʷínayɬ)
IV	16	Tillamook (Hutyéyu)*
V	Interior Salish	
	Northern	
	17	Shuswap (Secwepemctsín, səxwepməxcín)
	18	Thompson (Nlaka'pamuxcin, Nɬeʔképmxcín)
	19	St'at'imcets/Stl'atl'imx (Lillooet), Upper and Lower dialects
	Southern	
	20	Coeur d'Alene (Snchitsu'umshtsn, snčícuʔumšcn)
	21	Columbian (Columbia, Nxaʔamxcín)
	22	Colville-Okanagan (Nsyilxcn)
	23	Spokane-Kalispel-Flathead (Montana Salish)

* The language no longer has first-language speakers.

Note: The grouping of subgroups and languages in the Salish family is based on Czaykowska-Higgins and Kinkade (1998), P.D. Kroeber (1999), Thompson (1979), and Gerdts and Matthewson (2004).

similar in such geographically distant Salish languages as Nuxalk and Secwepemctsín, but they developed different meanings with time, which can nonetheless be traced back to earlier meanings that they must have had a long time ago. For example, the word *kúkwpi7* – sometimes spelled

Table 4.3 | Percentage of shared cognates between Secwepemctsín and other Interior Salish languages

Language	*Shared cognates with Secwepemctsín (%)*
Nlaka'pamuxcin	75
St'at'imcets	48
Nsyilxcn	50
Montana Salish	37
Columbian	34
Coeur d'Alene	32

Source: Adapted from Elmendorf (1965).

kúkpi7 – means "chief" in the Secwépemc, Lillooet, and Nlaka'pamux languages, but in ItNuxalkmc it means "grandfather." In comparing the different cognates of *kúkwpi7*, a word that goes back to the root form *kupi7*, we see that the ancient meaning of this word must have been something like "elder." In ItNuxalkmc it eventually evolved into "grandfather," whereas in the Northern Interior Salish languages, it came to mean "chief." Very likely, its ancient meaning points to the political advice and thus leadership that elders provided to the people in their social group, based on their wisdom (see Kuipers 2002). With time, the term *kúkwpi7* came to stand for the traditional leader of Secwépemc and other Interior Salish communities, whose position was partly hereditary and partly by appointment (see chapter 10).

As we discussed in chapters 2 and 3, there is good evidence that Proto–Interior Salish developed some 5,000 years ago at the onset of the archaeological Lochnore Phase through the incursion of Salish speakers into the Interior Plateau, whose language melded with the language(s) of the people who had lived there already for several thousand years, the new language being Proto–Interior Salish. Some 4,500 years ago, coinciding with the beginnings of the Shuswap Horizon of the Plateau Pithouse Tradition – that is, with Interior Plateau culture as ethnographic and archaeological sources have described it – the southern branch of Interior Salish separated from the northern branch and eventually split into the languages as we know them now: Okanagan-Colville, Kalispel (Montana Salish), Coeur d'Alene, and Columbian. The northern branch itself split into St'at'imcets (Lillooet) and Secwepemctsín/Nlaka'pamuxcin, with the latter two languages separating some 2,000 years ago (Elmendorf 1965). Linguist William Elmendorf (ibid.) has observed that the percentage of shared cognates among Interior Salish languages declines with geographic distance between languages, as well as noticeably declining where territories associated with languages are not adjacent.

Eventually, Secwepemctsín itself developed into two dialects: Eastern Secwepemctsín, spoken east of Kamloops at Adams Lake, Neskonlith, and

Little Shuswap, including these bands' communities near Salmon Arm, and also at Splatsín (Enderby) and Invermere; and Western Secwepemctsín, spoken from Kamloops west, north, and northwest, including at the Secwépemc communities on or near the Fraser and North Thompson Rivers. The dialect boundary between Eastern and Western Secwepemctsín appears to have run in the area around Monte Creek on the South Thompson River, some 20 kilometres east of Kamloops. This area was densely populated until probably the mid-1800s, when diseases wiped out many of the Secwépemc settlements in this area and when settlers were able to pre-empt and buy the land here at the exclusion of Secwépemc people (see chapter 12).

The Eastern and Western Dialects and Microdialects

The two dialects of Secwepemctsín – usually called Eastern and Western dialects – differ mainly in that the Eastern dialect changes certain *m's* and *n's* within words or at the end of words either into the vowels *a*, *u*, or *i* or into the glottal stop 7. Thus, whereas a Western dialect speaker would say "*kénem?*" ("what happened?"), a speaker of the Eastern dialect would say "*kána?*" The word for "mouth," *splútsen* in the Western dialect, is *splútsi* in the Eastern dialect.

Although Eastern dialect speakers use reduplication to make a diminuitive (little thing) out of a word, they do not use it to speak in the "I" and "my" form, like Western dialect speakers do. Thus, in the Western dialect, to say "I am Shuswap" one says "*Secwécwpemc-ken*" (reduplicating the *cw* before the stressed *é*), whereas Eastern dialect speakers say "*Secwépemc-ka.*" We explain more about reduplication below. In addition, a very small number of words are altogether different in the Eastern dialect, in most cases representing words that were borrowed or adapted from Nsyilxcn (Okanagan). Thus, whereas in the Western dialect the word for "flower" is *sweléńsem* (the nominalizer *s*, plus the root *wel* for "shiny," plus the lexical suffix *-eńs* for "ears" ["petals"], plus *-em* to indicate the intransitive verb), in the Eastern dialect it is *sts7e7kw* (a reduplicated form of the root *ekw* for "sparkle," with the inserted 7 producing a status form or inchoative, "getting sparkly"). The Western dialect word *xpé7e* (grandfather) is *slé7e* in the Eastern dialect, the latter borrowed from Okanagan.

In spite of these differences, speakers of the Eastern and Western dialects can communicate without difficulty, each maintaining their own dialect while understanding everything the other person is saying. As linguist Aert Kuipers (1989, 9) commented upon checking words with Western Secwepemctsín speaker Lilly Harry that he had initially recorded only in Eastern Secwepemctsín, "Of a list of 'new' words recorded in the ES dialect, many of them unknown to younger WS speakers, she was familiar with over 90%, showing that with the oldest speakers Shuswap is a more homogenous language than would appear at first sight."

Table 4.4 | Systematic sound changes between Western Secwepemctsín (WS) and Eastern Secwepemctsín (ES)

Syllabic m *(written* em/me*) and* ṁ *(written* eṁ/ṁe*) in Western Secwepemctsín*

- remains unchanged in ES after *p*, *m*, *m̓*
  examples: *t̓úpem* (s/he twists, wrings), *ep̓em* (s/he wipes; root *ép̓*) – both identical in ES and WS
- becomes *u* or *7u* after labialized consonants *kw*, *qw*, *xw*, etc.
  examples: WS *t.súnkwem* = ES *t.súnkwu* (island), WS *kwemtús* = ES *kwutús* (always), WS *yéwem* = ES *yéwu* (to dip-net), WS *tsecllúqwem̓* = ES *tsecllúqwu7* (to bail)
- becomes *e* (written *a*) or *e7 (a7)* in all other cases
  examples: WS *st̓emkélt* = ES *st̓akált* (daughter), WS *skem̓cís* = ES *ska7cís* (grizzly bear), WS *sem7é7em* = ES *sa7á7a* (wife)

Syllabic n (written en/ne) and ṅ (written eṅ/ṅe) in Western Secwepemctsín

---

- remains unchanged after *t*, *ll*, *n*, *n̓*, *l*, *l̓*
  examples: *sqlélten* (salmon), *mét̓ens* (s/he mixes it; root *met̓* = mix) – both identical in ES and WS
- becomes *i*, *7i* (or *a*, *7a*) after *ts*, *ts̓*, *s*, *i*, *7i*
  examples: WS *tsentés* = ES *tsitás*, *tsatás* (one fixes), WS *spéts̓en* = ES *spets̓i* (rope, Indian hemp), WS *sekúsen̓t* = ES *sekúsi7t* (star)
- becomes *e*, *7e* (written *a*, *a7*) in all other cases
  examples: WS *sk̓épqen* = ES *sk̓ápqa* (head), WS *stemtúmen* = ES *statúma* (dream), WS *t̓úpens* = ES *t̓upas* (s/he twists it)

Source: Based on Kuipers (1983).

The late Raymond Joe of Splatsín near Enderby, where the Eastern dialect is used, likewise observed, "The speakers from, say, Skeetchestn, and let's say the speakers from Enderby, if they were to get together, I understand every word they're saying because the meaning isn't changed the way it's pronounced … I and Ron Ignace [a Western Secwepemctsín speaker] could have a conversation in Secwepemctsín and we would understand one another." Based on fluent speakers' seamless ability to communicate across dialects, and on the very small number of different words between the dialects, which is estimated at less than 5 per cent, it is evident that Secwepemctsín has existed as a stable and homogenous language for some 2,000 years and across a homeland that spans several hundred kilometres. This stability leads us to suspect that the dialect split between Eastern and Western Secwepemctsín is no more than a few centuries old, and given that the dialect boundary between Kamloops and Chase does not constitute a boundary based on spatial separation by mountain ranges or watersheds or a boundary caused

4.2 | Raymond Joe of Splatsín (Enderby), 2000. He was a speaker of the Eastern Secwepemctsín dialect.

by population migration, the chances are that the dialect differentiation occurred due to an interest in *social differentiation* on the part of competing groups, expressed through different and distinguishing speech, namely the systematic change of the Western Secwepemctsín consonants *m*, *m̓*, *n*, and *n̓* to vowels and/or glottal stops in Eastern Secwepemctsín. James Teit (1909, 455) provided a clue to how this dialect development may have arisen from competing collective identities among local groups, noting that in the 1800s both the Stk̓emlúpsemc (people of and near the confluence of the North and South Thompson Rivers) and the Sexqéltkemc ("upstream" people of the Chase and Shuswap Lake area) vied for the self-designation Secwepemc7úw̓i ("real Shuswap"). It is possible that Sexqéltkemc speakers began systematically modifying their speech in the quest to mark social difference from the Stk̓emlúpsemc.

Aside from the two main dialects, each community or geographic area within Secwepemcúl̓ecw has unique speech patterns. A very small number of words – probably less than one per cent of the vocabulary – contribute to these differences. For example, speakers of the Northern Secwépemc communities call a porcupine *stsetśúy̓e*, whereas the Símpcwemc call it *setśúye*; and speakers of the Skeetchestn, Bonaparte, and Kamloops communities use an entirely different Western dialect term, *skú7pecen*, whereas speakers in the Chase area, Enderby, and Windermere use the Eastern dialect version of this term, *skú7paca*. Sometimes root words or lexical roots are slightly modified: in the Skeetchestn, Bonaparte, and Kamloops area, speakers of Secwepemctsín use the word *cetséẃs* to mean "get tired," whereas in Northern Secwépemc communities, the word *ctsetséẃs* is used, which involves a reduplication of the initial *ts* sound. Given these small differences, however, and the reduction of *n's* and *m's* into vowels in predictable instances in Eastern Secwepemctsín, it should be emphasized that the grammatical patterns of the language are identical across dialects, as long as we take into account basic systematic sound changes.

Aside from a limited number of words, the intonation pattern and subtle ways of pronunciation identify speakers of particular communities or areas. Thus speakers of the Northern Secwépemc communities in the Williams Lake area are known for their slow but melodic speech, locally referred to as *legtsínem* ("dragged-down speech"). By contrast, Secwépemc speakers of Tk̓emlúps, Skeetchestn, and St̓uxtéws speak quickly, and they also often substitute the short *e* vowel for the *r* (voiced velar fricative) sound and modify the pharyngeal or throat sound *g* into a glottal stop.

Interestingly, due to frequent intermarriage between neighbouring communities, Secwépemc communities at the intersection of dialects have long featured a mixture of neighbouring dialects. In the 1980s, some Secwépemc speakers at Simpcw (North Thompson Band) who had a parent or grandparent from the Chase (Eastern dialect) area had incorporated some Eastern Secwepemctsín into their speech. Others, who had parents and grandparents from Tsq̓éscen (Canim Lake), one of the Northern Secwépemc communities, spoke with intonation patterns similar to speakers of northern communities.

Features of Secwepemctsín

In Secwepemctsín's phonology (sound system), grammar (the way words are strung into a sentence), and lexicon (inventory of words and their meanings), there are many features that not only point to similarities with neighbouring Salish languages but also show its uniqueness and amazing complexity.

Sounds and Orthography

The number of sounds, or *phonemes*, in Secwepemctsín is forty-three (or forty-four, counting a very rare sound). These sounds include six vowels, eleven consonants that are very similar to consonants occuring in English, eleven plain consonants that do not occur in English, and sixteen additional consonants not occurring in English that are glottalized (made with an instantaneous "pinch" or "catch" in the throat). The Secwepemctsín inventory of sounds is similar to that of other Interior Salish languages, especially those that are closely related. Linguist Aert Kuipers used a linguistic alphabet similar to the International Phonetic Alphabet to write the language in his

4.3 | French Oblate priest Jean-Marie-Raphaël Le Jeune (1855–1929), ca. 1910. A missionary among the Secwépemc people between 1880 and 1827 while headquartered at St Joseph's Church on the Kamloops Indian Reserve, Le Jeune widely travelled to Indigenous villages throughout the Secwépemc nation and the Interior.

technical works *The Shuswap Language* (1974) and *A Report on Shuswap* (1989). In the 1970s, together with May Dixon of Canim Lake and other speakers of the language, he also developed a practical orthography to write the language on a typewriter using the letters of the English alphabet, together with apostrophies indicating glottalized sounds and the number 7 to stand for the glottal stop. This practical alphabet is widely used by Secwépemc people nowadays to write the language. Our chart of the Secwépemc sound system shows the ways that vowels and consonants are written in the practical orthography (see table 0.1).

During the late nineteenth and early twentieth centuries, the Oblate missionary Father Jean-Marie-Raphaël Le Jeune (1855–1930), who spent more than forty years among the Secwépemc, taught many Secwépemc, Nlaka'pamux, and Okanagan people how to write Chinook Jargon – a lingua franca widely used at the time between Aboriginal peoples of different languages and among Aboriginal and white people – using Chinook shorthand. Chinook shorthand is based on the Duployé shorthand system, which uses symbols of lines and dots to write syllables, and Le Jeune had taught himself to write it fluently as a young seminarian. After moving among the Nlaka'pamux people, a fellow priest, Father Dominic Chiappini, suggested that shorthand, rather than syllabics as they had become used among the Carrier during Father Adrien-Gabriel Morice's priesthood, might provide a feasible way to write Interior Salish languages. In 1891, at Coldwater, Father Le Jeune initially taught a young Nlaka'pamux man named Charlie Mayous how to write Chinook Jargon – then the widely used trade language among Aboriginal peoples and with non-Aboriginal people – using shorthand. Mayous, in turn, quickly realized he could write Nlaka'pamuxcin using shorthand. Le Jeune recorded, "Thereupon I conceived the idea of starting a school and assigned as teacher Charlie Alexis Mayous, for such was the name of the little lame man. He knew how to explain the sounds of the vowels and consonants to his students better than I could have done myself. At the same time, he learned to read fluently all of the prayers and catechism that I wrote for him. Not only the children but the adults too took an interest in Mayous' lessons" (trans. in Le Jeune and Poser 2011, 3). By the fall of 1891, accompanied by two Nlaka'pamux, Father Le Jeune was teaching shorthand, which the Interior Salish peoples called "Chinuk pípa" ("Chinook paper"), to write Chinook Jargon in numerous Secwépemc communities, and he began to publish his newsletter, the *Kamloops Wawa*, whose subscription quickly jumped from twenty-five copies to several hundred. Interestingly, Le Jeune built his writing lessons around the verses of hymns, noting that, "whereas previously it had practically been necessary to drag the most capable Indians by the hair, now the entire band worked eagerly at learning the shorthand." In other words, whereas people had been rather disinterested in taking in his catechism classes for the sake of converting to a new religion, they took enormous interest in the chance to learn to read and write – and to acquire new songs! During the winter of 1891–92, Charlie Mayous continued lessons with five or six Secwépemc learners in Kamloops, although he was very sick by that time, eventually passing away in the spring of 1893. It must have been during Le Jeune's lessons, or as likely during Mayous's lessons, that Secwépemc people began writing Secwepemctsín using Chinook shorthand.[6]

Within a decade, large numbers of adults of all ages were writing Secwepemctsín using shorthand, as attested by greetings and other writings submitted to the *Wawa*. With the help of two female Secwépemc assistants at Tk̓emlúps (Kamloops) – Angele Edward (Hyacinth Sisyésq̓t's daughter-in-law) and Emma Harry – Le Jeune continued publishing the *Kamloops Wawa*. During its publication run between 1892 and 1915, it had more than 1,500 subscriptions. In 1904 Le Jeune accompanied Chief Louis of Tk̓emlúps on a trip to France and Rome, which resulted in an audience with the Pope, where Chief Louis and a few others demonstrated their shorthand writing skills, winning a medal. Le Jeune himself published a prayerbook titled *Shuswap Manual* (1906) and a book titled *Studies on Shuswap* (1925), both written in shorthand.

Thus, more than a hundred years ago, many Secwépemc people were writing Secwepemctsín using the Duployé shorthand system. Using Secwepemctsín, other Interior Salish languages, and Chinook Jargon, Secwépemc people and those from neighbouring nations gained literacy and corresponded with one another and the priest, even writing want-ads, letters,

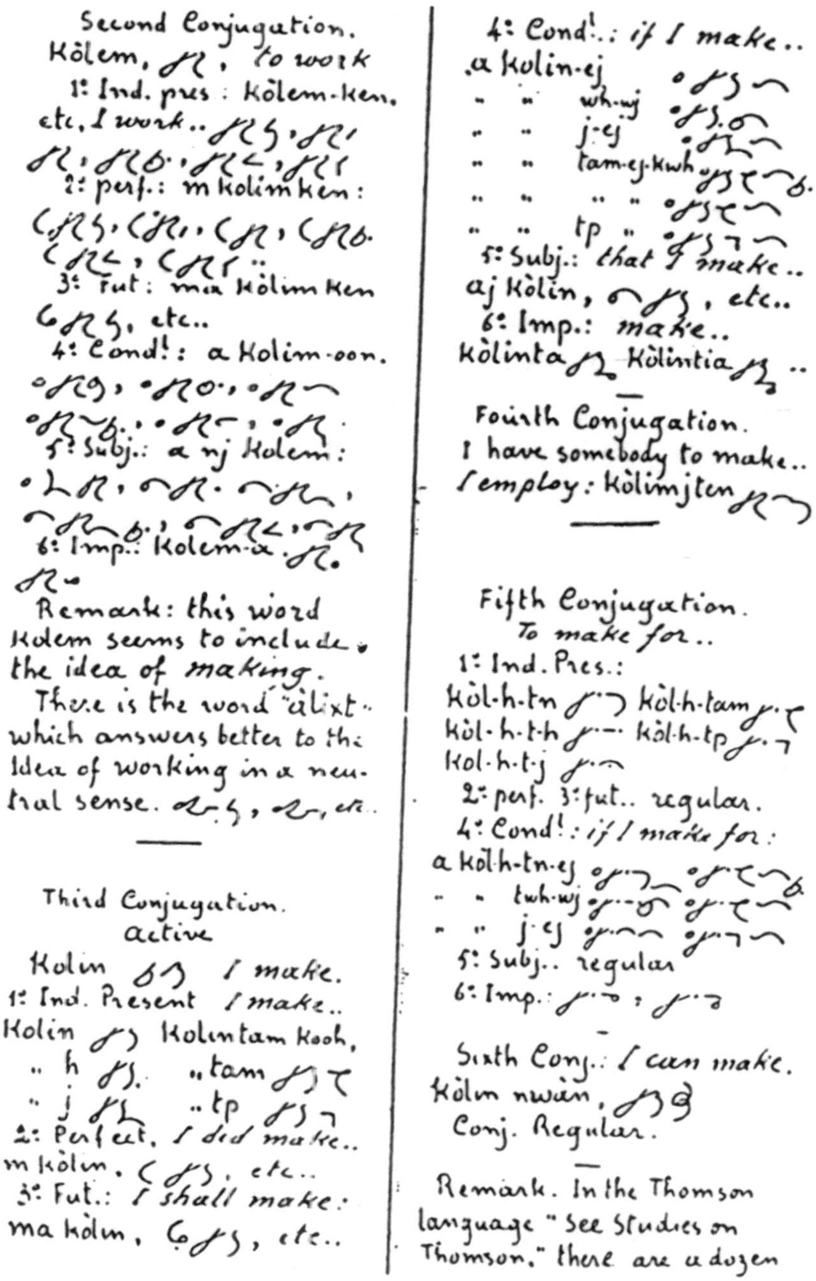

Second Conjugation.
Kôlem, , to work
1º Ind. pres : Kôlem-ken.
etc. I work..
2º perf.: m kolim ken :
3º Fut : ma kolim ken
, etc..
4º Cond! : a kolim-oon.
5º Subj.: a nj kolem :
6º Imp.: kolem-a
Remark: this word
kolem seems to include
the idea of making.
There is the word "ālixt"
which answers better to the
idea of working in a neutral sense. , , etc..

Third Conjugation.
active
Kolin I make.
1º Ind. Present I make..
Kolin Kolintam kooh,
.. h .. tam
.. j .. tp
2º Perfect. I did make..
m kolin. , etc..
3º Fut.: I shall make:
ma kolin, , etc..

4º Cond!.: if I make..
a kolin-ej
.. .. wh-wj
.. .. j-ej
.. .. tam-ej-kwh
.. ..
.. .. tp ..
5º Subj.: that I make..
aj kolin, , etc..
6º Imp.: make..
kolinta kolintia ..

Fourth Conjugation.
I have somebody to make..
I employ: kolimjten

Fifth Conjugation.
To make for..
1º Ind. Pres.:
kol-h-tn kol-h-tam
kol-h-t-h kol-h-tp
kol-h-t-j
2º perf. 3º fut.. regular.
4º Cond!: if I make for:
a kol-h-tn-ej
.. .. twh-wj
.. .. j-ej
5º Subj.. regular
6º Imp.: ;

Sixth Conj.: I can make.
Kolin nwān,
Conj. Regular.

Remark. In the Thomson
language "See Studies on
Thomson." there are a dozen

4.4 | A text sample from Father Jean-Marie-Raphaël Le Jeune’s *Studies on Shuswap* (1925), written in Secwepemctsín using the Duployé shorthand system.

4.5 | Linguist Aert Kuipers (1919–2012) of the Netherlands, 1983. He carried out extensive research on the Secwépemc language with elders in numerous communities between the 1960s and early 1990s.

and other correspondence, as well as reading and contributing to the *Wawa*. As Father Le Jeune and the whole generation of priests of his time retired and passed on, and when the church and government enforced children's attendance at residential schools starting in the 1920s and 1930s, not only did these institutions criminalize the oral use of Secwepemctsín at the school, and teach only English-language reading and writing, but they also hid the books and newsletters written in Secwepemctsín from students.[7] Today, almost no elders remain who know how to read Chinook shorthand, and throughout the decades when Secwépemc children attended residential schools in Kamloops and Williams Lake between the 1920s and 1970s, all literacy instruction involved the English language and Roman orthography. However, present learners and speakers of Secwepemctsín can still teach themselves and one another to read the words that their elders wrote in the language with the help of Father Le Jeune's *The Wawa Shorthand Instructor* (1896).[8]

Unlike the practical alphabet, Chinook shorthand does not accurately represent all sounds of Secwepemctsín. For example, it has no special symbols for the hard or glottalized consonants of Secwepemctsín (e.g., *ṗ, ṫ, k̓, tṡ, q̇, l̓, ṁ, ṅ, ẇ, ẏ, ṙ, ġ*) but writes them as plain, nonglottalized sounds. However, 100 years ago, this approach worked quite well because everyone still spoke the language and could pronounce words with the right glottal sounds or with sounds that were different from English rather than using the written language as a guide to pronunciation like learners of the language do nowadays.

Sentence and Word Structure

Secwepemctsín has interesting grammatical features, some of which it shares with other Salish languages and some of which are unique to Secwepemctsín. These features point to the connection between language, culture, perception, and cognition discussed at the beginning of this chapter. In its structure and lexicon, Secwepemctsín speaks to the dynamic relationships among humans, all other living things, the land, and the cosmos, and in doing so, it encodes the cultural knowledge that generations of past Secwépemc in turn inherited from their ancestors. As anthropologist and ethnobotanist Wade Davis (2007, n.p.) poetically phrases it, Indigenous languages represent "an old-growth forest of the mind, a watershed of thought, an ecosystem of spiritual responsibilities," offering us a different way of thinking about the natural and social world compared with the way that English or other European languages organize thought. These cognitive worlds, in turn, are born out of ancient experience on the land and are imminent not only in the words and word structure but also in grammatical features. Below, we discuss a few of these interesting features of Secwépemc grammar and word structure.

REDUPLICATION | Reduplication involves the "doubling" of individual consonants or all or part of the root of a word. Secwepemctsín uses the reduplication of a consonant-vowel-consonant or consonant-vowel root or partial root at or near the beginning of a word to express a plural or collectivity, although in Secwepemctsín this is done only when it is necessary to qualify that more than one person is involved in an action or event or that "each and everyone" of a group of people or things is involved in an action (distributive). For example, *sqéxe* means "dog," whereas *sqexqéxe* means "dogs"; and *pésellkwe* means "lake," whereas *pespésellkwe* means "lakes." This kind of reduplication also works with verbs. For example, *kitsc* means "arrive," whereas *ketskítsc* means "more than one arrives." In other instances, especially with verbs, this kind of reduplication expresses repetition, increased intensity of an action, or that someone or something has a certain quality "all over" or entirely. Thus *wíkem* means "to see" or "look in order to see" (but nothing specific), whereas *wekwíkem* means "to see or look all over, to repeatedly or continuously look." When we glottalize the *m̓* on the final resonant sound, thus saying *wekwíkem̓*, it means "seeing things" in the sense of "having a vision," seeing extraordinary things, or thinking one saw something but not being sure what it was – depending on context.

Yet another variation of consonant-vowel-consonant doubling, which adds the reduplicated part at the end of the word, expresses that a quality or state of being is in the process of becoming and increasing. Thus *petetét*, derived from the root *pet*, means "come to a boil"; *pecwúcw*, derived from the root *pucw* for "to blow," means "to swell up"; and *petát̓*, derived from the root *pat̓*, means "overflow," "boiling over," or bread "hanging over the edges" because the yeast dough rose too high.

A further kind of reduplication is consonant reduplication, where the consonant before the stressed vowel in a word is reinserted behind the stressed vowel. This kind of reduplication functions to make a diminuitive (little thing, quality, or action) out of a word. By extension, it is used to express actions, qualities, states of being, and feelings in the "I" and "my" form (first-person singular) of what in English would be considered verbs, adjectives, and nouns. Thus, when Secwepemctsín speakers speak use the "I" form, they actually express their actions, qualities, and possessions as *being little* – a way to humbly and respectfully speak about oneself when addressing others. Making one's actions, state of being, and possessions appear small increases one's acknowledgment of the social status of the person or people being addressed and thus acknowledges them as being important.[9]

Another function of consonant reduplication is to make a proper noun out of a word that functions like a noun, a feature that is seen, for example, in words for plants (see chapter 7) and for place names (see chapter 8). Thus the plant term *tseqwtseqwéqwelq̓w*, which comes from the reduplicated root word *tsiqw* or *tsewq* (red) and from the lexical suffix or shape classifier *-elq̓w* (stick), means "red-all-over sticks." The reduplicated consonant *qw*, however, changes the meaning to a certain kind of stick that is red all over, namely the plant name for red willow or red osier dogwood (*Cornus stolonifera*).

SPATIAL DEIXIS | All Salish languages, including Secwepemctsín, have a system of spatial deixis that employs very intricate categories beyond those that speakers of English are used to. Among these categories, demonstratives deal with the way a language expresses a speaker's orientation to spatial reference points and relations like "here" and "there" or "this one" and "that one." Unlike the English-language system, which gets by with an opposition between two points of reference, such as "this" versus "that" and "here" versus "there," Secwepemctsín spatial deixis includes three reference points: *here* (near the speaker), *there near you* (the addressee or person who is spoken to), and *way over there* (away from both speaker and listener). Thus *ye7éne* means "this one [near me, the speaker]," whereas *yeréy* means "that one, near you [the person I am speaking to]," and *yerí7* means "that one over there, away from both of us."

Deictic words and speech particles also provide information about whether the thing or person talked about is visible (present) or invisible (not present) in space and time. For example, *t̓lúne* means "over there" when referring to an area that is in sight or visible, whereas *t̓kllú7* or *t̓kllúne* refers to a place or area that is not in sight while someone talks about it and that "exists" because the speaker remembers it, imagines it, or knows about its existence. When Secwepemctsín speakers refer to people or things that act on one another, they also use the two articles (determiners) *re* and *le* (roughly translatable as "the") to distinguish between people or things that are present and those that are absent and invisible but remembered. For example, when one refers to deceased people, one uses the determiner *le* since deceased people are no longer present or visible but continue to exist in memory.

A third level of deixis, expressed by the determiner *t(e)k* or *k*, refers to hypothetical things. Thus, if I make the request "*kectsétsme tek sp̓íxle7cw!*" ("give me some fried bread!"), I am expressing the information that the fried bread that I am requesting exists only as a wish and that I am not sure there actually is any. If I ask "*t̓hé7n k ts̓i7?*" ("where is there a deer?"), I am wondering whether there is a deer that is in some kind of location, and thus the deer is not actually present or "real" in front of me, but I am thinking about where it might be and whether there actually is one.

In chapter 7, we show how the Secwépemc system of spatial deixis, in combination with place names and words for landforms, functions as a mental geographic-positioning system that allows speakers to convey very detailed information about the existence and location of things and processes on the land.

PRONOUN MARKING | Pronouns are words or particles that refer to persons or things (e.g., *he*, *it*, *we*, *us*, *you*, *I*, and *me*) without mentioning them by name. In a variety of ways, Secwépemc pronouns work differently from English pronouns. Rather than existing as independent words, they exist as particle words that are attached to an action word (verb), quality word, or noun. However, instead of a single pronoun ending, or suffix, there are several pronoun endings, and which one is used depends on whether the action someone carries out is aimed at another thing or person (transitive) or involves only a "doer," or agent, but no object or recipient of the action (intransitive). Another dimension of pronoun particle use is whether an action is the opening statement in a verbal "paragraph" or follows an initial previous statement by the same agent (the person who is doing the action or is the focus of the action). The use of pronouns in narrative – combined with the feature of passive voice (Boelscher 1990) – thus provides a way of tracking and foregrounding from whose point of view a narrative sequence is told, and it allows for switching perspective.

Finally, the meaning of Secwepemctsín pronouns is organized differently from the meaning of English pronouns. In Secwepemctsín, there is a single pronoun ending that means "he," "she," "it," and "they." Thus, unlike English, Secwepemctsín does not distinguish gender (male or female) in the third person. Elders who were raised with Secwepemctsín as their first language often generically use "he" when the person they refer to is female or when they are talking of a thing. However, Secwepemctsín makes up for its combination of third-person gender pronouns into a single one by having two different kinds of "we," namely one that *includes* the person I am speaking to and one that *excludes* the person I am speaking to. It also has two "you" pronouns for addressing one person ("you" singular) versus more than one person ("you folks" plural). Depending on the nature of the action a speaker expresses, these pronoun categories manifest themselves in several sets of particle words.

EVIDENTIALS | An interesting feature that Secwepemctsín shares with other Salish languages and many nonrelated Indigenous languages, but not with English, is what we call evidential suffixes. Evidentials are particle words that indicate the status of evidence of an utterance, as expressed in the grammatical categories of the language. When a Secwepemctsín speaker talks about a past event, he or she always reports whether the issue talked about is known to the speaker because he or she has firsthand experience of what happened, or because he or she knows that something happened from hearsay, or because of physical evidence that shows something has happened.

Consider the following examples. If someone says, "*Re Mary tscentés re tsitcws*," it means, "Mary fixed up her house." The verb *tscentés* has no further ending or suffix. Unless it is preceded by context information that establishes a narrative as based on hearsay information, this sentence is usually interpreted by speakers to mean that the person who reports the event personally experienced it, or in other words, was there when Mary fixed up her house.

If someone says, "*Re Mary tscentés-ekwe re tsitcws*," it could also be translated as "Mary fixed up her house." However, by adding the suffix *-ekwe* (pronounced "uka") to the verb, the speaker is indicating that he or she knows Mary fixed up her house *according to hearsay*. Someone who was there or knew Mary fixed up her house told the speaker about it. Thus *-ekwe* is an evidential suffix that indicates information according to what someone told the person who is the topic of the information.

If someone says, however, "*Re Mary tscentés-enke re tsitcws*," it means that the speaker knows from physical evidence that Mary fixed up her house. Perhaps, when he or she saw Mary's house, it was freshly painted, had new windows, and had a new roof. Thus *-enke* is another evidential suffix. Unlike the suffix *-ekwe*, which involves information that derives from being *told* about something, *-enke* involves knowledge derived from physical evidence or perception of one's senses. Such physical evidence can involve not only vision, as in the example above, but also smell or hearing. If I smell burnt toast and know Mary is fixing toast in the kitchen, I will say, "*M-q̓ust-enke re Mary re lekelét.s*" ("Mary's toast must have got burnt").

By using such evidential suffixes consistently in everyday conversation or in storytelling, Secwepemctsín speakers constantly remind one another of the status of knowledge or evidence that pieces of information have. In English, we can include such information by adding additional sentences. We can say, "someone told me he fixed his house," "I noticed that he fixed up his house," or more vaguely "it seems like he fixed up his house." However, these statements involve elaborations and choices of speech, which can also be omitted. In Secwepemctsín, the categories of grammar themselves encode this information and are an intrinsic part of the utterances made by speakers of the language. Many other languages have evidential particles, although each language has unique ways of expressing the evidentiary status of an utterance.[10]

LEXICAL SUFFIXES | One of the most fascinating features of Salish languages are their lexical suffixes. These are particle words that refer to concepts, or perhaps mental images, that invoke something's shape or kind of features, like human and animal anatomy or geographical features, the latter often derived from human body lexical suffixes. They also reference basic physical elements and cosmological shapes (fire, water, sky, land, mineral), botanical features (plant, shrub, bush, leafy part of plant, flower), and human-made things (house, campfire, conveyance or vessel, implement). Although it appears that they initially derived from free noun words, in many instances they no longer resemble those noun words. They can get attached to noun stems in order to form compound nouns and to verb stems, including verb stems that would be considered adjectives in English, in order to modify their meaning so as to incorporate nouns.[11]

Where they attach to verbs, free nouns can be used instead. For example, if we want to say "wash your hands!" we could say it just like in English, using the command *ts̓éwente* (wash), plus *re7* (your), plus *kelc* (hands), and thus say "*tsẻ́wente re7 kelc!*" In better Secwepemctsín, however, we would express this with a lexical suffix as "*tsẻ́wkstemce!*" ("wash," plus the lexical suffix *-kst*, which refers to hands, plus two more endings, *-m* and *-ce*, which refer respectively to an action and a command given to one person).

As they modify the meaning of verbs and nouns, many lexical suffixes have developed extended or metaphorical meanings. Thus many lexical suffixes that refer to body parts have extended meanings that refer to geographical shapes in the landscape as these are named in geographic terms and place names (see chapter 5). For example, *-tsin* (mouth) designates the mouth of a river, shore, or edge, as well as "speech, voice" and "language"; *-eqs* (nose) designates a land protrubrance; *-enk* (belly) refers to a rounded, relatively steep hill or "side hill"; *-ups* (buttocks) refers to a buttock-shaped point of land at a confluence; and *-iken* (back) refers to a mountain ridge. Lexical suffixes thus inscribe the shapes of the human body into the landscape (see chapter 7). Lexical suffixes can also tightly package together information found in vivid visual images about the shape, function, or nature of objects into a single compound word. For example, the word *c.wepúlecwem* means "[there are] weeds growing in/on the land." It includes the prefix *c* (inside), plus the root *wep* (hairy/covered with a hair-like substance), plus the lexical suffix *-úlecw/úl̓ecw* (land), plus *-em* to indicate the intransitive verb or action. Although in English it is usually glossed as "weed," it actually functions as a verb, thus making explicit reference to the action of growing. Other examples of deploying tightly packaged information with the help of lexical suffixes exist in the many Secwépemc language place names throughout Secwepemcúl̓ecw. Thus the place name Ck̓emqenétkwe is made up of the prefix *c* (inside), plus the root *k̓em* (two things come together at an angle), plus the lexical suffixes *-qen* (head) and *-étkwe* (water). Together, the word conveys the compounded visual imagery of this place, where the water of two creeks flows together (*k̓em*) on a high flat, or head (*-qen*), with the prefix *c* conveying the information that the name concerns the area "within" that is described by these shapes and substances. In chapter 7, we present more examples of the precise and uniquely encoded imagery conveyed by Secwépemc place names.

Other extended meanings or metaphorical uses of lexical suffixes involve *-ellts̓e* (insides, guts, or meat), whose meaning extends to character and feelings. Thus *ck̓eséllts̓e* describes someone of mean character. The lexical suffix *-us* (face) extends its meaning to "window," "fire," and "light." The suffix *-ékst* (hand or lower arm) extends to the notion of pointing, including the direction a wind comes from. Thus *secwepemcékst* refers to the east wind, and *pesxnmékst* ("wind from the direction of the dentalium shell people"), or Chilcotin country, refers to the west wind.

Secwepemctsín has more than a hundred of these lexical suffixes. As we can see from the examples above, they serve to express complex ideas about the shape and nature of things and about the ways that things and actions of certain shapes and kinds affect one another.

Lexical suffixes are also used as numerical classifiers to count different things according to their shape or kind. Thus the lexical suffix *-úse7* is used to point out small, round things, like berries or marbles. To point out four round things, like berries or basketballs, one says *mesúse7* (the root *mus* for "four" plus the lexical suffix *-úse7* for "round-shaped things"). The lexical suffix *-él̓tcw* (bark) is extended to sheet-like objects and used to point out and count pieces of paper. Thus *mesél̓tcw* refers to four sheets of paper. The lexical suffix *-éke7* refers to tree branches and antler-shaped things, and from there it extends to objects with protrusions, including cups or mugs, as they have a handle, and when the prefix *c* (inside) is added, the meaning extends to measures, like spoonfuls and cupfuls. The lexical suffix *-el̓qw* refers to trees, logs, and in general stick-like objects. Thus *mesél̓qw* refers to four trees or four pencils.

Importantly, like chemical elements in the periodic table, the combination of root words that bear meaning, lexical suffixes indicating shape and kind, which can be strung together, and other particle words serves to make up ever-new words in Secwepemctsín, including new words for new and introduced objects and concepts. Thus the Secwépemc word for "freezer" has been

Table 4.5 | A small selection of the more than 100 lexical suffixes of Secwepemctsín

Lexical suffix	*Meaning(s)*	*Independent noun/verb*	*Examples*
-ellcw, -llcw	"house," "dwelling," "building"	*tsitcw*	*tsewéllcw* (build a house) *cḱemtsenéllcw* (door) *sceńcéllcw* (packrat)
-ellp	"vascular plant," "tree," "shrub"	*tsrep* (tree)	*melénllp* (balsam fir, subalpine fir) *elkéllp* (kinnikinnik shrub) *qetśuye7é7llp* (yarrow)
-úl̓ecw, -l̓ecw	"land"	*tmicw*	Secwepemcúl̓ecw (Shuswap territory) *tspetkúl̓ecw* (hole in the ground, den)
-éke7, -ke7	"tree branch," "antlers"	–	*kelcméke7* (tree branch) *puméke7* (drumstick)
-qín, -qen, -qiń	"head," "at the head of"	*sḱépqen*	*tśéẃqnem* (wash one's head) *ctseq̓qínten* (hammer)
-tsín, -tsiń, -tsen	"mouth"	*splútsen*	Secwepemctsín (Shuswap language) *lectsín* (beautiful voice)
-éne, -éńe, -ne	"shoulder"	*tḱméne*	*tq̓upéne* (to break one's collarbone) *tkellpéne* (have a dislocated shoulder)
-élltśé, -lltśe	"meat," "inside"*	*tśi7*	*kenmélltśe* (bear meat) *xqwiyélltśem* (enjoy every morsel of a meal) *cḱesélltśe* (mean)
-íken, íkeń, -ken	"upper back," "spine"	–	*selíken* (two ridges) *tśelcwíkeń* (saddle)
-ílc, -íl̓c, -elc, -lec	"body in motion"	–	*ṫek7ílc* (to leave) *qwétśelc* (to warm oneself)

* The inside, or gut, is thought to be where feelings come from!

Table 4.6 | Words for Secwépemc hip and pelvic anatomy

cḱemíl̓ekp (pelvic bone or illium)
gloss: prefix *c* (inside), plus root *ḱem* (two surfaces come together at an angle), plus lexical suffix *-il̓ekp* (upper hip)
literal translation: inside area of two surfaces [bones] coming together at upper hip

cḱméṁqstcen (ischium)
gloss: prefix *c* (inside), plus root *ḱem* (two surfaces come together at an angle), plus reduplication, plus lexical suffix *-(é)qstcen* (lower hip)
literal translation: inside area of two surfaces coming together [bones connected by joint] at lower part of hip

n(e)xelqéqstceṅ (hip joint and acetabulum)
gloss: prefix *n* (on the inside), plus root *xelq* (ball joint), plus reduplication, plus lexical suffix *-éqstceṅ* (lower hip)
literal translation: inside ball joint at lower hip

tekteq̓yép (pubic bone and pubic symphysis)
gloss: prefix *tek* (on top), plus root *teq̓* (cross over), plus lexical suffix *-ép* (on bottom)
literal translation: at bottom of crossing-over [bone]

cḱemqenúps (tailbone)
gloss: prefix *c* (inside), plus root *ḱem* (two surfaces come together at an angle), plus lexical suffix *-qen* (round shape at top), plus lexical suffix *-úps* (buttocks)
literal translation: tail-like connected joint at buttocks

coined as *csúl̓men*, which derives from the prefix *c* (inside), plus the root *sul̓* (freeze), plus the lexical suffix *-men* (instrument or thing you do something with). In other words, a freezer is conceived of as a device or implement used to freeze things inside of it. The combination of multiple lexical suffixes is particularly productive in Secwépemc anatomical words, where lexical suffixes allow for very detailed descriptions of skeletal structures and organs by providing detailed visual and functional clues related to bones. Table 4.6 shows some examples of how they work to map out hip and pelvic anatomy very precisely and descriptively.

Some Secwépemc words allow glimpses into the cultural past. The word for "cold inside" (a dwelling or room) used today is *cts̓elltéṁ*, which consists of the prefix *c* (inside), plus the root *ts̓ell* (cold), plus the lexical suffix *-teṁ* (underneath). Why underneath? In the past, when Secwépemc people lived in underground pithouses, or *c7ístkteṅ*, being "inside" meant being underground. Likewise, the contemporary Secwépemc word *cḱmenkéllcw* can mean "ceil-ing" or "wall." Its meaning derives from the curved wall-ceiling of traditional underground pithouses. In short, the grammatical and word-building structure (morphology and lexicon) of Secwepemctsín serves to express, in an interesting and unique way, complex meanings and relations as experienced by the Secwépemc people, who have spoken their language for thousands of years while living in their homeland, Secwepemcúl̓ecw, and communicating with one another about their experiences.[12]

Secwepemctsín: A Critically Endangered Language

Like most other Indigenous languages in Canada, Secwepemctsín has become a critically endangered language in the past few decades. In the recollection of present and past Secwépemc elders, Indian residential schools – in Secwepemcúl̓ecw most notably the Kamloops Indian Residential School and St Joseph's Indian Residential School near Williams Lake – sought to stamp out Aboriginal languages, and between the 1930s and 1960s, two to three generations of children had the language literally beaten out of them. Many elders remember being strapped, put in solitary confinement, and forced to do physical labour. They were humiliated, chastised, and shamed by their teachers and supervisors for speaking Secwepemctsín on the school grounds. Some went to residential school for ten years, after being admitted at five or six years of age. Others attended for "only" five or six years. Although many Secwépemc who attended residential schools after first learning Secwepemctsín in the home as young children did not entirely lose their ability to speak it, their devastating experiences had major consequences for future generations. Just like the physical and sexual abuses suffered in residential schools continue to have ongoing impacts on the individual and collective well-being of Canadian Indigenous people individually and Indigenous peoples collectively, the assault on language and culture – what the Truth and Reconciliation Commission of Canada (2015b, 1) and Supreme Court Justice Beverly McLachlan (quoted in Fine 2015; see also McLachlan 2015) have called "cultural genocide" – has had lasting and ongoing impacts on the fabric of Secwépemc communities and on the very fate of our language. Cultural genocide, in the dimension of language, was linguicide.[13] Even as residential schools were being shut down during the late 1960s and 1970s, replaced by the Canadian government's policy of "integrating" Aboriginal children into mainstream schooling, the pervasive influence of English in the education system and in the workplace continued to erode the language and almost entirely disrupted and stopped intergenerational transmission. By the mid-1990s, merely 3.5 per cent of Secwépemc people, most of them elderly, were able to speak the language fluently. With the passing of many fluent elders since the mid-1990s, the number of fluent speakers raised using Secwepemctsín in day-to-day communication has further eroded and now represents less than 2 per cent of the population, or fewer than 100 individuals, nearly all

4.6 | Secwépemc language champion Mona Jules, 2008. She has dedicated the past thirty years to bringing the language back by teaching it and by mentoring younger learners.

of them in their sixties or older.[14] However, what gives hope for the future of Secwepemctsín are the efforts by the younger generation to learn and use the language. The past two decades have seen the emergence of a Secwépemc-language immersion school, Chief Atahm School, at Adams Lake, a small but dedicated number of younger adults have gained fluency and gained confidence in the language through intensive one-on-one learning with an elder who is a fluent speaker, and a few have been raised with the language in the home. These efforts speak to the persistence of a small but growing number of adults who are working hard to learn, promote, use, and teach Secwepemctsín in our communities, who are using what they have learned with their children and grandchildren, and who are thus keeping the language alive for present and future generations.

5 Re Styecwmenúl̓ecws-kucw

How We Look(ed) after Our Land

WITH NANCY J. TURNER

> What makes us a people is the common knowledge of living in Secwepemcúl̓ecw, knowing and using its landforms and resources, and talking about it in our language. (R. Ignace 2008, 164)

> Many of the old people say this is our land. When the creator placed us on this land he gave us land to look after, so that the land will look after us forever. And he also gave us languages to live in harmony with each other and in harmony with nature. (Michel 2005, 89)

As we saw in chapter 3, the cooling trend during the Shuswap Horizon of the Plateau Pithouse Tradition (3,500 to 2,400 years ago) increased salmon habitat and expanded the forests toward the valley bottoms, and then during the Plateau Horizon the climate and environment in the homeland of the Secwépemc became similar to what we know today. As these climate changes unfolded, throughout the past few thousand years, the ancestors of the contemporary Secwépemc spread out from their ancient homeland marked out by the transformers to the area beyond Xatšúll (Soda Creek), wintering on both sides of the Fraser River (Teit 1909), and to the Quesnel Highland and beyond. They moved far up Simpcwétkwe (North Thompson River), crossed the Yellowhead Pass, and continued to the Jasper area. They travelled into the area that is now Revelstoke and Upper Arrow Lake and crossed the upper reaches of the Canoe and Columbia Rivers, eventually settling in the upper Columbia basin. Throughout several thousand years, the Secwépemc developed ways to harvest, manage, and enhance the resources of their diverse environment, adapting to changing ecologies and fine-tuning the ways that plants, animals, and fish could be sustainably harvested. The practical ways of harvesting the resources of fish, meat, and plants that the land provided were accompanied and sustained by a belief system that imposed social and spiritual sanctions on people who did not treat all living things sustainably and respectfully. In this chapter, we detail the environment of Secwepemcúl̓ecw, the ways of resource harvesting and resource management, and the spiritual beliefs and values that comprise the traditional *stsq̓ey̓* (laws) written *on* the land that in turn sustain humans living *from and with* the land.

Although at its core Secwepemcúl̓ecw is characterized by the dry, arid landscape of the Interior dry belt and the adjacent rolling hills of the Interior Plateau, there are as many as nine diverse biogeoclimatic zones represented in Secwepemcúl̓ecw: the low-elevation (300–350 metres) river valleys in the Thompson and mid-Fraser regions as far as Farwell Canyon on the Chilcotin River and in the area around Soda Creek are the northern outliers of the bunchgrass/ponderosa pine zone, itself the very northern extension of the arid sagebrush steppe lands that extend from the arid plateaus and deserts of the Great Basin through the Columbia Plateau into the Okanagan and Similkameen Valleys of British Columbia. Besides bluebunch wheatgrass (*Pseudoroegneria spicata*) and other dry land grasses, these areas have abundant growth of big sagebrush (*Artemisia tridentata*), pasture sage (*Artemisia frigida*), tarragon (*Artemisia dracunculus*), common rabbit brush (*Ericameria nauseosa*), yarrow (*Achillea millefolium*), and prickly pear cactus (*Opuntia fragilis*), with sparse stands of ponderosa pine (*Pinus ponderosa*) and saskatoon bushes (*Amelanchier alnifolia*) along the gullies and drainages. A variety of edible root plants, including large-fruited desert parsley (*Lomatium macrocarpum*), mariposa lily (*Calocortus macrocarpus*), yellowbells (*Fritillaria pudica*), and arrow-leaved balsamroot (*Balsamorhiza sagittata*), also grow in this environment. Along the mid-Fraser River and adjacent watersheds, the rolling, grass-covered hills of the Cariboo region, with their slightly cooler temperatures, continue this habitat, reflected in the Secwépemc term *s̓temcúl̓ecw* (cleared or treeless land). Mule deer (*Odocoileus hemionus*) descend to the southwestern slopes of this habitat during calving season in spring, and the open grasslands are also home to coyotes (*Canis latrans*).

Away from the Thompson and Fraser Rivers, the valleys give way to arid rolling plateaus covered by open canopy of Douglas-fir (*Pseudotsuga menziesii*) growth with a dense undergrowth of grasses and herbaceous plants, creating a parkland setting in many locations. Large migrating herds of elk (*Cervus canadensis*) roamed these areas in the Thompson Plateau until some 200 years ago but have since disappeared, except in the upper Columbia River basin. Mule deer (*Odocoileus hemionus*), as well as increasingly white tail deer (*Odocoileus virginianus*), black bears (*Ursus americanus*), and various predator species, including cougar (*Puma concolor*), bobcat (*Lynx rufus*), and lynx (*Lynx canadensis*), live not only in this habitat but also across ecological zones and elevations.

At higher elevations of about 1,500 metres, the Interior Douglas-fir zone transitions into a belt of lodgepole pine (*Pinus contorta*) and, by about 1,600 metres, into the cooler and moister forests of Engelmann spruce (*Picea engelmannii*) and subalpine fir (*Abies lasiocarpa*). These high plateaus, called *t7íweltk* in Secwepemctsín, sustain habitat for mule deer and, since the early

5.1 | Billy Porter of St̓uxtéws (Bonaparte) examining tracks during a hunting trip in the *t7íweltk* (montane parkland) above Robertson Creek, a tributary of Upper Hat Creek, 1996.

1900s, for moose (*Alces alces*). These areas are also black bear (*Ursus americanus*) and grizzly bear (*Ursus arctos*) habitat. Highland lakes in these areas support populations of trout (*Oncorhyncus* spp.), whitefish, and other species. It is in the transition from the Douglas-fir zone to the higher-elevation lodgepole pine forests that soapberries (*Shepherdia canadensis*) are abundant. Higher up, huckleberries (*Vaccinium membranaceum*) and blueberries (*Vaccinium ovalifolium*, *V. myrtilloides*, and *V. caespitosum*), along with roots and bulbs like Indian potatoes (*Claytonia lanceolata*), tiger lily (*Lilium columbianum*), and nodding onion (*Allium cernuum*), are found in damp meadows and at forest edges. The wetter and cooler slopes and richer soils of the Shuswap Lake and Adams Lake highlands and the Quesnel Highland sustain a belt of western redcedar (*Thuja plicata*) and hemlock (*Tsuga heterophylla*) forests, stands of yew (*Taxus brevifolia*), and an array of herbaceous plants and shrubs that thrive in these wetter climates. At lower elevations than in other environments of the Interior, meadows feature abundant growth of Indian potatoes and edible lily species, notably glacier lilies (*Erythronium grandiflorum*). This environment also sustains large herds of ungulates and other animals.

The western, northern, and eastern parts of Secwepemcúĺecw feature the snow-capped high mountains of the Coast Mountains, the Selkirk, Monashee, and Rocky Mountains with their montane parklands, subalpine fir and white pine forests, subalpine meadows, and alpine areas that support additional root plants, including glacier lilies and a variety of medicinal plants (see fig. 7, colour section). These areas, snow-covered for eight months of the year, sustain a large number of high-elevation berry species, edible roots, and herbaceous plants in important summer plant and medicine-gathering areas and were the habitat of once abundant herds of migratory woodlands caribou (*Rangifer tarandus caribou*), which are now critically endangered. Other species include mountain sheep (*Ovis canadensis*), mountain goats (*Oreamnos americanus*), and smaller species like hoary marmots (*Marmota caligata*), along with their predators like wolves, eagles, cougars, grizzly bears, bobcats, and lynx.

In addition to these major biogeoclimatic zones, Secwepemcúĺecw includes many microhabitats created by drainages, soil types, and climate. These high-biodiversity areas were especially important for their plant and animal resources and provided "oases" for harvesting activities. The moist floodplains and riverbanks of the Thompson and Fraser Rivers and their tributaries provide lush growth of red osier dogwood and willow, along with Indian hemp, wild rose, scouring rushes, and common horsetails. Wetland marshes around the edges of lakes and ponds support a variety of reeds like cattails (*Typha latifolia*) and tule (*Schoenoplectus tabernaemontani*), along with edible root plants like water parsnip (*Sium suave*) and wapato (*Sagittaria latifolia*). These riparian areas are habitat for keystone species like beaver (*Castor canadensis*), muskrat (*Ondatra zibethicus*), otter (*Lontra canadensis*), and many species of waterfowl and birds. In moister areas at mid to higher elevations, stands of trembling aspen (*Populus tremuloides*), black cottonwood (*Populus balsamifera*), and paper birch (*Betula papyrifera*) occur, often with adjacent grassy meadows. Their rich undergrowth of grasses, wildflowers, and shrubs is a favoured habitat for songbirds, mule deer, moose, and in the eastern parts of Secwepemcúĺecw, elk. In mid to higher elevations, boggy areas support Labrador tea (*Rhododendron groenlandieum*) and trapper's tea (*Rhododendron columbianum*), as well as many edible berry species and medicinal plants.

Although Secwepemcúĺecw thus includes a vast geographic area and diversity of biogeoclimatic zones, it represents by and large a *shared habitat*, in that people from throughout Secwepemcúĺecw had access to, and knowledge of, the diverse range of areas that sustained plants and wildlife, as well as a common way of talking about it in Secwepemctsín.

Secwépemc people of the past had an understanding of the relationship between elevation level and what forest ecologists call *indicator tree species* within biogeoclimatic zones. The following story illustrates this point, showing how Senxwéxwlecw (Sk̓elép or Coyote) put his knowledge of biogeoclimatic zones to work in order to find his way home from the high mountains.

Xelxlíp, Xelxeléq | Coyote Juggles His Eyes

told by Ida William, recorded by Marianne Ignace, 1986

M-nes ne secplúl̓k̓w re Senxwéxwlecw.
Coyote went to a gathering.

M-séysus.
He gambled.

Ne xwexwéyt te stem m-ṫecwentéses re qelmúcw.
And he beat the people at everything.

Ṫcwum xwexwéyt.
He won everything.

M-k̓úcsentem yerí7 te qelmúcw.
The people envied him.

M-tsúnctem es neq̓citem te spipyúy7e es kwéctems te ckwṫústens.
The [bird] people wanted to steal his eyes and take them from him.

Yerí7 re Setsé7.
And there was Raven.

M-tsuns-ekwe es kwéctems te ckwṫústens re Setsé7.
It is said that Raven wanted to take his eyes away from him.

M-tsuns-ekwe, "Xelxlíp, xelxléq̓!"
He told Coyote, "Throw them up high and stick them back in!"

Kwéctem te ckwetk̓wtústens.
[Coyote] had his eyes taken from him.

Kllékstmentmes es pelq̓ílcs.
And they let him go [he was dropped] to make his way home.

M-plépes re Senxwéxwlecw.
And Coyote was lost.

Ṫ7ek telrí7,
He went along the way from there,

mesmúsens stém̓i k spepéns es k̓úlems te ckwetkwṫústens.

and he felt for something he could find to use as eyes.

Pelmíns re elk, re elkéllp te speqpéq.
He found some kinnikinnick, some kinnikinnick berries.

M-kwénses, xelxílqenses ne ckwt̓ústens.
And he took them and stuck them in his eyes.

M-wíkmes, k̓émell petéw̓s put k sle7s k swíkems.
He could see, but he couldn't see too well.

M-sesúxwenstes t̓e m-t̓7ek, m-séwenses re tsreprép,
And he went down along the way, and he asked the trees,

"Stém̓i ye7éne tek tsrep-kp?"
"What kind of tree are you?"

Emétctmes te skwest.s te tsrep: "Seléwll."
The tree told him its name: "White Pine."

T̓7ek telrí7 re Senxwéxwlecw.
Coyote went along the way from there.

T̓ri7 m-séwenses nerí7 re nek̓ú7 te tsrep,
He asked this other tree,

"Stém̓i tek tsrep-k?"
"What kind of tree are you?"

"T̓.sellp ren s7emetentsútst."
"Spruce is what I call myself."

Tsut re Senxwéxwlecw, "Yerí7, yerí7 ren sesúsxwenst!"
Coyote said, "That's it, I am going down!"

M-séwens cwú7tsem,
He asked someone again,

"Stém̓i ye7éne tek tsrep-k?"
"What kind of tree are you?"

"Melánllp."
"Balsam [Subalpine] Fir."

Ṫ7ek ṫe m-sesúxwenst, m-séwenses re tsreprép,
He went on down, and he asked [another] tree,

"Stéṁi tek tsrep-kp?"
"What kind of tree are you?"

"Mulc."
"Cottonwood."

"Yerí7, yerí7 ren sme7é7ey," tsut-ekwe re Senxwéxwlecw.
"That's it, I'm getting close!" said Coyote.

Yerí7 re st̓7eḱs, séwens neḱu7 te tsrep,
Here he came, and he asked another tree.

M-tsúntmes, "Q̇wlséllp."
He was told, "Willow."

M-sesúxwenstes cwúẏtsem,
And he went down once again,

m-sulltímcwes, "Stéṁi tek tsrep-k?"
and asked around, "What kind of trees [are there]?"

"Meltéllp."
"Trembling Aspen."

"Yerí7 ren sme7é7ey!"
"There, I'm getting closer!"

Qwetséts telri7 re sḱelép, telrí7 re Senxwéxwlecw.
Coyote, the one they call the "groundrunner," left again from there.

Telrí7 m-sulltímcwes, "Stéṁi ṫri7 tek tsrep-k?"
And from there he asked around again, "What kind of tree are you?"

M-lexéẏectem, tsúntmes, "Speqpqéllp."
And he was told, they told him, "Saskatoon Bushes."

"Yerí7 ren skíḱtsc!"
"I have arrived!" [he said].

Le-kítscwes, re spipyúy7e m-tsúnses, "Xelxlíp xelxléq."

When he had arrived, the birds told him, "Throw them up high and stick them back in!"

Must.s-ekwe.
Four times, it is said they did that.

Yerí7 re spelq̓cit.s te ckwetkʷẃústens.
And they returned his eyes back to him.

M-wíkmes cú7tsem.
And he could see again.

M-yews ri7 re sle7s re Senxwéxwlecw.
And Coyote was all right again.

M-w7écwes telrí7.
And he carried on from there.[1]

The Living Beings That Are Harvested

As we saw from the archaeological record discussed in chapter 3, the resource use of the Secwépemc and neighbouring Interior Plateau First Peoples, supported by this rich and diverse environment for the past 4,500 years, involved *hunting* of ungulates (deer, elk, caribou, and more recently moose), supplemented by trapping of smaller game. Of equal importance was *fishing*, especially the harvesting of salmon in the Fraser and Thompson River systems, along with various other lake and river fish. In addition, *plant harvesting* that included an extensive variety of more than a hundred plant species used as food, as well as many additional plant species used as medicines or for making tools, shelter, and clothing, was a crucial part of Secwépemc sustenance. Between 3,300 and 2,400 years ago, the sustainable management and harvesting of a variety of roots and bulbs that moreover required the chemistry of underground pit-cooking or steam-cooking became an important aspect of Plateau resource use, as is shown by the presence of large underground pit-cooking ovens in upland areas at that time (see chapter 3).[2] Although some argue that their use "disintensified" by around 800 years ago (Lepofsky and Peacock 2004, 134), with root processing shifting closer to village sites, the harvesting, processing, and consumption of root plants, including their *tsq̓elstém* (pit-cooking) continued to play an important role in the Secwépemc diet overall until into the twentieth century, as the memories of Secwépemc elders show us. In the section that follows, we discuss the species harvested by the Secwépemc, the methods and locations of harvesting them, and the ways that sustainable resource harvesting was supported by a moral system of responsibly and sustainably harvesting plants and animals, considered as living resources in an environment where humans were not masters over them but were part of the ecological network of all living things in a known yet changing environment.

The Myth of Living in Fixed Abodes versus Dwelling in the Landscape

In the process of "resettlement" of what is now British Columbia by colonizers (Harris 1997), the point that Aboriginal peoples, including the Plateau peoples and Secwépemc, had no "fixed abode" was often reiterated as a way to disqualify the Indigenous peoples on the land from valid occupation and livelihood in, let alone ownership of, their homelands. For example, Gilbert Malcolm Sproat, who was one of the commissioners of the Joint Reserve Commission of 1876–78, had noted in 1868 of the Nuu-chah-nulth, "any right in the soil which these natives had as occupiers was partial and imperfect as, with the exception of hunting animals in the forests, plucking wild fruits, and cutting a few trees to make canoes and houses, the natives did not, in any civilized sense, occupy the land" (quoted in Lillard 1987, xvi, emphasis added). A few decades later, Canada's poet laureate, Stephen Leacock (1941, 19), speaking from what some might call a naive Eurocentric perspective, expressed what we understand as internalized settler colonialism: "We think of prehistoric North America as inhabited by the Indians, and have based on this a sort of recognition of ownership on their part. But this attitude is hardly warranted. The Indians were too few to count. Their use of the resources of the continent was scarcely more than that by crows and wolves, their development of it nothing." Embedded in the ideological motives of these statements aimed at disavowing the legitimate and legal land tenure of Aboriginal peoples on the land is the Eurocentric notion that valid "living" takes place in "fixed abodes."

In Secwepemctsín, the concept of dwelling, staying, or "living" in a place, *mut* (singular/one person) or *tsyem* (plural/more than one person), is not confined to the idea of living in a fixed abode; instead, wherever people *stay* beyond being in transit is where they "live," including the periods of time they "camp" at annually visited resource-producing locations throughout the seasonal round. This idea of "living" is in contrast with the concept of *yist* (camping overnight), which designates en route camping while travelling to or from the location of a longer-term stay within a recurring seasonal round. Below, we discuss details of Secwépemc resource use with regard to fishing, hunting, trapping, and plant harvesting. We discuss them in line with our own and our colleagues' findings of not only resource harvesting or use but also management and stewardship practices, as they have been outlined in a broader context by ourselves and our colleagues (Berkes 2012; M. Ignace, Turner, and Peacock 2017; Turner 2014; Turner and Berkes 2006; Turner, M. Ignace, and R. Ignace 2000).

Fishing

The first Europeans to set foot in Secwepemcúlecw commented on the prominence of salmon fishing. Hudson's Bay Company chief trader Archibald McDonald (1827, 227) called salmon the "staff of life" of Secwépemc people in the vicinity of the Thompson River post at Kamloops. In a report to the Canadian government, Reserve Commissioner Gilbert Malcolm Sproat (1878) noted, "The salmon is the Indians' chief food, for the winter, and indeed at all times. No part of the fish is wasted. They prefer the salmon to beef, mutton, pork or to the vegetables which many of them now produce. At this season when the weekly coach leaves newspapers at my camp and the whites ask about politics and war the Indians crowd round to hear news of the salmon. Nothing will restrain them when the fish at last arrive. 'The salmon first and God next,' an old Indian said to me last year." In his ethnographic report on the Shuswap, George M. Dawson (1891, 15) noted, "Dried salmon ... before attempts at agriculture ... constituted the sole winter staple. The right to occupy certain salmon fishing places, with the annual visit to these of the more remote families, and the congregation of large numbers of Indians at specially favorable places, largely influenced the life and customs of the Shuswaps." Having visited Secwepemcúlecw during the summer months, and thus having become more privy to the fishing economy than to the hunting economy, Dawson may have downplayed the role of hunting. However, for the past 4,000 years or so, salmon had constituted between one-third and one-half of the protein consumption of Secwépemc people and thus played a key role in the livelihood of the Secwépemc.

SALMON IN THE PREHISTORIC DIET

An Ingenious method of estimating the proportion of salmon in the prehistoric diet of the Secwépemc and other Plateau peoples was devised by Brian Chisholm (1986). Chisholm put to use the fact that protein derived from marine (ocean) sources has a carbon isotope that is different from that of terrestrial (land) protein, allowing the lab researcher to measure the relation between the two. By measuring the proportion of marine versus terrestrial protein ingested by humans and animals throughout their lifespan and preserved in their remains, Chisholm was able to determine with a good degree of accuracy the proportion of salmon in the protein intake of the ancestors of Secwépemc and other Interior people, as the only stable marine protein source for Interior peoples would have been salmon. Using this method, Chisholm determined that Gore Creek Man ate less than 10 per cent marine protein and thus had very little salmon available. Human remains from the Clinton area – the Big Bar Lake and China Lake burials mentioned in chapter

2 – suggest that by 5,000 years ago, people derived around 37 per cent of their protein needs from salmon, and various analyzed samples dated to between 4,500 and a few hundred years ago show that 40 to 60 per cent of Secwépemc people's protein came from salmon (Chisholm 1986; Lovell et al. 1986). But not only humans sustained themselves by eating salmon; testing on dog remains from Keatley Creek on the mid-Fraser River near Pavilion (Crellin 1994; Crellin and Heffner 2000) has shown that even the dogs of Keatley Creek in good part subsisted on salmon!

Salmon were and are caught by Secwépemc as a vital and crucial part of who we are, our food, and our connection with those who give themselves to us. Many years ago, our ancestors figured out how to catch them with a variety of Indigenous methods highly suited to the particular species and to the nature of the river. Four species of salmon run in the rivers and tributaries of the Thompson and Fraser River systems.[3] The salmon species include, in order of seasonal availability in the rivers of Secwepemcúĺecw, *kekésu7* (spring salmon, Chinook, *Oncorhynchus tshawytscha*), *shéni7* (humpbacks, *Oncorhynchus gorbuscha*), *sqlelten7úẃi* ("ordinary/real salmon," sockeye, *Oncorhynchus nerka*), and *sxéyeqs* (coho, *Oncorhynchus kisuch*). In addition, *tṡolleníẃt* or *sgwigwle* (steelhead, *Oncorhynchus mykiss*) run in the Fraser and Thompson River systems to about Kamloops Lake. Before the Grand Coulee Dam destroyed Columbia River salmon runs starting in the 1930s, Secwépemc groups like the Shuswap Lakes and Splatsín people, along with people of the upper North Thompson River and Kinbasket, made use of upper Columbia River salmon, especially Chinook, utilizing fishing grounds at the salmon beds near Windermere and in the Big Eddy camp near Revelstoke, as well as at the Salmon Creek tributary to the Columbia not far from there. The latter grounds were remembered especially by elders of the Splatsín community.

Since the construction of some forty additional hydroelectric dams on the American and Canadian portions of the river during the twentieth century, no salmon have been able to return to the upper Columbia River.

Chinook salmon, or spring salmon, are by far the largest salmon species and reach 15 kilograms or more. Reuben Ware (1983, 9)[4] reports that into the early part of the twentieth century, Chinook were the dominant economic species among Interior and Coast Salish peoples:

> In terms of the Salmon fishery the primary food *and* commerical fish was the Spring Salmon, *not* the Sockeye. Ethnographic and documentary evidence describe that it was the Spring Salmon that was primarily caught in the 19th century. It was the early run of Springs in March and

April that broke the late winter doldrums and occasional food shortages and that brought thousands to the fishing grounds from Yale to Bridge River. As late as 1926, Spring Salmon was still the most important fish as the following "estimates" of Salmon taken by Indians in the New Westminster, Lytton, Lillooet and Williams Lake Agencies indicate:

Sockeye	5,600	31%
Spring [Chinook]	6,700	37%
Cohoes	4,500	24%
(Chum	1,500	8%)[5]
Total:	18,300	

In the mid-1980s, Secwépemc elders from Simpcw (North Thompson Band) remembered their own parents and elders catching spring salmon from a canoe by spear at the prolific fishing ground they called C7emtsíńten ("sitting down waiting for something" [salmon]) on the North Thompson River. Sammy Joseph recalled,

> I was pretty small when I used to watch them old-timers spearing them great big salmon, you know. The one that spears, he stands on the canoe, you know. I don't think I'd try my luck on it. Well, the guy that's on the back of the canoe there, he's gotta be pretty steady, you know. All they used is a long stick to steady that canoe, you know, probably just going like this, you know, it's kind of pretty fast, keep that canoe steady when the guy's spearing, when he gets one, well, he sits down. I used to watch 'em, he sits down and pulls the fish in, and oh, they get some great big ones there.

Tsecwésell (jacksprings) are male Chinook salmon who mature after only two to three years and average less than half the size of mature Chinook. Jacksprings were caught in the Thompson River near the mouth of Deadman's Creek in spring. This recurring run seems to have become extinct in the 1920s. Elder Celina Jules of Skeetchestn remembered,

> When they went by, *tsecwésell* they call them, a different kind of fish. The white people must have done something to them, they no longer go by, the *tsecwésell*, that's what the Indians called them. A big fat fish that went by in July, I think. I used to spear fish down the creek, that was all the work I had, spearing fish, and that was what I fed you all [her children], fish. I caught one or two, I walked, that's all the work I had, fishing, spearing fish … Gee, they're sure fat. They've stopped going by. I wonder what the white people have done to them, they must have locked them up or something …

5.2 | Celina Jules of Skeetchestn, 1986. She was one of the last monolingual speakers of Secwepemctsín.

> When the water rises, that's when *tśegwllníẃt* [steelhead] go by, those big fish. Sḱelép [her husband] stood in the creek, and then when they went by … he hooked them out, riding horseback in the water. (Translated from Secwepemctsín by Garlene Dodson, 1987)

Sqlelten7úẃi ("ordinary/real salmon," sockeye) are smaller, averaging about 3 kilograms. Sockeye runs, especially the large lower Adams River run, which is fished by the Secwépemc people of the Stḱemlúpsemc and Sexqéltkemc divisions, have very distinct quadrennial (four-year) dominance: the first year of four will have a very large run, whereas the next will be sharply reduced, and the remaining two years' runs will be smaller yet. The difference between dominant and low years will be as much as a ratio of several thousand to one. Large sockeye runs caught at Secwépemc fishing grounds at or near the communities on the mid-Fraser River include the Stuart Lake and Chilko runs and the Horsefly and Quesnel Lake runs. Teit (1909, 525) noted that in the 1800s "the rapids of Chilcotin River at the mouth of the Canyon were probably the most important salmon-fishery in the whole Shuswap country."[6] A small landlocked variety of sockeye are *ḱeknécw* (kokanee), which run in early fall in creeks at the outlet of numerous lakes in Secwepemcúĺecw.

5.3 | Ron Ignace and his son Joe Ignace gaffing salmon in the Thompson River near the mouth of Deadman's Creek, 2002.

Sxéyeqs (coho salmon) average about 3.5 kilograms. They migrate up the rivers in September and October and spawn in late November and December. Coho travel only during the night and hide to rest in protected pools and eddies of the stream during the daytime. Their age at maturity is normally three years. Like spring salmon, coho do not occur in cycles but return in similar numbers annually. Many tributaries of the Thompson River, including the South and North Thompson, and the Fraser River had and have spawning populations of cohos, although since the 1990s, stocks have declined.

Shéni7 (pink or humpback salmon) are the smallest of the Pacific salmon species, averaging between 1.5 and 3 kilograms. Pinks appear in large numbers in the Thompson River in alternating years. Their life cycle lasts only two years. Unlike the other species, they spawn on the edges of the main riverbed. On the spawning beds, the males develop a humped back, and both sexes change colour from bright silver to pale gray with a white to yellowish belly, blending with the stream colours. Humpbacks travel in shoals to the spawning grounds in late summer and early fall. They are and were the least economically desirable species of salmon, as their flesh is soft and not as tasty as that of the other species of salmon.

Throughout Secwepemcúlecw, fishing grounds have tended to be at or near back eddies where salmon rest or catch a ride during their migration

5.4 | Louis Matthew of Simpcw making a three-pronged fishing *wewtsk* (spear) from a pitchfork, ca. 1986.

upstream. In the fast, muddy waters of the Fraser River, the Secwépemc have long used *stúkwtsen* (dip-nets), made of *spétsen* (Indian hemp), with a frame made from the hard wood of juniper or yew. In the clear and relatively shallow waters of the main Thompson River and in the tributaries of the North Thompson, *ups* (gaffs) and three-pronged *wewtsk* (spears) supported by handles 5 metres or more in length were the most effective fishing method. Chinook or spring salmon continue to be caught with single- or double-pronged *meníp* (harpoon spears). Before metal was available, the tips of harpoons and spears were made from deer antler and bone, but since the time metal became available, Secwépemc people have forged pitchforks into three-pronged spears or forged metal rods into gaffs and have also made detachable harpoon tips from metal.

To be able to spot and catch the approaching salmon in the river, fishers built platforms on the banks and dropped white stones into the river, thus making the fish more visible in the water. Fishing platforms were also built on the steep and dangerous banks of the Fraser River, where people dip-netted. Besides the platforms, fishers often built out of boulders large circular holes 30 to 60 centimetres in height where the salmon emptied out of nets could be kept and killed with a club. Besides natural conditions produced by back eddies, fishing grounds thus involved an aspect of human labour and maintenance, and it was the individuals or families who built up and maintained such fishing areas or fishing rocks who were the first to harvest fish there.

In the clear and relatively slow waters of the South Thompson and main Thompson Rivers, the Secwépemc and Nlaka'pamux also used the method of lighting pitch-wood fires on canoes to attract the salmon and then spearing them from canoes. Daniel Seymour of Tk̓emlúps (Kamloops) remembered many people of his community and of Neskonlith and Chase fishing at Sq̓pe7, the prolific fishing ground east of Tk̓emlúps on the South Thompson River, where fish were also caught using this method, known by people in different parts of Secwepemcúl̓ecw as *tsétsk̓wem* (pitch-lamping or pit-lamping). Ike Willard, his wife Adeline Willard, and her sister Aimee August of Neskonlith, who remembered this method from their younger years, described it to Randy Bouchard:

> In the South Thompson river, pit lamping was done from canoes which were blackened on the outside so that the fish couldn't see them. The canoes were positioned in a parallel row diagonally to the riverbank as they drifted downstream. The man who sat in the stern and directed the canoe was called *mtap*. In the center of the canoe sat the man whose duty it was to spear or harpoon the fish. This man was called *tsects'lawt*. To be able to see the fish more clearly, this man blackened the area under his eyes with charcoal, and wore a buckskin or fur "blinker," called *ctselltṡellnáṅten* at his temples. The man who sat in the bow of the canoe and held the pitch wood torch was called *kwaṅp* "holding at the tail end." The pitch wood torch was approximately ten feet long and consisted of three-foot long pieces of pitch wood fastened onto the end of a green pole. The pole was constantly turned so that the pitch did not drip. A "head man" stood in the center of the canoe that was in the middle of the river, and called out which way the fish were swimming. The last "head man" among the Chase Shuswap people was Old August, Akís, who died in 1915. Pit lamping could only be done where the river was wide, smooth, and relatively straight. Therefore, one of the best places to pit lamp was between Banana Island, Tkweltáṁ, and where the Chase Bridge is situated today. (Bouchard and Kennedy 1975, 26)

Daniel Seymour and many other elders of Tk̓emlúps remembered their people fishing by torchlight at Sq̓pe7, a 5-kilometre stretch of the South Thompson River with sandy beaches starting from just east of the Indian residential school. Mary Thomas (interview with Rhandi Alphonse, 2001) remembered her parents fishing by torchlight for spring salmon on the Salmon River near Enderby:

> My Dad and them had a canoe, and they used to torch for salmon. Oh, nice spring salmon. In about July, great big salmon would come up, and they'd go up and get the pitch wood past the railway track. They'd

> bring the canoe up there, and at night they would torch for salmon, and they'd go down the river. By the time they got down to the lake, they'd have anywhere's from ten to twenty salmon. Then they'd take the horse and a little boat and they'd haul it home from the meadow. They had spears and a torchlight made out of pitch wood. They used the torch. They could see the salmon in the water and they'd spear them.

In addition, with the help of the strong fibers of *spétsen*, the Secwépemc made *ctálkweten* (gillnets), held up by floats made from animal bladders and anchored by round rocks as sinkers (see fig. 3.13). With the introduction of Western implements and materials, fishers in the 1900s began to use commercial netting, as well as various kinds of materials as floats and sinkers; however, as with fishing spears, the basic design and function of nets remained nearly the same. The Secwépemc also made a variety of conical or box-shape *mu7* (traps) that were efficient in the slow waters of the South Thompson River, on the upper Fraser River near Soda Creek, and at the mouth of tributaries to the main stem rivers. Finally, in different locations, like the mouth of Deadman's Creek and the mouth of the Barriere River, communities annually set up *tśelmíń* (fish dams) made of poles and a lattice of sticks to contain and then selectively harvest salmon as they migrated upriver. George M. Dawson (1891, 16) described the Barriere River fish fence, after which were named the Barriere River (Sṫyelltsecwétkwe) and the town of Barriere on the mid-North Thompson:

> Another form of trap, noted on the Barriere River, consists of two weirs or fences, each of which stretched completely across the stream. Both fences in this case sloped back up stream. The lower one was formed of upright parallel sticks, duly supported, and was provided with inlets below, consisting of converging sticks, which enabled the salmon going up stream to push through but prevented their return. The upper fence or weir consisted of horizontal poles and withes closely wattled in and supported by stakes. Between the two weirs the salmon remained till from time to time removed by the owner with a fish-spear of the usual type.

Born in 1899, the late elder Josephine Wenlock remembered that her grandfather, George Sisyúlecw, and "old-timers Old Casimir and Celesta and some of those younger guys" let the fish collect in the weir overnight and then speared them the next morning.

A similar weir existed on the north bank of the South Thompson River near Sk̓atsin until the early 1900s. Its construction was described to Randy Bouchard in detail by Ike Willard, Adeline Willard, and Aimee August. This weir had a well-engineered construction of poles and lattice weir that took advantage of the current. It also had trapdoors left open during the day, allowing salmon to proceed on to the spawning grounds (Bouchard and Kennedy 1975). After salmon had been trapped in the weir overnight, they were caught with scoop nets or spears the next morning, a method that also allowed the release of some salmon. Such weirs thus entailed selective harvesting methods and allowed for escapement of a part of the run. The remains of another weir were found during archaeological survey work 15 kilometres east of Kamloops on the South Thompson River between Monte Creek and Pritchard. This weir, or possibly a set of fish dams, was described by Bill Arnouse in 1991 as Skewkéw, "a 'major fishing area, one mile long' located along the north side of the South Thompson, extending as far east as the creek at the cement plant" (quoted in Bouchard and Kennedy 1991, 42). Its remains consist of dozens of sets of vertical stakes driven into the riverbed, along with remains of the lattice work of sharpened sticks, as well as the rows of rocks piled to hold the dam in place and to keep fish from escaping. Archaeologists George Nicholas and Catherine Carlson recorded and mapped this site as heritage site EdRa41 in 2002, noting the remains of 1,187 wooden stakes extending for 1,100 metres on the riverbed of the South Thompson. Through radiocarbon analysis, they were able to date samples of these stakes at between 120 and 1,560 years old, suggesting that the whole weir was used for a long period of time, with stakes and lattice work likely being fixed and replaced periodically (Nicholas 2002, 6–7; Nicholas, Jules Bonneau, and Westfall 2017, 97–102).

In the fall of 1869, settler A.L. Fortune found the outlet of Shuswap Lake near Sicamous barred by a large salmon weir held up by poles, the area being occupied by Secwépemc people. When they initially refused him passage, he threatened to destroy their weir, so rather than suffering damage to the weir, they eventually let him pass.[7] Hudson's Bay Company records for Fort Alexandria show that one or more such fishing weirs were also operated in the Fraser River above Xatśúll (Soda Creek) (Thomson and M. Ignace 2005).

With the growth of the non-Aboriginal commercial fishery off and near the mouth of the Fraser River, and even more so after the 1913 Hells Gate slide caused by Canadian National Railway construction above Yale in the Fraser Canyon all but depleted salmon runs in the Fraser and Thompson River systems, the federal Department of Fisheries began to monitor, curtail, and outlaw Aboriginal fishing during the first decades of the twentieth century.

A crucial aspect of the Interior Plateau peoples' reliance on salmon was the interplay of the dry climate conditions on the river, the lower fat content of salmon as they reached the mid-Thompson and Fraser River systems, and technology that was developed to process and wind-dry large quantities of salmon for winter use. With Secwépemc people relying on salmon for 40 per cent or more of their dietary protein, an adult would have consumed 200 to 300 salmon per year, dried and fresh. A family thus would have had to catch,

5.5 | Remains of a large fishing weir at Kew̓kéw on the South Thompson River west of Monte Creek, 2011.

5.6 | Fishing weir at Sek̓méw̓s (Sicamous), operated by the Secwépemc people of Splatsín (Enderby), ca. 1900. This is the weir that Alfred Fortune threatened to destroy and that, a few years later, the Splatsín Indians tried to protect from destruction by the game warden (see fig. 5.30).

process, and store in the order of 1,000 or more salmon per year. Sun-drying was the preferred method in the dry parts of the Thompson and mid-Fraser Rivers. In the wetter North Thompson and Eastern Shuswap areas, a combination of smoking and sun-drying was used. For drying, the fish were gutted, filleted, opened out, and then sliced horizontally at short intervals to let air penetrate, with the skin holding the sides together. With large fish (spring salmon), each side was split in half again and then sliced thinly before being hung on racks for three to four days. After the fish were completely dry, they were stored either in pits or in baskets above ground, although with the availability of gunny sacks, these were often preferred over baskets. Drying and smoke-drying were carried out not only for long-term (winter) storage but also for short-term storage throughout the spring and summer months. In other words, any fish, game, and plant product that was not for immediate consumption was dried for future use.

For immediate consumption, there existed a number of methods to boil, simmer, steam, bake, toast, and roast fish – as well as roots, fowl, and game. In the absence of pottery, the Secwépemc cooked their food in watertight baskets filled with hot stones. Another prominent cooking method was the roasting of food in pit ovens, the remains of which can be seen in many prehistoric

5.7 | Jack Sam and his wife at Squilax (Little Shuswap) with their drying rack full of dried salmon, 1940s.

sites. At the camping grounds, fresh fish was roasted above the campfire on sticks, a practice continued today.

It is important to emphasize that not only the fillets of salmon but also many other parts of the fish were eaten and preserved: the heads and backbones were dried along with the fillets and used for soups in winter. Salmon roe was consumed fresh as soup and also dried and preserved. Teit (1909, 517) notes, "Salmon-roe was wrapped in bark and buried; and salmon-oil was stored in bottles made of fish-skins, which were sealed with twine and glue." The preservation of salmon was a labour-intensive task and one involving expertise in, for example, judging the consistency and fat content of the flesh, choosing the proper wood for the fire, building a slow fire with a lot of smoke, tending to the fire, turning the fish when required, keeping dogs and insects away, and so on. Last but not least, it required skill and precision to gut and slice hundreds of salmon harvested during a night's catch with dip-nets, gillnets, or weirs. The Secwépemc First Salmon Ritual has long been the ceremonial cooking and *sharing* of the first fish caught in the season at a particular fishing ground.

Laura Harry of Esk̓ét underscored the significance of the Secwépemc reliance on salmon in the idiom of kinship: "*Re sqlélten, yerí7 re sxetéqst.s re stsmémelt-kt*" ("Salmon are our first children").

In addition to migrating salmon, the Secwépemc consumed and when necessary preserved a number of other fish species throughout the seasons. These included *keknécw* (kokanee, *Oncorhyncus nerka*), a small, land-locked variety of sockeye that was fished in numerous creeks at the outlet of lakes throughout Secwépemc territory during September and October. Various species of trout collectively named *písell* (*Oncorhyncus* and *Salvelinus* spp.) or indicated by the lexical suffix *-ésell* formed an important part of the protein supply. They included varieties of rainbow trout (*O. mykiss*), as well as *písell*, *xyemésell*, and cutthroat trout (*O. clarki*) (see below), which were fished with dip-nets in large quantities at the in-flow and out-flow of mid- to high-elevation lakes in spring as the trout prepared to spawn following the breakup of ice on these lakes. The spring trout fishery saw Secwépemc extended families camp at a succession of these lakes between late March and May, celebrating the abundance of fresh protein that became available, as well as visiting and trading goods and news. In the many large and small lakes of Secwepemcúl̓ecw, and in the main stem and tributary creeks of the Fraser, Thompson, and Columbia River systems, *stíq̓sell* (silver trout, *Oncorhyncus mykiss* ssp.), *q̓es7etnésell* ("Loon Lake trout," cutthroat trout, *Oncorhynchus clarki*), *sgwigwle* (lake trout, *Salvelinus namaycush*), fall run of lake-resident *k̓witésell* (steelhead, *O. mykiss*), *sem7ésell* (Dolly Varden trout, *Salvelinus malma*), and bull trout (*Salvelinus confluentus*) were also caught. The testimony of Secwépemc, Okanagan, and Nlaka'pamux fishers who were pushed out of Fish Lake (Pennask Lake or K̓emqenétkwe) in the 1920s due to a white millionaire privatizing the lake (Thoms 2002, 71) shows that in the 1920s, the Aboriginal trout fishery in this lake alone yielded 45,000 to 50,000 rainbow trout annually, apparently without harm to the trout stock.

Both *mámelt* (mountain whitefish, *Prosopium williamsoni*) and *xéxel̓* (lake whitefish, *Coregonus clupeaformis*) were caught in rivers and lakes of the Thompson, Fraser, and Columbia River drainages. Additional species of fish that were caught and eaten included *tseqwtsitsen* (peamouth, *Mylocheilus caurinus*), *tsq̓wmus* (longnose sucker, *Catostomus catostomus*), and *keléne* (bridgelip sucker, *Catostomus columbianus*). These species were often caught casually for meals, as people camped overnight or temporarily en route to major resource-producing locations, although suckers are known to be very bony fish and were not fed to children. Likewise, bottom fish like *ck̓emúlecw* (ling or burbot, *Lota lota*) were consumed, as was *xu7t̓* (sturgeon, *Acipenser transmontanus*), once common and known for their giant size in the Fraser and Columbia Rivers, although in the Columbia they vanished after the construction of hydroelectric dams in the 1930s. In 2003 even the oldest elders at Splatsín (Enderby) remembered hearing only from their own parents and grandparents about the once prolific sturgeon fishery on the upper Columbia (Secwepemc Fisheries Commission 2003, 18).

Hunting

For the mid-1800s, Teit (1909, 513) noted that "the meat on which they lived was of importance in the following order: deer, elk, caribou, marmot, sheep, hare, beaver, grouse, bear, moose, duck, goose, crane, squirrel, porcupine." Archaeological information (see chapter 3) attests to the kind and quantities of large ungulates, including elk, deer, mountain goat, mountain sheep, and caribou, that the Secwépemc hunted along with many species of small game. Moose did not arrive in the south-central Interior until the first decades of the twentieth century. Mule deer, white tail deer, and elk were hunted in the *t7íweltk*, the montane parklands of the Interior Plateau, usually 1,200 to 1,500 metres above the river levels. To track deer or elk, hunters often used dogs whose mouths and furs had been washed with *secwsqéqxe7ten* ("bathe dog in stuff," Hudson Bay tea or trapper's tea, *Rhododendron groenlandicum* or *Rhododendron columbianum*). The scent of *secwsqéqxe7ten*, which repelled dog odour and was infused with the fragrance of the montane parklands, was said to keep deer and other ungulates from smelling the tracking dogs.

In strategic areas between deer trails, deer licks, and travel corridors, including waterways, deer were driven into built deer fences, which, as human-made contraptions, were considered to be the property of their builders. Throughout Secwepemcúlecw, deer and elk fences were commonly used, and in the mountains of Wells Gray Park, the Styétemc (Canim Lake Secwépemc) and Tqéqeltkemc (North Thompson Secwépemc) who hunted there also used caribou fences. Fences were usually erected in areas where ungulates migrated during fall, often at crossings from one mountain to another, near licks, and at other well-chosen locations. Teit (1909, 521ff) reported that some of these fences, in use until the late 1800s, were from 800 to 1,600 metres in length. At strategic intervals, hunters placed snares triggered by strings that were released when the deer stepped on sticks on the ground. Another common method was for a group of hunters to drive ungulates along a gully. As the deer tried to escape up the slopes, they were shot down by marksmen positioned behind trees.

To facilitate driving game, Secwépemc hunters constructed hunting blinds in circular depressions with built-up semi-circular *tgéy̓menten* (rock walls). Such blinds were often constructed at high points overlooking elk and deer trails and crossings, especially in places where a steep gully funnelled animals up a predictable narrow route. Here, they could be ambushed and killed, the hunter hiding in the blind. The remains of one such hunting blind for elk, ideally suited to the fact that elk travel in single file following their lead bull, exist in the mid-elevation grasslands area near Jacko Lake south of Kamloops,

5.8 | Marshall Gonzales of Skeetchestn at an old hunting blind near Pipsell (Jacko Lake) south of Tk̓emlúps (Kamloops), 2013. This feature consists of three platforms with built-up stone walls, which allowed hunters to selectively kill elk as they were herded into a gully below, probably with hunting dogs. Elk were once prolific in the area but became rare after the arrival of cattle in the early 1860s.

where elk could be driven into a gully from the open grasslands with hunting dogs. A team of hunters was strategically situated and hiding behind a set of human-built rock walls and was thus able to pick out desired animals as the herd moved into the gully in single file. Other such hunting blinds existed in the grasslands south of there toward Douglas Lake (James 1994).

Although Teit (1909, 513) attributed the disappearance of elk from Southern Secwépemc territory in the 1860s to Secwépemc hunting with newly acquired firearms, it appears that there were other reasons for the demise of the elk. The late Herb Manuel of Sp'áxmen (Douglas Lake) remembered oral histories of large herds of hundreds of elk having gotten frozen on a lake around that time, with the local Aboriginal people killing and butchering many of them before the elk starved to death on the lake (James 1994). It is also very likely that the arrival of cattle in the grasslands south of Kamloops in the early 1860s brought in bovine diseases transmittable from cattle to elk but generally not to deer and moose (Blackstock and McAllister 2004; M. Ignace et al. 2014; Helen Swantje, personal communication, 2013).

Selcwéyecen (caribou, *Rangifer tarandus caribou*) and *sqwí7qwe* (hoary marmots, *Marmota caligata*), along with mountain goats in steep areas, were hunted in the higher subalpine and alpine areas, although caribou populations steeply declined after the 1930s, when moose came into the Interior.

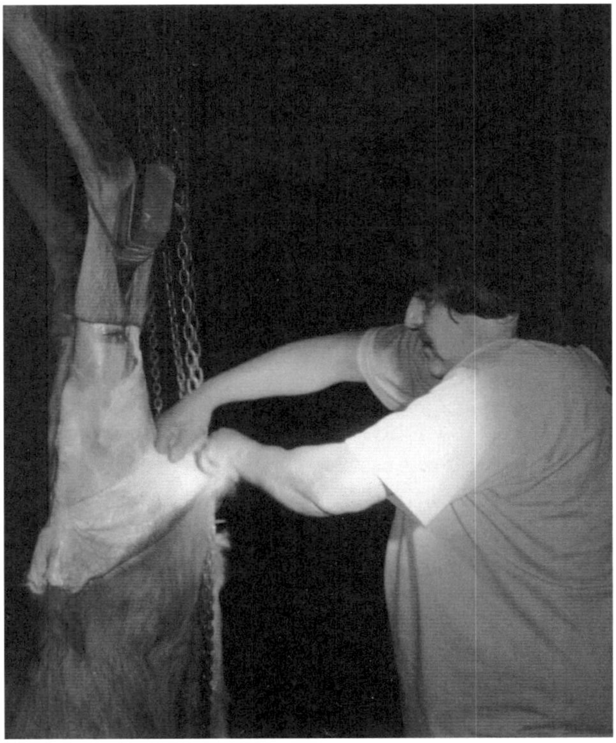

5.9 | Terry Deneault of Skeetchestn skinning a deer, 1996. As shown here, the correct way to strip the skin off the animal is to work it off in a downward motion with one's fists rather than cutting it off.

Among the North Thompson people, elders who were born in the early 1900s remembered hunting caribou, as did elders in the Canim Lake area, as members of both communities, often with brothers-in-law from communities connected by kinship, hunted the herds, whose scarce remnants still exist in and across the Quesnel Highland, upper Wells Gray Park, and Monashee highlands. Henry Celesta of Chu Chua remembered caribou hunting in his younger years, before the 1930s: "[Up Raft Peaks in Wells Gray Park and to Avola], that's where the people used to go, get a lot of that caribou them days, and they dry up a lot of caribou meat up there. There were lots of them [caribou] them days, you could count them by the hundreds. They eat lichen off the trees in winter. Them days there weren't many moose around." By the 1950s, he remembered, the caribou were gone.[8]

Hunting parties usually consisted of two or more brothers, cousins, or friends from interrelated families who would camp out in the montane parklands for two weeks or more at a time, travelling throughout the higher elevations. Thus Patrick Eustache of Chu Chua would invite his younger brother Manuel to go hunting: "Come with me, younger brother. I am going to hunt for you!" Besides feeding their own family with the meat they bagged, hunters distributed their meat among other relatives.

THE ART OF MAKING BUCKSKIN AND THE SECWÉPEMC DIVISION OF LABOUR

by Marianne Ignace

I learned how to tan buckskin, or deer hides, in the 1980s from Ida Matthew, Nellie Taylor, and Lizette Donald and her daughter, Virginia Donald. Ron Ignace, in turn, witnessed and participated in buckskin tanning with his great-grandmother Sulyén from the time he was a young child.

Interior Plateau buckskin tanning is a skill that exemplifies and celebrates women's work, but more than that, it expresses the complementary and mutually supportive division of labour between men and women. A workable hide, one that is above and beyond what a woman can chide her husband hunter for, is one that is cleanly worked off the hanging deer carcass by the hunter soon after he (or she) makes the kill. Instead of cutting off the hide, the skilful hunter makes only minor cuts, separating the skin from the meat and flesh by hand without leaving meat, gristle, and fat on the skin (see fig. 5.9). This step greatly reduces the amount of labour in the initial scraping process.

5.10 | A woman at Tk̓emlúps (Kamloops) tanning a hide on a stretching frame using a *sk̓etst* (stone-tipped tanning tool), photographed by Harlan I. Smith, 1897. The same implements and process of tanning are still used today.

5.11 | Virginia Donald of Simpcw lacing a deer hide onto a stretching frame in order to stretch and soften it, ca. 1995.

Since the hide is attached to the meat by one membrane and to the hair by a second membrane, the tanner dehairs the hide – often after soaking it in the cold water of a nearby creek for a few days – and then detaches the inside and outside membranes by working the hide on a scraping pole with a scraper made from the fibula or rib of a deer or moose – or nowadays sometimes with a dulled metal log scraper (see Teit 1900, 186). These scrapers, along with a shafted stone tool called a *sk̓ɛtst* (see fig. 5.10), are very similar to Nellie Taylor's 1986 tools and to scrapers we still use.

Once the hide is cleanly scraped, it is soaked in a solution of simmered deer brain, which releases a rich-quality mixture of fine fat and protein ideally suited to making the hide pliable and softening it. Nellie Taylor also liked to add a small chunk of old-style sunlight soap made from tallow and without perfumes or additives. After being soaked in this solution for about four days and being tested for "doneness" to determine whether the deer-brain solution has penetrated throughout, the hide is rinsed again in cold water, wrung out

/continued

(see fig. 5.26), and then laced onto a stretching frame (see figs 5.10 and 5.11). In the act of *ḱépem* (stretching and softening the hide), the tanner works the hide by poking it while leaning into it with a *sḱetst* tool (see fig. 5.10; and Teit 1909) on a broom-like handle for several hours as it slowly dries and gets stretched and softened in the process. Subsequently, the *sḱetst* is used to "fluff" the inside of the hide, further softening it (Teit 1900, 185). Finally, the hide is smoked briefly in cool smoky embers of pine cones or punky (rotten) fir wood. Especially the stretching and softening part of the process is arduous work, and a rest of even a few minutes will cause the hide to stiffen, making the whole stretching effort in vain. Big (male) winter hides are and were the most valued ones for high-quality protective garments and moccasins, and the neck and upper back part of the hide is the thickest and thus can be difficult to soften.

I had learned from both the literature and my elders' instruction that buckskin tanning was women's work, and I was therefore surprised when, during my apprentice effort to soften the neck part of the hide of a large buckskin, Nellie Taylor instructed me to get my husband, Ron, to help do the stretching. After I summoned him, he immediately and expertly started to *ḱépem*. When I asked where he had learned this skill, presuming still that this was women's work, I was told that Old Sulyén, who raised him, would routinely ask him and his mother's younger brother Greg to help out with that part of the tanning process. Like many other tasks, therefore, tanning exemplifies women's work, but in practice it involves the tacit support and complementary labour of men if and when needed.

After the men returned from the montane parklands and subalpine areas having made their kill, often deboning and even partially drying the meat for better ease of transporting it, they brought it down to the base camp, where the women would continue to dry and process it into large amounts of *sḱec* (dried meat). Thus, throughout two-thirds of the year, people were "on the go." While the families were encamped at base camps and while hunters were en route to hunting areas in the higher mountains, women made a *tsḱelélllcw* (lean-to) as a base camp and sustained their families by snaring, trapping, and hunting small game, including rabbit, marmot, groundhog, porcupine, beaver, and gophers, as well as waterfowl, grouse, and other species. As Ida Matthew remembered, "it seems you have to go out hunting for your meals."

Black bears were hunted or trapped, and their meat was made into *stṕúmenk* (smoked sausage). Bear grease was valued as a base for pitch ointment and other salves, as hair grease, and as fuel for lights. Grizzly bear hunting was a way to demonstrate courage and power, especially before guns

5.12 | Moose hunting by horse in Skeetchestn, 1950s. *Left to right:* Jimmy Peters Sr, Sam Camille, and Tom Peters.

were common. Bears, especially grizzly bears, were regarded as embodying powerful spirits and were considered the guardian spirits of twins. Among the Secwépemc and Nlaka'pamux, female grizzlies were also revered as protectors of their offspring – often twins themselves – who gave lullabies to women (see Wickwire 2001). Acknowledging the strong spirit power of bears, hunters who had killed a bear thus sang a mourning song expressing their sorrow. Ida William remembered that her father, Eddie Fortier, used to sing a song after he killed a bear: "I used to listen to him, you know, when he started to sing. He went outside and sit down and start to sing. Must be like that when a person dies. You have to sing a song for them, a hymn, something like that" (see also Teit 1909).

As the archaeological record shows, the bow and arrow became the important hunting weapon about 1,200 years ago, replacing the atlatl, or spear thrower. Bows were made from the wood of yew trees (*Taxus brevifolia*) – whose name, *tskwínek*, indeed means "bow" – or alternately from juniper wood. Up to a metre in length and with a string of sinew, bows were artfully dressed with quill work and covered with the skin of *llecwínek* ("dressed-up bow," bullsnake), flicker feathers, and cherry bark. *Tskwele7úẃi* ("real/ordinary ammunition," arrows) were made of saskatoon or rosewood using small side-notched points. They were grooved to allow the blood to flow after wounding an animal, thus making it easier to track wounded game (see Teit 1909, 518–19).[9] Teit (ibid., 520) noted that a distinguishing feature of Secwépemc arrows was red paint "half the length down the feahers."

Muskets, traded from the Hudson's Bay Company, supplemented the bow and arrow from the 1820s to the 1850s. By the 1860s, rifles had replaced bows and arrows, although older hunters continued to use them. Interestingly, to this day, Secwépemc hunters use the gesture of aiming with a bow, rather than pulling the trigger of a gun, to gesture hunting.

Simpcw elder Louis Matthew (see fig. 5.4) told a story about going hunting in his youth and about how people travelled, set up camp, and lived on small animals, like gophers – an animal cherished by the Símpcwemc – while they were at their base camp. It also shows that some women were expert hunters!

Le Q̓7éses re Spíxems re Nuxwnúxwenxw | Women's Hunting Long Time Ago

told by Louis Matthew, composed by Louis Matthew, Les William, Christine Simon, Marie Antoine, Clara Charlie, and Sarah Deneault, and transcribed by Marianne Ignace, 1997

Le q̓7éses ta7 k stsukw re sqélemcw k xexé7 ṫek píxem.
Long time ago, not only the men were good hunters.

Re s7i7llcw te nuxwnúxwenxw ell lu7 xexé7 te pexpíxem.
Some of the women, too, were good hunters.

Ren kyé7e Sulyén lu7 xexé7 te píxem.
My grandmother Sulyén [Julienne] was a good hunter.

Le tuwíwt-wen, m-wí7stmes re stcítsens re sṫye7 ren kyé7e ell re Katrín,
When I was young, when my grandmother and Catherine were finished cutting hay,

qwenén-ekwe es píxems ne Cmetqenétkwe7ten.
she said she wanted to go hunting at Foghorn Mountain.

E cwéṅwenes, m-qwetséts-kucw te Neqwéqwelsten, m-tsyéṁus-kucw.
Early in the morning, we set out from Chu Chua, and we camped.

Ta7 ey k screpqíns, m-yigépes-kucw ne q̓wmépst.s re sqeltús.
It wasn't noon yet, and we arrived by the foot of the mountain.

M-yews re sc7íllens-kucw ne tsecṫúgw.
And then we ate by the trail.

Le ptékes re crepqín, m-kítsc-kucw ne cpíxteṅ.
In the afternoon, we arrived at the hunting ground.

M-yéws re stntém-kucw re sqeq̓ú7s ne tsetsítcws re sesísk̓.

And then we took our traps into the gopher dens.

M-yews re stscentém-kucw re cyisténs, m-xgetsúlecwentmes re ntšesqéxe7s-kucw.
And then we fixed our camp, and we tied our horses to the ground.

M-qwetséts es píxems mell re Sulyén.
Sulyén had already left to go hunting.

Katrín ell re ntsétswe7 tscentém-kucw re cyistén.
Catherine and I fixed up the hunting ground.

M-yews re stšxentétenes re sqeq̓ú7s-kucw. Ta7 put k scw7its re sq̓7ums-kucw.
And then we checked our traps. We didn't trap much.

E nenénses m-tspelq̓ilcwes re Sulyén.
Later on, Sulyén came back.

M-tícwtše-ekwe te sexwlécken.
She said she had killed a buck.

M-kwens re ntšesqéxe7s es tspelqentéses re sxwlécken.
She took her horse to bring back the buck.

M-estúllentmes-kucw, m-neknílkentmes-kucw re tši7 es kécentem-kucw.
We gutted it and butchered it to dry it.

Kellésq̓t re syist.s-kucw.
For three days, we camped out.

E mesésq̓t m-nes es preniys-kucw re séme7 te w7ec te yecwmínses re sip.
On the fourth day, we visited some white people who were herding sheep.

M-c7eyentwécwes-kucw te súkwe ell te letí, m-kectémes-kucw te tši7.
We traded some sugar and tea from them, and we gave them some deer meat.

M-yístes-kucw tkllú7 neku7 te sítest, m-yews re stspelq̓ílcs-kucw te cyisténs.
We camped there for one night, and then we returned to our camp.

M-yews re syecs-kucw es tspelq̓ílcs te Neqwéqwelsten.
Then we returned to Chu Chua as planned [the part where the band office is now].

Yerí7 re stsukws.
That's the end.

Figure 10 (colour section) pictures the late Sammy Joseph of Chu Chua in his favourite hunting ground in the subalpine and alpine areas between Baldy and Foghorn Mountains.

Trapping

Although various methods of trapping and snaring large and small animals existed well before the beginning of the European fur trade in the early 1800s, the Secwépemc likely increased their trapping activity after the establishment of fur trade posts at Tk̓emlúps and Alexandria on the Fraser River. Especially beaver became a favoured trade item, and in fact the word for "beaver," *sqlew̓*, took on the new meaning of "currency" or "money," with beaver as an animal species being called *sqlew7úw̓i* ("real/ordinary currency") and *sqlew̓* becoming the word for "money." Other furbearing animals like lynx, marten, otter, coyote, wolverine, cougar, black bear, and squirrels were also trapped. From the Hudson's Bay Company records, it appears that within decades of the fur trade starting, beaver returns to the company's Thompson River post were declining, although the overall impact of Secwépemc trapping on game populations in the area throughout the nineteenth century is not clear. The decreasing returns between 1822 and 1826 reported by Archibald McDonald (1827, 230) could be due to fluctuating cyclical beaver populations or other factors.

During the mid-1920s, British Columbia authorities implemented a trapline permit system, and brokered by the local Indian agents, Secwépemc people registered their traplines. Invariably these traplines were located in the resource-producing territory associated with their home communities. Some traplines followed the course of creeks, whereas others were within arbitrarily demarcated areas. Between the 1920s and 1960s, trapping was integrated into an ongoing seasonal round that combined traditional resource-harvesting activities with gardening, agriculture, and cash labour. This system was also integrated into the already existing system of resource use and management discussed below.

Although trapping provided the opportunity to trade and buy staple foods and goods from the Hudson's Bay Company trading post in exchange for furs, and later from fur buyers, as remembered by Secwépemc elders who trapped in the first half of the twentieth century, trapping existed as integrated into the continuing reliance on game, fish, and plant foods, as well as into the continuation of *yecwmíňmen* (stewardship) of watershed-based resources. Joe Stanley Michel (2005, 89) explained it this way for people of the Adams Lake area:

> My grandfather, Alex Arnouse, and his father spent a great deal of time trapping in that area, but they did not register their trapline because the traplines were only registered about 1925 ... The people who usually

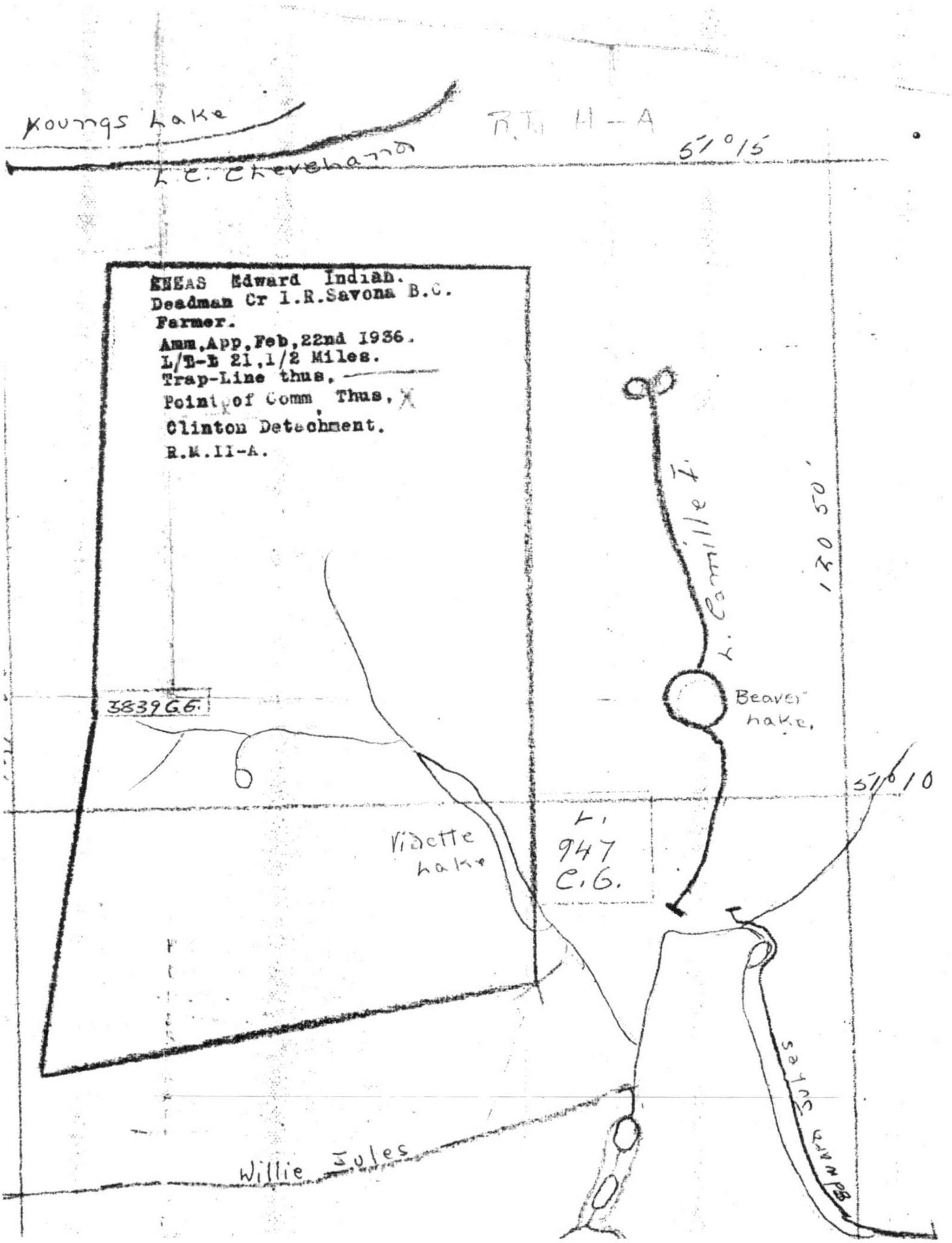

5.13 | Parchment map of Edward Eneas's trapline at Vidette Lake in the upper Deadman's Creek watershed, showing nearby traplines of Willie Jules, Edward Jules, and Louie Camille, all of Skeetchestn, 1936.

Table 5.1 | Beaver pelts traded at the Thompson River and Okanagan posts, 1822–26

Year	*Thompson River post*	*Okanagan post*	*Total*
1822	2,251	695	2,946
1823	1,625	584	2,209
1824	1,584	577	2,161
1825	882	512	1,394
1826	855	196	1,051

Source: A. McDonald (1827, 230).

Table 5.2 | Secwépemc words for “beaver”

Word	*Meaning*
sqleẇ	originally “beaver”; now “money” or “currency”
sqleẇ7éllp	“beaver par excellence,” *the* beaver, or powerful beaver, in stories
sqlew7úẇi	originally “real or ordinary beaver”; now “beaver as a species”
xqlewíẇelt	beaver babies: “offspring out of the inside of beavers”
tsméḿye or *tśmáṁlye*	one- to two-year-old beavers: “crybaby little beavers” (named for how they maintain communication with their mothers by making human-like sounds)
tsqwíqwqen	two-year-old immature beaver: “red head all over”
ṫemt	three-year-old beaver: “furry”
tetéṫemt	four-year-old (mature) beaver: “more furry all over”

> trapped in those had to look after that valley, as well, and lived up to – in my preface I said they were given the land to look after and they did it throughout the valley. So other families had other valleys as well, where traditionally they would trap and hunt and fish, but each of the families would have to, need to look after their own valleys, as well.

With beaver being the most important animal that could produce cash and trade goods since the beginning of the fur trade, Secwépemc trappers had an elaborate vocabulary for beaver in their various stages of life, as table 5.2 shows.

Plant Gathering

As we noted at the beginning of this chapter, the environments of Secwepemcúlecw sustain a large number of plants that the ancestors of the Secwépemc used for food, medicine, tools, clothing, implements, and shelters.

5.14 | Balsamroot meadow near Pinantan Lake, east of Kamloops, with "No Trespassing" sign, 2010. The Pencentén (Pinantan) area was a prolific root-digging ground of the Secwépemc.

Parallel to the hunting and fishing economy, Secwépemc plant resource use involved a number of intensely harvested, managed, processed, and stored high-yield staple plants, as well as the more casual use of a large variety of additional plants in season, some of which were dried if there was surplus but which were mainly consumed fresh while camping. Through research with Secwépemc elders Aimee August, Adeline Willard, and Ike Willard, Gary Palmer (1975b) identified 135 plant species remembered as used by these elders: 48 per cent for food, 53 per cent for medicine, 37 per cent for technology, and 22 per cent for ceremony. Further ethnobotanical research carried out since the 1980s by Nancy J. Turner, Marianne Ignace, Ron Ignace, their colleagues,[10] and many elders has revealed more than two hundred named plant species with Indigenous uses that show similar percentage distributions for categories of use, as well as revealing additional plants that serve as ecological indicator species (see M. Ignace, Turner, and Peacock 2017; and Turner, M. Ignace, and Loewen n.d.).

Of great importance in the diet of Plateau peoples, including the Secwépemc, were some sixteen "root" plants from different plant families whose starchy tubers, rhizomes, and bulbs were harvested for thousands of years in large quantities. Although garden root vegetables and traded rice and flour had increasingly replaced them by the early 1900s, the memory of their use and some harvesting continued throughout the twentieth century and into the present. In their raw state, many of these bulbs and tubers contain either inulin or other nondigestible starches that require human intervention by pit-cooking them, which turns the indigestible starch into digestible nutrients. In addition, sun-curing before pit-cooking them converts starches in the root or bulb into sugar (glucose, fructose, and sucrose), thus making them taste sweeter. One of the most prominent among the Secwépemc root plants is *tsétsẻlq* (balsamroot, *Balsamorhiza sagittata*). Its carbohydrate is mainly inulin, and the root becomes digestible and palatable only through prolonged *tsq̓elstém* (pit-cooking), as the chemistry of the pit oven converts the root's inulin into edible fructose and related compounds, while eliminating the turpentine-like pitch that oozes from its surface (Peacock 1998; Peacock, M. Ignace, and Turner 2017).

Another inulin root is *qwlḗwe* (nodding onion, *Allium cernuum*). Sun-curing and pit-cooking also enhance the nutritional composition of *scwicw* (glacier lily, *Erythronium grandiflorum*), another staple bulb (Loewen 1998; Loewen, Turner, and Thomas 2017). Lil'wat elder Alec Peters reported to Nancy Turner in 1984, "I know the grizzly bears, they dig it out too. They use their big claws like that [raking], and they just leave it like that in the sun, you now. I guess they must taste good when they're dry. They don't eat it right away. I've watched them. A long time, I've watched the grizzly bear, digging it out" (Loewen, Turner, and Thomas 2017). Secwepemc people also thought that bears taught people about sun-curing roots and bulbs to sweeten them. In 2014 Secwepemc elder Edna William reported several black bears digging up balsamroot near her home at Seseléltkwe (Two Springs), close to Upper Hat Creek, and then returning days later to eat it. Mary Thomas showed graduate student Dawn Loewen, who then chemically measured starch and sugar composition, that *scwicw* gets the optimal combination of sweetness and high edible starch content through a complex process that involves time of harvest and then sun-curing, followed by slow pressure-steaming or pit-cooking in underground pit ovens (see Loewen 1998; and Loewen, Turner, and Thomas 2017).

Additional important roots were *qéq̓me* (chocolate lily or riceroot, *Fritillaria lanceolata*) and *qweq̓wíle* (desert parsley or biscuitroot, *Lomation macrocarpum*), the plant associated with the "transformer" who explored the boundaries of Secwépemc and Interior Salish territory (see chapter 2). In the Secwépemc way of thinking, it is the meadowlark who tells Secwépemc people about the best time to harvest *qweq̓wíle*. In late April and early May, meadowlarks, who live in the same habitat as *qweq̓wíle*, call out to the coyote, "*Tucíctsemc ten qweq̓wíle*" ("You wasted my desert parsley on me"). Ecologists call the relationships between different living things in an ecosystem "ecological indicators," and they call the living things in these relationships "ecological indicator species." Secwépemc people incorporated the melodious song of the meadowlark into a saying associated with *qweq̓wíle*. Not coincidentally, the root is good to harvest only early in the growing season and at the time when the meadowlark sings. After that, it becomes bitter and in fact leaves a tingling sensation in the mouth.

TSQ̓ELSTÉM | PIT-COOKING

Archaeological evidence, as noted in chapter 3, shows that pit-cooking has existed as a cooking and plant-processing method for nearly 2,500 years in Secwepemcúl̓ecw. Various ethnographers and early visitors to the Secwépemc and other Plateau peoples reported on this method of cooking root vegetables in pressurized underground ovens, which, as the research cited above shows, not only cooked inulin roots and bulbs but also chemically converted their carbohydrates to maximize sugar and digestible starch content. In its edition of 15 July 1890, the gardening and botany journal *Garden and Forest Magazine* included a description of pit-cooking camas at Lower Arrow Lake, provided by James M. Macoun. By and large, this method was practised throughout the Plateau:

> While camping at Deer Park on the Lower Arrow Lake (an expansion of the Columbia River), a week since, I had an opportunity of witnessing the Indian mode of cooking *Camassia esculenta*. This species of *Camassia* is very abundant along the Columbia River, between the Upper and Lower Arrow Lakes, flowering there during the first weeks of May. The bulbs were collected by the Indians before the seed was fully matured, at which time they consider them at their best. The party I speak of had between twenty and twenty-five bushels of them at the lowest estimate. For two or three days before cooking was begun, the women of the party were engaged in cutting and carrying to camp branches of Alder and Maple (*Alnus rubra* and *Acer glabrum*). Several bundles of the broad leaves of *Lysichiton americanus* (Skunk-cabbage), and two or three of *Alectoria jubata*, the black hair-like lichen that grows in profusion on *Larix occidentalis*, had been brought with them. Everything being ready, the men of the party cut down a huge Pine for no other object, apparently, than to obtain its smaller branches, as no other portion of it was used. A hole about ten feet square and two deep was then dug in a gravelly bank near the lake-shore, which was filled with broken Pine branches. Upon these were piled several cords of dry cedar and pine, and this was covered over with small bowlders. The pile was then

/continued

5.15 | A traditional pitcooking at Cáclep (Fountain) on the Fraser River, 2000

lighted in several places, and left for some hours to take care of itself. When the Indians returned to it the stones lay glowing among a mass of embers. The few unburnt pieces of wood which remained near the edges were raked away, and the women with wooden spades banked up the sides of the pile with sand, throwing enough of it over the stones to fill up every little crevice through which a tongue of flame might be thrust up from the coals that still burned beneath the stones. Then the whole was covered with the Maple and Alder boughs to the depth of a foot or more after they had been well tramped down. Over these were placed the wide leaves of the Skunk-cabbage until every cranny was closed. Sheets of Tamarac-bark were then spread over the steaming green mass, and upon these the bulbs were placed. About half of them were in bark baskets closed at the mouth, and each holding about a bushel and a half. These were carried to the centre of the pile. The lichen of which I have spoken was then laid over the unoccupied bark, having been well washed first, and over it were strewn the bulbs that remained. The whole was then covered with boughs and leaves as before and roofed with sheets of bark. Upon this three or four inches of sand was thrown and over all was heaped the material for another fire, larger even than the first one. When this was lighted the sun was just setting, and it continued to burn all night.

> The next morning our camp was moved away, and I was unable to see the results of the day's labour. I was told, however, by one of the Indians who could speak a little English, that their oven would be allowed a day in which to cool, and that when opened the bulbs in the baskets would have "dissolved to flour," from which bread could be made, while those mixed with the lichen would have united with it to form a solid substance resembling black plug tobacco in colour and consistency, which could be broken up and kept sweet for a long time. (Quoted in Dawson 1891, 21)

Memories from elders like Mary Thomas and Lilly Harry of pit-cooking during their youth suggested a nearly identical method for cooking balsamroot and yellow glacier lily. These elders remembered using saskatoon branches, rose bushes, and shrubby penstemon as liner plants underneath and above the foods to be cooked. Before canvas was put on top to cover up the pit, a not too large quantity of water was poured along a stick onto the rocks, thus generating steam. The covered pit was then sealed airtight by covering it with a layer of sand. Temperature probe tests (Loewen 1998; Peacock 1998) have revealed that well-prepared cooking pits with red hot lava rocks will produce cooking temperatures of more than 150 degrees Celsius for several hours, with temperatures above the boiling point sustained for ten or more additional hours. On the importance of the "black hair-like lichen" (now *Bryoria fremontii*), see below.

Other important root plants included *skwenkwínem* (Indian potato, *Claytonia lanceolata*), which grows at mid to high elevations (1,000 to 1,800 metres), and *llek̓wpín* (bitterroot, *Lewisia rediviva*), which grows in select habitats in the dry terraces just above the river valleys and was a coveted trade item for *scpet̓ám*, one of the "national dishes" of the Secwépemc and surrounding peoples, a pudding made of saskatoon berries, bitterroot, fish eggs, and other roots and berries. Root plants also included *textsin̓* (peppery tiger lily), *k̓útse* (Indian celery), *cílcel* (silverweed), called "Indian spaghetti" by Esk̓ét elder Laura Harry, and a variety of edible roots that were harvested in wetlands throughout Secwepemcúl̓ecw and the Interior. These roots included *etsmét̓s̓* (water parsnip, *Sium suave*), the roots of *kwtellp* (bulrush), and *tsets̓elúl̓s* (wapato, *Sagittaria latifolia*), a potato-like root that Mary Thomas (interview with Rhandi Alphonse, 1997) remembered being harvested in the wetlands of Shuswap Lake near Salmon Arm during her youth: "The bulrush used to be plentiful along the lake, and the wapato. It used to be just thick in there, and my grandmother would go down and we'd go with her and we'd dig

5.16 (*left*) | Dr Mary Thomas of Salmon Arm with her birch-bark baskets, 1995; 5.17 (*right*) | Sarah Deneault of Neskonlith digging *skwenkwinem* (Indian potatoes, *Claytonia lanceolata*) at Mount Lolo, 1997.

them potatoes. She'd get a big basket full. They looked like little eyeballs with eyelashes. There used to be lots in here. And the water parsnip. Me and my granny used to dig up the roots, grab some, and run for the water and wash it clean, and we'd have a feed."

To ensure a good enough supply of high-yield starchy foods for the winter months, families would harvest and process several hundred pounds of root vegetables while camped at central root-processing areas in mid elevations, such as Petpút̓men (Upper Hat Creek) (see fig. 7, image b, colour section), Ck̓emqenétkwe (Scheidam Flats) above Kamloops, and Ck̓écse7ten (Back Valley) above Skeetchestn.

In the mid-1970s, Ike Willard estimated that around the turn of the century, when he was young, about 200 pounds (90.7 kilograms) of *scwicw* (glacier lily) would last a family for the winter months (Palmer 1975b, 54). Mary Thomas estimated that in addition, a family would dig as much as 100 pounds (45.4 kilograms) of *skwenkwínem* (Indian potatoes) (Turner, M. Ignace, and Loewen n.d., 153). This was at a time when families already grew potatoes and other vegetables in gardens, and the harvest of edible roots before the arrival of market

5.18 | Ron Ignace harvesting lodgepole pine cambium, 2001. This sweet-tasting spring food also has important cleansing, or detoxifying, properties.

starch foods would have been much higher. Eugene Hunn has estimated that on the Southern Plateau, where camas was the most important root plant, up to 50 per cent of the diet derived from root plants, whereas on the Northern Plateau, including Secwépemc territory, root plants may have been a slightly lesser part of the Indigenous diet (Hunn and Selam 1990).

In addition to roots, a large variety of fruits, vegetables, nuts, and seeds were harvested throughout the spring to fall months. The green shoots of various plants, including Indian rhubarb, fireweed, and balsamroot, provided welcome minerals and vitamins in early spring. The *st7íq̓wel̓qw* (cambium) of lodgepole pine and ponderosa pine has long been valued not only for its aromatic sweet taste but also for providing vitamins and minerals as well as for acting as a laxative-like "spring cleanser," or detoxifier.

Hazelnuts and pine nuts – often taken from squirrels' caches – as well as more than twenty species of berries harvested at different elevations throughout the summer, rounded off the diet. Important fruit plants included several species of *Vaccinium*, namely huckleberries, highbush and lowbush blueberries, and dwarf blueberries. The Secwépemc term for saskatoon berry (*Amelanchier alnifolia*), *speqpeq7úw̓i*, translates as the "berry par excellence" or "real/ordinary berry" and thus attests to the importance of this berry. Indeed, the Secwépemc distinguish three different kinds of what scientists

5.19 (*left*) | Bridget Dan of Esk̓ét (Alkali Lake) with the *sencweséllp* variety of saskatoon berry that grows by her house, 2014; 5.20 (*right*) | Cecilia DeRose with her harvest of highbush cranberries on the Sugarcane Reserve at the east end of Williams Lake, 2011.

call *Amelanchier alnifolia*: *speqpeq7úw̓i* have small seeds and grow on small- to medium-size bushes, often on or near old flood plains; *stséqwem* are very sweet with large seeds and grow on tall bushes in dry gullies; and *sen̓cweséllp* are a variety in between *speqpeq7úw̓i* and *stséqwem* and grow near Esk̓ét and Xgét̓tem by the Fraser River.

Additional important fruits were strawberries, raspberries, gooseberries, red and black currants, blackcaps, highbush and lowbush cranberries, chokecherries, black hawthorn, and even Oregon grapes and kinnikinnick berries, the latter eaten after they were fried with bear grease.

Of particular significance was, and continues to be, *sxúsem* (soapberry, *Shepherdia canadensis*), a bitter fruit high in vitamin C and iron that is *spem* (beaten off the bush), rather than *q̓wléwem* (picked), and is made into a thirst-quenching beverage or whipped into "Indian ice cream." A photo of elder Christine Simon, her grandchildren, and Katie Ignace beating *sxúsem* off the branches is shown in figure 11 of the colour section of this book.

Another integral part of the diet of Secwépemc and other Interior peoples was *wíle* (black tree lichen, *Bryoria fremontii*), which people raked off Douglas-fir, lodgepole pine, or subalpine fir trees at mid to higher elevations in early fall, although it could be harvested at any time of the year. After it was

5.21 | Dried cakes of *wíle* (black tree lichen, *Bryoria fremontii*), also called edible horsehair, 2006. This important traditional food of the Secwépemc and other peoples of the Interior Plateau was harvested in early fall in the montane parklands and then processed by prolonged pit-cooking.

5.22 | Clara Camille *(left)* of Xgét̓təm (Dog Creek) and Cecilia DeRose of Esk̓ét (Alkali Lake) harvesting prince's pine medicine in the montane parkland near Quesnel Lake, 2012.

washed to remove its outer layer of vulpinic acid, it was pit-cooked, shaped into loaves or cakes, and then dried for future use. The dietary importance of *wíle* was long considered to lie in its capacity to be an always available "starvation food." However, we are only just beginning to uncover the culinary chemical knowledge of the ancestors of the Secwépemc: recent experimental research by Stu Crawford (2017) has shown that in pit-cooking ovens, *wíle* absorbs sugars that are released from other plant foods during the slow pit-cooking process.

More than a hundred plants were used medicinally, most of them gathered in the *t7íweltk* (high wooded plateau) and subalpine meadow areas, often while people were on hunting trips. Medicinal plants included tonics and cleansing teas, such as those made from *sxúsem* (soapberry) sticks, *melánllp* (subalpine fir bark), and *secwsqéqxe7ten* (Hudson Bay tea or trapper's tea). Other medicines were *kíkwe* (Sitka valerian, *Valeriana sitchensis*), *qets̓uyé7é7llp* ("chipmunk tail," yarrow), willow bark, known for its analgesic salicylic acid, and a few highly potent and toxic plants like *tnílmen* (Indian hellebore, *Veratrum viride*) and *k̓etse7éllp* (devil's club, *Oplopanax horridum*). Numerous plants, sometimes complementing one another in a concoction as "partner plants," were boiled or steeped and used as poultices to soothe the pain of arthritis, sprains, and fractures.

Yecwmenúl̓ecwem | Plant Resource Stewardship

Elders of the Secwépemc nation and surrounding Plateau nations who experienced traditional plant gathering as they grew up during the first decades of the twentieth century maintain that root plants and other resources have actually declined in quality and productivity since the time when they were actively harvested. There are various explanations for this observed decline in productivity, and one significant factor is the severe impact of cattle grazing on root plant habitat. Another key reason for the decline in quantity and quality of root plants noted by many elders is that people are no longer *yecwmínem* (looking after) the plants as they did for many generations in the past. A growing body of ethnobotanical evidence suggests that Indigenous peoples in British Columbia and elsewhere in North America – people commonly described as "foragers" or "hunter-gatherers" – actively *managed* their environments to ensure a predictable, abundant source of the plants and animals they relied on, whether for food, implements, or medicines. For the Secwépemc and other Indigenous peoples, such practices combined economic motives of increased and reliable availability of important resources with deeply embedded spiritual beliefs and values about respect for living things and thus about the need to look after resources.

The Secwépemc practised a variety of management regimes that aimed at enhancing the habitat of individual plants and plant populations (plants in a

5.23 | A Salish woman with Shuswap basket demonstrating the operation of a root digger, photographed by Harlan I. Smith, 1898.

certain area) and at protecting them from predators and pests. For example, Mary Thomas remembered her father and the other Neskonlith men riding around their lands and setting fire to tent caterpillar colonies that were infesting the wild cherry trees, either *Prunus virginiana* or *P. pensylvanica.*

Another management technique mentioned by many elders included loosening or tilling the soil with digging sticks and weeding the root-digging areas in the process of doing this. In large-scale root-digging areas, such digging involved rolling back the grassy turf and then systematically digging trenches 30 to 60 centimetres in width to extract *scwicw* (glacier lily), *skwenkwínem* (Indian potato), *qéq̓me* (chocolate lily or riceroot), and other root plants. The removal of weeds and grass improved the habitat of the root plants. Les Williams of Salmon Arm remembered elders who would dig long root trenches through collaborative labour in the root-gathering areas of the Neskonlith Meadows. Areas for gathering root plants were thus carefully tended and tilled patches rather than "wild" habitats. In fact, such trench digging was an important aspect of the training of young girls. Digging stick handles from gravesites show incisions as emblems of trench-digging practice and skill, as do pictograph images (see fig. 3.12, items g and k).

There is evidence from the terms for "weeds" in Secwepemctsín and surrounding Interior Salish languages that the concept of "weeds" predated the origin of introduced noxious weeds. Before the latter were introduced, the term designated native plants that densely grew "hair- or fur-like" close to the ground. Thus the Secwépemc term for "weed" is *c.wepúlecwem* (the prefix *c* for "inside," plus the root *wep* for "furry, hairy," plus the lexical suffixes *-ulecw* for "land" and *-em* for "action"). In the days before noxious weeds invaded the interior, such plants would have commonly been grasses, which would have been cleared off by root diggers in the process of harvesting.

The skilful handling of the *pétse* (digging stick) allowed for selective harvesting and plant population management. Digging sticks were made of a hardwood like saskatoon berry or black hawthorn (*Crataegus douglasii*), with a fire-hardened pointed end and a cross handle, which long ago was often decorated with incisions indicating the trenches dug by its owner during *étsxem* (training). As George M. Dawson (1891, 20) observed of women digging with the *pétse*, "The women search the open woods and hillsides with crutch-like root-digging sticks in hand, and as each bunch of roots is extracted deftly toss it over the shoulder into a basket carried on the back." For roots that are deep in the ground, the use of the *pétse* allowed for the selective removal of bigger tap roots and bulbs while leaving smaller, immature ones undisturbed. Moreover, it was an extremely effective tool for extracting large taproots like balsamroot or desert parsley. The *pétse* also allowed resource gatherers to leave the "mother roots" of plants like balsamroot undisturbed, and as Aimee August of Neskonlith recalled, it thus allowed them to continue to propagate "daughter roots" from the "mother root." Mary Thomas and others explained that the best balsamroots to harvest were those that were carrot-size, generally those producing 5 to 15 leaves and perhaps 3 to 5 flower heads. The "mother" plants, in contrast, might have up to 50 or 60 leaves and 30 or more flower heads. Their giant taproots could extend a metre or more into the ground and would be far too tough to eat even after prolonged cooking. Harvesting the carrot-size roots while leaving smaller, immature roots as well as the largest roots was an excellent strategy for sustaining or even increasing balsamroot populations. In succeeding years, the smaller roots would grow to a good harvest size, while the "mother roots" would continue to propagate through seed that would germinate and grow in the tilled soil, as well as through sprouted roots. For root plants like *skwenkwínem* (Indian potato) that grow close to the surface, digging tools made from the antler of a mule deer facilitated sustainable harvesting as plant harvesters worked through the soil with the antler tool, extracting large size *skwenkwínem* but leaving the small young bulbs to regrow in the freshly tilled soil.

An additional propagation method remembered by several elders involved the replanting of the corms of *scwicw* (glacier lily). Sarah Deneault and Mary Thomas both remembered that when they were young girls, their mothers,

5.24 | The remains of an old cultivated patch of *spétsen* (Indian hemp) on the Kamloops Indian Reserve, 2007. This was once the site of a large village (see chapter 3).

aunts, and grandmothers would have them remove the corm buds from the *scwicw* bulbs after they had been harvested, collect them in baskets, and then return them to the tilled soil, thus propagating new plants from the harvested bulbs.

Similarly, people carefully tended their *spétsen* (Indian hemp) patches, especially those in productive locations near villages. As Beverley Bob of Merritt reported, she found some well-tended *spétsen* patches on the Kamloops Indian Reserve at the edge of a now drained wetland marsh where large pithouse village sites existed into the late 1800s. These patches had apparently been tended for generations by removing brush and undergrowth near the patch to ensure straight and thick growth of the perennial hemp shoots. Being a hemp weaver herself, she tended this patch for years to harvest hemp there, only to find one year that it had fallen victim to a bulldozer clearing land for a trailer park.

Ctálem (pruning) of berry bushes, especially *sxúsem* (soapberry, *Shepherdia canadensis*) bushes, was a commonly practised way of enhancing the growth of important plant crops. Since *sxúsem* are not picked but beaten off the bushes, many pickers remove the berry-laden branches and then, with whole families working together, beat them off the branches on a large canvas. Elders report that such pruning enhances rather than diminishes the productivity of *sxúsem* bushes in subsequent years (see fig. 11, colour section).

Root plant harvesting entailed plant selection, with those of optimal size being the preferred ones. Mary Thomas remembered that the preferred kind of *scwicw* (glacier lily, *Erythronium grandiflorum*) were those with three flowers rather than a single flower, predicting that those with multiple flowers would have larger bulbs (Loewen, Turner, and Thomas 2017).

Secwépemc people also had preferred locations, as they still do today, for a number of important food and medicinal plants. These were locations that were accessible from villages or in convenient locations along camping places and well-travelled routes within the seasonal round. For example, as Cecilia deRose and other elders of the Northern Secwépemc area showed, the *qwléwe* (nodding onion) patch at Blue Lake near Soda Creek, due to its rich soil and moist location, produced excellent *qwléwe* compared with nodding onions in poor soils and drier locations. Neskonlith Meadows was the area of choice for Secwépemc communities from the Sexqéltkemc division and even from surrounding communities to dig glacier lilies, chocolate lilies, nodding onions, and Indian potatoes. Medicinal plants like yarrow, which grow at different elevations, from river level to alpine areas, and in a variety of soils, were much preferred when harvested in the *t7íweltk* (high plateau) and *skwelkw̓élt* (subalpine and alpine) areas due to their higher potency caused by the short but intense growing season. Many of these preferred or choice gathering locations were identified by place names with the prefix *pell* (has), such as Pellcílcel ("has silverweed"), the name for Three Valley Lake; Pellskwakwíkwna ("has Indian potatoes"), which is near Monte Creek; the "Indian Range" above Chu Chua (Simpcw), whose Western dialect variant of the same name is Pellskwenkwíkwnem; and Pellqweq̓wíle ("has biscuitroot"), which is at the mouth of Tranquille Creek near Kamloops.

A crucial plant resource management technique among the Secwépemc and other Indigenous peoples of the Plateau and northwestern North America in general involved landscape burning to enhance the growth of berries and root plants, to control insects and invasive species like sage, to improve the forage for deer and elk, and to keep open meadows from growing over (Peacock, Ignace, and Turner 2016; Turner 1999; Turner and Peacock 2005; see fig. 12, colour section). Such burning took place on forested hillsides, especially on the margins of aspen groves; it also took place and continues to be practised in the sage- and grass-covered areas at or above the valley bottoms. Depending on the terrain and environment, such areas were burned in cycles of ten to twenty years. For example, in the sagebrush-bunchgrass areas, it appears that an optimum grass cover was reached within ten years, after which time the sagebrush took over again. Burning involved close timing of dry but not overly dry conditions in mid-spring (late March to early April), combined with favourable wind conditions. Such conditions typically exist from late March to early April, when gentle winds prevail in the valleys and often shift at midday, creating ideal conditions for burning in a contained area without the fires getting out of control, as the midday winds cause the fire to turn back and die out. Ron Ignace remembers his great-grandfather Edward Eneas and other elders of Skeetchestn lighting up patches of hillsides, aspen groves, and meadows near their trails during their hunting, gathering, and monitoring trips at that time of the year. Thus the "well-kept, park-like" appearance of the rolling hills around Tkemlúps (Kamloops) noted by Reverend George Grant (1873, 297), who accompanied railway surveyor Sandford Fleming on an expedition to the Interior in 1872, was due to the longstanding practice of fire management. Burning was designed to create and maintain productive parkland and forest areas and meadows, which did not constitute a naturally occurring "pristine" or "wilderness" landscape but were at least in part the result of human intervention and management. Settler D.S. Mitchell (1925, 4) of the Shuswap Lake area commented on the former practice of landscape burning:

> Formerly there was much semi-open country on the hills, showing great detail of cliff and gorge, now curtained over by the solid green of an almost impenetrable thicket of small firs, which has taken possession, for in those days the Indians ran fires at intervals of a few years, over the grassy slopes to check the encroachment of the forest on the patches where the women dried berries on bulrush mats, for winter food, or gathered edible roots; and where the men might hunt bears, when they came out to eat the fresh young grass and herbage in the spring.

Yecwmíṅmen | The Role of Resource Stewards

The idea of private ownership was foreign to us, but looking after things was not foreign. (Michel 2005, 85)

Beyond the practical strategies that the Secwépemc used to maintain and enhance plant resources as described above, there were individuals in any given community who functioned as appointed resource caretakers to enact a system of resource monitoring and taking inventory. On their way to plateau fishing grounds or in the process of travelling to hunting areas, experienced adult members of a community continually monitored the health of root-producing areas, berry patches, and medicinal plant patches throughout the seasonal round, with certain individuals functioning as *yecwmíṅmen* (Western Secwepemctsín) or *yecwmíṅma* (Eastern Secwepemctsín). Based on their skills and their experiences on the land, the latter were regarded as tacitly appointed by communities as experts who would assess the quality and quantity of a particular resource at known locations accessed by community members. *Yecwmíṅmen* took stock of the health and proclivity of salmon and game populations and communicated their findings to members of the community. In addition, it appears that they played the most active roles in the resource management strategies discussed above, particularly burning. Other *yecwmíñmen* took care of trails. Thus Ron Ignace (2008) remembers that one of the Skeetchestn adult males, Walter Humphrey, had the tacitly assigned task of clearing fallen trees and other obstacles from riding and foot trails in order to allow easy passage to and from resource locations by all members of the community. Based on the work of the *yecwmíñmen* as practical resource stewards, community chiefs functioned as decision makers who signalled the commencement of resource-producing activity, directed people to particular berry patches, and initiated the beginning of the salmon harvest. Thus Teit (1909, 573) observed how berry picking at prolific berrying spots was "looked after by the band in whose district they were situated," explaining that at several large saskatoon berry patches near Big Bar,

> the chief watched the ripening of berries, and deputed young men to watch and report on the various places. From time to time the watchman [*yucwmíñmen*] brought in branches and showed them to the chief. When the berries were about ripe, he sent out word that on a certain day the berrying would commence at a certain berry patch. Women would come from as far away as Alkali Lake and Clinton. The first day each woman picked only a little, about enough for herself and her friends to eat fresh during that day and night. After the first day they picked all they could and began to cure them. When they had finished one patch, the chief directed them to the next one which was ripe, and so on until they had finished all.

Resource stewardship was thus achieved through a combination of *yecwmiñmen*, who were specifically delegated to fulfil management and monitoring tasks involving game, fish, and plant resources within their habitats, along with political leaders of communities in whose area resources were gathered.

Considering this breadth of management regimes that improved the growth of plant populations, Mary Thomas, in fact, referred to Secwépemc plant management and harvesting as "just like a garden," defying the separation between agricultural "cultivators" and hunter-gatherer "foragers" often expounded by settler society since the late nineteenth century to denounce the Secwépemc's use of the land as "primitive" and thus to render their sense of land ownership illegitimate. In the words of Indian agent J.W. MacKay, "Some of the old Indians still maintain that the lands over which they formerly roamed and hunted are theirs by right. I have to meet this claim by stating that as they have not fulfilled the divine command 'to subdue the earth' their pretentions to ownership, in this respect, are untenable" (Canada, Department of Indian Affairs 1864–1990, "Kamloops Agency," in *Annual Report*, 1885, 92). For the Secwépemc, however, who were planting potato gardens in places like Cḱemqenétkwe (Scheidam Flats) and near Neskonlith on the South Thompson River by or before the 1820s (see table 11.2),[11] as well as growing a variety of garden crops, fruit trees, hay, and grains by the late 1800s, this cultivation was not perceived as a revolutionary way to get food but was incorporated into existing ways of thinking about managing plants, as is witnessed by the term the Secwépemc began using for gardening, *ḱweńllq* ("try out seeds"). In sum, Secwépemc traditional resource regimes, similar to those practised throughout the Interior Plateau and in all parts of northwestern North America,[12] involved practices of plant population management and habitat management that were in no way inferior to horticultural practices as they existed in other parts of the world.

The Traditional Seasonal Round

The months in the Secwépemc calendar (Dawson 1891; R. Ignace 2008; Teit 1909) reflect the seasonal activities shared by Secwépemc people. The number of years between events or in the lifetime of a person was measured as the number of *swucwt* (snows or winters). A seasonal round consisted of five seasons, called *neḱlltmicw* ("recurring changes of the land"), divided into thirteen lunar months. The five seasons included early spring (snow melting), mid- to late spring (root gathering), summer (berry and high-elevation root and medicinal plant gathering), late summer to early fall (salmon season), and mid- to late fall (hunting season). The calendar count started with the late fall "entering month," when animals moved into their dens and people moved into their *c7ístkteń* (winter homes), followed by *s7istk*, the stay-at-home period of winter, when men nonetheless hunted for game on snowshoes and trapped for different furbearing animals. They also went ice fishing on the lakes or fished from canoes using the *tsétsḱwem* (pitch lamp) method. In mid to late spring, people harvested different root plants at increasingly higher elevations as the snow melted between March and late May. During this time, they also pursued large runs of cutthroat trout and rainbow trout at many lakes in the middle to high plateaus, including Xixyúm (Hi-hium Lake), Teltsíḿten (Green Lake), Tṡpéten (Gustafsen Lake), Q̇es7éten (Loon Lake), and Sṗe7cwstwécwemstem (Bonaparte Lake). The time of the late spring freshet in the rivers and the arrival of swallows marked the beginning of salmon fishing, which began with spring salmon, followed by sockeye until early September. Then coho were fished, mainly in the tributaries, from mid to late fall. Not only did the catch from high-yield salmon and trout fisheries yield fresh protein between March and October, but significant portions were also dried for winter use. Throughout early to late summer, berries were picked as they ripened at higher and higher places on the plateaus. *Sxúsem* (soapberries), for example, ripen in the lower part of their range (1,000 metres) in early July but are ripe in the highest part of their range (1,600 metres) as late as the end of

Table 5.3 | Secwépemc calendar and seasonal round based on names and activities of the Skeetchestn area

Name	*Translation*	*Approximate month*	*Subsistence activities*
Pellc7ellcw7úllcwten	"entering month"	October/ November	people enter into their winter homes animals enter their dens hunting continues coho salmon run
Pelltetéq̓em*	"cross-over month"	December	winter solstice people live on stored provisions trapping
Pell7emtmín̓ Pellk̓well7emtmín̓	"stay at home month" "stay underneath month"	January	people live on stored provisions some ice fishing trapping
Pelltsípwenten	"cache pit month"	February	people live on stored provisions ice fishing fishing for steelhead with torch lights trapping
Pellsq̓épts Pesq̓épts	"Chinook wind month"	March	fishing at Loon Lake spring hunting for male deer first plants come out
Pesll7éwten	"melting month"	April	fishing at Tunkwa Lake digging of yellowbells, nodding onions, bisquit root, balsamroot
Pell7é7llqten Pell7ell7é7llqten	"root-digging month"	May	digging of balsamroot, Indian potatoes, and other roots spring (Chinook) salmon run fishing at Hi-hium Lake and Tunkwa Lake lodgepole pine cambium ready
Pelltspéntsk	"mid-summer month"	June	first berries ripe at end of month root digging spring (Chinook) salmon run

Name	Translation	Approximate month	Subsistence activities
Pelltqwelq̓wéľtem	"getting ripe month"	July	many species of berries ripe root and medicinal plant gathering salmon (Chinook) fishing in Thompson River
Pesqelqlélten	"many salmon month"	August	sockeye salmon fishing in Thompson River berries harvested at higher elevations chocolate lily and medicinal plants hunting season starts
Pelltemlliḱ̓t	"spawned-out month"	September	hunting season and drying of meat (deer and moose) for winter black tree lichen harvested salmon fishing continues
Pesllwélsten	"abandoning month"	October/ November	peak hunting season and drying of meat for winter tanning hides coho salmon run

* Dr. Aimee August of Neskonlith (interview with authors, 1991) told us that at the time of the winter solistice, people had their winter celebrations, and at that time children were allowed to play tricks on their elders, which was normally not allowed. The cross-over moon time, or solistice, was thus considered something like a liminal period, when normal activities and sanctions were temporarily suspended

Sources: Compiled from Teit (1909, 517–18) and Dawson (1891, 40). Additional names for months are given in Kuipers (1974) and, for the Chase area, in G. Palmer (1975a) and Bouchard and Kennedy (1975). Between 1995 and 2012, Marianne Ignace, Ron Ignace, and Mona Jules reviewed renditions, spellings, and translations of month names with several elders. Especially in the Chase area, some alternate names appear to be Pellscwícwem ("month when yellow glacier lilies grow," April) and Pelltqítq̓e7ten ("strawberry month," June).

August. From late July to mid-August, during the time the lupins are in bloom, people used to get marmots in the high mountains. The late summer to early fall period was the time for large-scale hunting of large deer, elk, caribou, and more recently moose, much of which was dried for winter use.

Often by mere allusion, the months of the Secwépemc calendar express the annual round of resource harvesting and the cyclical nature of the resource activities entailed in a year, called a *swucwt* (snow). The way that the thirteen-month cyclical lunar calendar was made to conform with a count of twelve named months was to extend and adjust the time of Pellc7ellcw7úllcwten ("entering month"), when humans entered pithouses and animals entered dens, bridging it into an annual calculation of some 365 days that matched the sun's journey as it entered the winter solistice Pelltetéq̓em ("cross-over month"). Pelltspéntsk ("mid-summer month"), which began with the summer solistice, marked the halfway point of the annual cycle.

Table 5.3 shows the seasonal round of resource harvesting for Secwépemc people in the Skeetchestn area. It involves the places most often habitually travelled, including the valley and shores of the Thompson River and Kamloops Lake, the plateaus on the north and south side of Kamloops Lake and the Thompson River, the Deadman's Creek Valley, and the valleys, plateaus, and mid-elevation mountains that frame it, along with the *t7íweltk* (high plateaus) of the mountains around Hi-hium Lake (at an elevation of 1,550 metres), Greenstone Mountain, and Battle Creek. As part of their seasonal round, Skeetchestn people have also long hunted in the watershed of the upper Bonaparte River and Bonaparte Lake. For plant gathering and hunting in subalpine and alpine areas, people would travel farther afield to areas like Skwelkwék̓welt (Tod Mountain). In addition, travels to engage in hunting, fishing, and camping with relatives would take people to other areas of Secwepemcúlecw on the Fraser and North Thompson Rivers or in the Shuswap Lakes area, although not as frequently.

For the Northern Secwépemc, an example of the seasonal round is Lilly Harry's account of annual hunting, fishing, and plant gathering in the area around Dog Creek on the Fraser River, along with travels to the alpine areas at Blackdome Mountain in the Camelsfoot Range on the west side of the Fraser, as well as to several lakes on the Plateau in order to harvest various fish species, including Gustafsen Lake and Lac La Hache. Although her account involves geographic locations that are different from the seasonal round of the people in the Skeetchestn area, the principle of alternating between seasonal resource-producing locations at different elevations is very similar, as is the mode of travel and practice of camping and living in resource-producing locations for weeks at a time. In both cases, annual seasonal round travel to resource-producing locations took place within a radius of some 100 kilometres.

Lilly Harry's Account of Annual Resource Gathering

from Kuipers (1989, 41–4), retranscribed and retranslated by Ronald E. Ignace and Marianne Ignace, 2008[13]

Te Tsentsneyk̓ ecwes re néses le q̓7es te qelmúcw es wéwlems tek sgwígwle.
The people long time ago went to Horse Lake to fish for steelhead.

5.25 | Lilly Harry of Xgéttem (Dog Creek) at Blackdome Mountain with medicinal plants, 1991. Blackdome Mountain is an important resource-harvesting location of the Western and Northern Secwépemc. A large open-pit copper mine near its peak destroyed much of the area in the 1970s and 1980s.

Xexyúm ri7 te swewll re sgwígwle.
The steelhead are very big fish.

Ec lu7 re wéwtskmes ṫ7éne ṫ7ek re swewll.
They fished them with three-pronged spears where the fish went by.

M-tseq̓mictmes ne llewt.s m-esṫéq.
They threw it [the spear] at their back where it stuck.

Le q̓7éses ta7 ri7 k qíṫe.
Long time ago there were no fishing rods.

M-nes te Nek̓úyt nu7 re m-wéwlemes te tseq̓wmús ell písell.
They went to Chimney Lake where they fished for sucker and rainbow trout.

Re Tṡpéten yerí7 re cwéw̓lemtens le q̓7es te qelmúcw.
Gustafson Lake [sic] was [also] the fishing place of the people long ago.

E m-yúcwtes re písell, nu7 m-lléqelcwes es wéwlems.
When the rainbow trout ran, the people camped [lived] there.

Te Txet́ínten t̓lu7 re m-wéwlemes te písell, swlle7úw̓i, ell q̓wé7k.
At Lac La Hache, they fished for rainbow trout, ling, and squawfish.

Te sllwélsten re keknécw t̓lu7 me7 tcwesétmenses.
In the fall they would travel there for kokanee.

Re tsem̓etúlecwstem te Cp̓estnétkwe, re Cteqtíq̓kwe, yerí7 t̓ucw ri7 re swelwéw̓lemtens.
The places that are called Flat Lake and Muddy Water, these were also their fishing grounds.

T̓lén te Tsxq̓elxétkwe nerí7 le Legwpél̓qs w̓7écwes re wéwlemes méte Tsepég.
Over at Round Lake, [elders] Legwpél̓qs and Tsepég used to fish.

Ne tk̓welltkwékweltks-enke mé7 ri7 re sxq̓weléw̓tens,
It must be below their berry-picking ground,

pyin re sts7em̓ét.stem Tektqwewq̓wewqín.
what they now call Timothy Mountain.

T̓lu7 yúmell ri7 le stext̓ex7ém w7écwes re w7écwes-enke.
Over there is where all the old people [elders] were, apparently.

Téke mé7e re skekéws w7ec re cwesétes-enke e nésmes k stem es penmíns.
See, they travelled far out when they went looking for things [resources].

E nésmes k stem, me7 penmíns éytsell me7 tspelq̓ílcwes.
When they went out, they found things and then came back.

Ta7 me7 scwesét.s tek nek̓w7ésq̓t me7 tskítscwes re m-cwesétes.
They wouldn't go off and return the same day when they went travelling.

Re m-cwesétes lu7 w7ec re styém̓wses ell me7 pellcteckeństqéxe7ten.
When they travelled, they travelled on horseback and with packhorses.

Me7 k̓wíncwes ri7 k syist.s éytsell me7 tspelq̓ílcwes.
They would camp overnight for several nights before they returned home.

Xexé7 lu7 te sw7ec. Xexé7 ri7 re sllek̓wmínems t̓ri7 te stém̓i.
They worked hard the way they lived. They had to work hard to remember lots of things.

Me7 tslexemstéc t̓hé7en k w7écwes k w7écwes ke7 stet̓ex7ém,
You had to know where your ancestors used to go and stay,

t̓hé7en k w7écwes k kénmes t̓ri7.
where they went and what they did.

Téke, len méme7 tl̓une te pestéwt tl̓u7 xwexwyúlecwem, w7écwes k w7écwes-enke
My mom went and stayed all over the country on the other side of the [Fraser] River

w7ec ne pexpíxmes.
with the hunters.

T̓lune ne tsem̓etúlecwstem tek Hawkeye, tl̓u7-ekwe w7écwes k w7écwes.
Over there at the place called Hawkeye, that's where she used to go and stay.

Kekéw ri7 t̓len te skwelk̓wél̓t.
Far away in the snowy mountains.

E m-nésmenses re sqwí7qwe, yerí7 tl̓u7 re m-qwetsétses.
When they went after [hoary] marmots, that's where they went.

Ne August m-kwemtús t̓7él̓ye re qel̓mucw, tíwel ri7 m-yews ri7 re st̓7eks.[14]
In August is when the people [from here] always used to cross over [to the west bank of the Fraser] but then they went on from there.

T̓lu7 re m-tsyémes wel m-ullcw re sqwí7qwe éytsell m-tsyét̓cwes.
And they lived [camped] there until the marmots went into hibernation, and then they came down [the mountain].

T̓len te tsqwemqwúm, re Pellsextsétṡey, re Pelltsq̓éy̓lecw, yerí7 re spíxten̓s le q̓7éses.
Off in the hills [in the range near Blackdome Mountain] at Pellsextsétṡey and Red Mountain ["has-markings place"],[15] those were their hunting grounds long ago.

Re tṡi7, re yegélecken, yerí7 t̓lu7 re m-píxens.
They hunted deer and mountain sheep over there.

Tekenú7s re Pesxwiyéy̓elst ne7élye re stslexéy̓ctsen.
The place I'm telling you about is on the other side of Blackdome [Mountain, "has sharp-edged rocks"].

Tsqwum, ne7éne tsqwum, ne stsetéwst.s m-pésellkus.

There is a hill, another hill from there, and in between there is a lake.

Nerí7 mé7e re w7écwes re swewll.
There are fish in there.

Nerí7 me7 w7écwes re qít̓mes re qelmúcw.
People used to fish there with hook and line.

Te skwelk̓wélt w7écwes re tsyémes, w7ec re pexpíxmes,
The hunting parties lived [camped] in the snowy mountains while they hunted,

ell w7ec re tkwenkwínmes.
and while they got Indian potatoes.

Tsplúk̓wst.s re scwicw t̓lu7, re skwenkwínem, re scwicw ell re sqwí7qwe w7ec re tsnésmenst.ses te kekewúl̓ecw.
They used to gather glacier lilies, Indian potatoes. It was the glacier lilies and the whistlers that they used to get from those faraway places.

As Ron Ignace (2008, 149) notes about the Secwépemc seasonal round, referring to research with Secwépemc elders during the 1990s,

> The elders whom I interviewed continued this sense of seasonal round throughout their life time, travelling between and among resource harvesting locations in the mountains, the high plateaus, the highland lakes, valleys, creeks and rivers. Our people continued to go on long camping trips to pick berries, riding on horseback up the mountains to the higher elevations, several thousand feet high. While women went on horseback picking huckleberries and blueberries, as well as *sxusem*, often snacking on raspberries, strawberries along the way, the men accompanied them and then traveled further to go hunting.

The basic division of labour, as described above, thus entailed women doing the plant gathering and processing while men carried out hunting and fishing. However, elders' observations and memories of resource harvesting in the early to mid-twentieth century (see Louis Matthew's story above) show that each community had one or more women who engaged in large game hunting as well as fishing,[16] and boys and men frequently took part in berry-picking and root-digging expeditions throughout their lives and, moreover, played an important role as *yecwmíňmen* (caretakers or resource stewards) in monitoring the health and productivity of berry patches, root-digging areas, and medicinal plant patches. The processing of foods, including the cooking and drying of fish and meat, and the often complex tasks involved in plant processing were by and large women's work. Thus men and women played complementary rather than separate roles and sometimes filled roles that transcended those typically associated with their genders. Men often helped out with women's tasks, including tanning, berry picking, and root digging, and women often carried out tasks usually associated with men, such as hunting and fishing by spear or net. Nellie Taylor and other elders noted that couples were partners who helped each other and complemented each other, summed up in the concept of *petne7éws* (the root *pétne7* for "partner" plus the lexical suffix *-ews* for "to one another" or "mutual"), their roles being reciprocal in helping one another out, or what we call *knucwentwécw* (they help out one another). As we saw above, the art of tanning deer hides, or buckskin, exemplifies and expresses the complementary division of labour.

Spritual Aspects of Resource Use, Management, and Stewardship[17]

In both a practical and spiritual sense, the careful and respectful management of resources involves numerous aspects, including not overharvesting animals, not wasting any part of an animal, and treating animals with respect, such as by carefully disposing of salmon bones, lest the fish stop returning. Respect is further shown by not spitting in the water and not leaving fish guts lying around. The story of Sk̓elép (Coyote) and the salmon, recorded by James Teit (1909, 743) from George Sisyúlecw of the Símpcwemc in the early 1900s, shows how Sk̓elép violated these norms of respect and thus lost his harvest of salmon, forgoing not only a valuable supply of food but also the social prestige he hoped to gain by giving a feast with his catch:

> Coyote built an underground house on the Upper North Thompson River, at a place now called Coyote's House. It was afterwards turned into rock, and may be seen there at the present day. He spent several winters at this place. One fall, salmon came up the river in great numbers, and he made up his mind to catch a large supply, saying, "I will dry very many, and then will invite all the people to a great feast." By the time the salmon ceased running, he had filled many sticks, and was delighted when he viewed the large amount of fish he had on hand. One day as he was passing underneath the sticks where salmon was hanging, his hair caught in one of them, and this made him angry. Four times this happened, and each time he became angrier. The last time he became very angry, saying, "Why can't I pass underneath these fish without their catching in my hair?" He tore down the offending salmon and threw it into the river. At once it came to life and swam away. Then all the salmon came down from the sticks and plunged into the river. In vain Coyote tried to stop them by catching them and clubbing them. In

5.26 | Ida Matthew of Simpcw wringing out a deer hide after soaking it in deer brains, 1987.

> a short time they had all disappeared, and he was left without supplies for the winter, and had to give up the project of giving a feast. Now he gathered up all the slabs of wood which he had used for splitting salmon on, and all the poles on which they had been hanging. He took them up to his house, and said, "I will boil them in the winter-time and have fish soup."

Ida Matthew remembered how she was instilled with respect for animals who helped out humans by letting themselves be caught:

> My mom would tell us that we were never to [play with animal parts]. We had to have respect, "*me7 eyemstéc we7stémes,*" because that's what we ate, so that we weren't allowed to play with it … It was pitiful enough that we had to kill them. She instilled in us that we were not to waste the food, that we had to kill the poor animal. With any kind of animal that we would hunt and eat, you have to respect them, too … We lived on a lot of fish-heads when we were kids. [My mother] would never

allow you to play with the fish-heads or any part of that. She didn't spill any of the *ékwen* [fish eggs].

Mary Thomas also learned lessons of respect and conservation from both of her grandmothers, who would carefully move salmon who had spawned back into the Salmon River, explaining that they would provide nourishment to their offspring in the following season (cited in Turner and Berkes 2006, 502).

There were other ways that people showed their respect for land animals, birds, fish, and plants by not wasting any part of them. Ida Matthew remembered her mother, Christine Eustache, telling her and her siblings not to "play" (wastefully) with animal parts, and Mona Jules remembered her grandmother Sulyén telling the grandchildren not to play with grouse they had just killed, saying "you don't make fun of them!"

To demonstrate the respect that all living resources thus deserve, the harvesting of all things in nature is connected to prayer that both thanks the Tqelt Kúkwpi7 ("Chief Above" or Creator) for providing the animals or plants that feed people and thanks the resources for giving themselves to people. By communicating with the spiritual world through tobacco that is scattered on the ground, the prayer also involves a gift to both the animal and plant, as well as to the Creator. Besides tobacco, Secwépemc people nowadays leave behind coins, or they will leave other tokens, like some grains for the squirrel who gives humans some hazelnuts or pine nuts from its cache. In Secwepemctsín, the terms for "thank you" are *kukwstsétsemc* (one person to another), *kukwstsétselp* (one person to many), *kukwstéc-kucw* (one person to group), and *kukwstép-kucw* (group to group), all of which derive from the root word *kukws* (to save someone). Thanking the Creator or the animal or plant who has given itself to feed a person thus acknowledges the role that living beings in nature play to avert starvation, suffering, and hardship. The act of praying, or *qweqwentsín* ("to show with your voice") that you are *qwenqwént* (poor or pitiful), thus demonstrates your humility to the powers in nature that provide for you (see also chapter 11).

Me7 qweqwentsín-kt | A Meal Prayer

Tqelt Kúkwpi7,
Creator,

Yerí7 re skukwstéc-kucw te skectéc-kucw ne7élye te s7íllens-kucw.
We thank you for giving us this food here.

Yerí7 re skukwstéc-kucw te skectéc-kucw te sqlélten, te teníye ell te tśi7 te kecmentsút es c7ell7íllens-kucw.

We thank you for giving us the salmon, the moose, the deer who all gave themselves up for us to have food.

Tqelt Kúkwpi7,
Creator,

Le7 re skectéc ne7élye te sk̓weńllq es ta7es k stektsíllens re k̓wséltktens-kucw ne7élye te melúlk̓w.
It is good that you gave us these garden foods so that our relatives who are gathered here will not starve.

Tqelt Kúkwpi7,
Creator,

Yerí7 re skukwstéc-kucw te skectéc-kucw te k̓wséltktens-kucw es le7es es k̓úlens ne7élye re tśi7, re swewll, re sk̓weńllq, xwexwéyt re stem ne7élye re sc7ell7íllens-kucw pyin te sitq̓t.
We thank you for giving us our relatives who harvested the deer, salmon, vegetables, and all the foods we have here today.

Wenécwem yerí7 te skukwstéc-kucw.
We really thank you.

Knúcwente-kucw es kwemtús es yecwentwécws-kucw ell es knucwentwécws-kucw es kwemtús ne7élye es le7es re sw7ec-kt ne tmicw-kt.
Help us to always look after one another and to help one another out so we can live well on our land.

Ṫucw tśílem.
May it always be so.

Thanking prayers thus connect people to the land and to the resources they harvested with the help of the Creator, as well as to their *k̓wséltkten* (relatives), reminding one another to *yecwentwécw* (look after one another) and to *knucwentwécw* (help one another). The animals who are harvested are incorporated into the realm of kinship. For example, "salmon are our first children" is an idiom that further strengthens human ties with them and responsibility toward them. Another significant aspect of the reciprocal relationship between living things on the land and humans is the requirement to pay tribute to them, thank them, and thus make them an offering. Such offerings often take place quietly and tacitly, as well as in a variety of ways. Sometimes tobacco is left, although tobacco was not nearly as ubiquitous until trading tobacco was introduced to the Interior. In some instances, elders gave coins, sage, or other tokens. Maggie Adolph of Cácl̓ep (Fountain) stated that she and her elders would leave a few grains of wheat or oats to replace the hazelnuts they had taken from the caches of squirrels.

In the Secwépemc belief system, the concept central to the relationship between an animal and the fisher or hunter who "bags" the animal is that the animal *kecmentsút* (gives itself) to the fisher or hunter. The hunter thus has to approach the animal with a clean mind and body, which includes having a *sq̓ílye* (sweat lodge) before the hunt to ensure spiritual cleanliness, as well as physical cleanliness by getting rid of his or her human scent. In the *sq̓ílye* the hunter prays to Scwelús, the spirit of the sweat lodge. Animals will often give themselves up to the hunter because they take pity on humans, especially in times of bereavement or in times of need. In Secwépemc communities, there are many memories of events when deer and moose gave themselves up to take pity on the mourners by not fleeing when approached by the hunter and by being found in unusual places close to human settlement. The Secwépemc ontology of the interrelationship of living beings on the land is thus informed by a concept we can call *reciprocal accountability* between humans, animals, plants, and place. Not only is it imminent in beliefs about the agency and animacy of all these beings, but it is also the underpinning of practical resource management and stewardship regimes. Hunting, fishing, and plant gathering are not only economic pursuits but also ritual and spiritual acts by which Secwépemc people enact and maintain relationships within an environment where everything is sentient, or as Richard Nelson (1983, 14) describes it among Northern Athapaskan people, where everything has a "watchful eye."

Another essential aspect of all resource gathering was the sharing among people of resources and labour, expressed in Secwepemctsín as *knucwentwécw* (helping one another). Members of interrelated families, including young children, would go on hunting, fishing, and plant-gathering trips, adults helping one another, sharing resources, and jointly providing for their families. Teit (1909, 572–3) notes that after a hunt, fat and meat were equally divided among the hunting party by the eldest hunter, and fish caught in communal fish traps were likewise "distributed among all the family who came there."

Skeetchestn elder Theresa Jules explained it this way:

Re m-yews mé7e m-cketscemnúcwes cú7tsem re sq̓wléwem te wenéx,
When the time came again to pick huckleberries,

yerí7 cú7tsem tl7élye re nuxwnúxwenxw ṫ7en xílem, tektékl̓em ri7.
again the women from here did the same thing, they made their lunches.

Ṫlu7 m-w7ec, m-qwelq̓wléwem, qwelq̓wléwem.
They would be out there, picking berries, picking berries.

Telrí7 re s7i7llcw m-xewentés re sq̓wléwems e cw7ítes.
Some of them dried their berries if they picked lots.

Ell ye7éne m-c7í7elcmens ri7.
And this they shared with others.

Ye7éne ṫ7en tṡílem m-c7í7elcmens lu7, m-ciláp.
With the whole works, they did the same, each with an equal share all around.

Ec cú7tsem ṫri7 m- ṫ7en re s7i7llcw cú7tsem ṫkllu7 m-tcúsem,
Again they would go about, some would go looking for more,

tcúsem ṫri7 ṫhé7en te speqpéq.
looking here and there for berries.

Swéti7 k xexé7 m-penstsíllen, m-cwiẏentwécw.
Whoever was smart enough to find food, they invited one another along.

Yerí7 ucw m-sqwetséts.s ucw.
So then off they'd go once again.

Re sxelxélwes ṫlu7 m-w7ec, m-pexpíxem ell ri7.
Their husbands were there, they also went hunting.

Ta7 ri7 k tlṫíltes.
They never stayed in one place.

In Secwépemc society and Plateau society in general, there existed a fine balance between the self-sufficiency required of individuals so that they were not a burden or *yéwyut* (nuisance) to society and the need to help one another. Nellie Taylor's story about Ant and Grasshopper (see chapter 9) shows the Secwépemc perception of the consequences of laziness in resource procurement and of the nuisance it produces among relatives, leading to those who are a *yéwyut* being rejected by their relatives and starving to death. Thus Secwépemc people practised looking after themselves and not being a nuisance to others, which meant not begging and not "freeloading" through everyday tasks and work, particularly during their *étsxem* (spirit guardian quest). At the same time, there was a strong ethic not to be *xwexwiyélesem* or *xeqxéqt* (stingy), especially with food, which was to be *c7í7elcmen* (shared out), and a strong ethic to be generous, connected to the idea of *knucwentwécw* noted above. Fishers and hunters who were stingy with their catch would experience not only social sanctions but also spiritual sanctions from the animals, who would subsequently refuse to give themselves to them. When fishers or hunters *te7óy̓e* (get skunked), the ultimate reason for this is their own behavior and attitude:

> Nellie Taylor often told of how she and her partner, Cecilia Peters, went to Hi-hium Lake (Xixyúm) to fish for rainbow trout. [On one occasion] two young men had set up camp and were roasting the fish they had caught without offering any to the Elders. "After that, the fish just quit running for them. They never caught any more," she remarked wryly. By violating the norm of sharing [especially with Elders] they had acted inappropriately and had brought about supernatural sanction of their behavior in that the fish stopped running for them. (M. Ignace and R. Ignace 2013, 426)

Thus, ultimately, although the reason for "getting skunked" can be attributed to the fisher's or hunter's disrespectful behaviour toward the animal he or she wants to harvest, it can also be attributed to disrespectful social behavior toward other humans. We see how human behaviour that is not respectful and responsible connects to spiritual sanctions whose consequence is to render one poor, pitiful, and without food. Inappropriate behaviour also connects to social sanctions, which entail the loss of social standing, good reputation, and companionship.

Secwépemc people also practised taking eggs from fowl, particularly mallard ducks and Canada geese, a practice called *c̓te7í7elt*, which can be translated as "hunting for eggs" but more appropriately as "stealing" or "taking" them from the breeding fowl. As Clara Camille remembered from her childhood – although keeping chickens was becoming the more common practice (see below) – nest hunters knew to always leave two eggs in the nest for each egg taken, thus not depleting the brood.

Much of the enactment of our Secwépemc laws, sustained by values and rules explained above, was carried out without public formal ceremonies and rituals. Instead, it involved, as it still does today, resource harvesters thanking the plants and animals who gave themselves to us – our *k̓wséltkten* (relatives), after all – and leaving offerings to assure good support from the land and the creatures it sustains. This was carried out quietly, matter-of-factly, and without announcement of ceremony. However, the resource allocation practices and the institutionalized ways of sharing much welcomed newly arrived resources, namely seasonal plants and fish, represent social institutions, backed up by the laws of responsible resource use that we explained above.[18]

The Secwépemc system of resource access, use, and management – practised for many generations in the past and derived from, and justified by, *stsptekwll* (ancient stories) and the past deeds of Secwépemc ancestors – is multidimensional. It entails practical strategies for living and practical resource management regimes, but at its core, it has always been sustained

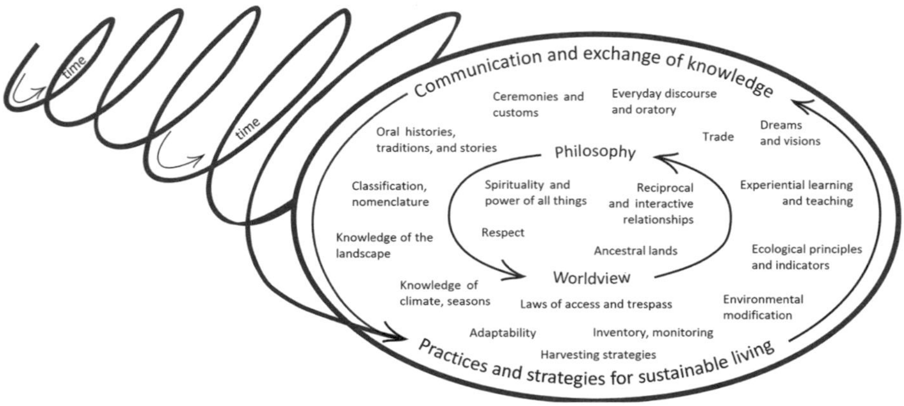

5.27 | Secwépemc traditional ecological knowledge and wisdom (TEKW), showing its components and their interconnections. The spiral represents the cyclical but also time-rooted and cumulative nature of TEKW.

by a system of spiritual beliefs and sanctions that underlie the laws of good conduct, access to resources, and trespass of land manifested in *yeri7 re stsq̓ey̓s-kucw* ("our laws"). It encapsulates the concept of an "ecology of the heart" (E. Anderson 1996) in that it combines spiritual aspects, Indigenous laws and protocols, and living resource management practices, along with their transmission and communication. It entails what Jeannette Armstrong (2009, 220ff) has called an "environmental ethic." Its components and the sum of its parts express and maintain *reciprocal accountability* with all living beings, underscored by a belief system and ways of transmitting knowledge about the land and its resources. It represents Secwépemc *institutions for knowledge* (Turner and Berkes 2006). These institutions fostered the conservation of plant and animal resources through time-built, fine-tuned, and adapted ecological understanding. By combining spiritual and moral lessons with sustainable practices of resource monitoring and management, as well as with social laws and institutions that provide sanctions against improper conduct, Secwépemc people maintained an integrated system of traditional ecological knowledge and wisdom. In its time dimension, it functioned like a *spiral*, evolving and adapting over the years, while following patterns of recurring cycles of seasons and the seasonal rounds of harvesting.

Changes in Resources and Resource Gathering during the Nineteenth and Twentieth Centuries

With the establishment during the early 1800s of fur trade posts at Kamloops, Fort Alexandria on the Fraser River, and Jasper House on the margins of Secwépemc territory, the Secwépemc supplemented their hunting, gathering, and fishing activity with trapping, notably for beaver, marten, and other smaller furbearing animals. However, especially during the early years of the fur trade, as shown in the report of Hudson's Bay Company chief trader Archibald McDonald (1827) for the Thompson River post at Kamloops, the fur traders not only relied on salmon supplied by the Secwépemc and neighbouring Interior Salish peoples for their sustenance but also purchased from the Secwépemc large quantities of berries, Indigenous roots, and hazelnuts, along with venison, bear meat, and wild fowl (see table 12.1).

Indeed, there is solid evidence that until the late 1850s, the Secwépemc maintained firm control over the harvesting of resources throughout Secwepemcúlecw (see Thomson and M. Ignace 2005). As we noted earlier, by the 1820s, the Secwépemc were selling substantial amounts of garden potatoes grown at Ck̓emqenétkwe above Tk̓emlúps (Kamloops) and at Sk̓atsín (Neskonlith) to the Thompson River post, and although the Hudson's Bay Company began its own vegetable and dairy farm operation in the Kamloops area in the 1840s, it continued to buy in the order of 12,000 to 20,000 salmon from the Secwépemc, Nlaka'pamux, and St'at'imc as the main source of protein for its traders until the early 1860s.

Following the influx of settlers into the Interior with the 1858 gold rush and the establishment of federal Indian reserves during the 1870s – which allocated a mere 1 per cent of Secwepemcúlecw as reserve land under the Canadian Indian Act – the Secwépemc increasingly supplemented their use of Indigenous plants and animals with garden produce. Garden potatoes continued to be grown for self-consumption and trade.

By the early twentieth century, gardening and small agriculture were practised in all Indigenous communities of the Interior. Supported by the parsimonious "peasant farming policy" (Carter 1990) of the federal Department of Indian Affairs – which aimed at "fast-tracking" Indians from what was construed as an evolutionary hunter-gatherer phase through a peasant-agriculture phase to "modern civilization" – Secwépemc were successfully gardening, ranching, and farming at this time, although settlers were increasingly competing for water rights and access. Throughout the first half of the twentieth century, Secwépemc people effectively carried out a mixed economy that involved waged work – often as ranch and farm labour – together with hunting and fishing, as well as the continued gathering of wild foods, although the use of root vegetables declined as they were increasingly replaced by garden potatoes and other vegetables, along with store-bought flour and rice. The mixed economy of this period is well illustrated in Ida Matthew's narrative below. She tells of her childhood memories of accompanying her parents as they camped on the land while her father was working as a ranch hand. Her parents provided for the family by gathering berries, catching gophers by flooding out gopher holes, catching fish in the Thompson River, and moreover drying surplus berries and gophers for later use.

Le q̓7éses well n-pépe7, Se7 méte Maryén w7ec-kucw re tsyémes ne Tsqeltqíqeṅ.
Long time ago, my father, Se7, and Marianne were all camping together at Tsqeltqíqeṅ.

Well ren pépe7 ell le Se7 w7ec re ṫíml̓ecwes ne Genier's.
My Dad, Se7, and them were clearing land at Genier's.

W7écwes well n-méme7 ell le Maryén qwelq̓wléwmes te stcwelcúcwel̓ ṫri7 ne scencénc, ell m-q̓wléwens stéṁi te tqwelq̓wélt te speqpéq.
My mother and Marianne were picking gooseberries around the rocks, and they picked any other kind of berries.

Ell m-wi7s re s7el7élkst.s, well n-pépe7 ell well Se7 m-ctekték̓ens re sisk̓ re ctsetsítcws wel re m-qwetṡt te séwllkwe.
And when they finished work, my father and them and Se7 and them filled the gopher holes until they were full of water.

M-tscwúytes re sisk̓, m-sepsṗ7élesqenses, m-yews yerí7 re skwens, m-c7íllentmes-kucw.
When the gophers came out, they clubbed them, then they took them out, and we ate them.

Ell héqen re s7i7llcw telrí7 xewentés well n-méme7.
And maybe some of them, my mother and them would dry.

Ell xwexwéyt te stem re sq̓wléwems m-xewentés.
And all the things they gathered, they dried.

Ell ren méme7 w7ec re q̓w7úmes te semtsétṡ.
And my mom was trapping groundhogs.

W7ec-kucw re tsknúcwstmes ren méme7 te sq̓wléwems, steṁi te speqpéq tsq̓wlewst.s
We were helping my mother pick whatever berries there were.

Tslexemstéten w7ec-kucw ṫucw re siséysus tekwmíte7.
I remember we were just playing all the time.

W7ec-kucw ṫri7 re tspelpélk̓stmes q̓7es te tsreprép.
We were knocking over old trees.

M-tsuns-kucw ren méme7, "Ta7ews ṫri7 k sxílltp!"
My mom told us, "Don't ever do that!"

Estqeyép e stsíq̓enwen̓tpes re wutscén!
The lizards will get startled if you dig them up!

Me7 kelkélents.s e r7áles. E wíkmucw tek wutscén e r7áles,
They'll chase you at night. If you see a lizard at night,

me7 llgwílcucw ne t7ikw, me7 ta7wes es c7úllcwments.s re wutscén.
you jump over a fire so they won't go inside you, the lizards.

Tslexemstéten cw7it-kucw re sc7íllens lu7,
I remember we had a lot to eat,

well n-méme7 qwelq̓wléwmes ell m-pexpíxmes, ell m-q̓w7úmes te sisk̓.
when my mom and them picked and when they hunted, and they trapped gophers.

Tekwmíte7-kucw re sc7íllens-kucw te ts̓i7.
We always ate meat.

Well ren pépe7 w7ec re ctálkwemes, w7ec le el7élkstes ne Genier's.
And my dad, he put a net in the river, while he worked at Genier's.

Ctálkwemes ne setétkwe, llumín̓s we7stémes.
He had his net out in the river, and he would spear whatever [fish] he could.

Ta7 k stselxemcícten stém̓i xwexwéyt re skwest.s re swewll.
I don't know what names all those fish have.

Tselxemstéten t̓ucw le7 te s7íllen.
I only know that they were good to eat.

Yerí7 re stsukws.
That's all.

At Hat Creek Ranch near Bonaparte – a ranch on St̓uxtéws land that was allowed to be pre-empted by settlers at the exclusion of the St̓uxtéws Secwépemc – generations of Secwépemc people from St̓ells (Ashcroft), St̓uxtéws, and other surrounding communities met to work and in fact ensured the profit of the ranch through their participation in "cowboying" and ranch hand activities. Bonaparte elder Billy Porter explained how, throughout his youth, many families from the surrounding Indigenous communities were encamped near the ranch, working together and socializing after work, while the women gathered berries and other plant foods to support their families.

As they harvested game, fish, and plants throughout the seasons, Secwépemc people continued to use horses or the horse and buggy for transportation. Domestic animals were added as travellers and passengers on trips to hunting, fishing, and berry-picking areas. In 1902 British Columbia's Indian commissioner, A.W. Vowell, described the way of life of Interior Plateau people: "On these nomadic excursions they are obliged to take their families with them, and frequently their domestic animals, consisting of dogs and cats as well, even ducks, geese and chickens are sometimes to be seen in the canoe, huddled up among the native impedimenta" (Canada 1902, 283).

Thus Ron Ignace's great-grandmother Sulyén would take the family's six to ten chickens, tied up in a gunnysack, along on these expeditions. Likewise, Cecilia DeRose, Bridget Dan, and Clara Camille remembered their parents and grandparents transporting chickens packed in crates or gunnysacks to their mid-elevation "meadows" – areas that combined traditional resource harvesting with hay making – where their families camped during summer. Hilda Jules and Elsie Hewitt reported how their parents would tie the family's milk cow to the back of the buggy as they went camping and berry picking at Six Mile on their way to visit relatives at Tk̓emlúps. As Hilda remembered,

> We used to camp on the road. We used to camp by that big ranch at Cherry Creek. Well, just on the other side of that little trailer, there is a spot in there, the road never used to go through that way, it used to go through up a steep little grade and down at the bottom there. That's where everybody used to camp. We used to camp there, maybe stay there a day or couple of days, and dad would go hunting. And from there we would move on and maybe we go as far as ah …, ah … Anyhow, it took us about two days to get there by wagon. On the way Dad and Mum would go off and … and it was a lot of fun. But we did fishing though, 'cause there was no fences, and there was no homes. The only home that was there was the Cherry Creek Ranch, and there was nothing from there … Then we used to camp at, what do you call it? We used to call it "Cornwall." I don't know what they […] that little place before you get to Kamloops there. Around in there [Sleepy Hollow], we used to camp there, too […] We used to fish from there … trout, used to catch fish, a lot of them would camp around there, and they'd go hunting. We used to smoke [the deer] and dry it there.

For their travels to berry-picking grounds, Secwépemc people from Simpcw (North Thompson River) and other areas began to use the way-freight – a passenger train attached to the Canadian National Railway freight train – to travel to berry-picking grounds, hauling back large quantities of blueberries and huckleberries from the upper North Thompson to their home communities.

5.28 | Hilda Jules of Skeetchestn, 2008.

Although the initial wave of land pre-emptions by settlers had occurred between the 1860s and early 1900s, it was during subsequent decades that more and more fences and "No Trespassing" signs went up and impeded our people's travels, hunting, and food gathering; as more and more of our traditional land areas became fenced in, the greater restrictions were felt by our people, who noted how their ability to hunt, fish, and gather was increasingly restricted. The words of Billy Porter (personal communication, 2006) of Sťuxtéws echo this feeling: "It's not like it used to be. It used to be wide open."

Hilda Jules also noted of Six Mile,

> Them *séme7* [white people], they used to kick us out of there. [Long before that] they kicked us out from Savona where we used to camp, lots of people used to camp. You know, the thing was, we used the place until they fenced all along in there [during the Trans-Canada Highway construction along Six Mile in the 1950s]. We used to go down by M.'s there. Dad would park the old wagon. We'd walk down the rest of the way … We'd go down there, maybe camp the night, and then from there, Dad would hobble the horses, and we'd camp … They'd always ask us, "Why did we give up our rights?" We had no choice, we were chased out. We were told we were "trespassing."

Her sister Elsie remembered one specific instance of getting "fenced out":

> I'd take my brother and my dad, take them out there to go hunt, and we were already had to open gates to get to hunt. So we had to open farmers' gates. So I told my dad, "Why should we not use our land to hunt in?" I said, "I'll go knock on [the farmer's] door and let him know that we are hunting on our land there." So I go down there and knock on his door, and [he said], "Go ahead, let your brother and dad hunt." He calls it his field now, but that was all our hunting areas. So there, we are slowly getting fenced out. Fences are really getting us."

Remembering a berry-picking trip with his grandfather around 1930, George Manuel of Neskonlith writes,

> suddenly there was a gate blocking our way with a barbed-wire fence running away from it in both directions into the bushes. On the gate there was a lock and a white board with black letters. I could not read them then, but they are still clear in my mind's eye today. My grandparents talked awhile in quiet voices. Then my grandmother held her skirts with one hand and lifted herself over the gate with the other hand. My grandfather looked at her strangely when he handed her the walking stick and baskets. But he followed her, and so did I. We were not a hundred steps beyond the gate when a white man came around a bend in the trail. As soon as he saw us he began to shout and wave his arms at my grandfather. Grandfather talked back to him in Chinook. I did not need to understand the words to know that they were both angered. Grandfather had put down his baskets when the man had begun to speak to him. He was just bending over to gather them up when my grandmother picked up her stick and began to chase the white man. She spoke only our own Shuswap language but she had made herself well understood. He left. We stayed. That woman was quite convinced that our people owned the land and that we had a special right to the bushes for which we were heading. No one had a right to fence it off. (Manuel and Posluns 1974, 48–50)

In the mid-1920s settler D.S. Mitchell (1925, 11) of the Shuswap Lake area commented on the destruction and slaughter of salmon with inadequate methods at the hands of white settlers during the early 1900s, which he contrasted with Secwépemc and settler methods of fishing:

> When the Indian struck at a salmon with his spear he got that salmon, and when he had enough he quit; not so the white men. They got after them with pitchforks, iron spikes, or pieces of thick telegraph wire fastened on poles, and with gaffs. After wounding several they would get one pinned to the bottom then lose it in trying to get it ashore. For each

> one that they got to the bank many got away with holes through them. For every ten they got, they injured a hundred that escaped. I have seen fish dying that had been slashed open as if with long handled shovels, and others leaking ripe eggs through holes torn in their sides. A fish could not spawn after having a pitchfork through her.

When Euro-Canadians intensified the large-scale commercial salmon fishery and canning operations near the mouth of the Fraser River in the 1880s, and as salmon runs dramatically declined following the Hells Gate slide during the construction of the Canadian National Railway line in 1913, the Secwépemc, far upriver from these events, experienced the curtailment of salmon fishing by the local government's appointed fish wardens. Ida William recalled,

> There used to be lots of people go in there and fish up there [at Barriere River], but since the game warden start bother the people, you know, they chase him away from there. They spoil everything, break all, they had some kind of little bridge where they sit down and fish, the game warden, fish warden supposed to come over and knock everything down, let it go in the water. This fish warden come around, get smart to the Indians, my mom used to say, "Geez, he's awful." This fish warden, two old ladies took him and threw him in the water. That fish warden come around, get smart to Indians, and after that kinda close everything for Indians. They can't go out and get some fish from where they used to fish. If you want to fish in the river, you have to get a licence or something like that.

Ida Matthew of Chu Chua remembered,

> Game wardens were pretty strict. We thought some of them were pretty mean, too. Trying to accuse a bunch of women from trying to shoot fish up at Raft River. And one of the ladies said, "What are we doing," talking in Shuswap, "listening to this old man? I'm going to tell him we're just going to take his pants off and we are going to make fun of him and throw him in the creek if he doesn't leave us alone." So, whoever was spokesman told him that "if you don't leave us alone, we're going to tear your pants down." And so he left them alone. He was trying to tell them that they were, they were in the creek, they were trying to catch a salmon so they could have their lunch, on their way to Avola [to pick berries]. They were in the wagon, travelling by wagon. But this is one of the incidents about. There were so many.

Ironically, while the fish wardens policed and interfered with the Simpcw people's fishing, serious damage was done to the salmon runs in the area

5.29 | Splatsín Indians waiting for the fish warden who was going to destroy their fish weir, photographed by C.W. Holliday, ca. 1892. The warden did not show up in the end, but the photo shows how serious the men and women of Splatsín (Enderby) took their rights to fish and make a livelihood at their fishing weir, which settlers previously had tried to take down and which was destroyed not long afterward.

through the construction of dams and other destructive measures. In the 1910s, the upper Adams River sockeye run had been wiped out by the construction of a sluice dam in the area, built to enable the Adams Lake Logging Company to chute logs down the river. In the process of transporting their logs, they all but wiped out the upper Adams sockeye run.

A decade or so after the Barriere River fishing weir was destroyed by the fish warden because of preposterous claims that the weir diminished the runs, the Barriere spawning grounds were all but wiped out by the construction of a power dam across the river:

> In 1931 a large number of salmon died in attempting to get past the Barriere dam. This evoked the rather sad comment that "several people have criticized the fish wardens for not rigging some method of transportation to take the fish from the pools to the lakes above. Perhaps next year they will do this if there is any kind of a run." It seems that criticism should not have been levelled at the fish wardens, but rather

> at the builders of the dam who gave no consideration to the needs of the fish. (R. Balf 1975, 125)

Despite all these impediments, Secwépemc people continued to fish what amounts they could get. It was not until the 1960s and 1970s that the use of Aboriginal resources began to decline severely, in part due to the decline of knowledge transfer caused by generations of residential school attendance and by the increasing reliance both on wage labour and on market foods. In addition, salmon runs continued to dwindle, and the federal Department of Fisheries and Oceans increased its regulatory power.

The landscape has changed as well. Increasing urban sprawl and the effects of cattle ranging, logging, mining, and other forms of industrial development have all impacted our ability to live off the land. Throughout the twentieth century, Secwépemc people experienced how settlers and newcomers, sanctioned by the property laws of government, increasingly impeded their access to resources by suddenly fencing off berry-picking, hunting, fishing, and camping areas. Then, with the construction of the new provincial highway system in the late 1960s, they saw further fences going up. Since that time, urban development, highway construction, the criss-crossing of Secwepemcúlecw by a growing number of transmission lines and gas pipelines, logging, mining, and other kinds of industrial activity have further escalated and impacted our ability both to live off the land and to have quiet enjoyment of the land for present and future generations. Mining companies are standing in line for environmental assessment permits that will allow them to make permanent changes to our landscape, which is imbued with the deeds of our ancestors, our stories, and our places. However, as the next chapter shows, beneath the contemporary freeways, highways, country roads, and logging roads are the Indigenous trails that give evidence of millennia of resource use by the Secwépemc and evidence of the network of transportation routes that enabled a flourishing trade between and among nations of the Interior.

6 Le Q̓7éses re Scwescwesét.s-kucw ell re S7eykemíṅems-kucw

Trade, Travel, and Transportation

MARIANNE IGNACE AND KENNETH FAVRHOLDT

We know from archaeological and historical records that extensive trading networks existed among North American Indigenous peoples for thousands of years before contact. By trading surpluses of their desired goods, such as foods, medicines, fibres, and materials, local groups could broaden the amounts and kinds of things that were available to them. In addition, through trading networks with distant groups, they could acquire desired and valued ornaments not locally produced. Chapter 3 referred to the existence of well-organized, extensive trade networks throughout the Interior Plateau that "moved large quantities of preserved food, textiles, medicine, stone, people, and other commodities for many hundreds of years" prior to the arrival of Europeans. Archaeological evidence shows that materials like basalt, obsidian, dentalium, and marine shells were traded from faraway places on the coast and in the Northern Interior as early as some 5,000 years ago.

Eỷkemiṅem | Secwépemc Trade Practices

James Teit (1909, 531–7) recorded some detailed information from Secwépemc people about trade among Secwépemc divisions and Indigenous bands, as well as about trade with neighbouring nations. In trade with outside nations, "gatekeeper communities" at or near the boundary of the nation were able to conduct trade and act as middlemen for goods not available to the Secwépemc. Teit noted that those of the Fraser Canyon division were great traders who acted as middlemen between other Secwépemc communities and the Tsilhqot'in, known as Pesxíxlemc or Pesxíxnemc ("have dentalium shell people"). In exchange for salmon and salmon oil, which they traded to the Pesxíxnemc, they obtained dentalium shells, which the Pesxíxnemc had obtained from the coast via the Carrier (Yúnecne); they also bought woven goat-hair blankets and belts, bales of dressed marmot skins, rabbit-skin robes, and snowshoes from the Pesxíxnemc. Some trading of salmon and salmon oil was done by the Soda Creek people with the Carrier; the Símpcwemc traded salmon and salmon oil with their northern neighbours, the Sekéwemc (Cree); and the Kinbaskets sold dentalium shells and other goods in exchange for buffalo skins to the Snépwen (Stony) and Tqisúllkemc (Ktunaxa). The Stkemlúpsemc and Sexqéltkemc traded with the Stśwéṅemc (Okanagan), obtaining roots (probably camas and bitterroot), horses, Indian hemp, and other items in exchange for snowshoes, dentalium shells, copper, and marmot-skin robes. The Stuxtéwsemc and Lower Fraser divisions at High Bar and Big Bar traded dentalium shells, skin robes, buckskins, and later horses to the St'at'imc (Fraser River Lillooet) in exchange for salmon, salmon oil, woven baskets, goat-hair robes, and plant fibres like mock orange and yew wood. Among people from all divisions and with foreigners, feathers were a sought-after trade item. The feathers of geese and swans, as well as the tail feathers of red-shafted flickers and hawks, were in demand, to be used as decorations. They were also a valued trade good. Most valuable, however, were feathers of adult golden eagles and the scalps of red-headed woodpeckers (ibid., 537).

Traded plants included locally available food plants like bitterroot or hazelnuts, as well as locally available fibres like yew wood, cedar root, white pine and birch bark, Indian hemp, and mock orange bark – all of which were available only in select environments and locations throughout Secwepemcúlecw. In addition, they included sought-after medicinal plants used in trade:

> [E]xamples of trade of ceremonial and healing plants include the exchange of Canby's lovage (*Ligusticum canbyi*), an important medicine for Interior Salish groups and Ktunaxa of British Columbia and Washington, and the occasional exchange of sweet grass (*Hierochloe odorata*) for ceremonial smudging, although the latter example may be relatively recent ... Often, too, medicinal healers would bring their own medicines with them when travelling to a patient some distance away. For example, when Annie York (Nlaka'pamux) was injured near Spuzzum in the Fraser Canyon, her great-aunt, a well-known "Indian doctor," gathered bags of the roots of poisonous water-hemlock (*Cicuta douglasii*), and brought them from Spences Bridge by bus to treat her. There are undoubtedly many other examples of this type of exchange in medicinal practices, but these are seldom recorded. A medical practitioner was often rewarded with gifts of foods or manufactured items that included plant products. (Turner and Loewen 1998, 57)

Throughout the many generations of contact and trade among the Secwépemc and their neighbours, not only were goods exchanged, but in a wider sense, trading networks also involved the exchange and transfer of technologies. We get glimpses of such ancient technology transfer from the *stsptekwll* (ancient story) of Skelép (Coyote) and the transformers explained in chapter 2, where we learn that the Interior people were taught fishing technology by coastal people, with the latter being taught about Indian hemp.

Cáclep (Fountain) on the Fraser River was known as a hub of trade, where people from different nations would convene to trade directly for salmon, especially when salmon were scarce in their own areas, and where those with kinship connections to the local mixed Secwépemc and St'at'imc population would participate in the fishery themselves. As Teit (1906) reports, they would also sell captives taken on war expeditions back to the St'at'imc in exchange for salmon. Another such trading hub was in the neighbourhood of Spences Bridge, where Secwépemc of the Fraser division, Ts'wéṅemc (Okanagan), Nicola Athapaskans, and even Carrier (Yúnecne) would come to trade. Peténi Valley (Botanie Valley) near Lytton, where thousands of people annually congregated to dig a variety of root plants, also served as a trading location for Secwépemc people, especially those who had access to Nlaka'pamux root-digging areas by virtue of family relationships (see chapter 9).

A well-known trading centre within the Secwépemc nation was Teltsíṅten ("place from where news is spread," Green Lake), which is in the heart of Secwépemc territory and at the intersection of most of the Secwépemc divisions. Here, while the trout were running in late spring, families from all Secwépemc divisions would camp for some weeks each year. As they fished, they held sports races and played games, found spouses for their children, and traded items desired by people from other Secwépemc divisions: "Here the [Shuswap] Lake Division sold some dried trout, nets, carrying-bags, some cedar-root, very dark marmot skins, and a few baskets, principally to the Fraser River bands, for dried salmon, salmon oil, and shells. The North Thompson band brought hazel-nuts to sell" (Teit 1909, 537).

Tk̓emlúps (Kamloops), at the confluence of the North and South Thompson Rivers, was another hub of trade, where people from different divisions of Secwépemc territory would gather, as was witnessed by the first Europeans who visited the confluence in 1811. Teit (1930a, 216) also noted trade and travel by canoe before the advent of horses and European trading companies: "The Shuswap, being at the northerly end of the trade routes from the south, would act as distributers in the same way as the Okanagon and Colville farther south; and, Kamloops being the nearest central point in their country, trade would gravitate to that place." When the Pacific Fur Company and subsequently the North West Company and Hudson's Bay Company established their forts at Tk̓emlúps, they encountered a well-established network and pattern of trade and exchange among communities in Secwepemcúl̓ecw, as well as between the Secwépemc and neighbouring nations. Whereas the exchange protocols among *k̓wséltkten* (relatives) were based on the values of generosity, reciprocity, and mutual care and support exemplified as *knucwentwécw* (helping one another) (see chapter 9), the protocols of *ey̓kemînem* (trade something in payment for purchases) and *eyentwécw* (pay one another) involved barter

6.1 | Teltsíṅten ("place from where news is spread," Green Lake), a major social-political gathering and trading place for people from all parts of Secwepemcúĺecw, 2013. Nowadays, as with many of the Interior mid- and high-elevation trout lakes, access to the lake for fishing is prevented by private property developments at the former fishing sites.

or profit seeking by individuals not closely related to the trader. They also involved the idea of profit making on items of surplus within one's own group in exchange for locally scarce items from groups that had a surplus of them, as well as the further selling of such items to third parties for added value. Trade and barter concepts on the Plateau also involved the idea of added value for processed and manufactured items. The journals of the Hudson's Bay Company traders from the early to mid-nineteenth century describe and often lament the astute bargaining of the Indigenous people who brought foodstuffs, including plants and salmon, to the company store.

Finally, in a detailed list of Indigenous items traded between Nlaka'pamux, Secwépemc, and other groups, along with Hudson's Bay Company items that entered the trade in the early nineteenth century (Teit 1900, 260–2), we see that the principal commodities that were traded had standardized currency values attached to them. For Indigenous trade items like salmon and salmon oil, Indian hemp, the dressed skins of deer, elk, moose, and buffalo, canoes, dentalium shells, stone tools, baskets, berries, and bitterroot, these currency values would have predated the arrival of the trading company. As horses were traded among Indigenous people and with the company, and as subsequently European staple goods like steel traps, cloth, tobacco, guns, axes, kettles, and blankets were traded in exchange for beaver furs and other dressed furs, the currency values attached to the Indigenous trade items became integrated into the currency values of European trade goods. Specific currency values included:

- a "stick" of dried salmon, which amounted to 100 sides of *scwik̓* (dried fish)
- a "package" of Indian hemp (*Apocynum cannabinum*)
- a fathom (or human wingspan) of dentalium shells
- a salmon skin full of salmon oil
- a dressed buckskin
- a dressed moose skin
- a dressed buffalo skin

Teit (ibid.) provided these examples:

½ stick of dried salmon would fetch 1 woven bag or 1 red or yellow stone pipe (catlinite stone);
3 sticks of salmon would fetch 1 tanned buffalo-robe without hair, or 1 large dressed buckskin, or 1 copper kettle;
5 packages of hemp would fetch 3 sticks of salmon;
10 cakes of saskatoon berries (service berries) or soap-berries were equivalent to 5 packages of Indian hemp or 3 sticks of salmon or 1 canoe;
for 2 pairs of long buckskin leggings one could get 4 tail feathers of golden eagle;
1 two-year old horse would fetch 6 sticks of dried salmon or 1 second-hand flintlock gun.

The above exchange values for articles of Indigenous manufacture and European manufacture as they existed in the mid-1800s suggest that a standardized system of currency exchange existed on the Northern Plateau during this time. Moreover, it shows that from the Indigenous perspective, European trade goods became actively integrated, or "plugged," into a pre-existing trade and exchange system rather than monolithically revolutionizing the nature of exchange as a result of the existence of fur trade posts (for a similar conclusion, see C. Carlson 2006).

Indigenous Use and Trade of Minerals: Copper, Jade, and Gold

Archaeological sites in different areas of Secwepemcúl̓ecw, at Nicola Lake in Nlaka'pamux territory, and in other locations throughout the Interior Plateau show evidence of the use of copper, particularly hammered copper pendants, earrings, and other ornaments, as well as tubular copper beads woven into men's breastplates (see Hayden 2000a; Rousseau and Rousseau 1978; H.I. Smith 1899, 1900; and R.L. Wilson and C. Carlson 1980). For the most part – with the exception of Plateau Horizon copper at Keatley Creek dated to between 2,000 and 900 years ago (Brian Hayden, personal communication, 2016) – these items have been assigned to the proto-contact or postcontact period, although perhaps too hastily. The Secwépemc mined native copper on the north shore of Kamloops Lake west of Tk̓emlúps before the arrival of trade copper. Franz Boas (1890, 85) noted that "Copper was obtained, partly by trade, but some was dug by the natives themselves. There was a digging at Kamloops Lake, which was worked up to the last generation, when a man was killed by a fall of rocks which buried the mine. Since that time it was never worked." When he passed through the Interior during his investigation of the resource extraction potential of the province, Lieutenant Richard Charles Mayne (1859, 123) took note of what came to be named Copper Creek on the north shore of Kamloops Lake, but he downplayed the Secwépemc's mining of their native copper: "Emerging from this pass, we descended to Lake Kamloops, along the side of which we held until night, camping at a spot called the Coppermine, where the Indians said they had found perfectly pure speciments of that metal. We made a very careful examination of the place, and although there were unmistakeable signs of the presence of copper, we saw nothing to cause us to doubt that the Indian's story was not, as usual, very much overcharged." Geologist George M. Dawson (1896, 16A) observed that "Copper Creek derives its name from the fact that the Indians have from time immemorial known it as a locality of native copper." The area in question is known as Painted Bluffs, now a provincial park to the east of Copper Creek on the north shore of Kamloops Lake. Skeetchestn elders know this area as Tsqweqwiyéyescen ("copper mineral rock place"), an Indigenous place for the "digging" of native copper.[1]

Harlan Smith's 1897–98 excavations at the "Government Site," the "Government Hill Site," and the large burial mound beneath what is now the Industrial Park on Kamloops Indian Reserve No. 1, subsequently known as EeRb 4 (R.L. Wilson and C. Carlson 1980)[2] show the use of copper ornaments as grave goods, including a set of copper earrings. In addition, the remains of dentalium necklaces with copper pendants were found at a Nicola Lake gravesite and were identified by Charlie Tsilaxitsa as "probably worn on the chest by the daughters of chiefs" (H.I. Smith 1900, 425). Tubular copper beads strung up in combination with dentalium shells were, according to Smith (ibid., 427), the remains of copper and dentalium breast shields. A similar breast shield was found with human remains at Deadman's Creek in the 1960s, as remembered by elders (M. Ignace et al. 2014). Smith's (1900, 334ff) descriptions of burials at all three sites – which in 1897–99 he claimed Tk̓emlúpsemc individuals did not associate with their immediate ancestors and which thus were very likely precontact – show copper ornaments and also lumps of "copper clay" in some of the burials (see chapter 3).

An accidentally exposed burial at Canoe Creek (EiRn 15) excavated by Eunice Rousseau and Mike K. Rousseau (1978) revealed a significant presence of copper. This burial – subsequently reburied – consisted of seven individuals, including three adults and four children ranging in age from newborn to approximately ten years of age. As the Rousseaus (ibid., 2) noted, "Several of the individuals had portions of their external soft tissue preserved due to the presence of copper salts produced from the large number of copper ornaments in association"; that is, the copper ornaments mummified parts of the remains that were in contact with copper. Copper ornaments in the burials included three types of cylindrical copper tubes. In addition to beads, the remains of a newborn infant sewn into a leather pouch included small copper plates, both corrugated and plain, sewn into the pouch. The Rousseaus (ibid., 23) attributed these copper beads and plates to European manufacture, noting that the corrugation on type 2 copper beads was too regular to be of Indigenous manufacture. A similar copper ornament was recovered at the Murray site in Lillooet (EeRb 1) (Stryd and Baker 1968) and was associated with a European brass button. However, a recently excavated burial at Teltsíṅten (Green Lake), which shows nearly identical tubular copper beads and plates, appears to include both European-manufactured copper and native copper (ARCHER CRM, personal communication, 2014). In sum, we have evidence of native copper procurement for the Copper Creek area, and we have the occurrence of copper ornaments, copper clay, and copper salts at burials throughout Secwépemc territory and in Nlaka'pamux and St'at'imc territory, thus pointing to the importance not only of copper as a trade good after contact but also of native copper as a prestige trade object throughout the Northern Plateau. Much more remains to be learned about the provenance, distribution, and manufacture of native copper associated with and mined in Secwepemcúl̓ecw.[3]

In addition to copper, archaeological sites show the use and trade of nephrite or *tskweléscen* (jade), predominantly in the form of certs or adzes, throughout the Plateau and adjacent areas. These were likely obtained from a prolific nephrite deposit on Bridge River, and it appears that they functioned not only as utilitarian tools but also as prestige objects (see Darwent 1998).

Some versions of the *stsptekwll* of Tllí7sa and his brothers references Tllí7sa wearing a shield of *swellwéll* (mica) when he approaches the supernatural "people eater" near Cherry Creek (see chapter 2, note 21). Mica, of course, is known for its anticonductor properties, and it is interesting that the Secwépemc, a long time ago, used it to protect themselves from the energy fields of supernaturals.

In addition, we know that Interior Salish people knew of gold deposits and mined gold. Kamloops trader Lolo St Paul's son led a group of explorers to a gold deposit on the Horsefly River, which eventually precipitated the Cariboo gold rush. The gold find at the mouth of Nicoamen Creek was made by a Nlaka'pamux person, and Tranquille River gold was successfully placer-mined by Secwépemc people and their relatives from other parts of the Plateau, with nuggets and dust sold to the Hudson's Bay Company's Thompson River post, as attested by the company's 1863–64 account book (M. Ignace et al. 2014, 204–6).[4]

Overall, we thus have ample evidence of gold, copper, nephrite, and other minerals used as prestige objects and in association with spiritual grave goods by the Secwépemc well before Europeans came into the country. In their "Memorial to Sir Wilfrid Laurier" (Chiefs of the Shuswap, Okanagan, and Couteau Tribes 1910), the Interior chiefs spoke of their use and ownership of gold: "At first they [the whites who came into the country about 1858] looked only for gold. We know the latter was our property, but as we did not use it much nor needed it to live by we did not object to their searching for it." Ultimately, although precious metals were connected to the prestige economy, this significance did not override the importance of the living resources in Secwépemc territory: air, water, animals, fish, and plants. These resources were what the Secwépemc valued and "needed," as stated above. It was these living resources that Secwépemc and Nlaka'pamux people tried to prevent from being damaged when placer-mining began during the 1858 gold rush on the Fraser River, and these concerns for living resources available for future generations – as opposed to short-term economic profit from mining activity with its environmental destruction – continue to shape contemporary Secwépemc concerns over mining.[5]

Travel Routes and Transportation

As they travelled between communities throughout Secwepemcúl̓ecw and beyond the nation, Secwépemc people relied on a network of overland trails, waterways, and portages. The network of waterways included the North Thompson, South Thompson, main Thompson, and Fraser Rivers, the Shuswap and Adams Lake systems and tributaries, as well as Canoe River, the upper Columbia River, and Upper and Lower Arrow Lakes. For the millennia before the arrival of horses on the Plateau changed travel routes and the capacity to pack items, these waterways were the "highways" of travel throughout the Plateau, connecting the Secwépemc divisions and communities, as well as connecting the Secwépemc with neighbours in all directions but especially with Salishan neighbours to the south. As Teit (1930a, 216) reported, "From the head of Okanagon Lake the Shuswap had only a short distance to carry their goods to the navigable waters of the Spallumcheen River, Shuswap Lake, and South Thompson River, to Kamloops, which was a central point. Trade followed navigable waters from here to Savona, and north by the North Thompson, at least 100 miles. This seems to have been an important route." Another trade route took people from the upper North Thompson by way of a portage across to the Canoe River and then down the Columbia to the Revelstoke area, where the Secwépemc of the Sexqéltkemc (Shuswap Lakes) division met the Sinixt and Syilx, with a canoe trade route leading down Upper and Lower Arrow Lakes to Kettle Falls in Colville territory in present-day Washington State.

Settler D.S. Mitchell (1925, 8–9) described trade routes between the Shuswap Lakes area and the Columbia River:

> It was only a twelve mile pack by Eagle Pass from sockeye salmon fisheries at Three Valley Lake, to the Columbia River, opposite where Revelstoke now stands. From there it required little effort to take baled dry salmon by canoe, away through a great region lying on both sides of the International boundary line. They could drift much of the way only using the paddle enough to steer. From Kum-tch-tche-tchin on the Shuswap River it was sixteen miles pack to Okanagan Lake. From Fish trap rapids on the Shuswap River to Okanagan Lake, twenty-two miles. The great horse route from the South Thompson River to Okanagan Lake was thirty-six miles. From the head of Okanagan Lake another great water route lay open. Another route, between the Shuswap Lakes and the upper Columbia River was by Schwn-e-meen, or Seymour, thirty miles. In the dry belt, horses were more plentiful than canoes.

The waterways were travelled with canoes made from large sheets of white pine bark or spruce bark turned inside out that had been stripped off a large tree in one piece in late spring. In areas that had stands of large paper birch (e.g. the Quesnel Highland and the Adams Lake and Shuswap Lakes areas) canoes were made of sheets of birch bark that were sewn and glued together. In addition, dugouts were made of good-size, straight-grained cottonwood trees and possibly became more frequent after the introduction of iron adzes. They were shaped and widened using steam produced by filling the canoe with water and inserting red hot lava rocks. Figure 13 in the colour section of this book depicts a canoe built with this method by Jay Coutts and the Ignace family in 2003. Rafts were also used to haul goods downstream, and the elders of Simpcw reported using log rafts to float down the North Thompson River from their fishing and hunting grounds to Chu Chua from the 1920s to 1940s.

It was from the 1920s to 1930s, as motor vehicle travel in the Interior materialized, and as highways were built up, that canoe travel rather suddenly declined. Joe Stanley Michel (2005, 86) of Adams Lake observed,

> [M]y brother-in-law, Harvey Jules, even though he's only six years older than I, said as a little boy he saw 40 canoes on the shore south of Adams Lake. The most I've seen, most canoes I've seen on the Adams Lake were 15. So the, I guess, it coincided with the roads coming into the Adams Lake area, wagon trails. The decline happened very quickly. But prior to that there were no roads. All the travel to the end of Adams Lake was done by canoe. Then they followed trails where they wanted to go in the mountains.

In addition to waterways, a network of trails connected communities across the plateaus and mountain passes, following river valleys, animal migration trails, or maintained and marked trails that allowed expedient travel on foot both between communities and between resource-producing locations. As historical geographer Kenneth Favrholdt (1997, 29–30) has noted about trade routes throughout Secwépemc, Nlaka'pamux, Carrier, and Tsilhqot'in territories described by early explorers like Alexander Mackenzie and Simon Fraser, "it is clear from the numerous references in the fur trade literature that an elaborate system of trails had been well used long before the first Europeans arrived in the region." Favrholdt (1997, 1999, 2009) also shows how, for the most part, throughout the nineteenth and twentieth centuries, wagon roads used by fur companies, gold seekers, and settlers were built on Aboriginal trails and eventually built up as highways and railways, finally becoming the main arteries of traffic we know today.[6]

In their "Memorial to the Hon. John Oliver, Minister of the Interior" (Chiefs of the Shuswap, Couteau, and Thompson Tribes et al. 1911), who was the federal minister then in charge of Indian Affairs, the Interior chiefs stated, "Good trails we had in plenty before the Whites came. The Whites are indebted to us for having them ready made when they came and allowing them to use them without charge." This network of trails was used to visit, trade, and exchange information between communities; other trails in mid and higher elevations were used to get to and from hunting grounds and plant-gathering areas. Trails were used by runners who travelled ahead to spread important news from one community to another.

On these trails, people walked on foot. Burdens such as bagged animals and baskets full of harvested plants secured by tumplines were transported on the backs of men, women, children, and dogs. For travel in winter, people used snowshoes made from mountain maple wood or sapling fir wood, with the cross-sticks made of birch wood and the netting made of caribou or deer rawhide (see Teit 1909, 534).

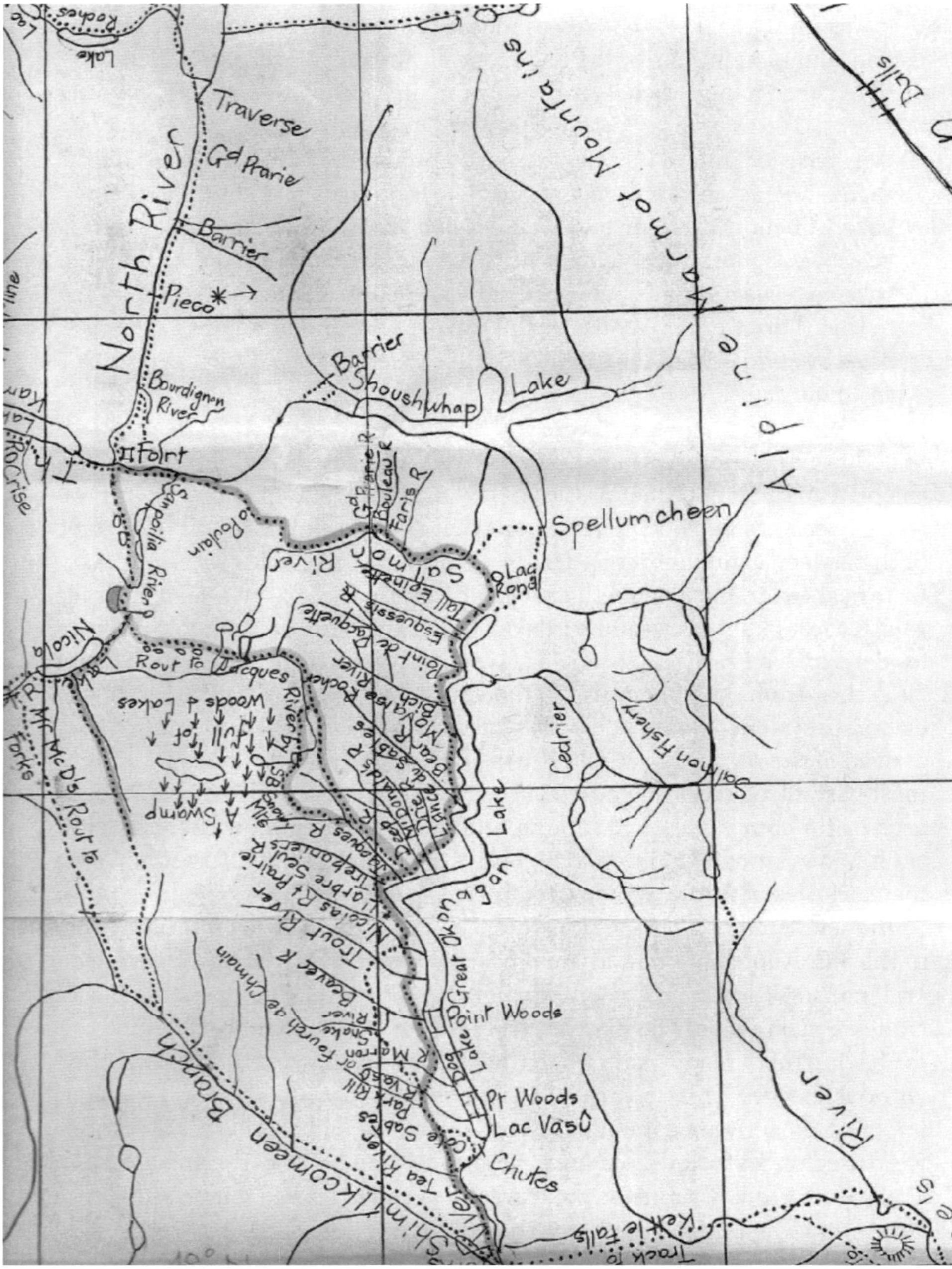

6.2 | A partial transcript of Samuel Black's map of the Interior, ca. 1833. The dotted lines show some of the Aboriginal trails that subsequently became Hudson's Bay Company brigade trails, many of which eventually became contemporary roads. The original map was identified by the late Bob Harris and Kenneth Favrholdt in the British Columbia Archives.

6.3 | Annual Unity Ride of the Secwepemc Gathering, which celebrates the interconnection of Secwépemc communities through old trails and horses, 2013. *Left to right:* Ron Ignace, Rob Miller, Sunny Lebourdais, Bonnie Leonard, Samantha Draney, and Leanne Tessier. After horses arrived on the Northern Plateau in the 1750s through trade with Southern Plateau trading partners and kin, horse culture became an integral part of Secwépemc culture, with Secwépemc people owning large herds of horses, breeding them, racing them, and using them for everyday transportation and packing of goods.

Horses arrived on the Northern Plateau in the mid to late 1700s from the south, originally traded from the Nez Perce and Shoshone to the Kalispel, Coeur d'Alene, and Flathead, who then traded them to the Okanagan and Secwépemc.[7] As Simon Fraser's account of his 1808 journey down the river named after him shows, horses had spread to the Northern Secwépemc area by this time, although it appears they were relatively rare and valued. Thus Xatśúll chief Cllúcwsem and his people were reluctant to loan or sell their horses to Simon Fraser's party.

The arrival of horses on the Northern Plateau in the late 1700s meant that the Indigenous peoples could haul larger loads and could travel faster to and between locations as long as the travel routes were suitable for travel on horseback. Although horses quickly became *the* mode of distance travel among the Stk̓emlúpsemc, Sextsínemc, Sexqéltkemc, and Fraser divisions, the densely wooded, steep mountainous terrain of the North Thompson did not always lend itself to horse travel, as even European visitors to the area like the Overlanders and Viscount Milton experienced in the early 1860s. The rugged mountainous terrain east of the Arrow Lakes apparently led to a decrease in traffic in that area following the introduction of horses; however, numerous trails connected the Arrow Lakes with the Shuswap Lakes area and with the area north to the Columbia River, including a Secwépemc "communication with the Columbia" through Eagle Pass, as was observed by numerous explorers, traders, and surveyors during the nineteenth century. Invariably, travel by canoe and travel on foot were connected in some areas: one notable trail, the Seymour or Moberly's Trail, connects the Seymour Arm of Shuswap Lake through Pettipiece Pass with the Columbia River near Downie Creek. Another important trail, which was still used by Simpcw (North Thompson) elders in the early decades of the twentieth century, led from the North Thompson River south of Blue River along the Finn Creek watershed, bypassing Tum Tum Lake, to the confluence of Canoe River and the Columbia at Boat Encampment. In 1817 this trail was explored by fur trader Alexander Ross, who was looking for a route between Kamloops and the upper Columbia. It is likely that other trails that followed the upper Adams River connected to the Columbia. Additional trails led to passes that crossed the Rockies. Thus, at Boat Encampment, artist Paul Kane met "White Capote, a Shuswap chief," who had come there from Jasper House to hunt, obviously having crossed Yellowhead Pass, as frequently did the Kinbaskets, who used a trail that connected Yellowhead Pass with the Canoe River and that, from there, continued upstream to Kinbasket Lake on the upper reaches of the Columbia River. The Kinbaskets, who had come to settle in the Columbia Valley, explored mountain passes leading across the Rockies to the east. Overall, for the area comprising the watersheds of the upper North Thompson River, Shuswap Lake, Adams River, and Columbia River alone – all at least partially within Secwépemc traditional usage – Kenneth Favrholdt (2009, 37–41) has identified at least thirty-six trails that provide shortcuts across mountain passes, connecting the core of Secwepemcúl̓ecw with resource-producing areas and trading groups to the east and southeast.

In areas where horse travel was expedient, it appears that the overland routes that subsequently became the well-travelled corridors not only of trade and communication among Indigenous people but also of the fur trade followed previously existing Aboriginal overland trails. Although some travel routes changed as a result of travel on horseback, horses were a natural extension of and addition to pre-existing patterns of communication and travel. Thus, as transportation of people and goods on horseback became common by the early to mid-1800s, the favoured route between Secwepemcúlecw and the Okanagan changed from the waterways described above to an overland route that now roughly follows Highway 97 through Monte Creek, Westwold, and Falkland to the head of Okanagan Lake. This was the route used by the Hudson's Bay Company brigades after 1826 en route down the Okanagan Valley to the lower Columbia River. Travel between Tk̓emlúps (Kamloops) and Skeetchestn followed a route along the south shore of Kamloops Lake through what is now Tobiano (formerly Six Mile Ranch). Another Indigenous travel route from Tk̓emlúps passed north of Kamloops Lake, crossed over the Criss Creek watershed, and traversed the Bonaparte Plateau to reach the Fraser River near Soda Creek. This trail also came to be used by the Hudson's Bay Company brigades after 1841, replacing another ancient trail and earlier company route up the North Thompson Valley to Little Fort and west across the Bonaparte Plateau to 100 Mile House. The arduous route is described in detail in company governor George Simpson's journal of 1828 (Favrholdt 1997, 287) Another network of Indigenous trails connected the Northern Secwépemc communities, including a trail from Llexwéxwewsem ("short cut trail," 150 Mile House) to Cmetém̓ (Deep Creek) near Soda Creek, as well as additional trails that led to the Quesnel Lake area and from there to Murtle Lake and across to the North Thompson.

The gold rushes on the Thompson and Fraser Rivers beginning in the late 1850s saw an influx of foreigners enter Secwepemcúlecw via the Okanagan Trail and travel to Tk̓emlúps and northward along the trails to the Cariboo region, the northernmost part of Secwépemc territory. The fur trade route to central British Columbia was soon supplanted by the famous Cariboo Wagon Road. Part of the wagon road was constructed in the 1860s along or on top of the ancient trail north of 100 Mile House. The improvement in some routes resulted in less use for other routes, but Secwépemc and other Interior peoples still used these trails for local travel.

During the twentieth century, some of these Indigenous trails became part of the network of contemporary motor vehicle highways, whereas other trails became overgrown or became criss-crossed by modern highways, logging roads, transmission powerlines, and other developments, making them difficult to find even for elders who travelled them in their youth. However, some trails have been rediscovered and some sections of trails have been partially restored. The Hudson's Bay Company brigade trail that went from Little Fort over the Bonaparte Plateau to Bridge Lake has been partially preserved by the provincial Ministry of Forests. Parts of the Okanagan Trail, used by company brigades, are preserved here and there. Other sections of the Aboriginal trails used by the fur traders and early settlers have the potential to be delineated and designated.

7 Re Stslexemúl̓ecwems-kucw
Secwépemc Sense of Place

As they travelled and lived throughout the different biogeoclimatic zones of Secwepemcúl̓ecw for generations and generations, the Secwépemc developed an intimate knowledge of all parts of the homeland, including the lay of the land as well as the places and environments where animals and plants could predictably be found throughout the seasons. Most of all, by means of communication in their language, Secwepemctsín, the ancestors of Secwépemc people developed and fine-tuned ways of communicating about the living landscape that enabled them to describe the lay of the land and to keep alive the memory of past things that happened in the landscape of Secwepemcúl̓ecw.

As we have seen, our *stsptekwll* (ancient stories) connect past events to places on the land whose names commemorate the ancient history of the land and connect it to the present. Stories also combine place names (toponymy) with ecological messages and with moral and social messages of events that happened in specific places associated with environments known to all Secwépemc, at least those of the past. Another important aspect of the knowledge, or cognitive map, that combines places and resources is Secwépemc topographic knowledge encoded in Secwepemctsín. The Secwépemc sense of landscape goes hand in hand with the way that the Indigenous language names and classifies, and thus shapes in the mind, the perception of landscape.

Terms for Landforms

Speakers of Secwepemctsín orient themselves in the landscape through the many terms for landscape forms that refer to places at different elevations, in different ecological areas, and in different geographic formations. For the ancestors of contemporary Secwépemc, who learned to live in this changing, but intimately known, landscape for hundreds of generations, these toponyms are more than speech labels for geographic locations. They imply an entire system of references and relationships in the landscape, where one term invokes the other and where people can predict what kinds of landforms they will encounter throughout their travels and what kinds of animals and

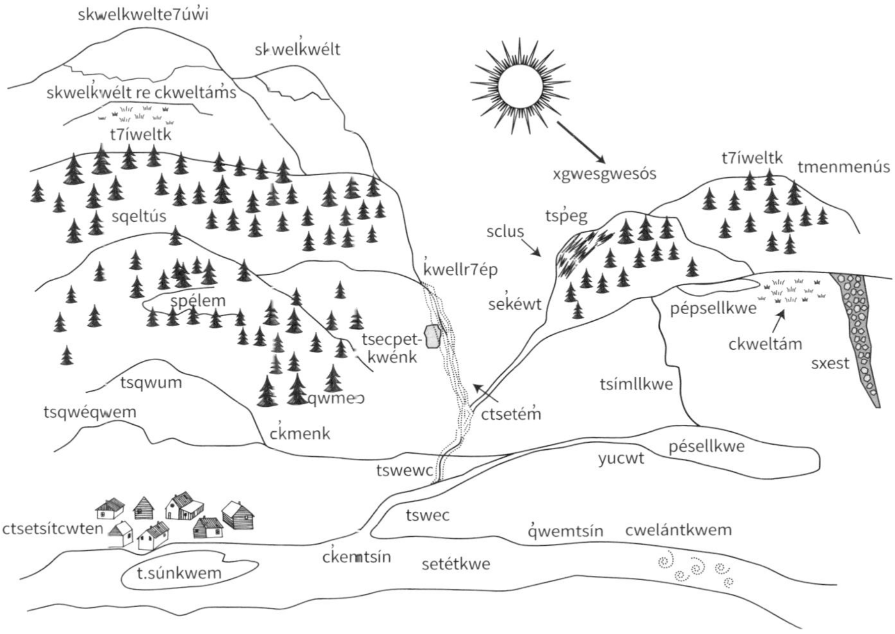

7.1 | Secwépemc landscape, showing geographical terms and typical features of the Interior Plateau.

plants, sources of water, and shelter can be found at or near a place that is mentioned. For example, as elders explained in mapping out these generic landscape terms, they knew that a plateau lake would have a *yucwt* (outflow), where you usually find trout after breakup in spring. Just like forest ecologists, Secwépemc resource users know that you would find certain plants on the *xgwesgwesós* (sunny southwest side of mountains) and others on the *cmenmenús* (shady and moister northeast side). Forested areas on the Interior Plateau would have included *ckweltáḿ* (moist meadows), often associated with aspen stands, which would in turn have provided pasture for horses, a nearby creek, and a good overnight camping location. These are also areas where deer still "hang out" and where a diversity of undergrowth and shrubs would have included edible plants. Along the rivers, *ctepṫúpkwem* (whirlpools) and *pelq̓étkwe* (back eddies) exist in predictable locations near rocky outcroppings and, as we have seen, are the locations for salmon-fishing spots. The geography of the Plateau itself is marked by a succession of *tsqwum* (hills), often preceeded or interspersed with *tsqwéqwem* (knolls), followed by *sqeltús* (mountains) that lead to the *t7íweltk* (high plateau) areas and eventually, in the highest areas, to the *skwelḱwélt* (snow-capped mountains).

Figure 7.1 presents a sketch of the generic Secwépemc landscape as it exists in the Stḱemlúps division – the Skeetchestn and Kamloops area. The generic landscapes of the Cariboo region and of the damper and more mountainous

North Thompson River and Shuswap Lake areas are slightly different from the Secwépemc landscape but are still recognizable in this sketch.

Secwépemc terms for landforms consist of a series of common basic root words for landscape features like "lake," "river," "mountain," and so on. In addition, by way of lexical suffixes that derive from shapes of the human (or animate) body, words for landforms inscribe the shapes of living things into the landscape. *Ckemk̓ménk* (rounded hillsides, plural from *ck̓menk*) resemble the shapes of curved bellies (*-enk* for "belly/curved shape"), *qwmep* (the bottom of hills) are their buttocks (*-ep* for "buttocks"), *ck̓emtsín* (the estuary of a river) is like the opening of a mouth (*-tsin* for "mouth"), *ck̓eméqs* (a pointed land form) is like a nose (*-eqs* for "nose"), and *ck̓emíken* (a ridge) is like the back of an animal (*-iken* for "back").

Table 7.1 lists and breaks down the most common Secwépemc landscape terms and provides their English meanings. In addition, it lists the set of lexical suffixes commonly used for landforms, among them several lexical suffixes derived from human body part suffixes. In words for landforms, these suffixes are used metaphorically to describe shapes in the landscape. The table also lists several lexical suffixes that specifically pertain to types of landforms.

Stsem̓túl̓ecwem | Naming the Land

Secwépemc place names – as opposed to the general words for landforms listed above – identify specific and unique locations or areas within Secwepemcúl̓ecw and connect these locations with memories of past events that occurred there, as well as with knowledge of environment, local resources, and landforms. They anchor Secwépemc history to the land in ways that connect people to the history of long ago, to the resources of the land, and to the lay of the land. They provide *oral maps* of the land, as past tricksters and transformers like Sk̓elép (Coyote), Qweq̓wíle, and Tllí7sa and his brothers shaped it and mapped it through stories.

In her ethnography of Esk̓ét elders' "maps of experience" articulated in stories and memories about place and travel throughout the area surrounding Esk̓ét, Xgét̓tem, and Tswécem̓c, Andie Diane Palmer (2005) recorded many narratives from Esk̓ét elder Angela George that connect specific named places – like Tsecyel̓kẇ, Cklutetétus, Spelpéplem, and K̓esétkwe – to past events. Christine Elsey (2013) uses the concept of "storyscape" to show how, particularly with St'at'imc and Nlaka'pamux stories of place as connected to place names, landscapes are poetically forged in the collective mind and thus remembered.

In anchoring places to stories by way of names, place names like Pesmémenc (Tobacco Mountain), Cwíẇesqen (Three Mile) on Lower Hat Creek Indian Reserve No. 2 of the St̓uxtéws (Bonaparte) Band, Sk̓emqín (the "head"

Table 7.1 | Secwépemc landscape terms and lexical suffixes

Landscape term	*Geographic feature*	*Gloss*
skwelk̓welte7úẇi	alpine area	root *sk̓welt* (snowy mountains), plus plural reduplication, plus *-uẇi* (par excellence, real, ordinary)
skwelk̓wélt re ckweltáṁs	alpine meadow	literally "snowy mountain's meadow"
t7íweltk	on the high plateau	"in the mountains"
sqeltús	mountain	*s*, plus root *qel*, plus *-us* (face)
tsqwum	hill	"mound, domed shape": *ts* (perpetual) plus root *qwum* (mound shape)
tsqwéqwum	little hill; knoll	root *tsqwm* (mound) plus reduplication for diminutitve
qwmep	bottom of a hill	root *qw(e)m* (mound shape) plus *-ep* (buttock, bottom)
spélem	prairie; clearing	nominalizer *s*, plus root *pel* (root?), plus *-em* (activity)
ckweltáṁ	moist meadow	"green" plus "bottom of valley": *c* (inside), plus root *kwel* (green), plus *-taṁ* (bottom, valley)
k̓wellr7ép	waterfall	"underneath of where it (water) stands upright": *k̓well* (underneath, among) plus root *r7ép* (stood up vertically)
tsecpetkwénk	cave	*tsec* (perpetual), plus root *petkw* (hole), plus *-enk* (belly/curved shape)
ck̓menk	hillside	*c* (inside of), plus root *k̓em* (two things coming together at an angle), plus *-enk* (belly/curved shape)
sek̓éwt	gully; canyon	includes *-ewt* (animal back; i.e., not upright but horizontal ridge)
tsṗ7eg	burnt-off area on mountainside (by landscape burning or natural fire)	*ts* (perpetual) plus root *ṗ7eg* (where the 7 is the status form "having begun to arrive in a state"); see *k̓wellr7ép* above
sxest	rockslide	nominalizer *s*, plus root *xes* (?), plus status form *-t* (completed state)

/continued

Table 7.1 | continued

Landscape term	*Geographic feature*	*Gloss*
xgwesgwesós	sunny side/south side of mountain	root *gwes* (sun shines on a place) plus -*us* (face of; here retracted to -*os*)
tmenmenús	shady side/north side of mountain	root *men* (shadow) plus -*us* (face of)
ctsetém̓	valley	*c* (inside of), plus root *tset* (?), plus -*tem̓* (at the bottom of)
pésellkwe	lake	This seems to come from *sewllkwe* (water) plus -*pes/pell* (has)
pépsellkwe	small lake or pond	consonant reduplicated (diminuitive) form of *pésellkwe*
pespésellkwe	area with many lakes	The Lakes Division area around Canim Lake can be characterized thus, as can the area south of Kamloops.
yucwt	out-flow; drainage creek of lake	The root *yucw* indicates the flushing out of something from above. The Northern Secwépemc also use the term *yucwt* to talk about giving birth (otherwise *k̓ult* in Secwepemctsín), thus indicating the flushing-out movement of a child from the womb.
ctsímllkwe	meltwater; runoff	*c* (inside), plus root *tsim* (to melt), plus *ll* (perpetual?), plus -*kwe* (water)
ck̓emtsín	mouth of river or creek	*c* (inside), plus -*k̓em* (two things come together at an angle), plus -*tsin* (mouth)
setétkwe	river	This may derive from an "unduplication" of the root *set'*, the word for the mid-Fraser River (Canyon) in Salish languages
t.súnkwem	island in river or lake	*t* (on top), plus root *sún* (*meaning unknown*), plus -*kwe* (water), plus -*em* (action)
tswec	creek	a root form
q̓wemtsín	shore	root *q̓wem* (?) plus -*tsin* (mouth)
cwelántkwem	eddy, whirlpool	root *cwel* plus -*ánt* (formative suffix?), plus -*kwe* (water), plus -*em* (action)

Table 7.1 | continued

Lexical suffixes (Kuipers 1974)	*Several lexical suffixes that occur in place names and names for geographic features derive from lexical suffixes that denote parts of the human or animal body*
-qin, -qiṅ, -qen	head, at the top of; dome shape at the top
-ekst, -kst	shape of hand with fingers
-tsin, -tsiṅ, -tsen	mouth (of a creek into a river)
-eqs, -qs	nose (nose shape)
-us, -s	face: a steep edge or side of a mountain
-éles, -éles, -les	chest; flat surface
-íken/-ikeṅ, -ken	back (ridge of a mountain)
-éws, -ws	middle, waist, side, elevated surface
-énk, -eṅk, -nk	belly-shaped, vertically curved, like a round hillside
-ep, -p	at the bottom of; buttock
-úpe7, -pe7	tail, bottom end
-ups, -ps	pointed buttock shape; confluence
Other lexical suffixes	*These lexical suffixes prominently occur in place names and generic toponyms*
-éllile	bushy area
-éscen	rock, mineral
-étkwe/-kwe	source of water, creek, river
-ewt	steep ridge (e.g., *sek̓éwt*, gully)
-min, miṅ, -men	instrumental: place where you do something with something
-taṁ/-teṁ	valley bottom; inside underneath (as in a pithouse)
-ten, -teṅ	instrumental: place where you do something, place for something

of Kamloops Lake) at Steelhead Park, Sk̓atsín (Neskonlith Indian Reserve No. 1) on the north bank of the South Thompson River, and Sqlewúl̓ecw (the Chasm) near Clinton still remind present generations of what happened there long ago during the travels of Tll̓7sa and his brothers, Qweq̓wíle, and Sk̓elép. During his geological survey of the British Columbia Interior in the 1880s, George M. Dawson (1891) recorded some 220 Interior Salish place names, many of which he subsequently entered onto his topographic maps of the Interior, including his "Kamloops Sheet" and "Shuswap Sheet." Through various research projects between the 1970s and 2000s, hundreds of additional place names were recorded in Secwépemc communities. Dawson's 220 names thus represent only a very small portion, probably less than 10 per cent, of the names that Secwépemc people had for places in Secwepemcúl̓ecw when Europeans came into the land.

Next to the place names associated with ancient transformer travels and deeds, numerous place names commemorate more recent events of warfare and altercations between Secwépemc and outsiders. Sekewmectét7us ("Cree's trail"), on the north shore of Kamloops Lake east of Copper Creek, is where a Secwépemc war party caught up to a Cree warrior who had advanced well into Secwépemc country and killed him (see below). Another place associated with past warfare is Tsq̓elentwécwten ("battle ground"), at the mouth of Raft River, where Símpcwemc (North Thompson Shuswap), helped by friends from Tk̓emlúps, fought against Cree. As Simpcw elder Chris Donald explained,

> The Cree Indians, they'd come all the ways through Tete Jaune. They come all the ways down, looking for all the people to have war. But they had their own war, battle ground, down at Raft River Creek. That's where they used to tell the people they gonna come down and have war. You know, they haven't got much of any kind, just a bow and arrow, spear. Cree would stay on the other side of the Raft River Creek, and the people from down this way, like Kamloops, Douglas Lake, and all the people who come from the lower [parts of Secwepemcúl̓ecw] they'd get together with these people, they started a war. The Cree, they said, "We'll stay on the other side of Raft River, and you guys stay on this side of Raft River. Whoever can make it across, get across." Well, they drive the other people back. The Cree usually mostly got beat up and killed off. I don't know why they used to want to go to war. Used to take the land, I guess. The Cree used to get cleaned up and nothing left. He'd leave one, he'd have to take his clothes off, take his shoes off, and tell him to go back for some more if you want a war again. To lose, to lose your life, you can come and have war. They say on the other side of Raft River, when the white people started clearing land and plowing it up, there are pieces of land where the earth is all white. It's where they piled all of the dead people and put wood on top of them and burn them up. That's what turned the earth white, the bones.

Other Simpcw place names that commemorate past battles are Kélentem ("being chased"), a place on Battle Mountain in Wells Gray Park where Sammy Joseph of Chu Chua remembered a Símpcwemc being "chased" down a gully on the mountain by Cree warriors, probably in the mid-1800s, resulting in a battle with a group of Cree. Chris Donald's story of Snine7éllcw ("owl's nest") near Vavenby on the North Thompson River, another site of a battle of the Símpcwemc against the Cree, also commemorates a battle with Cree invaders. Stseq.qíqeń ("park or put at the top") was the name for Balancing Rock near Savona, which Theresa Jules remembered in association with the Secwépemc and Okanagan having a contest there (see chapter 8).

Throughout Secwepemcúlecw, many other such place names exist that are inseparably connected to a story that not only explains the place name but also links that place and the activities of people in and around it to a larger landscape. One notable story about place is the *stsptekwll* of Sésq̓em ("open-mouth place"). The latter designates the long valley and lake in the upper Barriere River watershed and Vavenby on the North Thompson River, which George M. Dawson recorded on his Kamloops sheet map as "Saskum Lake." The shallow lake and long narrow valley produce eerie echoes as the wind sweeps the mountainsides. It is here that a *ṫkwilc* (Indian doctor) froze a deaf-mute girl into stone after her own family could not help her.

Story of Sésq̓em

told by Chris Donald, recorded, translated, and transcribed by Marianne Ignace, Mona Jules, and Ronald E. Ignace, 1986

Le q̓7éses re stsem̓túlecwmes Sésq̓em.
Long time ago, there was a place called Sésq̓em.

Meméws-ekwe w7ec te skwelk̓wélt.
A couple, they say, were up in the snowy mountains.

Tnek̓wé7 re sṫemkélts ta7 ri7 k sqwlútes.
One of their daughters couldn't speak.

Tnek̓wé7 re sṫemkélts ta7 ri7 k sqwlútes.[1]
One of their daughters couldn't speak.

Teklles-ekwe re nexwnúxwenxws, tnek̓wé7 re sqélemcws.
They say they had three girls and one boy.

W7ec ṫri7 mútes w7ec re siséysus.
She was sitting there as they were playing.

Ṫri7 re úq̓wis, ta7 penhénes re smetméṫelcs.
Her sisters, they never mixed with her.

W7ec re sqw7éles, stsqwelstémes, ta7 penhénes re stsqw7éles.
When they were talking, when she was spoken to, she never said a word.

Ṫri7 mut wel tsut-ekwe re kí7ces,
She sat there until her mother said,

"Me7 qwetséts.stem re sṫemkélt-kt te ṫhé7en tkllúne."

"We will take our daughter somewhere out there."

"Me7 llwélentmes ṫri7 te sqeltús."
"We will leave her up there in the mountains."

"Me7 plépes e qwetsetstsútes ṫri7 ṫhé7en."
"She will get lost when she wanders off somewhere."

"Ta7 k sxwexwistéten es púpelsten."
"I don't want to kill her."

"Put e kukwstsútes, newí7s," tsut-ekwe re sqélemcw.
"If she saves herself, that's fine," said the man.

"Me7 qwetséts-kp wellenwí7-emp, xwexwéytep re nexwnúxwenxw ell re tuwíwt."
"You go, all of you, all of you girls and the boy."

"Yerí7 wel qwetséts-emp te Sésq̓em ṫu7 le valley wel me7-kitsc-kp te pésellkwe."
"You folks start off for Sésq̓em through the valley until you get to a lake."

"Me7 répelc-kp telrí7 ne sqeltús-ekwe ṫkllu7."
"From there, you climb along the mountain they say is over there."

"Ye-ekwe me7 crepqín-emp nerí7."
"That is where you should stop for lunch."

Tsut-ekwe ṫri7 re sec7ítemc te sṫemkelt.s,
Said the oldest daughter,

"Me7 qwetséts-kucw ṫ7éne me7 q̓wléwmes-kucw te speqpéq."
"We'll set out over there, we'll pick berries."

"Me7 tsyem-kp nerí7 méte tuwíwt."
"You guys stay here with the young boy."

"Me7 llwellctp ṫri7 tek stem es ts7illens."
"You leave something to eat for him."

Yerí7 nerí7, tsuns es llwélens re sṫemkélts.
Here, there, they thought they'd abandon their daughter.

Tśílem-ekwe ri7 ṫe sqéxe re splútsens. Pellxlécw té seséle.
They said her mouth was like a dog. She had two teeth [fangs].

Yect-ekwe ri7 re tkmépe7sqens.
They said she had a long chin.

Wel w7ec-ekwe t̓ri7 k xexé7 te t̓kwilc, te tkwékweltks re Vavenby.
There was a smart Indian doctor there, down below Vavenby.

T̓ri7 t̓hé7en w7ec-ekwe re tsqeqnímenstmes t̓ri7 t̓e t̓kwilc.
Somewhere around there, an Indian doctor heard her.

Yerí7 te núxwenxw m-cwéyem, m-cwéyemes, cwéyemes, m-awt-ekwe ucw.
This girl barked, barked, barked, and howled again and again, they said.

Kúkwen sqéxe awtes.
Like a dog feeling sorry for itself when it howls.

M-tsut-ekwe re t̓kwilc, "T̓rey witsín olep-enke ri7."
The Indian doctor said, "That over there [near you] making a noise must be lost."

"M-llwélentem-enke. Me7 kúk̓len ell me7 tút̓lcten neri7 re mútes."
"She must have been abandoned. I will make her freeze into stone where she is sitting."

Tsqwmus-enke nerí7 re mútes.
She must have been sitting at the edge of a mountain.

Ri7 scenc, ri7 put yecyélqw. T̓silem t̓ucw te sqéxe nerí7 k mut.
That rock, it was quite long. Like a dog, she must have been sitting there.

Telri7éne re kelkélcs ner̓i7 ne lléqwlecw.
From there, her hands were down on the ground.

Re tkmepé7sqens t.séq̓em-enke, put w7ec k cwéyemes, k áwtes, wel t̓ulemí7 nerí7 te m-scenc.
Her chin, her mouth was wide open, just as though she were barking. She must have been howling, and that is how she was frozen there into a rock.

Nerí7 re núxwenxw ell re tuwíwt m-cwetsétses t̓kllu7,
Those girls and the boy left for [the area] over there,

t̓hé7en m-t̓7ékwes re st̓emkélt.s.
where the daughter had gone.

Tsut-ekwe re stemémc te núxwenxw, "Qeqnímen-tp-en ṫkllú7 k sqéxe?
The younger one of the girls said, "Do you hear over there, there seems to be a dog?"

"Nu7 k ṫkllú7 w7ec re cwéyemes, k áwtes, téke m-llwélentmes."
"It is barking out there, howling, because it has been left."

"Tsukw-enke nerí7 tek sqéxe téke m-cwéyem."
"It must have been only a dog barking."

"Ta7 me7 cwéyemes nerí7 ne tsitcw-kt, tsméṫelc nerí7 ne k̓wellqel̓múcws."
"She won't be barking anymore there, at our house, mixed up there among her people."

Qw 7élentém, m-qnúsem ṫucw.
Whenever she was spoken to, she would just nod.

W7ec-ekwe re cwéyemes, áwtes, plépes ṫhen-enke re sqwetséts.s.
They said she barked and howled, and got lost wherever she must have set out to.

M-tspepelq̓ílc, tsqwetséts, tsigáp.
They all came back, they set out and arrived this way.

M-tsigáp te stéq̓emes-enke nu7 k yerí7 ṫkwilc m-téq̓emstmes.
They arrived at the crossing, and there the medicine man helped them cross the river.

Téq̓tes nu7 wel tsúntem-ekwe te ṫkwilc,
When they crossed over, they were told by the medicine man,

"Qnímentpes k sṫemkélt-emp, yerí7 nu7, w7ec re cwéyemes, w7ec re áwtes."
"You should hear your daughter over there, she is barking and she is howling."

"Ta7 ri7 penhén ṫri7 me7 estqwíts.s nehé7e re mútes."
"She will never move from where she was sitting."

"Tśílem-enke te sqéxe re mútes, áwtes, cwéyemes."
"She is just like a dog, sitting, howling, barking."

"Nerí7, me7 ṫulemí7 nerí7, me7 scenc ri7 nerí7."
"There, she will be frozen there forever, she will be stone there."

"Pexyéwt put e ketscúses, ketscús t̓lune e llwélentpes, me7 répelc-kp es ts̓exentép kénem k sts̓exténs."
"Tomorrow, when it is just about time, it is time for you to abandon her, go up and see what she looks like."

Me7 tsukw-ekwe re sqélemcw kem répelc, ell tnek̓wé7 te sqélemcw.
Only the boy went up and the one man.

Téq̓em t̓u7 m-répelcwes.
They crossed the river and went up.

M-tkítscwes r̓ri7 te m-llwélentmes.
They arrived where she had got left behind.

Ta7-ekwe r̓ri7 k sqwetséts.s nerí7 kem llwélentmes.
She never left from where they had left her.

Nerí7-ekwe k mútes, m-áwtes, m-cwéyemes, m-cwéyemes, áwtes.
There, they said, she sat, howled, barked, and barked and howled.

M-qeqnímentem te t̓kwilc, m-k̓úlentmes nerí7 es ts̓elemí7s.
The medicine man had heard her and had frozen her into stone there.

Yerí7 te sqélemcw, tnek̓wé7 te sqélemcw, kítscwes r̓ri7 te m-llwélentmes yerí7 te núxwenxw.
That man, that one man, he arrived there, where the girl had been left behind.

R̓ri7 kem tsyémes, tspút̓em-ekwe ri7 ell tsut-ekwe ri7 tnek̓wé7 te sqélemcw,
They sat down when they came into the opening, and one of the men said,

"Yénke ri7 ne tsq̓wmus, héqen nerí7 le mutes, ts̓elemús te tken7éne."
"That must be at the cliff over there, maybe, where she is sitting facing this way."

Tsut-ekwe re qé7tses, "Yerí7-enke re scenc, yerí7 nerí7 nek le mútes, ne scenc."
His father said, "That must be the rock, there, where she is sitting, on the rock."

Nerí7 le mútes, cwéyemes, cwéyemes, áwtes.
She was sitting there, barking, barking, and howling.

Te t̓kwilc ri7 re k̓úlentmes.
The medicine man made her that way.

7.2 | Storyteller Chris Donald of Simpcw, 1985. Before passing away, he recorded a legacy of Simpcw place names, oral histories, and *stsptekwll* (ancient stories) with Marianne Ignace.

Nerí7 re stšelemí7s.
There, she was frozen.

Yerí7, ye7éne te séme7 yelxwentés yerí7.
There, these white people wrecked it.

Ṫri7 used to logmes ṫri, m-t7íkens-enke, k̓estwílcst.ses nerí7 xwexwiyúlecwem.
When they used to be logging there, they felled logs on it, ruining all the land there.

Ta7 put pyin k stšílems ne tsímelles
It's not the same as in earlier days.

Pelúqw-enke ṫ7éne te tkwékweltk re ckwetkwṫústens.
They chipped the bottom part of her eyes.

Like other elliptic place names, the name Sésq̓em makes a mere allusion to events that happened, thus inviting the story to be retold again and again in order to keep the events in memory and in order to keep the memory of the place itself in people's minds. That memory of place and its name, however, also encodes laws of social conduct.

As our ancestors lived and travelled throughout Secwepemcúlecw, they made history not only by naming places of historic and heroic events but also by naming places after the resources, including game, fish, and plants, that they knew they could harvest there. Pellcílcel ("has silverweed") reminds us of the occurrence of an important Indigenous root plant, *Potentilla anserina*. Pellskwakwíkwna reminds us of the Indian potatoes (*Claytonia lanceolata*) associated with a place above the South Thompson River. Tšotinéntkwe ("rattlesnake lake"), Pellstsetšúye ("has porcupines"), Pelltnílmen ("has Indian hellebore," *Veratrum viride*), Pellqweq̓wíle ("has large-fruited desert parsley," *Lomatium macrocarpum*) (see chapter 3), and Pelltím̓et ("has skunk cabbage," *Lysichiton americanus*) are further example of place names that give clues about animals and plants found there, in many instances demarcating choice harvesting locations. However, due to the effects of logging, mining, urban development, and other changes to the land, the resources commemorated in the name have disappeared from many of the areas in question. Others are threatened to be altered long term.[2]

Yet other place names give hints about human activity in certain locations, thus providing information about the plants and animals that are or were harvested in strategic, ecologically suitable locations. Cllemím̓en ("harpooning place") is the name of a salmon-fishing rock across from the mouth of Deadman's Creek, where salmon are speared with a *meníp* (harpoon spear). A similar harpooning place along the shore of the North Thompson River

7.3 | Pellqweq̓wíle ("has biscuitroot"), once a Secwépemc village west of Tk̓emlúps (Kamloops) at the mouth of Tranquille River, named after Chief Tranquille (Piqemús), 2015. This village became the site of a tuberculosis sanitorium in 1905 and then a home for the mentally handicapped from 1959 to 1984. As the Secwépemc name suggests, it was once a root-digging ground for *qweq̓wile* (biscuitroot).

near Birch Island was called Cllumíń (also "harpooning place"). C7emtsíńten ("sitting at the shore doing something place") on the North Thompson near Clearwater is the place where the Simpcw "sat at the shore" catching spring (Chinook) salmon until fishing restrictions were imposed by the federal Department of Fisheries and Oceans. S7emtúsa ("sitting at a rock face") is a cliff on the Adams Plateau where people did their *étsxem* (guardian spirit questing). K̓écse7ten ("drying-meat place") is a place near the northern boundary of the Skeetchestn Reserve where, on a well-ventilated southern exposure, people dried the meat from their fall hunt. It was also a village site, as several depressions still show us, and a tool-making area, as the evidence of large amounts of lithic flakes on the flat at K̓écse7ten shows. Just like the place names for battle sites, many place names that refer to human activity involve cryptic allusions to the activity. However, these place names evoke memories among current generations about the activities of ancestors and past people, about the use and occupancy of the land, and about how people travelled, lived on the land, and managed its resources. They also invite contemporary Secwépemc to continue the ways of the elders.

Place names connect the past with the present not only by pointing to resources but also by reminding us of the history of dispossession. As the resources disappear, giving way to logging, mining, and urban development, including golf courses, Secwépemc people can continue to remember what they did there as long as the stories are told and as long as the place names that invoke past activities are remembered. The effects of colonization and dispossession, and the struggle to overcome them by fighting for Secwépemc rights, are conveyed by the memories of what the past elders did on the land. As the Interior chiefs told the federal minister of the interior, Frank Oliver, in 1911, when asking him to settle the land question, "If a person takes possession of something belonging to you, surely you know it, and he knows it, and land is a thing which cannot be taken away, and hidden. We see it constantly, and everything done with it must be more or less in view" (Chiefs of the Shuswap, Couteau, and Thompson Tribes et al. 1911). Place names thus directly or indirectly tell stories about past activities in a cultural landscape that continues to have agency and, through the names, where we continue to be reminded of, and to perceive these human activities as, past *deeds.*

In addition, many place names give visual and relational clues about the shapes of geographical features and have thus served as a way for countless generations of Secwépemc from all communities to orient themselves in a landscape with common geological and geographic features, habitats, and ecologies. There is history in this naming practice, for as our people, over thousands of years, learned to use, know, and find their way in the environment during their seasonal rounds, the names for landscape features evoked memories, along with sentiment for the contours, smells, and activities associated with the land and with the previous generations who experienced that landscape.

Many, if not the majority, of Secwépemc place names creatively put to use the opportunities offered by the structure of the language to identify particular places by their physical shape, by the presence of bodies of water, bushy areas, or rocks, by the association of the habitat with plants and animals, and in the end, by the memories that places evoke of ancestors travelling this land. In short, the sense of Secwepemcúl̓ecw as organized and visualized in place names and landforms is tied up in an aesthetic experience of organized shapes of the land and in the memories of living and travelling in that familiar landscape of aesthetically organized shapes. These experiences and memories are what generate our collective sense of a historically created and inhabited Secwépemc landscape that connects people, animals, plants, and geography. The following presents some examples.

In chapter 4, we mentioned the Secwépemc place name Ck̓emqenétkwe, the flat area along Paul Creek above the Kamloops Indian Reserve that was renamed Scheidam Flats after an early pre-emptor. Like many other Secwépemc place names, it consists of a prefix, a root word, and lexical suffixes that together evoke a vivid image of the lay of the land. As a place name, Cḱemqenétkwe conveys the meaning and imagery, tightly bundled in a single word, of being inside a place on top of, or above, where two creeks flow together. There is no better way, including in many subordinate sentences in English, to describe what Cḱemqenétkwe portrays: a place that, once you are there, you are on the inside of as it extends before you, a place that features the coming together of waters (creeks) at an angle, and a place that is on top of, or above, other places. In tightly compressed visual images, it marks the coming together of creeks (Coal Creek and Paul Creek) to form the "water tap" of the Tḱemlúpsemc. Beyond the tight-knit image of strategic geography that is commemorated in the place name, Cḱemqenétkwe also commemorates both Secwépemc people's connection to land and our history of resisting settlers' appropriation. Like so many European settler names in Secwépemc lands, its English name, Scheidam Flats, bears the mark of the settler, the European pre-emptor who quickly left his mark on the landscape before selling his interests for profit in the 1860s and departing, as our people struggled to have lands allocated that would sustain us, despirte having never wavered about not having surrendered the rest of Secwépemc lands. Louis (Clexléxqen), chief of the Tḱemlúpsemc from the 1850s until his death in 1915, continually alerted provincial and federal governments to the fact that Cḱemqenétkwe represented the "hole in the table" of the Tḱemlúpsemc. Based on his unwavering raising of this issue, and the Kamloops Indian Band's pursuit of its title to this land, the band was eventually able to reincorporate Cḱemqenétkwe into its reserve in 1996. A good part of the land dispute surrounding it did not involve the few acres that Kamloops Indian Band members successfully argued they had continued to occupy by grazing their animals there and by living, camping, and existing there. Instead, the dispute involved the Tḱemlúpsemc insisting on their water rights and on the integrity of their watershed.

Foghorn Mountain in the Columbia Mountains above the North Thompson River has the name Cmetqenétkweten (the prefix *c* for "inside," plus the root *met* for "to camp, live, sit," plus the lexical suffixes *-qen* for "at the top," *-etkwe* for "water," and *-ten* for "place where people do something"). The name for this favoured and productive hunting ground and camping area describes another high valley characterized by creeks flowing together and thus implies a productive watershed in the lives of the Símpcwemc. As Chris Donald remembered, Cmetqenétkweten was "all the old people's hunting ground. People hunted deer, caribou, bear, and whistlers. They'd stay there a long time until they had enough of what they have there, then they'd come home. When they come home, they had to have packhorses to pack everything home. After that, some white people, you know, they'd turn a lot of sheep over there every year. Spoil all the hunting grounds. Any kind of animal, they'd look for it, they can't find them. Sheep spoil the ranges."

The Secwépemc word for Tk̓emlúps, usually translated as "confluence" or "meeting of the waters," has a visually vivid and interesting meaning that gives us clues about past Secwépemc ancestors' perception of shape and space. The word Tk̓emlúps derives from the prefix *t* for "on top of," plus the root *k̓em* for "two things coming together at an angle," plus the lexical suffixes *-l/ll* for "perpetual" and *-ups* for "pointed buttocks." The word invokes the kind of buttock shape that past Secwépemc people saw in the very shape of the confluence of the North and South Thompson Rivers, still visible from the bird's-eye view of an airplane or from the lookout on what is now Columbia Street in Kamloops. Tk̓emlúps, the village at the confluence – more recently, the "rez" – was in turn the "meeting place" where Secwépemc from different communities congregated, traded, camped among relatives and friends, and later met *séme7* (white people) (see fig. 3, colour section).

Other terms evoke travel and movement in the landscape and the intricacies of the Secwépemc language. Thus Pet̓mémnus (the root *pet̓* for "to come out into the open" plus the lexical suffixes *-men* for "instrumental or something you use to do something with" and *-us* for "the face of") marks the place near the northeast boundary of the Skeetchestn Reserve where, as people travel south along Deadman's Creek while coming home from the narrow gullies of the Criss Creek watershed, they "come out into the open" upon reaching the valley. In a song that Ron Ignace calls the "Secwépemc National Anthem," Nels Mitchell of Tk̓emlúps expresses the joy of coming home off the mountains on horseback and riding along the familiar gullies down to the lake:

Oh, re seksek̓éwt, re pespésellkwe.
Oh, the gullies, the lakes.

K̓eléňmentiye re íswell.
Listen to the loon, everyone.

Oh, cmump-ken nukw!
I am so lonesome [homesick]!

Yerí7 re spút̓em-kt te sek̓éwt.
Here we come into the open out of the gully.

Yerí7 re skitsc-kt ne setétkwe.
Here we arrive at the river.

7.4 | Nels Mitchell of Tk̓emlúps (Kamloops), a well-known Secwepemc singer and storyteller, ca. 1975.

Ne7élye me7 yístet.
This is where we camp.[3]

When returning from travels on horseback in the mountains, we feel the joy of coming home, the same as our ancestors did. The valley of our community, Skeetchestn, is a long, narrow, north-south valley framed by two mid-elevation mountain ridges. Elder Christine Simon has called the Deadman's Creek Valley and its east and west ridges "arms that stretch out to us when we come home into our valley from travels." Those ridges draw us home and evoke the memories we have of travelling there. Every sidehill reminds us of travelling there in the company of people who told us their stories of the land. In similar ways, the valleys and mountain ridges of all of our communities invite us home from travelling.

Place names are thus inextricably linked not only to the culturally filtered perception of geographic shapes but also to the history of specific places. More than that, they are connected to travel on the land. In 1984, when asked to remember place names in the North Thompson Valley, Chris Donald approached the topic of place names in the valleys and mountains he knew by going on a mental journey, later followed by physical ground-truthing journeys we took together with other elders, where he reiterated the names for places, also mentioning additional ones whose memory was triggered by seeing, hearing, and smelling the places of his earlier life. His way of naming the land consisted of mentally retreading familiar territory in order to identify a chain of place names throughout his seasonal round, which started in Chu Chua and moved up north to his trapline on the upper North Thompson River, accompanied by the remembrance of resource use, hunting and trapping expeditions, mishaps that had happened to past individuals, and stories of past battles and wars with outsiders that his own elders had told him about. As he remembered the past encoded in place names, he noted shapes in the landscape that give meaning to the names and connect words to history. Having named dozens of places from the vicinity of the Chu Chua Reserve to Little Fort, Clearwater, and beyond to Blue River and even Mount Robson, he described the places along the travel route up Simpcwétkwe (North Thompson River):

> The river before you come to Raft River is Clearwater River. Its name in Indian is Xeleq̓tsétkwe ["rolling water"]. Yeah, any old Indian hear that, he'd know where Xeleq̓tsétkwe is. And then you come to, what do you say, Raft River, Ctśwenétkwe ["drying-salmon river"][4] … and Cllq̓wetústen ["lying concealed, on one's belly, peering over a rock face"] near Clearwater, that's on a side hill. Old people, he say it used to be way to the top, he spying people, you know, strange people coming down. He call that after[ward] Cllq̓wetústen. And then, Birch Island, that's Cllumíṅ ["harpooning place"], and then you come to a place between Birch Island and Vavenby, Qwle7tút.s ["lodgepole pine rock face"]. And then [you] come to a place, Spelmáxtsk [the root *spél(e)m* for "prairie, clearing" plus the lexical suffix *-axtsk* for "Vavenby flats"(?)], and then [you] come to a place, and he calls [it] Snine7éllcw ["owl's nest"] [see above], and after that Tsk̓eqíqeṅ [the root *tsk̓e7* for "rock" plus the lexical suffix *-qiṅ* for "top of a mountain ridge near Vavenby"]. And from there you get to Nexexú7tem ["dry gully"]. It's a creek there where the people used to camp a lot long ago, Nexexú7tem, [or] Hole-in-the-Wall. And then you come to Snexléẇs [the nominalizer *s*, plus the root *nex* for "dry," plus the lexical suffix -éẇs for "ridge, path on a ridge"], that's Mad River. And after that Yexyexésceṅ ["dressed-up rock"]. That's where there's rocks with all the drawings and names of the places [pictographs on Highway 5 at McMurphy]. And then Sexqeltqín ["at the head of, on top of, upriver area," Wire Cache] and past that Pelltíṁet ["has skunk cabbage"], and then at Mile 16, Pesqlélten ["has salmon," Finn Creek], and from there you come to K̓wellr7ep ["waterfall," Little Hell's Gate at Wolfenden]. And [then] that Blue River comes from a river coming into this river. Just looks like milk. And it run like that for a ways before he changes [to] Cteqtíq̓kwe ["inside of a milky or clay-coloured creek,"

from the prefix *c* for "inside," plus the root *tiq̓* for "clay-like," plus the lexical suffix *-kwe* for "water"].

Likewise, when Leslie Narcisse and Chief Harvey Jules of Adams Lake remembered place names in the area around Adams Lake and Little Shuswap Lake in 1991, they recalled the names by way of imagined and remembered travels to places that they had encountered in sequence while travelling from the Adams Lake Reserve along the shores of Little Shuswap Lake.

For the people of Esk̓ét, as noted above, Andie Diane Palmer (2005) has shown how Secwépemc elders used narratives of personal and historical experience on the land to provide oral and mental maps that not only corresponded to the landscape but also "anchored" landscape to story.

Place names, in their connection to geographic and ecological knowledge and experience, as well as to memories of past generations' experiences on the land, represent an affirmation of the Secwépemc concept of *deeds* to land. As spots that are not isolated but are within the chain of "connected dots" and continuous agency on the land, they not only represent and confirm our emotional and historical connection to land but are also our evidence of *owning* the land we call Secwepemcúl̓ecw and having *title* to our land, as our ancestors continued to claim once they were shut out of our own lands in the latter half of the nineteenth century. As long as we maintain the connection between our landscape and experience by way of the stories we remember and the places we remind each other of, we will know where we come from and who we are as Secwépemc (see R. Ignace 2008, 180).

In the Secwépemc worldview, places are not named after great men, as they often are in European usage, witnessed by the way Europeans and Canadians renamed the landscape of Secwepemcúl̓ecw in honour of their own explorers and politicians. Nor do large bodies of land or water, such as Kamloops Lake, Shuswap Lake, and the Fraser River, have place names; instead, hundreds upon hundreds of place names exist throughout Secwepemcúl̓ecw for landmarks and spots along travel routes to provide points of reference for travellers and for a person who describes events in the landscape. Together with the imagery of generic Secwépemc words for landforms, they have allowed Secwepemctsín speakers for many generations to describe ecological relations, events, and travels in the landscape of Secwepemcúl̓ecw in precise terms, whether narrated in *stsptekwll* or recounted in more recent memories of humans travelling on the land, as well as to describe the connection of people's activities to the past history of Secwepemcúl̓ecw.

The Use of Directional Terms in Talking about the Landscape

In addition to the words that describe fixed features in the landscape or those that represent the intricate imagery of place names, Secwepemctsín has a

Table 7.2 | Secwépemc directional words and prefixes

Secwépemc root words	*Meaning*
wutémtk	downriver (in relation to speaker's location), thus also meaning somewhat down in altitude
s(e)xqéltk	upriver (in relation to speaker's location), thus also meaning somewhat up in altitude
t7íweltk	up the Plateau, the montane parklands
sextsíne	down to or by the river shore
(se)súxwenst (sing.), *yét̓elc* (pl.)	to descend a slope (one person/many)
répelc	to climb, to ascend a slope
kútse	to descend in a downstream direction, thus descending in elevation
cicúm	to ascend in an upstream direction, thus ascending in elevation
kúme, kúmelc	go ashore
Directional prefixes	*Meaning*
yi- (ye-)	this (pointing to)
ne-	in an enclosed or defined place
t̓-, t̓(e)k-	at, by, to a general area
t̓l-	at, by, to a fixed location
t(e)l-	movement from a place
tkn-	in the direction of
tktn-	in the direction away from speaker, "the other way"
Directional stems combined with above prefixes	*Meaning*
-én(e)	this one, close to the speaker or as the focus of attention
-élye	here (by speaker as focus of attention), also describes movement pertaining to right
-llene	there, that place or way

/continued

Table 7.2 | continued

Directional stems combined with above prefixes	*Meaning*
-lune	way over there, far yonder (invisible)
-llu7	over there (invisible)
-núne	over there (visible)
-nu7	on the other side, also describes movement pertaining to left
-ri7	that (away from speaker and addressee)
-rey	that near you (addresse)
Locational and directional prefixes	*Meaning*
c- (x-)	inside an area or place, movement into a place
t-, tek-	on top of, on the surface of
k̓well-	underneath, in a space underneath
ts-, st-	movement this way (hither), to speaker
xl̓-	ward-off, beat-off movement
pl̓-	"tagging along" movement
est-	sudden movement

large number of deictic words and particle words that speakers of the language deploy to convey meaning about the movement of humans or animals within the landscape. In relation to the person who tells the story and in relation to geographic features, this movement can be to or from a fixed place or within an area, such as up or down mountains, implying changes in altitude, upriver or downriver in relation to the current, across a body of water, out into the open, or into the forest. As we explained in chapter 4, deictics also convey information about whether the landscape feature mentioned is close to the storyteller or the listener or away from both, and they give information about whether the geographic features referred to are visible or invisible to the person who mentions them. These space reference words are a rich resource of the grammar of Secwepemctsín that allows a speaker to convey very detailed and precise information to the listener about the location of places, humans, and animals, as well as about the direction of their travel. Together with the detailed words and combinations of words for landscape forms and place names, they provide something like an oral geographic positioning system. Moreover, they enable a listener to visualize and vividly imagine movement in the landscape from the perspective of the storyteller.

To show how such terms are used in a narrative by a person who tells about events that happened in the landscape, we have included an excerpt from a memory of a hunting trip that Henry Squinahan of Esk̓ét told David Johnson around 1970, as recorded by linguist Aert Kuipers (1974, 107ff). After killing a large caribou in the subalpine area (*skwelk̓wélt*, "snowy mountains") between Esk̓ét and Tsq̓ésc̣en (Canim Lake), Henry Squinahan (Skwenícen), who was invited by his brothers-in-law of Canim Lake to accompany them on a hunting trip, travelled with his companions in the area.

Le pexyéwtes-kucw tskwnem te nts̓e7sqéxe7 es tecknemsqexemíntem.
The next day we brought some horses *[movement this way, to speaker's location]* to pack it [the caribou].

"Pexyéwt," tsut, "tlúne te Tyexqs me7 peqú̓lecwet t̓ekllune te Swepú̓lecw me7 w7écwet."
"Tomorrow," they said, "from over there *[specific area, visible to speaker]*, from Tyexqs ["dressed nose-like shape on top"] Mountain, we'll have a look around over there *[invisible area]* at Swepú̓lecw ["furry (for grass-covered) area"], that's where we'll stay."

T̓7ek-kucw t̓kllu7, nerey sllcílc, kucw t̓7ekwes te m-tswentsetsstqéxu7s, t̓7ek-kucw t̓ri7 yéske tspút̓em re selcwéyecen.
We were going along over there *[far, invisible]*, thick fog covered the area over there *[focus on listener]*, we went along trotting our horses, we were going along when a caribou emerged out into the open *[coming this way]*.

Stgetsgets.stém-kucw re swelmín̓ks, tsukw re ntsétswe7 re kllenwén̓ ren swelmín̓k, tsq̓élen re selcwéyecen yéske le m-púlstem-kucw.
We had strapped up our rifles, only I was able to get my gun out, I shot the caribou and we killed it.

Yerí7-kucw re m-s7estúllentem, m-qwetsétses-kucw, k̓woyí7se re stsmuxws.
We butchered it, and then we left, there was a dusting of snow on the ground.

T̓7ek-kucw tlri7, cuy̓, kellélls-enke te nt̓se7sqéxe7 t̓ek7éne le st̓ekcén.
We were going along from there *[movement from a place]*, look, what must be three horse tracks going this way *[movement from his side]*.

M-tsut le Moses, "M-pílemt-kt nukw, me yelpélc-kt tekten7éne."
Moses *[identified as deceased now]* said, "We're lost, we'll turn off this way *[away starting from Moses as speaker]*."

M-qwetsétses telrí7 cú7tsem, m-seláles le sllcwilc, pelq̓ílc-kucw le r7áles, m-wenécwmes te m-llcwilc.
We left from there again, the fog had lifted, and when we went back [to camp at Swepúl̓ecw] in the evening, it was really foggy.

M-q̓wempép le sllcwilc, t̓7en te spélem-kucw t̓7ek t̓7en ne cpeleménk, yéske t̓lu tsecnexwenstqín le skem̓cís.
The fog was gone, and over this way *[from position of narrator]* we went this way *[from position of narrator]* along a prairie, went along a prairie side hill, and a grizzly bear came running down the hill *[toward us]*.

T̓7ek t̓ek7éne wel re m- st̓7ek. M-tsúntsems, "Cuy̓, nésmente." Tsut, "Ne7élye kucw me7 re stseltśeléwtmes."
He went along that way *[general area moving closer to the narrator]* until he was coming *[toward narrator]*. They told me, "Hurry up, go to him." They said, "We will both stand here."

Yerí7 t̓ek7élye ren snes t̓lu7, estwéy-ken, ta7 t̓ri7 k stem wes k kénmes nukwll ne spéplem len cecále.
Then I went there *[to that area, focus on narrator]*, I arrived on top [of the hill], there was not a thing happening on the steep little prairie.

Mumt-ken nerí7. Yéske t̓ekcí7 estp̓en̓lléxw te tswetkúm te sisk̓, ec re k̓w7émes ec te illenes.
I sat down there *[in that spot]*. Then it emerged over there *[in an area away from narrator]*, holding a gopher in its mouth, it was chewing and eating.

Tsíqllcwens-enke t̓kllú7 m-úllcwes ell re estp̓en̓lléxwes ec re k̓w7émes.
It had been digging a den over there *[area invisible to narrator]*, and it had entered [the bush] and had come out, chewing.

Éytsell re tsqéq̓elnes, tsqéq̓len, m-leq̓wépmes, clentés re ck̓emllníw̓t.s, m-est̓íl̓ ucw.
Then finally I shot it, I shot it, it shrieked, bit its side, and stopped.

Tsqéq̓len cú7tsem, nerí7 m-clentés re ck̓emllníw̓t.s.
I shot again *[over there]* it bit its side.

Mus re stsqéq̓len pe tsqwetsétses tekten7élyus tékten stsqéq̓lenstnes.

Four times I shot it, and it took off this way *[coming toward me]*, in the direction where I had shot at it from.

Ṫucw nerí7 mut-ken yéske ṫek7éne sṫ7ek ṫri7 k stem ten cḱemímken.
I just sat there, and then something was coming this way *[focus on speaker's position, by his side]*, there, behind my back.

Tsut-ken tek snekú7s cú7tsem tek skemcís ṫek7éne k sṫ7ek, wel yéske le Moses Dixon re sṫ7ek, ṫ7ene re skemcís sṫ7ek, ṫ7ek nerí7 wel m-lleq̓út.
I thought there's yet another grizzly coming this way *[focus on speaker's position]*, but instead it was Moses Dixon who came, and over there *[toward speaker]* the grizzly was coming until he went face down.

Tsq̓élnem le Moses, .44 lu7 re stsq̓élens.
Moses shot, he shot it with a .44.

Estúllentem-kucw le skemcís, ptukw-enke cwem re sesṗéys nerí7 re stḱe7s le stskwils. M-tsútsen, "Ta7ews cú7tsem k stsq̓élenc k skemcís tek ḱwimemímnek, me7 pulst.ts k skemcís!"
We skinned the [deceased] bear, there was a hole where the bullet had penetrated its skin. He told me, "Don't shoot a grizzly again with such a small-caliber rifle, the grizzly will kill you!"

Past storytellers like Henry Squinahan and others knew how to expertly convey information about the movement of people and animals in the landscape of Secwepemcúl̓ecw using place name information and descriptions of landforms and features known among all Secwépemc and communicated in Secwepemctsín. In addition, they deployed an amazing number of deictic terms to communicate movement and location of people and animals on the land in fixed locations and areas in relation to the narrator and the audience. Finally, by communicating this information in a common language unique to Secwépemc people, storytellers were able to convey, for the benefit of present generations, a sense of how Secwepemcúl̓ecw as a living landscape is interconnected with our history of places, people, and living creatures, as well as with experienced events, all of which become the stories told to the next generation.

8 Re Stsq̓ey̓úl̓ecwems le Stet̓ex7éms-kucw

The Secwépemc Nation and Its Boundaries

> When they first came amongst us there were only Indians here. They found the people of each tribe supreme in their own territory, and having *tribal boundaries known and recognized by all.* (Chiefs of the Shuswap, Okanagan, and Couteau Tribes 1910, emphasis added)

Throughout the many years that our ancestors occupied the homeland on the plateaus between and adjacent to the Thompson and Fraser Rivers, they continued to expand the area where they lived and gathered resources off the land, justifying the name Secwépemc as it came to be used by insiders and outsiders. As we noted in the Introduction, the term "Secwépemc," derived from the root *cwep* for "spread out" and the lexical suffix *-emc* for "people," means "the spread-out people." Although archaeological data (see chapter 3) provide us with detailed information about places, timelines, and sequences of human occupation, and about the resources that ancient peoples pursued, it is difficult to determine the exact ethnic identity of past occupants, such as Secwépemc, Nlaka'pmux, Syilx (Okanagan), Tsilhqot'in, or Dakelh, let alone communities within these nations, or to determine the exact extent of territories occupied by the past ancestors of Indigenous peoples. As we showed in chapter 2, however, we can use a variety of data from historical linguistics, archaeology, oral histories, paleoecology, and population genetics to connect the emergence of the Secwépemc to deeds on the land now at the core of Secwepemcúl̓ecw.

The above quotation from the "Memorial to Sir Wilfrid Laurier" (Chiefs of the Shuswap, Okanagan, and Couteau Tribes 1910) shows that there emerged over time among our ancestors a sense of a finite Secwépemc homeland with boundaries that was perceived of as *stsq̓eyul̓ecw* ("marked on the land"),[1] whether through natural boundaries like mountains, watersheds, and other physical landmarks or through the deeded markings of ancestors immanent in physical features anchored to place names and stories. For example, Q̓wiyucénk (Cairn Mountain) marks the boundary among the Secwépemc, St'at'imc, and Nlaka'pamux; and a mound named Cwelcéscen at the headwaters of Bridge River marks the boundaries between the Secwépemc,

8.1 | Pillar Rock, north of Falkland, a story site and boundary marker between the Secwépemc and the Syilx (Okanagan), 2013.

8.2 | Coyote's Sweathouse, near Alexis Creek, British Columbia, an old boundary marker between the Secwépemc and Tsilhqot'in, 2013. It was moved by a settler-farmer, who perceived it to be in the way of cultivating his field.

St'at'imc, and Tsilhqot'in. In the east, Three Valley Lake was recognized as marking the boundary between the Secwépemc and Sinixt ("Lakes," Okanagan). Some of these markers are "Coyote rocks" and other geological shapes attributed to the deeds of shapeshifting ancestors or to more recent events.

To learn details about the Secwépemc's sense of a common homeland, Secwepemcúl̓ecw, including its external boundaries and internal divisions, we can turn to the rich record of Secwépemc oral histories, coupled with descriptions of Secwepemcúl̓ecw left by the *seme7úw̓i* ("real whites"), the first Europeans who came among the Secwépemc in the early nineteenth century during trips of exploration and the subsequent fur trade. These accounts give us instructive, although often incomplete, pieces of information about Secwépemc and surrounding nations' territories and boundaries as they were conveyed to the *séme7* (white) newcomers and perceived by them. As we will see in this chapter, between the 1600s and 1800s, and likely before that time, boundaries were not immutable but changed and shifted, at times expanding and at times contracting. Significantly, noting that the tribal boundaries of Indigenous nations were "known and recognized by all," the chiefs of the early 1900s, whose collective and individual memories reached back to the 1840s and before, also expressed common understandings maintained through sharing stories, knowledge of place names, and other kinds of discourse between and among nations of one another's territories. Nlaka'pamux head chief Sexpínlhemx (David Spintlum, 1812–87) is on record as defining what he called the "posts" of Nlaka'pamux territory. Not only does his account speak to the conscious knowledge of boundaries among Interior Salish chiefs, but it is also consistent with the Secwépemc boundaries we describe, and it addresses the unceded title to, and jurisdiction over, his homeland:

> One post up the Fraser at [Fountain] – one down the Fraser at Spuzzum – one up the Thompson River at Ashcroft – one up the Nicola River at Quilchena – one down the Similkameen River at Tcutcuwi'xa [near Hedley]. All the country between these posts is my country and the lands of my people. At Lytton is my centre-post. It is the middle of my house, and I sit there. All the country to the headwaters of all the streams running into the valleys between these posts is also my territory in which my children gather food. We extend to meet the boundaries of the hunting territories of all other tribes. All around over this country I have spoken of, I have jurisdiction. I know no white man's boundaries or posts. If the whites have put up posts and divided up my country, I do not recognize them. They have not consulted me. They have broken my house without my consent. All Indian tribes have the same as posts and recognized boundaries, and the chiefs know them since long before the first whites came to the country. (Quoted in James Teit, unpublished fieldnotes, cited in Hanna and Henry 1995, 5)

David Thompson's Map, 1792–1812

Alexander Mackenzie was the first European to visit the land of the Secwépemc, which he did on his brief trip through the very northwestern part of Secwepemcúlecw in the Soda Creek area en route to the Pacific. He entered information about the Indigenous groups of the area onto a sketch map, which was subsequently used by David Thompson of the Montreal-based North West Company in his "Map of the North-West Territory of the Province of Canada, from actual Survey during the Years 1792 to 1812." Thompson's map also includes information gathered during his own surveys of the Canoe and Columbia Rivers, where he may have encountered Secwépemc people on the eastern margins of Secwepemcúlecw, although his journals themselves make no references to individual Aboriginal people or groups of Aboriginals identified as Secwépemc. Thompson's journey to the Columbia took place just before and during the time of Simon Fraser's 1808 journey down the the big river that was subsequently named after Fraser himself. Thompson's map also incorporates information from David Stuart's and Alexander Ross's 1811–12

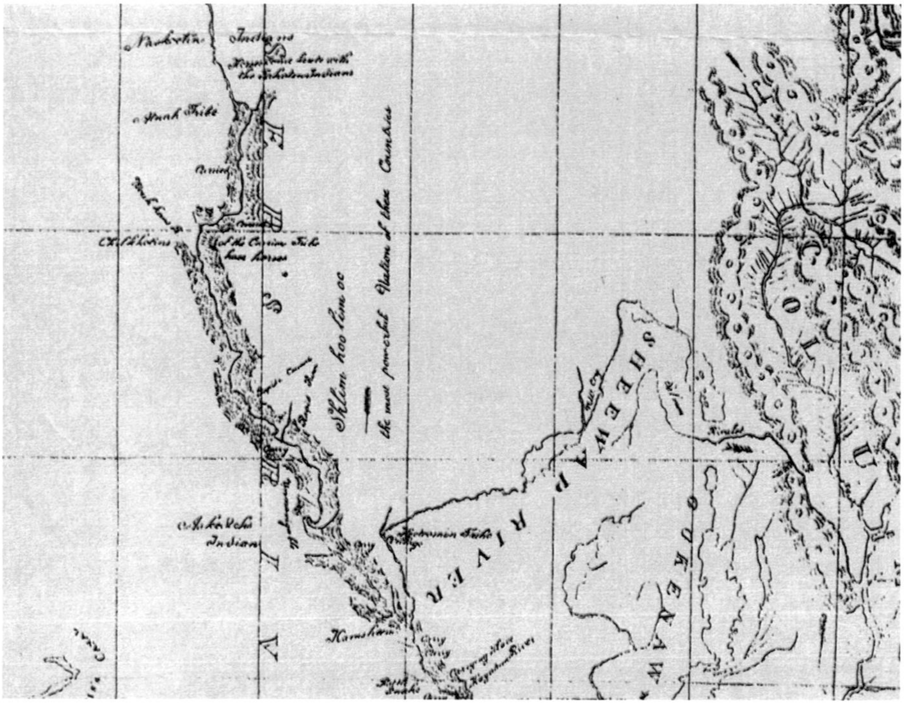

8.3 | An excerpt of David Thompson's "Map of the North-West Territory of the Province of Canada," based on information from Alexander Mackenzie and others, 1792–1812. It shows the "Shlim ho olim oo [Sṫemcúlecwemc], the most powerful Nation of these Countries," the Thompson River as the "Shewap River," and a "Koutumin" village near the present town of Ashcroft.

expeditions as employees of the Astoria-based Pacific Fur Company through the Okanagan to the confluence of the North and South Thompson Rivers at Tk̓emlúps (Kamloops). This expedition marked the first contact with Europeans by the Southern Secwépemc, particularly by the people of Tk̓emlúps and people from other communities encamped there at that time. Thompson's map gives information about the area associated with the Secwépemc and about the sense of boundaries between the Secwépemc and surrounding nations.

On his map, Thompson charts the "Athna tribe" inhabiting the area south of the Alexandria area, which is north of what is now Williams Lake. We must remember that Mackenzie and Fraser came from the north, that is, from Carrier country, and the latter refer to the Secwépemc as Athna, the term for "foreigners" in Dakelh, the Carrier language. North of the Soda Creek area are the "Naskootin Indians" (Nazko Carrier) and a note that "horses come hereto with the Tahotene Indians" (Lhtauten Carrier). This map thus locates the boundary between the Carrier and Northern Secwépemc along the Fraser River just above Soda Creek.

On the east side of the Fraser River are mentioned the "Sklim hoo lim oo," without doubt the Sṫemcúlecwemc – James Teit's (1909, 453) Slemxu'lExamux division – who are the Northern Shuswap people along the Fraser. They are noted as the "most powerful Nation of these Countries." On the west side of the Fraser River, opposite the "Sklim hoo lim oo," Thompson charts the "Chilkhotins" (Tsilhqot'in).

At a location that appears to be south of the mouth of the Bonaparte River, Thompson marked a "Kootoomin Tribe Village" – that is, an Upper Thompson or Nlaka'pamux village – which appears to be in the location of the present Ashcroft Band. The Thompson River, later named in his honour, David Thompson called the "Shewap River" (Shuswap River). South of "Salmon Rivulet" (Salmon River), at the head of Okanagan Lake, he locates the "Ookenaw-Kane" (Okanagan or Syilx). No eastern or northeastern boundaries with other tribes are indicated. Thompson's map indicates "NW Co." in the location of Kamloops, where the post was transferred from the Pacific Fur Company to the North West Company in 1817, subsequently becoming the Hudson's Bay Company's Thompson River post in 1821, after the North West Company and the Hudson's Bay Company merged.

Archibald McDonald's Map, 1827

The next historical map produced by early-nineteenth-century fur traders is Archibald McDonald's "A Sketch of Thompson's River District 1827." McDonald had succeeded John McLeod, the first Hudson's Bay Company factor at the Thompson River post in Kamloops, and in 1828 he accompanied company governor George Simpson on his inspection tour of New Caledonia in central-northern British Columbia and the Columbia and Thompson River districts.

John McLeod (1822–23), in fact, had provided a description of the "7 tribes" of the area served by the Thompson River post, and McDonald's map should be read in conjunction with McLeod's description:

> The first tribe are the Shew-shapps, which nation inhabits that part of the Country immediately in the vicinity of the post of Kamloops, their boundaries extends east to the Upper Lake or rather the first on Thompson's River above the fort, say 4 days march from the House and continues down the same Stream, till about ten leagues below the Fort, this nation consists of about 160 men able to work beaver, exclusive of women and children, they speak the same language with the North river Indians and bring in a proportion of the trade.

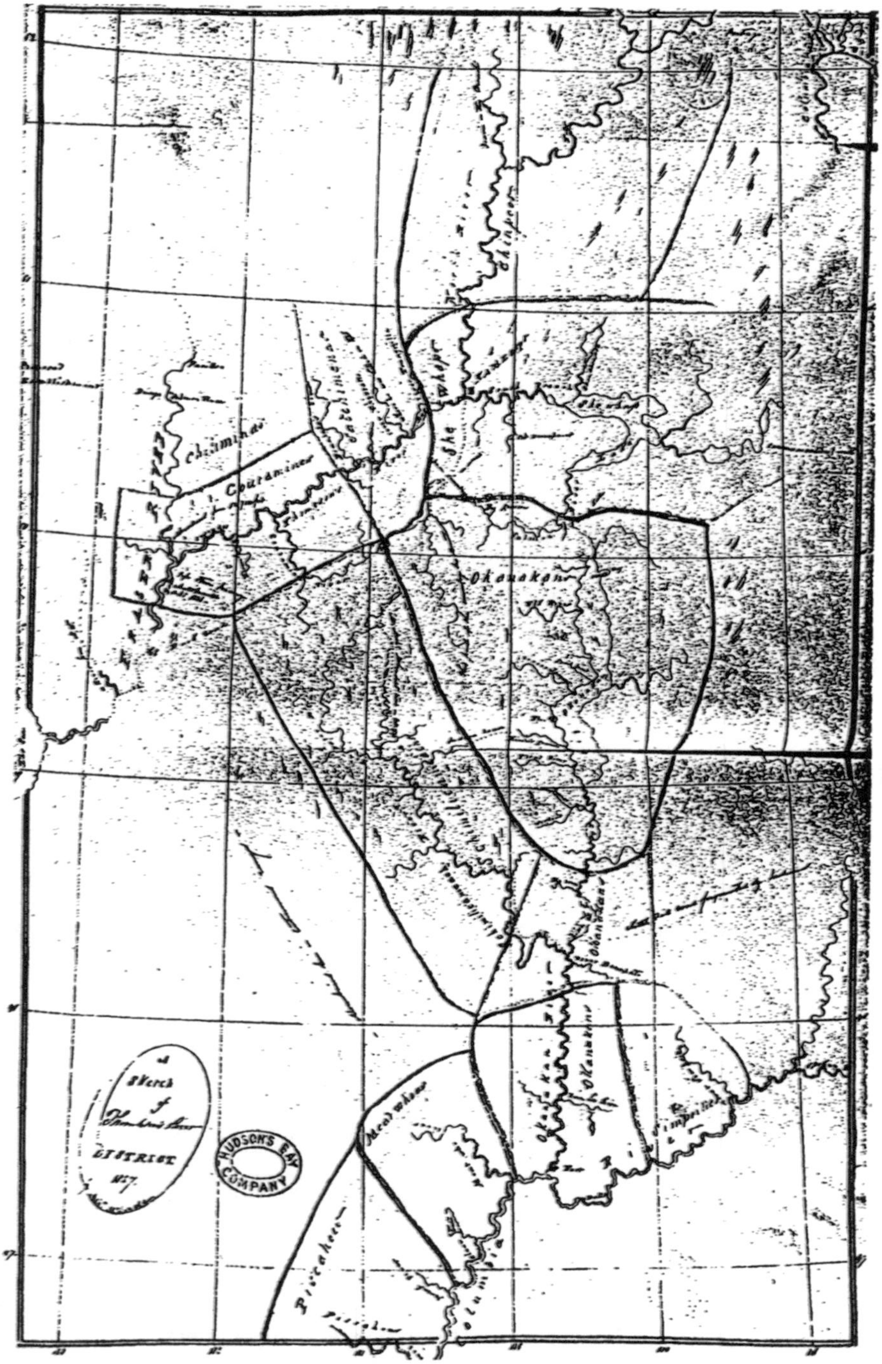

8.4 | Archibald McDonald's "A Sketch of Thompson's River District 1827." It shows various "divisions" of the Secwépemc and McDonald's understanding of the "Shewap" (Secwépemc) boundaries with neighbours.

He went on to list the other six "tribes," the second being "Cou-tu-min" (Nlaka'pamux), whose "Boundaries begin at the termination of that of the Shew-shapps and continues westward down the Banks of Thompson's River to ten Leagues below the confluence of Thompson and Fraser's Rivers." The third tribe was the "Si-mi-ha-ca-meachs," or Nicola-Similkameen people. The fourth tribe was the Okanagan. The fifth tribe he designated the "Stst-lam-chu" (St'at'imc?), or Fraser River Lillooet, including the people of Bridge River and Fountain, the latter of whom, as oral histories and place names have it, were at least partially Secwépemc, adding that "the greatest part of the salmon consumed at Kameloops is traded from them." The sixth tribe, said to live inland from the fifth tribe, was the "Spa-chil-quah," or Lower Lillooet of the Seton Lake and Anderson Lake area. The seventh tribe was the "Chin-poo" (Simpcw), or North Thompson Secwépemc.

Although McLeod's report and McDonald's map are inaccurate, incomplete, or inconsistent with regard to Secwépemc terms for or concepts of such groupings as they existed in the mid-1800s or more recently, they give some valid and useful indications not only of the names of Secwépemc divisions and approximate boundaries of these divisions but also of the boundaries of the Secwépemc nation with some of the neighbouring nations.

What McLeod and McDonald designate as the "Shew-shapps" or "She whops" apparently refers to the Kamloops and Shuswap Lake (i.e., Adams Lake, Neskonlith, Little Shuswap, and Spallumcheen) Secwépemc. Their area, according to the description and map, ran from the east shore of the Tranquille River along the lower North Thompson River west to where the lower Adams Lake would be, then south from Kamloops Lake to the northern end of Nicola Lake, then due west from there, with "Big Prairie" (the Westwold area) according to this map being Okanagan territory, then to Round Lake, and finally west from there to the Columbia River.

The second tribe, the "Cou-tu-min" or "Coutamine," is comprised of the Upper Thompson, or Nlaka'pmux, whose boundary, according to the map, extends to just southwest of the mouth of the Bonaparte River.

The third tribe, the "Si-mi-ha-ca-meachs" or "Schimilicameach," is comprised of the Nicola-Similkameen people, who, as McLeod correctly noted, formerly spoke an Athapaskan language related to Carrier and Chilcotin but had become absorbed by the Okanagan and Nlaka'pamux people of the Nicola Valley.

The fourth tribe, the Okanagan, according to McDonald's map, takes in the territory east and south of Nicola Lake, including "Big Prairie," as noted above.

The fifth tribe, designated by McLeod as the "Stat-lam-chu" and on McDonald's map as "Chiliminds," is comprised of the Fraser River Lillooet, or Upper St'at'imc. Under this name, McDonald also includes the Pavilion people, as well as the Upper Hat Creek people of the Bonaparte Band. As we will see below, Teit grouped the Pavilion people and Upper Hat Creek people with the St̓uxtéws (Bonaparte) people.

McLeod's seventh tribe, also noted on McDonald's map, the "Chin-poo," is comprised of the Simpcw (North Thompson Secwépemc). According to the map, their lands extend 50 to 200 kilometres up the North Thompson River and then over to the Adams Plateau.

One group not mentioned by McLeod but designated on McDonald's map is the "Satchimenas," without doubt the same people designated by Teit (1909, 456) as the "Zaxtci'nmux" (Sextsínemc, "shore people"). In Teit's terms, they constitute the Bonaparte division of the Shuswap (i.e., Bonaparte, Pavilion, and the people on the Thompson River below Skeetchestn). However, McDonald also includes with them the Skeetchestn people. According to his map, the boundaries of the "Satchimenas" run from the Tranquille River west to the Bonaparte River and south to Nicola Lake. The boundary between the "Satchimenas" and the "Coutamines," according to McDonald, runs a few kilometres southwest of the mouth of the Bonaparte River.

As McDonald's map is drawn from the perspective of the Thompson River post at Tk̓emlúps, it leaves open the northern and eastern boundaries of the Secwépemc. However, it is the first map that designates some of the internal divisions of the Shuswap as well as the distinct boundaries between the Shuswap and the neighbouring nations.

Alexander Caulfield Anderson's Map, 1867

Alexander Caulfield Anderson's large map of southern British Columbia, titled "Map of a Portion of the Colony of British Columbia compiled from various sources, including original notes from personal explorations between the years 1832 and 1851," was the most significant map of the region produced until the Province of British Columbia was created. It is signed and dated "Alex C. Anderson, 23rd May 1867."

During the 1830s and 1840s, Anderson was in charge of the Hudson's Bay Company's Fort Alexandria post on the upper Fraser River at Alexandria, south of present-day Quesnel. Later, he became fisheries commissioner for British Columbia and in the late 1870s was also one of the three members of the short-lived Joint Reserve Commission.

On Anderson's map, the northern and eastern boundaries of the Secwépemc nation are very distinctly marked. The boundary with the Carrier on the Fraser River is marked by a line titled "Northern Boundary of the Shewhapmuch Connexion called by the Tacully [Dakelh/Carrier] 'Atnahs.'" It locates what would be the Soda Creek and Fort Alexandria area as the "1st Atnah village." From just north of there, the boundary line runs southwest, crossing the Chilcotin River at or near Hanceville, and then on to the height of land that divides the Coast Mountains and the Interior Plateau.

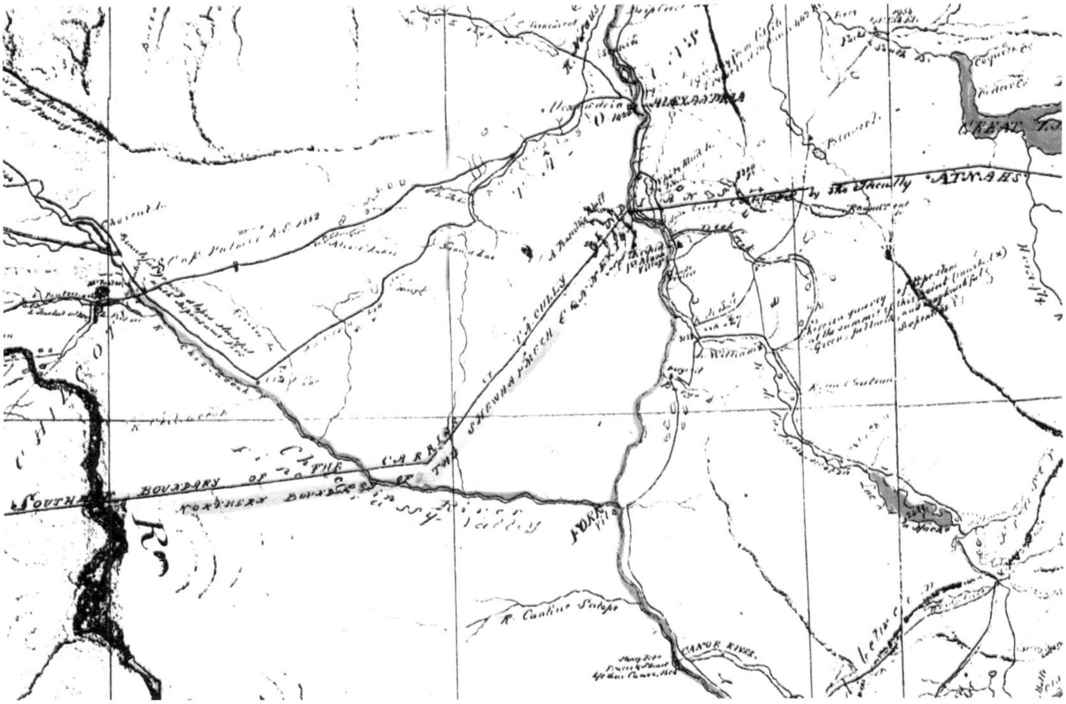

8.5 | An excerpt of Alexander Caulfield Anderson's "Map of a Portion of the Colony of British Columbia," 1867. It shows the Secwépemc-Carrier boundary on the Fraser River between Xatśúll (Soda Creek) and Alexandria.

East of Soda Creek, the line runs eastward, with Anderson specifically excluding Quesnel Lake – termed "Bun encha" ("it is a big lake") in Dakelh – from Secwépemc territory, then northeast past the mouth of the Atnah River into the Fraser near McBride, and then northeast to the height of land of the Rocky Mountains identified on the map as the junction of the Carrier, Sekani, and Beaver Indians with the Secwépemc. From there, the line runs southeast, past Cow Dung Lake, along what seems to be Robson Pass, then south along Sullivan's Peak to Mount Hooker and Punch Bowl, then along the Selkirk Range to Mount Balfour, then east of Upper Arrow Lake, and then south. The land to the east of this line is marked "Kootanai Indians."

Anderson does not indicate the southern or southwestern boundaries of the Secwépemc; instead, in the south and southwest, it appears that he lumps the Secwépemc together with the other Interior Salish nations, namely the Nlaka'pamux, St'at'imc, Sinixt ("Lakes," Okanagan), and Syilx (Okanagan) peoples and the Interior Salish–speaking Flathead, since he draws the southern boundary of what he calls "the extreme south-eastern Branch of the Shewap-much connexion" south of the 49th parallel at the headwaters of the

Flathead River. Nonetheless, Anderson's map is very valuable and detailed regarding the northwestern, northern, and northeastern boundaries of the Secwépemc with neighbouring nations. In addition, he clearly distinguishes them as *boundaries* between the Carrier and Shuswap nations, using the term "connexion."

George M. Dawson's Map, 1891

George M. Dawson's map is titled "Map Shewing the Limits of the Shuswap People of British Columbia with the Principal Subdivisions to Illustrate Dr. G.M. Dawson's Paper on the Shuswap People." The paper in question is Dawson's "Notes on the Shuswap People of British Columbia" (1891).

It must be emphasized that Dawson's term "Shuswap people" not only denotes the Shuswap, or Secwépemc, people proper but also includes the Nlaka'pamux, Okanagan, Sinixt ("Lakes," Okanagan), and St'at'imc. Among these five "divisions" of the Interior Salish people, he calls the Secwépemc people themselves the "Shoo-wha-pa-moo," or "Shuswaps proper" (Secwepemc7úw̓i) (see chapter 4), "from whom the name here applied to the group of related tribes is derived" (Dawson 1891, 5). He identifies the territory of the Secwépemc as follows:

> The people of this tribe and speaking an identical dialect, possess the largest territory, which includes the Shuswap Lakes and Adams Lake, the valleys of the South and North Thompson Rivers, and nominally extends northward to Quesnel Lake, though so few Indians inhabit or hunt in that region that it is difficult there to fix the limit exactly. The furthest northern point on the Fraser reached by the Shoo-wha-pa-mooh, is the vicinity of Soda Creek; but to the south of the Chilcotin River their country extends to the west of the Fraser, of which river they claim both sides as far down as, and including the village of Kwe-kwe-a-kwet (Bob's Village [Qwiqwíyqwiyt]), situated nine miles below Big Bar Creek. They thus spread westward to the north of the Lillooets, and are the only people of the Shuswap tribes whose boundary matches with that of the Tinneh [Dene]. The country about Clinton and the valley of Hat Creek is part of their territory, including the village of Skwai-luh [Tsk̓wáy̓lacw], on Pavilion Creek. To the south they are bounded by the Thompsons and Okanagans. They extend nearly to Ashcroft, on the Thompson River, but do not include the Stlahl [St'ells] village there, which is Thompson. Eastwards, the boundary runs thence nearly along the watershed between the Nicola and Thompson, but Trout Lake, at the head of one branch of Guichon Creek, is claimed by the Shoo-wha-pa-mooh. Grande Prairie belongs to the Okanagans, but all the lower part of the Salmon River, with

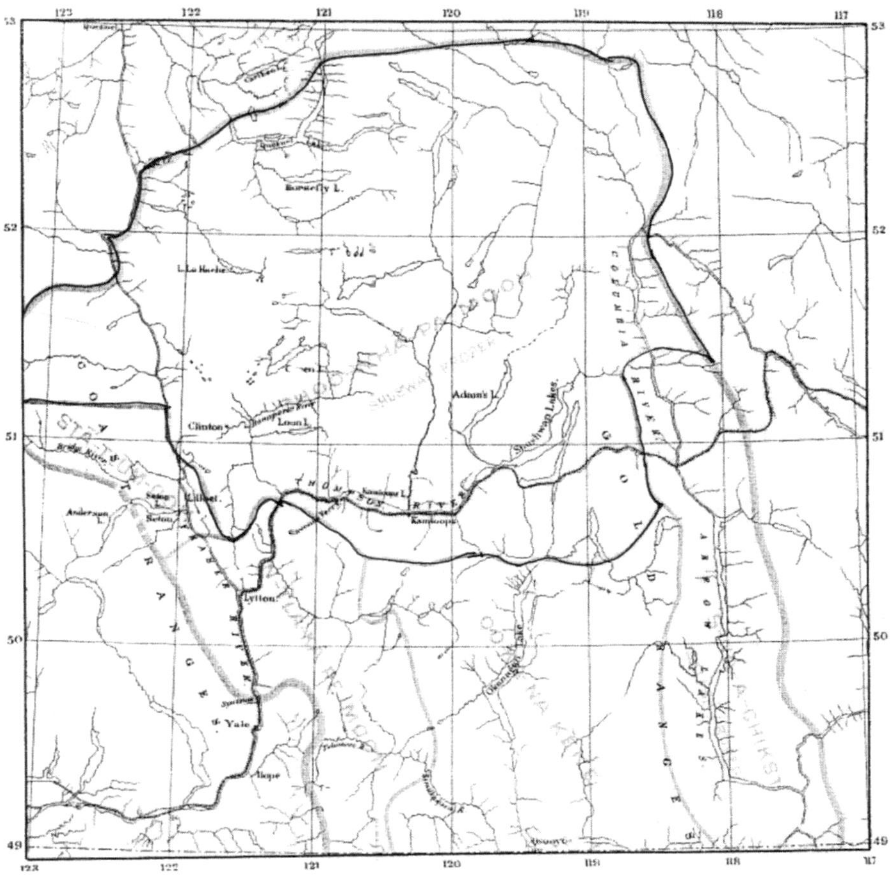

8.6 | George M. Dawson's "Map Shewing the Limits of the Shuswap People of British Columbia," 1891. It shows Dawson's understanding of the boundaries of the Secweépemc nation with neighbouring peoples.

> the Spallumcheen valley nearly as far south as the head of Okanagan Lake, is Shoo-wha-pa-mooh country. (Ibid.)

According to Dawson's map and description, Secwépemc territory takes in Quesnel Lake but not part of Bowron Lakes, and in the north the boundary is just short of 53 degrees latitude, leaving out the area toward McBride and Mount Robson, Yellowhead Pass being the northeastern-most point of Secwépemc territory. Dawson's map also does not include the territory in the Columbia River basin occupied by the Kinbaskets and does not include the Arrow Lakes, which were mainly occupied by the Sinixt, who were mostly of Okanagan ancestry. In comparing Dawson's map with Teit's 1909 map (see below), it is evident that Dawson's map includes only the area *exclusively* occupied by the Secwépemc during the mid-nineteenth century and leaves out areas of shared or overlapping use. The village Dawson records as "Kwe-kwe-a-kwet (Bob's Village)" is the same Qwiqwíyqwiyt ("blue all over") between Leon's Creek and High Bar on the Fraser River where Tllí7sa and his brothers became frozen into stone, and it is associated with Secwepemcúl̓ecw.

James Teit's Map, 1909

Teit's "Map Showing the Shuswap Territory" depicted Secwépemc territory and its boundaries with respect to seven named "divisions." The English term "division" is Teit's own. In Secwepemctsín, the names of the divisions all include a root word for a geographic area or location, combined with the lexical suffix *-emc* ("people"). Each division is comprised of a number of Indigenous "bands," which occupy a number of *ctsemtsyém̓ten* (ancestral villages), with one of these villages as its "headquarters."[2] Teit's list of Indigenous bands and villages in about 1850 shows thirty Indigenous bands, and he listed a "head-quarter" village for each of them, except the Arrow Lake Band (see below). Following the severe impact of mid-nineteenth-century epidemics, especially the smallpox epidemic of 1862–63, seventeen of these bands survived, and in the late 1870s and early 1880s, they became the bands that still exist as Indian bands under the Canadian Indian Act. The Secwépemc divisions named by Teit and associated with specific geographic areas of Secwepemcúl̓ecw include (as retranscribed from Teit's orthography into the Secwépemc practical alphabet):

- The Stk̓emlúpsemc/Stk̓emlúlepsemc[3] (Kamloops) division includes not only the Tk̓emlúpsemc, the people of the confluence of the North and South Thompson Rivers, but also the people of Skeetchestn in Deadman's Creek Valley near the head of Kamloops Lake. As main villages, Teit listed Tk̓emlúps and Skítsesten (Skeetchestn, "arriving place"), as well as numerous other historic villages at the mouth of the Tranquille River, at the mouth of Deadman's Creek, at Savona, along both shores of Kamloops Lake, and along the main Thompson River.
- The Sexqéltkemc[4] (Shuswap Lakes) division comprises the Secwépemc of the South Thompson River east of Monte Creek, Shuswap Lake, Spallumcheen, and Salmon River. "They hunt south along Salmon River, north on Adams Lake to the Columbia above Revelstoke, and east around Mabel and Sugar Lakes to Upper Arrow Lake" (Teit 1909, 455). They include the people at Sk̓atsín and Celéwt on both shores of the South Thompson River, at Cstálen on the west end of Little Shuswap Lake, at Qw7ewt on the eastern shore of Little Shuswap Lake, and at Splatsín (Spallumcheen) near Enderby. Teit (ibid.) also included the "Lakes," or Sinixt, in this division, a statement

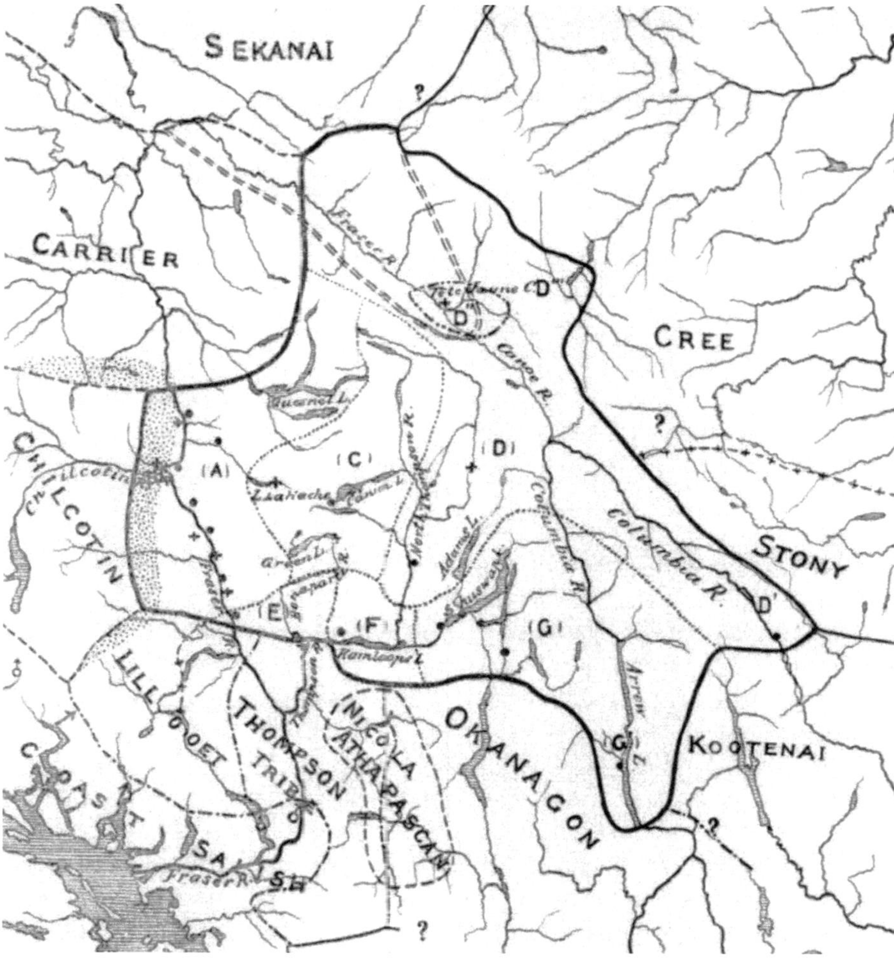

8.7 | James Teit's "Map Showing the Shuswap Territory," 1909. It shows "divisions" and external boundaries of the Secwépemc according to hunting and resource-harvesting territories described to Teit by Secwépemc people.

he later corrected (see below). Additional villages were in the densely settled Monte Creek to Pritchard area and in the Salmon Arm and Sek̓wméw̓s (Sicamous) areas.

- The Tqéqeltkemc comprise "people of the Upper Reaches" of the North Thompson River as far as Tete Jaune Cache and Jasper, as well as the Simpcw, the people of the mid-North Thompson River. The main villages were Tseqwtseqwélqw (part of the present reserve at Chu Chua near Barriere) and Pesqelqlélten on the upper North Thompson near Finn Creek. Additional members of this division had village sites at Tete Jaune Cache, and some wintered east of Yellowhead Pass as far as Jasper House. Teit also reckoned the Kinbaskets (Kenpésq̓t) of the Columbia River Valley among them, although they were also composed of families from the Adams Lake and Shuswap Lake, whose dialect prevailed as they settled on the upper Columbia (see below).

- The Sṫemcúlecwemc ("people of the cleared land or grasslands," describing the Cariboo area) are the people of the Fraser River area between Clinton and Soda Creek – comprising the villages of Pelltíq̓t (Clinton), Qwiqwíyqwiyt (High Bar), and Steq̓éws (Big Bar), whose members merged with the High Bar people – as well as the people of Xgéṫtem (Dog Creek), Tswécem̓c (Canoe Creek), Ṫéxelc (Williams Lake), Xatṡúll (Soda Creek), Cmetém̓ (Deep Creek), and Esk̓ét (Alkali Lake). Formerly, a large village with more than fifty pithouses existed at Kelly Creek. In addition, the Empire Valley Band, comprised of the Tsecwéptemc, who nearly all perished in the 1862 smallpox epidemic, was part of this division, living on the west side of the Fraser River.
- The Séṫemc (Canyon) people – *seṫ* apparently being the word for a deep, carved canyon like Farwell Canyon – included several Indigenous communities on the west bank of the Fraser River at the mouth of the Chilcotin River Canyon. Being more sedentary than all other communities and divisions, they suffered the greatest impact of the smallpox epidemic and as a division became "extinct," with the survivors settling among their relatives in neighbouring villages, mainly at Xgéṫtemc (Dog Creek) and at Esk̓ét (Alkali Lake) among the Sṫemcúlecwemc. The Esk̓ét people still refer to their ancestors and elders who lived or were born on the west side of the Fraser River as the Pestéwtemc ("across the river people") and do not think that this part of Secwépemc territory was relinquished. According to Teit (1909) the Séṫemc of the mid-1800s, before their dramatic population loss during the 1862–63 smallpox epidemic, had close relationships through intermarriage with Pesxíxnemc (Tsilhqot'in) people who lived among them.
- The Styétemc are the people of the Lake Plateau between the North Thompson and Fraser Rivers, including the village at Tsq̓éscen (Canim Lake) and formerly also Texṫlínten (Lac La Hache) and Pelltseq̓wmús ("has suckers," which was named after a lake on the upper Bonaparte River), whose survivors settled at Tsq̓éscen after the smallpox epidemic.
- The Sextsínemc are the "people of the lower shore," including the people of Sṫuxtéws (Bonaparte Band) on the main Thompson River and the Nek̓w7étkwemc ("people of the one river"), or Main Thompson Band, who lived on both sides of the Thompson River between Rocky Point and below Cornwalls just south of Ashcroft. Like the Séṫemc, their numbers were severely decimated as a result of epidemics, and the survivors joined their relatives at Sṫuxtéws and Skeetchestn. Teit also reckoned the people of Tṡk̓wáy̓lacw (Pavilion) as part of the Sextsínemc. In the 1980s Secwépemc

elders from Sť̓uxtéws also noted that the people of Sť̓ells (Asḥcroft)[5] used to be considered Secwépemc. Whereas the people of Tš̓kwáy̓lacw became St'at'imc due to increased intermarriage with Lillooet communities, Sť̓ells became reckoned as a Nlaka'pamux village due to continuous intermarriage with the latter.

THE SETTLEMENT OF THE KINBASKETS IN THE INVERMERE AREA

The following is Kinbasket elder Sheilagh Dehart's account of the migration of the Kinbaskets to the upper Columbia River Valley, which took place in various stages between the early decades of the 1800s and about 1845–46:[6]

> The young men at Adams Lake would go hunting. The first year, they took an old trail along Seymour Arm, went across the Columbia River and made camp at Downie Creek and then sailed up the Columbia River, when they came to a big lake, which was later named Kinbasket Lake. They did this journey each spring and returned to their winter homes at Adams Lake in the fall. A year or so later, the men were joined by two or three other young men from Chu Chua, one of which was named Yelheelna Kinbasket. This time when they arrived at Kinbasket Lake, they went up to Canoe Reach and on to Valemont, and explored both sides of Kinbasket Lake. They arrived at the Columbia River, and camped at Downie Creek where it enters the Columbia River. When they went home, they told the people about it, and the Elders told them "That's Kootenay Country, very dangerous." But the young men continued to explore. On the next trip, another group joined them and they made it to Boat Encampment. Boat Encampment junction became "Home" and the Indians lived there on and off.
>
> When the young men first started exploring, they didn't have a chief and they needed a leader so Chief Yelheelna Kinbasket became their chief. He was the first chosen Shuswap chief in the Columbia Valley. From the Boat Encampment they kept exploring south, eventually they got to Beavermouth. Eventually they found another route through the mountains which they cleared so that they could take their horses on the seasonal trek. This route went through Albert Canyon, Revelstoke, Eagle Pass (Spelqwax) and on to Adams Lake. They made another trail from Beavermouth to Revelstoke and then brought their horses, women and children from villages around Adams Lake. Over time, they moved their camp south of Golden near Parson and then to the vicinity

/continued

> of Reflection Lake, on the shore of the Columbia River and a few miles towards Spillimacheen. This is where Chief Yelheelna died.
>
> Yelheelna's son, Paul Ignatious Kinbasket was the next Shuswap Chief for the group. His Indian name means Fire. Shortly after Paul Ignatious became Chief, there was trouble among the men of the tribe. So the new Chief gathered his family and a few friends to trek to Kinbasket Lake to make it a permanent home. After staying near Reflection Lake for a while, they moved towards Brisco and then on to Edgewater. Their final move was to an area between Dry Gulch and Invermere, where they continued to stay in the pithouses in the wintertime. Chief Paul Ignatius brought the last big group of people over from the Chu Chua country. After that they came one by one.
>
> Paul Ignatius Kinbasket's son Pierre took over as Chief when Paul Ignatius was bothered by a "shortness of breath." Pierre had married Marianne on their last trip to Adams Lake, and they had their first child a year after he became Chief. Chief Pierre Kinbasket was the third and the last of the hereditary Shuswap chiefs in the Columbia Valley. His house was the first built but he found it too windy living by the church so he built a new three roomed house down at Stoddart Creek where the Setetkwa golf course is now. (Quoted in Shuswap Indian Band 2008, 26)

What were the reasons for the migration? In all likelihood, the area settled by the Kinbaskets had been at least intermittently occupied by Interior Plateau people for several thousand years, as is witnessed by numerous pithouse sites in the area. The move of the Kinbaskets into the Windermere area was thus more of a "resettlement" than a new migration outward. As Sheilagh Dehart's narrative indicates, Sexqéltkemc (Adams Lake) and Simpcw hunters had regularly travelled, camped, and hunted in the Columbia Valley previously. Family disputes in their home communities were one reason that Shuswap Band elders gave for the migration, as were the rich resources of the area, notably salmon, deer, and elk. The large elk herds of the area must have been especially tempting since elk had nearly disappeared from the core areas of Secwepemcúĺecw after the mid-1800s. Kinbasket elder Xavier Eugene added, "They were just more or less doing their thing, and they got in the middle of being here permanently when the Indian agent made the reserves ... So that's the only way that I can see it ... such a small number of our people came over. Because they happened to be here at the time when the reserves were designated" (Shuswap Indian Band 2008, 31). In other words, not long after the move of Secwépemc families into the Columbia Valley and Windermere area, the federal government's allocation of Indian reserves contributed to the Kinbaskets being regarded as "settled" there. It is important, however, to acknowledge the evidence, albeit scant, of Interior Salish pithouses in the area – which were not used by Ktunaxa people – and the ethnohistoric and ethnographic references to a Kinbasket Secwépemc presence in the area for resource use, camping, and travelling. Throughout their presence in the upper Columbia Valley, the Kinbasket frequently intermarried with the Ktunaxa, who occupied the same and adjacent areas.

Sheilagh Dehart's account associates the origin of the families who settled the Columbia Valley with the Secwépemc at Adams Lake and Chu Chua (Simpcw). Teit (1909, 460), who had not visited the Kinbaskets, noted that "the ancestors of these people belonged mostly to the Upper North Thompson Band. It seems, however, that some of them belonged to the Lower North Thompson Band, and a few came from the Adams Lake and Shuswap Lake area." Teit included them in the Tqéqeltkemc (North Thompson) division, stating that "their hunting-country extends on both sides of the Columbia, north to beyond Golden," as well as noting that their name Kenpésq̓t came from their former chief. Before the construction of the Mica Dam, the North Thompson people connected to the Canoe and Columbia Rivers by way of a trail from the North Thompson River near Avola that bypassed Tum Tum Lake.

The Secwepemctsín dialect of the Kinbaskets is a variety of Eastern Secwepemctsín associated with the Shuswap Lakes division rather than a variety of the Western Secwepemctsín dialect spoken by the Símpcwemc. This distinction suggests that the majority of the Kinbaskets may have been from the Adams Lake, Shuswap Lakes, and Splatsín areas.

Based on information from his Secwépemc consultants mainly between 1900 and 1903, Teit (1909, 450, 453–6) defined the external boundaries of the Secwépemc according to the "hunting grounds" described by the members of the different divisions. These formed the basis for his map of Secwépemc territory. The boundaries as thus described reflect the extent of Secwepemcúlecw in the late 1700s to mid-1800s. As discussed below, however, boundaries were by no means static over time but changed as a result of warfare, intermarriage, and peace treaties among nations led by local groups. Thus, in the west, the Sét̓emc "claimed the country back to within a short distance of Hanceville – some say to a place called Pestat [Pestéwt, 'across the river'] near the junction of Deer Creek and the Chilcotin River" (Teit 1909, 453), sharing the northern extent of their hunting grounds with the St̓emcúlecwemc. Near the Hanceville trail, a landmark rock called Xq̓ilyeteń re Sk̓elép (Coyote's Sweathouse) – different from the one encountered by the Qoa'qLqaL transformers on their journey up the Thompson River – marked the western boundary with the Pesxíxlemc (Tsilhqot'in) (see fig. 8.2).

As mentioned above, south of there, Cwelcéscen ("plenty of roots"), a mound on a tributary of Bridge River, was considered the boundary marker between the Secwépemc Sṫemcúlecwemc, the Tsilhqot'in, and the St'at'imc (Teit 1909, 453). The southwestern boundary of the Sextsínemc with the Nlaka'pamux and the St'at'imc was "near Ashcroft on the Main Thompson ... the lower part of Hat Creek, through Marble Canyon, to Pavilion and both sides of the Fraser near there" (ibid., 456). Finally, the southern boundary of the Secwépemc with the Tṡwéṅemc (Head-of-the-Lake Okanagan) and the Nlaka'pamux ran through the plateau near Stump Lake, south of the Thompson River and Kamloops Lake.

The Sṫemcúlecwemc, besides hunting on the east of the Fraser River between Xatṡúll and below High Bar, "claim as hunting grounds the country west of the Fraser for over thirty miles back, including some of the feeders of the Bridge River, all of Big Creek and other creeks emptying into the Fraser, north to Churn Creek," as well as Empire Valley, the Ground Hog Mountains, and land opposite Xatṡúll and Williams Lake on the west bank of the Fraser (Teit 1909, 453).

In the north and northeast, or the "upper reaches" of Secwepemcúl̓ecw, Teit (1909, 454) described the boundary of the Tqéqeltkemc (North Thompson people) as extending to the upper reaches of the Fraser River, to Robson Pass, and beyond to what is now Jasper. Teit (ibid., 546) was also told that the "country of the Upper Fraser River was part of the Secwépemc hunting grounds, and abounded in game and fur-bearing animals." On his map, he charted the area on the upper Fraser River between roughly the Bowron Lakes area and Tete Jaune Cache as "temporarily occupied by the Sekani" (ibid., 450). This "temporary occupation," according to the oral histories of warfare he recorded, happened as a result of the intrusion into Secwepemcúl̓ecw by parties of Sekani (Tseyk̓ene) during the latter part of the eighteenth century. After a major ambush by Sekani at Pesqlélten, the Tqéqeltkemc fishing ground on the upper North Thompson River, where the Sekani killed many people and took many of the women as slaves, a large group of warriors from the Sṫemcúlecwemc division and the Stk̓emlúpsemc division pursued and then attacked the Sekani, killing many of them and beating them back, thus reclaiming this part of the territory. Teit's 1909 map and territorial description also include all of Quesnel Lake as within Secwépemc territory.[7]

The Stk̓emlúpsemc hunted "in the country south to Stump Lake, in all the territory around Kamloops Lake, and along part of the South and main Thompson Rivers" (Teit 1909, 455). They also hunted to the headwaters of the Bonaparte River and north on the North Thompson to near Louis Creek (ibid., 456). The Sextsínemc "claim the valley of the Bonaparte River to near Ashcroft, and the lower part of Hat Creek, through Marble Canyon to Pavilion, and both sides of the Fraser River there" (ibid., 455).

Teit (1909, 455) also gave a detailed description of how far the Sexqéltkemc (people of the Shuswap Lakes and Enderby areas) travelled and hunted, bordering on the land used by the Okanagan and Sinixt ("Lakes," Okanagan) peoples: "They hunt south along Salmon River, north on Adams Lake to the Columbia above Revelstoke, and east around Mabel and Sugar Lakes to Upper Arrow Lake. Sometimes they hunted even beyond the latter in the mountains east of Lardeau and Nakusp."

In sum, during the first part of the 1900s – the time to which Teit's and Dawson's data pertain, in that they record memories of elders who were alive during the late 1800s and into the 1900s – there was thus a sense of distinct boundaries of the Secwépemc with neighbouring nations. This sense of a distinct territory with boundaries existed not only among European visitors and traders but also among the Secwépemc and neighbouring nations. Such boundaries were marked by watersheds and mountain ranges; in many cases, however, there existed arbitrarily established boundary markers. These markers, usually accompanied by distinct place names, often commemorated events of past conflict or peace treaties where the Secwépemc ancestors had settled disputes. In addition, boundaries often included overlapping areas of land use, especially in "border town" areas that featured intermarriage between neighbouring groups.

WHO ARE THE SINIXT ("LAKES") PEOPLE?

In his book on the Shuswap, Teit (1909, 455) mentioned the "Arrow Lake band" as a "small band of Shuswap located on Lower Arrow Lake, where they have a reserve, and hunt the country as far north as Revelstoke," adding them to the Shuswap Lakes division. He also noted that the "Arrow Lake band" "intermarried a great deal with the Kootenai, and formerly sometimes with the Okanagon of the Columbia." While gathering the information for his Shuswap monograph, Teit had, in fact, not visited the Arrow Lakes area. In his fieldnotes for 1910–13, after he had visited the Arrow Lakes and Okanagan areas, he corrected his earlier statements:

> In my paper on the Shuswap I allowed the Shuswap the territory along the Arrow Lakes almost down to Robson. I had not then been in that district, and was misled by some statements of the Shuswap of the Shuswap Lake region, which appeared to be corroborated by white testimony, to the effect that the Arrow Lake country was former Shuswap territory, partly occupied in recent years by Colville Indians chiefly for

/continued

> hunting and trapping purposes. This was not correct. The Lake tribe occupied from very early times all the country in British Columbia as outlined on the accompanying map, and I have been unable so far to collect any evidence that any part of the territory was ever occupied by other tribes. Further inquiry among the Shuswap confirm this. The only part seemingly in doubt is the extreme north, the old Revelstoke band having been much mixed with Shuswap. (Quoted in Bouchard and Kennedy 1986, 78)

In these fieldnotes, Teit also wrote,

> The Kootenay mouth people say emphatically that the Arrow Lake Band are their own kin and speak the exact same language as themselves. They have intermarried from time to time with Shuswap and in a less degree with Kootenay. At the present the Arrow Lake Band is made up of some 24 who may be called Lakes and one Shuswap (from Spallumcheen [Splatsín]) and one Kootenay (from Kootenay Lake), both women married there, making about 26 altogether. They were all mentioned by name to me and some of them are cousins and other relatives to the Kootenay mouth band (the latter number 11: 10 Lakes and 1 Thompson). (Quoted in Bouchard and Kennedy 1985, 10)

Of the northern boundary of the Sinixt ("Lakes"), Teit noted, "Lakes – all country along both banks [of] Columbia … up to beyond Revelstoke. Only men went above Revelstoke for hunting and trapping – considering near border [with] Shuswap both tribes hunted and trapped river above Revelstoke but Lakes most numerous" (quoted in ibid.). In a letter to Franz Boas dated 20 May 1909, Teit observed, "They also had no permanent camps north of Revelstoke although they claimed the right to hunt and trap a few miles north of Revelstoke, but the country a little north of Revelstoke (about 15 miles N and beyond) was considered Shuswap … Numbers of them [Shuswap] came across the mountains to Revelstoke where sometimes in the fall there were as many Shuswap as Lakes" (quoted in ibid.).

Known as Sinixt – from Collville-Okanagan Sngaytskstx ("people of the Dolly Varden trout") – the (Arrow) Lakes people should be considered a different and distinct Interior Salish people. Having already been reduced in numbers due to epidemics by the time that the 1846 Oregon Treaty established the 49th parallel as the border, many Sinixt remained near their traditional fishery at Kettle Falls and eventually settled on the Colville Reserve in the United States. With few Sinixt remaining in Canada, and with many of the remaining Sinixt having intermarried among the Secwépemc and Ktunaxa and having thus lost Indian status in their community of origin, the Arrow Lake Band was officially declared "extinct" as a band under the Canadian Indian Act in 1956. Since the 1980s, descendants of Sinixt on both sides of the border have fought for their recognition as a distinct Aboriginal group, much of whose land is in British Columbia, and in 2008 they launched a lawsuit claiming Aboriginal title to Crown lands in the West Kootenays, including the Arrow Lakes north to Revelstoke and the Slocan Valley (see Bouchard and Kennedy 1985, 1986; Kennedy and Bouchard 2009; and Pryce 1999).

Secwépemc Laws of Land Tenure and Access

> [The first white people] found the people of each tribe supreme in their own territory, and having tribal boundaries known and recognized by all. The country of each tribe was just the same as a very large farm or ranch (belonging to all the people of the tribe) from which they gathered their food and clothing, etc., fish which they got in plenty for food, grass and vegetation on which their horses grazed and the game lived, and much of which furnished materials for pipes, utensils and tools, etc., trees which furnished firewood, materials for houses and utensils, plants, roots, seeds, nuts and berries which grew abundantly and were gathered in their season just the same as the crops on a ranch, and used for food; minerals and shells, etc., which were used for ornaments and for plants, etc., water which was free to all. Thus, fire, water, food, clothing, and all the necessaries of life were obtained in abundance from the lands of each tribe, and all the people had equal rights of access to everything they required. You will see the ranch of each tribe was the same as its life, and without it the people could not have lived. (Chiefs of the Shuswap, Okanagan, and Couteau Tribes 1910)

As we noted at the outset of this chapter, the above quotation from the 1910 "Memorial to Sir Wilfrid Laurier" by the Interior chiefs mentions "boundaries known and recognized by all," thus indicating a conscious sense of a defined territory with marked boundaries. In addition, it invokes important principles of the land tenure of each nation. By referring to the land as a ranch "belonging to all the people of the tribe," the chiefs spoke of their vital connection to their homelands as sustaining their peoples. The chiefs also insisted on the principle of *collective land tenure* at the level of the "tribe," or nation, as opposed to land ownership resting with the village group or with families, let alone with individuals. In fact, in referring to distinct territories of tribes with recognized external boundaries, along with a system of "tribal," or common, land tenure, the Interior chiefs strongly invoked the concept of Aboriginal or Indigenous *nationhood*. Their words conveyed the concept of the Secwépemc, Nlaka'pamux, St'at'imc, Syilx (Okanagan), and others as distinct *nations*, thus refusing to surrender to the nucleation of these nations into "bands" imposed by the Canadian government in the 1876 Indian Act.

Teit (1909, 572) explained the Secwépemc concept of land tenure, which was largely shared with the other Interior nations: "All the land and hunting grounds were looked upon as tribal property all parts of which were open to every member of the tribe. Of course, every band had its common recognized hunting, trapping and fishing places, but members of other bands were allowed to use them whenever they desired … Fishing places were also tribal property, including salmon-stations … At the lakes every one had the privilege of trapping trout and erecting weirs."

Teit (1909, 573) also noted that "berry patches were tribal property, but picking was under tribal control. All the large and valuable berry spots were *looked after* by the chief of the band in whose district they were situated" (emphasis added). Of root-digging grounds, Teit (ibid., 582) stated that they were also "common tribal property. Some people of the Northern Fraser River bands laid a claim on the root-digging grounds of Quesnel Lake, where very large lily-roots grow, but these claims were not recognized by the rest of the tribe." In other words, like the chiefs of 1910, Teit emphasized a tribal, or nationwide, system of land tenure and access to resources, with the chiefs of local bands, on behalf of their communities, acting as resource stewards, or caretakers, for the benefit of all people of the nation. Thus it was not the Indigenous communities, or "bands," that had exclusive rights over resources; rather, by descent or blood, all the members of a nation had access to the resources within the nation. Local communities, headed by their chiefs and specifically appointed resource stewards, called *yecwmíńmen*, were considered to be the caretakers of resources and tracts of land where their people lived.

In his discussion of Nlaka'pamux land tenure, which he regarded as identical to Secwépemc land tenure, Teit (1900, 293) provided further details: "Of course each [Nlaka'pamux] band had their usual hunting-places, naturally those parts of the country nearest to their respective homes; but Indians from other villages, or other divisions of the tribe, frequently hunted in each other's hunting-grounds without being considered intruders; and sometimes hunting-parties representing two or three tribal divisions would hunt over the summer hunting-grounds of another division without rousing any feelings of resentment." After citing an instance of such resource use, he concluded, "The hunting-territory seems to have been common property of the whole tribe. Among the Spences Bridge and Nicola Bands any member of the Shuswap and Okanogan tribes who was related to them by blood was allowed full access to their hunting-grounds, the same as one of themselves … If, however, a person who was not related to a Thompson Indian were caught hunting trapping or gathering bark or roots, within the recognized limits of the tribal territory, he was liable to forfeit his life" (ibid.).

To substantiate his argument for common, or Secwépemc-wide, ownership of and access to resources, Teit (1909, 572) mentioned a case of the Northern Secwépemc trying to assert exclusive control of their hunting areas at some point in the past, likely during the early 1800s. The Southern Secwépemc challenged them on this assertion, causing the Northern Secwépemc to abandon their claim to exclusive ownership of a part of Secwepemcúl̓ecw. From what Teit (ibid., 575) tells us, this insistence on exclusive control of hunting grounds by a smaller group within the nation coexisted with the Northern Secwépemc's adoption of a clan and crest system imported from the coastal tribes, apparently not long before the arrival of Europeans in Secwépemc country (see also Furniss 2004).

Among the communities of the Fraser Canyon division, and subsequently Soda Creek, Dog Creek, Pavilion High Bar, and the neighbouring Styétemc (Canim Lake) division, a system of ranked classes and crest groups was being established during the early 1800s. Adapted at that time by these communities from their western neighbours – who had previously adapted these crest groups from coastal peoples – and having spread to all the St̓emcúlecwemc and Sét̓emc communities by 1850, this system included a ranked "class of nobility" as "clan chiefs" and hereditary clan crests, along with ornaments, dances, and ceremonies enacted at festivals. Membership in the crest groups of nobles was by initiation, "which followed a short period of fasting and training, in a manner similar to novices of religious societies. These groups of the nobility were strictly hereditary" (Teit 1909, 576). The "nobility" included "chiefs" and "chiefs' descendants" in both the male and female line, and they comprised one-half to two-thirds of the population. The crest groups in existence in the Fraser Canyon division included the Grizzly Bear, Raven, Wolf, Eagle, and Beaver, and their emblems were displayed on fishing grounds, graves, houses, and other property. The other groups were "commoners," who comprised a variety of crests, such as Black Bear, Moose, Caribou, Elk, Deer, Sheep, Goat, species of grouse, Frog, Salmon, Service Berry, Rain, Rockslide, and others. From Teit's (1909, 575ff) description, it appears that these "commoner" societies were not hereditary but were by association and interest group, involving a short initiation. Thus hunters belonged to the big game societies, whereas women joined the Service Berry society. Finally, those of the lowest rank were slaves, who were people captured in warfare and raids; however, unlike the slaves of the North Pacific Coast, whose enslavement cast a long-lasting stigma on their ranked status, the slaves of Interior Plateau society became integrated into the communities of their captors and intermarried with them.

The rank and crest group system, it appears, involved a short-lived adaptation from coastal societies mediated by the neighbouring St'at'imc and Tsilhqot'in societies, which had immediate ties to the coast:

> It seems certain that the whole system outlined above was originally foreign to the Shuswap tribe, and has been introduced from the … Chilcotin and Lillooet tribes, who themselves have borrowed these customs from their neighbors of the coast … the Chilcotin mainly from the Bella Coola, and the Lillooet principally from the Squamish … Although the method of dividing the people into three classes originated at an earlier date than the crest groups and societies, still I think there is no doubt of its being derived from the same sources. Probably the original families of each band, perhaps only the chief and relatives, became the nobility; while all accessions to the band were classed as common people, without any rights to land or fisheries. (Teit 1909, 581)

It appears, then, that this hereditary rank and crest system, headed up by "chiefs" of families, was a device at a given time to move away from the system and laws of collective ownership of and access to Secwepemcúl̓ecw and toward a system of exclusive, hereditary, small-group property rights. However, it was short-lived and restricted to the communities in the Fraser River, Fraser Canyon, and Canim Lake divisions, and having come into existence over no more than two generations in the early to mid-1800s and thus lacking a long or deep tradition, "these customs soon dropped out of use" (Teit 1909, 582) following the decimation of the Northern and Western Secwépemc communities by smallpox in the early 1860s, especially the Fraser Canyon division. Little was remembered about them by the early 1900s, and elders in the 1980s and 1990s did not remember this stratified system.

Franz Boas (1890, 86), whose own Secwépemc research consisted of a few days of work with unknown informants while travelling through the Tk̓emlúps (Kamloops) area in 1888 and again in 1894 and 1897, thought that there were "family owned" hunting grounds among the Secwépemc, but he gave no details or examples that substantiate this claim. Likewise, George M. Dawson (1891, 14) wrote of "hereditary" hunting grounds, "each family having its own particular hunting place," and noted that he received much of the information on "customs" from J.W. MacKay, the local Indian agent (ibid., 13). Like Boas, he provided no details or examples. Yet another reference to hunting and trapping grounds "belonging" to families as "allotted estates" was given by settler D.S. Mitchell of the Shuswap Lake area. Mitchell (1925, 4) noted, "They had Chiefs, councillors, and held Courts. Their tribal country had been sub-divided or apportioned among the different Indian families, as trapping, or hunting grounds: each family had an allotted estate. The Sa-how-ya, or north east arm, had belonged to the Sinastin family. The Kowatnimh-at-kwa, from Sicamous to Mara, had belonged to the Katl-noo-mat family. The Finn settlement at White Lake had belonged to Noohk-Kwiout. The Schwn-a-meen or Seymour Arm, had belonged to the families of Sil-sa-leitsa, and Silpachn, and so on." Mitchell, who admired Secwépemc culture and resource use and deplored settlers' destruction of salmon runs and habitat (see chapter 5), was trying to understand and express Secwépemc land tenure in terms that would make Europeans value it. Thus he described "families" with "allotted estates" as well as winter residences and summer resort-like residences, similar to the Scottish gentry! At the same time, the quotation above includes somewhat accurately written Secwépemc names of individual men alive during the late nineteenth century according to baptism records, like Sil-s-leitsa, Silpachn, and Katl-noo-mat. So what do we make of this account? Given Teit's decades of residence, travel, and research in Interior Salish territories, his knowledge of the language, and the general high quality of his ethnographic work, he appears to be the more accurate and reliable source. It is quite plausible that Mitchell was actually referring to the traplines that by the mid-1920s had become registered to individuals and their families in Eastern Secwépemc territory, as in other parts of Secwepemcúlecw. It is also possible that what he was aware of and thus referred to was the fact that particular families headed up by male individuals were considered to be the *yecwmíńmen* (caretakers) of particular areas, although not at the exclusion of others harvesting resources in those areas. Adams Lake elder Joe Stanley Michel (2005, 85) echoed this idea when he remarked,

> It's whatever needs to be looked after. Sometime the game would have left the valley all together. There is no game. And with some negotiation they can ask the people in the other valleys permission to trap and fish and gather food material in that valley. And this was no big deal. It happened quite often that some valleys would have no animals in it, or the plants in that valley would not grow that well that year. So the whole area was – in just by friendly negotiations they said, "Come over. Maybe all the deer have come over this side of the mountain and you, you don't have any in your valley." So there's a friendly way of looking after each other.
>
> The idea of private ownership was foreign to us, but looking after things was not foreign. I don't know if you can understand the difference between the two.
>
> And this is where we ran in to conflict with the new settlers when they began fencing off areas and saying, "Now this is private land." And we, our People were puzzled by this, and some even said "How come you left your private land across the ocean, left your cemeteries, left your traditions, left your people, and now you come tell this is private land." So there was conflict in that area, and still is.

Access to fishing resources was no different: all individuals who were born into a nation or who had ancestors from that nation were allowed to fish for

8.8 | Joe Stanley Michel of Cstálen (Adams Lake Band), ca. 2000. He was a well-known storyteller and champion of the Secwépemc language.

salmon and other fish on the fishing grounds of that nation. This principle extended to resource access on the basis of intermarriage. As the late elder Sam Mitchell of Cácl̓ep (Fountain) explained to Steven Romanoff (1992, 251) about the Bonaparte Secwépemc's access to the productive Cácl̓ep fishery on the Fraser River, "If the head guy has daughters who marry out, the sons-in-law live there because that's how they fish and gather. That's how they get grouped up … That's how Shuswap came here. They came down and saw lots of fish and girls." Although, especially among the St'at'imc and some Fraser River Secwépemc, there is documented "family" ownership of fishing rocks (Bouchard and Kennedy 1992; Romanoff 1992), this individualized system of ownership could well be related to the high-maintenance efforts required of fishing rocks. These efforts entail the building and maintenance of platforms, throwing white rocks into the river to create better visibility of fish where the water is clear, and the clean-up of the site. Sam Mitchell's testimony implies that the "owner" of a fishing rock was also its main caretaker and that he allowed others the use of the fishing site after his family had harvested fish.

The Secwépemc and Nlaka'pamux system of land tenure and access to resources, which extended to the entire Interior Plateau, thus involved *joint access* to the common territory of a nation, based on blood and kinship ties, which then extended to the territories of other nations, in a secondary sense, by way of having relatives in those nations. Angelo Anastasio (1972) recognized how this system of resource use and access among nations functioned to accommodate seasonal variations in game, plants, and fish by providing individuals and thus their extended families with a network of access not only to resources within their own Indigenous nation of birth but also to resources in other nations where they had ancestors and relatives, as long as these ties were kept alive and thus recognized.

James Brow (1972), an American anthropologist, carried out brief research with Northern Secwépemc people in 1966. Some of his consultants were Esk'ét (Alkali Lake) elders David Johnson, Alice Belleau, and Pierre Squinahan, all born before 1900. Brow did not ask these elders whether they had any concept of Secwepemcúlecw as a commonly held territory in a political, social, or economic sense, assuming a "boundary" between the Northern Secwépemc and Kamloops area Secwépemc. When Brow (ibid., 49) asked David Johnson, "before the Europeans came, where was the boundary between Kamloops Shuswap and Shuswap territory?" he was told, "there was no fixed boundary. Each band had its special fishing places and places where it used to build its winter villages, but the land … belonged to all the Shuswap and anyone could hunt where he wanted," the latter referring to the habitual, but not exclusively owned, fishing places and ancestral villages of the Indigenous bands.[8]

Among Eastern Secwépemc elders, the same concept of common Secwépemc land tenure prevailed. At a national unity meeting in 1983 where members of all parts of the nation explored ways of working together as a nation, the late Chief Harvey Jules of Adams Lake reminded everyone that Secwépemc territory was jointly owned and shared by all Secwépemc.

Likewise, Secwépemc elder Mary Thomas (2001, 20) of Neskonlith also unequivocally referred to the same idea when she stated, "We traveled a lot. There was no such thing as private property. All the Secwépemc dialect people shared the whole territory of the Secwépemc Nation. Nothing was private property: we always shared."

In recent years, Secwépemc elders, many of them deceased now, continued to state that the use of resources in Secwépemc territory, in the late elder Billy Porter's words, was "wide open" to all people of Secwépemc ancestry and that no band or community exclusively owned resource-producing areas at the exclusion of other Secwépemc bands and individuals. Neskonlith elder Sarah Deneault also commented on the Secwépemc as one people, who were, however, split up into separate governing units, or bands, by the federal Department of Indian Affairs:

Kellklláw̓sis re qelmúcw m-emátntlses ṫek band.
Splitting up the people and calling them by *band*.

Yerí7 westám ṫe tsqwatstn.[9]
Nowadays, those are the groups of people we have.

Yerí7 Kamloops Band *rí7 nek̓ú7 t̓e tsqwatstn.*
The Kamloops Band are one group of people.

Neskonlith ri7 nek̓ú7 t̓e tsqwatstn.
Neskonlith are one group of people.

Adams Lake *rí7 nek̓ú7 cú7tsa.*
Adams Lake are yet another group.

Yerí7 kellklláw̓sis re Indian agent, Indian Affairs, *tsam̓át.sta.*
Those were separated by what is called the Indian agent, Indian Affairs.

K̓all le q̓7ásas, e t̓hánas ri7 re tsqwatstn ri7 nerí7.
But long ago, wherever they were, they were one group of people.

Nek̓úsa ri7 t̓e tsyam t̓lu7 wa7 t̓hánas.
They were one group of people wherever they lived.

Yerí7 t̓e tsqwátstn ri7.
They were one group of people.

Thus, overwhelmingly, the historical and ethnographic evidence, combined with the testimony of living and recently deceased Secwépemc elders, suggests that the Secwépemc concept of land tenure in the nineteenth and early twentieth centuries was defined by a concept of nationhood. It entailed the collective ownership of and access to all resources within Secwepemcúl̓ecw by all people of Secwépemc ancestry, with particular communities or Indigenous bands, led by their chiefs, acting as the local caretakers and protectors of land and resources. To further underscore this point, if the Secwépemc had had a sense of exclusive Indigenous band ownership during the late 1800s and early 1900s, there was no reason for them not to indicate such a concept of exclusive smaller-group ownership in their "Memorial to Sir Wilfrid Laurier" (Chiefs of the Shuswap, Okanagan, and Couteau Tribes 1910). Instead, they strongly emphasized the collective nature, at the Secwépemc nation level, of land tenure.

Boundary Maintenance: Treaties, Wars, and Intermarriage

Our tribal territories, which we have held from time immemorial, often at the cost of blood. (Chiefs of the Shuswap, Couteau, and Thompson Tribes et al. 1911)

The oral history record gives abundant evidence of the ways that boundary disputes between the Secwépemc and neighbouring nations were settled long before the arrival of Europeans. Throughout the centuries before Europeans arrived in Secwepemcúlecw, in numerous instances, the Secwépemc made treaties with outside nations to put an end to a dispute and to settle disputed boundaries. Teit's (1930a, 229ff) posthumous monograph on the Okanagan, Flathead, and Coeur d'Alene provides details of a pre-Confederation treaty that redefined the boundary between Secwépemc and Douglas Lake Okanagan territory, describing how Pelkamulox III (Pelk̓múlecw, "he rolls over the earth"), the chief of the Douglas Lake area, who had succeeded his father and grandfather of the same name, and Chief "Kwolila" of Tk̓emlúps negotiated a peace treaty after several generations of warfare and raids between the Secwépemc of the Tk̓emlúps division and the Secwépemc of the Okanagan:

> Pelkamulox [the son of a chief of the same name who had moved north from Spokane territory to live among the Okanagan] became a noted chief and was known far and wide. During his early life he was much engaged in war. These wars commenced in his father's time or before and continued for many years – many Okanagan as well as people of other tribes being killed. Salixw, where he made his headquarters was considered the chief seat of the Okanagon tribe (or at least of the northern division). The old name of the place is said to have been Okanaqen. Pelkamulox built a fort here of stone and afterwards the place became generally known as Salixw [Salíllcw], "heaped-up [stone] house," with reference to the fortifications of stone … This place is said to have been impregnable and war parties of Thompson, Shuswap, Kutenai and others who assaulted it were easily beaten off. Kwolila,[10] the Kamloops chief, had heard of the many attacks by enemy war parties on Pelkamulox and determined to go and see him. His people tried to dissuade him, telling him it was very dangerous for any one to visit him, for his people had been attacked so often that they trusted no one and attacked all strangers on sight who approached their place. Seeing that Kwolila was determined to go, the Shuswap and the people of Nkamapeleks who were at the time a mixture of Shuswap and Okanagon, offered to accompany him in an armed body, but he refused their offer, saying he would go alone. As he was leaving, his people told him, "Pelkamulox's people will kill you before they know whom you are, and even if they know, they may kill you." Kwolila answered, "I am Pelkamulox's brother, and I will go and see him alone." Arriving on the open ground before Pelkamulox's house, the people ran out to meet him in battle array. Pelkamulox recognized him and was glad to see him. He took him to his house and kept him as his guest for a long time. Kwolila advised Pelkamulox to forsake Salixw and go north with him. He told him, "Salixw is a bad place to live in. You will always have trouble as long as you stay there." Pelkamulox was persuaded. It was early summer, and he and his people traveled north with Kwolila to Komkenatkwe [K̓emqenétkwe, "headwaters"],

> now called Fish Lake, in the Nicola country. This place was at that time in Shuswap territory, for the Shuswap claimed the country south of Kamloops around the head of the Nicola River. Stump Lake, Douglas Lake, Fish Lake, and Chaperon Lake were all in Shuswap country. This country at that time was full of elk and deer, and there were also many sheep, bear and other game. Prairie chicken, grouse of all kinds, and waterfowl were plentiful, and the lakes teemed with fish. Here at Fish Lake Kwolila made a lasting agreement with Pelkamulox, giving him the perpetual use over all the Shuswap territory of the upper Nicola Valley, south, east and west of Chaperon Lake, comprising Douglas Lake and Fish Lake … Kwolila said, "you will have the country for yourself and your people as your own. I will live as your neighbor at Toxoxitcen [Tsec7uc7ú7tsen, "place where they came to an agreement," Chaperon Lake] and will retain all the country from there north. You will make Fish Lake your headquarters in the summer and I will summer at Chaperon Lake so that we may be close neighbors part of the year. You will give me your daughter, Kokoimalks [Qwiqwimélqs, "blue robe"?], to be my foster child, and she will always live with me, but your son you will keep with yourself.

This treaty is remembered to this day by the people of Sp'áxmen (Douglas Lake) and the Secwépemc people of the Stk̓emlúpsemc division as the Fish Lake Accord.[11] Teit's (1930a, 170) list of Okanagan area place names mentions "Fish Lake" as being at the headwaters of the Nicola River, the name of a small settlement there being Komkona'tko (K̓emqenétkwe, "head waters").[12] Information presented by J. Michael Thoms (2002) suggests that the "Fish Lake" of the accord is Pennask Lake, situated at the headwaters of the Nicola River, and he also mentions its Indigenous name as being "K̓emqenétkwe," as remembered by a Douglas Lake elder in the 1960s. In 2013 the late Clarence Jules Sr of Tk̓emlúps verified Pennask Lake as being identified with the Fish Lake of the accord.

Genealogical connections of various families to Kwolila and Pelkamulox continue to be recognized. The Fish Lake Accord tells us important things about the existence of precontact treaty making among Indigenous nations of the Plateau and about the mechanisms by which Interior Salish nations approached, negotiated, and maintained such treaties. Notably, Pelkamulox and Kwolila reminded each other that they were brothers, in that both were the sons of the second Pelkamulox, the Douglas Lake chief being his son by a Spokane Okanagan mother and the Kamloops chief being his son by a Tk̓emlúpsemc (Kamloops Secwépemc) mother. Reminding each other of their close blood ties as *uq̓wiyéws* (siblings of same sex to each other) is what allowed them to reconnect and to establish a political relationship on the basis of blood relationship. As one of the terms of the treaty, Kwolila surrendered

8.9 | Chief Clarence Jules Sr of Tk̓emlúps (Kamloops), 2012.

part of the area his people had advanced into but at the same time established an area of overlapping boundaries and land use with his half-brother. Living side by side during the summer season allowed them to implement the shared boundaries, to monitor each other's access to resources, and to maintain peaceful relations in the spirit of relatives. In exchange for giving up part of the land that the Secwépemc had advanced into, Kwolila asked Pelkamulox to surrender his daughter, but not his son, to him, to be adopted and raised by him. Having been raised among the Tk̓emlúps Secwépemc, Kokoimalks would marry into the Secwépemc nation, thus further consolidating the kinship alliance between the two groups.

Another instance of this kind is the treaty recorded in 1895 between the Secwépemc, Stony, and Ktunaxa regarding their respective hunting grounds in the area where the Kinbasket Secwépemc had established themselves by

8.10 (*overleaf*) | Genealogy of nine generations of the Secwépemc descendants of Chief Pelkamulox I (born ca. 1670) and his grandsons Pelkamulox III and Kwolila, who negotiated the Fish Lake Accord in the 1760s or 1770s to re-establish peace between the Secwépemc and Douglas Lake Okanagan. Through the younger generations in the genealogy, most families in Skeetchestn and Tk̓emlúps (Kamloops) and some families in other communities connect to these ancestors, as do many in the Syilx (Okanagan) and Nlaka'pamux nations.

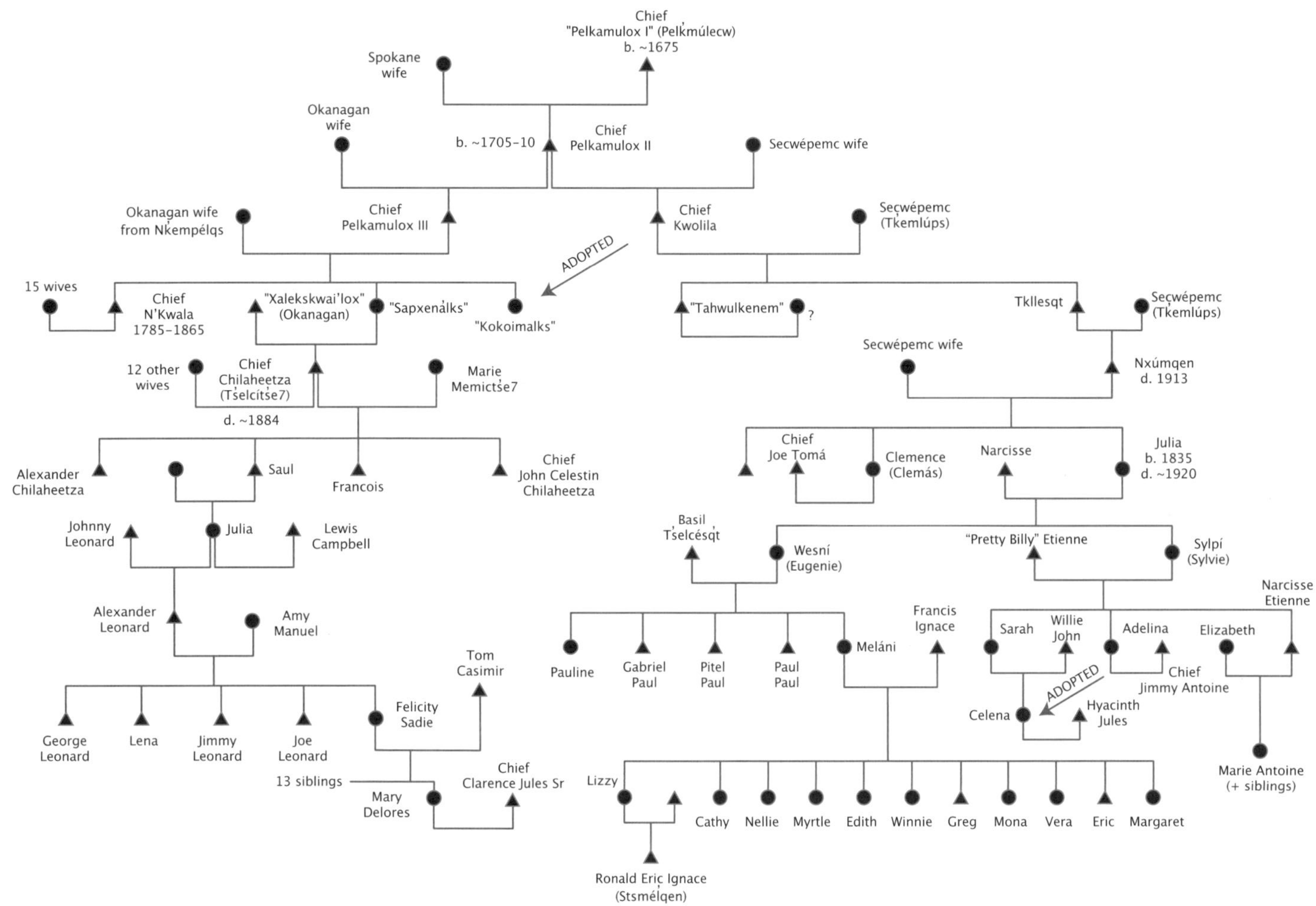
Chief
"Pelkamulox I" (Pelk̓múlecw)
b. ~1675
Spokane wife
Okanagan wife
b. ~1705–10
Chief Pelkamulox II
Secwépemc wife
Okanagan wife from Nk̓empélqs
Chief Pelkamulox III
ADOPTED
Chief Kwolila
Sec̓wépemc (Tk̓emlúps)
15 wives
Chief N'Kwala 1785–1865
"Xalekskwai'lox" (Okanagan)
"Sapxenálks"
"Kokoimalks"
"Tahwulkenem"
?
Tkllesqt
Sec̓wépemc (Tk̓emlúps)
Secwépemc wife
Nxúmqen d. 1913
12 other wives
Chief Chilaheetza (Ts̓elcíts̓e7)
d. ~1884
Marie Memicts̓e7
Alexander Chilaheetza
Saul
Francois
Chief John Celestin Chilaheetza
Chief Joe Tomá
Clemence (Clemás)
Narcisse
Julia b. 1835 d. ~1920
Johnny Leonard
Julia
Lewis Campbell
Basil Ts̓elcésq̓t
Wesní (Eugenie)
"Pretty Billy" Etienne
Sylpí (Sylvie)
Alexander Leonard
Amy Manuel
Tom Casimir
Narcisse Etienne
Francis Ignace
Sarah
Willie John
Adelina
Elizabeth
Pauline
Gabriel Paul
Pitel Paul
Paul Paul
Meláni
Chief Jimmy Antoine
ADOPTED
Celena
Hyacinth Jules
George Leonard
Lena
Jimmy Leonard
Joe Leonard
Felicity Sadie
Chief Clarence Jules Sr
13 siblings
Mary Delores
Lizzy
Cathy
Nellie
Myrtle
Edith
Winnie
Greg
Mona
Vera
Eric
Margaret
Marie Antoine (+ siblings)
Ronald Eriç Ignace (Stsmélqen)

8.11 | Ike Willard, here in a First World War uniform, and his sister Agnes Jules, 1918. He was from Tk̓emlúps (Kamloops) but married Adeline Willard of Neskonlith and lived there most of his adult life.

or before the 1840s (see above). As George M. Dawson (1891, 5) found out, "The emigrants made friends with some Stoney Indians who were in the habit of crossing the Rocky Mountains by the Howse Pass, for the purpose of taking salmon in the Columbia. Supported by these allies, the Shoo-wha-pa-mooh [Secwépemc] colonists were able to hold their own till the influx of the whites occurred and prevented further overt acts against them." By the 1890s, however, game had become scarce on the eastern slope of the Rocky Mountains. In the presence of Indian agent Robert Leslie Thomas Galbraith, the chiefs and spokespeople of the three nations – Chief Pierre Kinbasket, Chiefs Abel, Patrick, and Pielle of the Ktunaxa, and Chief John Cheneka of the Stony, along with some other "Kootenay and Shuswap Indians numbering in all about 25" – discussed the issue in 1895 and decided, in the words of Patrick, the headman of St Mary's Reserve, that the "Stonies may come and hunt in these parts, but do not want them to cross the Columbia River, and they must also attend to their fields and cattle during the seven months closed season" (Shuswap Nation Tribal Council 2015, 14). Likewise, Chief Charlie Kinbasket – brother of Pierre Kinbasket – agreed, "I know that the Stonies' heart must have been sore when they heard they could not hunt this side of the Rockies. They have come here to make a new arrangement and when they return home, they will feel good for we will not object to their hunting in these parts, provided they do so only in the open season" (ibid.). This agreement thus allowed the Stony seasonal access to the Ktunaxa and Secwépemc hunting grounds in the area occupied by the Kinbasket.[13]

The oral history account that the late Ike Willard of Tk̓emlúps and Sk̓atsín provided of warfare between the Tsẃeńemc (Okanagan) and Secwépemc in the Adams Lake, Kamloops, and Simpcw area is another case in point. After an era of feuds that involved two young Secwépemc men from the Adams Lake area as "spies" among the Okanagan, the Okanagan and Secwépemc met on the Thompson River near Tk̓emlúps to affirm peace and to acknowledge one another's boundaries. Unfortunately, the published account of this feud, titled "ATAM and Wul-PA-han [Wulpáxen]," omits the peace making and reduces the narrative to a generic, historically decontextualized "story" of two bad boys (Bouchard and Kennedy 1979, 93–6). A close listening to Ike Willard's narration in Secwepemctsín reveals the political and historical significance of the story. It reveals not only how the Secwépemc dealt with traitors but also how neglect on the part of the community turned young men into traitors against their own people. In addition, it shows the ability and desire to put an end to bloodshed by engaging in peace treaties.

Atahm ell Wulpáxen | The White Arrow of Peace

told by Ike Willard, recorded from Ike Willard and published in abbreviated and rewritten form by Randy Bouchard and Dorothy Kennedy (1979, 93–6), retranscribed by Ronald E. Ignace, 2008

There was a couple living at Adams Lake who had two little boys, Atahm and Wulpáxen. There was some kind of sickness who took over the old man first, and then the old lady died. Just the two little boys was living, and so Atahm was the oldest little boy. He took his little brother and went to his aunt, oh, for a few months and exchange over to his uncle and round about. Pretty soon none of them liked the two boys. They wanted them to live the ways, the ways of the Indian ways of living, to go out and do their own, like on their own, so they pushed them around and pushed around Adams Lake; people would move down by around Chase above there.

Atahm was old enough to know something was [going on], but he kept his little brother. He wanted to delay him while he planned. He told his little brother, he says, "We live up here, there is a cave in there somewhere, and we will live in there, and at night we will go out, and they are making salmon now, meat and dried meat, the elders." Atahm went to work and stole food at nights and stored it up for the winter in the cave. They lived there for several years. They were grown up and grown up. They thought it was a cruel way that they was treated by his people.

8.12 | Adams Lake pictograph, showing the events told in the White Arrow of Peace, 2012.

One day there was enemies come in, invaders, invaded Adams Lake, eh Chase, invaded there, the people … kikwillie hole there, people, about one hundred people or more, enemies. He set fire to the kikwillie hole, he does, enemies did. Atahm and Wulpáxen were sitting way up on that side hill watching all this. He told his little brother, he says, "Hey," he says, "I think we better give up to them enemies. If they don't kill us it will soon be winter anyways. If they don't kill they might take us along and we will go with them, and later on when we grow up as men, we will come back and kill our people on account of the way they been treating us, pushing us around." His little brother says, "Okay." He was young.

Atahm told his little brother, "You stay here and if you see a fire swinging above around and around, that will be me calling you to come. So Atahm went down, he was just about to be killed when he got down there by the warriors. So he told his intentions to an interpreter. Yeah, they take him to where the chief is and find out what he intend to do. They took Atahm towards Princeton way somewhere, and when he got there and told the chief what these two boys intend to do, the chief said, "That will be fine, that is what we want, we want to get their trails where they living."

They kept the boys and raised them up, look after them good, and when they grow up into men, Atahm and Wulpáxen were men, they came up to

Kamloops, [then] Chua Chua, right up to Adams Lake. Shuswaps were beaten up bad and they got what they want, so they went back [to the Okanagan] and when they got there, the chief gave his daughter to Atham. Atahm got two wives. They were there around for two or three years, something like that. He was a hard man to get, he always get away. Some time he tells his little brother, "Let's let our people kill these people here, you know their revenge and get out of it." They sneak away from the warriors and back up there on Neskonlith Lake, up on the side hill stayed sitting down there, watching the people fighting. When the Shuswap people kill all the Princeton people, they come down. They holler from there, "We just give you a chance to kill all those people for revenge. I am Atahm and Wulpáxen," and a fella told him to prove it. There is a rock back in there, a big white rock and grey. Wulpáxen drew a picture of his brother, draw a picture the way he is standing, and the next will be Adams Lake, and he drew an arrow above his head, still standing today. He left from there and went to Princeton way.

Two, three years, a few years after, Wulpáxen said, "It is not right to kill our own people. I will go down and try to make peace. We've been killing our own people for many years. Very few times we give them a good chance to fight, to have a good fight with them, to kill enemies, their enemies." Atahm said, "I don't think it is right, I don't think you'll live if you go down there." [Wulpáxen said,] "I'll live all right, I will talk to them." So finally, for a week, he [Atahm] told his brother, "All right, if you want to go you can go, but don't stay too long for I will be missing you, and I will want to know what has become of you." So a few days after, Wulpáxen come down, that is the youngest brother, come down to Kamloops. There was nobody around, but he was already seen himself, seen him coming. The brother took off from there and told that there is a man coming, one, and it looks like Wulpáxen, Atahm's youngest brother. The story he was coming already, was already up to Chu Chua. Wulpáxen was sitting around there [Kamloops] and wondering, maybe said he, "I will go to Chu Chua first." He left Kamloops and went across the Thompson River and went on to Red Willow, and he found there was a bunch of people there, they were ready for him, and he come right into their homes. "You're Wulpáxen?" [He answered,] "Yes, it is me." Oh, they treat him good. The old womens come in there and welcome him, fed him and treat him good. An old fella come up and said that the peoples are out hunting, they will be back maybe tonight or tomorrow. Wulpáxen wasn't scared since he was treated real good but he already fall. One Old fella come in and said, "You must be tired, you had a long ways coming." [Wulpáxen answered,] "Yes, I am getting that way," and says we will go into the sweathouse. He took Wulpáxen into a sweathouse, and he had two little boys at the entrance, and the old people told them, "Boys, when he wants to come out, just open the entrance, just little nook to cover his head." The old man said, "The real warriors are out fighting somewhere." Nobody seen but two spears. [Wulpáxen said,] "I wanna go out and have a swim," and the boys were told to open the sweathouse. "Your uncle wants to come out." Wulpáxen slowly went to the river for a swim and he was looking around, forever watching everything. The old fella said, "Come in, there is nobody around, come in, there is nobody around!" The second time he come out, he was getting slower and slower, slow come out. He went down the river for a swim, and when he went in for the third time, and the old fella was putting more water on the rocks making more steam. He said, "I want to go out for a swim, open the door!" The warriors were already by the entrance, and grown up people, as he was coming out slowly, they open it up just enough to cover his head coming out slowly halfways out. They put the two spears into his ribs on each side, and he made a jump, but it was too late. The tomahawk was right on him by the head, laid him down dead.

Then they come out there, we got Wulpáxen dead now. "What we going to do?" Everybody come out and see Wulpáxen laying there. [They said,] "We are going to have to move out of here. If Atahm heard about his brother we will all be dead. Let us get out of here and gather up some place where we might have chance to get him." One of them says, "I am pretty sure there is a lot of us gonna die off!" So they moved, took a short cut trail down from Red Willow [Tseqwtseqwél̓qw, the old reserve at Chu Chua] to Chase. I assume towards Chase. "That is where we are going to die if we are to die." So everybody moved over and told everybody to get ready. Wulpáxen is dead and Atahm didn't come after two or three weeks after they sent out scouts all over these little points around, where they can see miles away. They described what Atahm looked like: with two women and two little boys. So the scouts see them two women and two little boys. "That's him, Atahm comes!" So everybody send out a word right up to Kamloops, Atahm is coming, so everybody moved and dug themselves in, buried them up and waited for him. They know exactly what day of the year, and I am pretty sure the next day Atahm hollered across, hollered out. The first time he come down to Kamloops, he did not see any people there, so he left his wife there and took off to Tseqwtseqwél̓qw. "There might be some people there," [he said,] so he left his kids and his wife.

So when he got there [Tseqwtsqwél̓qw], there was nobody around. He seen a little island where the people making a sweathouse and he see a black object over there. He walked into the water halfway up, but the water was too swift and was dragging Atahm down. And so he said, "I think it is too strong a current!" And so he come back to shore and he had to let it go. It was his brother laying there, so he took off from there and he did not know what that black thing was across there. He left from there towards and joined up with his wife in Kamloops and went towards Chase. He got into [place], he was already spotted, then he went over to [the place]. They mention certain places, people coming in there, and then they come to Qw7ewt. Around Qw7ewt he was coming up the river. He [knew] exactly … where he will come out, and sure enough, he come out by himself, right out in the open, and he hollered across and one old fella answered, "Who is that?" and Atham answered. [The old fella said,] "That is good, we will get you across, Atahm!" And two boats to be sent out, one for him and one for the women. They were going to fight him right on the water. They send out good swimmers, but they find out Atahm could swim better than anybody. Oh, they didn't take a chance, they got across. Atahm got on with his two little boys on one boat, he came across, and he had his spear ready any minute to use his spear. But it was all old people there. They said, "There is nobody around, all the younger people left, so it is just old people, you know, the rest are out in the hills." And he said, "I want to know where my brother is!" [They answered,] "Oh your brother has got two wives, and they took him up to the mountain, up to the plateau, and they have been up there for two or three days. They liable to be back today or tomorrow, for sure." Oh, they say that the girls was just after Wulpáxen! So he was kinda satisfied that his brother is still alive out hunting, and he had two wives, so then one kid come in and said that the sweathouse is ready for uncle, if he wants to come in. "Yeah," old fella says, "yeah, we will take Atahm, he has come a long ways, he might need to go in the sweathouse to loosen himself up." Atahm say, "Yes, I need a sweathouse!" So he went, he went over to the sweathouse, and there was the sweathouse, the rocks was red hot. He went in, and in a few minutes he wants to come out, and as soon as he lifted the entrance, he made a leap and two jumps from there, and he was in the water. He made a good dive and he was looking around, looking around about him, but there was nobody. He come to the shore and went back to the sweathouse and went back in. The old people told him, "There is nothing around, you're with your own people here." So he kind of relaxed a little bit, so Atahm come out a second time. The third time he come out, the people was kinda scared of him, and they want him to go back in the sweathouse. The fourth time he went in, they put more water, more steam in the sweathouse, tire him out. That is the time, the fourth time he comes out, the old fella push the arrow that was beside him out to warn the warriors that it was time to come, and the two little boys leave the entrance, so the boys told what they seen the arrows coming out. The warriors run over with spears, with spears and tomahawks, three of them come out and waited for him to come out on each side. Atahm says, "I want to go out, getting that way to have a little swim to go out," so Atahm slowly coming out, just halfway out, the two spears enter his side. Atahm made one leap and busted one spear, broke one, but it was too late, the third man jump on him and roll him to the ground and told him, "Too late Atahm, you know what you done to your people, don't you, all these years? You've been fighting your people. Now it is no use that you live, you are going to die. Your brother is already dead, don't say nothing about him!" And the tomahawk come down on his head and he laid there, and [they] pulled him out to the little flat, and the people come down and look at the body of Atahm and seen him laying there.

They had a meeting of their own. One old fella says, "You know, they got two little boys who is old enough to know something about it. If we are going to let them boys live when they grow up, they come back after us to revenge for their father." The rest of them say, "What we going to do with them, we are going to have to kill them!" So they club the boys with tomahawks, laid them beside his father. Man, that was a real good meeting. They told the women, "Don't be scared, we are not going to touch you women, we are going to send you back, don't be frightened!" The interpreter was there to interpret to the women. The women's two sons was taken, I guess the womens felt bad, so they kept the womens there for a few days. They told everybody to get everything ready, some cooked, some raw. All them roots and salmon to pack, that takes eight men to pack all those things, and to take those womens back. "Take the older men, not too old, the middle-aged old fellas to take them back to Princeton way." They went on for four days before they reach from where the womens left his father, who was the chief. The first kikwillie hole was the biggest kikwillie hole they had ever seen, and the women kept right on going to the corner of that building where his father was laying. He told his father what happened, he told everything, the father just lay there and never said a word. The people from Adams Lake there were just like enemies, the people just sitting there with their arrows and spears. Anytime they want to go out, there would be three or four going out with them with spears and arrows, ready to kill them any minute.

The chief never said a word for four days. He got up and told them peoples, "Put them weapons away, put everything away!" So everybody had to lay their arms down. He says, "You know, this is the best word I've ever heard about making a peace terms among ourselves." He says that "we are going to join up with the Shuswap Indians at Tk̓emlúps, not this year, next year, but there will be no more killing after this." So he sent the packers with food, and he told the chief, "You're going to meet all the chiefs from Princeton, to meet to tell [the] Tk̓emlúps[emc]!" And they waited the next year until all the berries were ripe, and they move to this side of the river, all the Shuswaps. And the next day, they seen all the Princeton Indians coming in on the other side, and they put up their teepees and stayed there for a couple more days more, before they met one boat coming across from one side and one boat from the other side. And they meet in the middle of the river. They tie up there and they made the peace there with one white arrow. No more killing of a man with a different language, you can try to make signs with them, you can make peace with them, but no more killing after this.

That was their promise together. So they pull out and their chief went across to the other side and said, "All our womens, all the girls, can marry your men. You can take him wherever he wanted, and the father can come and visit their daughter whenever he wanted, and the girls can visit their fathers back home and go about into one." So the Shuswaps accept all that. Now mostly Okanagan people settle to Shuswap ways into Adams Lake, into Kamloops. Same way with others, Merritt bunch. The peace was declared among them. Just a matter of a few years after, when they seen the first white man in Kamloops. That is all.[14]

Teit's (1909) work on the Secwépemc includes a detailed section on "warfare" between the Secwépemc and surrounding nations, consisting of oral history narratives by unnamed Secwépemc people. He noted that "wars" were carried out until 1860 or 1862, the most "war-like" divisions being the Tk̓emlúps and the Fraser River divisions. The oral histories of "wars" that he heard from Secwépemc consultants contain accounts of raiding parties of outsiders, including St'at'imc and Lil'wat (Lower Lillooet), Sekéwemc (Cree), and Sekani, who in each case entered Secwépemc country, trying to occupy fishing locations or hunting areas, and in other cases raided for women. At various times in history, the Secwépemc themselves penetrated into neighbouring nations' territories, including southward into the Okanagan, especially for a time between the 1300s and the 1700s. Teit (1930a, 221–2) noted that, during this time, most of the Shuswap war parties against the Okanagan came from Savona and Kamloops:

> Long ago, about 1700, the Shuswap had wars with the Okanagon. Once a large Shuswap war party from Savona and neighborhood was defeated at Namtusten ("place of ambush") and nearly all of them were killed. Another Shuswap war party had many men killed by falling over a cliff [McIntyre Bluff] below Penticton. It seems that this war party came over the plateau to the bluffs above the valley, which they reached in the evening. Here they halted to observe some camps in the valley below. They were noticed by some Okanagon scouts, and in the night time were surrounded by a strong party of Okanagon, who shortly before daybreak attacked them suddenly. Many of the Shuswap, not knowing the locality, fell over the precipice in the dark. Some of the others escaped to isolated rocks, where steep cliffs cut off their retreat, and they were shot there after daylight. A number of others escaped through the Okanagon in the dark, and reached home. Their war chief was killed.

The late Theresa Jules of Skeetchestn connected the outcome of Okanagan-Secwépemc warfare to a landmark called Balancing Rock on the south shore of Kamloops Lake, about 1 kilometre to the west of Six Mile Point (see fig. 8.13). Her grandfather K̓estmíc (ca. 1840 to ca. 1950) told her the oral history of a war between the Ts̓wéñemc (Okanagan) and the Secwépemc. The Secwépemc beat the invading Okanagans. One of the Okanagan men then challenged the Secwépemc to pick up a rock and throw it on top of a pillar. The Okanagan person tried and failed. The Secwépemc man picked up the rock and threw it on top of the pillar. Adding her oral comments, she explained that this was a true story, told to her "by my grandfather Ḱestmíc, and also by Ḱwetmémelcken and Annie Ṕáxa7, as well as Julienne and Edward Eneas," who were Ron Ignace's great-grandparents. All of these elders, she said, knew this story. It was there that a party of Okanagan attacked the Secwépemc. The Secwépemc used to have to be watchful when passing through this area. Secwépemc people had powers, which helped them to know when their enemy was coming. *Ṫkwilc* (Indian doctors) were known for such powers, she added. They had the power to sense things before they happened. The Secwépemc's *ṫkwilc* thus dreamed the coming of the Okanagan, and they prepared for war by getting their weapons ready and hiding their children. In those days, the women would stay in hidden places and wait until more arrows were needed. Then they would prepare the arrows and take them to the men. The Secwépemc went and met the Okanagan at the place now called Balancing Rock, where there is a little mound with a rock balancing on top. After driving out the Okanagan, the Secwépemc men imitated the sound of wolves – which people say could be heard in that area – and thus signalled to the women and children to come out of their hiding places and return to their homes, which were pithouses and tents.

Theresa Jules (see fig. 11.6) noted that the Secwépemc name for Balancing Rock is Stseq.qín or Stseq.qíqeṅ ("large heavy object put on top"). She added, "Our *ṫkwilc* froze the rock so that nothing will happen to it, so it won't fall." After their defeat, she noted, the Okanagan and Nlaka'pamux moved out of this country to an area farther away.

Stseq.qíqeṅ | Story of Balancing Rock

told by Theresa Jules to Ronald E. Ignace, 2000

Ne7éne te tmicw ne q̓wemtsíns re pésellkwe, te-m tśelílcucw, xwent yerí7 re swiktc re Tḱemlúps, m-yews-ekwe le q̓7es te qelmúcw, ye7éne te Secwépemc ell re Stśwéṅemc, tśniqwsensmens-ekwe ye7éne te tmicw e swéti7 nerí7 es wecwcstés, es westés.
In this land here, by the shore of the lake, when you stand there you can see Kamloops. Long time ago the Secwépemc and Okanagan fought over this land and over who would get to keep it.

Tśníqwtes-ekwe … xexé7-ekwe re stsetśníqwt.s. Ḱwíncwes-ekwe te sitq̓t yerí7 re stsetśníqwt.s, ye7éne Secwépemc ye7éne re stsq̓élenmens re tskwíneks, m-yews ri7 re nuxwnúxwenxw nerí7 re snesnést.s, nerí7 re skectés ye7éne re Secwépemc te sqelqélemcw te stsíllens ell te stskwils.

8.13 | Balancing Rock on the south shore of Kamloops Lake, 2009. This rock feature commemorates the Secwépemc winning a war against the Syilx (Okanagan), according to a story told by Theresa Jules of Skeetchestn.

They were fighting … they fought hard. I don't know how many days they fought. These Secwépemc they were shooting their bows and arrows. And the women went there and they brought food and arrows for the Secwépemc men.

Yerí7 re sk̓úlems es kectés m-ta7ews nerí7 re sxenwéllens es pulsentwécwes. M-yews yerí7 re stsut.s, "Yéwske ri7 re swi7s es ts̓níqwtels me7 kwéntmes ne7éne xexé7 te sqélemcws re Stś̓wén̓emc ell re Secwépemc."
And they couldn't beat one another. That's when one of them said, "So that we can end the fighting, let's take one strong man each from the Secwépemc and the Okanagan."

"Yehé7wes ye7éne es xenwén̓s es cwentés ye7éne te xyum te scenc ell cwentés ne7éne, es tntés ne7éne ne tqeltks ne7éne te tsqwum, nerí7 me7 t̓cwúmes ne7élye te tmicw." M-yews yerí7 re stsunm̓ékstmens ye7éne te xyum te Stswén̓emc.
"Whichever one of the two is able to lift up this big rock on top of a mound [pillar] will win the land." And then they pointed out a big Okanagan.

M-k̓wénses nerí7 ye7éne te scenc es cwentés, es tntés ne7éne te tsqwum. Ooooh, k̓ékmell-ekwe re sxenwéllens es tntéses. M-kellpékstmenses, m-plek̓es.
He took that big rock to lift it up, to lift it onto the pillar. Oooh, but he couldn't put it on there. He let go of it, and it rolled down.

M-yews yerí7 re stsuns ye7éne te sqélemcw te Secwépemc, "Yéwske yerí7 re newí7 k k̓wenc es xenwén̓c es cwentés ye7éne te xyum te scenc."
And then they said to this one Secwépemc man, "You should try to lift up this big rock."

M-néses nerí7 ye7éne te sqélemcw, m-cwentéses, ooooh, xmenk-ekwe, w7ec nerí7 re m-sxenwéllenes-ekwe, yerí7 re stntés ye7éne te xyum te scenc ne tsqwum.
That man went there. Oocohh, it was heavy! But he was able to lift that rock up and put it on the pillar.

Telrí7 yem-ekwe re st̓cwums re Secwépemc ne7élye te tmicw es Secwepemcúl̓ecws. M-yews yerí7 re sqwetséts.s re Stś̓wén̓emc es llwélent.s ye7éne te tmicw, es ta7ews cúy̓tsem es ts̓níqwtsentels.
That's how the Secwépemc won this land as part of Secwépemc country. And the Okanagan left to abandon this land, so they wouldn't fight over it any more.

Telrí7 yem-ekwe wel westés pyin ye7éne te tmicw es q̓iyét.s yerí7 re Secwepemcúl̓ecw. Ye7éne pyin re stsem̓étstem ye7éne te Sk̓elép te scécen̓c.

And it's written on the land that it is Secwépemc territory. Nowadays, they call that a Coyote rock.

During the 1700s, the Secwépemc also expanded northward into the McBride area, driving out the Sekani who had previously moved into this area claimed by the Secwépemc. "War parties," as Teit noted, included anywhere from two or three warriors – in this case, representing a raid rather than organized war – to large war parties of up to 200 or 300. War chiefs were the leaders in strategy and tactic, "versed in the science of war" (Teit 1909, 542). Often, a *ṫkwilc* (Indian doctor or medicine man) also accompanied the war party. For example, a place called Snine7éllcw ("owl's nest"), on the North Thompson River east of Vavenby, commemorates a battle where a party of Cree attacked some Simpcw. Before the attack, one Cree warrior hid in a tree hooting like an owl to communicate with his friends, but he was detected by a *ṫkwilc* accompanying the Simpcw and was shot down. Subsequently, the rest of the Cree party was killed as well.

Snine7éllcw | Owl's Nest

told by Chris Donald, recorded by Marianne Ignace, 1985, translated and transcribed by Marianne Ignace and Mona Jules

Yerí7 k stseṁetúl̓ecwstem te Snine7éllcw.
That place called Owl's Nest.

Cw7it-ekwe ri7 nu7 tsyem ne sextsínes re setétkwe.
They say that there used to be lots of people who lived by the shore of the [North Thompson] river there.

Yerí7 re s7ímnemes nu7 re sníne nu7 ne sqeltús re tsq̓wmust.s.
That was where an owl was hooting up on a cliff on a mountain.

Yerí7 lu7 le medicine man *tsut-ekwe, "Ta7 ri7 k snínes ṫri7 ec k ímnemes."*
They say that a medicine man there said, "That isn't an owl hooting."

"Me7 kwenkwéntp re tskwínek-emp, me7 xwexwéyt-kp."
"You must take your bows and arrows, all of them."

"Me7 cw7it k stskwele7úẇi-emp me7 trépelc-ep."
"All of you must take lots of arrows and climb up there."

"Ṫkllúne me7 ṫekmíṅtpes ṫkllu7 ṫe ck̓míkeṅs."
"Over that way is where all of you should approach them, from behind."

"Sekéwemc ri7."
"They are Cree people."

"Qwenmíns es t̓íqwentels nerí7 e tsyémet e r7áles."
"They want to kill us all over there, right where we will be staying after dark."

"Me7 nésmentp es t̓íqwentp xwexwéyt."
"All of you must go after them and kill them all."

"Yihé7en ri7 ec k ímnemes, ri7 me7 xetéqs me7 tsq̓élentp."
"The one doing the hooting, he is to be the first one you guys will shoot."

"Tnk̓we7-ekwe ri7 tq̓wemút nu7 ne tqeltks re q̓wmust.s re rock bluff, *yerí7 re ímenmes t̓e sníne."*
"One of them, as you can hear, is sitting on top of the rock bluff, and he is the one hooting like an owl."

W7ec-ekwe ell ri7 t̓ri7 tsyem cw7it t̓e Sekéwemc, tsnínect.s nerí7 ne seckéwelc.
They say that there were many Cree people camped there, hooting at their people farther down below [to signal them].

Tsúntem-ekwe yerí7 tek tnk̓we7 te stet̓ex7ém.
They say that that elder told them about it.

Xexé7 t̓e xeltsq̓él̓nem.
He is a good shot.

E w7ec k t̓úcwtes k stem me7 xeltsq̓élens. Me7 ciyúcwt.
If there is something in flight, he can shoot it. It falls to the ground.

Ecwes k núxwes k ts̓i7, me7 xeltsq̓élens me7 qémens.
If there is a deer running, he shoots and will hit it.

Xexé7-ekwe t̓ek sxemqenélt ne tskwírek.
They say that he was an excellent shooter of arrows.

Ri7 mé7e nu7 tq̓wemút,
So the one who had climbed up and sat there,

kekéw-enke k tsrépes, yulqw t̓e llq̓elqw,
it must have been quite a ways, up a big tree,

teq̓wmút-ekwe nu7, tekwnéṁkstses ne tseck̓úẏeqens re sqwí7qwe.
they say that he was perched up there hanging onto a marmot's den on a bent-over log.

Tsrépctem-ekwe ṫ7éne te ck̓wellck̓mékst.s te arrow.
They say that he was pierced by an arrow under his arm.

M-pult-ekwe le ck̓wellq̓ékseṅtem,
They say that the one who was shot under the arm lay there,

k̓ell m-leq̓wépem-ekwe te m-ciyúcwt ṫe tsektṡús,
but they say he let out a cry as he fell from the cliff,

le tseck̓úẏeqens re sqwí7qwe.
from the den [bent-over tree] of the marmot.

Ṫmépctem-ekwe ṫ7éne te k̓wellk̓mékst.s te arrow.
They say that the arrow chopped off his arm.

Re m-pult-ekwe le ck̓wellq̓ékseṅtem,
They say that the one shot under his arm lay there,

k̓émell leq̓wépem-ekwe te m-ciyúcwt le ckwellq̓éksentem le tsecqúẏeqens re sqwi7qwe.
but they say that when he got shot under the arm, he let out a cry as he fell from the marmot's den.

Qiyéṁes-ekwe ṫ7éne le tsyem.
They say that the ones [other Cree] camped there were scurrying about.

Tseltṡelíl̓c.
They all stood up.

Put e ṫhen-ekwe ṫri7 k tsq̓élentmes, te stskwele7úẇi.
They were shot here, there, and other places with arrows.

Westém-ekwe nerí7 wel q̓wempstém yerí7 Sekéwemc.
They say that they [the Simpcw Secwépemc] fought those Cree until they were all gone.

Q̓wempstém ṫlu7 m-k̓well7éxwmentem xwexwéyt.
They were all shot and their remains thrown down the cliff.

Kweckwéctem ṫe stectéckens ṫri7 stskwele7úẇis,
They took all their backpacks and arrows,

m-k̓well7éxwemctem xwexwéyt.
and every last one was thrown down the cliff.

Pílk̓ctmes ṫri7 ṫe sxtśey te yelyúlqw.
They rolled big fat sticks and logs down on them.

Re m-tsúntmes, "E wi7 ṫ7en k sk̓úlctem ṫe stsyéqwneṅtem ṫlu7,
They were told, "When we have finished with the fire preparations,

ne tkwékweltks, me7 yéṫelcwet teke me7 tsertsrentém."
down below, we will go down there and set fire to them."

Yerí7 pyin nu7 re Snine7éllcw.
Nowadays that place over there is called Owl's Nest.

Tśílem wiwéy nerí7 scenc, k tsyéqwes-enke,
The rock is sort of visible, where there must have been a fire,

ne tkwékweltk, ne tsqúmes-enke re Sekéwemc.
down below, where the Cree people were piled up.

Tsertsrentém wel re m-tselék̓ xwexwéytes.
They were all burned until there was nothing left of them.

Ta7 ṫri7wes k estkéṅmes.
There was not a sound from any of them anywhere.

Tsq̓elentwécw ṫucw ṫri7 wel re m-q̓wempstém.
They fought one another until the other side was gone.

Ta7 ṫri7 k swelmíṅks.
There were no guns.

Q̓7es-ekwe ṫri7 lu7 le lléptes le wuxépes.
They say that the fires burned for a long time before they went out.

Tsigrápes telrí7 le qwetsétses, tsut-ekwe,
When those who went away arrived back home, they said,

"Ta7 mí7 ṫri7 k stem ṫri7 k sk̓lékstmentem-kucw."
"We never let anyone go."

"Ṫíqwentem-kucw xwexweyte7úy."
"We killed them all."

"E kesenwéńtem ri7 cú7tsem ṫek cw7it tek Sekéwemc, me7 tcúsem ri7."
"When lots of the other Cree become aware that they are missing, they will come looking."

Xwexwéyt nu7 le tsyem ne pestéwt tsúns-ekwe,
All of those living on the other side of the river were told,

"Me7 teqtéq̓em-kp ṫlune ne pestéwt me7 yístet."
"You cross the river to the other side and that is where we will camp."

"E kesenwéńtem ṫrey te k̓wséltktens."
"It's possible that their relatives will miss them."

"Héqen e ta7-enke k skekéws, me7 tcúsem!"
"Maybe they aren't far off, they will begin looking!"

Ta7-ekwe ri7 k skítsentem ṫe k̓wséltktens.
They say that the relatives of those beaten never caught up to them.

Ṫlú7-enke ṫucw ṫlúne ṫe, t7éyentmes cu7tsem ṫek cw7it te soltes.
It must have been way up there somewhere, where they were met by many [Secwépemc] soldiers.

Ṫíqwentem ṫri7 xwexwéyt le Sekéwemc.
The Cree people were all killed.

Tnk̓we7 telrí7 re sklléikstmentem.
One person was let go.

Tsúntmes e tspelq̓ílcwes e stskwnem-k ṫri7 ṫek cw7it ṫek soltses.
He was told, if he returned, to bring many of his soldiers.

Ṫri7 tscwiyúlecw-ekwe ri7 m-tsútes ṫri7 k ṫkwilc,
When it was the break of dawn, one of the medicine men said,

"Me7 yecwementwílc-kt xwexwéytet."
"Let's all watch over one another."

"Ta7 ṫri7 me7 estcéy-kt wel me7 kitsc-kt núne, núne ne Mosquito Flats."
"We will not stop until we reach over to Mosquito Flats."[15]

"Ne qelmucwúl̓ecw, nu7 me7 estcéyet."
"Over there at the reserve, that is where we will stop."

On one occasion, a group of Cree attacked the Simpcw as they were camping and fishing at their Ctśwenétkwe (Raft River) fishing grounds. They killed all but one young man, Peter Moyís, also called Peter-One-Eye, who was Chris Donald's "grandfather."[16] Chris Donald recalled, "They were up there to do some drying of fish. They were up there to dry up some fish when the Crees coming. They [the Cree] kill them off and they took my grandfather Peter." Peter was captured as a slave and taken across the Rocky Mountains by them. He made his escape and eventually returned to his people at Tseqwtseqwélqw.

Judging by the approximate birth date of Old Peter and others mentioned in Chris Donald's narrative, this battle and subsequent capture occured after the 1860s – probably in the 1870s. The narrator also mentioned that, in his own time, there was an area with "white ash" at the mouth of Ctśwenétkwe from the cremation of war casualties after this battle.

Although at times Secwépemc war parties consisted of members of single communities, in many instances they included support from neighbouring communities. It is notable that all instances of Secwépemc warfare involved Secwépemc against, or in defence against, non-Secwépemc intruders or Secwépemc intruding into other nations' territories. In one instance, reported in Teit's (1906, 237–9) ethnography of the St'at'imc, a group of Secwépemc warriors penetrated deep into the centre of Lillooet territory in the centre of the Lillooet and Anderson Lake area, occupying the rich fisheries there and taking women and young boys as slaves for a period of several years. They were eventually beaten back by two St'at'imc brothers who had quested for powers and then lured them into a bog, where most of the Secwépemc warriors perished. Subsequently, the St'at'imc brothers offered them peace. Teit's oral histories of warfare include three instances of what appear to be "wars" or feuds of Secwépemc against other Secwépemc. On close inspection, however, each of these wars represents an instance of enforcing criminal justice, where an individual from one Secwépemc community or extended family engaged in continuous serious criminal behaviour against members of his own community and was deemed beyond rehabilitation. In each case, the perpetrator's relatives gave licence to the victims to kill the perpetrator (see chapter 9).

Another oral history about conflict and warfare, but based on the ordeal of an individual captured by outside invaders, is the story of Tessie,[17] one of the ancestors of Ida William and Josephine Wenlock of Simpcw.

Story of Tessie
told by Ida William, recorded by Marianne Ignace, 1986

Le q̓7éses re qelmúcw w7ec re cwesétes t̓hé7en t̓e kekéw, pexpíxem.
Long time ago, people were travelling far away, they were hunting.

Yesyíst t̓hé7en.
They were camping out there, wherever.

Kítsentmes t̓e k̓ist t̓e qelmúcw.
They were caught up by bad people.

Stq̓wiycénemc. T̓iqwctmes t̓e k̓wséltktens.
They were Blackfoot Indians. They killed their relatives.

Kwéntmes re tutwíwt t̓e nuxwnúxwenxw, m-qwetséts.stmes.
They took the young women and set out with them.

T̓íqwentem t̓ri7 re s7i7llcw.
Some of them were killed.

T̓hé7en t̓ri7 xwistés k nuxwnúxwenxw, t̓ri7 m-kwénses.
There, they took the girls they liked.

Te kekéw t̓e tmicw m-kwéntmes.
They took them to a faraway land.

Yerí7 re kyé7es-kucw m-kwéntem. Tuwíwtes ey.
They took our grandmother. She was young yet.

Le skwest.s Tessie. Yerí7 re m-swestém nek̓u7 t̓e swucwt.
Her name was Tessie. She was kept there for one year.

St̓ek7ílc. K̓úlctmes t̓e túm̓es cw7it t̓e silltśu7.
She took off this way. Her aunt [who had also been captured] made her lots of moccasins.

T̓ek7ílc t̓e k̓ist re qelmúcw.
She ran away from the bad people.

Tspelq̓ílcwes.
She returned.

Tstektéklles te tmicw-kt.
She made it back down to our country [crossing the Rocky Mountains].

Pelmíntmes t̓e k̓wséltktens, tspelq̓entémes.
She was found by her relatives and brought back.

8.14 | Ida William of Chu Chua (Simpcw) in a berry patch near Ctśwenétkwe (Raft River), 1985.

M-tskítscstem ne7éne ṫe tmicw-kt.
She was brought back to our land.

Ne7éne ne Tseqwtseqwél̓q̓w,[18] *yerí7 re stsemtúl̓ecws.*
Here, to Tseqwtseqwél̓qw that's what they call the place.

Neri7 re tskítscstmes m-séwentmes ṫe k̓wséltktens,
When she was taken over there, her relatives asked,

"Ṫhé7en k xílmes es stspelq̓ílcs?"
"What did she do to come back?"

Lexéẏens xwexwéyt.
She told them everything.

Yerí7, ta7 me7 re scwúytsem k swet ks kwéntem penṫlu7s,
And that was it. Since then, no one has ever been taken by them,

k skwéntem ṫe k̓ist ṫe qelmucw k sxílltem ṫri7.
taken by the bad people, and no one was ever treated like that again.

As we showed in chapter 7, Simpcw elders remembered additional stories they had been told by their elders of battles with Cree who came down the North Thompson. These battles took place at the mouth of Raft River, on Battle Mountain, and in Wells Grey Park, and they are commemorated in place names.

Francis Ignace of Skeetchestn remembered a war between people from Skeetchestn and Tsilhqot'in people who came to seize fish from Skeetchestn Secwépemc fishing grounds at the mouth of Deadman's Creek:

> At Lemonade Flats, there's the mouth of the creek, the other side, that's where the Indians camp in the fall time. And the Indians from way somewhere come over to fight. They were sitting around in there, and the scout saw them … They seen them, they come way over … The boy went around, tell them people [the Shuswap], "There's a bunch of different Indians up there" … There was still hundreds and thousands. They all fight. And that's where they killed them all. My granny was telling me that. But I seen that, too. All the arrows, arrows, knives, broken.

According to Francis Ignace, there were further battle grounds at the Criss Creek bluffs, the Thompson River, and Walhachin. He said, "Even up Deadman's Creek, they had a big war once in a while."

Another battle site is near the mouth of Copper Creek on the North shore of Kamloops Lake east of Savona. Shortly before he passed away, Francis Ignace (recorded by Ron Ignace and Marianne Ignace, 1987) showed us the location of a place where Secwépemc warriors caught up to an invading Creek warrior and killed him, pointing to the location now called Indian Point on the north shore of Kamloops Lake:

> Copper Creek, there's lots of fight at that one. There's lots of Indians at Copper Creek, yeah … There's some Indian camps there. And there's, there's some Cree coming in, from Calgary. And they start fighting them. They killed [many of them]. They shot one in the leg, [he] fell down, clubbed him in the head. And they put rocks over the head, put rocks there, how tall [he] is. I seen it … I know just where it is … My granny [Cecile Melmenétkwe] showed me how tall that was.

This incident is also related by Teit (1909, 550–1), who identifies the place where the Cree warrior was killed as Sekewmectét7us ("Cree's trail") (see chapter 7), a place on the north shore of Kamloops Lake east of Copper Creek where a party of Cree who had come down the North Thompson River were pursued by Selpáxen and his party from the Tk̓emlúps area:

8.15 | Francis Ignace at Copper Creek, showing the location of Sekewmectét7us ("Cree's trail"), 1986. Here a Cree warrior was brought down long ago.

One of the Cree made the sign of a woman's privates to the Shuswap, who were leading. After a long and hard run, the fleetest of the latter drew near to the slowest of the Cree, and the two parties commenced to shoot arrows at one another as they ran. One of the Shuswap hit a Cree, and the two parties commenced to shoot arrows at one another as they ran. One of the Shuswap hit a Cree in the foot with an iron-tipped arrow, which disabled him so much that he was soon left behind by his party. When the Shuswap came up with him, they clubbed and killed him.

He was a very tall man, and had extraordinarily long hair. They stretched his body full length on the ground, and drove in two pegs – one at the soles of his feet, and one at the crown of his head. They also stretched his hair out full length from his head, and drove in another peg where the tips of his hair reached. After scalping him, they buried him at this spot, close to the trail. Many people afterwards visited this place to see the length of the body and hair of the Cree warrior that had been killed. His scalp was kept for many years and exhibited, to show

> the wonderful length of the hair. From this event the place was named SEqaumuxṭê´tus ("Cree little trail") [Sekewmectét7us].

Splatsín elders remembered hearing oral histories of Ktunaxa people invading their country, probably in the 1840s or 1850s, to take fish from the Salmon River. On several occasions, they were beaten back. On at least one other occasion, Nespélem people came up from the south to invade into the hunting and fishing grounds of the Splatsinac but were beaten back by the latter.

While travelling to Ottawa with James Teit during the Indian Rights Movement, probably in 1908, Chief Basil Dick (Basil David) of Sṫuxtéws gave Teit (1898–1910, n.p.) a detailed account, "perhaps about 80 years ago," or around 1830, of an invasion by a Cree war party into the Xatśúll (Soda Creek) area. It tells us something of the extent of territory that the Secwépemc travelled, how they moved, and how they patiently strategized a counterattack against enemies who took their women – not immediately, but carefully and slowly, over more than one season. Notably, this incident happened in June, and the Cree kidnapped two women and took them across Yellowhead Pass into their country east of Jasper. Although the Secwépemc pursued them, and the women had left signs for their relatives to find them, the Secwépemc lost their tracks and returned home. After the salmon season was over, and the Secwépemc had provisions of dried salmon that they could take and cache along the way, they organized a party to bring the women back and then travelled beyond Yellowhead Pass, where they found an infant, to which one of the women had given birth, killed and impaled on a sharp stick. Again, they eventually lost the tracks of the Cree and their Secwépemc captives. They set out one more time, with a larger war party "bent on revenge" in the fall of the following year. As they reached the Rockies beyond where they had previously ventured, heavy snow fell. While making large numbers of snowshoes, they killed large amounts of game, which they butchered, dried, and cached, thus ensuring provisions for the trip home and snowshoes for travel in the deep snow. As they systematically fanned out and canvassed the vast country for Cree, they eventually came upon a Cree camp, where the Cree group and their Secwépemc captives, now a year later, were camping. One of the Secwépemc women, as she sang a song while fetching water, communicated with one of the Secwépemc warriors, singing to him in Secwepemctsín of the Cree party's intentions to break camp the next morning. The Secwépemc men then instructed the women to "enjoy themselves" during the night. When the Cree men eventually were soundly asleep, the women scattered the men's snowshoes and fled from the camp, which allowed the Secwépemc to ambush the Cree and kill them.

Similarly, Chief Louis of Kamloops told of Blackfoot people attacking the Kinbasket Secwépemc and also taking women. Among the Kinbasket

Secwépemc was a warrior named Kwistá, who had obtained a metal star from the missionary who had come among them. When he reached the Blackfoot camp, Chief Louis told Teit (1898–1910, n.p.), Kwistá "pointed to the star on his breast and told [the Blackfoot] to look at it. They kept looking at it and their power of attacking him seemed to disappear. They were the same as hypnotized by the star and by his audacity. He took the women home and delivered them to their friends."

Our Secwépemc elders thus viewed the oral history stories of warfare, as well as the places and people commemorated in them, as evidence of their own ancestors' defence of the Secwépemc homeland and of the Secwépemc people's continuing rights to that land, which they had defended with their own blood. This warfare is what the chiefs referred to in their "Memorial to the Hon. Frank Oliver, Minister of the Interior" (Chiefs of the Shuswap, Couteau, and Thompson Tribes et al. 1911) – part of their eloquent defence of Aboriginal rights and title to land – when they talked of the land that had been stolen by the settlers and that their ancestors had defended "at the cost of blood." As we have seen, in some cases, physical boundary markers, such as Stseq.qíqeṅ (Balancing Rock), or pictographs commemorate instances of warfare and defence of territory against outside intruders, as well as the restoration of peaceful relations. Most knowledge survives in oral histories, and as long as the stories stay alive, future generations will remember what the defence of Secwepemcúlecw meant to Secwépemc people of the past. It must have been in this spirit that Chief Louis and Chief Basil Dick remembered and told to James Teit the stories of past wars, until now buried in the archives, as Teit accompanied them to Ottawa, where they sought to deal with the land question and to achieve a just settlement of the lands that settlers had taken from them, enabled by the laws of the colony and Canada.

Make Love, Not War

Another mechanism for the peaceful maintenance of the nation's boundaries was intermarriage across borders at the periphery or boundary of the nation. We have evidence of this for all Secwépemc boundaries and nations bordering on the Secwépemc. In the northeast, especially in the area from Tete Jaune Cache to Jasper House, the Secwépemc intermarried with the Cree, to the extent that the population of that area was of mixed Cree-Secwépemc ancestry, which is still acknowledged by the descendants of these people who live at Chu Chua on the North Thompson River. During the early 1800s, and likely well into the early 1900s, the Secwépemc and Cree population in this area further intermarried with Sekani who came down the McBride corridor from the northeast and with Iroquois who moved out west with the North West Company fur trade at the outset of the nineteenth century. At the northwestern boundary of Secwepemcúlecw, the Fraser River Secwépemc intermarried frequently with the Tsilhqot'in and Carrier, resulting in many people of mixed Secwépemc and Carrier-Tsilhqot'in ancestry, especially in the Xatśúll (Soda Creek) area. Indeed, Teit (1909, 457n1) recorded that the village of Kalaxústen near the trading post at Alexandria had a mixed Secwépemc, Carrier, and Tsilhqot'in population.

At the southwestern boundary, in Splatsín, but also among the people of the Tk̓emlúps division (Kamloops and Skeetchestn), the Secwépemc intermarried with the Syilx and Nlaka'pamux, resulting in many people with ancestry from different nations. The Fish Lake Accord gives us details of how Secwépemc people cemented peace treaties through the intermarriage of chiefs' children and through the adoption of a chief's child into the other nation. Teit's (1930a) genealogy of the interrelationship of Secwépemc and Okanagan people shows 300 years of continuous intermarriage among these nations, including also the Nicola-Similkameen people, a group of Dene (Athapaskan) speakers in the Similkameen Valley who, as their language became extinct by the 1850s, were absorbed by the Okanagan and Nlaka'pamux peoples in the area. During the latter part of the nineteenth century, Chief Hyacinth Sisyésq̓t of Skeetchestn arranged for the marriage of his daughter Pauline into the Douglas Lake Okanagan. To this day, the descendants of her family and the Skeetchestn and Tk̓emlúps Jules families recognize their connection.

At the western boundary, the Secwépemc of Qwiqwíyqwiyt (High Bar) and Sṫuxtéws frequently intermarried with the St'at'imc, especially the people of Cácl̓ep (Fountain) and Tśk̓wáy̓lacw (Pavilion). In fact, for some time until the early 1900s, Tśk̓wáy̓lacw and Cácl̓ep were considered partly Secwépemc communities, and it appears that the Sṫuxtéwsemc's access to the fisheries at Bridge River and Fountain was due to the high frequency of intermarriage among these groups.

Finally, at the southern boundary on the main Thompson River in the Sṫells (Ashcroft) area, Secwépemc people from Sṫuxtéws and Sṫells itself (see above) intermarried with the Nlaka'pamux of Ashcroft and Oregon Jack. We will see below how, within the laws and protocols of access to resources through salmon fishing, large game hunting, and plant harvesting in significant areas, marriage with members of the Secwépemc nation gave a person access to Secwépemc resources. Likewise, Secwépemc who married among surrounding nations obtained resource-harvesting rights in those nations for themselves and their descendants. Intermarriage thus constituted a peaceful way of maintaining good relations in boundary areas and, through its continued practice over what were likely long periods of time, resulted in mixed populations in these areas. Over time, however, practices of intermarriage also resulted in changes of ethnic affiliation in these areas. Whereas Tśk̓wáy̓lacw was in good part Secwépemc during the late nineteenth century and into the early twentieth century, its population is more St'at'imcets-speaking than

Secwepemctsín-speaking at present, and it appears to consider its political and ethnic affiliation as primarily St'at'imc. The same holds for Fountain and for the people of Sẗells, who appear to have once considered themselves more Secwépemc than they do now.

This chapter has provided information about the system of land use and access among the Secwépemc, as it existed between the late 1700s and the first half of the 1800s, before the colonization of Secwépemc by Euro-Canadian settlers. As we have seen, the prevailing sense was that the Secwépemc had equal access to all the resources of the nation. This chapter has also documented how, before the arrival of Europeans and in the decades following, the Secwépemc defended their boundaries against intrusions from neighbouring Aboriginal groups and at times themselves expanded into others' territories. The common thread of these oral histories of warfare is that on many occasions, seemingly the most important ones, Secwépemc people from neighbouring communities joined together to push out strangers or to pursue retribution against outsiders who had taken or killed their women and their kin – including children in their own villages – and who had tried to invade resource grounds. As the documentation shows, in some of these instances, Secwépemc people from communities separated by hundreds of kilometres, such as Soda Creek and Kamloops as well as the upper North Thompson River and Kamloops-Skeetchestn, joined together to fight back intruders in organized warfare expeditions.

Next to warfare, formal peace treaties and political alliances, as well as intermarriage, especially in boundary areas and areas of overlap with other nations, provided mechanisms for peaceful coexistence. The memories of how boundaries with neighbouring peoples were maintained through intermarriage and peace treaties or were changed over time through warfare and raiding are what we call *tsq̓eyúlecw* (what is written on the land) and are thus part of the law of the nation.

As the accounts of feuds, wars, peace treaties, and marriage alliances presented in this chapter show, there existed among the Secwépemc and their Salish and non-Salish neighbours a definite sense of territory and territorial boundaries, along with *stsq̓ey̓* (laws) of trespass and access. Such Indigenous laws also existed among the neighbouring peoples. Thus Chief Sexpínlhemx (David Spintlum) of the Nlaka'pamux referred to the southern, eastern, western, and northern "gates" of his nation in the 1870s, placing the gate with the Secwépemc at Ashcroft (Hanna and Henry 1995, 5). Throughout history, however, boundaries shifted and changed, with Secwepemcúlecw at times expanding in various directions and at times yielding territory either directly to neighbours or through treaties that reset boundaries or created joint territorial ownership and use.

9 Ḱwseltktenéws-kucw

How We Are Relatives to One Another

Tsecwmíntlmen ren ḱwséltkten.
I greet all my relatives.

Te kekéw re steṫ7ék-ep!
You have come from far away!

Penhénes-enke ne setétkwe k steṫ7ék-ep
Whenever you come to the river,

te stsqwemqwúm, te sekseḱéwt,
from the mountains, from the gullies,

le7 re swíktelmen ey xwexwéyt-ep!
it is good to see you all!

Yerí7 me7 sucwentwécw-kt!
Let us acknowledge one another!

Nels Mitchell, "Secwépemc Welcome Song"

We have seen that the fundamental concept behind the Secwépemc laws of land tenure is the *common use of and access to Secwepemcúlecw* for all people of Secwépemc ancestry. We have also seen how intermarriage among nations, followed by rights of access established for the children of such marriage alliances, allowed access to other nations' resources. This system existed throughout the Interior Plateau through a network of ties and connections of mutual access to resources.[1] Particular communities, or Indigenous "bands," within the Secwépemc nation were the *yecwmíńmen* (caretakers) of lands and resources in their surroundings, and they defended their areas against outside intruders, as the oral histories of Secwépemc warfare show us, often supported by their friends and relatives from surrounding communities. In this chapter, we discuss the social, political, and spiritual aspects of how the Secwépemc recognized, respected, and honoured one another as family and relatives throughout Secwepemcúlecw. In other words, we describe the laws and protocols that supported the social fabric within and between our communities, as well as with outsiders beyond our nation.

What gives a person rights to live in Secwepemcúĺecw and reap its resources is the connection through blood to other Secwépemc, called *k̓wseltktenéws* (being relatives to one another). This relationship can also be established through formal adoption of both individual children and adults or through formal treaties between our nation and others that incorporate adoption, such as the Fish Lake Treaty and the White Arrow of Peace (see above). Sk̓elép's (Coyote's) way of guiding the salmon into the rivers of Secwépemc country (see chapter 2) reminds us of the powers of kinship, for he not only procured salmon as an economic resource but also fixed the mutual bonds between the Wutémtkemc ("downriver people," Lower Nlaka'pamux) and the Secwépemc by impregnating the two *t̓kwilc* (medicine women) who guarded the fishing weir at Spences Bridge and thus turning them into in-laws. In addition, it caused Sk̓elép to have children in the neighbouring nation, giving them access to the resources of that nation. As long as the memory of the story stays alive, these bonds are acknowledged and support resource sharing. Moreover, Sk̓elép took on the spiritual power of these women – their way of dreaming and predicting as well as their ability to cause things to happen – and incorporated them into the ways of his children and offspring.

Me7 xyemstém re k̓wséltkten-kt (Let Us Honour Our Relations) | Secwépemc Social Organization and Kinship

Secwépemc social organization has been described by ethnographers as being inherently "loosely organized" and flexible, connected to a Plateau-wide system of ensuring access to resources where local resources were not available or occurred in cycles. However, for the ancient inhabitants at the large Keatley Creek village between Fountain and Pavilion, archaeologists have claimed an emerging "corporate group" organization based on rank within and between groups (Hayden 2000a, 2000b; Hayden and Schulting 1997; Hayden and Spafford 1993). For the Columbia Plateau, anthropologist Lilian Ackerman (1994) has claimed "nonunilineal descent groups" – that is, definite clan-like groups based on membership through the father's or mother's side or through both. It could be argued that in Secwépemc country such groups exist in family groupings connected to specific communities, like the Jules, Arnouse, and Johnson families, many individuals primarily identifying with one of these groups even though, through intermarriage, they are connected to more than one of them. Elizabeth Furniss (2004), in discussing Northern Secwépemc social organization, notes the inherent tensions between family groupings within a community and the greater collective of the community as a whole, as shown through records since the late 1900s – an issue that certainly continues to exist in contemporary communities.

In the decades or century before Europeans began to appear in Secwepemcúlecw, Secwépemc society was undergoing a period of change not only in terms of warfare, migration, and territory but also in social organization, specifically in the western part of Secwepemcúlecw along the Fraser River. Notably in the Fraser Canyon division, people had begun to incorporate aspects of a clan and crest system adopted and adapted from coastal societies by way of the Carrier and St'at'imc (see chapter 8).

In the oral histories surrounding wars and treaties, we have already seen two important principles that existed among Secwépemc people, at least according to genealogies that extend to the 1670s (Teit 1930a). First, the chiefs of communities, especially important "hub" communities throughout the Interior Plateau at Tk̓emlúps (Kamloops), Sp'áxmen (Douglas Lake), Yucwt (Williams Lake), and Lytton, had multiple wives from their own and surrounding nations, thus ensuring ways to maintain political and territorial alliances. Second, the children of important political chiefs were adopted out to cement political alliances or were married back into the nations and communities with whom peace treaties needed to stay active.

K̓wséltkten (being relatives) is what bonds the Secwépemc as a people and bonds us to our allies and friends in neighbouring nations. Being born of particular parents defines membership in a network of people who are seen as connected and belonging together. Kinship connects a person to a community of origin and to other communities with which that person is associated, placing him or her in a network of obligation and cooperation throughout life. Marriage, social control, and the production and distribution of goods – in short, all aspects of individual and collective behaviour – are organized by, and in turn reflect on, a person's kinship ties. Each Secwépemc person has ties of kinship and ties with in-laws that, if enough generations and connections are remembered, literally extend throughout Secwépemc territory. Ultimately, the "glue" of Secwépemc kinship is a significant factor that enables the existence of the nation in perpetuity because it binds each and every Secwépemc person to others within the nation. This web of kinship stretches across bands, or communities, throughout the nation and beyond, and in many ways it is the essence that holds the entire nation together. For countless generations, Secwépemc people have associated with one another on the basis of kinship ties. If people visit another community, they are identified in terms of their relatives. Even when people do not personally know anyone in the other community, they will invariably have close or remote ties with the elders of that community through one or more of their own elders' past network of kinship and marriage. In that sense, Secwépemc persons are never just individuals unto themselves but are always thought of as someone's relatives. The term *k̓wséltkten*, always used with a possessive pronoun, means someone's "family," "relatives," or "kinfolk" – that is, everyone who can be traced as related to an individual on either parent's side of the family and who thus shares rights of access to land and resources and has to help one another out and support one another (see chapter 5). The oral history of the Fish Lake Accord peace treaty between Chief Pelkamulox of Sp'áxmen and Chief Kwolila of Tk̓emlúps, discussed above, attests to the conscious power of kinship relations in maintaining peaceful social and political relations among communities and across the whole nation, enacted through the chiefs of these communities. Indeed, in Secwépemc usage, the term *k̓wséltkten* sometimes has the connotation "friend." Likewise, the term *stemét*, which is usually translated as "one's friend," can also mean "cousin" in reference to a relative of the same generation as oneself because awareness of mutual kinship entails friendship in the sense of mutual respect and the mutual obligation to help one another.

The notion of one's *k̓wséltkten* is egocentric rather than sociocentric since it does not involve a definite and finite social descent group, extended "family," or "clan" with exclusive membership; instead, one's network of relatives is conceived of from the point of view of a particular person. Depending on the nature and purpose of an individual's connection with others, the net of one's relatives, including blood relations and all relations through marriage, can be cast wide or can be cast more narrowly.

Individuals or sets of people who identify and think of one another as relatives call each other *k̓wseltktenéws*, a term that roughly translates as "being relatives to one another." The term that is used for close relatives, or the members of a person's extended rather than nuclear family, is *k̓wseltkten7úẁi* ("real relatives"). Again, who is counted among one's *k̓wseltkten7úẁi* is, at least to some degree, a matter of one's upbringing and personal preferences. In general, one's parents, parents' siblings, first or sometimes second cousins, children, siblings' children, and own grandchildren are counted as *k̓wseltkten7úẁi*.

Kinship involves the notion of descent (who a person's ancestors are), relationship (the siblings of ancestors, one's own siblings, and their descendants), and marriage. It deals with blood relationship among people, as well as affinal (in-law) relationships, yet these relationships are not strictly defined by biology but are culturally categorized.

Secwépemc Kinship Terms

At the heart of the Secwépemc sense of family and relationship is the "system of kinship" used to organize members of extended families and to refer to one another as relatives. The Secwépemc set of kinship terms provides words for different kinds of relatives that are used to refer to them or to address them. These terms, in turn, are connected to the mutual roles of *k̓wséltkten* and to expectations about how they should behave toward one another. Secwépemc terms for relatives are organized differently than English kinship terms. First,

Secwépemc kinship terms are used in an extended or classificatory sense; rather than applying only to immediate relatives, they tend to be used for all members of a generation connected to an individual by blood or through marriage. Thus, whereas in English the term "grandmother" is used only for one's actual mother's mother and father's mother, in Secwépemc all individuals known to be related to a person two generations up are classed in Western Secwepemctsín as *kyé7e* (grandmother) or *xpé7e* (grandfather) and in Eastern Secwepemctsín as *kyé7e* (grandmother) or *slé7e* (grandfather), thus including what in English are called "great-aunts" and "great-uncles." The children of all persons called "grandparent" are called "aunts" or "uncles"; hence the Secwépemc term for "aunt" includes a grandparent's sibling's daughter or a great-grandparent's sibling's grandchild. The terms for sibling are extended to all relatives in one's own generation; although the terms for one's own children differ from the terms for one's siblings' children (classed as "nieces" and "nephews"), the latter are extended to parents' siblings' children's children (i.e., one's cousins' children). Finally, the term for "grandchild" covers not only a person's actual children's children but also a person's siblings' and cousins' children's children, thus standing for any child related to oneself two generations down. In this way, Secwépemc kinship terms group relatives together on the basis of generation.

Secwépemc kinship terms also group certain relatives on the basis of gender, including that of the speaker and that of the person addressed or referred to. Thus the terms for "brother" and "sister" are based on whether a sibling is of the same or opposite sex as the speaker; terms for "aunt" and "uncle" are also based on this principle in that the terms for parents' same-sex siblings are different for males than for females, whereas the terms for parents' opposite-sex siblings are the same for the males and females using them.

In addition to the basic terms listed above, there are further variations of kinship terms that are used to address relatives, especially elder relatives. These often include a stop or glottalized consonant in the middle of the word. Thus, when calling to a maternal uncle, one says, "*si7se!*" and when calling to a maternal aunt, one says, "*tuṁe!*" which are actually "calling to" terms rather than the terms for "maternal uncle" and "maternal aunt," which are *síse7* and *te(t)ṁe7* respectively. Additional slight variations include talking about "my" or "your" relative. There are also endearment terms for some relatives, some of which derive from baby talk, and other such terms for young children. For example, *téte7* is used to refer to one's *tsétse* (little sister), *iṁke* is used to refer to one's *imts* (grandchild), and *túṅce* is used to refer to one's *stunc* (nephew or niece).

As table 9.1 shows, Secwépemc kinship terminology is quite complex when it comes to the terms for aunts and uncles, where males and females use different terms for maternal aunts and paternal uncles, although both males and females share a term for maternal uncles (*síse7*) and paternal aunts

Table 9.1 | Secwépemc kinship and in-law terms

Term	*Refers to*	*Translation*	*Used by*
túpe7	FFF, FMF, MFF, MMF, etc.	great-grandfather	male/female
qné7e	FFM, FMM, etc.	paternal great-grandmother	male/female
kye7e7úẃi	MMM, FMM, MMMZ, FMMZ, FFZ, FMZ, etc.	great-grandmother (lit. "real or ordinary grandmother")	male/female
xpe7e7úẃi	FFF, FMF MMF, MFF, etc.	great-grandfather (lit. "real or ordinary grandfather")	male/female
kyé7e	MM, FM, MMZ, MFZ, FMZ, FFZ, etc.	grandmother	male/female
xpé7e (Western Secwepemctsín)	FF, MF, MFB, MMB, FFB, FMB, etc	grandfather	male/female
slé7e (Eastern Secwepemctsín)	FF, MF, MFB, MMB, FFB, FMB, etc	grandfather (also great-grandfather in Western Secwepemctsin)	male/female
qé7tse	F	father	male/female
qe7tse7éẏe	step-F	stepfather	male/female
kí7ce	M	mother	male/female
ki7ce7éẏe	step-M	stepmother	male/female
méqse7	FB, FFBS, FFZS, FZBS, FZDS, FZHu	female's paternal uncle	female
léẃe	FB, FFBS, FZBS, FZDS, FZHu	male's paternal uncle	male
tíkwe7	FZ, FFZD, FFBD, FMZD, FMBD, FEWi	male's and female's paternal aunt	male/female
túm̓e	MZ, MMZD, MFZD, etc.	female's maternal aunt	female
ḱúẏe	MZ, MMZD, MFZD, etc.	male's paternal aunt	male
síse7	MB, MMED, MMZD, MFBD, MFZD, MZHu	male's and female's maternal uncle	male/female

/continued

Table 9.1 | continued

Term	*Refers to*	*Translation*	*Used by*
úq̓wi	female: Z, MBD, FBD, FFBDD, etc. male: B, FBS, MBS, MZS, etc.	sibling or cousin of same sex as speaker	male/female
uq̓wiyéws	two males who are brothers or cousins to each other two females who are sisters or cousins to each other	siblings or cousins of same sex as each other	male/female
smé7stem	male: Z, FBD, MBD, etc.	siblings or cousins of opposite sex as speaker	male/female
(s)me7steméws	male and female who are siblings or cousins to each other	to be siblings or cousins of opposite sex as each other	male/female
kic	oZ, oFZD, oMBD, etc.	older sister or cousin	male/female
qetsk	oB, oFBS, oMZS, etc.	older brother or cousin	male/female
tsétse	yZ, yFBD, yMBD, etc.	younger sister or cousin	male/female
síntse	yB, yFBS, yMZS, etc.	younger brother or cousin	male/female
sqwsé7	S	son	male/female
st̓emkélt	D	daughter	male/female
qwsé7	ZS, BS (female speaking only)	female's nephew	female
stunc	female: ZD, BD male: ZS, ZD, BS, BD	nephew or niece	female/male
sxélwe	Hu	husband	female
sem7é7em	Wi	wife	male
scwnémt	any in-laws	in-laws	male/female
s7étstem	female: HuB male: WiZ	brother-in-law of female sister-in-law of male	male/female
lltsetsék	WiM, HuM	mother-in-law	male/female
sexéx7e	WiF, HuF	father-in-law	male/female
sépen	SWi	daughter-in-law	male/female

Table 9.1 | continued

Term	*Refers to*	*Translation*	*Used by*
snek̓llcw	DHu	son-in-law	male/female
sekéw, skew	HuZ, BWi	sister-in-law	male/female
stśect	ZHu, WiB	brother-in-law	male/female

Abbreviations: F (father), M (mother), Z (sister), B (brother), S (son), D (daughter), Hu (husband), Wi (wife), oB (older brother), yB (younger brother), oZ (older sister), yZ (younger sister), thus FF (father's father), FFF (father's father's father), MFB (mother's father's brother), DHu (daughter's husband), and so on.

(*tíkwe7*). The technical term that anthropologists use for this kind of kinship system reflected in words for relatives, especially aunts and uncles, is "bifurcate collateral."

Interestingly, the Secwépemc term *léẇe*, used by a male for "father's brother," is cognate with,[2] or similar to, the Okanagan term *lew*, for "boy's father." Likewise, the Secwépemc term *túm̓e*, used by a female for "mother's sister," is cognate with the Okanagan term *tum*, used by a female for "mother," as is the term *k̓úẏe*, used by a male for "mother's sister," which is cognate with the Okanagan term *sk̓uy*, used by a male for "mother." A boy's paternal uncle is thus thought of as like an additional father, and a girl's maternal aunt is like an additional mother. These relatives, indeed, would have been the most likely relatives to raise a child whose actual mother or father passed away. In addition, as many Secwépemc elders have observed, it was quite common for a parent's sibling, especially a mother's sister, to take in and raise some of her nieces or nephews.

More than fifty years ago, William Elmendorf (1961) noticed that among groups in the Salish language family, kinship terminologies of particular languages comprised two types: (1) a simpler lineal Coast Salish "bifurcate merging" type, which includes Nlaka'pamux (Thompson) and St'at'imc (Lillooet) terminologies, and (2) a more complex Interior "bifurcate collateral" type, which includes Okanagan and other Southern Interior Salish terminologies, along with the way the Sahaptin family terms are organized, although the actual terms are very different from the Interior Salish ones. By contrast, the Nlaka'pamux and St'at'imc terms, especially for "aunt" and "uncle" and for "niece" and "nephew," are similar to the Coast Salish "bifurcate merging" type. At the time, no complete set of Secwépemc kinship terms had been recorded, but as the many terms that refer to parents' siblings show, the Secwépemc kinship terminology is closer to the Interior bifurcate collateral type. Elmendorf made a convincing argument that the Interior bifurcate collateral system is the more ancient system. Thus it appears that, although Salish won out as the language spoken subsequent to the migration of people from the coast, the pre-existing kinship system persisted among the Secwépemc, Okanagan, and our southern neighbours.

Respect for Elders and Kindness to Younger Ones

Another important aspect of the Secwépemc kinship system is the respect that is due to an older relative. The Secwépemc term *stet̓ex7ém* is used for "elders" but is also used to refer to any senior adult family member. All persons older than oneself are to be treated with respect. The word used in Secwepemctsín for this is *xyemstéc* (you honour someone). What happens when an older person is not treated with respect is illustrated in Mary Thomas's story about Muskrat (Seklácwa7 in Eastern Secwepemctsín and Skelécwe7 in Western Secwepemctsín). She tells this story in the Eastern Secwepemctsín dialect.

Seklácwa7 | Story of Muskrat

told by Mary Thomas,[3] recorded by Marianne Ignace and Ronald E. Ignace, May 1994

Nerí7 spút̓as-ekwa re lacús te núxwuxw.
It was the time when a pretty girl appeared.

Acwas-ekwa neri7 sácwmas, m-ust-ekwa ucw.
She was there bathing, she would dive under the water.

T̓ri7 t̓e tkekák̓wal̓tk-ucw m-t̓7ak-ekwa re senxwúxw … re Seklácwa7!
Coyote, no the Muskrat, went along out there at a distance, the Muskrat!

Kwatsútas re sk̓úlmas as la7s-ekwa k s7ístkas.
As he packed away things to store so that he would have a good winter.

Wikt.s-ekwa re seslá7s ucw.
She saw that old man [Muskrat] again.

Re m-ust-ekwa-ucw re núxuxw t̓7ána sták̓walc-ekwa ucw.
The woman would dive into the water as before and float to the surface again.

Ts̓xatám-ekwa-ucw re Seklácwa7, "Tsecwes7úw̓isas a seslá7!"
She would look toward Muskrat [and say], "The old man has a scary face!"

Re m-ust-ekwa ucw ri7 núxuxw sták̓walc-ekwa-ucw.
The woman would dive again, then float to the surface of the water.

Ṫ7an ṫri7 ṫ7ak ucw, "Tsecpullníṅut re seslá7!"
She would go by again [and say], "The old man is dried up around the hips!"

Oh! Ṫri7 sṫ7ak-ekwa-ucw, "Wetswetscáca7 re seslá7."
Oh! She would come back around again [and say], "That old man has lizard legs."

Kwak̓wáṅmas-ekwa ṫlu7 ṫe tsecwesus7úẁis, wetswetscáca7, tsecpullníṅut!
She was looking the old man up and down, [describing him as] scary-faced, dried up around the hips, and having lizard legs!

Xwexwéyt ṫlun te sk̓ápqas kwak̓wáṅmas-ekwa re seslá7a wel púṫa.
Right from the top of his head down, she looked him up and down until each time he came up.

K7ápes-ekwa re ṗúsmas re Sekláċwa7. (chuckle)
The Muskrat became very sad. *(chuckle)*

"Ta7 ṫri7 k stam k stsqúqwa, stsqwnckstmastn k k̓wsaltktn all wel xílltsas re núxwuxw ṫe k̓estsínmatsas, qwanqwánmatsas!"
"I haven't done anything to torment her relatives for the woman to be that way toward me, for her to swear at me, to talk pitifully about me!"

"Ah ri7, háqa ma7 guyt ri7 tka7 wi7 re skwak̓wáṅmatsas."
"Oh well, maybe she'll get tired of making fun of me."

Ta7a ṫri7! Sṫ7ak-ekwa mall ucw, westám-ekwa! "Tketkaṫmúṁpa re seslá7a!" (laughter)
Not at all! Along she came again, still after him! "The old man has a dirty tail!" *(laughter)*

Oh! Kítsitmas-ekwa te s7gayċp.
Oh! Then he got very angry.

Tsut-ekwa, "Ma7 tpapqstn."
They say he said, "I will teach her a lesson."

Ts7úst-ekwa te tkwékwaltk re Seklácwa7 lek wel e, tsqwaẏmínta re núxwucw, qwmánksta! (laughter)
The Muskrat dove under water and then he took advantage of the woman, got her pregnant! *(laughter)*

Ta7-ekwa k stslxastás.
She didn't know about it.

Ená! Ṫucw wel xyawílc yi7ána stsqwmanks.
Oh no! She began to become big from her pregnancy.

Ḱultíl̓a-ekwa, tuwíwt-ekwa re skúyas.
He made a child, they say he had a little boy.

Tsut-ekwa má7a re pellsṫakált, sáwatm-ekwa re núxwuxw, "Swáti7?"
The one whose daughter it was asked the woman, "Who is it [the father of the child]?"

Tsúntm-ekwa, "Swáti7 k xillt.s-enka?"
They said to her, "Who did this to you?"

"Ta7 ya ṫri7 k stselxastátn, swátas-nka."
"Well I don't know, I don't know who it was."

Tsúntm-ekwa ṫ7ána, "Plúk̓watiya xwexwáyt, re sqálqlacw re stam."
They told the people, "You people gather together everyone of the men and all that."

Tsut-ekwa, "E swat a qwíṫsmas yi7ána sk̓wimáṁlt yerí7 ma7 pallsa7á7a."
They said, "Whoever the baby smiles at, he will be the one to get [her for] a wife."

Lacús-ekwa ri7 núxwuxw.
They say that the woman was very pretty.

Ixw! Re senxúxwlacw ya-ekwa k xetáqse7úẁi.
Strutting smartly, Coyote was the very first to go.

"Yerí7 ma7 yac ra tsáwa7 k pall-sa7á7a," m-tsut-ekwa-ucw. (laughter)
"It will be me who gets a wife," he said. *(laughter)*

Oh! Put a stam-ekwa re ska7cís e tsúwat.s, tá7 ṫri7 re sk̓wimáṁlt k s7astqwíṫs.
Oh! He acted like a grizzly bear. The baby didn't smile.

Re m-tclupa7tsút-ekwa m-paplk̓ilc, m-paplk̓íl̓c-ekwa re senxúxwlacw.
Coyote bit his tail and rolled around.

"Re m-astqwíṫ! M-astqwíṫ!" "Tá7a ṫri7!"
"He smiled! He smiled!" "No, no way!"

Oh! Te m-xíla, ta7 ṫri7 k swat!

Oh! And so it went, there was no one!

Wel a tsut-ekwa ṫ7ána:
And then they said this:

"Ta! k̓all tnk̓wa7 k l-ta7 k astwáy̓s! Tsqwlentákwiya!"
"Hey! There's still one other [Muskrat] who hasn't come forward! You folks go and call him!"

Tsut-ekwa re kúkwpi7, "Tsqwlentákwiya!"
The chief said, "You guys call him!"

"Xwexwáyt re swat ma7 tsnas."
"Everyone is to come here."

Tsut-ekwa ucw re Seklácwa7,
And so they say that Muskrat said,

"Ah, ṫlan k stsqwatsítsimactsalp!"
"Ah, you guys quit saying pitiful things about me!"

"Re ntsáwa7 re sen7awít.s sxwexwáyt.s re stam. Ye-ekwa put ra tsáwa7, tá7a ṫri7!"
"I'm the last one in the line up of everything! As if it had to be me, no way!"

"Ta7 ṫri7, tk̓wnm7ípla7tals re kúkwpi7. E tsnasucw-ekwa."
"Not at all, the chief has given his orders to us. He said for you to come."

"Cuy̓ yam!" gaypatsútas-ekwa. Ya-enka k sáma7 k tsut "Got a guilty feeling." *(laughter)*
"Okay!" he said angrily. I guess that's what the white man calls "Got a guilty feeling." *(laughter)*

Tsqwatsáts-ekwa re Seklácwa7.
So they say that Muskrat came forward.

Yerí7 ṫri7 n tsyámas-ekwa yi7ána txlcatáṅs re tsyeláṗ, neri7 re sk̓wimáṁlt.
Where the people lived, there was a stepladder made from bushes, that was where the baby was.

Hu! Xílmas-ekwa re Seklácwa7, re klkákalcs na7ána,
Hu! And so Muskrat had his little hands here [on his hips],

"Q̇utsetsútsu7, Q̇utsetsútsutsu7, Q̇utsetsútsu7, Q̇utsetsútsutsu7."

"Little Fatty, Little Fatty, Little Fatty, Little Fatty."
(Muskrat sings and dances, with hands on hips.)

Cyánmas-ekwa yerí7 melcámas re Seklácwa7. (chuckle)
Muskrat goes round and round dancing. *(chuckle)*

Mus-ekwa re smelcáms, every round m-tsut-ekwa-ucw,
He danced four rounds, every round he would say,

"Q̓wetsetsútsu7, Q̓wetsetsútsutsu7, ya-ekwa ri7 le tsecpullníńut."
"Little Fatty, Little Fatty, they say that it's the one who is dried out at the hips."[4]

"Q̓wetsetsútsu7, Q̓wetsetsútsutsu7, ya-ekwa ri7 le tscwesus7úẃis!"
"Little Fatty, Little Fatty, they say that it's the one with the scary face!"

Ṫri7 m-cyánm-ekwa.
He would circle around again.

"Q̓wetsetsútsu7, Q̓wetsetsútsutsu7, ye-ekwa ri7 le tsckaṫtmúḿpa!" (laughter)
"Little Fatty, Little Fatty, they say that it's the one with the dirty tail!" *(laughter)*

"Q̓wetsetsútsu7, Q̓wetsetsútsutsu7," ya-ekwa ṫe m-smust.s re stscyánas,
"Little Fatty, Little Fatty," they say that on the fourth time that he circled around,

tsem7áy-ekwa re núxwucw ya-ekwa re stsut.s, "Q̓wetsetsútsu7, Q̓wetsetsútsutsu7, tsún all lu7 k yaws!"
he came close to the woman and then said, "Little Fatty, Little Fatty, I thought I was the one!"

"Q̓wetsetsútsu7," satsínas-ekwa. Ne smust.s ṫe stsut.s, "Yúmall lu7 k syá-enkas!"
"Little Fatty," he sang. On the fourth time, he said, "I thought that was the one!"

Huuu! Re sk̓wimáḿlt, sqexwqwáq̓wxwt.s, ya-ekwa re sxílas u7líla.
Huuu! The baby's little feet did this [danced in the air], he laughed.

Ṫek7ílc re Seklácwa7.
Muskrat ran away.

"Xeltskwántiya!"
"Grab him, you folks!"

"Swáti7 kwawáńtmas Seklácwa7 yerí7 ma7 pallnúxwuxw."
"Whoever can catch Muskrat will be the one who gets the woman."

Xixw! Re senxúxwlacw ya-ekwa.
Strutting forward, they say, was Coyote.

Telri7ána xílm-ekwa Seklácwa7, ctkelcátkwa-ekwa.
They say that Muskrat did this, he ran into the water.

Ṫri7-ekwa senxúxwlacw, ust-ekwa.
Coyote was right behind him, he dove in.

Re m-xílm-ekwa, m-kwa7wállna7-ekwa te skwa …
They say he did this, he caught something a …

Ṫ7ána m-xílm-ekwa, "M-kwawáẃa! M-kwawáẃa!" Sxtṡay-ekwa ṫe yact. (laughter)
They say that he did this, "I caught him! I caught him!" They say that it was only a long stick. *(laughter)*

Llxup-ekwa le Seklácwa7. (laughter)
Muskrat got away. *(laughter)*

Xwexwáyt re stsptákwll ri7 re stsmámelt re stseptákwla7stmas.
All of the stories were told to the children.

Ec re stsúnstmas re stsmámelt, "Tákwiya má7a! Ta7us pahán, wa7 ṫhánes a tṡílmas k stṡxatáp ra7 staxṫax7am, ta7us pahán k skwak̓wánma-tp."
The children were told, "See that! Never ever, no matter how you look at your elders, don't ever look someone up and down."

"Ma7 qwaqwatwílc-kp."
"You will become pitiful."

"Eyastákwiya, xyastákwiya ra7 staṫax7ám."
"All of you, respect and honour your elders."

"Ma7 tcwlpílcmatlas a xa, kapcítpas ṫe cptíńastns ra7 staṫax7ám."
"If you hurt the feelings of elders, it will come back on you."

"Táka re Seklácwa7, kwak̓wánmata, geyáp, qwmankst.s re núxwuxw." (laughter)
"See Muskrat, they made fun of him, he got angry, he got the woman pregnant." *(laughter)*

"Qílqalt táka re Seklácwa7." (laughter)
"See how funny the Muskrat is." *(laughter)*

"Ta7us pahán re staxṫax7ám k s7awátn-tp ṫe skapcítp ṫe ṗúsmas."
"Don't ever say things to an elder, to make them feel sad."

This fascinating story expresses in humorous terms what can happen if a young person insults and verbally "torments" (*qwnákstmas* in Eastern Secwepemctsín and *qwnékstmens* in Western Secwepemctsín) an older person who should be treated as an elder – in this case, one of the opposite sex. The taunts that the pretty young girl uses with Muskrat are full of allusions that he would find particularly insulting. The remarks she calls out *about* him rather than directly *to* him not only call him "scary-faced," or very ugly, but also allude to him being impotent, or "dried out around the hips" (from *tsec* for "perpetual," plus the root *pull* for "dried out," plus reduplication of *-níẇt* for "hips, sides"), adding his "dirty tail" to the insult. The reference to *wetswetscáca* (lizard legs) not only comments on the short crooked legs that muskrats indeed have but also subtly alludes to the role of lizards in the Secwépemc belief system, as they are said to have evil powers to invade someone's body by crawling up someone's legs and invading the body through that person's anus, driving him or her crazy (see Ida Matthew's mention of lizards in chapter 5).[5]

The words that are used to describe how the girl treats this elder emphasize her violation of important cultural protocols of interaction with elders and relatives. She "looks him up and down" (*kwak̓wáńmas* in Eastern Secwepemctsín and *kwenk̓wéńmens* in Western Secwepemctsín) while uttering her remarks about him, perceived as a seriously insulting way to interact with an elder. When wondering why the girl torments him like this, he not only considers the fact that he himself as an individual has never treated her badly to bring this behaviour about but also ponders that he never did anything to her *k̓wséltkten* (relatives), thus perceiving of the cause of her action both as between individuals and as involving the family or group.

The consequence of her insults is that he impregnates her, not without himself subsequently having a "guilty feeling." Thus stories like this one invite the audience to ponder the consequences of misbehaviour toward elders, as Mary Thomas concludes at the end. In addition, they do not involve unequivocally "good" and "bad" actions but show the consequences of going against Secwépemc law.

The story of Chipmunk and Owl addresses the same issue. Here, in a story revolving around a pun, young Qetṡwéẇye (Chipmunk), whom we know is a female from her role in other *stsptekwll* (ancient stories), insults her *xpé7e* (grandfather), Sníne (Owl), by saying, "Your balls are wrinkled!" When questioned, however, she quickly corrects herself to the phonetically very similar line "Your kinnikinnik berries [which they have been picking] are wrinkled." When she repeats this four times, Owl charges after her, and as she almost escapes, he leaves the scratch-mark that Chipmunk has down her back, which becomes the characteristic stripe of chipmunks, thus reminding us to this day of her breach of law when she insulted the old man.

Re Qetśwéẇye ell re Sníne | The Chipmunk and Owl Story[6]

Mut-ekwe re Qetśwéẇye méte xpé7es, re Sníne.
Chipmunk lived with her grandfather, Owl.

Nek̓ú7 te sitq̇t m-cuyt es tq̇wlustsíń te elk.
One day they left to pick kinnikinnik berries.

W7ec re tq̇wlustsińmes, re Qetśwéẇye m-tsúnses re xpé7es,
While they were picking into their mouths, Chipmunk said to her grandfather,

"Yerí7 re7 stsqepq̇ipusél̓cken!"
"Your balls are wrinkled!"

M-tsúntem te Sníne, "Enwét-k?"
Owl said to her, "What did you say?"

Tsut re Qetśwéẇye, "M-tsúntsen, 'Tsqeq̇ipúse7 re7 elk!'"
Chipmunk said, "I told you, 'Your kinnikinnik berries are wrinkled!'"

M-yews re scwelpílcs re stq̇wlustsíń cú7tsem.
Owl turned around and picked some more.

M-tsut cú7tsem re Qetśwéẇye, "Tsqeq̇ipusél̓cken-k."
Chipmunk said again, "Your balls are wrinkled."

Raltsíńmentmes te Sníne, "Enwét-k?"
Owl said sternly, "What did you say?"

M-tsunses re Qetśwéẇye, "Tśecwlemtsíńmentsen! Tsutst-ken en stsutst, 'Tsqepq̇ipúse7 re7 elk!'"
Chipmunk told him, "I had a slip of the tongue! I meant to say, 'Your berries are wrinkled!'"

Mus-ekwe re stsúntem. Le must.s-ekwe, m-geyépentmes te Sníne, m-t̓éxelcmentmes re Qetśwéẇye.

Four times he said that. On the fourth time, Owl got angy and charged at Chipmunk.

Kéḱmell yerí7 re sllxups ne tspetkúl̓ecws, ḱémell m-tś̓legwegwéẃkentmes te Snine.
Chipmunk almost escaped into her hole, but she got scratched on her back by Owl.

Telrí7 wel tsegwtsugwíken re qetś̓wéẃye.
That's why the chipmunk's back has a stripe on it.

On the topic of respectful behaviour toward relatives, Mary Thomas also told the story of Tś̓qíqse7 (Chickadee). It deals with the kindness that should be shown to younger siblings and with the consequences of being *gít̓kstmen* (purposefully mean to someone). Tś̓qíqse7's story is part of a multifaceted epic story told in its most detailed version by Charlie Draney of Skeetchestn and recorded by Aert Kuipers (1974, 116–30), who titled it "The Trout Children and Their Grandparents." Another version, written down by George M. Dawson (1891, 33–5), very specifically connects this *stsptekwll* to a location – Pípsell (Jacko Lake), located in the grasslands above Tḱemlúps (Kamloops) – and connects it to an additional location, the remains of a prayer tree called Ḱecúseṁ ("tears well up in someone's eyes"), which were not far from the lake (see fig. 6, image e, colour section).

The entire story is about a woman who, having lost all her relatives, creates a daughter from a stick (a tree!). The daughter meets a handsome man at the lake where she lives and goes under the water with him, for it turns out that he is a trout man or otherwise described as one of the *xqelmecwétkwe* (water people). They have two children, who subsequently long for their grandmother and swim up to the surface of the lake to visit their grandmother's place but are too shy to face her. Having observed and recognized them, she prepares medicine to turn them permanently back into humans, and when she spills it on them, she fully douses the boy, who becomes human, but she is only able to partially douse the girl, who becomes a puppy. In the translation of Charlie Draney's version of what happened,

> The boy changed into a human being, but the girl changed into a little dog. Then their grandmother consoled both of them, she consoled the boy saying, "I am your grandmother. Long ago your mother left from here. I got (drenched) you well, but I didn't get your sister well, she only became a little dog. Remember for the future, whatever your sister does, if she runs away with your game, or no matter how angry you are at her, never whip or kick her. Always, as long as the two of you live here, if you are hunting or whatever your are doing, if she runs away with the

> game you killed, or eats it, never whip your sister, nor do anything else to her." So the boy lived there, his sister followed him everywhere, he hunted, the old woman taught him what to do when hunting and made arrows for him. Once she (his sister) ran away with his game – he had shot an excellent bird – and the boy became angry and whipped the little dog. The little dog yelped and ran away, it ran and ran, and finally it flew up and said: "Your sister, your sister, your sister" [re7 tsétse, re7 tsétse, re7 tsétse], changing into a chickadee. The boy ran after the chickadee and called out to him, but it kept saying to him, "Your sister, your sister, your sister." Finally the boy returned, crying, and came home to his grandmother; the latter already knew what had happened, she had long since sensed it. His grandmother asked him: "Why are you crying?" and then he told her. She said to him: "There you are, I told you not to whip your sister whatever she might do. And now she has left you, you don't have a companion any more." (Kuipers 1974, 127–8)

Mary Thomas interpreted the boy's loss of his sister's companionship as follows:

Ec ma7 tśúmas wel ma7 yews la tsátsas.
He will cry forever for his little sister.

Oh! Every time ucw lexáy̓act.s-kucw len kyá7a ucw m-kák̓mall wes a lqwaq̓wtes.
Oh! Every time that our grandmother told that story, we would almost start to wail.

Pyin e qnímanc ay ac re tcúsmas t̓ek tsátsas. Every story, every legend, has a lesson.
Now when you hear it, it's still looking for his little sister. Every story, every legend, has a lesson.

M-tsuns-kucw len kyá7a, "Tákwiya má7a! Tá7us us k xaxnantwácwep!"
My grandmother would say to us, "See that now! Don't go hurting one another!"

Ec k lá7-ep, ac k yucwmntwácwep.
Be good all of you, look out for one another.

E tsháqas a k̓ult-kp t̓ri7 t̓ek stam.
Things happen, you could be transformed into something.

Ma7 pelpstép ra7 tsátsa7, ra7 síntsa.
You'll lose your little sister, your little brother.

Yecwmíntiya ra7 setsetatamámc.
Look after those younger than yourself.[7]

This ethic of respecting the elderly and taking care of younger family members also supports the cohesion of the entire extended family to whom this applies. Medicinal charms both symbolized and empowered the cohesion of families, where old and young supported one another. Thus Mary Thomas talked of *tseptspáq̓* (sweet-scented bedstraw, *Galium triflorum*) as a plant that mothers would tie into their medicine bundles. "And that was to wish that their family stay close together, never to argue or go against one another. That was the idea of that little medicine bag, that they keep the family strong together."

Adoption

As a custom, "adoption" can refer to traditional practices that create an officially (or publicly) recognized parent-child bond between two persons not naturally related as such. The Secwépemc language has a term for adoption, *skwentél̓e* or *skwen̓le*, as well as *kweníl̓e* – all derived from the root verb *kwen* for "take (in)" plus the lexical suffix *(i)l̓e* for "offspring" and all referring to the concept of "taking in and raising as your own," very similar to the *Oxford English Dictionary*'s definition of adoption as "taking up and treating as one's own."

Secwépemc adoption principles and practices can best be explained as integrated with the overall values and principles of Secwépemc social organization and culture. In Secwépemc society, the emphasis is on the sharing of parental roles among parents and their siblings (aunts and uncles of their children), as well as grandparents, rather than on exclusive parenting within the nuclear family. The extended family in the past provided – and to some extent, continues to provide – for joint nurturing and training responsibilities. Grandmothers, aunts, uncles, and older siblings took an effective part in the parenting and supervising of younger relatives. Such informal fostering or joint rearing of the children of close relatives had an important function in the pursuit of resource-harvesting activities. When mothers accompanied their husbands on hunting, trapping, or fishing expeditions, they sometimes left younger children in the care of a sister, mother, or older daughter. Elders reported that a nursing woman was sometimes asked to babysit and nurse infants other than her own. Such shared nurturing responsibilities were not considered to be adoptions, as they were both temporary and informal. However, like adoption, the concept of joint nurturing is based on values and concepts associated with kinship roles.

In all cases of actual formal adoptions that elders reported to Marianne Ignace in the mid-1980s, the adopted person was a relative of the adopting parent, although the genealogical relationship was sometimes rather remote. Because women were seen as primary nurturers, it was generally women who adopted. The cases cited below took place between around 1900 and the 1940s.

To understand the Secwépemc notions and practices regarding traditional adoption, we examine a few cases of adoption remembered and told by elders in the 1980s that date back to the early 1900s. All of the cases listed below were thought of as the *sk̓wentéle* (taking-in) of a child. All adoptees were infants or children when taken in.

Example 1 involved the adoption of a child fathered by the adopting parent's husband born from a liaison with another woman. When the child's natural mother died, his father's wife took him in, thus integrating him into his natural father's family.

Example 2 involved the adopting parent taking in two of her grandchildren. One was orphaned after his mother died and his father was unable to care for him alone. And one was the child of a daughter who was severely disabled after an accident and was subsequently unable to raise her daughter.

Example 3 involved a child who was adopted by his mother's husband's father and wife but who took on the identity of a recently deceased child of the couple who had had the same name. He was thus adopted by social, not biological, grandparents but took the role of their son. The adoption took place after he was orphaned and had been living "from place to place" for a while. As the section below on names and name giving explains, people perceived a deep connection between the name children were given or had and the social persona that they had and were to develop. Moreover, a name could revive a role in the kinship network that matched the previous person who had had that name. Implicit in this idea are notions of rebirth.

Example 4 involved a child who, after her mother died, was adopted by her *tum̓e* (mother's sister), who was the local chief's wife. Her father remarried and subsequently had twelve children by his second wife. The adopted child was consequently raised as the chief's daughter, although she maintained her relationship with her deceased mother's relatives and, to a lesser degree, with her father's new family. Her adoptive mother also arranged her marriage when she was sixteen, as well as her second marriage (which was a "levirate" in the wider sense of the term) (see fig. 9.3).

Example 5 involved a young man who was adopted by his maternal grandmother's sister – classed as his *kyé7e* (grandmother) – after his own mother died. The reason given for this adoption was that his father married a widow with a large family and thus lacked the resources to take care of him, so his *kyé7e* took him in and raised him as her own.

Example 6 involved the same adopting parent of example 5, who also raised another male youth. The mother of this youth wanted to marry, and his father was married to another woman, so his paternal grandfather's sister, his *kyé7e*, took him in, adopting him.

Example 7 involved a woman who, after being born out of wedlock, had been adopted by her maternal grandmother's father's sister, Púle7, who was her *kyé7e* (or *kye7e7úw̓i*, "real grandmother"). Púle7's own "granddaughter," the daughter of her brother's daughter, later adopted this woman's daughter, as well as her daughter's daughter and later that daughter's daughter.

Example 8 involved a young man in his late teens who lost his mother, after having previously lost the grandmother and great-grandmother who had raised him. His great-grandmother's niece (the daughter of his paternal grandmother's father's brother's daughter) stepped in to adopt him, although he was a young adult, providing him with mentorship and with social and political support in his quest for leadership in the community.

In numerous other cases that involve adoptions well into the late 1990s and 2000s, grandparents' siblings stepped in to claim their *im̓ke* (grandchild) as their own close grandchild when the actual maternal or paternal grandmother of a younger child passed away. In yet another scenario of adoption, grandparents or even great-grandparents adopted grandchildren by "claiming" them and then giving them a destiny to be raised by an elder, with the elder passing on knowledge, stories, and practices to the chosen grandchild. Thus, as Ron Ignace remembered, he was "claimed" by his great-grandmother Sulyén Eneas. Already in her late sixties when he was born, she raised him as a young child, "claiming" him from his own mother, Lizzy Jules.

We see that in all of the above cases, the "taking-in" of a relative is the result of a natural mother not being able to care for a child for physical or social reasons. The adopting parent takes in the child because the adopting parent is a *k̓wséltkten* of the actual parent. In examples 5 to 7 above, the adopting parents were women who were unable to have children of their own. In addition, Secwépemc elders have frequently mentioned that when a woman had many children, she might pass one or more of them on to a sister who had none. Example 8 involves a young man beyond the age of needing immediate guardians, yet the adoption marked the replacement of his deceased mother with a related elder of similar age who would give advice and lend support to the young man.

In addition to such circumstances, the case of the Fish Lake Accord (see chapter 8) also points to the traditional practice of adopting out children for political reasons. Like marriage, raising the child of a former enemy cements a political alliance. In the case of Kamloops chief Kwolila's adoption of his young niece Kokoimalks, the child of his half-brother Okanagan chief Pelkamulox, the adoption involved not a stranger but a close relative, yet it occurred in circumstances where the two families, and the communities and nations behind them, had become enemies. Adoption among chiefs also involved a chief's political guardianship of an allied chief's son. Thus, when Pelkamulox lay dying after he was mortally wounded by a St'at'imc chief during an altercation at Cáclep (Fountain), he charged Kwolila with the guardianship of his son, Hwistesmetxe'qen ("walking grizzly bear"), and asked him to see that his son avenged his death (see chapter 8). Hwistesmetxe'qen (ca. 1780–85 to 1865) (Teit 1930, 231), better known as Chief Nikwalá, or N'Kwala, was to play a key role in interactions with fur traders during the first half of the nineteenth century.[3]

Traditional Secwépemc adoption was formalized through a publicly witnessed announcement and by virtue of the adopting parents visibly taking on the public and practical role as supporters, guardians, mentors, and caretakers of a child or young adult. It appears that when missionaries established themselves among Interior Plateau peoples in the late 1960s and instituted child baptism soon after that, a form of traditional adoption practices continued in the form of godparenting. Like the adopting parents in oral histories of adoption, Secwépemc godparents invariably were aunts, uncles, or other senior relatives of a child who went on record – in this case, even the written record – as mentors and guardians of a child.

Skwentéle, the traditional practice of adoption, can be understood as having both social and political functions. It assured a home and parentage for children whose birth parents could not raise them for a variety of personal reasons, including health problems, as well as sharing out children among related women who could not have children of their own. In addition, among chiefs, it supported political alliances and had functions of political mentorship and protectorship. As shown by the examples of adoptions between around 1900 and the 1940s, traditional, or "custom," adoption was carried on among Secwépemc people well into the twentieth century.

Marriage and Residence Patterns

In his ethnography of the Secwépemc, James Teit (1909) noted the flexibility of community membership between Secwépemc and other Interior Salish peoples in that many people moved between communities rather than being continually and perpetually associated with a particular community of birth. This seeming flexibility, or "disorganization," of Secwépemc kinship and village arrangements can be explained by the protocols of resource ownership, sharing, and family obligation that emerged over time in Interior Plateau society, also evident in the kinship terms used for in-laws. When a young man married, he was expected to move in with his parents-in-law for a few years as a kind of "bride service." The very term for "son-in-law," *snekllcw* ("the changing of abode/dwelling"), makes reference to this custom: the son-in-law, upon marriage, was expected to reside in the community of his wife's family, learning to hunt, fish, and gather there, while getting to know his new relatives. Eventually, after some years, he and his wife would move back to his family of origin. Nonetheless, they were expected to return throughout their life, such as in times of cyclical fluctuation of salmon, in times of hardship, and in times of mourning (when a close relative died), as well as periodically to go on hunting and fishing trips. A man would count on being invited by his brothers-in-law (his wife's brothers or cousins) to hunt in the part of Secwepemcúl̓ecw associated with his in-laws, thus benefiting his wife and children by getting to know the terrain and its resources. Teit (ibid., 591) also mentioned another kind of marriage, where a young man "touched" a young girl on the breast or heel, after which she had to marry him.

As the case of the Fish Lake Accord shows, marriage of the children of chiefs between different nations served the purpose of building political alliances. Marriage records from the mid-nineteenth century show that marriages were also frequently contracted between faraway communities, although the majority of individuals appear to have found spouses from nearby – either their own community or a neighbouring community. As remains the case today, marriages were prohibited between individuals who were known to be related. Teit (1909, 591) noted that the incest taboo encompassed first and second cousins. However, given that the terms used for *smé7stem* (cousins of the opposite sex) were extended to all the individuals to whom a person was related, the taboo of marrying a relative was extended to all the people to whom a person was remembered to be related – or more aptly, to one's elders! Thus today the rules and prohibitions involving marriage are closely connected to the "remembering" work that elders carry out, which entails the memories of past marriages and relationships, the children produced by them, and so forth. As shared and collective memories, both kinship and marriage practices are connected to our sense of history.

Upon marriage, and following the "bride service" of the *snek̓llcw* (son-in-law), a couple's main place of residence, in most cases, was in the husband's village, and hence it was in their father's Indigenous band or community where most children were predominantly raised and socialized, thus getting to know the land and its resources. Throughout life, however, by way of maintaining ties with their mother's relatives and other relatives from previous generations who had married out, they would continually visit these places and harvest resources with these relatives. At least in the nineteenth and early twentieth centuries, in a small number of marriages, it was actually the husband who moved into his wife's village. In such scenarios, there were prevailing political, economic, or social reasons. For example, in the early 1900s, Chief André Tyenmésq̓t of the Símpcwemc (North Thompson), who had only one remaining daughter after losing his sons to sickness, arranged for Cucwéll (Tapít or David Casimir) of Tk̓emlúps to move to Chu Chua to marry his daughter by offering him the chiefship of the village. Cucwéll, of course, was also Chief Louis's grandson, so his marriage to Lizette (Eliza), Chief

Tyenmésq̓t's daughter, had the additional purpose of alliance between the two chiefs and their families.

In Secwépemc society, polygyny (a man having more than one wife at the same time) was sanctioned, although it was mainly chiefs and leaders who were able to maintain and support any number of wives, in good part for reasons of political alliances with neighbouring nations. The story of the Fish Lake Accord, along with Teit's (1930a) detailed genealogy of Chief Pelkamulox and his descendants, shows the existence and function of intermarriage among nations, including the polygynous marriages of Pelkamulox. Various chiefs throughout Secwepemcúl̓ecw are remembered by present elders as having had numerous wives. For example, Chief Spyu7 (Eagle) in the Esk̓ét area is remembered as having had as many as seven wives. It appears that by the late 1870s, most men who had had multiple wives had given up all but one senior wife, at least for the public record. The 1877 census undertaken by the Joint Reserve Commission during the allocation of reserves in the Interior lists a single male, the subchief Tswélne of Tk̓emlúps, as having two wives. All other unions, at least for the record, were monogamous. Upon his baptism, Chief Louis of Tk̓emlúps, who had several wives, gave up all but his oldest wife, Victoire, including his youngest wife, Marie, whom he arranged to be re-married to Abraham LaRue of Tk̓emlúps. Upon Victoire's death and Abraham LaRue's death, Louis remarried Marie, thus fulfilling his obligation to take care of her. Unlike other chiefs at that time who sent their additional wives home to their own communities, Louis, so it was remembered, kept his wives in the Tk̓emlúps area, continuing to provide for them (Jeanette Jules, personal communication, 2013).

Another custom of Interior Plateau society was *sk̓élpem*, whereby a widow married the *úq̓wi* (sibling or cousin) of her deceased husband – a practice called "levirate" by anthropologists who have observed it in many societies – which ensured that she would have a hunter-provider, a father for her children, and a continuing spousal relationship within a community that she was often not born in but had married into. A widower, likewise, would be expected to marry his deceased wife's sister or cousin, a practice called "sororate," thus acquiring someone who could raise his children, carry out female chores, and provide companionship. This caretakership through *sk̓élpem* extended not only to the actual sibling of a deceased spouse but also to any first or second cousins of the same sex.

Of traditional marriage, Teit (1909, 591) noted, "Marriage by presents and marriage by betrothal were the most common and honorable methods." The arrangement of the marriage itself, or the engagement, was a formal affair. It involved a meeting between the relatives of the bride and groom during which the "appointment" to marry was announced as *emútctem̓-ekwe te s̓temkélt.s-kucw* ("he is appointed [sat down] to marry our daughter"). Members of both families would then make speeches citing the good ancestry (pedigree) of the bride and groom, as well as the qualities of each that made them fit to be good spouses, mentioning their domestic, hunting, and fishing skills. This arrangement and meeting formalized the marriage and announced it to the public. It thus made the engagement and alliance between the two families official. The wedding itself usually involved a small feast and give-away, although in some instances the arrangement meeting seems to have been the only official part of the marriage arrangement. It is noteworthy that this traditional arrangement of marriage and ceremony continued on into the 1920s and 1930s; although, superficially, marriages were legalized through the Catholic Church, the internal ways of arranging marriages and officiating them through arrangement meetings continued. Most elders who married before the 1930s and some who married as late as the 1940s had marriages arranged in this manner.

In the narrative below, Sarah Deneault (recorded by Ron Ignace, 1997) of Neskonlith remembered how marriages were arranged in her youth, during the 1930s and 1940s, and told her own story.

Ma7 tqwalmíns re staxt̓ax7áms yi7ána,
The elders/parents of those involved talked it over,

re tuwíwt e cacácu7tmas ec xílmas t̓ri7 ec k negwílcwas.
the boy or young girl doing that, sneaking around.

Tqwelmíns re staxt̓ax7ám:
The elders talked about it:

"Yerí7 cwuy̓! Yi7 yi7ána. Cwi7 má7a!"
"Let's do that! Yes this one. Let's carry it out!"

"Well newí7-mp pyin ma7 ma7 yecwmntwácw."
"From this day forth, you will care for one another."

Put 'em together, they're married! *Meryí ri7.*
Put 'em together, they're married! They're married.

Kectám te staxt̓ax7ám e stámas.
Their parents/grandparents gave them something.

Es kectám es knúcwata núna tuwíwt es knúcwata yi7ána t̓e núxwuxw.
To give to the boy to help him to help this woman.

"Yi7 yi7ána ec ren sápnas."
"This is my daughter-in-law."

Nek̓ú7 t̓e ntša7sqáxa7 re st̓amált e stámas.
One horse, a cow, or something.

Ron Ignace: Re skectém te stet̓ex7éms?
Ron Ignace: Given to them by their parents/elders?

Mhm. Horse, one family, one side family, give 'em a horse. A horse and a horse and a colt, and same a cow or a calf from the other side.

All t̓i7 stam, cllúqwmn̓ all le n …
And other things, a cup and …

They didn't, ta7t̓ri7 k pat̓lu7 tšelcwílap, ma7 stsunt.s,
They didn't, in those days there were no chairs, for them to say,

"Yi7ána letáp, yi7ána tšelcwílap, yi7ána spul̓tn." No no!
"Here's a table, here's a chair, here's a bed." No, no!

Well newí7s ri7 ma7 pamíns t̓há7a ma7 atícwas,
They themselves would find a place where they would sleep,

t̓ha7 ma7 xílmas t̓ha7a ma7 …
what they would do, what …

Re tuwíwt tsúnta te staxt̓ax7áms, "Cwi7 má7a!"
The boy was told by his parents, "On you go!"

Re tuwíwt yerí7 mell ri7 llq̓mntam t̓lúna.
The boy was already trained out there [knew how to provide for his wife].

Te staxt̓ax7áms tsún̓macta t̓e spíxa, t̓e swáwla te stam, xwexwáyt.
He was taught by his parents to hunt, to fish, everything.

Tselxastás mell ri7.
He knows those things already.

Yi7ána cecácu7ta tselxastás ri7 xwexwáyt.
This young girl knows how to do everything.

Ma7 k̓weltsentsút, ma7 qwítšam.
She cooks, washes clothes.

Ma7 ma7 stam xwexwáyt ma7 k̓úlas ne tsitcw.

She would do everything around the house.

All t̓ucw, t̓ucw ri7 kwelkúk̓walt le q̓7ásas le,
And as soon as they were born, long ago,

staxt̓ax7áms re stsmált.s, t̓ucw kwalkúk̓walt mall ri7 m- …
the parents of the children, as soon as they're born, they already are …

put 'em together, *mall ri7 m-tqwelmíntem yi7ána t̓e stat̓ax7áms,* both parents.
put 'em together, they have already been betrothed by the parents,
both parents.

Yi7ána ri7 e tutwítas ri7, tslexastás mall yerí7.
This one when he grows up, they already know.

E tutwít!
When they both grow up!

K̓ult te núxwuxw yi7ȧna cecácu7ta, yerí7,
A woman, now this young woman, that one,

"Yerí7 kwánt-iya má7a."
"The time has come, you people take her now."

Yerí7 tk̓wanm7ípla7tns le q̓7ásas.
Those were the laws long ago.

K̓ámall pyin!
But now!

T̓lu7 waw7ác t̓lu7 cacácu7ta t̓lu7 m-peskúya.
Young girls are out there and have a child.

T̓lu7 w7ac m-nas ne tnk̓wa7 m-peskúya.
They are out there and go to someone else and have a child.

T̓lu7 m-nas ne swat t̓lúna, tlri7. (inaudible)
They go to someone else out there somewhere. *(inaudible)*

Ron Ignace: So you didn't, in them days, you didn't marry for love?

You didn't marry for love. You love, you loved him, when you were told, "Go with him." "I behave."

Tá7 ṫri7 ntsáwa7 k skácmatsla nek swat.
I myself wasn't given to anyone.

I was twenty-one when I left home. They were gonna …

Tsúntsas lu7 nstaxṫax7ám e skácmatslas ne one, nek̓wá7.
My grandparents were going to give me to one person.

Staxṫax7ám put ṫe sqálacw.
He was an older man.

He lost his wife. So then they ask me,

"Ma7 lá7an neri7 ṫa7 snas?"
"Will you be alright to go there?"

I was seventeen or eighteen or whatever so.

All lu7 má7a, yi7ána sqálacw, had three kids.
And he had, this man, had three kids.

Re stsmalt.s tekallás.
Three children.

Ac lu7 tsyecwmníl̓astnas.
I used to care for them.

Yi7ána tuwíteṅtsas ra slá7a re sa7á7as,
The one who raised me, my grandfather's wife,

sṫakált.s, sṫakált.s re pll-sxáłwa.
her daughter, her daughter had a husband.

Qwtsaq má7a le sṫakált.s, m-pes-stsmáltas ya te tekallás.
Her daughter had died, she had three children.

Yerí7 m-re stsúntsas lu7 len twítentsas ṫen máma7,
So then my foster mother said to me,

"Kána ma7a ks la7s ka7 ṗúsma ṫa7 snas?"
"Will you be happy to go there?"

"Ma7 la7 téke," tsut, "e yecwmíncwas well ra7 qwsa7, well ra7 stutnc."

"Look, it would be good," she said, "if you took care of your nephews, your little niece."

"Two boys and a girl, *put lu7 tsetsítsma7t.*"
"Two boys and a girl, they are quite small."

Oh, oh! Put e syacs ntsáwa7.
Oh, oh! As if it had to be me.

Ptínasma. "No! *Tá7ṫri7 tá7a.*"
I thought about it. "No! Never, no."

Ra úq̓wi yam.
You see, she was my sister.

Although in this case Sarah Deneault decided not to follow the suggestion to *sk̓élpem* (follow the custom of levirate), many marriages that occurred until somewhere during the late 1940s and perhaps beyond that time in Secwépemc country were in some way arranged, or at least suggested by elder relatives. Others were strongly discouraged on the basis of a young man and woman being considered too closely related.

We have shown how in political accords like the Fish Lake Accord, and in the arrangement of other chiefly marriages for the maintenance of peaceful relations at "border communities," marriage across nations played an important role in building and maintaining alliances. This strategy of marriage alliance was employed by the Secwépemc when the first whites came into our country, the *seme7úẁi* ("real whites"), who were the largely francophone Hudson's Bay Company or North West Company personnel. Many of these men engaged in marital alliances with Secwépemc women, often with the daughters of chiefs. From the perspective of the Secwepémc, this network of marital alliances turned the *seme7úẁi* into friends rather than strangers and thus into relatives and allies who became part of the economic and social network. Moreover, from the point of view of Secwépemc society, relatives could be controlled and politically influenced.

Several European and Metis Hudson's Bay Company traders and middlemen in the trade had common-law wives in Secwépemc communities. Among them were Joe Bourke (see fig. 9.2), who had a Skeetchestn wife but additional children in several communities by Secwépemc women, as well as Fred Griffin and Metis Charles Fortier (see fig. 9.3), Pierre Boucher (Bushy) of Kahnawake, and several others. In the same way that the Secwépemc saw themselves as having obligations toward their white sons-in-law, the latter were implicitly conceived of as having reciprocal obligations of, if nothing else, goodwill

9.1 | Jean Baptist ("Lolo") St Paul of Tk̓emlúps (Kamloops) with his wife and two daughters at the Thompson River post, ca. 1865. The photo's original caption described St Paul as the "most celebrated Indian Chief in British North America."

toward their Secwépemc in-laws. Having married into Secwépemc families, they had become more than guests and thus entertained the goodwill of their Secwépemc in-laws. In Secwépemc tradition, besides enjoying the protection of the families they married into, they thus gained access to the land and resources of the Secwépemc – not for their own benefit but for the benefit of providing for their wife and offspring. For example, Lolo St Paul (see also chapter 11), of mixed French and Iroquois background, came to Tk̓emlúps as early as the 1820s. Working as an interpreter and packer for the Hudson's Bay Company, he was a valuable liaison between the company and the Tk̓emlúps Secwépemc. Not surprisingly, he married a Tk̓emlúps woman, thus being allowed to settle in the Tk̓emlúps village at the confluence. Some of his children subsequently married among the Tk̓emlúpsemc. One of his daughters, Sophie, subsequently married trader John Tod. However, different from Lolo St Paul, who took up lifelong residence among the Secwépemc, she joined Tod after he left the Thompson River post to take up residence at Fort Langley and then Victoria. Their children became members of *séme7* (white) society rather than staying connected with their Secwépemc ancestors.

John McLean, son of Hudson's Bay Company trader Donald McLean, the latter having met his end in the Chilcotin War of 1862, married among the St̓uxtéws people and established a roadhouse on the Hat Creek wagon road, settling on the reserve, his offspring by and large maintaining an identity as

St̓uxtéws Secwépemc by continuing to live at Hat Creek after it was established as a reserve in the 1870s.

As settlers poured into the Interior following the gold rush of 1858, and as colonial and provincial land ordinances would eventually exclude Indians from land ownership, Secwépemc women continued to marry settlers. From the perspective of Secwépemc laws of access and use, these *séme7* sons-in-law were allowed to take up residence near or among them and to utilize the resources of the land for the benefit of their offspring. As shown in chapter 11, however, once the colonial and then provincial land ordinances first legislated in the 1860s specifically excluded Indians from owning land, intermarriage would serve as a way to dispossess Secwépemc of their lands while tracts of land were being pre-empted by their white sons-in-law, some of whom subsequently separated from their Secwépemc wives and then sold the land that their Secwépemc in-laws had trusted them to look after for the benefit, in Secwépemc custom, of their wives and children. Due to Secwépemc people subsequently being excluded from the lands occupied by these sons-in-law who had come in as guests, there was a growing sense of betrayal among Secwépemc people that emerged at the time.

Theresa Jules remembered that when she grew up in the 1930s, her elders warned her about marrying white men:

Mé7e, tsúntsems lu7 ren xpé7e le K̓estmíc,
Yes, my grandfather K̓estmíc said to me,

"Imts! E t̓xem̓wílc-ucw, e ketsnúcwes te7 st̓xemwílc,"
"Grandchild, when time comes for you to be grown up,"

"e yews te7 st̓x7em, e yews te7 stqwlútemt.s t̓ri7 k sqélemcw e smeryís t̓ri7,"
"when you become an adult, when a man comes to speak about marriage,"

"ta7 penhén k st̓inúcwenc k séme7, tá7a!"
"don't ever wish to be with a white man, no!"

"Me7 sesésu7t.st.s ri7!"
"They will make you a slave!"

"E wi7es re e sesésu7t.s ri7 k sesésu7t.s, me7 tseq̓mínt.s."
"When the master is through with his slave, he will throw you away."

"Me7 ts̓ílem tsut telrí7."
"It will be like that."

"E tslék̓es k sílltsu," tsut, "wel me7 tseq̓mínc."

He said, "Like a worn out shoe that you throw away."

"Me7 xillt.s," tsut, "ṫri7."
"That is what he will do to you."

Spouses as Petne7éws (Partners)

Aside from the social and political functions of marriage, and the fact that many marriages in the past were arranged marriages, Secwépemc elders have commented on the way that husband and wife complemented each other in roles, with the husband having a more formal role outside of the household, whereas the wife had the leadership role in the domestic, or home, sphere. Elders have also noted how spouses, as *petne7éws* (partners),[9] were expected to treat each other with respect, to support each other, and to help each other along as they raised their children and looked after future generations. Mary Thomas's parable about the male and female salmon wisely illustrates this concept.

Re Sqlélten | Story of the Salmon

told by Mary Thomas, recorded by Marianne Ignace and Ronald E. Ignace, 1994, transcribed by Mona Jules

"Ená ucw!" tsuns-kucw re staṫax7ám,
"Oh no!" our elders would say to us,

"E k̓ultas re swawll ṫ7ána tsatsítsl̓a."
"When the fish are born they are little."

N7ána ri7 ac re tsclálqas ac re s7í7llnst.as ṫe ák̓wa, w7á7cwas.
This is where the food of fish roe is stuck, when they are about.

Tśíla ṫi7 stsmámlt, ma7 pell-yecwamíńma e tsatsítsma7tas.
That's the way it is too for children, they have someone looking out for them when they're small.

Ená q̓upáp n7ána re s7í7llans telrí7 ma7 xyawílcwas.
When their bit of food is all gone, from that they begin to grow.

Ṫri7 tśíla re stsmámalt able to help themselves a little.
Children are the same way until they're able to help themselves a little.

Tsut re swawll es qwetsátsas, oh! Qwámqwat!
When the fishes begin to leave, oh! They're so beautiful!

Ená wu7állas re sesṗays.
Their skin glitters.

Ṫri7 tśíla ri7 re cacácu7ta, re tutuwíwt.
That's the way it is with little girls and boys.

Tá7 ri7 k stsetśucwlá7s.
It isn't wrong.

Yi7ána ri7 re tutuwíwt m-wucwqína, kllu7sána.
Those boys would comb their hair, parting it.

Yerí7 re stcúsas tek nuxwnúnwanxw.
Then begin looking for girls.

Ell yi7ána nuxwnúnxwaxw m-násmas re tutuwíwt m-tsntás ucw (laughter) ṫri7 m-kúpem.
And those girls would go to the boys and strike them *(laughter)* or begin to push.

Ah! That's normal *ri7!*
Ah! That's normal, it is!

You know that's what life is all about. That's nothing wrong with that.

Yerí7 re sqwetsáts téka swawll.
See the fishes continue to go on.

Oh! Twítas wel re skitsc núna ne xyum ṫe pásellkwa.
Oh! They continue growing until they get back to the big lake.

W7ácwas nu7, w7ácwas, xaxyawílcwas.
They're there, there until they grow very big.

Oh! Kítscwas ne7ána ṗúsmas re skwnams re tnak̓wá7s.
Oh! Then it's in their hearts to take one companion.

Ená, nuxwnúxwuxw all re sqáqalqlacw, sm7á7astwacwas.
Those girls and boys begin to look for a spouse.

Yerí7 ac te sáysus, nu7 te c7íllnas, qwatsq̓útsas.
They're there playing, eating, and getting fat.

Qwetsátsas m-tsútas yi7ána núxwuxw,

They begin their swim upstream, and the woman says,

"Oh! Yerí7 nukw sem7áys as pukwmín ra ák̓wan."
"Oh! I sense that the time is getting close for me to lay my eggs."

"Yáwska ri7 k scetáps a sqwetsáts-kt."
"It should be about time for us to be moving on."

Yerí7 memáws re sqwetsqwatsátsas.
Then the couple sets out.

La7 re sṫektáṅs ne séwllkwa, tkítsi7s re relralátkwa.
Their journey in the water is good, they get to the rapids.

Oh, xmank yi7ána núxwuxw.
Oh, the woman is heavy.

Me7 tsuns ri7 re sxálwas, "Ctsetsáẇs-ka, gúyt-ka nukw."
She says to her husband, "I'm getting tired, I'm sleepy."

Me7 tcláĺqwam-ekwa ucw n7ána ne tsecrápla7cw ne tsack̓úykwa re sqálacw.
They say that he would grab onto a stick in the water with his teeth.

Re m-tsuns re sa7á7as,
He would say to his wife,

"Tlúnus qwetqwát ra7 súpa7 k tqwenm̓qs-ucw."
"Hang on over there with your soft tail."

Neri7 m-xíla, m- mállelcwas.
She would do that and rest.

Xmank re núxwuxw.
Well the woman was heavy.

Yirí7 re m-sm7áll.lcs, m-tsut re núxwuxw,
When she was feeling better, the woman would say,

"Cuẏ! Yerí7 nukw ra sm7áll.lcs, kekáw ṫe sw7ac-kt ṫe qwetsáts-kt."
"Come on! I'm rested now, we have a long way to go."

Tlri7 m-qwetsqwatsátsas.
Then they set out from there.

Scanc t̓7ána séwllkwa, ac ts̓ílmas t̓e petatát.
The water was full of rocks, it was like it was boiling.

Ma7-k̓wincwes re smállelcs cum yigráp núna ne sclel̓cs.
She would rest a number of times before reaching the spawning grounds.

Yigáp nehá7a k pukwmínsas re ák̓was.
They arrive to where the eggs would be layed.

Re sqálacw t̓7ána m-xillct.s t̓e súpa7s narí7 nehá7a re ák̓was t̓e pukwmíctmas.
The male would do this with his tail, there wherever they [her eggs] would be layed.

Qúqwta7st.s nawi7s a t̓hánas a ts̓ílmas re stségragt.s yi7ána re sesp̓áys.
He doesn't care about himself and how torn up his skin gets.

K̓úlas nerí7 nehá7a t̓e pukwmínsas re ák̓was re núxuxwas.
He makes the bed where the female will lay her eggs.

Knúcwas neri7, yacwamíns, m-knúcwasas.
He helps her there, he looks after her, he helps her.

Yerí7 núxwuxw, wi7 re s7ak̓was, yerí7 re st̓qwewst.s re sqwlap.
When the female finishes laying her eggs, they both spawn, then die.

Yerí7 re stsut.s le staxt̓ax7á, re stsptákwlls.
That's how the story of the elders were.

"Tákwiya má7a! re tutuwíwt."
"You people see that! You young people."

"Ma7 xílap-kp ri7, ma7 tutwít-kp ri7."
"You will do the same way, you will grow up."

"Ma7 ptínasmen-tp a skwnam-kp t̓ek núxwuxw."
"You think about taking a woman."

"Ma7 la7 k syacwamín-tp, a tnk̓wa7 a sk̓úlctls yugwyúgwt t̓ek stsmámalt."
"Take good care of the one so that she can bear you strong children."

Táka tsut re swawll, qúqwta7st.s nawi7s t̓há7a k ts̓ílmas re sts̓xtáns.
See what was said about the fish, he didn't care about how he looked.

Núna ṫe squqwstá7st.s re sa7á7as, m-tclálq̓wu n tegwṫegwt ṫe sextśey.
Out there, he didn't care when he felt for his wife, he bit into hard sticks.

Ne sxwaxwáyt.s re sxílas ṫ7ána xílmas re skwṫust.s,
Everytime he did that his face went like this,

ṫlúna re sṗsaqst.s re sm7úyst.ses ṫe clálq̓wmas.
his nose bending from biting into sticks.

Qúqwta7st.s ri7 a ṫhánas a tśílmas nawí7s k cḱúltns.
He didn't care about his looks or ways.

Tsukw ṫucw a sḱúlcta ṫek yegwyégwt ṫek stsmált.
Just so long as he got strong children.

Names and Name Giving

The system of Secwépemc name giving accompanied the sense of kinship. Children were given hereditary names from a "remote ancestor" (Teit 1909, 570), usually a person of the child's grandparent's or great-grandparent's generation. The belief was, as it is today, that the child who received a name from a grandparent made the *yerí7 re swumécst.s le xpé7es* ("deceased grandparent come alive"). Not passing on our ancestors' names to our children is like turning our backs on our ancestors. As we say, "*E ta7es es kectéc re7 stsmémelt te Secwepemcéske7s re steṫx7éms, tśílem te7s tmélcmenc*" ("When you do not give your children the names of their ancestors, it is like you are turning your back on them"). In a spiritual sense, the child is believed to be a rebirth of that ancestor and, in a social sense, maintains continuity with the past. Teit (1900, 291) noted that during the late 1800s, names were formally announced by giving a feast: "The most honorable and satisfactory method of giving a name is that of calling the neighboring people together, giving a feast and proclaiming before them the name by which the child is to be known." Within a given band or community, even within the same division, no two people had the same name, although across divisions the same names would commonly recur. In fact, many ancestral names – he figured between one-third and two-thirds – were shared among the Secwépemc and Upper Nlaka'pamux. "Either they were one people originally, or they have intermarried often. Even in bands that, so far as the tradition goes, have never lived close together nor had any direct intercourse, – like the Lytton band of the Thompson tribe, and the Shuswap bands of High Bar and Big Bar" (ibid., 570). Given that these Secwépemc and Nlaka'pamux names, as Teit himself noticed, were of ancient origin and had existed for many generations, it appears that at least some of them may date back more than 2,000 years, when the two languages were still one! Male and female names are recognized by their endings, or lexical suffixes: male names typically end in the lexical suffixes *-ésq̓t* (day), *-éscen* (mineral rock), *-élst* (rock), and *-qín/-qen* (head), whereas female names typically end in *-étkwe* (water) and *-iṅek* (bow, derived from the bow shape of a pregnant belly). Other suffixes like *-ítśe7* (skin or blanket), *-el̓qs* (robe), and *-eṁt/iṁt* (skin or dress) can involve either male or female names.

Table 9.2 shows some hereditary names that existed in Secwépemc communities during the second half of the nineteenth century and into the early twentieth century, as derived from elders' memories or in some cases retrieved from baptismal records and cross-checked with elders. Some of the names below continue among present and recently deceased individuals, and to some degree, traditional naming has been revived in recent decades. However, as Teit (1900, 1909) noted, one of the legacies of the epidemics of the mid to late 1900s was that numerous names were forgotten and were not passed on to keep the memory of the previous bearer alive, although people at the time tried to avert this loss by harbouring the names of several ancestors to keep their memory alive. In the first generation of Secwépemc people baptized by the Oblates in the 1860s and 1870s, the Indigenous names of individuals were recorded, as were the names of their parents in many cases, with the missionary recording the Secwépemc hereditary name of a person as that person's surname, the new baptismal name being entered as the first name.

The Secwépemc and Interior Salish system of naming embodies both a cyclical and chronological sense of history. Throughout Secwépemc history, the particular names of ancestors were recycled every two to three generations. As they do today, names also served to keep track of chronological time in that the practice of naming also embodied the particular appearance and personal characteristics of an ancestor, and with the name went the knowledge of the life history of that ancestor. When individuals were baptized beginning in the 1860s (see chapter 11), the French baptismal names they received became "indigenized" by being pronounced the Secwépemc way. Thus, for example, the name Jules – given to different and not closely related males at Skeetchestn, Simpcw, and Cstálen – became pronounced Sul, Victoire became Mektwál, Fidèle became Pitél, Edouard or Edward became Etwá, Marie or Amélie became Melí, and Eugénie became Wesní. Like the hereditary Secwépemc names described above, these baptismal names were consequently, and into the present, passed down in alternating generations to keep the memory of the previous name bearer alive. Since Indian agents struggled to write the Indigenous names as last names, they assigned a person's father's name as the new last name in the next generation, with this last name often changing again as new first names were assigned to males as last names. Thus Ḱwenéye7 of Simpcw, born in about 1830, received the name Jules when he was baptized in 1867. One of his sons was baptized as Celestin,

Table 9.2 | Secwépemc personal names

Secwépemc female name	*Gloss*
Melmenétkwe	root *məl(a)men* (medicine) plus *-étkwe* (water)
Ts̓elpínek	root *ts̓el* (standing up), plus *-p* (completed), plus *-ínek* (bow)
K̓wetmém̓el̓cken	root *k̓uwétem* (walk), plus *-él̓cken* (body, small animate thing)
K̓wetemétkwe	root *k̓uwétem* (walk) plus *-étkwe* (water)
Wecwpétkwe	root *wecw* (come alive), plus *-p* (arrived in that state), plus *-étkwe* (water)
Ests̓elmét̓el̓cken	root *ests̓el* (stand up suddenly), plus *-met̓* (mix together), plus *-el̓cken* (body)
Xyemétkwe	root *xyem* (big) plus *-étkwe* (water)
Semecél̓qs	root *sem̓éc* (life force, spirit power), plus *-él̓qs* (clothing, be dressed)
Ts̓elpíts̓e7	root *ts̓el* (stand up), plus *-p* (arrived in that state), plus *-its̓e7* (blanket)

Secwépemc male name	*Gloss*
Tyenmésq̓t	root *tyém̓nem* (circle around) plus *-esq̓t* (day)
Sisyésq̓et	root *séy̓se* (play) plus *-ésq̓et* (day)
Sisyúlecw	root *séy̓se* (play) plus *-úlecw* (land)
K̓wenéye7	root *k̓wen* (try out) plus diminuitive *-ey̓e* (possibly a nickname)
Llík̓wstem̓t	root *llik̓w* (tattered) plus *-stem̓t* (clothing)
Táxwelst	root *taxw* (hanging down) plus *-elst* (rock)
Súk̓welst	root *suk̓w* (blown away) plus *-elst* (rock)
Selpáxen	root *selp* (be excited, in a hurry) plus *-áxen* (wing)
Ts̓elewtqín	root *ts̓eléwt* (stand up) plus *-qin* (head)
Ts̓elcésq̓et	root *ts̓elc* (stand up) plus *-ésq̓t* (day)

Note: The analysis we provide includes a breakdown of the root and what is usually a lexical suffix, which in most, but not all, cases of names is tied to gender. The metaphorical and storied meaning of most of the names is more elusive, and although it is tempting to think of the literal translations as all there is to these names, we need to be mindful of the fact that in most cases they are ancient hereditary names that go back to past name holders' *étsxem* (spirit guardian quests) and thus bear subtle and hidden messages beyond what is in the literal translations.

pronounced Celestá, and went on record as Celesta Jules; another son was baptized as Casimir, becoming Casimir Jules; and a third son was baptized as Abel, pronounced Abíl, becoming Abile Jules. Celesta's son Emile became Emile Celesta, with the Jules dropped, and Emile's son in turn was baptized Henry Celesta. Casimir's children and subsequent offspring retained the name

Casimir, whereas Abile's offspring's name was Anglicized to Abel in subsequent generations (see fig. 9.3). A few family names are Anglicized versions of Secwépemc names: Ṫcum became Calhoun, and in Dog Creek, Tséltṡel was Anglicized to Saul-John in one family and to Chelsea in another family, whereas Skwenícen became Squinahan (see figs 9.3 and 9.4).

Some individuals were known by nicknames, often derived from their physical characteristics or events that had happened to them, although some names that originated as nicknames were then passed on to descendants of the original name bearer to keep that ancestor's memory alive. Thus a man in Skeetchestn was named Spéṗẇe7sqen ("hit on the back of the head"), a name he apparently inherited rather than it commemorating something that had happened to him. Other names refer to characteristics of an animal that the bearer physically resembled or that the bearer's behaviour reminded people of. Examples of such names are Klé7cwe (Muskrat, vocative form of *klecwé7*), Sceṅcéllcw (Packrat), Sunéc (Willow Grouse), Sk̓elép (Coyote), and Sxwéẏlecken (Buck, from *sxwlécken*). However, as Teit (1900, 291) noted, some names that refer to animals and natural phenomena derive from the name bearer's spirit guardian quest (see chapter 11). Other names, like Kúle7, Se7, and Púle7, appear to be names derived from baby talk or affective language. The genealogies at the end of this chapter in figures 9.2, 9.3, and 9.4 illustrate the pattern of name giving and show how both Secwépemc names and baptismal English or French names were kept alive in families.

K̓wseltktenéws | Sharing and Cooperation in the Extended Family

As remains the case today, the extended bilateral family, what we call a person's *k̓wseltkten7úẇi* ("real relatives") on both the mother's and father's side, was the core unit of Secwépemc economic production and social interaction. Although a pervasive ethic of sharing between and across families, as well as throughout the whole community, existed in Secwépemc society, it was the extended family, situated around a group of interrelated households, that was the core productive unit of Secwépemc society: people provided food for all the members of the extended family who lived together. Food-gathering task groups usually included interrelated members of connected families and varied depending on the task. Hunting task groups were often composed of two or three brothers or cousins, their wives, and their children, whereas plant-gathering task groups involved related females and their children. Furthermore, the extended family functioned as a flexible and inclusive, rather than exclusive, group that acted in social and political solidarity, which at various times resulted in factions and competing interests among groups within a community or band. For the Northern Secwépemc, Elizabeth Furniss (1995) discusses the inherent tensions between the interests of family groups and the interests of the larger community. Based on research with Aboriginal groups on the Southern (Columbia) Plateau, Lillian Ackerman (1998, 516) documents the emergence of "nonunilinear descent groups" since "at least the 1900s and likely before that." Members of such a group reckon their group membership through descent on either the mother's or father's side from a common ancestor, and this dscent "provides an individual with his or her identity" (ibid.). However, she noted the flexible nature of such affiliation: "A person could grow up in a particular extended family that reared either his mother or father; after adulthood, a person may choose to change his affiliation from his mother's extended family to his father's extended family (or vice versa), or to some other relative; or a person may marry into a family and affiliate himself to his spouse's people" (ibid., 516–17).

Another significant aspect of Secwépemc extended family life was, and continues to be, the importance of sharing and *knucwentwécw* (helping one another), on the one hand, and the importance of personal self-sufficiency and autonomy, on the other hand, embodied in and sustained by the *étsxem* (spirit guardian quest) of young adolescents (see chapter 11). Although elders throughout their narratives talked about the many ways that their own elders and ancestors helped one another by sharing in food-gathering tasks and by sharing the fish that were caught, the game that were bagged, and the berries that were picked, they also emphasized the fine line between *c7í7elcmen* (sharing) and individual *q̓en7ə̓lt* (freeloading) – that is, helping out and being helped versus lacking self-sufficiency and thus being a burden to others, or a *yéwyut* (nuisance).

To balance the values of *knucwentwécw* (helping one another) and *yecwentwécw* (looking after one another), self-sufficiency was another important core value of Secwépemc society. The theme of self-sufficiency, not being a *yéwyut*, and working hard is embodied in Nellie Taylor's favourite story, the one about Ant and Grasshopper.[10]

Re Scwicwéye ell re Skelklécs | Story of Ant and Grasshopper
recounted by Nellie Taylor, 1987, as told by her great-grandmother Agathe Llecwpusétkwe of Skeetchestn

Re Scwicwéye ell re Skelklə́ts.
Ant and Grasshopper.

Le q̓7éses ren kyéy7e re slexéy̓ems ucw,
Long time ago, my grandmother used to tell me,

w7ec re scwicéye élkstes.
[the] ants were busy working.

K̓wiyusmes all summer welem sllwélsten.

They were suffering all summer until fall.

Kell w7ec re skelkeléts tigáynekmes.
But the grasshoppers were playing guitar.

Xq̓wiyelltṡem ṫri7 te sqweq̓wyílc.
They had fun dancing.

Ṫri7 stem re tsúwets.
They had all kinds of activities.

S7istk.
It was winter.

Yerí7 re stektsíllens.
There, they starved.

Yerí7 re stekṫéxelcmens-ekwe re scwicwéye.
They charged over to the ants.

Yerí7 re scpupéẇtsens-ekwe.
There, they knocked on their door.

W7ec-ekwe re ckelltsictmes te scwicwéye.
They opened the door for them, the ants.

Ts7ullcw-ekwe.
They entered.

Qwenqwént-ekwe yéwses re s7ucw7úcwtes ṫucw.
They were very pitiful when they were freezing.

Ta7-ekwe pell-stektsúsems re skelkeléts.
They didn't have wood, the grasshoppers.

Kítsentmes re scwicwéye te skelkeléts, q̓en7élt.
When they got to the ants, the grasshoppers, they begged for food.

Tsúntem-ekwe ṫ7éne:
They were asked this:

"Kénem-k?"
"What's the matter with you?"

"Yerí7 ṫucw well re7 qwse7 re stektsíllens."
[They were told,] "There, your nephews are starving."

"Kénem ke7 pell-stsillen es metéc-kuc?"
[The grasshoppers asked,] "Do you have any food to feed us?"

"Ah, ṫri7 tigáynekcte!"
[The ants said,] "Ah, there, play guitar for them!"

"Tigáynekcte ṫri7 me7 letwílc."
"Play guitar for them, then they will feel better."

"Me7 meqméq̓."
"They'll get full."

Qwenqwént ṫri7, yerí7-enke kem sxwayts re skelkeléts.
The poor things, the grasshoppers must have all died.

Sexlítemc | Guests, Not Relatives

In Secwépemc culture, a *sexlítemc* (guest) is distinguished from all people who are our *ḱwséltkten* (relatives). Sexlítemc are strangers without resource rights who come into our country. They are at the mercy of their hosts to feed them and provide them with shelter. As our elder Nellie Taylor stated, because they have to rely on their hosts and are thus a *yéwyut* (nuisance) rather than self-sufficient, "*qwenqwént yerí7 re sexlítemc*" ("guests are pitiful"). The tacit law in the Secwépemc nation, however, is that to acknowledge the pity their hosts take on them, guests reciprocate the favours and help extended by their hosts. From this perspective, our ancestors looked at the trade goods that Europeans offered not only as commercial trade goods but also as tokens of the guests' reciprocity. When the new wave of settlers came into Secwépemc country following the gold rush, the guest-host relationship was severed, as the Interior chiefs emphasized in their "Memorial to Sir Wilfrid Laurier" (Chiefs of the Shuswap, Okanagan, and Couteau Tribes 1910) (see chapter 12).

Secwépemc Genealogies

Genealogy is the study of the history of families and the tracing of their lineages back in time. Genealogies map out a person's ancestors and relatives, often expressed in a family tree or genealogy chart. Figures 9.2, 9.3, and 9.4 provide different examples of genealogies of Secwépemc individuals and interconnected groups of relatives from different areas of Secwepemcúlecw. They show how people of different communities intermarried throughout

Secwepemcúlecw and how – with the help of elders' memories, church baptism and marriage records, Department of Indian Affairs census data and band lists, Hudson's Bay Company records, and Canada Census data from the late nineteenth and early twentiety centuries – one can trace the family history of many individuals to the late 1700s, which is literally before the first Europeans arrived in Secwepemcúlecw. Furthermore, many Secwépemc individuals and families can connect their ancestors to individuals who appear in a detailed genealogy of Okanagan, Secwépemc, and other Plateau people connected to the family of Okanagan chief Pelkamulox, who signed the Fish Lake Accord with Chief Kwolila of Kamloops (see chapter 8), thus extending the time depth of these genealogies back into the 1600s. The genealogies also show how chiefs' children were married into neighbouring nations to maintain peaceful alliances among nations. They also illustrate the pattern of name giving discussed above, where personal names recur in alternating generations, thus causing a deceased ancestor to come alive and keeping that ancestor in memory. Besides oral memories of kinship relations recorded with Secwépemc elders between 1884 and 2017, we relied on interpreting and checking baptismal and marriage records with elders wherever possible. These records are dated 1866–82 (Williams Lake area baptisms), 1867–82 (Kamloops area baptisms and marriages), 1882–90 (Kamloops Diocese baptisms), and 1882–1900 (Kamloops Diocese marriages). All of these records are listed in the References under Oblate Missions of British Columbia. An additional source was some baptismal records from the Okanagan (Pandosy) Mission at what is now Kelowna (Oblate Missions of British Columbia 1859–60).

9.2 (*opposite*) | Genealogy showing the ancestors of co-author Ronald Ignace (Stsmél̓qen) on his maternal and paternal sides. His grandmother Meláni *(right)* further connects to the Fish Lake Accord genealogy. The oldest ancestors traced were born in the 1780s and 1790s, before Europeans came into Secwepemcúlecw. The older generations would have included additional siblings, but these were the generations severely affected by the 1862–63 smallpox epidemic.

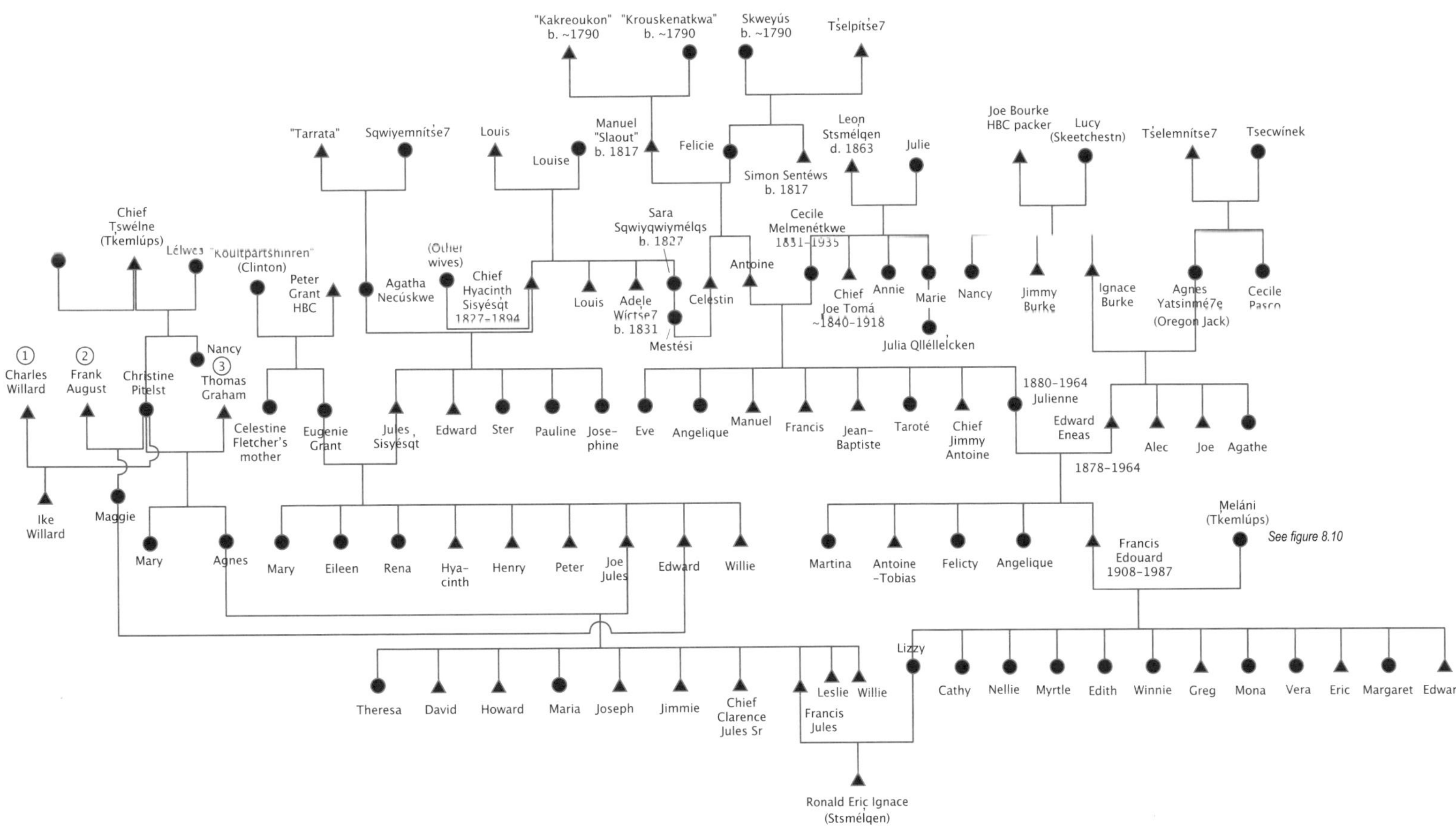
"Kakreoukon" b. ~1790
"Krouskenatkwa" b. ~1790
Skweyús b. ~1790
Tselpitse7
"Tarrata"
Sqwiyemnítse7
Louis
Louise
Manuel "Slaout" b. 1817
Felicie
Simon Sentéws b. 1817
Leon Stsmélqen d. 1863
Julie
Joe Bourke HBC packer
Lucy (Skeetchestn)
Tselemnítse7
Tsecwínek
Chief Tswélne (Tkemlúps)
Lélwes
"Koultpartshinren" (Clinton)
Peter Grant HBC
(Other wives)
Agatha Necúskwe
Chief Hyacinth Sisyésqt 1827–1894
Louis
Adele Wírtse7 b. 1831
Sara Sqwiyqwiymélqs b. 1827
Mestési
Celestin
Antoine
Cecile Melmenétkwe 1831–1935
Chief Joe Tomá ~1840–1918
Annie
Marie
Julia Qllélleĺcken
Nancy
Jimmy Burke
Ignace Burke
Agnes Yatsinmé7e (Oregon Jack)
Cecile Pasco
1 Charles Willard
2 Frank August
Christine Pitelst
Nancy
3 Thomas Graham
Celestine Fletcher's mother
Eugenie Grant
Jules Sisyésqt
Edward
Ster
Pauline
Jose-phine
Eve
Angelique
Manuel
Francis
Jean-Baptiste
Taroté
Chief Jimmy Antoine
1880–1964 Julienne
Edward Eneas
1878–1964
Alec
Joe
Agathe
Ike Willard
Maggie
Mary
Agnes
Mary
Eileen
Rena
Hya-cinth
Henry
Peter
Joe Jules
Edward
Willie
Martina
Antoine -Tobias
Felicty
Angelique
Francis Edouard 1908–1987
Meláni (Tkemlúps)
See figure 8.10
Theresa
David
Howard
Maria
Joseph
Jimmie
Chief Clarence Jules Sr
Francis Jules
Leslie
Willie
Lizzy
Cathy
Nellie
Myrtle
Edith
Winnie
Greg
Mona
Vera
Eric
Margaret
Edward
Ronald Eric Ignace (Stsmélqen)

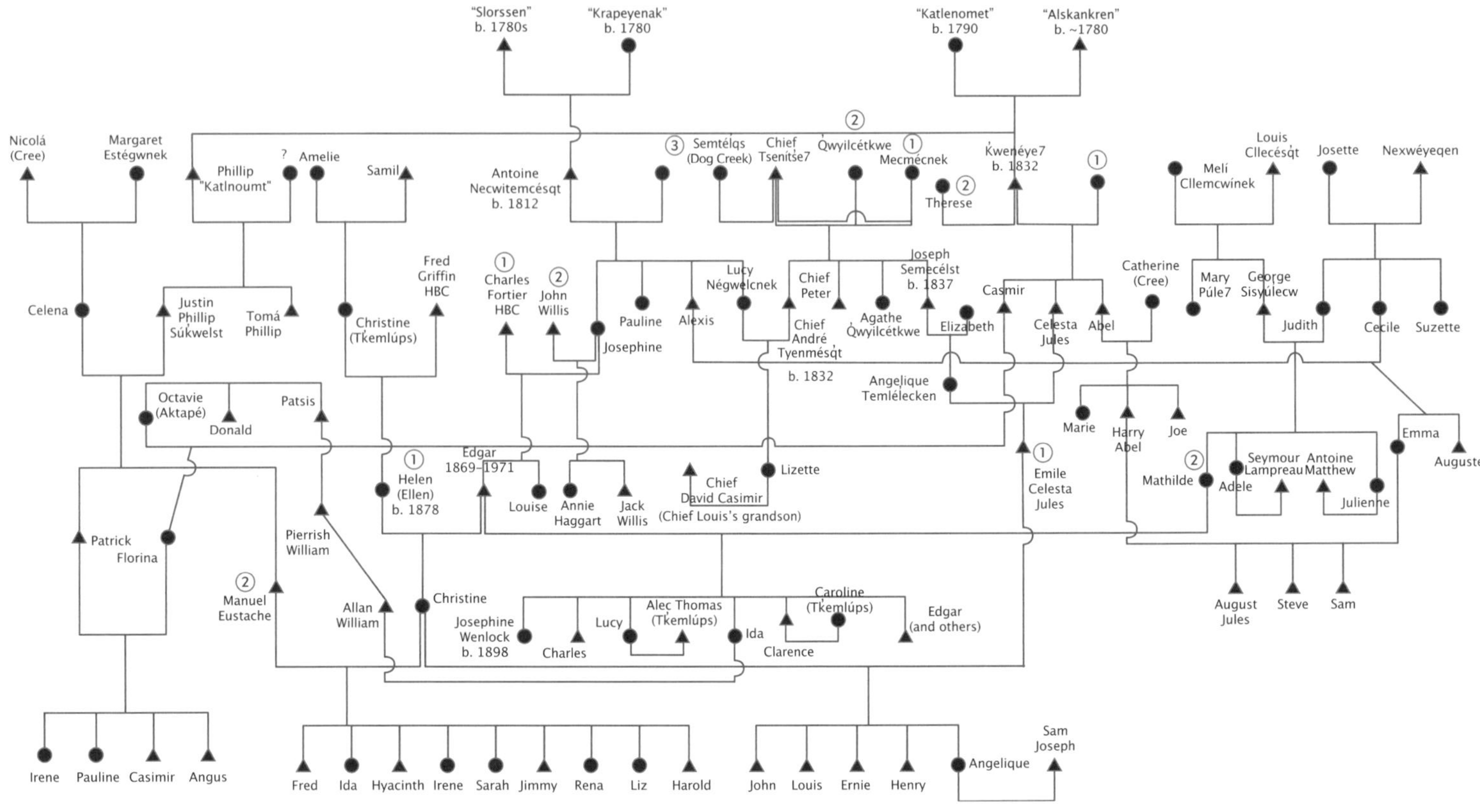

9.3 | Genealogy of six generations of members of interconnected Simpcw families dating back to the 1780s. The transition to baptismal English (or French) names in the late 1800s is illustrated, as are adoptions and intermarriage of Simpcw with Tḱemlupsemc, Cree, Metis, and Hudson's Bay Company workers. Also shown is how individuals are named after ancestors, usually in the grandparent generation.

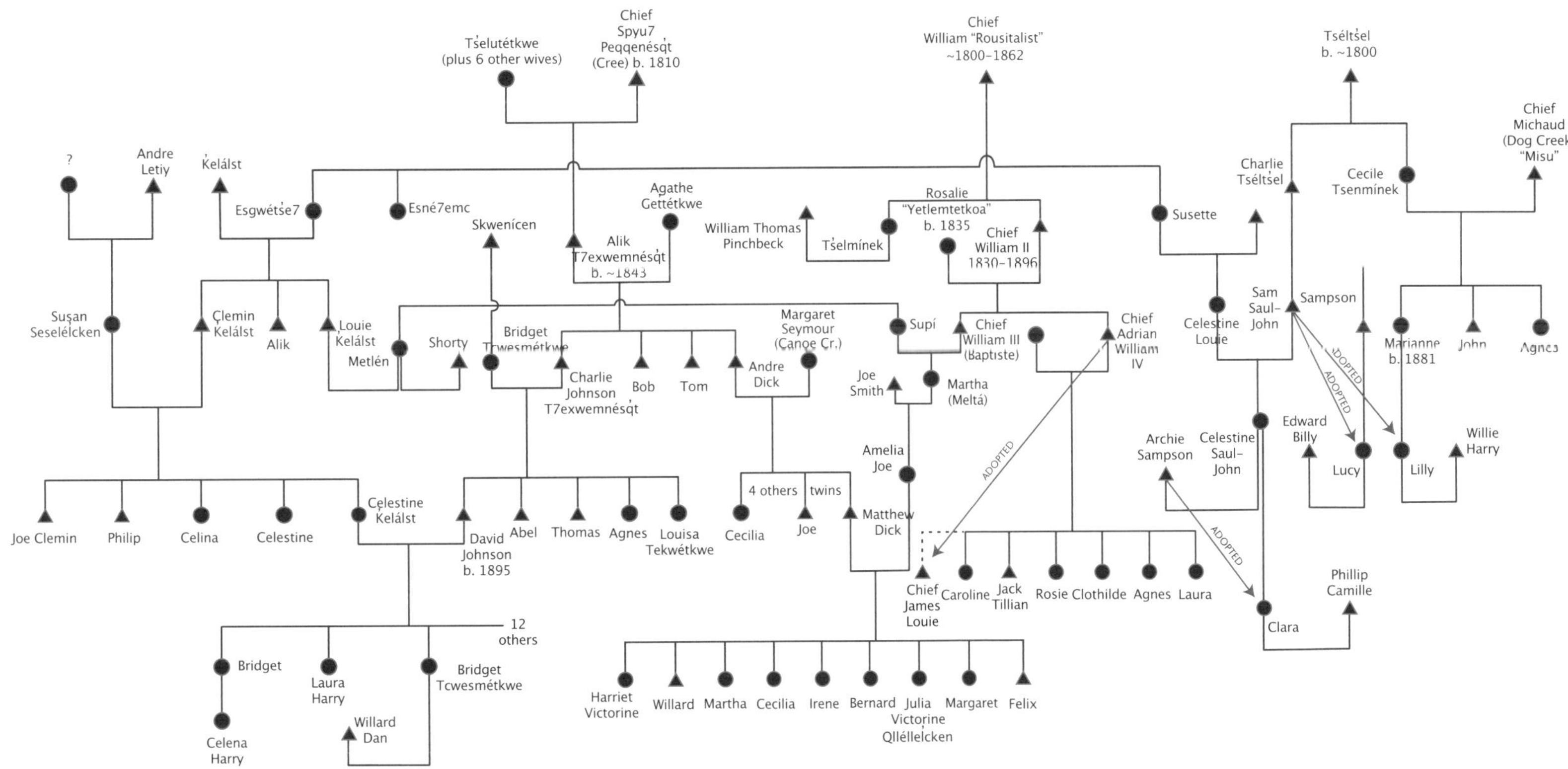

9.4 | Genealogy of Bridget Dan and Cecilia DeRose of Esḱét (Alkali Lake) and Clara Camille of Xgéṫtem (Dog Creek), showing the interconnection through kinship across communities and generations. Similar to what figures 9.2 and 9.3 show, English names for the most part replaced Secwépemc names in the late 1800s, with some exceptions. Julia Victorine Qllelleİcken received her Secwépemc name from Julia Qllelleİcken (see fig. 9.2), whose mother was from Skeetchestn and married into the Ṫéxelc (Sugarcane) community. Both Bridget and Cecilia are descendants of "Chief Spyu" (Peqqenésq̓t, "sun rising over mountains day"), who moved to Esḱét from Cree country, which probably explains his name. Also shown are descendants of Chief William of Ṫéxelc and Chief Michaud ("Misu̓") of Xgéṫtem.

10 Re Kukúkwpi7s-kucw ell re Tk̓wenm7íple7tens

Secwépemc Chiefship and Political Organization

In Secwepemctsín, the term *kúkwpi7* refers to leadership of the localized Indigenous community – James Teit's (1909) "band" – without any paramount leadership at the level of the nation. We can learn about principles of Secwépemc chiefship, but also about processual history of chiefship, from oral histories told by elders who remembered successions to chiefship and histories of chiefs dating back to the late 1800s and earlier. Information recorded in the works of James Teit (1909), Franz Boas (1890), and George M. Dawson (1891), along with ethnohistorical information about the comings and goings of chiefs throughout the nineteenth century and early twentieth centuries adds to the picture of the role and functions of chiefs and chiefly succession during the 1800s and 1900s.

There was no paramount chiefship at the level of the nation; instead, throughout the nineteenth century and well into the twentieth, Secwépemc society existed as a segmental or confederated political entity, composed of equal parts, namely the traditional communities, or "bands" in Teit's sense. There existed different types of chiefs for different roles and situations. Teit (1909, 569) noted that the Secwépemc "had war chiefs, hunting chiefs, and chiefs of dances, who were men elected as the best qualified to fill these positions." We believe that what Teit calls "hunting chiefs" were actually what we previously referred to as *yecwmíṅmen* (caretakers) of fish, game, plant resources, and trails. The roles performed by the *yecwmíṅmen* were based on a person's experience and knowledge, and they involved an assigned and recognized role within the community.

For example, Ron Ignace and elders in Skeetchestn remember that Ron's great-grandfather Chief Edward Eneas – who was appointed by custom as chief of the Skeetchestn community between about 1940 and 1950 – was also in charge of tending the various ecosystems in the areas above the community through fire management. Another community member, Walter Humphrey, who succeeded Edward Eneas as chief, had the task of clearing and repairing trails in the high mountains, plateaus, and valley bottoms frequented on horseback by Skeetchestn people.

In addition to these resource caretakers, there were what Teit (1909, 569) called "hereditary chiefs": "The Shuswap had one hereditary chief for each band, the office descending in the male line." The role of the chiefs was as follows:

> Chiefs had no special privileges, and their only duties were to look after the general welfare of the band, regulating, when necessary the gathering of the food-supply, so that all could have an equal chance, and admonishing the lazy and quarrelsome. They also gave their advice on all-important matters, and were the agents of the band in dealing with strangers. The chief was looked upon as a kind of father and leader of the people, and was expected to set a good example, and to act fairly in all matters. (Ibid., 570)

On the one hand, therefore, within the context of the egalitarian essence of Secwépemc society in the immediate precontact and early contact period, chiefs were equal among their advisors and community members. They were expected to lead by example and, save for the brief interlude of hereditary ranked crest groups in the Fraser River, Fraser Canyon, and Canim Lake divisions (see chapter 8), represented no higher rank or class than their community members. Moreover, as Teit (1909, 569) acknowledged, despite the ideal of patrilineal succession personal skills and merit played an important role in selecting a chief, especially when more than one possible heir existed or when no sons existed: "Sometimes all the immediate male relatives of the deceased [chief] held a meeting and *elected the son considered best fitted to occupy the position,* and he was announced by them to the band as chief. Soon afterward he gave a small feast to all the members of the band, to which visiting strangers were invited. At this feast the people addressed him as chief, and henceforth recognized him as such until his death" (emphasis added).

Chiefly succession was therefore not automatic, but the successor was established on the basis of descent from, or kinship ties with, the previous chief and, most of all, on the basis of fitness for the position. We know very little about actual chiefs during the centuries preceding first contact. However, by tracing the succession of chiefs who interacted with explorers and fur traders in the early 1800s, and subsequently with colonial and government agents, we see that in many instances, chiefly succession did *not* take place in the paternal line.

As Teit (1930a) notes, Kwolila, who was chief of the Tk̓emlúpsemc at the time of the Fish Lake Accord during the 1760s or 1770s, was preceeded by Taléxen, who was killed in a war expedition that drove the Sekani out of the upper North Thompson River and McBride areas (Boas 1890). It appears that Q̓wíyemtscen ("rainbow") succeeded him, and Nels Mitchell of Tk̓emlúps (Kamloops) – who had the same inherited name, Q̓wíyemtscen – mentioned

10.1 | Chief Peṫmíṫse7 (Joe Tomá) of Skeetchestn, ca. 1915. He succeeded Chief Hyacinth Sisyésq̓t, appointed by the latter as his successor around 1894. Peṫmíṫse7 was chief at Skeetchestn during the Indian Rights Movement until his death in 1918 during the Spanish flu epidemic.

that Q̓wíyemtscen's daughter was Chief Louis's first wife. The Hudson's Bay Company journals and correspondence of the 1820s to early 1840s, however, mention "Court appatte" as chief at Tk̓emlúps. By the mid-1850s, Chief Louis Clexléx̣qen – whose father had the same Secwépemc name – was chief of the Tk̓emlúpsemc until his death in 1915. Near the end of his life, Chief Louis had no surviving son who could become his successor. Louis wanted to pass his chiefship to his grandson, Seymour Pitel (see chapter 12), but the Indian agent disqualified him because he had not reached the age of majority at the time of Louis's passing in 1915. Thus Louis's chiefship passed to Eli LaRue, who was Chief Louis's son-in-law, Eli LaRue's mother having been Chief Louis's youngest wife, whom he gave up after the arrival of the missionaries. Another son-in-law, Joe Jules (himself the grandson of Hyacinth Sisyésq̓t; see below), although initially designated as successor by Chief Louis, declined to become chief, choosing instead to become a *tk̓wenm7íple7ten* (advisor).[1]

Leslie Jules (personal communication, 1987) of Kamloops remembered hearing that Hyacinth Sisyésq̓t, chief of Skeetchestn between the early 1860s and his death in 1894, rose to the rank of political chief from being a war chief. Sisyésq̓t himself apparently succeeded "Nowelsghut" (Nexwéylesq̓t) as chief of "Boute du Lac," the area at the west end of Kamloops Lake (see M.

10.2 | Chief Basil Dick (Basil David) of St̓uxtéws (Bonaparte), photographed by James Teit, ca. 1916. The original caption describes him as "wearing a traditional costume."

Balf 1980). Before his death, Hyacinth Sisyésq̓t designated his niece Clemás's husband, Pet̓mítše7 (Joe Tomá), as his successor. As explained by Skeetchestn elder Nellie Taylor, Hyacinth Sisyésq̓t considered Joe Tomá, his son-in-law, to be most fit for office. It is significant that Sisyésq̓t's appointment of a successor came at a time when Secwépemc people and leaders were beginning to notice the growing impacts of white settlement on Secwépemc lands and were feeling increasingly betrayed by the federal and provincial governments with regard to the land question.

In St̓uxtéws the chief between the 1890s and 1930 was Ts̓elcwíw̓elst ("the rock that came to be stood up"),[2] or Basil Dick, as he was locally known, although the public record knows him as Basil David. He succeeded Adam Seynsút, who was not a close relative. Seynsút had been St̓uxtéws chief during the late 1860s and at the time of Peter O'Reilly's allocation of reserves in the early 1880s. Basil Dick was the son of Sqéqxe, a well-known ṫkwilc (Indian doctor) baptized as Gaspar Kekra the same day his son Basil was baptized in May 1871 at age twenty. Basil became a prominent spokesperson for the Interior chiefs during the early decades of the twentieth century. With a delegation that included Chief Capilano of North Vancouver and Simon Pierre of Katzie on the lower Fraser River, he went to London in 1906 to meet the king of England (see chapter 12) and took part in delegation visits to Ottawa in 1908, 1912, and 1926, continuing to act as spokesperson for the Interior Tribes and then for the Allied Tribes right up to its bitter and unjust end in 1927 (see chapter 12). In 1926, when he travelled to London with Pierrish William of Neskonlith and John Chilaheetza of Douglas Lake to again seek an audience with the king in order to address the land question, London newspapers mentioned that he had served in the First World War and lost an arm (*Daily Chronicle* 1926; *Daily Graphic* 1926; *Daily Herald* 1926).[3] Aside from the qualities that made him a well-respected leader, including his ability to speak English and the fact that he could read and write, he had an additional, little-known credential: according to the late Clarence William of Sṫuxtéws, Basil Dick had trained as a *ṫkwilc* (see chaper 11).

Basil Dick, supported by his community, appointed his son Tony Basil to become his successor in the 1930s when he passed away.

André Tyenmésq̓t, chief of the Símpcwemc from 1864 to 1918, had apparently succeeded his brother Peter "Tenemasket" (Tyenmésq̓t), who had died in 1862 during the smallpox epidemic (Manson 1860–62, entry of 2 September 1862). Chief André "Tayemaskret" (Tyenmésq̓t) is listed as the son of "Tseyenetssa" (Senitṡe7 or Tsenitṡe7, ending with *-itṡe7* for "blanket, hide"), himself mentioned as chief at "La Barriere" on the North Thompson by Alexander Ross in the late 1810s. André's mother was "Kwilratkwa," presumably Q̓wyilcétkwe ("dancing water"), and he had a brother, Joseph Semecélst, and a sister, Agathe, whom the baptism records recorded as Agathe Kwilratkwa, based on her mother's Secwépemc name (see fig. 9.3). Chief André lost most of his children to disease during the late nineteenth and early twentieth centuries and by then had a single surviving daughter, Lizette (Eliza). Having no male heir, he appointed his son-in-law Cucwéll (Tapít or David Casimir), enticing him to move up to Simpcw country and stay there, becoming chief. David Casimir, in turn, was the son of Chief Louis of the Tk̓emlúpsemc, which created an alliance between the Simpcw and the Tk̓emlúpsemc.[4]

In the Northern Secwépemc area, at the time of the arrival of Simon Fraser, a prominent regional chief was Cllecwúsem ("cover up one's face"), who wore a mask when he encountered the first Europeans. His status is attested by the fact that he met Fraser and his party at the northern gateway of Secwépemc territory near Alexandria and put himself in charge of securing them safe passage through the Secwépemc communities on the Fraser River, before meeting with the St'at'imc chief at Ṫiṫq̓et (modern-day Lillooet), outside of

10.3 (*left*) | Chief Baptiste William ("Will-yum") of Ṫéxelc (Williams Lake), photographed by Edward Sapir, ca. 1916; 10.4 (*right*) | Chief François Selpáxen of Squilax (Little Shuswap), photographed by Edward Sapir, 1915.

Secwépemc territory, to hand the visitors over to the St'at'imc (see chapter 12). In the Ṫéxelc (Williams Lake) area, the title of "Chief William" ("Will-yum") was passed down from the first chief of that name, born in the early 1800s, who died of smallpox in 1862 and is buried at Glendale, a Secwépemc settlement that was taken away by land pre-emptions (see chapter 12). The second Chief William, likely his son, was chief from 1862 until 1888, when he was replaced by his *tk̓wenm7íple7ten* (councillor) "Tomabusket." After the latter died, William resumed his chiefship until his death in 1896. His son Baptiste (see fig. 10.3) succeeded him, and after Baptiste died in 1917, his brother Adrian William succeeded him (*Secwepemc News* 2013; see also Gilbert n.d.).

In the South Thompson and Shuswap Lake areas, Nesqénell emerged as a powerful leader during the mid-1850s. In turn, related to the Adams Lake chief Gregoire of Atahm and to Chief Táxwelst of Squilax (Little Shuswap), Moise "Neskonlith" (Nesqénell) was one of the chiefs of the Sexqéltkemc and the "western gatekeeper" of the Sexqéltkemc (Shuswap Lakes) division at the time when settlers began to come into the country in the early 1860s. He was the chief who, with colonial surveyors giving him instructions that the surveyors themselves failed to follow, marked out the Neskonlith Reserve, still disputed by the federal government despite a specific claim by the three communities in the area (see chapter 12). Nesqénell was succeeded by his son Leon Nesqénell, who was chief during the 1878 Joint Reserve Commission and, in turn, was succeeded by his youngest brother, Maxime Nesqénell. Maxime was then succeeded by Leon Nesqénell's daughter's husband, William Pierrish, who served in the First World War and accompanied Basil Dick to Ottawa and London. William was followed by his brother Francois, who was the father of Aimee August and Adeline Willard, wife of Ike Willard. Elder Sarah Deneault was also raised by Francois and his wife, Lucy.

Thus, at least throughout the nineteenth and early twentieth centuries, chiefship in many instances was not automatically hereditary. It is difficult to determine how chiefship was impacted by epidemics and the serious and devastating changes brought about initially by the fur trade and subsequently by white settlement, missionaries, and colonization.

Tk̓wenm7íplem̓ (Giving Advice) | Authority and Decision Making

As Teit (1909, 569) noted, within Secwépemc communities there existed a *council*, or group of *advisors*, to the chief called *tk̓wenm7íple7ten*,[5] who were instrumental in selecting and/or verifying a chief. By consensus among the heads of extended families, these *tk̓wenm7íple7ten* "appointed," or put forward, a person as chief and thus verified and legitimated his appointment.

This council also had an important function in all other matters regarding the making of decisions. Composed of elder males from the extended families, it acted as an "advisory group" for the chief. As such, it was the decision-making body in all matters involving collective welfare and collective action of the band. Within the egalitarian nature of Secwépemc society, chiefly authority was accompanied by the consensus of the extended families. The chief's authority did not flow vertically but was one of building and maintaining consensus and listening to community members. Robert Manuel, son of the late Chief George Manuel, explained this important aspect of traditional chiefship as creating consensus, noting that, according to what his father had told him, the *kúkwpi7* (chief) was expected to appear as though he "rubberstamped" decisions. That is, he had to carefully control and steer decision making toward consensus and be such a skilled intervener that to his followers it appeared as though he merely "rubberstamped" decisions, agreeing with everyone else. Unanimous consensus thus had to be skilfully and carefully created and managed. Decision making was – and in some form continues to be – a process of negotiation and listening. In addition, it is our understanding that in past Secwépemc society, women played a significant role behind the scenes. Although even into the middle of the twentieth century women were absent from political meetings (Christine Simon, Nellie Taylor, and Mary Thomas, personal communication, 1994), they had behind-the-scenes influence in that they gave advice to their husbands, sons, cousins, and nephews who were *kúkwpi7* or *tk̓wenm7íple7ten*. Their advice was given in the home, within the domestic domain, but it found its way into decision making among the leaders in the public domain. The beginning of the Tllí7sa *stsptekwll* (ancient story) exemplifies this contribution by women (see chapter 2). Tllí7sa's aunt has knowledge about how to vanquish the *tśecelemc* (dangerous powers) on the land, and she gives him advice, but it requires his physical, mental, and spiritual powers to carry out the deeds. She does not accompany Tllí7sa and his brothers in their pursuits.

There are numerous modes of action and communication that played a part in traditional political decision making. These methods included the lobbying of support through unofficial consultation, as well as "testing the wind" by mentioning a matter in public or semi-public. A chief was expected to be in consultation with his people at all times.

Although the goal of traditional Secwépemc political behaviour, as we understand it, was to strive toward political and social unanimity, there were numerous ways that discontent and dissent were voiced, often implicitly. One of these ways was absence, which amounted to a tacit voice of protest or disagreement. By being absent from a meeting, *kúkwpi7* and *tk̓wenm7íple7ten* voiced their dissent, and their absence was understood in this manner by others.

Another principle of political action involved letting people "do it to themselves." Rather than removing a person from office who made decisions that community members felt were unjust and not in their interest, the community would wait for the leader eventually to expose his behaviour as unacceptable and then to leave or resign. In other cases, as Nellie Taylor explained, especially in small communities, people would leave, and the chief would have no one to be chief over. Again, authority extended only as far as the will of the people to be guided and the ability of the *kúkwpi7* to take advice from his people.

Paramount Chiefs and Chiefs as Spokespeople for the Nation

Although each community had its *kúkwpi7*, there were chiefs who, at least since the time when the first Europeans came among us, exerted influence and acted beyond their communities. We show in chapter 12 how Chief "Xlosem" (Cllecwúsem) of Xatśúll (Soda Creek), as noted above, accompanied Simon Fraser through all the Secwépemc communities along the Fraser River, apparently recognized, or at least tolerated, by the chiefs of other bands and villages along the way. Throughout the fur trade, some chiefs exerted their influence beyond their communities. Thus when the fur traders appointed Chief N'Kwala of Douglas Lake as the caretaker of Fort Kamloops during the 1820s, the Tk̓emlúpsemc chiefs challenged him (see Thomson and M. Ignace 2005, 14). In the early to mid-1820s, this led to the Secwépemc chiefs of the

Tk̓emlúps area entering the post to claim their local authority. As trader Archibald McDonald (1826–27, entry of 9 September 1826) reported,

> Not being too well satisfied with the conduct of the two [Secwépemc] chiefs (Court Apotte & Tranquille) here last spring, the Key to the Post, contrary to Custom, was not given to the former, but to Nicholas [N'Kwala], another chief of the Okanagan Tribe which gave some umbrage to the [Secwépemc] & the consequence, as might be expected, was not the entire security of the Fort & the few little things left therein … With respect to the Fort however, it cannot be said they have acted with any wanton violence for at best 'tis but a frail concern & as such we find it.

Court Apotte (Court Apatte) was the local chief of the Tk̓emlúpsemc by or before 1822 and was still alive in 1843, known by trader John Tod as the "old chief Court Apotte." He thus would have been regarded as the caretaker and steward of the land and resources where the fort was situated. Chief Tranquille, who went by the Secwépemc name Pacamoos (Piqwemús) and whose village was near the mouth of Tranquille River on the northeast end of Kamloops Lake, was allied with him. By giving the key of the Thompson River post to Okanagan chief N'Kwala, the traders had violated Secwépemc laws of land tenure and indeed had insulted Court Apotte and his neighbouring chief, Tranquille. At the same time, Secwépemc political and kinship protocols constrained their response. As we remember from the Fish Lake Accord, N'Kwala was a close relative of the Tk̓emlúps chief, and in Secwépemc protocol it was compromising to contradict a close relative, especially one who was an honoured chief. The Secwépemc would have been insulted by the traders giving N'Kwala the keys to the fort, but they were in a delicate position with regard to maintaining harmony with a related group (Thomson and Ignace 2005, 14n45).

Within the nation, at least as things emerged throughout the second half of the nineteenth century, certain chiefs were able to exert a more dominating role than others. Chief Louis (Clexléxqen) of Kamloops was noted to be influential, as was Chief Sisyésq̓t of Skeetchestn (see Oblate Missions of British Columbia 1866–74). Chiefs Nesqénell and Atahm were spokespeople among the Eastern Secwépemc. Sarah Deneault of Neskonlith called "Neskonlith" (Nesqénell) the "keeper of gate" at the eastern boundary of the Neskonlith Reserve, and Joe Stanley Michel stated that Nesqénell was "appointed as … main spokesman of the people in negotiations with governments" (quoted in Canada, Indian Claims Commission 2008, 25). Of course, it was Chief Nesqénell who staked out the Neskonlith Reserve for the Secwépemc in the Shuswap Lakes and Adams Lake areas (see chapter 12). Above, we have described the traditional political apparatus of the Secwépemc as confederate or segmental – that is, composed of equal parts that consulted with one another regarding decisions for the mutual benefit of a number of bands or the entire nation, as well as acting as a joint political body in interactions with the outside. From the ethnohistorical record, we have numerous references both to the consultation that went on among the Secwépemc chiefs and to joint political meetings and action.

As noted in chapter 6, Green Lake, situated in a central location within Secwepemcúl̓ecw on the plateau between the North Thompson and Fraser Rivers, was an annual gathering place for people from all parts of Secwepemcúl̓ecw, where not only trade, athletic competition, and visiting took place during the trout run in late spring but also political consultation among the chiefs of the many divisions and communities that gathered here. The meaning of its Secwépemc name, Teltsíńten ("place from where news is spread"), speaks to its important role in this respect.

Joint meetings among Secwépemc chiefs were also reported during the early period of the fur trade. John McLeod, the first trader at the Thompson River post in 1822–23, voiced his concern over the Secwépemc and their Okanagan allies, led by Chief Nicola, taking over the fort to hold their meetings, including their war council to avenge the death of his father, Chief Pelkamulox (see chapter 8).

On 20 December 1826, Archibald McDonald witnessed and described a major gathering at Kamloops attended by more than 300 people. Although he admitted that he had no clue as to what was being discussed at the meeting because neither he nor his company men spoke or understood Secwepemctsín, he reported the details of Secwépemc eating etiquette and foods consumed at this large gathering. Moreover, he observed that "during this rendezvous it is also an object with them to pledge their friendship with each other" (A. McDonald 2001, 53) – doubtlessly an expression of social and political alliances between the chiefs at this meeting. Here is McDonald's (ibid., 53–5) detailed account of the gathering:

> Wednesday 20th – Everything being prepared to commence the grand banquet, we all had an invitation from Court Apath this afternoon, but for the present myself only and one of the Canadians attended. It is much to be regretted that the object of this kind of jubilee (not uncommon among the Natives here) is not better understood by the Europeans, & am sorry to say that I am not likely to throw any additional light on the subject – not a word of the Native language here can anyone attached to the Company's service speak. All our little dealing with them is done thro the medium of the Okanagan … On arrival at the camp I saw for the first time the Basin [hollow depression] the Chief

had constructed for the express purpose of this entertainment – its dimension at base is 45 feet square with an upright wall of about 4, and then the roof running to a point in the centre, to answer the purpose of a door. To this aperture is fixed up nearly perpendicular, a stout stick of about 18 ft. notched at convenient distances to serve as a ladder … [A] gang of stark naked fellows actively engaged in lowering down by means of slings from 20 to 25 of their waterproof baskets, smoaking hot with thin soups, none of them less than 10 gallons & some considerably more. In mean time as many were already busily employed below cutting up the most excellent dried Beaver & venison laid up at the expense of much labour & privation to themselves solely for the purpose since autumn – bear's fat, both raw and melted … & roots of every description peculiar to this part of the country ready for distribution. The guests, near upon 300 men, sat upon the ground as thick as they could … round & round this subterranean habitation, leaving very little space for the attendants, who by the bye let it be observed were not the most contemptible of the Shewhaps & even Court Apath himself was by no means an idle spectator altho his labour did not extend beyond mere superintendence. Every man was furnished with the cheekbone of salmon for his spoon, & the soup kettles, consisting of berries, roots, grease, pounded fish, salmon roe, &c &c being planted here & there among them, they fell to & soon emptied their dishes. These spacious reservoirs the Shewhaps Chief & other personages in attendance made it a point to taste a portion of each before the hungry visitors commenced the attack.

The next course was each a lump of suet, after which the Beaver & venison with a raw piece of bear's fat; & lastly the roots. This ceremony occupied about two hours, when I enabled them to resume the pipe, which being some time indulged in, the devouring organs were again called to action & to continue alternately with the pipe for at least 24 hours.

It is a universal rule with them on such occasions that the guest must eat all put before him, & if this task be too much another is imposed – that of carrying it with him. This (being liberally supplied with the most substantial part of the eatables) was unluckily the case with myself today, but the constant dry salmon at home rendered [it] more agreeable than painful. Those who come from a distance are by this law much beholden to their good appetite & to their still better powers of digestion, but I believe before the feast is over seldom the latter is found capable of performing its functions, & the consequence is what naturally might be expected. This heaving up scene affords the host (evidence absolutely necessary) the most convincing proof of their being treated to their heart's content.

> They have been dancing for the last 48 hours, which I believe necessarily carries with it a system of fasting. During the dance presents were exchanged. The Coutamines gave 3 or 4 horses, Guns & Hayques [haiqua shells used as currency].[6] The Shewhaps returned the compliment with Guns, Robes, Beads & a few Beaver traps. I observed hung up in the Banquet Hall what they told me were appendages belonging to some of the deceased relations of Court Apath & friends, which in the progress of the dance were often saluted with loud peals of mourning & lamentations.
>
> During this rendezvous it is also an object with them to pledge their friendship with each other, altho religion is no doubt the primary consideration.
>
> Before quitting this grand affair, I acknowledged the good behaviour of the Coutamines when I was among them [and] intimated our intention of soon going that way again for salmon, & the probability of the whites by & bye passing thro their country with Boats &c &c, all of which seemed to leave them with sentiments of additional regard for us. The rest of our people crossed to the camp in the evening. None of the Okanagans attended & but very few of the Schimilicameach [Similkameens].
>
> Thursday 21st – A few of the Coutamines left the camp early this morning, but those good fellows that swallowed most of last night's emetic are still on the ground.
>
> Friday 22nd – The six principal Indians from below came across this morning to see us before their departure – took their names & gave each a ½ yard green Beads, a corn scalper & ½ head leaf tobacco.

During the 1870s and 1880s, the Oblate Missionary Father Charles Grandidier, in his correspondence and letters, gave us numerous clues as to the often implicitly and clandestinely political nature of social gatherings. In 1873 he reported, "The Chief of the Bonaparte has assembled all the Sauvages from Lytton to Clinton and all the Secwépemcs, under pretext of giving them a holiday (festival). I don't know what it is but I fear that there is more to it than meets the eye" (Grandidier to d'Herbomez, 16 November 1873, in Oblate Missions of British Columbia 1866–74).

A year later, in further correspondence with his bishop, Grandidier also voiced his opposition to the give-aways among the Bonaparte, Clinton, and Upper Nlaka'pamux, which signified the witnessing and sanctioning of political decisions. He wrote, "They conduct their business under the guise of festivals, horse races, etc. but in the meetings the chiefs alone gather to discuss subjects which the people do not hear" (Grandidier to d'Herbommez, 6 September 1874, in Oblate Missions of British Columbia 1866–74).

Chiefly Authority, Social Control, and Criminal Justice

In addition to control over resources, Secwépemc law also prevailed in matters regarding criminal justice. The Secwépemc way of dealing with a serious crime was to hold a council presided over by the *kúkwpi7* and *tkwenm7íple7ten*, often called "Indian court," where evidence was heard from both sides to establish what happened and who was at fault, leading to a verdict, a sentence, and a determination of retribution, often in the form of compensation. As reported by Alexander Caulfield Anderson, the Hudson's Bay Company officer at Fort Alexandria during the 1840s, "In case of individual acts of aggression or outrage, and especially in the case of murder, retribution was inflexibly exacted. But punishment was visited not only on the guilty; and then usually through the medium of the tribe, or with their approval and cooperation" (quoted in Thomson and M. Ignace 2005, 27).

The victim's extended family had a role in achieving retribution by giving its cooperation and advice. The perpetrator's family also gave its consent to the sentence, especially in cases of serious crimes that involved the death sentence of the perpetrator, as shown by the stories of Secwépemc internal war mentioned in chapter 3, or what J.P. Reid (1993, 31) refers to as "privileged killing" in order to revenge murder.[7]

For the members of the perpetrator's social group to disregard this principle of consent by not surrendering the criminal offender in their ranks was to *eyemstsút* (neglect to meet one's obligations), and the family of a victim would come to torment the guilty person as well as his or her kin. The responsibility to deal with crime not only fell on the offender but also involved the social responsibility of his group.[8]

The evidence from the fur trade journals again shows that in cases of theft and murder, the traditional Secwépemc justice system prevailed. When an Aboriginal person murdered a white fur trader, the Hudson's Bay Company officials understood that it was their responsibility to respond in terms acceptable to our people as their "hosts." Although "Europeans were loath to accept compensation in payment for the murder of one of their own," and the rhetoric of fur trade journals emphasized a desire to "pursue judicious, firm and conciliatory measures" (Thomson and M. Ignace 2005, 29), actual instances of criminal justice show that the company invariably followed Indigenous legal protocols (ibid.), according to which, from the Secwépemc perspective, the traders were *sexlítemc* (guests) in Secwepemcúlecw and the Secwépemc were their hosts.

The 1841 murder of Hudson's Bay Company officer-in-charge Samuel Black at the Thompson River post in Kamloops by a "Kiskowskin," a young Secwépemc who was the nephew of Chief Tranquille – who had inexplicably died soon after being refused a gun by Samuel Black, with Chief Tranquille's widow suspecting Black had committed an act of sorcery – shows how

Secwépemc principles of criminal justice were involved in the aftermath of Black's murder. They involved the local Secwépemc chief Grand Gule not only agreeing to retribution but also seeking consent from the perpetrator's family to deal with the culprit (Thomson and M. Ignace 2005, 30–2). The crucial condition of Chief Grand Gule surrendering the perpetrator was a payment made to the Secwépemc chief, arranged by Black's successor, trader John Tod, after previous attempts to extort the perpetrator from his group by means of violence had failed.[9]

In their attempts to convert Secwépemc people to Catholicism, missionaries tried to put the Indigenous institution of already existing "Indian courts" to use, interpreted by them as "public confessions" that led to the "punishment of sinners." They thought that these "courts" represented an existing institution on which to build private confessions. Between 1858 and 1875, public confessions were commonly advocated and used as part of the "missionary method." Bishop Pierre-Paul Durieu stated, "The public confessions and public penitence could become an excellent means to root Catholicism among the Indians near the Pacific," adding, "The first act of the missionary is to put vice in its place" (quoted in Dionne 1947, 91, our translation). It was of central importance to deal with "sin" and "sinners" by instituting "fear" of the holy sacraments of confession and communion.

However, as Father Grandidier and his associates in Tk̓emlúps (Kamloops) and other Secwépemc communities began to realize by the mid-1870s, the institution of "Indian courts" was a far cry from private confession and the idea of sin as a personal offence against God. Within a few years, they realized that the "*sauvages*" had "no fear of the Holy sacrament" and that "Indian courts" were social tribunals involving criminal justice matters rather than confessions of conscience. One priest lamented that during "Indian courts," the accused "only say what they absolutely can't deny" (quoted in Dionne 1947, 98, our translation).[10] Initially, they had thought that the Indigenous institutions were not that dissimilar from European confessions. However, after a few years, they realized that the Indigenous "Indian courts" dealt with the taking of admissible and provable evidence, as opposed to confession on the basis of conscience. After the mid-1870s, public confessions took a diminished role, with the Oblates realizing their social, rather than religious, functions (Dionne 1947).[11] As "Indian courts" that dealt with criminal offences within the community, they continued to exist. Theresa Jules remembered them as follows:

Ta7 k slegwtsínem, ta7 ṫri7.
There was no gossip, no.

Ta7 k slegwtsínment.s ṫl̓un k swéti7.
No one out there gossiped about anyone.

E legwtsínmes ṫri7 k swet, m-kwéntem ne7éne ne xwqwentsíṅten, m-cíṫlcstem.
If someone did gossip, that person was taken to the church here and made to kneel down.

Re m-séwentmes, "Kénem mé7e ṫri7 wel xílem ye7éne?"
The person was asked, "Why did you behave this way?"

"Ṫri7 stwelíl̓menc re7 úq̓wi, e k̓estsínmenc?"
"Why did you make fun of your sister or brother, swear at them?"

"Ta7 k stśkénemst.s."
"They did nothing to you."

"Me7 eyentsút-k me7 nerí7."
"You make amends now right there."

Re m-k̓úlentem yerí7 re s7elkst.s ṫri7 ṫhé7en ṫri7.
The person was made to do work out there somewhere.

Ye-enke k tsuns pyin ṫ7en re séme7 the "law."
Nowadays, I guess that's what the white man calls "law."

Stéṁi lu7 k stseṁét.stem?
What was it called again?

Ron Ignace: Gossip?

Mé7e.
Yes.

Ron Ignace: Cw7it-en lu7 k stk̓wenm7ípleṅstsut.s ne7élye re qelmúcw?
Ron Ignace: Did the people here have lots of advice about implementing traditional laws?

Mé7e cw7it, tk̓wenm7ípleṅtem.
Yes lots, the advice was laid down for them.

Xexé7 lu7 le q̓7éses le kupkúkwpi7.
The chiefs long ago were smart.

E tsútes es cplul̓k̓ws ... me7 ... me7 nek̓wésq̓t tśílem k sxetéqs,
If they needed to have a meeting ... then ... it would be one week before,

me7 temtéw̓s yehé7en k k̓welmétentem.
the one asked to tell others would carry the message by horseback.

Me7 tsqwetséts yerí7 te wutémtk,
He started from downstream,

me7 lexéy̓em, lexéy̓em, lexéy̓em,
he would relay the message from house to house,

nu7 m-t̓7ek te Ck̓écse7ten.[12]
all the way to Back Valley.

In addition, Ida William of Chu Chua (Simpcw), Louisa Basil of St̓uxtéws, and Nellie Taylor of Skeetchestn remembered various instances from the 1920s and 1930s where the chief of the community held "Indian court" to deal with theft, insults, and other disputes.

Remembering the way of life of the 1920s to 1950s, Secwépemc elders born between the 1890s and 1930s also talked of the social order, which included some degree of continuing independence from the institutions of the dominant society, as well as from the seeming rigidity that the Durieu method brought to the social sanctions of the old "Indian courts." Sarah Deneault, like other elders, interpreted these "courts" as a sign of an era when Secwépemc people were united rather than split up into nucleated bands, when chiefs had authority in their communities, and when our people were relatively autonomous.

Until changes were made to the Indian Act, which imposed a biannual election system throughout the Secwépemc nation, community chiefs continued to be appointed and affirmed by consensus among the members of a community. In some cases, chiefly succession continued to be patrilineal, as was the case in St̓uxtéws when Basil Dick's son Tony Basil succeeded his father in the mid-1930s. In other cases, there was no patrilineal succession, but successors were still appointed on the basis of some kind of notion during this era. At least throughout the 1930s and 1940s, according to elders' testimony, "Indian courts" continued to be held by the chief. Using the titles of the Durieu system, but interpreted as Secwépemc tradition by elders, the community chief was assisted by his *tk̓wenm7íple7ten* (captains or advisors) and by his law enforcers, the watchmen. The "tin-tin man," or bellringer, was the local messenger who spread news about deaths in the community and other events. The chief himself would act as judge. Nellie Taylor of Skeetchestn recalled a case from her childhood where a woman accused of having stolen another's buckskin out of the creek was ordered by the chief to make restitution. Sarah Deneault also remembered "whipmen" in communities, who would discipline children who did not obey their elders.

The powers of chiefs to maintain order in the community thus extended well into the twentieth century. Although the provincial government had asserted its own control over legal and criminal justice matters since the 1860s by establishing magistrates and courts, it is interesting that this assertion of legal authority was not always enacted. As we see from the above instances of "Indian courts," matters pertaining to the reserve community continued to be internally adjudicated by the chief and his watchmen until at least the 1930s. However, a 1914 case at Hat Creek within the area associated with the St̓uxtéwsemc (Bonaparte) that did not transpire on a reserve sheds some light on the degree to which outside authorities continued, at least in some instances, to recognize the local authority and autonomy of chiefs.

On 22 October 1914 Adelina August of St̓uxtéws (Bonaparte) was killed by Charlie Pierro, also of St̓uxtéws, at Hat Creek Ranch, while men and women from Bonaparte and surrounding communities were encamped there during the potato harvest. Pierro fled the scene. A criminal investigation was launched by the local police, without turning up Pierro. On 30 October 1914 the local Indian agent, John Freemont ("Nigger") Smith,[13] met with local provincial police and with Chief Basil Dick and his "principal men." It was agreed that Chief Dick would search for Pierro for thirty days, without further police involvement. On 18 November 1914 Chief Dick and his men handed Pierro over to the authorities (Canada, Department of Indian Affairs 1914). What is significant about this case is that, as late as 1914, the local community's authority was recognized to bring a suspect – against whom evidence by witnesses from the local Secwépemc community was strong – to be charged and tried. It shows how, despite settler society asserting that it had established its laws and criminal justice institutions in Canada, these institutions themselves ceded a certain amount of continuing authority to local chiefs, if for no other than practical reasons, namely that the local chief and community were in a better position to find a suspect, and gather evidence, especially where the victim was also a member of the local community.

This chapter has thus shown how Secwépemc leadership, principally enacted through the role of political chief and advisor roles, functioned both in traditional Secwépemc society and well into the twentieth century, in the face of government agencies and the church attempting to undermine it and lessen traditional authority. Chiefly authority was not strictly hereditary but relied in equal parts on the chosen successor's fitness to lead his community, create consensus among community members in collaboration with *tk̓wenm7íple7ten* (councillors) from the community, deal with outsiders, and represent the community in joint and common political action against outside forces. Last but not least, community chiefs, together with their council, had an important role in maintaining law and order in the community and in administering justice. What they knew to hand down, of course, involved the principles laid out by the teachings in the stories they knew.

1 | Pictographs at Stemqín (Savona Mountain), 2001. Here Secwépemc people went *étsxem* (spirit guardian questing). The pictographs are on the ceiling of a cave that is on a steep rock slope about 1,200 metres above the valley. Courtesy of Marianne Ignace.

2 (*overleaf*) | Tskwiḱúý ("logs lying down"), the mouth of Scotch Creek on the north shore of Shuswap Lake, 2015. Here the journey of Tllí7sa and his brothers began. Courtesy of Marianne Ignace.

3 | Tk̓emlúps (Kamloops), the confluence of Secwepemcétkwe (South Thompson River) and Simpcwétkwe (North Thompson River), 2015. Here Tllí7sa vanquished a powerful grizzly bear who lived with Sk̓elép (Coyote). The confluence was the site of a large ancient village where 2,000 people met the first European visitors in 1811. Courtesy of Marianne Ignace.

4 (*opposite*) | Tsmeltám̓ (Marble Canyon), 2012. Here a supernatural bald-headed eagle tried to kill Tllí7sa by smashing him against the rock face, with Tllí7sa spitting out red ochre that he pretended was his blood. Courtesy of Marianne Ignace.

5 (*above*) | Qwiqwíyqwiyt (High Bar Canyon), 2007. Here the journey of Tllí7sa and his brothers ended when they were *ṫult* (frozen into stone) by Chipmunk Girl, who was on her *étsxem* (spirit guardian quest) across the Fraser River. The brothers, in turn, froze her into stone. Chipmunk Girl is visible as the rock column on the right bank of the river, and the three brothers are visible as three rock columns on the left bank. Courtesy of Steve Allen.

6 | Southern Secwépemc territory landscapes: (a) eastern Shuswap Lake, looking southwest, ca. 2004; (b) Monte Creek locality in the South Thompson River Valley, looking south, ca. 1985; (c) South Thompson River Valley near Pritchard, looking north, 2010; (d) South Thompson River Valley east of Kamloops, looking east, 1985; (e) Pípsell (Jacko Lake) locality in the uplands south of Kamloops, looking west, 2013; (f) Kamloops Lake west of Kamloops looking east, ca. 2000; (g) Thompson River Valley near Walhachin, looking southeast, 1985. Courtesy of Mike K. Rousseau (a, b, c, d, and f) and Marianne Ignace (e).

7 | Western Secwépemc territory landscapes: (a) Bonaparte River Valley north of Cache Creek, looking north, ca. 1995; (b) Upper Hat Creek Valley, looking northwest, 2006; (c) Keatley Creek locality in the mid-Fraser River region, looking northeast, ca. 1985; (d) Churn Creek locality in the mid-Fraser River region, looking west, 1990; (e) the Dog Creek locality in the mid-Fraser River region, ca. 1990; (f) upper mid-Fraser River region looking northwest, ca. 1990. Courtesy of Mike K. Rousseau (a, c, d, e, and f) and Sandra Peacock (b).

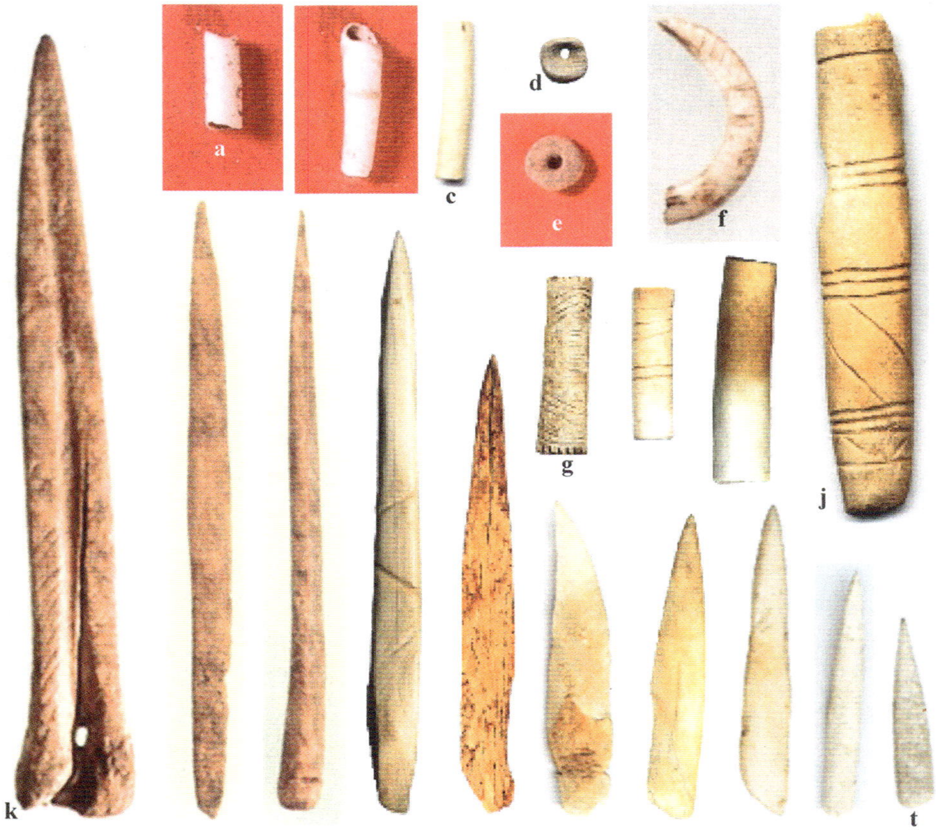

8 | Examples of common bone, antler, and shell artifacts found in Plateau and Kamloops Horizon occupations 2,400 to 200 years ago: (a–c) marine dentalium shell beads obtained through trade with Northwest Coast groups; (d–e) bone beads; (f) incised beaver tooth; (g–j) gaming pieces; (k–t) basketry needles, awls, and small bone "unipoints" used for tipping projectiles, fish hooks, fish gorges, and leister barbs. Courtesy of Mike K. Rousseau.

9 | Subalpine meadows at Trophy Mountain in Wells Grey Park, an important hunting ground used by the Simpcw and Tsq̓éscen Sɛcwépemc, 1991. Courtesy of Nancy J. Turner.

10 (*opposite*) | Simpcw elder Sammy Joseph in the alpine at Qelqeléscen (Baldy Mountain) high above the mid-North Thompson River, 1987. Dunn Peak is in the background. In these areas of high mountain peaks and valleys, Simpcw people hunted caribou, deer, whistlers, and other game. Courtesy of Marianne Ignace.

11 (*above*) | Skeetchestn elder Christine Simon harvesting *sxúsem* (soapberries) with her grandchildren Candice and Tyson, joined by Katie Ignace *(right)*, 2007. Courtesy of Marianne Ignace.

12 | Landscape burning at Skeetchestn Reserve, 2015. For Secwépemc and other Indigenous peoples of northwestern North America, landscape burning was a crucial aspect of managing grasslands and forests. Courtesy of Marianne Ignace.

13 | The Ignaces' dugout canoe at Sk̓emqín on the shore of Kamloops Lake, 2003. That year the Ignace family – including Jay Coutts, Greg Ignace, Ron Ignace, Marianne Ignace, George Ignace, and their younger children – built a cottonwood dugout canoe 4.5 metres in length, subsequently navigated on Kamloops Lake. Courtesy of Marianne Ignace.

14 | St Joseph's Church on the Kamloops Indian Reserve, ca. 1998. Built in 1912, this church was Father Jean-Marie-Raphaël Le Jeune's residence and attracted Secwépemc people from the area, although surrounding communities also had their own smaller churches built in the same style. All of them were preceded by small log churches built in 1866–67. Courtesy of Christan Beharrell.

11 Re Tyegwyegwténs-kucw ne Tmicws

Secwépemc Spirituality and How It Was Hidden in the Church

In the preceeding chapters, we have explained how ways of living on the land and ways of understanding interactions of humans, animals, plants, and landforms must be understood within a Secwépemc ontology that views all beings on the land as having agency (acting upon one another) and as having feeling (being *sentient*). This way of seeing, as we explained in chapter 5, engages humans, plants, animals, and the land itself, including the weather, or sky, as *reciprocally accountable* to one another. To explain the Secwépemc actions and reactions to traders, missionaries, and colonizers, as these outsiders increasingly shaped Secwépemc existence starting in the latter part of the nineteenth century, we elaborate on some central concepts of Secwépemc spiritual beliefs previously addressed in chapters 2 and 5. We then show how Secwépemc people adapted to, syncretized, and navigated the big changes that happened when so many lives were lost during epidemics in the early 1860s and soon after missionaries came into Secwepemcúl̓ecw.

In chapter 2, we discussed the role of Sk̓elép (Coyote) in his historical and social-moral dimensions. According to the Secwépemc belief system, it was Senk̓éwelc (Old One), the "chief of the ancient world" (Teit 1909, 596), who sent Sk̓elép to "travel over the world and put it to rights" during that period a long time ago when the earth "was much troubled with great winds, fires and floods" (Secwépemc elders' handed-down knowledge, ca. 1900–04, quoted in ibid., 595–6). Often equated with the Tqelt Kúkwpi7 ("Chief Above" or Creator), Old One, who was "all powerful," put the sun, moon, weather, and seasons in place, introduced many of the animals into Secwepemcúl̓ecw, and taught the people how to harvest and preserve them. He introduced use of the *sq̓ílye* (sweat lodge) as a custom that sets humans apart from animals. Behind the Salish people's movements into different parts of the Interior Plateau was Old One's guiding hand or power. It was Old One who reminded people to be *respectful* to all living things. We saw in chapter 6 how this notion of respect, communicated as *xyemstém* ("[let us] be respectful") or *me7 xyemstéc* ("be respectful"), is at the core of Secwépemc beliefs about human interaction with the land and all living things on the land, and it is profoundly connected to resource management practices and laws.

As we explained in chapter 5, central to the relationship between an animal and the fisher or hunter who "bags" the animal is the concept that the animal gives itself to the fisher or hunter, what we call *kecmentsút*. Plants as sentient beings also give themselves in this manner.[1] Therefore, the harvesting of all things in nature presupposes prayer that thanks the Tqelt Kúkwpi7 (Creator) for providing the animals or plants that feed people, as well as thanking the animals or plants for giving themselves to people. The sanctions for disrespectful behaviour extend beyond the animal or game resource into the realm of social relations, entailing a law of respectful conduct and resource management.

Beyond what zoologists and botanists would consider living things, the notion of sentient powers that rest in the land also extends to specific places in the landscape. Especially the places visited by the *stsptékwle* (transformers) are imbued with powers. They continue to be *medicines* that can act on people. They can harm people if one shows disrespect or carelessness. They will benefit people when they are treated with respect. All parts of the Secwépemc land and environment are thus thought of as a "sentient landscape."[2] The land communicates with people, and people communicate with it in song, prayer, story, and thought. As Secwépemc people, we communicate with its powers, and the landscape communicates with us in a continuous reciprocal relationship where we are required to be accountable to the land and all of its beings and powers.

Certain places were thought of as being inhabited by "powers that interacted with people by producing sudden violent changes in the weather if people who travelled through these areas did not show their respect to these places with prayers and offerings" (Teit 1900, 344). The concept of *x7ensq̓t*, translated by Secwépemc elders as "the land will turn on you,"[3] expresses the sentient power of particular places. In his ethnographies of the Secwépemc and the neighbouring Nlaka'pamux, James Teit (ibid.) explained,

> They also made offerings to peaks and to the genii of certain places in the high mountains, especially peaks or hills, [which] were considered sacred, being the residence of land mysteries. Some of these places, when trodden upon by human foot, were always visited by snow or rain. In other places, snow or rain fell only when they were trodden upon or visited by a stranger for the first time. Indians, therefore, when hunting in the vicinity of these places, visited them, and appeased the spirits by making an offering to them, thus insuring good weather during their stay, and good luck while hunting. These offerings generally consisted of a lock of hair, a rag from the clothing, a little powder, a few shot, a piece of tobacco, a stone, and so on. The women, when picking berries or digging roots on certain mountains, always painted their faces red. In general, they paint their faces wholly red before coming in sight of

> certain lakes, that they may be favored with good weather and good fishing. The paint is considered as an offering to the spirits. Sometimes, when they came in sight of these lakes, they made the sign of goodwill or blessing … and prayed to them to give them good weather and plenty of fish. They also did this to some of the mountain-peaks near their hunting-grounds.

These instances are expressions of the concept of *x7ensq̓t* as still known by elders who were taught about it as they accompanied their own elders on the land. *X7ensq̓t* expresses the respect for places on the land imbued with spiritual power that derives from past events and experiences of ancestors, which present generations regard as *deeds.* Such respect is shown by blackening one's face and making offerings that express gratitude to the powers inherent in these places. One such place is Ḱecúsem̓, the stump on the trail from Knutsford to Nicola Lake at the crossing of Peterson Creek, identified by George M. Dawson (1891, 33) as connected to the *stsptekwll* (ancient story) about the trout children at Jacko Lake (see chapter 9). It is in the vicinity of the site of a proposed open-pit mine. Another place mentioned as imbued with such powers is Pelúkwes (Deadman Falls) at the headwaters of Deadman's Creek.

The powers in the Secwépemc universe also include past ancestors – that is, the deceased – who can act on us and influence the course of events. Hence people pray to deceased loved ones to help them in times of hardship.

Another important concept in Secwépemc spirituality is that of personal power, derived from the different sources of "spirit power" or the "guardian spirits" with which some humans are born. Sometimes they receive them from their elders as young children, and they can find them as adolescents and adults by questing or "practising" for them. These powers then protect and guide them for life, becoming part of their identity and essence. Skeetchestn elders referred to the guardian spirit with which a person is born as his or her *sk̓últen* (what you are born with). Often before they *tslexemwílc* (came to their senses) at the age of five or six, young children were blessed, or *melámentem* (doctored), with the spirit power of one or more animals. Thus, as Ron Ignace remembered, as a young child he was doctored with two powers that were to guide him throughout his life (see Introduction). On the one hand, his great-grandmother doctored him with the grease and paw of a *skem̓cís* (grizzly bear) so that he would have that animal's strength and power to guard the land. To complement the awesome power of the grizzly bear, his grandmother Meléni doctored him with the power of the *tsecwyáńst* (woodworm),[4] which, although small in size, persistently, patiently, and steadily drills its way through the trunk of a tree.

Clothilde Thomas of T̓éxelc (Sugarcane) and Laura Harry of Esk̓ét confirmed the practice of people being doctored with the powers of the *tsecwyáńst* in their area. Splatsín elders also remembered that a property of the *tsecwyáńst* was its ability to withstand cold, not unlike the mountain pine beetle (*Dendroctonus ponderosae*), which in people's recent memory defied human attempts to get rid of it. Laura Harry remembered that her brother was doctored up "with the beak and feet of a hummingbird – he could run and whistle real well." Other elders remembered their own parents or grandparents rubbing a child with a *tṡqíqse7* (chickadee) so that the child would be a good talker or with part of a *sqleẇ* (beaver) so that the child would become a hard worker.

During their adolescence, young people acquired spirit powers derived from forces in nature, "practising" for them by going on their *étsxem* (spirit guardian quest). At the onset of *llxumc* (puberty), girls began their training in a small lodge away from their homes but supervised by their grandmother, mother, or aunt, practising endurance tasks like sewing and embroidery, basketry, and making rope from *spétṡen* (Indian hemp). They also practised digging trenches to hone their root-digging skills (see chapter 5), as elders like Nellie Taylor remembered. Secluded from males, they "spent every night in the mountains roaming about, exercising and praying" (Teit 1909, 587). Young boys began their training "when the voice changed, or when they commenced to dream of women, and canoes" (ibid.), separating themselves from the community for days or weeks at a time over a period of one year to several years.

By going "up in the mountains," a young person had to live in solitude for days, potentially weeks and months, often on more than one stay. Through *étsxem*, which included fasting and prayer in solitude, individuals found their personal *seméc* (spirit guardian power). They were told, "*Me7 etsxemíncwes re7 seméc*" ("You should train for your guardian spirit power"). *Seméc* is thus conceived of as a spiritual quality and essence that does not exist accidentally or automatically but instead can be obtained and channelled by training and working hard for it. While away from the distractions of community and other people, young people on their *étsxem* went through rigorous fasting and physical training that allowed them to communicate with the spirits of animals. Songs would come to them, given by an animal or a force of nature, like fire or water, that thus showed itself to the person questing and transferred its spirit power. These acquired *seméc*, embodied as a certain animal or a force of nature, would come to people, often during their dreams or while they were in a trance state. These *seméc* would become part of them, giving them special powers derived from the characteristics of the animal spirit or force of nature they received.

In addition, *étsxem* entailed a social dimension in that it removed young people from the community, requiring them to subsist on their own and to become economically and emotionally self-sufficient rather than being a burden on people, or what is called a *yéwyut* (nuisance). Returning home to the community, young people who had completed their *étsxem* also had more of a sense of appreciation for their elders, their family, and the social life of the community. Especially for females who trained to excel in resource-harvesting tasks that required persistence and patience, the symbols of their achievements were painted with ochre onto rocks, or in the case of digging trenches for root gathering, they were notched into their digging stick handles as "trench marks."[5]

Here is how the late Leslie ("Lesím") Narcisse of Adams Lake explained *étsxem*:

> You go, by gosh, when you practising, you gotta hide. You're not gonna see nobody for three, four months. You gotta be … If you hear somebody talkin' far away, you're gonna have to run away. And you know what kind of lunch they get? Dried meat about that big. That's gotta last you three, four months. You're not going to eat it, [laughs] but you gotta smell it, you gotta taste and rub it up and put it away for you all the time. And you gotta swim. And you not supposed to swim like, like now, in day time. When you practisin', you can't swim till the sun goes right down. You have your rocks and everything ready, right here on top of your wood. And as soon as … as soon as the sun goes down and it's dark, you gotta be hidden away too. Right in the forest where [not] anybody can see your fire or smoke or anything. And then you fix your sweathouse. Put your rocks in there. And that's where you wait for … for your power to come in. And you got to swim hard and you got to pray. You not gonna go just walk right in, without asking Jesus Christ or to God or your angel to help you. That's the way you got to go. You're not just going to run in there and stay. And you're not going to be two, three people. Just yourself. And you got to hike. And if you don't do that, nothing will come to you. It's time, I guess what I'm saying, when it's going to help you. And somebody maybe through the night will be talking to you. The language, you know, it will speak to you. Okay, you look out. It wasn't a human. It was a deer, or a chicken or whatever. Whatever wants to help you, that's the one to call you from outside. Now, what are you gonna do? He'll tell you, "If you need my power, this is what you gotta do and this is what you gotta say." And if he's gonna give you a song, he'll give you a song. And if he don't, well you'll just have to … just have to … well, you just kind of think about them, you know, and then you holler, and whatever he is, and you just call him, "I need your help right now!" And they'll help you. That's your power. He's watching you all the time after that. That's the way it goes.

He went on to comment sarcastically about how difficult it has become to find places to *étsxem* with the increasing resource development and settlement throughout Secwepemcúl̓ecw: "Only place I guess guys can get to practise

11.1 | Leslie ("Lesím") Narcisse *(foreground)*, in his late eighties, telling stories of *étsxem* (spirit guardian questing), 1991. *Background left to right:* Simon Fraser University students Denise Michel, Truman Jones, Russell Leonard, and Luc Duchesne.

is way back in … pretty close to [the] North Pole, I guess. It's the only place the Indians can practise right now. You can't, you can't practise nowhere, you know, what they used to do. There're so damn many people right now." In other words, with Secwépemc people fast losing the ability to *quietly enjoy* their homeland, Secwepemcúl̓ecw, the parents and grandparents of younger generations realize how increased settler populations, including their "back country" recreational vehicles, urban development, logging, and mining, have impeded the ability of present and future generations of young Secwépemc to follow the laws of our ancestors by conducting *étsxem*.[6]

Although some *seméc* guardian spirits were inherited, those that a person fully understood and could interact with were the ones that had been acquired during *étsxem*. Teit (1909, 606) noted that most men had several guardians, "but generally one was much more powerful than others. Those of some men were wholly helpful, and could not be used to harm any person; while others had exactly the opposite properties." Powerful guardians were tobacco, pipe, the dead, cannibal, fox, coyote, and water, as well as grizzly bear, wolf, eagle, thunder, loon, pinto horse, white horse, weapons, hunger and famine, mountain goat, otter, beaver, hare, owl, fire, rain, blood, woman, black bear, deer, scalp, man, and boy. People who had acquired a certain *seméc* partook of the character of their guardian. They were instructed by their guardians to paint their face or body in a certain way to embody the guardian spirit's power.

The emblems and signs of young males who had completed their *étsxem* were also depicted in pictographs, in personal tattoos, and on amulets. James Teit, in his books on the Nlaka'pamux (1900) and Secwépemc (1909), as well as in his early work on female Nlaka'pamux rock painting (1896) and in his posthumous work on Plateau tattooing and face and body painting (1930b), showed numerous sketches of body painting that displayed a combination of symbols representing guardian spirits and instructions for designs from guardian spirit helpers.

Ṫkwilc | Indian Doctors

In Secwépemc society and Interior Plateau society in general, individuals who showed special powers young in life and who then trained for long years in seclusion to practise their special gifts, often acquiring additional *seméc*, were the *ṫkwilc*, often referred to as "Indian doctors." *Ṫkwilc* had powers to predict and foretell, to cure illness in the wider sense of restoring physical, spiritual, emotional, and mental well-being, and to inflict harm when their own powers were threatened. *Ṫkwilc* could turn energy (from humans and animals) into matter by "freezing" animate beings into stone, a process referred to as *ṫult*, as shown in the Tllí7sa transformer epic (see chapter 2).

Leslie Narcisse told of the powers of *ṫkwilc* a long time ago: "Long ago what makes it danger for younger people … what they call 'big Indian doctors.' They … they're not mad. But their power is too strong. And then if … if they see anything, you know, like a little bit wrong. Boom, you're you're you're gone. If … if you're not strong enough in your power, they'll kill you. That's how it goes." Men or women could become Indian doctors, and as Secwépemc oral histories from diverse communities tell, *ṫkwilc* and their work were an important aspect of the fabric of Secwépemc communities until several decades after missionaries arrived and began to baptize people.

Each Secwépemc community had several adults who had trained as *ṫkwilc* and were practising Indian doctors whose powers were evident in extraordinary actions, as recounted in the stories that tell of their deeds. In fact, from the memories about *ṫkwilc* who were alive and active in the late 1800s and early 1900s in numerous communities, it appears that during that time at least 10 per cent of adults had trained to become *ṫkwilc*. It appears that the natural gifts, but likely also the preparedness and support for lengthy and arduous training, ran in families.

Ṫkwilc had certain places where they were known to practise together. Thus Lizette Donald of Simpcw mentioned that "at Vavenby, about two miles this side [toward the Chu Chua Reserve], my mom used to show me where them guys used to practice," adding that the Canadian National Railway "got that all down." In other words, they destroyed not only the physical attributes of this place when they put through the railway track but also its spiritual

11.2 | *Ṫkwilc* (shaman) Cecile Melmenétkwe *(left)* of Skeetchestn with Madoline Simon and Melanie (Meláni) Paul, ca 1935.

quality and essence. Another such place was Skweṫúse7 (Face Lake) in the highland valley near Logan Lake. As Mary Uslick and Christine Simon remembered being told, Secwépemc and Nlaka'pamux *ṫkwilc* would gather there to practise together, and the people from both nations would come there to be cured of their ailments. Sarah Deneault of Neskonlith knew of Tkweltám̓ (Banana Island), in the South Thompson River just west of Neskonlith, as a place where *ṫkwilc* "did their work" and practised together.

There are also known places throughout Secwepemcúl̓ecw where young people, particularly those who became *ṫkwilc*, completed their *étsxem*. One such place was at Pelúkwes (Deadman Falls), where a cave underneath a 50-metre waterfall into a ravine streambed served as a place of *étsxem*. Another place was a steep cave near the summit of Stemqín ("place of dreaming," Savona Mountain), where to this day pictographs attest to past sojourns of people on their quest, which is also the case at many other places throughout Secwepemcúl̓ecw where faint pictographs remain or where at times they have been exposed and defaced (see fig. 1, colour section).[7]

Guided by their guardian spirits, *ṫkwilc* could channel their powers to do good work, to overcome their own sickness, or to heal others' sickness brought on by being *q̓éwentem* (put under a spell) by those who used their powers in a bad way.[8] Guided by one or more of their innate *sk̓últen* and

11.3 | *Ṫkwilc* (shaman) K̇estmíc of Skeetchestn (born ca. 1850) at age ninety-four with his granddaughter Adele Peters (née Bob), ca. 1944.

acquired *semée*, they could *lens* (sense) events that were happening in faraway places; they could predict events and thus avert dangers, and by channelling their powers, they could even save people from death. For example, George Sisyúlecw's mother, Cllemcwínek, was a known *ṫkwilc* who dreamed that her daughter was being murdered, which subsequently happened. She then put a curse on her daughter's husband, whom she saw killing her daughter in her dream, or vision, and he died within the year. As explained by Simpcw elder Josephine Wenlock, "He fall down outside when he's drunk and they lose all the bottom feet [soles of his feet, probably from frostbite]. And that's what kill him: he didn't last very long, cold weather kill him."

Leslie Narcisse remembered how Sqéqxe Tomá, a *ṫkwilc* in the Chase area, killed a deer with his powers:

> Right in a big crowd that old Tomma. It was wide open country, you know. And now they got lots of trees all over. There was lots of people there. There was some kind of fun going on there. There was a big buck going right through the open, quite a ways too. And them boys were saying, "Gee, that's a big, big deer going through." And then the old, old

> guy says, "Oh you boys want that deer?" He [they] said, "Yeah we want 'em." He just went like this with his finger [motion of shooting a bow and arrow]. And that deer was … just his finger. And he said, "Shwoo." He dropped the deer. [laughs] Those boys went up there and drag 'em, bleedin' … Look at where he was shot. Get quiet. Yeah, that's the power, boy.

Nellie Taylor remembered how Ster, who was a *ṫkwilc* and the daughter of Chief Hyacinth Sisyésq̓t of Skeetchestn (see chapter 9), used her powers to save her son, Hyacinth Taylor, who was Nellie's husband, from drowning:

> When Ster was a child, and when [she] was playing with her brother Jules [Sul], Sul hit her in the eye with an arrow, and she lost the eye. This is why she was blind [in one eye}. The old chief, Hyacinth Sisyésq̓t, pulled out the arrow, and in the process of that, he caused it to give her power. She could predict things and had dreams that forecast events. Later, one time, she saved her son, Hyacinth Taylor, with the power that she had received. He was at Walhachin riding his horse when the [Thompson] river was high. He went down to try to cross it. Just when he decided that the water was too high, he saw people standing up high above the other bank, watching him. Not wanting to appear cowardly, he went in with his horse anyway, and they got caught in a back eddy. It was Ster who saved him by hollering and staring at the horse. Another time, someone was caught [in danger] when his horse took off on him. Ster started hollering at the horse, and the saddle belt snapped, saving the rider.

Leslie Narcisse remembered an incident in his youth (probably in the 1920s or 1930s) where a young man fell off his horse in a horserace and was badly hurt, but a *ṫkwilc* instantly restored him:

> The race horses was goin'. And that first guy tumbled over. All the horses just run, run right over 'em. Break his bones. And I believe the old policeman … they all run for that guy from the horses. One young fella. Oh, he must be about twenty, twenty years old. Maybe younger than that. He must've put a little feather on his on his uh … He said, "If you guys can't help that guy," he says, "get away. I'll help him." He said, "Anyway, you're gonna … you have to run away from here." He hollered for Jesus Christ right, right now. He said, "I need your help right, right now. I need to help this guy. I want him up." It was real hot, sunshine, and a few seconds it wasn't sunshine. Boy, the heavy rains just come right down. Everybody has to run away. It was so heavy rain, and me and that one old guy, we just watch right there. We was underneath one …

> one lumber. We just wanted to get away from the rain. The rain quit [after] 'bout five minutes, ten minutes, I guess. Here them guys were standin'. And that, that guy that was hurt bad, he was on the next races already. See, that's how powerful long ago. He must've been from down there [Skeetchestn/Savona] somewhere, that young fella that time. [The *ṫkwilc*] helped the guy. Make him stand up. He was going strong again.

Ṫkwilc could also use their powers to harm people, whether in self-defence or in acts of aggression. Thus Josephine Wenlock remembered that one of her uncles was killed by a *ṫkwilc* named Ellnús when he was twenty-five years old. Ellnús was playing a *sllekméẃes* (bone game) with her uncle and another young man and was caught cheating by the two young men. She explained, "The two gave him a licking, [so] the *ṫkwilc* cursed them to die." Subsequently, her uncle became sick and died after three months. The other young man was said to have got crippled hands from where he hit the *ṫkwilc*. What Ellnús did was put a *q̇éwens* (spell or curse) on the young men.

Leslie Narcisse spoke of an incident where the Sexqéltkemc *ṫkwilc* mentioned earlier, Sqéqxe Tomá, averted such a curse with his own superior powers and in retaliation caused the death of the other *ṫkwilc*:

> From Merritt, three Indian doctors wants to kill that old guy from around here. He was a big Indian doctor, too, this guy from here. These guys here they come to kill that old, old, old guy. He never fight with his hands. He fight with their powers. Seeing that old guy, that old Sqéqxe Tomá, you know. These guys were drummin', these three guys that come from Merritt. That old guy [Sqéqxe Tomá] comin', comin' in like that. That was just full of feathers what they had in there. That's not too much, you know. But then he … he just blowed the thing, and then things goes all over just like a real heavy fog inside … Boy, that one guy he was drummin', and he started rolling on the on the floor. [laughs] And that old Sqéqxe Tomá he just goes like that. All that feathers come right in his hand again, and walk out. And here that guy that was rolling around already and not too long, he died. And that other guy, he made it halfways home and he died. And the other third one, he made it home, but he was gone. See that's how, they never fight with their hands or anything. They wouldn't shoot one another, but it's just, just the power.

As noted above, to manifest his or her powers, a *ṫkwilc* could *ṫult* (freeze into stone) or *ṫultemí7* (freeze forever into stone) a person or animal, thus *transforming living energy into matter*. In chapter 2, we saw how at the time of the *tellqelmúcw* (transformers), those powers existed among the *tellqelmúcw* themselves and among the powerful beings that challenged them, as attested by the marks in the landscape that show their encounters or at least showed them until resource development destroyed them. There are memories of *ṫkwilc* having used their powers to "freeze" moving objects in the twentieth century. Chris Donald of Simpcw remembered that the *ṫkwilc* Old Moyís (Pílsi) "used to make the train stop, and he made the steam-boat stop, because he couldn't stand the noise. One time he stopped a car, too. Four white guys got out and were wondering what was wrong with it."

The concept of a person's *seméc* (spirit power) also involves a set of taboos that entail violations of a person's aura of spirit power. Thus, in Secwépemc tradition, a person, especially a young person, must not *ta7 me7 re spetkúseṅc* ("pass in front of someone's face"), lest one cause harm to that person's *seméc*, and for the same reasons, one must not *ta7 me7 re spetkíkeṅc* ("pass behind a person unannounced"). *Twéxem* (stepping over) a person who is lying down has the same implications in that it can interfere with the *seméc* of the person over whom one steps,[9] thus unleashing that person's spirit power and potentially harming the person who steps over someone. Thus not only does such behaviour potentially harm the spirit power of the person in front of or behind whom one passes, as well as over whom one steps, but it can also do harm to the trespasser because the person treated carelessly can cast a powerful spell on the trespasser. Secwépemc people were thus always taught to announce their passing in front of or behind someone by saying, *ṫ7e7k-ken* ("here I come").

Péxwem | Ways to Heal

[Secwépemc *ṫkwilc*] cured people by exorcising the disease, by incantations, by certain prescriptions, by laying on of hands, by massaging parts of the body and by sprinkling water on the head, and by blowing it over the body. (Teit 1909, 612)

The source of illness, especially in cases where a person inexplicably fell sick without physically detectable cause, was perceived as the sick person having been *q̇éwentem* (put under a spell) by a *ṫkwilc* who had used his or her powers in a bad way. The work that the *ṫkwilc* undertook to exorcise a sickness and restore physical and mental health to the victim of a *q̇éwentem* (bad medicine spell) is called *péxwem*. Garlene Dodson recalled how, perhaps in the 1950s, a member of her family had fallen victim to such a spell. Her mother, Celina Jules, summoned a *ṫkwilc* from the Nespélem area, Mary Pierre, to come and restore her health. "When she came, she worked on us. She had a basin with water, and she was singing. While she was singing, you could hear it in this whole valley [Deadman's Creek]. The water started bubbling." Awaiting the visit of the *ṫkwilc*, Celina Jules had gathered hides from her male relatives and made her daughters tan about fifteen hides through hard work. These tanned hides were the payment for the *ṫkwilc*'s work. As she explained, a *ṫkwilc* never asked for payment. Instead, the person who called the *ṫkwilc* paid voluntarily as he or she saw fit.

The physical work of blowing or sucking disease out of a victim, as well as massaging and touching, was complemented with the use of *melámen*, which were plant substances that could exorcise a spell and could restore health and balance. Among these *melámen*, for Secwépemc and other Plateau peoples, *sek̓epleṅllp* (rosebush) has the well-known function of achieving this effect, as well as returning the spell to the source. In the words of Garlene Dodson,

Ec re tsútes ren kí7ce, "E k̓ístes re sq̇éwems re ṫkwilc, me7 ṫult-k, me7 yecwestsút-ucw."
My mother [Celina Jules] used to tell us, "If an Indian doctor casts a bad spell, he will 'freeze' you, and you have to take care of yourself."

E ta7es es tslexemstéc ṫhé7en re7 sxílem ye7éne es kllep stéṁi7 es k̓úlens, nerí7 me7 ṫult, me7 ṫultemí7-k, me7 qwtseq-k.
If you don't know how to take off what he did, you will get "frozen," frozen for ever, and you will die.

K̓émell ye7éne wellenwí7-kt wenécwem7úẇi re melámen-kt, tikwemtús re qwel7éẏenes re nuxwnúnxwenxw, m-tsútsnes, "Wellenwi7-kt wenécwem7úẇi re melámen-kt ne7élye."
But this here is our real medicine. I always tell the girls, I tell them, "We have the real medicine right here."

Re sk̓epléṅllp ri7. Yerí7 welllenwí7-kt re melámen-kt te m-sq̇7es m-kwéntem, m-wellqentém, m-tṡéwentem re tsitcws.
That's the rosebush. That's our real medicine. Since long time ago, they gathered it, they boiled it, they washed their house with it.

Ṫri7 me7 k̓úlentem, me7 sté7ntem. me7 íllentem ye7éne te sekwéẇ, kwéntem ye7éne te sweléṅsem, yews ri7 re skwéntem me7 tntémes me7 xewentémes, ne7éne me7 kwéncwes, me7 tntécwes ne7 stemstíteṁt.
You take some of it, you drink it, you eat the rosehips, you take the flowers. And after you get them, you dry them, and you put it in your clothes.

Ec lu7 tsútes ren kí7ce, "Wenécwem7úẇi ye7éne re melámen-kt, re sk̓epléṅllp!"
My mom used to tell us, "That's our real medicine, the rosebush!"

Sq̇ilye | Sweat Lodge

That's the biggest thing for Indians long ago. You can't make fun of it. If there's any big Indian doctors around, and you make fun of the sweathouse, goodbye. You might not get out of there. Find your *seméc* [guardian spirit] in there. Now today [people will say,] "Oh, we sweat, we sweat." Gee whiz … No, they [didn't] make sweathouses anywhere, [only] where it's clean, and where it's hardly anybody runs around. Like way up. Halfways up the hill or

11.4 | A contemporary *sq̓ilye* (sweat lodge) at Cḱemqenétkwe (Scheidam Flats) above Tk̓emlúps (Kamloops), 2016.

somewhere else. Them old people, that's where they make their sweathouse ... Yeah, that's uh ... that's how much I seen. (Leslie Narcisse)

Among the most ancient and original gifts that Old One made to the Secwépemc, it is said, was the *sq̓ilye* (sweat lodge). It is said that Old One spoke to the spirit of the *sq̓ilye* and told it, "when they pray for relief from pain for health, long life, lightness of body, fleetness of foot, wisdom, wealth, and success in hunting, gambling, and war, pay heed to them, and grant their desires. Gather their sickness when they are in the sweat-house, take it from their bodies, and cast it to the winds" (quoted in Teit 1909, 643). Then he went and spoke to the spirit of the fir boughs, telling it to help the *sq̓ilye* spirit. And he told the water spirit likewise, as well as the fire spirit and the earth spirit. We are told that the spirit of the *sq̓ilye* is Scwelús, whose name is a reminder of what the sweat accomplishes, as it refers to approaching the sweat with a clean conscience and revealing or opening oneself up to truth and understanding. In turn, the spirit of the sweat will reveal itself to us so that we are able to gain insights and strength.

The *sq̓ilye* thus became the institution that separated humans from the powerful animal beings of the ancient world, allowing humans to acquire powers that would enable them to vanquish those of animals by praying and through spiritual and physical cleansing. It is no coincidence that in the Secwépemc story about Sníne (Owl), the latter being one of the most powerful beings, it is the sweat lodge that enables people to subdue and channel the power of Sníne.

Sníne | Story of Owl[10]

told by Ida William, recorded by Marianne Ignace, 1986, translated and transcribed by Mona Jules and Marianne Ignace

Le q̓7éses re qelmúcw w7ec-ekwe, peskúye te k̓woyí7se.
Long time ago, there were people around here, and they had a small baby.

M-yístes t̓lu7 te tmicw, k̓woyí7se-ekwe re pépis.
They camped over there on that land, their baby was tiny.

M-kénmes-enke, tsec.cít.s te qéwtens.
I don't know why, but [the woman] was fixing his [her husband's] hair.

Tcwíqnem, tcwíqnem. Tsec.cit.s re sxélwes te qéwtens.
Brushing his hair, brushing his hair. She fixed her husband's hair.

Re sk̓wimémelt m-ts̓7úmes. Yéwsens.
The baby was crying. They found it a nuisance.

Kwens-ekwe re xqwllíntens, m-tsk̓empéllcwens ne sk̓empéllcws re letént.
She took its birch-bark cradle and set it outside the tent.

Tsyem-ekwe ne tsitcws, ne leténts.
They were staying in their home, their tent.

Ta7 ks necwentsút.s es ts̓exentés re sk̓wimémelt.
She didn't make an effort to check the baby.

M-estúkw. Estúkw re sk̓wimémelt.
It was quiet. The baby was quiet.

M-q̓7éses m-stp̓enlléxwes, ts̓exentéses. M-skik̓éys.
After a long time, she went out, she looked. There was nothing.

Tsukw re xqwllíñten nerí7 stseq.
Only the cradle was sitting there.

Re Sníne tsnésmens, m-kwénses re skwiméṁelt.
The Owl had come, and had taken the baby.

Qwetsétses ne k mútes-enke.
It had taken him to wherever it must have lived.

Píxct.ses ṫri7 tek stem. Seqwyits, ṫri7 stem, kwéctses te s7íllens re baby.
It hunted different things for him. Rabbits, whatever, and took them for the baby to eat.

M-twites re twiwt, sqéqlemcw.
The child grew, became a young man.

Ptínesmens kénem mé7e wel westém te Sníne.
He thought about it, and wondered why he was kept by the Owl.

Séwens re Sníne telhé7e k tskwéntmes.
He asked the Owl where he was taken from.

Lexéẏectem te Sníne, "Yéwsens re7 steṫex7ém, tsk̓empéllwents te tsk̓empéllcw."
He was told by the Owl, "Your parents found you a nuisance and set you outside."

"Qeqnímentsen te7 stṡ7úmucw, wel tskwéntsen."
"I heard you cry, that's why I took you."

K̓ulcts te tskwínek ell re stskwil̓s.
He made a bow and arrows for him.

W7ec re píxmes le tuwíwt, w7écwes te kekéw.
He used to hunt, the young boy, going far.

Re Sníne m-tsúntem,
He was told by the Owl,

"Ta7ews penhén ke7s kucénucw."
"Don't go too far."

Nexéll es pelq̓entém te steṫex7éms.
It was afraid that he would be returned to his parents.

Must.s.
Four times [he said that].

Kénem wel ta7 k snecwentém te Sníne es kucéns.
He wondered why he wasn't allowed by the Owl to go too far.

Q̓wmiw̓s m-negwílcwes.
He was wild and he was hiding away.

Negwílcwes es ta7es es wíktmes nerí7 te tsyem te qelmúcw.
He was hiding away, so he wouldn't be seen by the people camped there.

Kell yerí7 re stet̓ex7éms.
But they were his parents.

Pelq̓ilc cwú7tsem ne Sníne e r7áleses.
He returned again to the Owl that night.

Lexéy̓ect.s re Sníne, "M-wíwkem-ken te qelmúcw."
He told the Owl, "I saw people."

Tsúntmes te Sníne, "Ta7ews cwú7tsem t̓kllu7 ke7 snes."
He was told by the Owl, "Don't go over there again."

Ta7k sk̓él̓nems.
He didn't listen.

Tsnes cwúy̓tsem nerí7, sesúxwenst ne tsyémes re stet̓ex7éms.
He went over there again, he came down to where his parents were camped.

Wíktem-enke te qé7tses, wel re m-kwéntem.
He must have been seen by his father, and he was taken.

Tsúntmes te stet̓ex7éms es pulst.s re Sníne.
He was told by his parents to kill the Owl.

K̓ulcts ts̓ílem te xq̓ílye7ten.
He made something like a sweathouse for it.

Nerí7 tntéses k xixéyt tek scenc.
And there he put hot rocks for it.

Ts̓ílem-enke t̓7éne ks tncit.s te xiyéscen̓.

And it must have been like that, that he put hot rocks in there.

Re sqéqlemcw m-néses t̓lu7 ts̓ilem ne "fly."
The boy went in there through the flap, like a "fly."

W7ec re sícwmes te séwllkwe ne scenc.
He was spilling water on the rocks.

Llegwllgwílc ne xwiyúl̓ucw t̓ri7 t̓hé7en.
[The Owl] was jumping all over the hot ground, everywhere.

Ta7 k sxenwéllens es p̓enlléxws t̓e xixyúl̓ecwtens te xixeyt te scenc.
It could not get out from that hot place, the hot rocks.

Qwtséqes.
He died.

Re tuwíwt m-sqwetséts telrí7, pelq̓ílc ne stet̓ex7éms.
The young boy set out from there, he returned to his parents.

Twiw̓t-enke put re sxyemwílcs.
He must have been grown up some, he had become bigger.

Púlst.ses re Sníne, qwnékstmens.
He killed the Owl, he ruined it [took away its power].

Yerí7 m-kwéntmes te stetex7éms, yerí7 m-sw7ecs ne stet̓ex7éms tikwemtús.
Then he was taken back by his parents, then he stayed with his parents all the time.

Ell m-pulst.s re Sníne.
And he had killed the Owl.

Yerí7.
That's all.

The *sq̓ilye* (sweat lodge) is one of the fundamental institutions of Secwépemc society. It allows individuals to cleanse in a physical and spiritual sense, to pray with a clean mind, and to share and communicate with others with a clean and honest mind.

Secwépemc men and women sweated separately, each in their own *xq̓ílye7ten* (sweat lodge or sweathouse). Because females, especially those who are fertile and menstruate, have the power to cause harm to men's powers, women's sweat lodges must be downstream from men's. Sweat lodges, as Leslie Narcisse explained (see above), are along creeks, in remote places, and thus away from the village and human traffic. They are relatively small, conical structures that are made from bent-over sticks of red willow or willow (*Salix* spp.) and that are covered with bark or, more recently, with canvas. Traditionally, some sweat lodges were semi-underground structures.

The short text below explains the process of preparing a *sq̓ilye* (sweat lodge) and the process of *q̓ilye* (having a sweat),[11] also called *sq̓ilye* and *ctsreṁ*.

Ctsreṁ | Having a Sweat
by Bridget Dan, 1999

Me7 tsq̓íw̓lep-k.
Your make fir boughs.

Me7 kwnem-k tek cgwláṅkten, sestı́kw̓, leméts ell tek stektsúsem, tgeýtsem-k ell me7 yéqwllpem-k.
You get kindling, fire starter, and firewood, you stack them up and you light it.

Tsecyéwem-k me7 tektsqúseṅcwes.
You pack water and you put it on the fire.

Me7 tntec k melámen – k k̓etse7éllp ell k sqwi7qwe7ellp.
You put medicine on it – devil's club and mountain avens.

M-xyep re scenc tek tseqwéscen̓, me7 cpleṁ-k.
You heat the rocks until they are red hot and put them in the sweathouse.

T.sicwésceṅ-k me7 necentsiṅcwes.
You splash water on them and close the entrance.

Tkllentsútce me7 t.secwnentsútucw tek melámen ell me7 sté7encwes.
You wash yourself off with medicine, you drink some.

Me7 qwentsíctc re tmesékst te snewt, me7 sérencwes k smenc ne tsyeqw.
You pray in the four directions of the wind, you sprinkle tobacco on the fire.

Me7 ullcw-k, me7 líq̓wem-k, me7 qwentsín-k ell me7 setsínmucw.
You enter [the *sq̓ílye*], you spill water on the rocks, you pray and you sing.

Yerí7 re sq̓ilye-kt, me7 ta7 ews ke7s llxup.
This is our way of having a sweat, don't rush off.

E Llwélentmes re Qelmucw te Swemécs | When the Life Power Leaves a Person's Body

The people say, "*E qwtséqes m-llwélentem te semécs, m-llwélentem te sk̓últens*" ("When someone dies, their *seméc* leaves them, their *sk̓últen* leaves them"), and their spirit powers separate from their body and travel to the other side.

K̓estmíc was a powerful *t̓kwilc* who had several *skwelk̓ulten* (plural of *sk̓últen*) with which he was born and several *seméc* that he worked to acquire. As a twin, he had the power of the black bear from birth. During twenty-six years of *étsxem* as a young man and adult, he aquired several *seméc* that gave him his extraordinary powers as a *t̓kwilc* throughout his life. Theresa Jules told a powerful story of how when K̓estmic was being attacked by a grizzly bear, he communicated what was happening to him across many miles of mountains to his "sister" (cousin) Cecile Melmenétkwe, also a *t̓kwilc* and training a great distance away.

As K̓estmíc's great-grandson James Peters remembered, when K̓estmíc prepared to die many years later at the age of more than 100, he felt he was losing control of his many powers. During many nights before he died, he could be heard wrestling with his powers, making different animal sounds. Eventually, to be able to die and pass over to the other side peacefully, he kept just one of his powers, the *sníne* (owl). The owl, in turn, despite its all-encompassing powers having been curtailed many, many years before in the *sq̓ilye*, continued as a messenger of death. As James Peters said, "When you hear an owl, two or three days ahead, someone is going to die." K̓estmíc's power of the owl therefore lives on in the present power of owls to foretell events, especially death, just as he kept the owl to let him know when he was about to pass to the other side.

The Secwépemc ways of dealing with death connect to the ways that the spiritual powers of a person exist and manifest themselves during one's lifetime, as well as to how that power lingers and then travels to what we call the "other side," although it can be mobilized to help the living. Teit (1909, 592–4) provides us with a sparse account of diverse customs surrounding burials, somewhat dissociated from the integrated social and spiritual system of which they are a part, although we recognize certain customs in present ways of dealing with the deceased and burying them.[12] Below is an account from Ron Ignace of the events in the aftermath of a person's death, based on handed-down information from Skeetchestn elders and lifetime experiences. The ways of doing things vary slightly among communities but are very similar:

> When a person has taken his last breath, it is said that his or her *sk̓últen* (spirit) lingers on for four days (three in the case of children) before passing to the "other side." The person's still-living spirit is symbolized

11.5 | Chief Louis's funeral at St Joseph's Church, Kamloops Indian Reserve, April 1915. The original caption includes, "He was 87 years old, and had been Chief for 60 years."

and manifest in a fire that is lit as soon as word is spread of the passing. This fire must be kept burning clean, without people putting garbage or debris into it. The fire is also the way to communicate with the deceased, and food offerings are made daily at mealtimes to feed the deceased as his or her spirit still lingers among the living. The body is washed and dressed and then laid out on fir boughs. Each community has individuals who take care of the deceased and the rituals of handling the deceased, the wake, and the funeral. In Skeetchestn, Sam Camille was charged with the task of handling funerals for many years before he passed away in 2003. He would ring the bell four times to spread the news, three times if a child had died. He would consult with the family about where to bury the deceased in the graveyard and would supervise the digging of the grave by hand rather than by machine. He would tell the young men to go hunting in order to feed the family as well as the many members of the extended family and the friends from near and far away who would gather at the house of the deceased for the wake.

The women will come into the house where the deceased has lived and clean it from top to bottom with juniper and rosebush before the deceased is laid out on a bed of fir boughs for the wake. Fir boughs, as decreed by Old One when he gave people the *sq̓ilye* (sweat lodge), are spirit helpers. All *k̓wsəltkten7úw̓i* (members of the family) are asked to stand back without taking part in any of the tasks, and the community does everything for them. This custom is meant to lift the burden of their bereavement and to ensure that they do not have to worry about the basic tasks of feeding themselves and their children, cleaning house, and so on. At the end of the fourth day, before sunset, the deceased is buried after a ceremony to honour the person's memory. Then the person will join his or her ancestors on the "other side," which mirrors the life of people on this earth. There, the deceased play bone games with their ancestors, and they hunt and fish with their ancestors. Thus, besides the food that is offered to the deceased through the fire in order to provide nourishment for their journey, the deceased are provided with all the necessities of life, which are placed by their side in the grave, such as hunting implements, digging sticks, fishing harpoons, and baskets. Personal charms, amulets, and items that attest to one's identity and spirit are also included.

Immediately after the burial, the grave is swept with fir boughs, and a spokesperson for the family invites everyone who has attended the burial to a feast where they are served game and fish provided by the men and garden foods provided by the women of the village but not by members of the bereaved family itself. This custom is meant to thank the guests and honour them for sharing in the family's grief. Following this feast, the possessions of the deceased, like a horse, a saddle, and guns, are put up in a *sllekméẃes* (bone game), thus enacting a social insurance policy where the individual's wealth is redistributed among members of the community, rooted in the law of reciprocity. At that point, and after the deceased has again been fed through the fire, the fire is extinguished because the spirit of the deceased has left for the other side. In the months and years to come, foods are offered to the deceased and to other ancestors in order to appeal to their spirits. At times of difficult decisions and in times of hardship, they are asked to make their spiritual presence and guidance known at a meeting or in a sweat lodge in order to help and guide.

For four days following the burial, the immediate family members of the deceased visit the gravesite to examine it for "tracks," which may be deer tracks or other animal tracks, and sometimes small footprints are noticed. These tracks and the directions they point to give clues to the family members about events that will happen.

If throughout their life individuals have committed an impropriety, they are stuck wandering this land as a spirit and will seek someone to help them cross over. That is when people will see them appear as a *sqweqwyém* (ghost).

The clothes and immediate belongings of the deceased are burned. If there is an article or item of the deceased that a person wants to keep, it has to be cleansed with juniper and rosebush in order to wash off the tracks of the deceased and separate it from the person's spirit. After one year, it can be used.

11.6 | The Sṫuxtéws (Bonaparte) team during a *sllekméẇes* (bone game) tournament at Chu Chua (Simpcw), 1987. *Left to right:* Ann Morgan, Theresa Jules, Louis Morgan, Felix Morgan, Emily Morgan, and Roger Porter.

> During the year following a person's death, especially among widows and widowers, various taboos have to be observed, such as abstaining from hunting red meat, and various protocols have to be followed, such as sleeping above a bed of fir boughs as well as sweating and bathing early in the morning. Family members cook and hunt for these people, as well as feeding them small amounts of grease so that they will not be poor and suffer down the line.

These observations and descriptions of ceremony attest to the ways that Secwépemc beliefs about the reciprocal and mutual interaction of powers in nature are part of the powers of humans. As Skeetchestn elder Daniel Calhoun remarked, "The *seméc* chooses you, and you choose it through working and practising for it." The ceremony surrounding funerals attests to, manifests, and reproduces the spiritual connection between people and ancestors, whose power still lingers among the living; by way of *seméc*, the ceremony manifests the connection between people and all forces in nature, which are seen as having spirit; and it reinforces the laws of reciprocity among humans. The sequence of events described above, practised at funerals throughout Secwepemcúlecw with slight variations, has continued as an organized way of enacting laws and protocols, surviving in some fashion the onslaught against

Secwépemc institutions during the past 150 years. Below, we describe how the Secwépemc had to hide their religion in the church in order to save it.

Hiding Religion in the Church: Syncretism after the Arrival of Catholic Missionaries

Close on the heels of the invasion of strangers during the gold rush and Fraser River War, as well as the devastating smallpox epidemic of 1862–63, Catholic missionaries of the Oblates of Mary Immaculate established themselves in Secwépemc territory. To the Secwépemc, European priests were not an entirely unknown entity. As with the prophesies about the coming of the *seme7úw̓i* ("real whites") and infectious diseases (see chapter 3), there had been predictions about the coming of "black robes" – hence the name *q̓wéy̓leqs* ("black robe") for priests and missionaries – both by the Secwépemc's own ancestors and by Metis of the fur trade who predicted hard times ahead:

> Long before the arrival of the first white miners, a Hudson Bay half-breed told the Shuswap that after a time strange men would come among them, wearing black robes (the priests). He advised them not to listen to these men, for although they were possessed of much magic, and did some good, still they did more evil. They were descendants of the Coyote, and like him, although very powerful, they were also very foolish, and told many lies. They were simply the Coyote returning to the earth in another form. If the Indians paid attention to and followed the directions of these "black-robes," they would become poor, foolish and helpless; and disease of all kinds would cut them off. If they avoided them, they would remain contented, happy and numerous. Some Indians believed what was told them, and for this reason called the first priest whom they saw "Coyote." At the present time some Indians wonder whether, if they had taken the half-breed's advice, it would have turned out as he said, and whether it is really the priests and their religion that are the cause of the people dying so much, and not being so well off as they might be. (Teit 1909, 621–2)

Itinerant missionaries had travelled through Secwépemc country in the 1840s. In 1842 the Jesuit priest Father Modeste Demers also travelled through the Interior, eventually arriving at the Hudson's Bay Company's Thompson River post in Kamloops to explore the possibility of setting up missions in the Interior. He carried on to Fort Alexandria on the Fraser River, where he wintered and built a small chapel, making several expeditions to the Carrier north of there and to the Atnah (Secwépemc) south of there. Another Jesuit, Father Pierre-Jean De Smet, travelled to the source of the Columbia River, to Boat Encampment, and to the Jasper House area in 1845–46. He was accompanied by Father John Nobili, who in the summer of 1846 returned to the Okanagan Valley and from there travelled through Secwépemc territory. Father Nobili recorded,

> On the 27th of July, I baptized nine children at Fort Okinagane – the children of the chief of the Sioushwaps were of the number. He appeared full of joy at seeing a Black-gown direct his course towards their country. On the 29th I left Okinagane, and followed the company. Every night I prayed with the whites and Indians. On the road three old men came to me, and earnestly begged me to "take pity on them, and prepare them for heaven!" Having instructed them in the duties and principles of religion, and the necessity of baptism, I administered to them, and to forty-six children of the same tribe, what seemed to be the height of their desires, the holy Sacrament of regeneration.
>
> On the 11th of August, a tribe of Indians, residing about the Upper Lake on Thompson's River, came to meet me. They exhibited towards me all the marks of sincere and filial attachment. They followed me several days to hear my instructions, and only departed after having exacted a promise that I would return in the course of the following autumn or winter, and make known to them the glad tidings of salvation.
>
> At the Fort of the Sioushwaps, I received a visit from all the chiefs, who congratulated me on my happy arrival amongst them. They raised a great cabin to serve as a church, and as a place to teach them during my stay. I baptized twelve of their children. I was obliged, when the Salmon fishing commenced, to separate for some months from these dear Indians, and continue my route to New Caledonia.
>
> I arrived at Fort Alexandria on the 25th. All the tribes I met manifested towards me the same emotions of joy and friendship. To my surprise I found at the Fort a frame church. I returned in the fall and remained there a month, engaged in all the exercises of our holy ministry. The Canadians performed their religious duties – I joined several in marriage, and administered to many the Holy Communion. Twenty-four children and forty-seven adults received baptism. (Quoted in De Smet 1847, 274)

Father Nobili next travelled north to the Carrier and then, by way of the Tsilhqot'in, returned to the Secwépemc, among whom he said that he "succeeded in abolishing polygamy": "After my return to the Sioushwaps, I baptized forty-one persons, of whom eleven were adults. I visited five more villages among the neighboring tribes, amongst whom I baptized about two hundred persons. I performed the ceremony of the planting of the Cross, in eight different places, and founded four frame churches which were constructed by the savages" (quoted in ibid., 277–8). Despite the zealous number of baptisms during this short period – which, unlike the Oblates, they performed without prior religious instruction – neither Demers nor Nobili maintained a presence in the Interior but instead returned to Oregon Territory and went south from there.

As the stories have it, Sk̓elép (Coyote) was believed to have *gone to the East* after he finished his work, perhaps to return one day. When missionaries came into the Interior Plateau, *arriving from the East* – although in the northern Plateau, technically, thy arrived from the south – there were some associations between the promise of Sk̓elép's return and the arrival of missionaries. As we know, Sk̓elép could show up in ever-new shapes. James Teit (1909, 612) found out that "when the Indians saw the first priests, they believed them to be Coyote and his assistants, presaging this important event."

In the late 1850s, and before establishing themselves at Kamloops and Williams Lake, the Oblates set up a mission at Okanagan Lake, and as the baptism records of the Okanagan Mission show, a few Secwépemc people of the Kamloops region came to get baptized (Oblate Missions of British Columbia 1859–60). In addition, between 1859 and 1866, the Okanagan missionary Father Charles Pandosy of the Oblates of Mary Immaculate also travelled to "Fort Thompson" on occasion to baptize people there. The list of his and his associates' baptisms includes Hudson's Bay Company Metis and Scottish employees of the Thompson River post at the time, such as Antoine Lamprant, the various children of trader Donald McLean by his Aboriginal wives, the children of "Corbeau," and a few "*sauvages*" brought by their Secwépemc parents to be baptized. Among the adults baptized either by the earlier Jesuits or by Pandosy at the Okanagan Mission must have been Chief Hyacinth Sisyésq̓t's parents, who are listed in the 1866 baptism book of the Kamloops Diocese as "Louis" and "Louise" – that is, with French baptismal names, which they had obviously obtained elsewhere, either at the Okanagan Mission or in the previous decade from Fathers Nobili or Demers on their trips through Secwépemc territory.[13] During this time, Chief Louis of Kamloops must have received baptism, subsequently acting as a witness at the church wedding of Jean-Baptiste Lolo St Paul and his Tk̓emlúpsemc wife, Marie, also at the Pandosy Mission (see Oblate Missions of British Columbia 1859–60).

In 1867 the first permanent missionary, Father Florimond Gendre, set up headquarters at Tk̓emlúps, followed by Father Charles Grandidier in 1871, who had previously been at the Okanagan Mission, and then by Father Jean-Marie Lejacq in 1880 (Gurney 1948; Oblate Missions of British Columbia 1866–82). Besides the superior priest, two to three "*assesseurs*" (junior priests) were usually at the mission, some of whom stayed only for a brief time. Shortly after Father Gendre's arrival, the Tk̓emlúpsemc built St Joseph's Church at their main village northeast of the confluence, on the site of the earlier Jesuit chapel, a small log-cabin structure. Within months, each of the Southern Secwépemc communities had its own church building.

The Skeetchestn church was St Mary's (Ste Marie), the St̓uxtéws (Bonaparte) church was St Louis, the Simpcw church was St Jean-Baptiste, the Adams Lake church was St Croix (Holy Cross), and the Sk̓atsín (Neskonlith) church was St Peter and Paul (St Pierre et Paul).

At the same time, the Oblates also set up headquarters 20 kilometres south of Williams Lake, establishing another mission they called St Joseph's (Whitehead 1981), which served the Northern Secwépemc, Southern Carrier, Tsilhqot'in, and Northern Lillooet communities. As in the Southern Secwépemc area, local churches were soon built at Canoe Creek, Dog Creek, Canim Lake, Sugarcane, and Soda Creek. As early as 1842, Father Demers had built a small log chapel at Chimney Creek near Williams Lake, which, however, burned down ten years later, with only the chimney remaining.

It is all too easily assumed that with the arrival of the first missionaries in Secwépemc country during the 1860s, Secwépemc people "converted" to Christianity and uncritically endorsed this new way of thinking without so much as reflecting on it. As we know, these early days of missionaries' presence and teachings led to the collective and individual trauma our people suffered in the Indian residential schools. Endorsed and eventually financed by the Canadian state, missionaries engaged in an effort to eradicate both our collective knowledge of the past and our ability to talk about it in our own language and on our own terms.[14]

In comparing Secwépemc spiritual, or religious, continuity with that of the Nlaka'pamux, Teit (1909, 459) commented, "The Shuswap seem to be less conservative than the Thompson Indians, and have been quicker to accept the teachings of the missionaries, and to discard their old ways of life." However, it is not clear whether Teit merely compared the elaborate displays in the Tk̓emlúps stagings of passion plays in the early 1990s with what he saw near his home among the Nlaka'pamux or whether his statement was based on more detailed observations and experiences. The question, in the end, is one of spiritual syncretism – the melding of different spiritualities, including the Indigenous – as opposed to one of readily adopting, or being pressured into adopting, an outside religion.

The baptism records in both the Kamloops area, which would become the Kamloops Diocese, and the Williams Lake area give interesting insights into missionary procedure and this emerging syncretism. These records show the baptism of adults throughout Secwépemc communities beginning in fall of 1866 and continuing after that date. Initially, there were a few adult and child baptisms. From 1867 onward, baptisms seem to have become systematic efforts by the priests; for example, on 20 October 1867, Father Gendre arrived at "Ste. Marie" (St Mary's), the newly built small log church at Skeetchestn, and baptized eleven adults between the ages of eighteen and fifty, including Sisyésq̓t, the chief of the community, his *tkwenm7íple7ten* (councillors), and his adult relatives. Following the baptism of men, the adult women of the community were baptized, starting with Sisyésq̓t's wife, Necúskwe, who took the French name Agathe. The missionary wrote down each person's Indigenous name, and the new names were apparently perceived as being received *in addition to* the hereditary Secwépemc names.[15] Although some of the Indian names have still been passed down to younger generations, the baptismal European names are also remembered as handed-down names. Given the role that name giving has always had in our society (see chapter 9), our ancestors who received names from the priests would have perceived the bestowal of new and exotic names as an honour, a gift from the black robe visitors. We cannot help but think that missionaries realized the advantage of bestowing names as gifts in the spirit of gift giving, especially since their vows of poverty meant that they had little to offer by way of material gifts. After all, as hosts to the visiting *séme7* (white) guests, our ancestors had waited for their kindness to be returned for some time but in vain.

The Oblates were formed as a Catholic order in France soon after of the French Revolution. Their philosophy was not dissimilar to Jesuit philosophy; they regarded themselves as "soldiers of the Pope" (Whitehead 1988, 5), and their objective was to "stir up the faith which is dying among the poor" (ibid., 6) by holding "missions." The latter adhered to a formula of prayers and preaching to be conducted on a predetermined set of days in order to convey the basic tenets of the Catholic faith (Gurney 1948; Whitehead 1988). Oblate statutes included rigid daily activity and scripture study, meditative prayer, recitation of the rosary, and examination of "conscience" to conquer one's sins, which were regarded not as social digressions but as personal offences against God. By the mid-nineteenth century, after arriving in northwestern North America, the Oblates had developed a "strict, rigid plan for both conversion and control of Indian spiritual development" (Whitehead 1988, 13). Whitehead (ibid., 14) noted that, different from the Protestant churches, "Catholic missionary efforts aimed at producing not so much pseudo-Europeans as devoted Roman Catholics, and permanent missionary control was an important component of this plan." To achieve this kind of control, the Oblates apparently drew inspiration from the self-supporting agricultural missions known as "reductions" that were established by the Spanish in Paraguay during the nineteenth century (ibid., 15), further supported by the initial reception the Jesuits experienced on the Columbia River in the 1840s.

Among the procedures practised by the missionaries, the first act was baptism, as the continuing practice of adult baptisms throughout the 1860s and 1870s shows. Baptism occurred with only minimal indoctrination into the Catholic belief system, which followed later, with the missionaries staying in one place for a few days at a time to hold "missions," or retreats, at which they imparted the sets of concentrated teachings offered to the Indigenous village community. The dioceses operated by the Oblates stationed at Kamloops and Williams Lake covered a huge terrain. After 1886 parts of their travels along the South Thompson, main Thompson, and Fraser Rivers could be made by Canadian Pacific Rail train, but since many Indian villages were off the beaten track, they additionally had to travel by horse, by horse and buggy, by sleigh, and occasionally on foot. The work of the missionaries who served the Kamloops Diocese extended from the North Thompson River down to Kamloops, east to the Shuswap Lakes area, even occasionally covering Windermere on the upper Columbia River, along the Thompson River to Bonaparte, occasionally north to Clinton and High Bar, and south to Spences Bridge, as well as comprising the Nicola Valley. As the baptism books reveal, a missionary would visit each village perhaps three times per year for a few days. For the rest of the year, our people were left to their own devices.[16] Throughout these trips, the missionaries carried out baptisms, initially with adults and, by the 1870s, increasingly with young children; in addition, they taught the catechism and prayers, as well as holding confessions and communion. Father Jean-Marie-Raphaël Le Jeune's (1892) letter to his bishop, reiterating a visit to the Chu Chua (Simpcw or North Thompson) Reserve, gives insights into this practice:

> Having arrived here Saturday, 27 March, I will be staying here until Thursday, 4 April. During my visit, the schedule is as follows: at 6 a.m., I rise, mass at 6:30 a.m., followed by a sermon about the Stations of the Cross. At 7:30 a.m., free time for breakfast until 10:30 a.m. Meeting of the Natives [*sauvages*] at the house of the chief to talk with them about the sermon of morning mass, and to go through their catechism prayers with them, etc., and at the same time to teach them to read and write … After having spent two and a half hours with these exercises, everyone retires to the church at 1 p.m., to recite the rosary, followed by instruction in confession and communion. Following this, there is free time until five o'clock, so they can gather their firewood and attend to other domestic chores. At five o'clock, we go through the Stations of the Cross, instruction of the Stations of the Cross, celebration of the Holy Sacrament, and evening prayers. From 7 p.m. until 8:30, free time for supper. At 8:30 p.m., meeting at the chief's house for catechism, etc., until 11 p.m. (Our translation)

From the late 1860s until the mid-1920s, following this frenzied and concentrated missionary indoctrination over concentrated short periods, people in Secwépemc communities were without religious instruction for the next several months, save for their own occasional visits to Tk̓emlúps and other communities to visit with relatives, at which time they occasionally got their children baptized, as the records show.

In their missionary practices, the Oblates initially tried to put to use existing Indigenous practices and institutions. Thus they advocated that their priests use handshakes in meeting and greeting Indigenous people (Dionne 1947). A second Indigenous institution the Oblates tried into put to practice was that of the existing "Indian courts" (see chapter 10), interpreted by the priests as "public confessions" that led to the "punishment of sinners." For them, these courts represented an existing institution on which they could build private confessions. Between 1858 and 1875, public confessions were commonly advocated and used as part of the "missionary method."[17]

During this time, as the missionaries learned the Indigenous languages from the local people, core religious concepts were translated into Interior Salish languages, facilitated by their interpreters. Early missionaries like Fathers Gendre, Grandidier, and Lejacq had for the most part relied on Chinook Jargon to preach and teach the new religion. Their Chinook Jargon sermons, in turn, were retranslated into the Aboriginal language by a local interpreter bilingual in Chinook Jargon and the local language. In his reminiscences published in the *Kamloops Wawa* in 1915 (see also Gurney 1948; and Robertson n.d., 255–60), Father Le Jeune himself remembered several anecdotes of misunderstandings (cited in Robertson n.d.) where the interpreter mistook the word *chapelet* (prayer beads) for *saplel* (sack of flour) or used the word "snow" instead of "year" in literal translation from Secwepemctsín (see chapter 5). There was much room for knowledge, let alone meanings, to get lost in translation.

Among the Interior missionaries, Father Le Jeune stands out as having learned as many as eight Indigenous languages and was known for being able to preach in the different languages. By all accounts, among Secwépemc elders, he was remembered as fluent in the Secwépemc language, although Tessie Dillabough of Kamloops, probably his last housekeeper before he retired, remembered him replacing his plain *p's* with glottalized *p̓'s*, which created some amusing mispronunciations. In Secwepemctsín, situations around fixing a bed or room as opposed to someone's privates can be imagined!

After having first learned Nlaka'pamuxcin while staying in Lytton, and then Secwepemctsín with the help of local Secwépemc who knew Chinook Jargon, Le Jeune set out to translate prayers, hymns, parts of the catechism and liturgy, and portions of the Bible into Secwepemctsín and neighbouring languages (see chapter 4).

The translations of spiritual concepts are revealing. The terms for a number of Catholic religious concepts were borrowed from Chinuk Wawa (Chinook Jargon), although they originally derived from French. These terms included *lekrés* (grace), *lasakristí* (sacristy), *lesós* (angels), *lepík* (bishop), and *lakaristí* (Holy Eucharist). However, with Le Jeune's growing reliance on Secwepemctsín, many crucial words of prayer and religion became Secwépemc words. Inevitably, these words carried the "baggage" of the pre-existing Secwépemc worldview, spirituality, and spiritual practices. The word for "bless" or "baptize" became *melámen(t)*. Its semantic field was already taken, as it was the word for "to doctor someone," what a *ṫkwilc* did. The word for "to pray" became *qweqwentsín*, the pre-existing word for prayer in Secwepemctsín. Literally, it means "to express one's pitiful state with words," indicating the Secwépemc concept of praying with humility, which involves showing, in a social and spiritual sense, that one is pitiful and needs help.[18] The term for "holy" was the borrowed Secwépemc word *xexé7* (power[ful], smart), which is connected to notions of spirit power and guardian spirit questing. On close scrutiny, many of the Secwépemc words that entered the Catholic prayers in Secwepemctsín reflected pre-existing values of spiritual and social relationships working together, and pre-existing spiritual connections, as much as the theological concepts of the church. The term *ḱestentsút*, chosen as the word for "sin," maintains the flavour of our fundamental belief in the social responsibilities people have to one another, as opposed to private, religious "fear" of God. Whereas the Catholic catechism defines "sin" as a "personal offence against God," the word *ḱestentsút* means "to do something bad to yourself," thus entailing the issue of social reciprocity and the concept that, by harming others, you "do it to yourself" and lose face in the end, as the community loses faith in you. Implicitly, it goes with terms like *yéwyut* (to make a nuisance of oneself) in that the sinner is a *social* burden on the community.

Catholic Prayers in Secwepemctsín

As not only words but whole prayers became translated, they also maintained the connection with *our* way of thinking and *our* spiritual and social laws. The Secwépemc translation of the Catholic Act of Contrition shows this connection:

Oh, Tqelt Kúkwpi7-kt,
Oh, our Chief Above,[19]

necwéẏmentsútstmen ren sḱestentsútst.
showing remorse I am telling on myself that I did bad to myself.

Ta7 ks xillts es nésmens ne tqeltk te tmicw.
It won't happen that I go to the land above.

Yerí7 re skestentsút, me7 néstsems ne xyum te t7ikw.
When I do bad to myself, it will take me to the big fire [purgatory].

Tuxwt necwéẏmentsútstmen cú7tsem le7 ṗúsmen.

I am also feeling remorse, telling on myself, to your heart.

Re newí7 xexé7 te Tqelt Kúkwpi7,
You, the Chief Above,

necwéy̓mentsútstmen ren sk̓estentsútst.
I truly feel remorse, telling on myself, for doing bad to myself.

Nerí7 me7 yegwentén ren p̓úsmen,
I will strengthen my heart,

es ta7ews cú7tsem ens k̓úlem te k̓ist.
so that I will not do bad any more.

Le7 re sqweqwenstsnémcwes.
May you take pity on me.

Likewise, the Secwépemc version of the Lord's Prayer invokes specific social notions:

Llepéncte-kucw re sk̓éstentsút-kt,
Forgive us for us doing bad to ourselves,

tšilem te sllépenctem-kucw te k̓wellqel̓múcws.
as we forgive our neighbours.

Ta7 ews ks necwentéc es t̓ecwentés-kucw te k̓ist.
Don't allow that the bad wins over us.

Tseclegentéke-kucw te k̓ist.
Drag us away from the bad.

Aside from the concept of *k̓estentsút*, we find here terms like *t̓ecwentés* ("to win" over somebody or something), which invokes gambling and thus the supreme spiritual power associated with gambling contests. In Secwépemc prayer, rather than being "delivered from evil," one much more graphically begs the Chief Above, or Creator, to "drag us away" from bad things.

The first line of the Secwépemc Lord's Prayer makes reference to eschatological entities that are rather different from those in the English one:

Qé7tse-kt, ne kllén mútucw,
Our Father, who lives [is camped] in a place that's invisible,

xwexwéytes re qelmúcw xexecít.s te7 skwest.
all the people [Indians] imbue your name with power.

Here, we have the Secwépemc concept of living and camping in place, *mut*, discussed in chapter 5, along with not an entity like "heaven" but "a place out there that's invisible." Rather than reciting "hallowed be Thy name," Secwépemc people do honour to the Creator, "our Father," by imbuing his name, in its genealogical and spiritual essence, with power. Again, the concepts of *xexé7* (power[ful], smart) and *skwest* (name) were not neutral for Secwépemc people but were already filled with meaning that connected humans, living things, the land, and potential supernatural powers. As these words, already filled with prior meaning, became part of Catholic prayers, the old meanings continued to live in these prayers. That is why, as long as our people prayed in our language, the meanings that Secwépemc ancestors had defined and known continued to survive. Used today by elders who still pray in Secwepemctsín, prayers derived and translated from Catholic prayers are not signs and evidence that the Secwépemc gave up their worldview. Instead, we continue to uphold this worldview within the churches that our people built to welcome and accommodate the new religion.

Likewise, the Secwépemc interpreted receiving holy communion within the terms of reciprocity between hosts and guests. As one missionary lamented, expressing his own prejudice about our ancestors' hunting-fishing-gathering livelihood, "they look at communion as a good thing, it's an honour to the person who receives it … they would gladly receive it every day, if one gave it to them, as they live a lifestyle of fishing, of negligence and laziness" (quoted in Dionne 1947, 116, our translation).

Another notable theme in syncretized Secwépemc religious concepts that unfolded during that time was the role, widely spread throughout the Interior Plateau, of the Virgin Mary as guardian spirit and helper who could take pity on those who prayed to her (*qweqwentsícte-kucw*, "take pity on us"), thus bestowing gifts of power. As Laura Peers (1996, 289) concluded in her analysis of Salish perceptions of the Virgin Mary, the use of "pity" and "guardian" in the Marian hymns of the Plateau "is thus a direct continuation of traditional Native perceptions and expectations of powerful things." Peers also notes the way that men prayed to trees as female, life-giving powers, encircling them and asking the tree's pity to enhance their social powers. As we saw in chapter 2, Coyote's first wife was a tree.

It is notable that the lists of individuals baptized between 1866 and the 1870s, when adolescent and child baptisms replaced adult baptisms, record many individuals, remembered and well known to elders in the 1980s, who were born in the 1840s to 1870s and baptized during that time, sometimes during the first years of adult baptisms in the 1860s and early 1870s. However, twenty or thirty years after their baptism, the stories that circulated among Secwépemc people told of their deeds as *ṫkwilc* (Indian doctors). The term for being baptized, *melámentem*, is also the term used for being "doctored" by a *ṫkwilc*. According to elders' memories, there continued to be practising *ṫkwilc* in Secwépemc communities well into the mid-nineteenth century. Although they supposedly bowed their heads to the new religion, succumbing to the theology of Catholicism, the stories remembered about their lives and deeds show that they also continued to know and practise the powers and spiritual ways of the people before them. In all communities, Secwépemc people continued to pray in Secwepemctsín, and the ways that they "embraced" or took part in Catholic rituals did not, in their minds, manifest surrendering either their lands or their souls to the colonizers.

In fact, many elders who were immersed in the ways of expression, the metaphors, and the rituals of the Catholic religion also continued to readily embrace our ways of living on the land, rather than becoming "civilized" and sedentary, our ownership of and title to our lands, and our spirituality as it had existed before. However, they did not necessarily think that each of the two worldviews and knowledge systems had to remain "pure" or that they were mutually exclusive. They picked what they wanted from Catholicism, adapted what they chose, used religious discourse for political purposes, and in the end "hid our own religion, the most precious of all parts of our existence, in the church" (R. Ignace 2008, 256). This was done to protect it. The meaning of prayer and religion was closely connected to the social fabric of the community.

Among these people who were baptized yet continued to be *ṫkwilc* was Ron Ignace's great-grandmother Julienne's own mother, Melmenétkwe, who took the baptismal name Cecile. Theresa Jules's grandfather Ḱestmíc received baptism and became Abil (Abel) but continued his work as a *ṫkwilc*, as attested by oral histories of his work until his death in the 1950s (see fig. 11.3). Likewise, other communities had their baptized *ṫkwilc*. In the North Thompson, Pílsi was a known *ṫkwilc* who had powers to foresee things and the power to *ṫult* (freeze into stone). As Ida William reported, he would tell Father Le Jeune that he "was his own priest" rather than attend church. Hyacinth Sisyésq̓t's daughter Ster, as we saw above, was a well-known *ṫkwilc*, although she took baptism and acted as godmother to many throughout this period (see Oblate Missions of British Columbia 1866–82). As we saw, Ster continued to act as a *ṫkwilc* despite her "conversion" to Catholicism.

During this period, symbols of the Catholic Church became freely incorporated into Secwépemc rituals. Thus Ida William reported that her mother, Mathilde, when she was sent on her *étsxem* (spirit guardian quest), took along her prayer beads and rosary, after people, according to Ida's sister Josephine Wenlock, told her, "You better quit that crazy work." Although her own elders had planned for her to become a *ṫkwilc*, she "didn't last" in her *étsxem*.

However, the powers she did acquire before she interrupted her *étsxem* allowed her to foretell things and to dream about future events. The narrative below by Theresa Jules, which explains the ways that her *ṫkwilc* ancestors Cecile Melmenétkwe and Abil Ḱestmíc prophesized hard times, also shows how Theresa Jules's belief system integrated these ancestors' Indigenous prophesies of the resurrection of Secwépemc lifeways along with Catholic concepts of apocalypse.

Mé7e yem xexé7-enke le q̓7éses yerí7.
Well I guess that it must have been hard times long ago.

Kítsentmes-enke w7ec re stektsíllens yem.
I guess the people were experiencing a time of starvation.

Q̓wempépes-ṫk7e …
When it was all gone …

Swéti7 me7 lu7 lexéxy̓ectsems ṫlúne le w7é7cwen te Chase?
Who was it that told me about it, when I was over there in Chase?

"Ta7a pyin k tṡi7."
[She said,] "Today there are no deer."

Le q̓7éses tsut, "Tṡi7 ṫri7 moose ṫri7 ṫ7en."
Long ago, she said, "The deer, the moose were all around."

"Ṫri7 stkelyál, ṫri7 ṫhé7en me7 wíktem-kucw," tsut.
"There were herds of them, we saw them here and there," she said.

"Yerí7 pyin," tsut, "tṡílem re skey̓s."
"But now it seems," she said, "there aren't many around."

M-yews tken7éne.
And again over that way.

Yerí7 re stsut.s, "Sṫ7ek tsut te kenkín," tsut.
She said, "That's creeping along slowly our way," she said.

"Me7 re sléntem," tsut, "k stektsíllen-kt-ekwe ri7."
"We'll notice," she said, "times of starvation."

Stektsíllen me7 kwenwéńtem-ekwe.
They say that the times of starvation are coming.

E ta7 e syecs re stektsíllen me7 ṫíqwentls,
If it isn't starvation that kills us,

ye7éne xyum te t7ikw, e tsrépes re tmicw.
there will be a big fire, when the world begins to burn.

Yerí7 Tqelt kúkwpi7 e yews re stk̓wenm7íplem̓s,
When the Creator lays down the law,

re t7ikw me7 ṫíqwentls, ṫqupt xwewéyt ye7élye.
the fires will kill us, everything here will explode.

Ta7 me7 ṫhen me7 pesxílem-kt.
There will be nothing we can to do about it.

E ta7-ekwe ri7, me7 yec ye7éne cúẏtsem nek̓ú7.
If that doesn't happen, it will be this other thing.

Me7 lleptnúcw-kt ne7éne tsék̓wscen̓.
All of the lights will go out on us.

Tå7 ṫri7, ṫ7éne coal-oil nukwll ta7 ṫri7 me7 sts7ek̓ws.
Not even the coal oil will make light.

Me7 ṫpep re tmicw, ta7 ṫhen te7 swíkem.
The earth will be in darkness, you won't be able to see a thing.

Ta7 me7 swiktc k stem me7 tepṫépt.
You won't see anything, there will be darkness.

Tsukw-ekwe ye7éne yi, ye7éne yerí7 te tsek̓wscen7úẇi,
They say that only the, this, the candle,

ṫ7éne [candle], yerí7, blessed candle.
that candle, blessed candle.

Ta7-ekwe penhén yerí7 e stá7es te7 swecém ne7 tsitcw.
They say that you should never be without this in your house.

Tsukw-ekwe yerí7 me7 knúcwentls, Ronnie.
Ronnie, they say that will be our only help.

Ta7ews llépenc, me7 tslexemstéc.

Don't forget that, remember that.

Me7 kwnem-k, nes-k ne bishop, me7 tskectsís.
You take some, go to the bishop, he will give it to you.

Me7 xlitc-k tek tsek̓wscen7ú̇wi, blessed candle.
You ask for candles, blessed candles.

Me7 yews yerí7 ec sténes, me7 tskwi̇les ṫri7.
So you can have some all the time, have it ready.

Xexé7-ekwe ri7élye me7 skénems re tmicw.
They say that great disasters will happen here on earth.

Wenécwem ri7 ṫri7 me7 sxílems.
Those things will really happen.

E ta7wes k snecwentsétsemc, e ta7wes es necwentéc, me7 wiktc yerí7.
If you don't believe me, if you don't believe it, you are going to see it.

Xwexwéyt me7 tśílem me7 qeqitsínem ṫri7 stémi,
Everthing will make strange noises like,

me7 egwmúp, me7 cwescwestsín.
it will, it will be frightening noises.

Ell me7 yews k sxillt-kt.
And then these things will happen to us.

Nerí7 me7 wéyelcwes le q̇7es te m-llwélentls tl7élye.
Those who have passed on before us, will appear before us.

E ts7ék̓wes-ekwe nehé7 tek sitq̇t, nri7 k stsq̇ey̓s,
They say that someday, when the world once again becomes day, when it is supposed to be that way,

me7 ts7ek̓w cú7tsem ye7élye.
there will be light again all over.

Me7 ṫíqwentelt me7 xweyt-kt.
We will be killed, we will all perish.

Cú7tsem telrí7 me7 tswumec-wílc-kt.

And again we will become alive again.

Me7 kectélt cúỷtsem e súp̓em-kt.
We will be given another chance to breathe again.

E ptékes mé7e telrí7, Ronnie, ta7 cú7tsem e skénems k stem.
So then, Ronnie, when all that has passed, nothing more will happen.

Xwexwéyt me7 pelq̓ílcwes te ts̓ílmes le q̓7éses-enke.
Everything will go back to the way it must have been long ago.

Es le7s ye7élye tmicw.
So that the world will be good again.

Me7 ts̓ílem-ekwe t̓ri7.
They say that is how it's going to be.

Yerí7 ri7 re slexéxỷectslem.
That was what I was told.

Ta7 lu7 le xpé7e-kt le K̓estmíc ell le Cecile lu7 wes k school*-es tá7a, ne7éne.*
Our grandfather K̓estmíc and Cecile never went to school, no [right here].

E lexéỷenses lu7 k stem, tuxwtúxwt re sts̓ílems t̓ri7.
If they predicted something, it would be exactly that way.

Ta7 t̓ri7 k stslegws k stem.
None of the facts were held back from anyone.

Xexé7 lu7 te tsqwétsten.
They were powerful relations.

Throughout this period of syncretic worldviews, it appears that at times we had compliance from missionaries and that at other times we did not. Among the missionaries themselves, some, especially Father Le Jeune, or "Persén" (Père Saint in French), were highly respected among the many Secwépemc communities they served. Le Jeune, like most priests of his generation, not only supported the use of Secwepemctsín in liturgy, translating hymns and prayers into our language, but also taught the ancestors of present Secwépemc people to read and write Secwepemctsín by means of the shorthand writing system of the time, the Duployé shorthand system (see chapter 4). Thus, throughout the late 1800s to early 1900s, there was a brief and flourishing period of literacy among the Interior Indigenous people. It was during

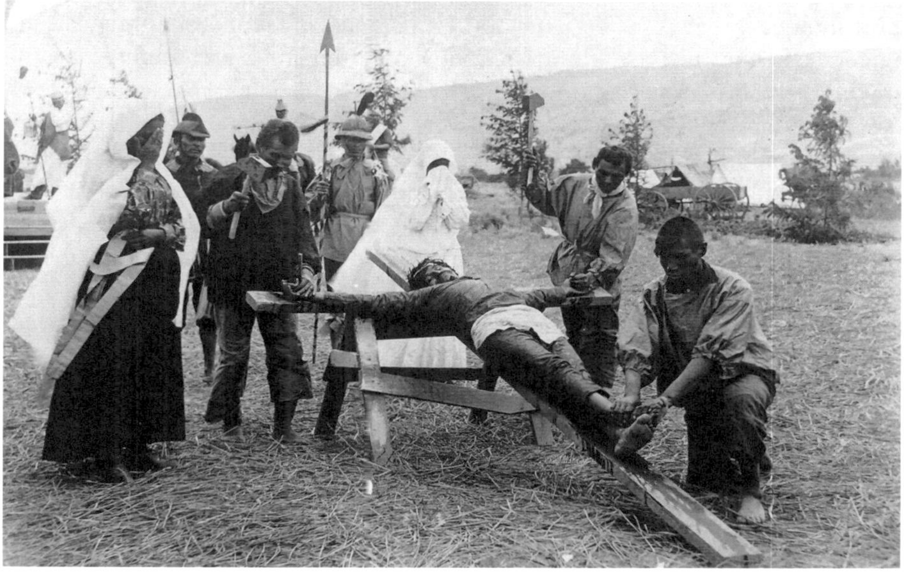

11.7 | Passion Play at the Kamloops Indian Reserve, directed by Father Jean-Marie-Raphaël Le Jeune with the assistance of Fathers Eugene Casimir Chirouse and Victor Rohr, along with a "Squamish Indian named Laket Joe," 22 June 1901. The original caption included, "Commencing Saturday, June 15, Indians began arriving from all directions by steamer, canoe, light and heavy wagons and horseback until 700 were assembled. Leading up to the main event, and by way of preparation for the tableau, mass and other services were held each day, morning, afternoon and evening. A week later, June 22, the tableau was produced with great success. This was followed by services on Sunday and an early mass on Monday, after which visiting priests were farwelled and the celebration concluded."

Le Jeune's tenure in Kamloops in 1893 and again in 1901 that the Tk̓emlúpsemc staged elaborately acted Passion Plays, or "tableaux."

On various occasions, Le Jeune also wrote letters to support Secwépemc chiefs in the pursuit of the title question and more adequate reserves. As reported in the *Kamloops Sentinel* on 26 August 1910, it was also Le Jeune who, in James Teit's absence, read the English version of the "Memorial to Sir Wilfrid Laurier" (Chiefs of the Shuswap, Okanagan, and Couteau Tribes 1910), after Chief Louis of Kamloops had presented it in a speech (presumably in Secwepemctsín) to the prime minister and his entourage (see chapter 13).

Other priests more sternly pursued the missionizing regime and methods of the Oblates (see Furniss 1995), communicating in the language but trying to actively instill the strict "*méthode missionaire*," which included kneeling before the church-condoned chief, as well as various methods of chastisement and corporal punishment. In at least one instance in Nlaka'pamux country, a local priest was eventually removed as a result of supporting corporal punishment (see ibid., 244–5). In another instance, in Lillooet territory, Father Eugene Casimir Chirouse, along with the local chief and his watchmen, was imprisoned after severely and repeatedly whipping a young man and girl for "sinful activities" (Le Jeune, *Kamloops Wawa*, 8 May 1892, cited in Robertson n.d., 13). Chief "Kramousalist" of Soda Creek, upon consulting with Father J.M. McGuckin, flogged two married women of his community who had spent a night with white men at a nearby roadhouse, McGuckin noting that "the chief admits that he had never flogged any of his women before" (quoted in Furniss 1995, 243).

At least one of the priests, Father Charles Grandidier, operated in an ambivalent role. On the one hand, like other priests and as condoned by the Oblate order (see Blake 1998), he variously wrote letters to government officials in order to help Aboriginal peoples in the Interior in their pursuit of getting adequate reserves. He even noted to Bishop Louis-Joseph d'Herbomez, "There are great disorders; and the *sauvages* almost everywhere want to lead the priest rather than to be led by him" (Grandidier to d'Herbomez, 26 September 1873, quoted in ibid., 34). On the other hand, as his correspondence with d'Herbomez and with government officials shows, he divulged intelligence to these officials about Aboriginal peoples' political meetings, intentions, political alliances, and actions, having secured the help of two "half-breeds" as informers. It was also during Grandidier's tenure in Kamloops, during the mid-1870s, that he reported the Secwépemc reverting to "gambling, dancing and feasts" (Grandidier to d'Herbomez, 22 February 1875). Grandidier was trying to use the Durieu system of social and religious order to restrict the political power of the chief and his councillors, but on various occasions he noted the "hypocrisy" of chiefs in accepting the religion and stated that "their motives are nothing more than some caprice, and most of the time they are like a bunch of sheep" (Grandidier to d'Herbomez, 28 June 1873).[20] Elizabeth Furniss (1995) notes that Williams Lake priests reported a similar resurgence, or at least hesitance to fully embrace the Catholic religion, among the Northern Secwépemc. In all likelihood, this reverting to traditional custom was attributable to the grave concerns regarding the land question that were surfacing at the time. Given Father Grandidier's advocacy of reserve allocation, it is also possible that he chose to report these things to alert his bishop, and the federal and provincial authorities to whom the bishop reported, to the urgency of dealing with the issue. However, unlike Father Le Jeune, who appears to have been clearly on the side of the Indigenous peoples, Father Grandidier's correspondence and interventions played into the hands of the federal and provincial authorities and served to undermine the chiefs' political action and quest for land rights rather than serving them.

Last but not least, a significant aspect of Catholic religion was the dual worldview of good versus bad, exemplified in a set of further oppositions, which most notably included that between God and the Devil. The concept of God as a benevolent, spiritually omnipresent, but physically absent "Creator" was one that reasonably integrated with our idea of Old One as the Tqelt Kúkwpi7 ("Chief Above"). One could speculate that the idea of Jesus as Sisi Kri, where Sisi reputedly was one of the ways of referring to Sk̓elép (Coyote) (see chapter 2), makes tacit connections between the Messiah and the trickster. Moreover, as the biblical story of the New Testament narrates, and as our people would have interpreted it, Sisi Kri departed but said that he would come back one day, as did Coyote. Thus, in more than one way, there are resemblances between Jesus and Sk̓elép, who nonetheless does not personify everything that is good but acts as a trickster. The association of the first missionaries with Sk̓elép further speaks to this resemblance. Of central importance in the conveyance of the new religion and worldview, of course, was the very idea that where there is a God, there is a Devil as his opposite. Moreover, the Devil is the very personification of "evil" in opposition to "good." The term for Devil that made its way into our language is Tseq̓mínten (Castaway), obviously after Lucifer. However, there remains the issue of whether the Devil as the dualist antithesis to God exists in the Secwépemc worldview. Among one another, and in the Indigenous language, Secwépemc people reflected on this issue.

Among the narratives by Secwépemc elders was a story about a certain priest that not only raises the issue of the character of priests and their role among the Secwépemc but also invites us to rethink the dialectic of religions and worldviews:

Re Q̓wéy̓leqs ell re Síntse7 | The Priest and the Altar Boy
told by Ida William, recorded by Marianne Ignace, 1986, transcribed by Marianne Ignace and Ronald E. Ignace

Re q̓wéy̓leqs tsúntem-ekwe te qelmúcw,
The priest was asked by the Indians,

"Stém̓i ri7 w7ec k sts7íllenstses núne re tswiwéy ne ctswiwéy̓ten,
"What do the dead corpses eat over there in the graveyard,

w7ec k illenes t̓ek stem?"
when they eat things?"

Qeqnímens-ekwe re qelmúcw le t̓7ékwes t̓ri7.
The Indians heard it when they went by there.

W7ec-enke k íllenes t̓ek stem ne ctswiwéy̓ten.
There was something eating in the graveyard.

Nerí7-enke k qelmúcw, héqen, k íllentem t̓ek stem, ne tsliq̓.
It must be people, maybe, that were eaten by something, among the buried.

Re q̓wéy̓leqs tsuns re síntse7,
The priest told the altar boy,

"Me7 kwékwentsemc ṫlu7 e r7áles pexyéwt!"
"Take me there tomorrow night!"

Qwetséts.stem ṫe síntse7 e r7áles.
When it was night, the altar boy set out with him.

M-tsut-ekwe, "Héqen yenke re Stšeq̓mín̓ten w7ec k sts7íllenst.ses re qelmúcw!"
He [the priest] said, "Maybe it is the Devil that is eating the people!"

Ṗé7ntmes ṫe sintse7 m-qwetséts.stmes ṫe ctswiwéy̓ten.
He was piggybacked by the altar boy and was taken to the graveyard.

Le kitsc-ekwe ṫlu7, m-kóso-ekwe nerí7 w7ec re ts7íllenst.ses re xelxlélcw.
When they arrived there, there was a pig there, so they say, eating corn.

Nexéll-ekwe re q̓wéy̓leqs, ye-ekwe re kóso neri7 k w7ec.
The priest was scared because there was a pig in there [in the graveyard].

Re kóso m-ṫek7ilc telrí7, m-kwṫep.
The pig ran from there and got away.

Ṫ7ek ṫe m-tseq̓él̓qwmentem re síntse7.
As they were going along, he was bumped into [by a pig], the altar boy.

Re q̓wéy̓leqs m-temtéwses ne kóso.
The priest [slid off the altar boy's back and] rode on the back of the pig.

Ṫek7ílcmentmes-ekwe te kóso,
The pig took off with him,

m-kekéw-ekwe wel re m-xwiyúcwtes re q̓wéy̓leqs.
it was a long ways before the priest fell off.

Tuxwtúxwt welílem-enke re síntse7.
The altar boy must have laughed really hard.

"Kwéntem ṫe Stseq̓mín̓ten re q̓wéy̓leqs!"
"He was taken by the Devil, that priest!"

M-kitsc ne xqweqwentsín̓ten.

He arrived at the church.

M-séwentmes ṫe qelmúcw, "Kénem?"
He was asked by the people, "What happened?"

Tsut re síntse7, "Ta7 ri7 ks Stseq̓míṅtens."
The altar boy said, "It wasn't the Devil" [or "there is/was no devil"].

Re kóso m-ullcw-enke ne ctswiwéy̓ten, íllenes re stem.
A pig must have gone in there, and was in there eating things.

Yerí7 re stemtéwsmens re q̓wéy̓leqs m-ṫek7ílcstmes.
The priest rode on its back and it took off with him.

Kekéw-ekwe wel re m-xwiyúcwtes re q̓wéy̓leqs!
They went far before the priest fell off!

Ta7 k skwens re síntse7 cúy̓tsem es p̓7éṅtem!
He didn't take the altar boy again to piggyback him!

"The Priest and the Altarboy," which Ida William emphatically told as a *true story* – something that was told to her second hand as having happened in a previous generation's memory, although apparently not in her home community of Chu Chua – is an interesting narrative that tells us the Secwépemc side of the encounter with missionaries and Western religion. It refutes the image that Aboriginal peoples were passive recipients of this new religion. It shows instead that the ancestors of the present generations consciously reflected on the content and purpose of Catholicism as embodied by the missionary. They maintained their own ways of experiencing and explaining the world in the face of the new religion; in doing this, they resisted missionaries' ways of explaining the world, and as this story shows, Secwépemc people kept their sense of humour as they engaged in all those things. Like other good stories, "The Priest and the Altarboy" has different layers. First, it deals with the concept of the Devil itself. The missionary seizing on an opportunity to prove the existence of the Devil is put in his place: the Devil turns out to be a pig! The sentence "Ta7 ri7 ks Stseq̓míṅtens" carries an ambiguous message. It means, "It wasn't the Devil," referring to the fact that what the missionary and he encountered in the graveyard was a pig rather than the Devil. But the sentence can also mean, "There is no devil," with the episode being taken as theological proof of the nonexistence of the Devil (R. Ignace and M. Ignace 1999, 53–7).

There is an additional important message in the story. The word for "altar boy" is *síntse7*, derived from the word for "little brother" (see chapter 9).

However, the "little brother" has to piggyback the priest. This image evokes the notion of our burden as colonized people, bearing the burden of the church on our back. By exposing the priest's false intentions, the Indigenous "little brother" sheds the burden of the priest.

Other stories could be told about the priests, our altar boys, our prayers, our *ṫkwilc*, and the period in which Secwépemc people accommodated, but also reflected on and at times resisted, the new religion. During the 1920s the situation changed. With the changes to the Indian Act imposed under Deputy Superintendent of Indian Affairs Duncan Campbell Scott in 1920 and 1930, residential school attendance became compulsory. A new generation of priests replaced the old ones, priests who burned the books that had taught Secwépemc people to read (Les Williams and Louis Matthews, personal communication, 1998; see also chapter 4). More and more, under the increasingly oppressive collaboration of church and state, Secwépemc people lost the physical and mental spaces to reflect on the Secwépemc's own worldview and that of the missionaries, so they were no longer able to integrate, on their own terms, what they saw fit of the outsiders' religion.

12 Telrí7 re Semséme7 m-Neq̓wcit.s te Tmicws-kucw

The Unfolding of Dispossession during the Nineteenth and Early Twentieth Centuries

The previous chapters have focused on the laws and practices of Secwépemc land use and occupancy as they emerged in the distant past and as they were enacted, adapted, and reshaped in the nineteenth and early twentieth centuries after European traders and then settlers came among the Secwépemc. In this chapter, we provide a more systematic and detailed account of the impacts of traders and then of settler society on the Secwépemc, chronicling the devastating population losses brought on by disease and the subsequent dispossession of land wrought on the Secwépemc by colonial, provincial, and federal policies and practices. Together, these interventions produced a lasting and integrated system of oppression, coercion, and "tutelage" (Dyck 1991), as well as a subsequent system of "cultural genocide," as the final report of the Truth and Reconciliation Commission of Canada (2015b, 1) calls it.

The Secwépemc and surrounding peoples of the Interior Plateau experienced influences and signs of Europeans well before they physically encountered them. As early as the 1750s, horses – initially introduced to the American Southwest by Spanish explorers and then traded and bred among Indigenous peoples – made their way to the Plateau.[1] In addition, European trade goods obtained through chains of trade among Indigenous nations, including copper (see chapter 6), obsidian, shells, and beads, had made their way to the Plateau well before the 1700s.[2]

Even before the actual arrival of Europeans in Secwepemcúĺecw, our ancestors experienced the first traumatic consequences of encounters with these foreign newcomers. By the 1770s and early 1780s, European-introduced diseases had arrived in northwestern North America, with a smallpox epidemic spreading northwestward from the Mississippi River at that time, which apparently caused grave illness and, in all likelihood, took lives on the Interior Plateau (Boyd 1994; see also chapter 3, boxed text). It is uncertain how many people succumbed to it. In 1808 Simon Fraser (1960, 94), who would have been well aware of the marks of smallpox left by survivors in European society, noticed a man on the Fraser River who had smallpox scars.

The first European on record to set foot in Secwepemcúl̓ecw was Alexander Mackenzie, who met Northern Secwépemc in the area from Alexandria to Williams Lake during his 1793 journey to find the Pacific Ocean. He travelled down the Fraser River from the land of the Carrier, briefly crossing through the very northern part of Secwepemcúl̓ecw in the area near Xatśúll (Soda Creek). Using the term "Athna" – the Carrier term for "foreigner" – for the Secwépemc, Mackenzie (1970, 314) noted that the Atnah lived in "subterraneous recesses" (pithouses) and had in their possession "iron, arms and utensils which they had traded from their neighbours to the Westward." This account points to the then-existing trade networks along the "grease trail," so named for the trade of oolichan grease from the coast, and to trade routes that involved the Tsilhqot'in, Ulgatcho, Nazko Carrier, Kluskus Carrier, and Coastal Nuxalk, as well as to other coastal peoples trading with the Nuxalk, who had already had indirect or direct contact with Europeans through the maritime fur trade since the late 1770s.

As noted in the previous chapter, from the information that James Teit (1900, 366) recorded more than a century ago about the Secwépemc and other Plateau societies, we know that even before the first coming of *séme7* (white people), the Indigenous people of the Plateau reported *ṫkwilc* (Indian doctors) having visions that "foretold the coming of White people, the advent of epidemics, the final extinction of the Indians, the introduction of whiskey, stoves, dishes, flour, sugar, etc." Some people thought that the first white people were the Coyote people returning. In fact, the term *séme7* itself appears to derive from the Salish root *sem* for "to tell stories." It speaks to the initial perception by Interior Salish people, manifested in dreams and visions by *ṫkwilc* at the time, that the white people were "storied beings" from the past. Another term for the first whites seen, "the employees of the Northwest [North West] and Hudson['s] Bay Companies" (Teit 1909, 452), which the Secwépemc provided to Teit in the early 1900s, was "*spetekl*" (*stsptékwle*), the term used for the ancient transformers, or "*speteklo'e*" (*stsptekwle-úẇi*, "real transformers").

Before the *séme7* arrived in Secwepemcúl̓ecw in the early 1800s, their appearance further south cast a tragic shadow on local Aboriginal people. When Chief Pelkamulox of Douglas Lake, who had made the Fish Lake Accord with his half-brother Kwolila of Tk̓emlúps (Kamloops) (see chapter 8), travelled among his Salish friends and relatives in what is now Montana around 1800, he encountered two Europeans among them, Finan McDonald and Charles Legace, traders of the North West Company who were exploring the area. Upon his return to his home country, Pelkamulox travelled to the communities of his Secwépemc relatives with news and stories of the white men, their appearance, and the tools and implements they had. He travelled to Splatsín, among the Sexqéltkemc, and then to Tk̓emlúps, eventually venturing as far west as Cácl̓ep (Fountain) on the Fraser River, where a local St'at'imc chief from Seton Lake killed him in an argument about the truthfulness of these events, which must have appeared extraordinary and *qwémqwemt* (marvellous). Some twenty years later, this murder led Pelkamulox's son N'Kwala (Nicola), who had become the protected adopted son of Tk̓emlúps chief Kwolila, to revenge his father's death. Helped by his Secwépemc and Nlaka'pamux relatives, he killed and captured some 300 Lillooet from the Seton Lake and Anderson Lake area.[3]

In the first decade of the 1800s, the Secwépemc encountered white people who arrived in different parts of Secwepemcúl̓ecw. In 1807–08 David Thompson's journey across the Rocky Mountains to the Columbia River took him to the eastern boundaries of Secwépemc country along the upper Columbia and Canoe Rivers. In late May 1808, Secwépemc people met Simon Fraser above Xatśúll on the Fraser River, communicating with him through the Dakelh (Carrier) language with the help of a young boy whose mother was Dakelh. It was "Xlosem" (Cllecwúsem), the "Old Chief" from Xatśúll, who first received him and then guided Fraser's party through all the Secwépemc communities along the Fraser River, as Fraser and his men, who were trying to descend the river at the worst possible time – the spring freshet – proceeded on their journey.

Cllecwúsem must have heard about the *séme7* travellers before their arrival. Commemorated in the name Cllecwúsem ("cover up one's face"), he masked himself, thus averting harm that might befall him if exposed with a naked face to the powers of the newcomers.[4] Although Fraser and his party portaged and floated their canoes and belongings to avoid some of the worst rapids, they nearly perished on several occasions. As Fraser's party struggled to descend the river, the Old Chief from Soda Creek kept pace with them, at times riding ahead to notify the next village of the group's impending arrival. Fraser (1960, 65) noted the hospitality shown by the Secwépemc: "They brought us dried Salmon and three different kinds of roots with which they regaled us all." The Old Chief accompanied them for two weeks into "Askettih" (St'at'imc/Lillooet) territory. At T̓it̓q̓et, what is now the Thunderbird Reserve on a flat outside of the present town of Lillooet, the Old Chief left them, returning home and leaving Fraser and his party among St'at'imc guides. Some ninety years after this encounter, "Setse'l,"[5] a Secwépemc elder of the Dog Creek area, told Teit of Simon Fraser's visit and identified the Old Chief by name as "Xlosem" (Cllecwúsem), as well as recalling the names of the chiefs of neighbouring communities at the time, thus anchoring Simon Fraser's visit in Secwépemc genealogical memory and sense of historical reckoning. The memories of "Setse'l" (Tséltšel) also both corroborate Simon Fraser's (ibid., 72–84) journals, which mention gift exchange, and prophetically connect his arrival to the return of previous transformers, specifically the ancient "cannibals" who were vanquished by the ancient transformers. In Teit's (1909, 449) words,

> [Simon Fraser's] visit is remembered by a very old man, Setsél by name, who was born in the village Peq on Riskie Creek, and was still living at Alkali Lake in 1900. He was a small boy when Simon Fraser's party came down Fraser River with canoes. Xlosem [Cllecwúsem], the Soda Creek chief, accompanied the party as guide, and interpreted for them. Kolpapatci'nexen was at the time the chief of the Canoe Creek band, and Haxkwe'st was a noted war chief and a wealthy man. He had three wives, and was tall, and wore only a breech clout, excepting in the winter-time. Some of the Soda Creek Indians were the only Shuswap who had seen white men prior to Fraser's party. In many places the people thought the strangers were transformers, mythological beings, or cannibals [*tśecélemc*, people eaters], and consequently were very distrustful of them. Fraser gave presents of tobacco, beads and knives, to almost all the Indians he met. The tobacco was black twist, and much stronger than the native tobacco. And many men who smoked it became sick.

The first interactions with *séme7* in the Southern Secwépemc area occurred in 1811–12, when Alexander Ross and David Stuart of the Pacific Fur Company, an American enterprise based at Astoria on the mouth of the Columbia River, came to Tk̓emlúps (Kamloops) after having founded Fort Okanogan. In the fall of 1811, Stuart and three companions "explored up the Oakinacken – till we reached its source, then crossing a height of land fell upon Thompson's River after travelling for some time among a powerful nation called the She-waps" (quoted in Ross 1855, 158). They remained with the Secwépemc in the Tk̓emlúps area during the winter of 1811–12, trading beaver skins and promising to set up a permanent post. The following spring, Alexander Ross (1849, 200) visited the area again, entering in his journal that they "encamped at a place called by the Indians Cumcloups [should be "Cumeloups" for Tk̓emlúps][6] near the entrance of the North branch … The number of Indians collected on that occasion could not have been less than 2,000."

In 1812 the North West Company also built a post near the confluence, and in the following year the Pacific Fur Company sold out its interest to the North West Company. The first factor of the North West Company was Joseph LaRocque, who, in the fashion of making political alliances through marriage, married an Indian woman of the area, Chief N'Kwala's sister Suk̓wmél̓qs. In 1821 the Hudson's Bay Company (HBC) merged with the North West Company and continued under the HBC name. However, it retained most of the North West Company personnel, mainly French-speaking white people and Metis, as well as Mohawk people who had come west following the War of 1812.

On the northwestern boundary of Secwepemcúl̓ecw, the Hudson's Bay Company established Fort Alexandria at the intersection of the Carrier, Tsilhqot'in, and Secwépemc nations and their pre-existing trading routes. Through a network of brigade trails that traversed the heartland of

Secwépemc territory along the Fraser River and then across the Bonaparte Plateau to the north shore of Kamloops Lake, Fort Alexandria was connected with the Thompson River post, with Fort Okanogan at the confluence of the Okanagan and Columbia Rivers, and ultimately with a post at the southern end of the Okanagan where it meets the Columbia.

The Tqéqeltkemc (North Thompson Secwépemc), in the area from Tete Jaune Cache to Jasper House, traded at the small HBC outpost at Jasper House intermittently occupied between the 1820s and 1840, interacting and meeting up there not only with the few HBC personnel in the area but also with Cree and Stony people who lived in the general area and to the east and southeast.[7]

By and large, it was the dealings and interactions with the Hudson's Bay Company that marked the relationship between the Secwépemc and whites until the late 1850s.

Following the 1821 merger of the Hudson's Bay and North West Companies, when Governor George Simpson travelled to the posts of the newly merged company to carry out a feasibility study of HBC posts, it became clear that the principal purpose of the Thompson River post or Fort Kamloops was not the trade in furbearing animals. Instead, the rolling hills of bunchgrass surrounding the fort provided ample pasture for brigade horses and allowed the company to keep and breed a good number of them. Of equal importance was the fact that the salmon bought *from* the Secwépemc at Tk̓emlúps and from surrounding nations who came there to trade, as well as the salmon brought to Tk̓emlúps by brigade from the Fraser and lower Thompson Rivers, ensured the sustenance of the HBC personnel. This trade in salmon was extensive. Between 1822 and the 1850s, as witnessed by surviving HBC journals, the company annually traded between 12,000 and 20,000 fresh and dried salmon from the Secwépemc and surrounding nations. About one-half to two-thirds of this amount was obtained from the large-scale fisheries at Fountain and Thompson Landing (Nicoamen) in Nlaka'pamux country; the remainder was obtained fresh or dried from local Secwépemc communities on the North Thompson, at the head of Kamloops Lake, at Tk̓emlúps itself, and on the "Upper Lake" (Adams Lake and Shuswap Lakes).

Dried salmon became the staple food for HBC personnel throughout the northwest. As trader Archibald McDonald's (1827) report to Governor George Simpson tells us, it was rationed at the rate of three dried salmon per day per man, two per woman, and one per child. Much of the salmon bought at Tk̓emlúps was redistributed among posts in the whole district, including Fort Okanogan, Fort St James, Fort George, and so on. The overwhelming evidence from HBC trading post journals recorded in Interior Salish country shows that the company abided by the Secwépemc's and other Interior Salish peoples' sense of resource ownership within their own territories. Duane Thomson and Marianne Ignace (2005, 6) show that, "With the HBC operating 'by sufferance' – as Alexander Ross had termed it – among the Salish, company personnel necessarily either submitted to local resource tenure regimes or negotiated exceptions to local regulations." As we pointed out in chapter 6, the Secwépemc laws and protocols of resource ownership and access excluded all people not related to Secwépemc. Traders and *sexlítemc* (visitors) were thus not automatically entitled to harvest valued resources in Secwepemcúlecw, except those who married Secwépemc women. The HBC records show that the company in all cases *bought* salmon rather than catching and processing it themselves. This practice could be explained by the fact that the traders not only lacked the Secwépemc's and other Interior peoples' expertise in fishing and processing fish, as well as the related technology, but also had few women available to slice and dry the salmon. However, as the work by Thomson and Ignace (ibid.) on the fur trade era on the Plateau shows, the Secwépemc continued to assert their ownership of the river and of salmon.

In one instance at Fort Alexandria on the Fraser River just above Soda Creek, local Aboriginal people – Secwépemc, judging by their names – confronted the traders on the river as the latter were trying to harvest salmon with a weir they had set up. It was only after the HBC personnel agreed to pay for the salmon that they were allowed to keep their weir in the river:

> On October 5, 1827, after the HBC men had finished moving the weir to a better and unoccupied position in the Fraser River, nearly all the Indians opposed our departure. The Capot Blue on this occasion distinguished himself in the eyes of his countrymen and Canadians by remarking our Weir should not be set below, and raising the skin from one of his hands said the Chief, meaning me, was not invulnerable but flesh and Blood like themselves. Giving a war hoop he got himself under arms, and this appeared to be the signal for Mischief. The most insignificant scoundrels showed a temper to second their Leader. I sent for the old Chief, Chin-las-ket and represented the absurdity of his countrymen in opposing us, in a cause where certainly there was no ground for open hostilities. The place was unoccupied (and not likely to be occupied this season) and I thought there could be no insuperable objections. Salmon we must have as the Indians would give us none. The noise was quieted, the chief returned after having consulted with his friends and said we might set our weir below. Who-las-ket, being the proprietor of the spot would not come when I sent for him but returned a message we might have the place. (Traders George McDougall and J. McGillivrary, 1827, quoted in Thomson and M. Ignace 2005, 19)

In this instance, Who-las-ket's subsequent permission to the traders to carry out some fishing was on the condition that the traders provide him with ammunition. However, still dissatisfied with the arrangement, members of Who-las-ket's group eventually cut a 4.5-metre hole in the company's weir.

As Thomson and Ignace note in discussing this series of events, Who-las-ket and Chin-las-ket, described as supplying "his countrymen with Salmon but the whites he seems to consider as of no account" (ibid.), only "did what was expected of him in Secwépemc law (i.e., supply fish to his own people, for whom he was the caretaker, and thus maintain his own social and political standing)" (ibid., 18).

As the HBC's presence continued at the Thompson River post from the 1830s to 1850s, the company continued to rely on foods bought from the Indigenous peoples. Archibald McDonald's (1827) dispatch to George Simpson shows the quantities and types of Indigenous foods purchased by the company from the Secwépemc. It includes not only salmon but also deer meat, beaver meat, bear grease, hazelnuts, ducks, geese, and a number of gallons of unspecified native "roots" – the Indigenous root plants described in chapter 5 – along with garden potatoes (*Solanum tuberosum*), which were apparently already grown by Secwépemc at that time (see table 12.1).

Hudson's Bay Company records show that throughout the 1830s and 1840s, the Secwépemc continued to grow garden potatoes at Cķemqenétkwe, at Neskonlith, in the Adams Lake area, and probably in other locations, selling significant quantities to the company (see Black 1836; and Tod and Manson 1841, 1842, 1843).[8] Until the 1850s the HBC annually continued to trade in the range of 10,000 to 20,000 salmon, fresh or dried, from the "Upper Lake" (Adams Lake and Shuswap Lakes), from the "Lower Lake," or "Bout du Lac" (Sķemqín at the outlet of Kamloops Lake), and from the Nlaka'pamux and Fraser River Lillooet fisheries near Fountain and Bridge Lake, all of which had to pass through Secwépemc territory by brigade.

What held for salmon fishing, namely that "the surviving Thompson's River journals from 1822 to 1858 contain not one reference to an HBC employee fishing [for salmon]" (Thomson and M. Ignace 2005, 21), also appears to hold for hunting, at least at the Thompson River post, since aside from a few instances of HBC employees shooting a few ducks near the post, there is no indication that the HBC personnel at the post hunted for their own meat. At HBC posts that were in the territory of peoples with different resource tenure regimes, the company routinely had a "hunter" who provided meat for the post's employees. In fact, like many HBC posts in the Northwest and on the Prairies, the Jasper House post on the margins of Secwépemc, Stony, and Cree territory had its own hunter. By contrast, the HBC records for the Thompson River post mention neither company hunters nor significant hunting activity on the part of the traders. This fact provides further evidence of the continuing enforcement of Secwépemc ownership and control of resources. Although HBC personnel planted potato and vegetable gardens starting in at least the 1840s, it was only in the early 1860s that the HBC was finally successful in providing for itself by operating a dairy farm and growing larger gardens north of Kamloops.

Table 12.1 | Foods traded to the Thompson River post by Secwépemc and surrounding Aboriginal peoples, 1826

Food traded	*3 officers 3 women 2 children*	*12 men*	*8 women 10 children*[a]	*Starving Indians*[b]	*Total*
dried salmon	1,340	9,838	238	670	12,086[c]
fresh salmon	163	347	229		739
fresh venison (lbs)	799	344	125		1268
horse-flesh (lbs)	116	284			400
dogs		16			16
swans	4				4
geese	13				13
ducks	74				74
partridge	97				97
rabbits	29				29
badgers	64				64
fresh trout	19				19
eggs	300		270		570
roots (gallons)	10	23	15		48
suet or grease (lbs)	25				25
beaver tails	6				6
dried beaver (lbs)	4				4
fresh bear (lbs)	25				25
nuts (gallons)	5				5
berries (quarts)	372	645	154		1,171
potatoes (bushels)	20	20			40

[a] The original table states "no rations" (for non-officers' women and children), although the figures indicate that some foods were provided or sold to the employees for their families.

[b] The reference to "starving Indians" is interesting, as there is no evidence in the 1825–28 journals of any "starving Indians" among the Aboriginal peoples who camped in the vicinity of the post. Perhaps this reference involved the Hudson's Bay Company making alottments for feasting and feeding Aboriginal peoples who visited and traded.

[c] In addition, 6,325 salmon were sent to the Okanagan post to feed the officers and employees there, for a total of 18,411.

Source: A. McDonald (1827).

As we saw in chapter 10, throughout the Hudson's Bay Company trade era during the first half of the nineteenth century, Secwépemc laws also prevailed in matters pertaining to criminal justice and social order in interactions between traders and Secwépemc. "Indian courts" – apparently derived from Indigenous traditions before missionaries and settlers arrived – were ways of settling criminal justice matters, and the authority of chiefs and councillors played a crucial role in this process. As Thomson and Ignace (2005, 29) maintain, a close look at actual instances of criminal justice show that the HBC invariably followed Indigenous legal protocols between the Secwépemc hosts and the traders as *sexlítemc* (guests) in Secwepemcúlecw.

After 1858: Change in Political and Economic Relations

> If a person takes possession of something belonging to you, surely you know it, and he knows it, and land is a thing which cannot be taken away, and hidden. We see it constantly, and everything done with it must be more or less in view. If we had nothing, or the British Columbia Government had taken nothing from us, then there would be nothing to settle, but we had lands, and the British Columbia Government has taken them, and we want a settlement from them. (Chiefs of the Shuswap, Couteau, and Thompson Tribes et al. 1911)

Although the Secwépemc and other Interior chiefs remembered their dealings with the fur traders, the *seme7úẁi* ("real whites"), in a positive light, the 1858 gold rush and events it set in motion profoundly changed the relationship between Indigenous peoples, settlers, and the Crown. In the "Memorial to Sir Wilfrid Laurier" (Chiefs of the Shuswap, Okanagan, and Couteau Tribes 1910), the Interior chiefs told of their memories of the coming of the "other whites" after the initial period of the fur trade, when their lands, resources, social fabric, and laws had been respected by the newcomers and had largely remained intact:

> Just 52 years ago the other whites came to this country. They found us the same as the first or "real whites" had found us, only we had larger bands of horses, some cattle and in many places we cultivated the land. They found us happy, healthy, strong and numerous. Each tribe was still living in its own "house" or in other words on its own "ranch." No one interfered with our rights or disputed our possession of our own "houses" and "ranches," vis. our homes and lives.
>
> We were friendly and helped these whites also, for had we not learned the first whites had done us no harm? Only when some of them killed us we revenged on them. Then we thought there are some bad ones among them, but surely on the whole they must be good. Besides they are the queen's people. And we had already heard great things about the queen from the "real whites." We expected her subjects would do us no harm, but rather improve us by giving us knowledge, and enabling us to do some of the wonderful things they could do.
>
> At first they looked only for gold. We knew the latter was our property, but as we did not use it much, [and did] not need [it] to live by, we did not object to their searching for it. They told us, "your country is rich and you will be made wealthy by our coming. We wish just to pass over your lands in quest of gold."

> Soon they saw the country was good and some made up their mind to settle it. They took up pieces of land here and there. They told us they wanted only the use of these pieces land for a few years and then would hand them back to us in an improved condition; meanwhile they would give us some of the products they raised for the loan of our land.
>
> Thus they commenced to enter our "houses," or live on our "ranches." With us when a person enters our house he becomes our guest and we must treat him hospitably as long as he shows no hostile intentions. At the same time we expect him to return to us equal treatment for what he receives.
>
> Some of our Chiefs said, "These people wish to be partners with us in our country. We must, therefore, be the same as brothers to them, and live as one family. We will share equally in everything half and half in land, water and timber, etc. What is ours will be theirs, and what is theirs will be ours. We will help each other to be great and good."
>
> The whites made a government in Victoria – or maybe the queen made it. We heard it stated both ways. Their chiefs dwelt there. At this time they did not deny the Indian tribes owned the whole country and everything in it. They told us we did. We were hopeful.
>
> We trusted the whites and waited patiently for their chiefs to declare their intentions toward us and our lands. We knew what had been done in the neighboring states, and we remembered what we heard about the queen being so good to the Indians and that her laws carried out by her chiefs were always just and better than the American laws.
>
> Presently chiefs (government officials) commenced to visit us and had talks with some of our chiefs. They told us to have no fear, the queen's laws would prevail in this country, and everything would be well for the Indians.
>
> They said a very large reservation would be staked off for us (southern interior tribes) and the tribal lands outside of this reservation the government would buy from us for white settlement. They let us think this would be done soon. Until this reserve was set apart and our lands settled for they assured us we would have perfect freedom of traveling and camping and the same liberties as from time immemorial to hunt, fish, graze and gather our food supplies where we desired; also that all trails, land, water, timber and so on would be as free to access as formerly.
>
> Our chiefs were agreeable to these propositions, so we waited for treaties to be made, and everything settled.

In 1846, without the input or participation of Aboriginal peoples, the United States and British governments established the 49th parallel as the boundary between US-claimed and British-claimed territories west of the

Rocky Mountains, with the exception of Vancouver Island, which stayed under British control as the chief trading post of the Hudson's Bay Company. In the early 1850s, after a British royal charter had granted Vancouver Island to the HBC in 1849 and after it had been established as a British Crown colony in the same year, Governor James Douglas engaged in a series of fourteen treaties with Aboriginal groups on Vancouver Island. Dated 1851–54, the Douglas Treaties were in line with the Royal Proclamation of 1763, which was aimed not only at purchasing lands in Aboriginal peoples' recognized possession for the purpose of non-Aboriginal settlement but also at protecting Aboriginal village sites as well as ongoing hunting and fishing rights from encroachment by incoming European traders and settlers. Under the terms of the fourteen Douglas Treaties, Governor Douglas, representing the British Crown, bought 930 square kilometres of land for white settlement in exchange for cash, clothing, blankets, and other trade goods, while guaranteeing the Aboriginal groups their continuing right to hunt and fish on unoccupied Crown lands and ensuring that they could retain existing settlements.

During the time of the Douglas Treaties, the Mainland was not yet a colony, and after the initial treaties, the British Crown purported to run out of money to settle further treaties. However, the 1858 gold rush played a key role in the pace of settlement of the Interior, not only transforming its physical landscape but also having profound impacts on the political, social, and economic history of the area.

Gold was initially found by Indigenous miners on Nicomen River near Lytton in 1857 and subsequently at the mouth of Tranquille River near Tk̓emlúps. The finds were reported to Governor James Douglas (1857a), who noted the Indigenous peoples' resistance to white miners' intrusion into territory and taking of minerals:

> A new element of difficulty in exploring the gold country has been interposed through the opposition of the native Indian tribes of Thompson's River, who have lately taken the high-handed, though probably not unwise, course of expelling all the parties of gold diggers, composed chiefly of personnel from the American territories, who had forced an entrance into their country. They have also openly expressed the determination to resist all attempts at working gold in any of the streams flowing into the Thompson's River, both from a desire to monopolize the precious metal for their own benefit and from a well-found impression that shoals of salmon which usually ascend those rivers and furnish the principal food of the inhabitants, will be driven off and prevented from making their annual migration to the sea.

Similarly, Douglas (1857b) expressed to Hudson's Bay Company governor George Simpson,

> The Indians object to the entrance of white men into their country and will not permit them to work the auriferous streams, partly with the view of monopolizing the precious metal for their own benefit, and partly from an impression that the salmon will leave the rivers, and be prevented from making migrations from the sea. That disposition on their part is altogether in favor of our interests and I cannot help admiring the wisdom and foresight of the Indians; and have given directions to the officers in charge of the Company's Posts to respect their feelings and to permit them to work the gold for their own benefit and to bring it in as an article of trade.

Douglas thus not only took note of the Indigenous assertion over lands and minerals but at the time also thought of our peoples' actions as protecting the trade monopoly of the Hudson's Bay Company and the interests of the British Crown vis-à-vis American intruders.

In 1858, when gold was discovered on the Fraser River near Yale, it was Douglas himself, ironically, who passed the news on to California about the find. Throughout the spring and summer of 1858 – with Douglas being instructed by the Colonial Office not to impede the influx of foreign miners as long as they abided by British law – several thousand miners poured onto the Fraser River, coming up from the Okanagan inland, up from the coast, or through the Lillooet area. As Robin Fisher (1992, 97) states, "hundreds of bustling miners came to get rich, and to do so quickly. They were intolerant of anything that stood in their way." By late 1858 the number of miners invading the Fraser River had increased to between 20,000 and 30,000, prompting the British to establish the Mainland as a colony that same year. As the gold rush unfolded in the Fraser Canyon, it became what historian Daniel Marshall (2000) has called the "Fraser Canyon War."

As the influx of foreign miners unfolded, not only did the gold seekers' mining operations on the Fraser River interfere with Aboriginal salmon fishing, but gold seekers also plundered Nlaka'pamux villages, and a number of Nlaka'pamux from the area were killed. Another party of miners on their way to the Fraser River ate and destroyed Okanagan villagers' stored winter provisions and then brutally killed a group of unarmed Syilx (Marshall 2000, 205). When gold seekers raped a Nlaka'pamux woman, the Nlaka'pamux retaliated by killing several miners in the Kanaka Bar area, throwing their bodies in the river (ibid.). As thousands of miners retreated to Spuzzum and Yale, they formed militia brigades of miners from the United States and other regions who had previously fought in Indian wars, many of them being of the persuasion that "a good Indian is a dead Indian." Many of them voiced their intent to annex the Interior of British Columbia, even though the Oregon Treaty had established the 49th parallel as the boundary between the British Crown and the United States. As Marshall (ibid., 233ff) recounts, the Nlaka'pamux, led by Chief Spi̓ntlam (Cexpe'ntlEm̓, Sexpínlhemx), were holding a war council to beat back the miners at Nk̓emtsín (the confluence of the Thompson and Fraser Rivers) in company with allied chiefs from the Secwépemc and Okanagan nations.[9] With Spi̓ntlam urging that they make peace rather than go to war, the chiefs and their people who had gathered at Nk̓emtsín were approached by the American captain of the Pike Guards, H.M. Snyder, accompanied by another militia leader, John Centras, heading up a large, more peace-minded militia. As Snyder recounted in 1858,

> [W]e ware on our march by sunrise. This day we made pease with 4 different Chiefs and camped within seven miles of the Thompson River. Here we was met by Spintlum. The war chief of all the tribes for some distance up & down Frazer [*sic*] River … Here I proceded at once to hold our grand counsil which consisted of Eleven Chiefs and a very large number of other Indians that had gathered from above and below. We stated to them that this time we came for pease, but if we had to come againe, that we would not come by hundreds, but by thousands and drive them from the river forever. They ware much supprised and frightened to see so many men with guns & revolvers. For marching along in single file they looked to be three times the number their was … I feel well satisfied that the Treaty was the best that could be made under the circumstances, and think it will be held sacred by the Indians. (Quoted in ibid., 199)

From Snyder's narrative, it appears that as many as eleven treaties – none of which exist in written form – were made with the chiefs of local Indigenous communities as he worked his way up the Fraser River from Spuzzum to Lytton (ibid., 230–4; see also Hauka 2003, 89–90; and Harris 1997, 112).

The importance of the Fraser Canyon War and subsequent treaties lies in the fact that the British colony abdicated its duty to defend its boundary and all but let Americans annex the Fraser Canyon area. Because of the peace treaty that the Nlaka'pamux, together with their Interior Salish allies, including the Secwépemc and Nsilx, entered into with the Americans, law and order was restored. It was thus the action and intervention of the Indigenous peoples of the area that maintained the Crown's sovereignty.[10]

Governor Douglas eventually arrived in the area, horrified and embarrassed that it could have been annexed by the American militias and embarrassed that the Crown itself was late to avert this possibility, instead leaving it to the Indigenous people to solve the issue. In the end, the Mainland became a colony in 1858, being joined to Vancouver Island as the Colony of British Columbia. From 1862 to 1867 another large gold rush unfolded in the the Cariboo region, which precipitated the construction of the Cariboo Wagon Road, built at least partially on the bed of already existing Indigenous trails (see chapter

6), and a small gold rush occurred on the Big Bend of the Columbia River, an area now beneath the reservoir of Mica Dam.

Within a year or two of arriving in the gold fields, miners became eager to pre-empt land, realizing the potential for farm and ranch land that Nlaka'pamux and Secwépemc territory held, specifically the Fraser and Thompson Valleys. Additional settlers came on the heels of gold seekers. The Aboriginal trails east of the Fraser River and along the Thompson River became the new wagon "super highways" of the Interior. With the British Crown refusing to allocate further funds for treaties, and the new joint colony of Vancouver Island and the Mainland being devoid of funds, Douglas did not enter into additional treaties but instead opted to establish reserves on the Mainland in order to protect Aboriginal interests in land, instructing his surveyor, William Cox, who was the assistant commissioner of lands and works, to lay out reserves "as severally pointed out by the Indians themselves," providing them with as much land as they wanted (quoted in Fisher 1992, 153). Specifically, the reseves were intended to protect Indian settlements, cultivated fields, fishing stations, and graveyards, along with "every piece of land to which they had acquired equitable title through continuous occupation, tillage, or other investment of labour" (Canada, Indian Claims Commission 2008, 21).[11]

Although Douglas's "pro-Indian" attitude in the negotiation of treaties and subsequent intent to establish "Douglas Reserves" has been hailed as well intended, the downfall for British Columbia Aboriginal peoples was Douglas's neglect to codify his intents in the form of laws that protected Aboriginal title (see Canada, Indian Claims Commission 2001; Harris 1997; and Tennant 1990). In addition, as we will see with regard to the Douglas Reserves in Secwépemc territory, Cox made the fatal error of not following through on reserve designations, in violation of Douglas's instructions. The first colonial land ordinance of 1861 legislated under Douglas did not exclude Aboriginal people from pre-empting land but instead stipulated that "from and after the date hereof, British subjects and aliens who shall take the oath of allegiance to Her Majesty and Her successors, may acquire the right to hold and purchase in fee simple unoccupied, and unsurveyed, and unreserved Crown Lands in British Columbia, *not being* the site of an existent or proposed town, or auriferous land available for mining purposes, or *an Indian Reserve or Settlement*" (Pre-emption Consolidation Act of 1861, sec. 3, emphasis added).

Significantly, this acquisition of land through pre-emption permitted settlers to get land almost for free by simply living on the land and making "improvements" like tilling the soil, erecting fences and buildings, and planting crops. In the Interior, a settler could pre-empt up to 320 acres of unsurveyed Crown land, as long as the land was not an "Indian Reserve or settlement." Despite Douglas's proposal to set aside reserves for Aboriginal people, the racist and appalling action of the colonial government initiated at this time resulted in land that had never been ceded by Aboriginal people being given away to settlers without treaties and without any follow-up on imperial policy to acquire land by treaties and purchase, as the Royal Proclamation of 1763 had legislated. As strangers invaded Secwepemcúlecw, the chiefs of our communities took whatever measures they could to protect our lands and made their objections known to colonial personnel who travelled through Secwépemc territory. In response, the assistant commissioner of land and works, William Cox, was sent to the area to investigate matters, to set aside any lands claimed by the Indians, and to inform the settlers not to interfere with Native land.

As early as 1860, "Cox was ordered by Douglas to mark out distinctly all the Indian reserves in his district, define their extent as pointed out by the Indians themselves, and report back to [Richard Clement] Moody," the commissioner of lands and works (Canada, Indian Claims Commission 2008, 21). In 1861 Cox demarcated a reserve at the head of Okanagan Lake; however, it was not until the fall of 1862 that Cox travelled to the Interior, initially to investigate a complaint at Cherry Creek by a Secwépemc Indian identified as Shimtikum, "whose cultivated fields were under threat by two settlers. Cox was asked to mark out Shimtikum's lands and inform the settlers that they could not encroach" (ibid., 22). He subsequently marked out a reserve at Cherry Creek with posts and drew a sketch map.

During this time, Cox also staked out a reserve on the Bonaparte River, although no map apparently exists. At Tk̓emlúps, he met with Chief Louis, who asked him to mark out a reserve, and consequently, in a letter to Moody dated 24 October 1862, Cox provided a brief description of the reserve as "Situated at Kamloops, and extends along the North River, east side, for about 6 miles and along the Thompson River to the east for about 12 miles more or less, running back to the mountains in both cases. The soil in some places is of the best description and the pasture excellent – a quantity timbered with pine and willow" (British Columbia 1875, 26). In addition, he gave Chief Louis instructions to put up posts advising settlers of the reserve. During this trip, Cox was also approached by Chiefs Gregoire and Moise Nesqénell of the Sexqéltkemc at the South Thompson River and Shuswap Lake to demarcate reserves for them since settlers were encroaching on their lands. Cox subsequently gave Chief Nesqénell notices to post, but he did so without visiting the area to mark out a reserve on a sketch map and without producing a detailed description. He thus left it up to Nesqénell to carry out these tasks, and Nesqénell and his people marked out a reserve comprising some 600 square kilometres that started at Monte Creek in the west, ran along the South Thompson River and Little Shuswap Lake to Scotch Creek on Shuswap Lake, and from there extended to the lands north of Adams Lake. Cox did not return to the area to verify the reserve or to survey it. It was not until after Douglas retired in 1864 and Frederick Seymour became governor, appointing Joseph Trutch as

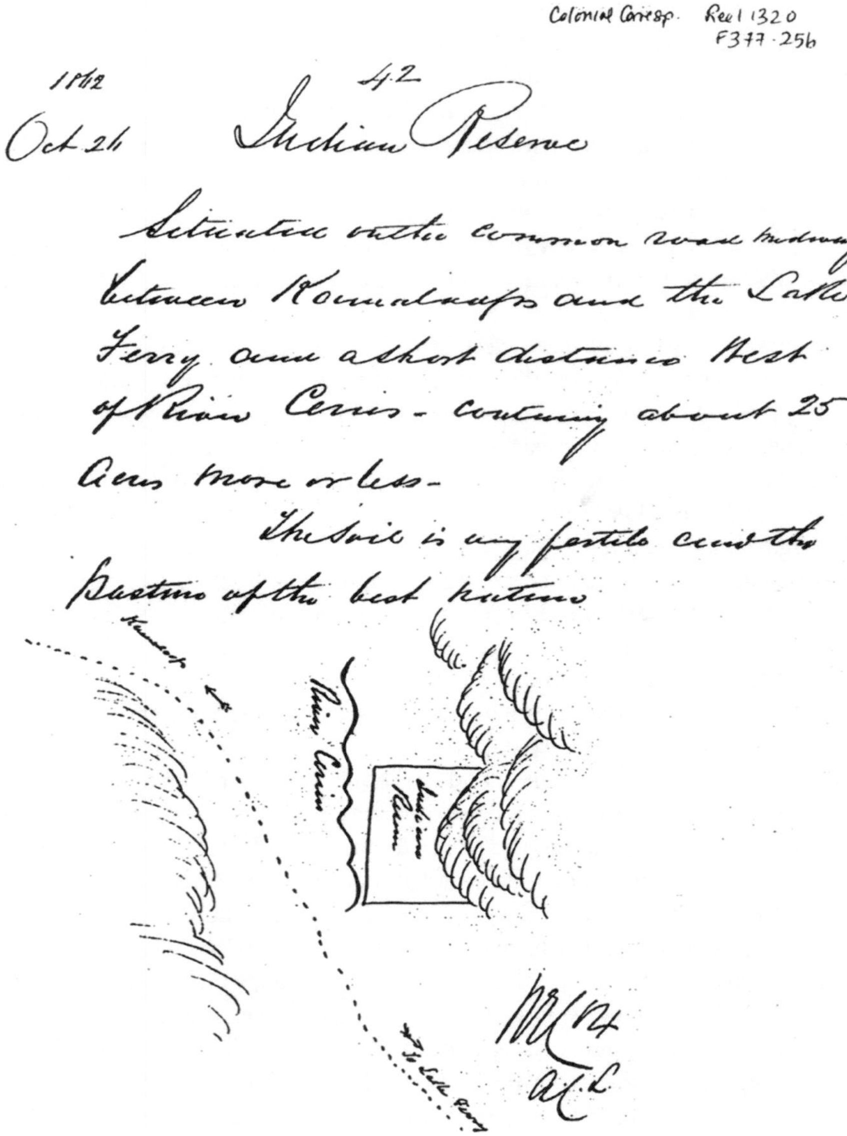
Colonial Corresp. Reel 1320
F377.25b

1862 42

Oct 21 Indian Reserve

Situated on the common road midway between Kamloops and the Lake Ferry and a short distance West of Rivière Cerises – containing about 25 Acres more or less –

The Soil is very fertile and the Pasture of the best nature

12.1 | William Cox's sketch map of a 25-acre Indian reserve at Cherry Creek, 1862. Cox was sent by Governor James Douglas to lay out this reserve in order to protect the cultivated field of an Indian of Skeetchestn from pre-emption by settlers. Like all of the "Douglas Reserves" promised at the time, the Cherry Creek reserve was never formally allocated and surveyed. It was subsequently pre-empted by two settlers married to Secwépemc women, and these settlers then sold the land to another settler.

surveyor general and chief commissioner of lands and works, that attention was again turned to the reserves that Cox was to have allocated. Noting that the Kamloops and Shuswap Reserves were entirely disproportionate to the numbers and requirements of Indians, Trutch ordered Walter Moberly to investigate "whether in your opinion arrangements can be made to reduce the limits of these Reserves, so as to allow part of the lands now uselessly shut up in these Reserves to be thrown open to Preemption" (quoted in Canada, Department of Indian Affairs 1885, 865).

Significantly, Trutch's instructions reduced Douglas's broad notion of the areas that reserves should include to only "cultivated lands" (Canada, Indian Claims Commission 2008). Moberly, who was told by Chief Nesqénell that Cox had already arranged for the marking out of the reserve, subsequently drew a sketch map that showed the "Indian claim" without verifying it or surveying it. In September 1866, Edgar Dewdney, surveyor for the Royal Engineers, who were tasked with reserve surveys, was sent to demarcate and survey three much smaller reserves, which he sketched out but did not actually survey.[12]

After marking out the reserve at Cherry Creek, Cox additionally proposed a reserve for the Sẗuxtews people in the Bonaparte River Valley and a reserve for the Skeetchestn people at the head of Kamloops Lake, but these reserves were unaccompanied by maps and only briefly mentioned in correspondence. The Skeetchestn Reserve was to consist of "about 9 miles on both sides of the Thompson River, commencing at the foot of Kamloops Lake" (British Columbia 1875, 51), a claim that was ignored by Reserve Commissioner Peter O'Reilly when he visited the Skeetchestn Band in 1868, although Chief Sisyésq̓t reminded him of Cox's promise. The initial reserve at Cherry Creek, marked out and described by Cox in 1862, was soon afterward given away as a pre-emption to two settlers who had married Secwépemc women of Skeetchestn.

During the crucial period between 1861 and April 1864, when Douglas retired, in all areas of our territory, settlers began pre-empting lands in defiance of reserve lands that had supposedly been set aside. For example, the Esk̓étemc (people of Alkali Lake) had been promised a 40-acre parcel situated at their traditional village at Esk̓ét. However, in 1861, two settlers, H.O. Bowie and Philip Grinder, had already registered a pre-emption claim "for land at the head of Alkali Lake running north-west from the creek." With Bowie subsequently buying out Grinder, and acquiring a further pre-emption in 1867, the settler's pre-empted land increased to several hundred acres; the Esk̓étemc, numbering around 150 people, were supposed to make do with 40 acres in total (Canada, Indian Claims Commission 2001, 24–5)!

Similarly, the Williams Lake (Sugarcane) Band lost a large part of the land it occupied on and around the present city of Williams Lake to the pre-emption of another settler, Walter Pinchbeck (Canada, Indian Claims Commission 2006), who had married Chief William's daughter but then abandoned her and bought up adjoining pre-emptions, eventually getting fee simple title to

12.2 | Surveyor Walter Moberly's sketch map of the proposed "Douglas Reserves" at Tk̓emlups (Kamloops) and Neskonlith, 1865.

nearly all of present Williams Lake at the exclusion of the people of T̓éxelc. The same fate befell proposed reserves among other Secwépemc communities on the Fraser River and at Bonaparte. In all cases, the areas in question were pre-empted by settlers after being vaguely promised by Douglas's envoys.

The St̓uxtéws people lost their proposed Douglas Reserve when the most valuable lands of the Bonaparte Valley were pre-empted and subsequently turned into the Hat Creek Ranch.

As the Secwépemc chiefs expressed in their "Memorial to Sir Wilfrid Laurier" (Chiefs of the Shuswap, Okanagan, and Couteau Tribes 1910), "our land is the same as our life." Reserve Commissioner Gilbert Malcolm Sproat came to the same conclusion, stating in a letter to the superintendant of Indian Affairs in Ottawa, "I do not exaggerate in saying that some of these Indians die if they lose their land: they take it so much to heart" (quoted in Fisher 1992, 103).

Another devastating impact of the period of the gold rush and land pre-emption was the smallpox epidemic that struck the Interior in 1862–63, wiping out at least one-third of the Secwépemc population. Along with other epidemics of the nineteenth and early twentieth centuries, this smallpox epidemic had a profound and catastrophic impact on the Secwépemc at a time when the gold rush and rampant settlement had already made the Indigenous peoples vulnerable.

THE DISASTROUS IMPACT OF DISEASES IN THE NINETEENTH CENTURY

As Cole Harris (1997), Robert Boyd (1994, 1999a), and Robert Galois (1992) have suggested, the depopulation of northwestern North America, including the Secwépemc homeland, began before Europeans physically arrived. The earliest recorded smallpox epidemic to affect the Indigenous peoples of the Interior Plateau struck in 1782.[13] It entered the Columbia and Fraser River plateaus after it had devastated the Indigenous populations of Central America, the American Southwest, reaching the upper Missouri River, the Great Lakes, and the Northern Plains in the previous two years. Father Adrien-Gabriel Morice (1904, 308) reported that in late 1862 smallpox "afflicted the southern parts of New Caledonia and almost converted it into an immense graveyard," adding that two white traders were reported to have sold smallpox-infected blankets to the Tsilhqot'in (ibid., 317).[14] As noted above, in 1808 Simon Fraser (1960, 55) reported seeing a man with smallpox scars during his trip down the Fraser River. The disease this man had contracted and survived was likely the 1782 smallpox epidemic that affected Indigenous peoples on the Columbia River and portions of the Northwest Coast, as well as in at least parts of the Interior. Teit (1900, 176) noted that "small-pox has appeared but once among the Upper Thompson Indians; but the Lower Thompsons state that it has broken out three or four times in their tribe. Its first appearance was near the beginning of the [nineteenth] century." Of the Secwépemc, he reported, "this disease has visited portions of the tribe twice" (ibid., 463).

The Hudson's Bay Company journals of the 1830s and 1840s report occurrences of typhoid fever and other infectious diseases at or near the Kamloops post. Galois (1996) characterizes the 1847–48 measles epidemic as the first modern pandemic to strike western North America.

The most deadly epidemic to reach the Interior First Nations during the nineteenth century, however, was the 1862 smallpox epidemic, which started in Victoria harbour and soon spread up the West Coast and into the Interior, where it ravaged until 1863. Teit (1900, 176) reported,

> It was brought into the [Interior] country in 1863, and thousands of Indians throughout the interior of British Columbia succumbed to it. If the evidence of the old people can be relied on, it must have carried off from one-fourth to one-third of the tribe. In many cases the Indians became panic-stricken, and fled to the mountains for safety. Numbers of them dropped dead along the trail, and their bodies were buried, or their bones gathered up, a considerable time afterwards. Some took refuge in

/continued

> their sweat-houses, expecting to cure the disease by sweating, and died there. It was early in spring when the epidemic was raging, and most of the Indians were living in their winter houses, under such conditions that all the inhabitants were constantly exposed to the contagion.

Teit was told how near Spences Bridge, all the occupants of a group of winter houses died, and their friends or relatives buried the deceased by collapsing the roof of the houses on them, eventually removing their bones and burying them in the local graveyard. Of the 1862–63 epidemic among the Secwépemc, Teit (1909, 463) remarked, "The population of the [Shuswap] tribe … is now probably less than one-third of what it was fifty years ago. Small-pox epidemics have been the prime cause of this decrease. This disease has visited portions of the tribe twice; and in 1862–63 it was especially severe, wiping out whole villages."

Teit (1909, 457–62) described how nearly the whole population of the Chilcotin Canyon division (Sét̓emc), where the disease had first been contracted from the Tsilhqot'in, perished in the epidemic, the few survivors moving in among their relatives at Esk̓ét (Alkali Lake). Other communities that were severely affected by the epidemic included the Tseckecwénk, or Buckskin Creek Band, on the west side of the Fraser River just south of Xatśúll (Soda Creek), the people of the Beaver Valley east of there, the Tsecwéptemc, or people of Empire Valley, the people of Llenllenéy̓ten (near Big Bar), and the people of the Snek̓we7étkwemc on the main Thompson River between Walhachin and Ashcroft.[15]

Fur traders, government agents, and visitors to Secwepemcúl̓ecw also reported on the 1862–63 epidemic. In the Northern Secwépemc area, Cariboo gold commissioner Thomas Elwyn (1862) observed, "The small-pox has been raging amongst the Indians throughout the District (with the exception of Williams Lake). At Beaver Lake nearly fifty have fallen victims & one Indian now represents the tribe," adding that "the sufferers can obtain no reliable [medical] advice." A few weeks later, Elwyn (1863) reported to the colonial secretary again, revealing the unwillingness to provide funds for medical help: "I have to report that the small pox is raging fearfully amongst the Indians at this place. Over sixty men, women & children of this tribe have already fallen victims to the terrible disease. The propriety or otherwise of extending to these poor creatures some slight Government relief has been the cause of great anxiety, but I felt that in the face of disallowances which already reach a very heavy sum, I could not take the responsibility of such a slip."

At Fort Alexandria, the Hudson's Bay Company journal entry for 1 January 1863 notes, "Two Atnahs [Secwépemc] arrived from the Rapid, gave martens and $20.00 in cash. They report the Indians of said place dying by the dozens, the smallpox is playing havoc amongst them. Some whites also died recently at Beaver Lake." In his account of the Overlanders' trip down the North Thompson River near Mad River, M.S. Wade (1981, 114) wrote that "the Overlanders passed a large potato patch from which the Indians had been driven off by small pox and which afforded an agreeable variety to the monotony of jerked beef."

Although HBC trader William Manson (1860–62, entry of 26 June 1862) reported that he had vaccinated Indians against smallpox at the Thompson River post, he also reported the death of numerous Secwépemc of the area: "It is reported that Sill-pah-han (from the North River) and some other of his band have died of smallpox. He is a loss to us as a hunter as well as an influential and well disposed Indian towards whites" (ibid., entry of 25 July 1862). Likewise, in 1862 Peter (Chief Tyenmésq̓t) of the Simpcw (North Thompson) died of smallpox (ibid., entry of 2 September 1862), as did the Secwépemc wife and children of Antoine Lamprant, a Metis HBC employee (ibid., entry of 28 July 1862).

The Overlanders, and a year later Walter Butler Cheadle (Milton and Cheadle 1865), noted an entire village in the vicinity of Clearwater wiped out by the disease, decaying dead bodies lying among the abandoned pithouses.[16] Because there were so few survivors, few specific oral histories remain of the smallpox epidemic, although there exists, unspoken, the collective memory of a wave of death. A few specific stories survive. Augusta Evans, born in 1888, remembered,

> It must have been about 1860, that smallpox time. My grandmother told me. She lived through it. Not many did.
>
> She said that lots of Indians lived on this high bench and that's where they are all buried. They died like flies, yes.
>
> And for years after, a flag used to wave above the graveyard, but that's gone now. But no one goes near it anyhow. No one wants to go near it. How they got it she says was from a man on foot coming through the country. A white man. A miner, maybe, in those days. He camped near the Indians and they gave him food and were good to him. And I guess he thanked them by giving them this nice blanket – a Hudson's Bay blanket, my grandmother says.
>
> Well, that man didn't have smallpox – no, he didn't have it. But they figured out later that he must have carried it with him in that blanket. They all got it anyway after he left. It cleaned them out.
>
> Well, my grandmother's younger brother got this smallpox. They were young in those days. She didn't get it because she stayed away from the others. She was living in an underground house. (Quoted in Speare 1973, 30)

/continued

Ida William of Chu Chua (Simpcw) recalled, "Long ago, supposed to be lots of people, Indians. My mom used to say, both sides of the river, lots of people got places like that. Right from here across, right up to Little Fort, right from Kamloops. And these people give those Indians some kind of diseased blanket, smallpox. Lots of people died from that … Yeah, suppose lots died, no doctor or nothing to help them. So many in one big place like that died from that sickness. Must be lots of bones buried all over the country." Andie Diane Palmer (2005, 37ff) has recorded stories about the 1862–63 smallpox epidemic from elders at Esk̓ét (Alkali Lake). In one incident, members of one village community kept away others whom they believed to be infected by rolling boulders down a hillside to prevent them from coming near.

Throughout these stories, as among those told by many different Indigenous peoples in North America, we hear of the diseased blankets. Augusta Evans believed they were not purposely passed on to Indians, whereas Ida William's account suggests that they may have been knowingly and purposefully given to Indians to spread the disease.[17] Although a smallpox vaccine had been in existence for several decades, in only a few places, and to only small groups of people, was it made available. In the end, not only did smallpox have a deadly impact, taking the lives of at least one-third of the Secwépemc population, but it also occurred at a crucial time, namely when white people were coming into Secwepemcúl̓ecw and pre-empting its most valuable areas to the exclusion of the Secwépemc themselves, enabled by the policies of the colony.

Reserve Allocation and the Land Question in Secwepemcúl̓ecw, 1866–82

From 1864 to 1869, following Douglas's retirement, the Indian land policy of Governor Frederick Seymour was enabled by the overtly racist land policies of Joseph Trutch, the commissioner of lands and works, who, as we saw above, struck down or hugely reduced the reserves previously proposed by Douglas. Trutch adamantly denied that Indians had ever possessed title, and he argued that they were not *using* their land: "the Indians really have no rights to the land they claim, nor are they of any actual value or utility to them" (British Columbia 1875, 42). Trutch epitomized the settler ideology that true ownership of land could be acquired only by agricultural pursuits, and he set out on a policy to systematically reduce previously proposed or allocated reserve lands (Canada, Indian Claims Commission 2001, 2006; Fisher 1992; Tennant 1990),[18] employing his brother-in-law Peter O'Reilly as reserve commissioner to reduce or simply ignore the previously proposed reserves. He did this by callously misinterpreting Douglas's instructions, even lying about them (Fisher 1992; Foster 2007; Tennant 1990).

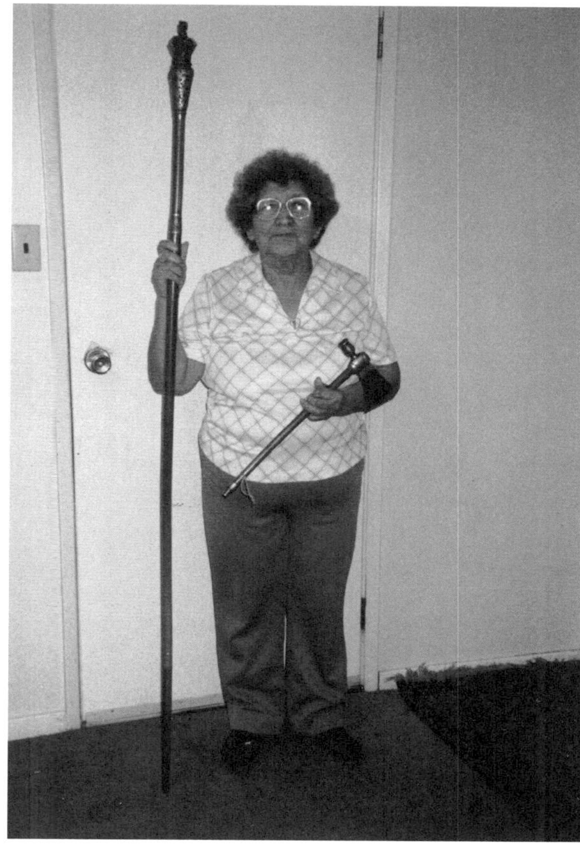

12.3 | Nellie Taylor with the chief's staff and hatchet pipe that in 1867 were given to Hyacinth Sisyésq̓t, her husband Hyacinth Taylor's grandfather, 1990. This staff and hatchet pipe, along with the picture of Queen Victoria that accompanied them, were used to make replicas that are now on exhibit at the Secwepemc Museum in Kamloops.

The 1866 colonial land ordinance, subsequently consolidated and amended in 1870, which was legislated during Trutch's tenure as commissioner of lands and works and Seymour's tenure as governor, specifically excluded "any of the Aborigines of this Colony or the Territories neighbouring thereto" from pre-empting or buying lands "except to such as shall have obtained the Governor's special permission" (Pre-emption Ordinance of 1866, sec. 1; Land Ordinance of 1870, sec. 1). Throughout the Interior of British Columbia, settlers were able to pre-empt 320 acres of Crown land, and upon showing "permanent improvements" to the value of $2.50, they were able to obtain a Crown grant for the land they had pre-empted, thus acquiring fee simple title to the land at the exclusion of Aboriginal people.

Seymour himself, while endorsing Trutch's policy regarding reserves, sought to demonstrate the Crown's supreme authority through "pageants," inviting Indigenous chiefs from throughout British Columbia to come to Government House in New Westminster to celebrate Queen Victoria's birthday. In 1865 he ordered from London "one hundred small cheap canes with

12.4 | Chiefs at New Westminster, 1867. *Standing left to right:* Chief Ta O'task of Tswécem̓c (Canoe Creek) and the first Chief William ("Will-yum") of Ṫéxelc (Williams Lake). *Sitting left to right:* Chief NaNah of Xgéṫtem (Dog Creek), Chief Quiltquarlsin of Esk̓ét (Alkali Lake), Chief Se-askut (Hyacinth Sisyésq̓t) of Shuswap, Chief Timpt Khan of Babine Lake, Chief Silkosalish of Lillooet, Chief Kam-oo-Saltre of Xatśúll (Soda Creek), and Chief Sasastunpt of Bridge Lake.

silver gilt tops of an inexpensive kind, also one hundred small cheap English flags suitable to canoes 20 to 30 feet long," subsequently presenting a staff of office and the other regalia "to each friendly tribe" (Fisher 1992, 158). Among others, a number of chiefs from the Secwépemc nation and the neighbouring Interior nations were presented with these regalia. They included a staff or cane, a hatchet pipe, a picture of Queen Victoria, and a Union Jack. Seymour organized these theatrical events, including the regalia that were distributed, to symbolize the submission of Aboriginal groups to British sovereignty and authority.

Among Aboriginal peoples of the Interior, however, a different interpretation emerged and was passed on to contemporary generations. The regalia were seen as symbols of the Crown's *recognition* of Indian sovereignty and were thus regarded as affirming the rights to land, to resources, and to self-governance of the Aboriginal groups, including the Secwépemc. Consequently, they are displayed in the Secwepemc Museum, where they are guarded and kept by the descendants of the original recipients. In Skeetchestn Nellie Taylor had inherited the regalia from her husband, Hyacinth Taylor. The meanings and discourse associated with them are significant. They reflect the "symbolic capital" invested in them and actualized in them by pointing to Secwépemc sovereignty over land, to the existence of Secwépemc *stsq̓ey̓* (laws), and thus to our rights and title. They also reflect changing meanings over time.

Hyacinth Taylor – named after his grandfather – was the son of Esther (Ster) Sisyésq̓t, herself the daughter of Hyacinth Sisyésq̓t, who was the chief of the Skeetchestn people at that time. As we explained in chapter 10, Sisyésq̓t did not follow the model of patrilineal succession of chiefship but instead appointed his son-in-law (niece's husband) Pet̓mítse7 (Joe Tomá) as his successor. However, old Sisyésq̓t willed the staff of office he had received to his daughter, Ster, who was a *t̓kwilc* (medicine woman), rather than to his political successor. The staff thus remained among Ster's descendants during the twentieth century, removed from the political office.

As Robin Fisher (1992, 159) has shown, the chiefs who attended Seymour's "pageants" in New Westminster used the occasion to voice their complaints regarding settlers taking up their lands, but they received evasive replies. At home, in our communities, the chiefs used their own measures to keep land-hungry settlers off our land. As A.G. Pemberton (1866) wrote to Trutch,

> Dear Sir, – would you be good enough to tell me in what time the Government intend fixing upon the Indian Reserves in this District, and also when we may expect to see some one up to settle the Indians and make them understand which land they are to have, and which they are to give up, as under the present circumstances they will not allow anyone to do anything on the land they claim, which is most inconvenient to the settlers. They prevented us from even cutting down trees, and say they don't want anything to be done until they see you … The same inconvenience is felt down at Savona's Ferry. The Indians have there driven off the cattle. They are also burning off the grass in every direction, which will make feed very scarce for hundreds of cattle which winter upon the Thompson.

This burning was Sisyésq̓t's initiative. As large cattle-drives were being brought into the Interior grasslands instigated by former gold seekers turned settlers, Sisyésq̓t defended our people's tenure of our lands by burning the grasslands, thus temporarily disabling cattle herds and asserting ownership of the area. This intervention was what earned him the name Sq̓wexúlecw ("smoke coming out of the ground") (see Introduction).

Following British Columbia's entry into Confederation in 1871, when article 13 of the Terms of Union stated that a "policy as liberal as hitherto" was to be pursued by the federal government with regard to Indian lands,[19] to be instigated by Trutch, the provincial and federal governments argued over the size of federal reserves in the province. Given British Columbia's refusal to create reserves that were even a fraction of the size that had been allocated in central and western Canada under the post-Confederation treaties, by 1874, Canada's minister of the interior, David Laird, had noticed that "the liberal policy heretofore pursued by the Local Government, seems little short of a mockery of their claims" (British Columbia 1875, 152). Not long afterward, the governor general of Canada, the Earl of Dufferin, reminded the BC government that it was Canada's practice to extinguish title and lamented, "In British Columbia this principle seems never to have been acknowledged" (Canada, Indian Claims Commission 2008, 94).

During the mid-1870s, Indian groups continued to protest the government's refusal to address their land question, and in 1875 the Secwépemc of Tk̓emlúps, Skeetchestn, Bonaparte, North Thompson, Neskonlith, Adams Lake, and Little Shuswap sent a petition to the federal minister of the interior protesting the entirely inadequate size of their reserves. This time it was the attorney general of British Columbia, George Walkem, who shot back that the federal government, in asking for larger reserve allocations, "did not understand the physical structure of this country and of the habits of the Indians" (Canada, Department of the Interior 1876, 79).

As settlers continued to pour into the Interior and pre-empted most of the available agricultural land, several years passed without any reserves being set aside. The Secwépemc and other Aboriginal peoples of the Interior continued to find ways to let their grievances be known. Missionaries, by and large, acted as allies of the Indians in the pursuit of the land question. On 28 August 1874 Father Charles Grandidier, then at the Okanagan Mission, wrote in the *Victoria Daily Standard*,

> The whites came, took land, fenced it in, and little by little hemmed the Indians in their small reservations … Many of these reservations have been surveyed without their consent, and sometimes without having received any notice of it, so they could not expose their needs and their wishes. Their reserves have been repeatedly cut off smaller for the benefit of the whites, and the best and most useful part of them taken away till some tribes are coralled [*sic*] on a small piece of land, as at Canoe Creek or elsewhere, or even have not an inch of ground, as at Williams Lake. The natives have protested against these spoilations, from the beginning. They have complained bitterly of that treatment, but they have not obtained any redress. (Quoted in Canada, Indian Claims Commission 2001, 28)

Father J.M. McGuckin (1878) of the St Joseph's Mission at Williams Lake wrote to the superintendant of Indian affairs,

> The Indians in this section are becoming very discontented and using threatening language on account of the delay in settling their reserves. I have used all my endeavours to keep them quiet up to the present, but it is evident that they will not heed me much longer in this matter. If something is not done for them immediately it is thought that they will even take possession of the land of some of the settlers together with the crops thereon this season. An attempt of this kind would be disastrous to all concerned, but on account of the small number of settlers, these would be the first and greatest sufferers.

It was also Father Grandidier who during this period mentioned the Secwépemc and Okanagan plotting to go to war against the settlers. More than individual communities protesting the insufficiency of their reserves, the threat to go to war as a united Secwépemc nation, and in alliance with the Okanagan, is significant in that it shows the political will and motivation of the Secwépemc as a nation. Thus Father Grandidier wrote to Bishop Louis-Joseph d'Herbomez,

> From two sources I have received the same intelligence,[20] that the Indians are thinking of war. One of them is Chief Nskantlin [Neskonlith?] who disclosed to Ross, a neighbouring farmer, that the Chief of Kamloops had promised to join him in making war and recovering their land. Ross told another farmer who repeated it to me. The other source was Mme. L. Campbell who told me that Cissiesket [Sisyésq̓t], Chief of the Lake Head [Skeetchestn/Deadman's Creek] himself had acknowledged that Louis, the Kamloops chief, wanted to unite all Indians to make war and retake their lands. I give it to you as it was given to me. It is this trend in my opinion gives more force to the manner in which these trips are incessantly made by the different chiefs to other chiefs' homes. Lastly there was a huge meeting at Osooyoos Lake which the chief of Kamloops and of Nicola Lake attended, arriving there they learned that the meeting had been dissolved and they returned home. They conduct their business under the guise of festivals, horse races, etc. but in the meetings the chiefs alone gather to discuss subjects which the people do not hear. (Grandidier to d'Herbomez, 6 September 1874, in Oblate Missions of British Columbia 1866–74)

Grandidier's and other Oblate missionaries' correspondence make numerous references to political gatherings "under the guise of festivals" and also throw some light on the church's efforts to impose its own structure on and control over the political system by way of the Durieu system, which distributed religious and secular offices such as chief, captain, and watchmen within the community.[21] We know that Chiefs Louis and Sisyésq̓t were allies as chiefs of Kamloops and Skeetchestn, two closely related and allied communities that comprised the Stk̓emlúpsemc division. They were also linked to the Okanagan at Douglas Lake by the Fish Lake Accord and to the Okanagan of the Osoyoos and Penticton area by the White Arrow of Peace and by reaffirmed marital alliances throughout the 1800s and into the twentieth century (see figs 9.2, 9.3, and 9.4).

With the newly appointed regional superintendent of Indian affairs, Israel Powell, obviously disturbed by the threat of an Indigenous alliance and war, the Joint Reserve Commission was formed in 1877 and began to carry out its work of allocating reserves in the southern part of the Secwépemc nation and in the Okanagan in 1877.

Again, at the outset of the commission's work,[22] commissioners Gilbert Malcolm Sproat and Alexander Caulfield Anderson mentioned the danger of an Indian war. As Sproat and Anderson (1877) stated to Minister of the Interior David Laird, "Indian situation very grave from Kamloops to the American border – general dissatisfaction – outbreak possible." They continued, "There was talk that the Indians were contemplating linking up with Nez Perce insurgents in the United States. Indians among the Shuswap claimed to have recently come from Chief Joseph's camp, and they gave accounts of the battles that the Nez Perces had fought … There was a meeting of Indians to discuss problems and tactics at the head of Okanagan Lake in late June or early July" (quoted in Fisher 1992, 192).

When they met the reserve commissioners, the Secwépemc chiefs from the southern communities sought to display their unity as a nation. As a group, riding in formation, they met the commissioners on horseback with flying banners – likely the Union Jack, the flag that they interpreted as symbolizing a bilateral relationship in which they were equals with the Crown (Canada, Joint Reserve Commission 1877). As elder Nellie Taylor of Skeetchestn maintained, each of the chiefs who had received the staffs from Governor Frederick Seymour had also received a Union Jack.

The Joint Reserve Commission's correspondence gives us some clues about how the commissioners proceeded and how they played chiefs against each other (Canada, Joint Reserve Commission 1877). Knowing that Chiefs Louis and Sisyésq̓t as allies were opposed to the allocation of reserves without treaties, let alone of the size envisioned by the commission, they settled with "some small tribes up the North Thompson, Adams Lake and Little Shuswap" to begin with. They settled with André Tyenmésq̓t on the North Thompson, whose area was yet less affected by settlers' pre-emptions than the areas around Kamloops. Having laid out a reserve at Simpcw (North Thompson), together with several very small reserves in the area, they settled with the chiefs in the Chase and Salmon Arm area. After settling with them, the commission returned to the Stk̓emlúpsemc (Skeetchestn and Tk̓emlúps) chiefs, eventually allocating reserves at the confluence of the North and South Thompson Rivers and west of the head of Kamloops Lake, with the main Tk̓emlúps Reserve at the confluence comprising 35,000 acres and the Deadman's Creek Reserve comprising just over 20,000 acres, both much larger than the main reserves on the North Thompson (5,000 acres) and those in the Chase area (6,400 to 7,200 acres). Commissioner Anderson (1877) explained the government's concern about the "confederation" among the "several tribes" – that is, their sense of national unity – and blamed the Indigenous groups from the south for stirring up trouble:

> [A] confederation has, we have reason to know, been entered into the heads of the several tribes, the object of which is, apparently, to urge their land claims the more forcibly through union. Whatever the nature of this combination, however, there can be no question that the counsels of the envoys from the insurgent septs South of the Line, have served to intensify previously existing discontents. Our object has been by prudent and cautious action to break up, if possible the union, and to deal in detail severally with the various questions in issue. In this we have already partially succeeded; our proceedings up the North River having served to detach the Chief André from the rest, leaving as we believe, him and his people well satisfied with their appropriations.

After the commission's dissolution in 1878–79, Sproat continued to allocate further reserves. However, the continuing delays of reserve allocation in the face of continuing land pre-emptions propelled the Secwépemc in the Williams Lake area to seek the help of their local justice of the peace, William Laing-Meason, who wrote to Sproat on 7 March 1879,

> The Indians in this vicinity have requested me to address you in their names, and to explain to you how much [they] are in need of more agricultural land … At Canoe Creek – The Indian Reserve does not contain more than ½ an acre to each [adult]. At Dog Creek – The Tribe is small but the reserve is too small in proportion. At Alkali Lake – The land is nearly as small in proportion to the number of Indians as that of Canoe Creek. At Williams Lake – There is no Indian Reserve, and the Indians do not own a single [acre] of land. They are living on land belonging to the Catholic Mission of that place … All the above Indians are very discontented on account of the Commission not having visited them before this time.
>
> I have tried to explain to them that the Commission had not time to come here last year, and that they would certainly not be neglected, but

> it is impossible to make them understand such reasons. If it is in your power to send the above tribes some assurance that you will visit them this season it would, I feel sure, help much to remove the great discontent which at present exists among them. (Quoted in Canada, Indian Claims Commission 2001, 43)

Writing again to Sproat on behalf of the Williams Lake area Secwépemc on 21 April 1879, Laing-Meason stated that the Secwépemc were in such a desperate state that they were considering destroying the crops of settlers (cited in Canada, Indian Claims Commission 2001, 44). Chief William expressed his sorrow about settlers taking his people's land and about the poverty of his people:

> The land on which my people lived for five hundred years was taken by a white man; he has piles of wheat and herds of cattle. We have nothing – not an acre. Another white man has enclosed the graves in which the ashes of our fathers rest, and we may live to see their bones turned over by his plough! Any white man can take three hundred and twenty acres of our land and the Indian dare not touch an acre. Her majesty sent me a coat, two ploughs and some turnip seed. The coat will not keep away the hunger; the ploughs are idle and the seed in useless because we have no land. (Quoted in Canada, Indian Claims Commission 2006, 16).

With Sproat's subsequent resignation as reserve commissioner, it was left to Joseph Trutch's brother-in-law, Peter O'Reilly, to complete reserve allocations throughout Secwépemc territory in the early 1880s. Taking until 1882 to set up reserves in the area, he found that virtually all of the fertile land had been pre-empted and that irrigated fields were impossible to get for the Indians amid the pre-emptions surrounding them.

The Joint Reserve Commission's census data on the Southern Secwépemc communities show the degree to which the Secwépemc were engaged in the ranching and cattle industry. The Tk̓emlúpsemc (Kamloops Band), with a population of 234 at the time of the commissioner's visit, had 979 horses, 278 head of cattle, 153 pigs, 2 work oxen, and 775 fowl, along with a good range of farming implements. The people in Skeetchestn, numbering 88, had 437 horses, 235 head of cattle, 13 pigs, and 215 fowl. On the North Thompson, the people numbered 144 and had 121 horses and 47 head of cattle. At Neskonlith, where James Douglas's surveyors had noted in the early 1860s that community members had large numbers of cattle and horses, the population was 140, with 228 horses, 33 head of cattle, 20 pigs, and 14 fowl. Other communities had similar numbers of horses and cattle (Sproat 1877).

Thus, by the early 1880s, Indian reserves had been established in all of the seventeen communities in the Secwépemc nation, although legal surveys of these reserves were not conducted until some twenty years later. By the late 1880s, following the smallpox epidemic and further epidemics of measles, tuberculosis, and other diseases, coupled with the continuing influx of settlers, the non-Aboriginal population in the province had outgrown the Aboriginal population. The chiefs of the Interior continued to use every occasion to raise the land question, although they had few occasions to do so. Despite Lord Dufferin's statement that he thought the Aboriginal people of British Columbia had land title and that this issue should be solved, the public discourses of the federal and provincial governments of the time refused to address the title question and continually sought to transform the issue of our nation's collective title and rights to Secwepemcúlecw into a question of the size of individual bands' reserves. None of the Secwépemc were able to read and write, and very few of them spoke any English. Thus the Secwépemc had to rely on the help of missionaries, their local Indian agent, and other possible advocates as they continued to protest restrictions on fishing rights (see Ware 1983), the ongoing cut-offs of reserve lands, and other injustices. Aside from what we can glean from the scant written documents that state Secwépemc concerns, little by way of the Aboriginal side exists in the written record. In the creation of Interior Aboriginal people's collective consciousness about the colonizing efforts, storied discourses existed and were told by word of mouth. Without doubt, they circulated in our communities. Occasionally, they were told to white officials, who wrote them down. Thus, during his delegation's meeting with Prime Minister Robert Borden in 1912, Douglas Lake chief John Chilaheetza noted, looking back,

> I wish to tell you a little of what the Government officials spoke to my father and the fathers of the other Chiefs of the old days. They told the Chiefs that they came there as the Spokesmen and the mouthpieces of the Queen, and they told my father that they wished to talk to him regarding the lands and other matters … There were four of them, and the last was a Mr. Sproat. So my father and the other Chiefs there said they would speak to these commissioners who said that what was said would be taken to the Queen. They said they proposed to give the Indian tribes reserves, large pieces of land, and that they would be set apart and posts set in the ground and these posts would be the same as a high fence around them. And they said the Chiefs would be set down there as heads of these places and everything upon these lands which would be posted would be the real property of the Indians – the gold and silver and everything. They explained to the Indians that it would all be done for the safety of the Indians, as many whites would come to that country and wish lands, and they wanted the Indians to have a certain amount of their own country kept for them and saved from settlement by these whites. My father and the other Chiefs asked them what about

> these lands outside of the reserves, and the commissioners said, "We will discuss these lands later." (Indian Rights Association of British Columbia 1912)

Beginning in the late 1870s with the establishment of the Kamloops-Okanagan Agency, which was subsequently divided into the Kamloops Agency and the Okanagan Agency, the Secwépemc nation was split into agencies that combined some Secwépemc communities with Syilx, others with Nlaka'pamux and Lillooet, and Northern Secwépemc with Tsilhqot'in and Carrier. Indian agents began to assert their control over individual communities and continued the nucleation of the nation into bands and reserves. As attested by the annual reports of the federal Department of Indian Affairs, along with Indian agents' correspondence from the 1880s through the 1920s, Indian agents were beginning to meddle with the political authority vested in chiefs (see chapter 10).

This practice had already begun during the Joint Reserve Commission, when the commissioners suggested refusing to acknowledge Sisyésq̓t as chief and threatened to deal instead with Pierre Te7iken, one of the *tkwenm7íple7ten* (councillors), who may possibly have vied for chiefly power. Further examples from the late nineteenth and early twentieth centuries are the dismissal under the Indian Act of Chief Francois Selpáxen at Little Shuswap and the Indian agent's insistence on appointing Eli LaRue as chief of the Kamloops Band against the choice of Chief Louis to have his grandson Seymour Pitel succeed him (Jeanette Jules, personal communication, 2015).

Historian Robin Fisher (1992, 173–4), echoing the words of US historian Robert F. Berkhofer (1965, x), has referred to the loss of Indigenous political authority during this time as "probably the most significant turning point in the acculturative history [of Indian tribes]." Although it is clear that through the Indian Act and whatever means available, white authorities undermined the authority of chiefs in their own communities, it should be pointed out that the chiefs who continued to lead in our communities were experienced leaders who were born at or before the mid-1800s. The temporary force of the Indian Rights Movement of the early part of the twentieth century shows that it was in good part the courage and persistence of these chiefs that sustained the Secwépemc's efforts to address the land title issue with the federal government. Paul Tennant (1990, 84), commenting on the generation of Indigenous leadership that emerged in British Columbia following the passing of the chiefs born in the first half of the 1800s, has called them "neo-traditional" leaders. It should be noted, however, in reflecting on what we know about the old chiefs' attempts to appoint trained and suitable successors (see chapter 10), and about the calculated interference of Indian agents in this process as enabled by the Indian Act, that this was a daunting process. As communities and their leaders sought to maintain the integrity of their process and outcomes of appointing leadership according to traditional laws and protocols, they were subjected to an onslaught of interventions and manipulations on the part of Indian agents enforcing federal policies.

Throughout this period, further diseases continued to take their toll on the Secwépemc, with frequent outbreaks of often fatal measles, as well as influenza, mentioned in the Indian agents' reports of the 1880s and 1890s. The report of 1882 states that there had been an outbreak of measles in the Kamloops Agency during the winter months, which "raged with considerable virulence," resulting in a decrease of population in many bands (Canada, Department of Indian Affairs 1884, lxiv). In 1888 "an epidemic of measles of a virulent type was very prevalent in quite a number of Indian Bands of this province, and in many instances fatal results followed an attack of the disease" (Canada, Department of Indian Affairs 1889, lxxxi), with Indian agent William Laing-Meason, previously justice of the peace in the Williams Lake area, reporting numerous outbreaks in the Williams Lake Agency (ibid., lxxxvi). During the same year, there were also outbreaks of typhoid fever (ibid). In 1891 "'La grippe,' that virulent type of influenza was very prevalent among these Indians [of the Kamloops and Okanagan Agencies] as was also an epidemic of measles. A considerable number of them fell victims to these diseases" (Canada, Department of Indian Affairs 1892, xxii). According to Simpcw elder Ida William, in approximately 1910, a measles epidemic exacerbated by pneumonia killed more than fifteen children of the North Thompson Band. Finally, the 1918–19 Spanish influenza pandemic killed nearly one-third of the population in many Secwépemc villages. Elders born in the late 1800s or early 1900s, who as children or young adults survived the flu epidemic, vividly remembered the trauma of losing loved ones, parents, children, elders, nieces, and grandchildren. Josephine Wenlock described its consequences in her community of Chu Chua (Simpcw): "When everything was over, no old ladies, no, and all the old men is gone. That was fifty-nine people got killed."[23] Fifty-nine victims represented one-third of the community's population at the time. The dozens of small and large graves in our graveyards are reminders of the loss of thirty or more people of all ages during the epidemic. In Skeetchestn, Ron Ignace's great-grandmother Julienne (Sulyén) lost three of her siblings; her uncle, Joe Tomá, who was chief of our community, also died. Virtually all families lost parents, grandparents, and children during the influenza epidemic. Many children were orphaned and lost not only parents but one or both grandparents during this time. Some families were entirely wiped out.

The loss of parents and grandparents, as well as aunts and uncles, nieces and nephews, and children and grandchildren of all ages, had a serious effect on the transmission of our culture since there were few elders left to pass on cultural knowledge and skills. From a more personal perspective, the loss of so many family members and relatives was a devastating and traumatic event

12.5 | Josephine Wenlock (1899–1990) of Chu Chua (Simpcw), who was an expert genealogist and oral historian, 1987.

for those who survived. During the early 1900s and well into the 1940s, tuberculosis and pneumonia contributed to the much higher death rate and lower life expectancy of Aboriginal people in Canada in general, including among the Secwépemc.

These historical events and processes, then, are what the Secwépemc faced before and after 1858, beginning with the arrival of the first *seme7úw̓i* ("real whites"), who, as the chiefs from that time remembered, by and large left our institutions and our control over our lands intact. As the chiefs acknowledged in 1910, their circumstances began to worsen with the influx of the "other whites" throughout the gold rush (Chiefs of the Shuswap, Okanagan, and Couteau Tribes 1910), which was followed by the deadly smallpox epidemic and by some four decades of frustration as racist land ordinances and government policies disabled our ancestors' access to their own lands. During this time, as the government procrastinated on the establishment of reserves, more settlers acquired fee simple title to all of the most productive lands within Secwepemcúlecw under land ordinances that excluded our people from following the same process.

Throughout the last decade of the nineteenth century and the first decade of the twentieth, the frustration in Secwépemc communities grew as settlers who arrived in ever-greater numbers entirely surrounded reserve lands and continued to ask for the best arable tracts of land to be "cut off" from our reserves because the "Indians were not using them," as they frequently stated. Although the provincial government continued to claim its "reversionary interest" in any lands that were deleted from reserve lands – a question that was not settled until 1938 – the federal government failed in its trust obligation to Aboriginal peoples by not legally surveying reserve lands for two decades following the 1878 allocations. In more cases than not, despite initial meek protests that surrenders could not take place without the consent of the members of the band, cut-offs from reserves in favour of settlers were enabled by the federal Department of Indian Affairs, resulting in a number of specific claims subsequently being filed by Secwépemc communities, some of which have been refused, whereas others remain dormant.

The Skeetchestn Band experienced a cut-off of its reserve land when a settler named Chris Pumpmaker took over a portion of the best arable land on the northeast boundary of our reserve. Following Pumpmaker's assertion, the Secwépemc, led by Chief Sisyésq̓et, insisted on the boundary that the Joint Reserve Commission had established and indeed showed surveyor William S. Jemmett that Pumpmaker had moved the reserve boundary post that had been established in 1877. As Jemmett noted in a letter to Edward Mohun dated 8 July 1878, when he reversed this move, "I made the alteration, as directed, on the West boundary line, along the stream which seemed to please the chief very much. These extra bits I marked out clearly on the ground" (quoted in Canada, Department of Indian Affairs 1878).

Despite this, Pumpmaker subsequently received his land, which the Secwépemc never surrendered. In the absence of legal land surveys until

/continued

1906, it was these temporary markings "on the ground" (e.g., blazed trees that could be felled or heaps of stones that could be moved) that were the sources of grief in our communities. It was this distrust of marking things "on the ground" that our elder Theresa Jules referred to when she recalled that all the elders before us had warned one another not to trust transactions that were merely "marked on the ground" rather than settled with legal surveys and land designations. This was what she meant by "don't mark it on the ground" (see chapter 13). The incidence of Pumpmaker's claim – which the Skeetchestn community settled as a specific claim in the early 1990s – is but one small instance of reserves being struck off the map, as was the case in Cherry Creek, Bonaparte, Esk̓ét, and other places, or being severely diminished by settlers' encroachments, to which the federal government yielded.

The decade of the 1910s saw an increase in immigration to Canada and thus a further increase in settler land pre-emptions throughout the Interior. Adeline Willard mentioned about her husband, Ike, who volunteered in the First World War, "Isaac [Ike] went into the army and when he came back, where there was Indian land, there were all settlers there. He went in the Army in 1914, and then, when he came back in 1918, there was white settlers already around where the Indians' camping grounds were" (Adeline Willard and Ike Willard, interview, 1974, Secwepemc Museum and Archives).

By 1912, when the McKenna-McBride Commission was established to resolve the ongoing question of reserve allocation in British Columbia, Secwépemc water rights had also become a contested issue. From the late 1870s to the early 1880s, while establishing reserves in the Interior, the federal government had recorded Secwépemc access to water rights. For example, in establishing Kamloops Indian Reserve No. 1, the Joint Reserve Commission acknowledged that the "prior right of the Indians as the oldest owners and occupiers of the soil to all the water which they require or may require for irrigation and other purposes from St. Paul's Creek, and its sources, and northern tributaries, is, so far as the Commissioners have authority in the matter, declared and confirmed to them" (Canada, Joint Reserve Commission 1877). The commission granted 500 "miners inches" of water to the Tk̓emlúpsemc, but the federal government never registered these water rights, and in the early part of the 1900s, the province began to assert authority over water rights through legislation, at the objection of Secwépemc people, who vigorously but in vain expressed their need for access to water during the hearings of the McKenna-McBride Commission (Canada, Royal Commission on Indian Affairs for the Province of British Columbia 1913–16). In a 1921 BC Court of Appeals decision regarding Tk̓emlúpsemc water rights, the court dismissed the validity of Reserve Commissioner O'Reilly's 1869 written allocation of Tk̓emlúpsemc water rights as the "then rights of the Indians," which the court deemed no longer valid! In the meantime, settler ranchers were constructing dams and ditches throughout waterways in Secwepemcúl̓ecw, diminishing the flow of creeks, water levels in lakes, and most of all, Secwépemc people's access to water.[24]

Despite what historian Sarah Carter (1990) shows were deliberate policies on the part of the Department of Indian Affairs aimed at "civilizing the Indian" by enforcing "peasant farming" activities rather than competitive agriculture, by the 1910s and 1920s Secwépemc people had become successful farmers. According to the department's report of 1922, the Secwépemc people in the Kamloops Agency harvested 18,888 bushels of wheat, 48,540 bushels of oats, 11,075 bushels of peas and beans, 185,010 bushels of potatoes, and 6,211 tons of hay (Canada 1923, 38). In the provincial total of Native agricultural production, they harvested about 32 per cent of the wheat, 39 per cent of the oats, 39 per cent of the peas and beans, 58 per cent of the potatoes, and 28 per cent of the hay (Canada, Department of Indian Affairs 1923; see also Knight 1978; and Matsui 2005). It was during this time, however, that settler ranchers increasingly asserted and were granted water rights over the objections of Secwépemc chiefs, with the Department of Indian Affairs only occasionally and without acumen enforcing water rights that had been promised to Secwépemc communities (Matsui 2005, 2009).

In summary, this chapter has shown how, during the traumatic and devastating period between 1858 and the early twentieth century, the gold rush precipitated the influx of land-hungry strangers, with the Indigenous people, led by the Nlaka'pamux, who suffered at the hands of the whites, themselves averting the annexation of the Fraser River area by Americans during the Fraser Canyon War. Subsequently, as the mainland of British Columbia became a colony and then entered Confederation, colonial and then federal and provincial policies and laws, notably the land ordinances, enabled settlers to pre-empt and get possession of the most fertile parts of Secwepemcúl̓ecw at the exclusion of our people. As smallpox and other diseases ravaged the Secwépemc, the settler population multiplied, gaining access to ever more land and resources. Upon our peoples' protests and desperate measures to fight back by joining up with Aboriginal peoples south of the boarder, the Canadian government in the late 1870s and early 1880s set up reserves that consisted of a fraction of what had been promised, or even what had been allocated and then rescinded, during the early 1860s, and then it further reduced these reserves. In the next chapter, we discuss the early-twentieth-century movement among the Secwépemc and neighbouring Indigenous peoples of British Columbia to protest, to insist on their never-extinguished rights to land, and to voice their protest in memorials and petititions, as well as in narratives among themselves.

13 Tṡelílcstem re Stsq̓ey̓s-kucw

The Indian Rights Movement of the Early Twentieth Century

Early in the twentieth century, chiefs of the Interior began a concerted effort to address their grievances about land and rights, resulting in various delegations that travelled to Europe and to Ottawa to press our peoples' title and rights issue as Aboriginal or Indigenous nations, not as nucleated bands, as the federal Department of Indian Affairs would have it.

In 1904 Chief Louis of Kamloops, together with Okanagan chief John Chilaheetza,[1] accompanied Father Jean-Marie-Raphaël Le Jeune to Rome and France, meeting the pope and winning a medal for his accomplishments in writing Chinook shorthand at a Vatican competition. On this occasion, Chief Louis also accompanied Father Le Jeune to his homeland in Brittany, France, meeting Le Jeune's sister and relatives. They tried to get an audience with King Edward VII but were unsuccessful.

Kamloops elder Tessie Dillabough (personal communication 1989), at ninety-one years old, remembered,

> I was in school when that was going on. But I remember when they used to all gather and talk about this land claims. And then they would all chip in so much money, and they would pick out whoever was the smartest, could speak English, and they'd send them to Ottawa. And then there was times, too, one year, Old Chief Louis went along with them, they went to England, and they wanted to see the queen, and they told them that they can't see the queen, but they insisted, but they never even did see the queen. They just went so far and they came back. They didn't get no results anywhere at all from England. And very little from Ottawa.

The notion of the queen representing the Crown – as opposed to the king, her son Edward VII who had succeeded her in 1901 – is interesting, reflecting the nineteenth-century discourse around the queen as the representative of the Crown.

In 1906 Chief Isipaymilt of the Cowichan Tribes, Chief Basil David (Basil Dick) of Bonaparte, and Chief Joe Capilano of Squamish went to England to see

13.1 | Tessie Dillabough (1895–1992) of Tk̓emlúps (Kamloops), 1988. Tessie was Nels Mitchell's sister and experienced the time of the Indian Rights Movement as a young woman. She was also Father Jean-Marie-Raphaël Le Jeune's housekeeper in the late 1910s and early 1920s.

King Edward VII, also accompanied by a young interpreter of the Katzie tribe, Simon Pierre. As Keith Carlson (2005, 6) notes, "The delegates who traveled to London in 1906 seeking promises from King Edward VII were not asking for new protections. Rather, they wanted confirmation that existing Royal promises would be honored. They believed that during the colonial period Governor James Douglas had both verbally and in writing entered a 'covenant that all land from the Indians should be paid for.'"

The chiefs released the text of their petition, which asked the Crown to keep its promises of the Douglas era, to the British Columbia media, including the *Victoria Sentinel*, just as they departed.[2] A few days after arriving in London, the delegates managed an audience with the king, but their visit was tightly controlled by the Canadian Embassy, and it is unclear whether they were able to present the king with their written petition on behalf of all of British Columbia's Indigenous peoples. Although in what survives of the written public record there is no reference to the content of their meeting with the king, Carlson (2005, 29–30) infers that their own impression was that they had communicated their petition to the king and had extracted promises from him to address their grievances about how the Crown's promises made in the 1850s and early 1860s, during Douglas's tenure, had been derailed. In

1912, during a meeting with Canadian prime minister Robert Borden, Chief Basil Dick would say of his visit to London in 1906,

> It is now seven years since I was asked by the people of my country to come in search of the Great Chief of the Whites, and my people gathered money together, and with two other chiefs I went to England to see the King. As we laid before the King over there all the disadvantages which the Indians in British Columbia were suffering from and Lord Strathcona told us that we must return and come to Ottawa and there lay our grievances before the Chief at Ottawa [the prime minister]. (Quoted in Shuswap Nation Tribal Council 2015, 38)

When asked by Prime Minister Borden, "Did you see the King?" Basil Dick answered, "Yes. We spoke of our country and we talked over matters continuously for two or three hours" (quoted in ibid). This account is quite different from that of Canadian Embassy officials, who left the impression that it was a very short audience.

In 1908 a larger delegation of chiefs from throughout British Columbia, which also included Chief Louis, Chief Basil Dick, and Chief Chilaheetza, went to Ottawa and met with Prime Minister Wilfrid Laurier and his government. Subsequently, the Interior chiefs also aligned themselves with the Nisga'a and the Coastal Indian Rights Association. Bonaparte elder Louisa Basil remembered the circumstances of the 1912 Ottawa visit, which again included Sṫuxtéws chief Basil Dick, her husband's paternal grandfather, noting the meetings prior to the departure of the delegation, which the missionaries had described as political gatherings "under the guise of festivals" (see chapter 12):

> All I know is that it was ten days those people were in Ottawa. I guess there were sure a lot of Indians. All the Indians had cows a long time ago. They are not like we are nowadays and have hard times. Every day someone would kill a cow. The next day when that was gone they would kill another. They must have killed about ten cows before the people left, maybe more, because there were so many people. You could see tents way down the other way and way back this way. Gee, sure was a lot of people. Gee, the drums all night and all day. Stick game. All the chiefs were having meetings and all the rest of the people doing different things.

The chiefs' delegation visits to London and Ottawa in 1906 and 1908 and their petitions asking the federal government to address the land question, as well as a subsequent uprising by the Gitksan on the Skeena River, eventually prompted a response. In April 1909 under Laurier and Interior Minister Frank

13.2 | *Left to right:* Chief Louis of Tk̓emlúps (Kamloops), Chief Basil Dick (Basil David) of St̓uxtéws (Bonaparte), and Chief John Chilaheetza of Sp'áxmen (Douglas Lake), ca. 1906–08. Either this photo was taken in 1906 before their planned visit to London in order to see King Edward VII (in the end, Chief Louis did not go), or it was taken in 1908 at the time of their delegation visit to Ottawa.

Oliver, who was in charge of the Department of Indian Affairs, the government appointed lawyer Tom MacInnes "to investigate and report upon the nature and present status of the Indian Title to Certain lands known as 'Indian Lands' in Canada, with special reference to British Columbia" (quoted in Foster 1999, 177). In his detailed and succinct opinion on the issue of the land question, MacInnes determined that Canada and British Columbia had utterly neglected to address the land question since the early 1860s and continued to do so. He recommended that the Laurier government address the issue of BC Indigenous land rights, demonstrating that, upon entering Confederation, neither party had ever taken steps to seek extinguishment of Aboriginal land title.

TOM MACINNES'S LEGAL OPINION

Legal historian Hamar Foster (1999, 195) has called Tom MacInnes's legal opinion "a remarkable document. Not only did he search out and analyse sources hitherto largely ignored (notably the 1875 *Papers Connected with the Indian Land Question*) [British Columbia 1875], he also brought to the task considerable legal ability and a willingness to follow premises through to their obvious – and, for some, uncomfortable conclusions."

MacInnes, neither before his 1909 legal opinion nor subsequently, concerned himself with matters of Indigenous rights and laws. He was a published poet, just like Duncan Campbell Scott, the federal deputy superintendent of Indian affairs, who was a nemesis of the Indigenous people during this critical period.

The highlights of MacInnes's legal opinion are as follows:

- He iterated the legal weight of the Royal Proclamation of 1763 and therefore of the continuing imperial obligation to extinguish title, as described in the proclamation. Therefore, it makes full sense that our Indigenous nations' representatives insisted that the "Queen" (Victoria), in their memory and gifts, and subsequently the "King" (Edward VII) were in a position to help set right the wrongs that had occurred since the time of Josepth Trutch's tenure as surveyor general and chief commissioner of lands and works.
- He detailed, some sixty years before historian Robin Fisher (1992) did so, the crucial role that Joseph Trutch played in denigrating Indigenous title, let alone in relentlessly reducing Indian reserves. Across the continent, the Treaty at Niagara (Borrows 1998) reiterates the Indigenous perception of the Royal Proclamation.
- Rather prophetically, drawing on his conclusion, contrary to lawyer Samuel H. Blake, that it was "policy, not law" that had induced the French government to grant to the French Canadians the right to their own laws, religion, and language, MacInnes wrote, "It is conceivable that the French Canadian population of Canada will, a century from now, be small. Yet their rights will be as sacred then as now" (quoted in Foster 1999, 194).
- MacInnes's final conclusion was that "the Indians today are technically correct in making appeal direct to the King … whenever they think their

title is being infringed [by the province] or ... Their trustee, the Dominion Government, is not properly protecting their interests and title" (quoted in ibid., 195).

- MacInnes recommended that the federal government bring the parties before the court and, on the basis of the evidence he had researched, adjudicate the issue of Indian title by way of a reference case involving the Indigenous people on the Skeena River – prophetically the area and people who would file the *Delgamuukw* court case in the mid-1980s, which would eventually acknowledge and define Aboriginal title in 1997.

In July 1910 the Interior chiefs gathered at Spences Bridge north of the confluence of the Thompson and Fraser Rivers and, assisted by James Teit, wrote "The Declaration of the Indian Chiefs in the Southern Interior of British Columbia" (Shuswap Nation Tribal Council 2015, 16–18), obviously aware of Laurier's impending visit to the Interior and northwestern British Columbia, with Laurier at the time apprised of MacInnes's legal opinion. During Laurier's campaign visit to Kamloops on 25 August 1910, the Interior chiefs presented him with a memorial that again addressed their grievances.[3] According to coverage in the local *Kamloops Sentinel* on 26 August, Laurier met with a large number of chiefs, "among them the 102-year-old chief of the Fountain Indians," at the Oddfellows Hall in Kamloops, "where one of the Chiefs on behalf of the delegation made an oral presentation [of the memorial], with Father Le Jeune [the resident missionary at the St Joseph's Mission] serving as interpreter."[4] The "Memorial to Sir Wilfrid Laurier" (Chiefs of the Shuswap, Okanagan, and Couteau Tribes 1910) has become an important foundational document that addresses the Interior chiefs' grievances and offers a solution of Aboriginal title and rights. It is our "Magna Carta," as Ron Ignace calls it. In Kamloops and at another stop on the Skeena River, Laurier vowed to address the issue, noting that it was a legal matter that the Judicial Committee of the British Privy Council would have to address.

On 10 May 1911, after Laurier's election defeat to the Conservative Party the previous fall, the Interior chiefs presented a "Memorial to the Hon. Frank Oliver, Minister of the Interior" (Chiefs of the Shuswap, Couteau, and Thompson Tribes et al. 1911), emphasizing and elaborating on their grievances and again asking the Crown to make good on the promises of Douglas's time. A few weeks prior to that, on 3 March 1911, the Indian chiefs had met with BC premier Richard McBride, who had flatly refused to address their issues.[5] In his written submission to Laurier, dated 9 March 1911, McBride stated, "The position taken by the local administration is, I trust, made clear to you and your colleagues that the Government has decided there is no question to submit to the Courts" (quoted in Roy 2012, 360).

In January 1912 representatives of the Indian Rights Association, including several Interior chiefs – among them Chief Louis, by then eighty-two years old, Basil Dick, Francois Sellpahan (Selpáxen), Baptiste William, and James Raitasket – went to Ottawa and presented a petition to Prime Minister Borden, recounting their previous attempts to seek justice on the issue of their unceded title and rights to land and reminding him of Laurier's promise to take the issue to the Supreme Court and to the Judicial Committee of the British Privy Council. They asked, "If you have neither power nor inclination to help us in the obtaining of our rights, then please recommend to England that they settle the case for us" (Indian Rights Association of British Columbia 1912).

During the 1912 Ottawa delegation visit, Chief Basil Dick told Borden, "I come to lay before you our right to the lands and the evil treatment of the Indians received at the hands of the British Columbia Government, for the food has been stolen from the wives and the orphans of the Indians" (Indian Rights Association of British Columbia 1912). Chief James Raitasket of Lillooet reiterated, "the whole country has been taken from us without treaty or agreement and without compensation of any kind, and the citiers have come later, and the railways later, and these things have been built on our lands" (ibid.).

Subsequently, the BC and federal governments established the 1913–16 Royal Commission on Indian Affairs for the Province of British Columbia (McKenna-McBride Commission), which refused to address the overall question of unsurrendered Aboriginal title. Once again, the Interior chiefs sent a statement of protest to Borden, asking that their claim be referred to the Judicial Committee of the British Privy Council. During the McKenna-McBride Commission's hearings in the reserve communities of the Interior, chiefs tried to address their concern about the land question in their opening addresses to the commission. Below, we present some of the ways particular community chiefs in the Secwépemc nation addressed their concerns in line with Indigenous ways of speaking, which were nonetheless brushed off by the commissioners. The commission hearings, in addition, went a long way toward threatening and devaluing Secwépemc chiefs' own presentations. When Sam Pierre of the Splatsín Reserve questioned the commission about its mandate, he was reminded by commissioner Edward Ludlow Whetmore, "We are not here to be examined by the Indians … we are here to examine the Indians. Do you know that we could place you in prison for not answering our questions?" (Okanagan Agency, in Canada, Royal Commission on Indian Affairs for the Province of British Columbia 1913–16, 10–11; see also K.D. Smith 2009).

Without considering the wider question of title, the McKenna-McBride Commission instead recommended approving 87,000 acres of new reserve land and cutting off 47,000 acres of existing reserve land. The chiefs of what had become the Allied Tribes of British Columbia – the joint association of coastal and Interior chiefs that had been formed in 1915 – submitted a "Statement of the Allied Indian Tribes of British Columbia for the Government of

13.3 | Interior chiefs' May 1916 delegation to Ottawa. *Standing left to right:* Chief Elie Larue, Chief John Tetlenitsa, James Teit, Chief Adolph Thomas, and Chief William Pascal. *Sitting left to right:* Chief James Raitasket, Chief John Chilaheetza, Chief Paul David, and Chief Basil Dick (Basil David).

British Columbia," which protested the findings of the McKenna-McBride Commission on two principal grounds: (1) "that the additional lands set aside are to a large extent of inferior quality and their total value is much smaller than that of the lands which the Commissioners recommend shall be cut off"; and (2) "In recommending that reserves confirmed and additional lands set aside be held for the benefit of bands, the Commissioners proceeded upon a principle which we consider erroneous, as all reserved lands should be held for the benefit of the Tribes" (Allied Tribes of British Columbia 1919, 7).

The statement then set out the problems that needed to be addressed in order to settle the Aboriginal title issue and proposed a resolution process. In 1924, ignoring these proposals, Parliament legislated the changes to BC Indian reserves recommended by the McKenna-McBride Commission. Finally, in 1927, upon continuing pressure by the Allied Tribes, Parliament established a Special Joint Committee of the Senate and House of Commons to "enquire into the claims of the Allied Indian Tribes of British Columbia as set forth in their petition" (quoted in Tennant 1990, 104). The Allied Tribes, represented by their lawyer, Arthur Eugene O'Meara, made their representation to the joint committee, although both the provincial legal team and the federal representative refused the chiefs of the Allied Tribes and their legal counsel access to the *Papers Connected with the Indian Land Question* (British Columbia 1875), a seminal document of evidence for their submission (Tennant 1990) and one upon which MacInnes's 1909 legal opinion, indeed, had relied. In 1926 several chiefs again went to Ottawa to address their concerns. And that year Basil Dick, accompanied by Chief Chilaheetza and Pierrish Williams of Neskonlith, again went to London, hoping for an audience with the king, only to be turned back when the king turned out to be on holidays. In 1927 Basil Dick went to Ottawa to attend the joint committee hearing, accompanied by Peter Kelly of Haida Gwaii and Andy Paull of Squamish, both of them younger activists. Without allowing the Allied Tribes access to *Papers Connected with the Indian Land Question*, the joint committee subsequently rejected the Allied Tribes' claim and legislated section 141 of the Indian Act, which made the raising of funds by Indian groups for the purposes of advancing land claims, filing such court cases, and retaining lawyers a criminal offence.[6]

The "Secretary": James Teit

James Teit played a crucial role during the Interior peoples' Indian Rights Movement (see the Introduction). Having lived and worked in proximity to the Aboriginal people of the Interior, he was recruited by Franz Boas to carry out ethnological work in the Interior under the auspices of the Jesup North Pacific Expedition (see Teit 1900, 1906, 1909; see also chapter 1). He was subsequently recruited by Edward Sapir to conduct work for the National Museum in Ottawa. Aside from his ethnographic studies in the Interior, Teit began to assist the Interior chiefs in their political struggles in the early part of the century and continued to do so throughout the formation of the Interior alliance of chiefs and their subsequent alignment with the coastal nations as the Allied Tribes of British Columbia, on whose executive committee he held a seat until prior to his premature death in 1922 (see Wickwire 1998; and P. Campbell 1994).

Teit acted as a "secretary," or scribe, in writing and presenting all of the memorials, declarations, and presentations of the Interior chiefs, and he acted as a "witness," either explicitly or implicitly, to their pursuit of the land question. Moreover, he acted as an "interpreter" when, subsequent to the memorial to Laurier, a delegation of chiefs appeared before BC premier McBride in 1911,[7] as well as before Prime Minister Borden in 1912.[8]

Teit's prominent dual role in ethnographic writing and in the Indian Rights Movement of British Columbia begs the question of the authorship of the memorials and petitions. A reading of the political texts in comparison with Teit's ethnographic writings – the latter edited by Franz Boas – reveals a striking difference: whereas Teit's ethnographic monographs, including his summaries and renditions of Shuswap myths and oral histories (Teit 1909, 571ff), are written in the style of Victorian prose at the turn of the century rather than reflecting either the speech conventions of the Interior Salish language or the Aboriginal peoples' conventions of English speech, the memorials easily translate into the Aboriginal languages and make use of English terms, meanings, and concepts familiar and common in the Aboriginal languages. Although the Laurier memorial and the other documents of the time survive in written text only in English, they reflect the way of speaking of the Interior Aboriginal peoples. This is clear from the simple but eloquent style of speech, the expressions and metaphors used, and, of course, the concerns that are addressed. Wendy Wickwire (1994, 17) has commented on the issue of Teit's authorship of this memorial: "Just because the words appear in English, a language foreign to the chiefs, they do not represent the views of an outsider. Quite the contrary: in addition to all we can distil from the political history of the period and the commentaries on that history, the style and content of the surviving documentation has strong links to its Native signatories."

Wickwire (1994) also shows that Teit's use of metaphor – such as the land as the "life" of a people and the "house" that represents the Indigenous nation – matches the language use of Interior chiefs at the time who made speeches during their delegations' visits to government. In addition, at least the memorial to Frank Oliver shows a long list of actual signatories who would have read the document and signed as part of a large group of political leaders who felt they were represented in the document. In sum, Teit did not compose the documents as an agitator but functioned as a scribe for the chiefs during the Indian Rights Movement.

The Chiefs

Whereas the memorial to Laurier itself bears no individual signatures, the memorial to Frank Oliver, written ten months later, has a list of sixty-eight signatory chiefs attached. Beyond the Nlaka'pamux, Secwépemc, St'at'imc, and Okanagan chiefs, this list includes chiefs of the Sto:lo, Ktunaxa, and Carrier nations. Paul Tennant (1990, 84) ascribes the rise of the inter-nation Indian Rights Movement among British Columbia's Aboriginal groups during the early 1900s to the rise of "neo-traditional" chiefs. The lists, however, show that during the early 1910s, the chiefs representing the various bands as portions of Indigenous "tribes" were by and large elderly chiefs born during the 1830s and 1840s. Among them were Chief Louis, who had been chief of Kamloops since the 1850s, and likewise of this generation were André Tyenmésqt of North Thompson, Baptiste William ("Will-yum") of Williams

Lake, James Capel (Gabriel) of Clinton, Antoine Chelhautken (Ts'eléwtqen) of Adams Lake, and Samson Soghomigh (Sxuxumíc) of Esk̓ét, all of whom had personally experienced the gold rush, smallpox, the arrival of missionaries, the Joint Reserve Commission, and the usurpation of their lands by settlers. Others, like Petlamitsa (Petmítše7, Joe Tomá) and Basil David Ratskola[9] (Basil Dick), were in their fifties but had experienced much of the latter part of the nineteenth century firsthand. The narrative of events during much of the nineteenth-century contact as told in the memorial to Oliver embodies their firsthand experiences and thus their witnessed and lived knowledge.

In all cases, according to contemporary memories of past chiefs and according to written documentation of the era, the chiefs who supported the memorials and declarations were representatives who had arisen out of Indigenous modes of succession and selection (see Canada, Department of Indian Affairs 1864–1990; Manson 1860–62; Oblate Missions of British Columbia 1866–74; Sproat 1877; and Teit 1930a).[10] Significantly, the elders we interviewed in the 1980s and 1990s either remembered these chiefs or had been told about them and were thus aware of these chiefs' genealogical connections to present people.

Themes of the Memorial

In their "Memorial to Sir Wilfrid Laurier," in light of the prime minister's own francophone background, the chiefs refer to the first Europeans who came among them as the "real whites": "We speak to you the more freely because you are a member of the white race with whom we first became acquainted, and which we call in our tongue 'real whites'" (Chiefs of the Shuswap, Okanagan, and Couteau Tribes 1910). Without doubt, this term is the English translation of the term for the first "white people" still employed by Secwépemc and other Interior Salish people in their languages, which is *seme7úẃi* in Secwepemctsín.

As we saw in chapter 4, the first whites credited with "first contacts" among the Interior Aboriginal people were the North West Company's Scottish employees Alexander Mackenzie and Simon Fraser on the Fraser River and English employee David Thompson on the Columbia River, as well as the American Pacific Fur Company's Scottish employees David Stuart and Alexander Ross. Possibly, there was a sense that the former were sent by the North West Company. More significantly, perhaps, the subsequent fur trade as carried out by the Hudson's Bay Company employed mainly French Metis and Iroquois Metis workers, who were often the ones to interact with the Native people. Thus there was an association between the first *seme7úẃi*, who had respected our boundaries, resources, and laws, and Laurier himself as being one of those people. The memorial thus addressed him in the style of Secwépemc oratory to remind him to carry on the traditions established by his forebears.

"A Ranch of our Own"

On the ownership of lands and resources as they perceived it, the Interior chiefs themselves refered to our homelands as a "ranch":

> When they first came amongst us there were only Indians here. They found the people of each tribe supreme in their own territory, and having tribal boundaries known and recognized by all. The country of each tribe was just the same as a very large farm or *ranch* (belonging to all the people of the tribe) from which they gathered their food and clothing, etc., fish which they got in plenty for food, grass and vegetation on which their horses grazed and the game lived, and much of which furnished materials for pipes, utensils and tools, etc. …
>
> You will see the ranch of each tribe was the same as its life, and without it the people could not have lived. (Chiefs of the Shuswap, Okanagan, and Couteau Tribes 1910, emphasis added)

There is significance in the very metaphor of the *ranch* used by the chiefs. Since the 1870s, the federal Department of Indian Affairs had tried to impose the policy and ideology of agriculture as the only viable livelihood (see Carter 1990), while refusing to grant reserves sizable and arable enough to support agriculture. As the chiefs themselves noted, and as the nineteenth-century documentary record reveals, Interior Aboriginal peoples had indeed practised ranching and horticulture to supplement their livelihood since at least the mid-nineteenth century. Moreover, as shown in chapter 5, the regimes of plant and animal harvesting and resource stewardship were such that ranching and farming were not actually revolutionary but were akin to already existing practices. By referring to the Secwépemc homeland as their "ranch," the chiefs deployed a metaphor that made their land use regimes compatible with the settler ideology, which disqualified Indigenous land use as mere "foraging" and privileged agriculture and ranching. However, for the Interior chiefs, the concept of the "ranch" entailed far more than arable pre-empted lots; rather, they used the term "ranch" for the entire Aboriginal territory of the nation (tribe), every part of which contributed to gaining a livelihood and every part of which had a history and was imbued with the deeds of their ancestors and with the power of all living things and the land itself.

The chiefs of 1910 unequivocally noted the collective ownership of lands and resources by "tribes" – in modern usage, "Aboriginal nations" (see Canada, Royal Commission on Aboriginal Peoples 1996a, 1996b) or increasingly "Indigenous nations." As shown in chapter 7, the collective and joint sense of ownership of the "ranch" of Secwépemc territory expressed in the memorial matches the converging lines of evidence of the ethnographic literature on resource and land tenure, as well as matching the sense of territorial and resource ownership expressed by elders throughout the latter part of the twentieth century.

About the circumstances surrounding the government policies that enabled the alienation of our homelands, as well as the government's utter disregard for Indigenous laws and jurisdiction, the chiefs noted:

> At this time [when the whites formed a government in Victoria], they did not deny the Indian tribes owned the whole country and everything in it. They told us we did. We Indians were hopeful. We trusted the whites and waited patiently for their chiefs to declare their intentions toward us and our lands … Gradually, as the whites of this country became more and more powerful, and we less and less powerful, they little by little changed their policy towards us, and commenced to put restrictions on us. Their government or chiefs have taken every advantage of our friendliness, weakness and ignorance to impose on us in every way. They treat us as subjects without any agreement to that effect, and force their laws on us without our consent … They have broken down our old laws and customs (no matter how good) by which we regulated ourselves. They laugh at our chiefs and brush them aside … They have knocked down (the same as) the posts of all the Indian tribes. They say there are no lines, except what they make. They have taken possession of all the Indian country and claim it as their own … They have never consulted us in any of these matters, nor made any agreement, nor signed any papers with us. They have stolen our lands and everything on them and continue to use same for their own purpose. (Chiefs of the Shuswap, Okanagan, and Couteau Tribes 1910)

The memorial to Oliver expressed the same firm stance of the diverse nations, or "tribes," on their unsurrendered ownership of and unextinguished title to their entire respective lands. The chiefs staunchly maintained that they had never surrendered their lands to either government, noting the lack of consultation and agreement – and thus the theft of Aboriginal lands. Poignantly, they added, "If a person takes possession of something belonging to you, surely you know it, and he knows it, and land is a thing which cannot be taken away, and hidden. We see it constantly, and everything done with it must be more or less in view" (Chiefs of the Shuswap, Couteau, and Thompson Tribes et al. 1911).

Written a year after the memorial to Laurier, the tone of the memorial to Oliver is more urgent. The chiefs refer to their ranches and homelands as the land on which their own blood was spilled: "our tribal territories which we have held from time immemorial, often at the cost of blood, are ours no longer" (Chiefs of the Shuswap, Couteau, and Thompson Tribes et al. 1911). The association of blood with Indigenous lands had also been used by Chief

Basil Dick in his presentation to Borden during the chiefs' visit to Ottawa in 1912. This association, of course, invokes our people's emotional and historic ties with Secwepemcúlecw, namely its landscape and resources and our memories of living on the land. Moreover, it invokes the past sacrifices that our people made for this land. For Secwépemc people, this notion also evokes the history of warfare with surrounding nations. As shown in chapter 7, stories of ancestors captured in warfare during the mid-1800s and of the defence and defeat of invading war parties were a vivid and important part of Secwépemc oral traditions and collective memories. Places where people a long time ago gave their lives in battle continue to have special spiritual and symbolic meaning, connecting present people to the land via the ancestors who fought for that land and died on the land. The blood spilled on this land symbolizes the Secwépemc's continuing ownership of their "ranch," or homeland, derived not only from occupation but also from defence of the homeland and from collective sacrifice.

Premier McBride, in response to the 1910 "Declaration of the Indian Chiefs in the Southern Interior of British Columbia" (Shuswap Nation Tribal Council 2015, 16–18), had claimed that the Indians, "in common with the whites, enjoyed all the advantages arising from building of railways and the large amounts expended for the building of roads and trails as well as other government utilities" (quoted in ibid., 26). To this statement, the chiefs answered in the Oliver memorial,

> Perhaps we do, but have we not assisted in building them, and have they not been built up from the direct robbery of ourselves and our country? We claim that these things are rightfully ours, and yet we are made to pay for using them. Had we never assisted in the making of these railways and roads; had this Government paid us for all our timber that was used, and all our fifty millions of gold taken out of this country, and all our salmon that has been caught, and destroyed, and many other things which might be mentioned that went into the making of these roads … then the British Columbia Government might speak of our sharing in the benefits of roads to which they infer we are in no way entitled. (Chiefs of the Shuswap, Couteau, and Thompson Tribes et al. 1911)

On the curtailing of hunting, fishing, and gathering, the chiefs wote to Oliver:

> We pointed out in a petition signed by fourteen of our chiefs and sent to your Indian department July 1908 … the severe restrictions put on us lately by the government re hunting and fishing; the depletion of salmon by over fishing of the whites, and other matters affecting us. In many places we are debarred from camping, traveling, gathering roots and obtaining wood and water as heretofore. Our people are fined and

> imprisoned for breaking the game and fish laws and using the same game and fish which we were told would always be ours for food. Gradually, we are becoming regarded as trespasser over a large portion of this our country. (Ibid.)

Five years later, during the McKenna-McBride Commission hearings in the communities of the Interior nations, the chiefs in their opening statements referred to how they and their "children," or community members, had become poor and how the seasonal rounds of the resource economy had become restricted. In his statement to the commission on 15 October 1915, Chief André Tyenmésq̓t of Símpcwemc (North Thompson) noted,

> You know how poor I am, just like as if I was tied up – therefore I am kind of poor. It seems as though I cannot help myself to better myself, like as if I were afraid all the time. Everything seems to be locked up now, different from what it used to be a long time ago. It used to be that everything was open to me, a long time ago. That is what I want. I want to be more free, so that I can get along better. I want to know who ever is the Chief that is going to help me on that point, to help me on what is good. (Canada, Royal Commission on Indian Affairs for the Province of British Columbia 1913–16)

Joe Tomá, chief of Skeetchestn (Deadman's Creek), stated before the commission on 29 October 1913: "The grievance of all the Indians in British Columbia, that the white man has kind of spoilt us and locked us in. The white men have taken all the land and claimed all the water rights, and stopped us from hunting, fishing, etc." (Canada, Royal Commission on Indian Affairs for the Province of British Columbia 1913–16).

Chief Francois Silpahan (Selpáxen) of the Little Shuswap Band stated before the commission on 25 October 1915, "It is not on our reserve only that our hard feelings commence; it is for lands outside the reserves where the whitemen have stopped us. They stopped us from getting deer and birds, stopped us fishing. That is what we have told the Government in Ottawa … When the Indians were here a very long time ago, and able to look for their own food all over, the Indians used to increase, and they used to have good living" (Canada, Royal Commission on Indian Affairs for the Province of British Columbia 1913–16).

In these statements, the chiefs clearly expressed their concern over the lands beyond the reserves, where they had experienced the curtailment of their harvesting of traditional resources. In each case, the commissioners of the McKenna-McBride hearings immediately steered the topic back to the "use" of reserve lands.

"Borrowed Land"

In the Laurier memorial, the chiefs noted that the first white settlers who stayed on after the 1858 gold rush had told them that they wanted the use of the land only "for a few years": "Soon they saw the country was good, and some of them made up their minds to settle in it. They commenced to take up pieces of land here and there. They told us they wanted only the use of these pieces of land for a few years, and then would hand them back to us in improved condition, meanwhile they would give us some of the produce they raised for the loan of our land" (Chiefs of the Shuswap, Okanagan, and Couteau Tribes 1910).

The notion that the tribal land owned by the Aboriginal people was *loaned* to settlers was still in the collective memories of various elders during the 1980s and 1990s. Christine Simon of Skeetchestn remembered her father, uncles, and other elders of the community making hay at Six-Mile Ranch – by then fee simple land pre-empted by a rancher. After making hay, the people of Skeetchestn took home half of the crop, leaving the other half to the settler. Christine Simon remembered being told by her elders that the understanding at the time with the white rancher was that he was just *kwllén* (borrowing) the land from the Indians at Skeetchestn: "He was just borrowing the land, 'cause why would my Dad, Louis Deneault, Buckskin Louie get a load out of there, Hyacinth Taylor. They all had wagons. They put their hay on and brought it back. That's what I know" (our translation from Secwepemctsín). Although the settler may have believed that he paid the men from Skeetchestn in hay for their labour, we think that our elders interpreted their payment in the spirit of the way the chiefs who penned the Laurier memorial remembered the covenant with settlers: "We will share equally in everything half and half in land, water and timber, etc. What is ours will be theirs, and what is theirs will be ours. We will help each other to be great and good" (Chiefs of the Shuswap, Okanagan, and Couteau Tribes 1910).

The Memorial as Oratory: Style and Meanings

A common practice of ethnohistorians has been to reduce extremely complex and culture-specific discourses to a residual of "historical fact" or to "cherry-pick" them for historical truth. Oral historians, in the meantime, have alerted us to the importance of understanding the social practices and cultural meanings underlying discursive practices. Robin Ridington (1990a, 1990b; Ridington and Ridington 2006), writing of the Dunne-zha, has drawn attention to how particular Indigenous knowledge systems and the experiences they engender embed particular discursive practices. Bruce G. Miller (2011), Julie Cruikshank (1998, 2005), Elizabeth Tonkin (1992), Andrew Martindale (2006), and others have alerted us to the social conventions and structure of narratives about the past as they are embedded in particular ways of experiencing the natural world and social relations. This embeddedness, in turn, means that understanding their messages requires careful interpretation from within the protocols of speech and the laws of conduct of particular Indigenous groups.

Compared with the literature on Northwest Coast oratory, predominantly a feature of the potlatch (Dauenhauer and Dauenhauer 1990; Halpern and Seguin Anderson 2000; M. Ignace 1992; Seguin Anderson 1985), relatively little has been published about the style, content, and conventions of oratory on the Interior Plateau. Nonetheless, we know from early accounts that oratory, or "palaver," was a significant facet of public feasts or gatherings, as observed by early traders, such as Simon Fraser, Archibald McDonald, and David Stuart. The Hudson's Bay Company's journals for the Thompson River post and Fort Alexandria make numerous references to formal speeches by chiefs of the Secwépemc nation or other nations who visited the post.

In its oratorical and discursive dimensions, the Laurier memorial follows the conventions of speechmaking common in western North America in that it begins by establishing a connection with the audience. In this case, as noted above, Laurier's French background is emphasized as connecting him to the *seme7úẁi* ("real whites"), who respected the Aboriginal peoples' land tenure, culture, and political organization. Thus symbolically linking him to the *seme7úẁi*, the chiefs asked Laurier to come "full circle" by entering into treaties to settle the land rights and political rights of the Interior Aboriginal peoples.

The discursive and symbolic meanings expressed by the Interior chiefs also emphasized the Aboriginal cultural meanings attached to the relationships between *k̓wséltkten* (relatives) and nonrelatives, as we explained these meanings in chapter 9, as well as between guests and hosts. The chiefs noted,

> With us when a person enters our house he becomes our guest, and we must treat him hospitably as long as he shows no hostile intentions. At the same time we expect him to return to us equal treatment for what he receives. Some of our Chiefs said, "These people wish to be partners with us in our country. We must, therefore, be the same as brothers with them, and live as one family. We will share equally in everything half and half in land, water and timber, etc. What is ours will be theirs, and what is theirs will be ours. We will help each other to be great and good. (Chiefs of the Shuswap, Okanagan, and Couteau Tribes 1910)

We must understand the meaning associated with these statements about the connection of guests and hosts in light of the Interior chiefs' understanding of how guests and hosts interacted. In Interior Salish society, *sexlítemc* (guests) are *qwenqwént* (pitiful) for lacking access to resources in order to provide for themselves and for lacking relatives whose duty it is to support them. Given the "pitiful" position of guests, who are expected to reciprocate the kindness of their hosts, the phrase "We treated them as [guests], and then waited to see what they would do" implies the Interior Aboriginal peoples' law of reciprocity (Chiefs of the Shuswap, Okanagan, and Couteau Tribes 1910). Within Aboriginal society, when a person treats someone or a group of people as guests, it is understood that the guests will at a later date return the favours they received. Hospitality is expected to be reciprocated without needing reminders. This expectation is at the crux of the relationship between the Interior peoples as hosts and their white guests: from the perspective of the former, the fact that they allowed the white guests into their land and acted as their hosts created a binding obligation on the part of the guests, which the whites did not honour in subsequent years. The chiefs themselves noted this expectation: "We expect him to return to us equal treatment for what he receives … They say the Indians know nothing, and own nothing … This is how our guests have treated us the brothers we received hospitably in our house" (ibid.).

The history of political control by federal and provincial governments is thus perceived as based on failed reciprocity due to the neglect and denial of the obligations incurred by guests vis-à-vis their hosts.

The Legacy of the Memorial: The Past in the Future

More than a hundred years have passed since the Interior chiefs wrote and presented the Laurier memorial. Subsequent decades saw the entrenchment of Indian administration as set out in the Indian Act and the carving-up of the Indigenous nations of the Interior through Indian agencies and band administration. We have shown that the Laurier memorial represents a carefully crafted text that reflects the oratory and voices of Interior Aboriginal peoples and that lays out our own view of history as it has unfolded with the arrival of newcomers since the early 1800s. Moreover, in its content and message, the Laurier memorial is rooted in our own *stsq̓ey̓* (laws), which address fundamental principles of relations between nations, of land tenure and ownership, and of relations between guests and hosts. Thus the Laurier memorial is connected to our *stsptékwle* (ancestors), who wrote our laws on the land, and to the *stsptekwll* (stories) themselves.

For the past two decades, the Laurier memorial has given a new voice to those seeking to reunify the Secwépemc nation. Told in the words of the past chiefs and elders, it articulates the underpinnings of Indigenous nationhood, a collective sense of ownership and use of the nation's resources, the need for just and adequate treaties, and the injustices of the nineteenth and twentieth centuries. The Secwepemc Museum in Kamloops prominently houses a display on the memorial, which includes explanatory plaques as well as replicas

13.4 | Chief Wayne Christian *(left)* of Splatsín (Enderby) and Nlaka'pamux chief David Walkem of Spences Bridge at the ceremony on the Kamloops Indian Reserve to commemorate the 100th anniversary of the "Memorial to Sir Wilfrid Laurier," 2010.

of the staff of office, hatchet pipe, and picture of Queen Victoria that were given to the Interior chiefs on the occasion of the queen's birthday in 1865. The Laurier memorial, as authorized by all the chiefs in the nation, provided an ideological basis for the re-establishment of Shuswap gatherings during the mid-1980s. These annual gatherings of members of the whole nation, like the "festivals" described and undermined by Father Charles Grandidier, bring the nation together to renew its sense of joint culture, language, and kinship, while bringing the chiefs together to engage in dialogue. In August 2010, to mark the 100th anniversary of the Laurier memorial, the Shuswap Nation Tribal Council and the Nlaka'pamux Tribal Council hosted ceremonies to re-affirm the spirit and message of the memorial, as well as to recite it in light of its continuing role. The Shuswap Nation Tribal Council also issued a booklet that presents the text and context of the memorial.

The Laurier memorial is powerful in the sense that it was composed by our ancestors and reminds us of the history of the nineteenth century, but like any good ideological tool, it also lays out solutions to the present struggles over lands, resources, and governance that the Secwépemc nation and other Interior nations are facing. Although the memorial has become a cornerstone at public unity meetings, in presentations to governments, and in land and resource agreements, it remains to be seen whether its words are a prophetic missive from the past that will come to shape the future of the Secwépemc and surrounding nations.

Other Voices from the Early Twentieth Century: Stories about the Crown

Although the discourse of the memorial to Laurier, the memorial to Oliver, and other petitions of the time represents our people's way of asserting to government our inherent rights to the land, our sense of Indigenous nationhood, and our deplorable social and economic conditions, there were other voices questioning historical injustices, the behaviour of the representatives of the Crown, and the fate of our people. These voices were articulated within our communities, rather than to the outside, and they existed in satirical stories involving characters of the past and present. These stories existed in our communites as voices of opposition against the theft of our land. Unfortunately, the few that happened to be recorded were hardly understood as such for the longest time. However, since more than a century ago, these satirical stories have been used by our elders to give new shape to our old stories, deploying their characters and symbols to question and challenge Euro-Canadian oppression. In this process, they have enabled us to make what anthropologist Julie Cruikshank (1998, 128) has called "intellectually consistent sense of disruptive changes."

During the 1960s, linguist Aert Kuipers recorded a short story about a man named "Peteség" that was told to him by Seymour Pitel of Deadman's Creek (Skeetchestn) as one of his examples of texts that could serve as a source for linguistic analysis of Secwepemctsín.[11] This story was subsequently circulated in Secwépemc communities as part of *A Western Shuswap Reader* (Dixon, Palmantier, and Kuipers 1982) and then published in a linguistic publication of Secwépemc narratives produced by Kuipers (1989, 32), who mentioned that "only minor editorial changes were made … these include a few cases where an English word on the tape was replaced by a Shuswap one." However, when we eventually listened to the original tape recording of Seymour Pitel – a Skeetchestn elder who lived from about 1900 to 1970 – it became clear that, in his eagerness to delete English words from the text, Kuipers or his editors had changed the entire meaning of the story. Published without an interjected sentence at the end of the first line that was omitted from the written transcription, the story reads like any funny anecdote about a person, here a chief, who is duped by another person. With Pitel's interjected sentence, "That's the king he met from the Old Country, Peteség," we suddenly know that this is a story that involves not a local chief but the *king of England*. Told among Secwépemc people in their communities, the story of Peteség (pronounced "Petesá") outwitting the king of England is a story of protest, apparently composed and told by people in the middle of the Indian Rights Movement.

W7ec re Peteség, t7éyentmes te xyum te kúkwpi7.
There was a man named Peteség, who was met by the big chief.

That's the king from the Old Country [England] that Peteség met.

Yerí7 re stsúntem re Peteség, "Ṫhe7e k tskwéncwes xwexwéyt te7 ntśe7sqéxe7, xwexwéyt te7 tspenpíntu te ntśe7sqéxe7, cw7it re7 sṫaṁált, cw7it re7 kóso?"
Peteség was asked, "Where did you get all those horses, all those pinto horses, and your many cattle and pigs?"

Tsútes re Peteség, "Ctseq̓menétkwentsems ren uq̓wi ne ctsetíkens re pésellkwe. Tntsems," tsut, "ne qw7ep, m-ctsq̓mnétkwentsemses."
Peteség said, "My brother threw me in the water in the middle of the lake. He put me," he said, "in a sack and threw me in the water."

"Yerí7," tsuns, "w7ec, w7ec neri7, tskwékwen ye7éne tspenpintu te ntśe7sqexe7 te ck̓emúl̓ecws yerí7 séwllkwe, re pésellkwe."
"There," he said, "there were, there were, I took these pinto horses from the bottom of the water, the lake."

"Tqéyen re koso, sṫaṁált, xwexwéyt yerí7 pyin re tswiktc ne7éne, Kúkwpi7, tl̓u7 ri7 re tsqéyenes te séwllkwe, te ck̓múl̓ecws re séwllkwe."
"I rounded up the pigs, cows, everything that you here see now, Chief, I drove them this way out of the water, from the bottom of the lake."

Yerí7 re m-stsuntem te kúkwpi7, "Cwecuẏ, tśkénem me7 re sctsq̓mnétkwentsemc, me7 tskweném-wen tek tspenpintu tek ntśe7sqéxe7, tek sṫaṁalt ell koso tśilem me7 scw7it.s, scw7it.s te7 stskwném."
Then the chief said to him, "Come on, how about you throw me into the water, [that way] I'll get pinto horses, cows, and pigs, just as many, as many as you got."

Tsuntem te Peteség, "Exték, cwecuẏ!"
He was told by Peteség, "That's right. Okay, let's go!"

Qwetsétstem re xyum te kúkwpi7 ne7éne put ne súten te nexléẇsten, ne stsetéwst.s.
He took the chief right to the middle of the bridge.

Yerí7 tsúntem yerí7 xyum te kúkwpi7, "Cuẏ, úllcwe ne7éne te qw7ep, me7 yegíṁtsentsnes, me7 ctsq̓mnétkwentsnes!"

Then he told the big chief, "Come on, get into this sack here, I'll tie it up and throw you in the water!"

Yerí7 re m-sqwetséts es tsq̓mnétkwentem.
Then they left to threw him in the water.

Yerí7 re snecwmí7s le kúkwpi7.
And that was the end of the chief.

Seymour Pitel continues in English at the end of the story: "That's a short one. And the big chief, he couldn't come out, he couldn't come out of that sack. You know, Peteség told him a good one. That's a good little story, though."

Seymour Pitel, or "Simú" (ca. 1900 to mid-1960s), was one of the elders in the Skeetchestn community during Ron's childhood. Ron remembers that he walked with a severe limp, having been shot in the hip after he was caught in bed with another man's lady. He was well known as a lady's man. A funny story told by past elders is remembered about him. One of the ladies he was having an affair with was the lady who led the Secwépemc prayers in our church. One Eastertime, as she was leading the prayer of the stations of the cross, she made a Freudian slip, as her mind must have been on other things. Instead of beginning her prayer with "O sisi kri," she began with "O Simú," thus giving herself away. As in the stories of Sk̓elép (Coyote), the sacred and the profane were closely connected, even in our church!

Stories aside, Seymour Pitel had a connection to the Indian Rights Movement of the Secwépemc chiefs during the early part of the century. As Tessie Dillabough recalled, Pitel's grandmother Annie, who died during the 1870s or 1880s, was the daughter of Chief Louis of Kamloops, and he was thus Chief Louis's grandson. According to Tessie, Pitel's grandfather Chief Louis raised him after his mother's death. Pitel thus would have lived in Chief Louis's household during his youth and would have heard about, and witnessed, our people's Aboriginal rights and title concerns as a member of the household. In all likelihood, Chief Louis himself would have told him about the issues, rendering the Indian Rights Movement part of Pitel's historical consciousness. Tk̓emlúps knowledge keeper Jeanette Jules was told by her elders that Chief Louis had picked Pitel as his successor, but the Indian agent, invoking the Indian Act, dismissed Pitel as not quite being of legal age – something that would not have stood in the way of his succession under traditional Secwépemc law since the *tkwenm̓7íple7ten* (councillors) of the community would have provided him with protection and advice until he matured. In the end, the Indian agent installed Eli LaRue as chief, who was Chief Louis's stepson.

It is highly likely that Chief Louis himself told Seymour Pitel the story about the man named "Peteség," although it appears that this story circulated among our communities. In 1909 James Teit recorded another Peteség story as the "Story of Butcetsā′ and White-Chief," probably as told by elder Sxwéy̓lecken of Dog Creek. Of Butcetsā′, Teit (1909, 733) noted, "He is said to have been an Indian. The meaning of his name is unknown."

Rendered in Teit's (1909, 733–5) own words, the story begins, "Butcetsā′ was a lad who lived in a certain village. Far away in another country lived many people whose chief was noted for his wisdom and magic. One day Butcetsā′, who had great magical powers, told his friends that he intended to go and steal the wife of White-Chief; but his friends told him that White-Chief [said to be a *séme7*] was possessed of great wisdom and magical powers, and would certainly discover and kill them" (ibid., 733). Asking the wind for help, Butcetsā′ transforms himself into a pinto tomcat,[12] which White-Chief's wife takes in. When White-Chief leaves for a great feast and his wife refuses to go, saying she has to look after her cat, Butcetsā′ changes back to a human and induces the woman to run away with him. After White-Chief finds his wife gone, he pursues her, but Butcetsā′ changes her appearance, so her husband does not recognize her.

White-Chief subsequently marries again, and Butcetsā′ decides to steal his second wife, changing himself into a rooster. When White-Chief's wife is in her separate house while menstruating, he reveals his human form and induces her to flee with him. As in the first episode, White-Chief pursues them, but does not recognize his wife when he sees her because Butcetsā′ has changed her appearance. Following that, Butcetsā′ took the second wife to his own country, and thus he now had two wives. "He said, 'The noted White-Chief has neither wisdom nor magic.'" (Teit 1909, 734).

Butcetsā′ then contrives to steal the chief's horses. One night, he rounds them up and drives them away. When White-Chief pursues him, Butcetsā′ conjures up a European house along the trail and changes the colour of the horses to white. Again, White-Chief does not recognize his horses when he sees them. After Butcetsā′ herds them to his own country, he steals a second herd, this time transforming them into pintos. Again, the Chief does not recognize his horses. Butcetsā′ takes a third herd, changing them into black horses, and a fourth herd, changing them into buckskin-colour horses.

White-Chief, who "could not be a great chief without having plenty of horses" (Teit 1909, 734), decides to buy new horses. Butcetsā′ drives the stolen horses, still in changed colours, back to White-Chief's country and sells them back to him. When White-Chief asks him how he obtained so many horses, Butcetsā′ tells him that he found them on the bottom of the lake. In the final episode, as told by Seymour Pitel, Butcetsā′ dupes White-Chief into jumping into a sack and being thrown in the lake, where the chief subsequently drowns. At the end of the story, "Butcetsā′ drove away the horses he had sold, and joined his two wives. White-Chief's people said they were glad that he had disappeared, for he was foolish; and they elected another chief, who had more sense" (ibid., 735).[13] As Seymour Pitel revealed in his telling, White-Chief is the king of England.

Yet another such story is one that Aert Kuipers (1974, 110–16) titled "The Gambler's Son and Red-Cap," which was told by Seymour Pitel in Secwepemctsín and translated by Kuipers with the help of his Secwépemc consultants at the time. It begins,

> There was a rich man here at Deadman's Creek [Skeetchestn]. His land was large, a big plain, it was filled with his cattle, many hundred heads of cattle. He had many race-horses, much money, much cattle, many young men were working for him. There came to him, having heard of him, a great chief from across the great lake, whose name was Red-Cap.[14] He came to race against him, to make bets. The old man lost, he lost his land, he lost all his money, he lost his cattle, he was cleaned out. The old man and his wife were left with nothing at all. Rich as he was, the old man had lost all his possessions. They lived there, having lost all their belongings. So he was living there, trapping squirrels and rabbits, he was trapping them to keep alive. Well, he had a son, he called his son Tllí7sa. (Ibid., 113–14)

With the help of a pitiful colt, "a pitiful colt so hairy, with a dragging tail, pot-bellied" (Kuipers 1974, 114), Tllí7sa then challenges Red-Cap to a horserace. The latter, upon seeing the pitiful colt, thinks he can win even with a slow workhorse, but Tllí7sa wins. They continue horse racing, and Red-Cap subsequently bets the possessions he had gained from Tllí7sa's parents, riding a saddle horse, then a race-horse, and finally a white horse. Tllí7sa wins the final race and wins back his parents' money and cattle.

Then Red-Cap tells Tllí7sa, "Go way over the big lake, beyond the edge of this country, there you will cross the big lake [Atlantic Ocean], and visit me in my house there" (ibid.).

Tllí7sa sets out across the land, coming to a great prairie with tipis (the Plains), where "his grandmother" warns him, "you are on a risky errand, [going] to the big chief, risky, risky! If he defeats you, you'll die!" (ibid.).

Tllí7sa gets to the "big lake" (ocean) and crosses the water on the back of a golden eagle (our most sacred animal). The eagle warns him, "I'll tell you, you are on a dangerous errand; if you can't win against chief Red-Cap, he'll kill you. I'll tell you: He has two daughters. If you can catch the younger one and take her yellow garter [*tq̓elsxétemcen*], then you'll win" (ibid., 115).

Upon arriving on land (i.e., Europe/England), Tllí7sa sees two women who are bathing in a lake. Tllí7sa steals the younger girl's garter, apparently her source of power. She begs him to return it but eventually says, "alright, I'll help you in all the tasks my father gives you to perform. However difficult the task, I shall finish for you, if you think of me and do not forget me. If you forget me, you will suffer greatly" (ibid.).

Tllí7sa then goes to see her father, who puts him to tests. He first tells him to move the lake to another place and, in its old place, to plant grain, including oats. Tllí7sa does this with the help of the girl. Next, he is asked to clear a mountainside of trees and stones to plant crops. He again does this with the help of the girl. His third test is to sleep in a pigsty, apparently the hardest feat. Again, the girl helps him and he succeeds. Red-Cap then says, "Alright, take my youngest daughter as your wife" (ibid., 116). During a great feast, where all sorts of guests "came and looked at the clever Indian named Tllí7sa who had won against the great chief" (ibid.), the girl suggests they flee to his country.

With the father behind them making a thunderous noise as he pursues them to kill Tllí7sa, they flee on Red-Cap's white horse, which is the source of Tllí7sa's *seméc* (spirit power). As they flee with Red-Cap in pursuit, the girl takes hair from her head that she throws on the ground, and it becomes a thorn bush that entangles her father. As he pursues them again, she takes more hair from her head, which becomes ice, and Red-Cap struggles to free himself from the ice. Still hearing him in pursuit, Tllí7sa and his wife change into loons with Red-Cap shouting, "oh, now you have defeated me, Tllí7sa. Return home from here" (ibid.).

What do we make of these stories? They imagine resistance to the powers of the Crown, here presented as land-hungry and out to get Secwépemc people's possessions. Beyond that, the above story presents the Crown not so much as possessing political and economic powers but ultimately as resting on spiritual powers since the land is won from the Aboriginal people in a bet, the outcome of which in the Secwépemc way is seen as resting on the spiritual powers of the bettors. Tllí7sa is warned about the supreme spiritual power of Red-Cap. In the end, however, it is Tllí7sa's power, helped by Red-Cap's daughter, that prevails. Tllí7sa, the Aboriginal person, defeats the Crown by way of his spiritual power. In doing so, he puts to use the loon, which must have been his previously acquired *seméc* (spirit guardian power), and for his escape he uses the white horse, acquired when he vanquished Red-Cap. As we saw in chapter 11, both the loon and white horse are considered powerful spirit guardian helpers.

There is a prophetic side to this story: not coincidentally, the hero of the story is Tllí7sa, who in the ancient world had beaten the "people eaters" and dangerous powers in our country, ridding it of the monsters and powers that harm us as humans. In the above stories, Tllí7sa was brought back in name, but also in persona, to deal with new "people eaters," namely the Crown, which was leading and enabling European settlers to take Secwépemc land. In the words of Chief Basil David, addressing Prime Minister Borden in January

1912, "I come to lay before you our right to the lands and the evil treatment of the Indians received at the hands of the British Columbia Government, for the food has been stolen from the wives and the orphans of the Indians" (Indian Rights Association of British Columbia 1912).[15]

As we noted above, Teit (1909, 733–5) includes the story of Butcetsā′/Peteség among dehistoricized "mythologies." Wendy Wickwire (2005) has shown how Franz Boas's editorship of Teit's work during the early part of the twentieth century in general involved the removal of references to Interior Salish people's political and historical concerns. Teit, in contrast, throughout his activity in the Indian Rights Movement, was keenly aware of the political concerns and struggles of the Interior peoples, functioning as their "secretary," as we have seen. In additional stories he recorded from Nlaka'pamux and Okanagan storytellers during the very time he assisted the chiefs as "secretary" of the Interior Tribes and then the Allied Tribes, we see further reflections and satirical comments on political changes and events. One such narrative, quoted and discussed in chapter 2 (p. 62), involves Sk̓elép (Coyote) losing the "paper."

> Coyote once met Old One or Great Chief. Old One said, "You have used your excrements as a counselor for a very long time. However, this method is very inconvenient. Each time you desire advice, you have to defecate. Also there is danger of your excrements getting cold. I will give you a paper. Carry it with you. When you need advice, consult it." Coyote carried it in his hands for several days, but he did not like to carry anything in his hands. One day when he was defecating, or otherwise engaged, he laid it down and forgot about it. Several days later he wanted advice about something and found he did not have the paper. He went back a long way and searched for it, but could not find it. Perhaps the wind had blown it into some hidden place. Coyote had to resort to consulting his excrements again for advice.
>
> This is how Coyote lost the paper. If Coyote had not lost it, the Indians would now know writing, and the whites would not have had the opportunity to obtain written language. It was because of the foolishness of Coyote. (Teit 1937, 173)

This short story represents a reflection about the worth and value of paper, or the written word, as providing *tk̓wenm7íple7* (advice), which is the input and information that a judge and advisor to the chief gives based on understanding circumstances, knowing evidence, seeing, and even predicting. Teit (1937, 173n3) comments, "Coyote's use of his excrements for advice occurs frequently in tales of the Salishan tribes. It was one of the magical powers given to Coyote by Chief," according to the Okanagan tale "Coyote," and was perhaps our way of saying that Coyote relied on his own "bullshit." The paper, what we call *stsq̓ey̓* (laws), which also signifies the Indigenous rights that Coyote loses, comes from Old One. At least in this version of events, the loss of the paper, and thus of our rights, is all Sk̓elép's fault. However, there is another layer to Coyote as scatologist. Just as in the modern context of trickster stories we might be compelled to think of the connection between excrement and paper as involving bullshit, we need to look at the message implicit in the use of excrement in the act of giving advice, or *tk̓wenm7íple7* (counselling), which in turn guides decisions. In the Secwépemc hunting past – and still among those who are contemporary hunters on the land – it was extremely useful to have a detailed understanding of what excrement can tell us since, from the excrement of game (and humans!), we can detect what the animal ate, where it last was, what state of health it was in, and in what direction it was travelling. Far from bullshit, Coyote's scatology involves a detailed reading of nature. He (along with us) thus questions whether recordkeeping on paper in all aspects improves on scatology, itself a metaphor for experiential knowledge gathering and making sense of evidence. Skeetchestn elder Theresa Jules emphatically echoed our reluctance to rely on the authority either of paper or of the legal marking of land rights through posts on the ground:

Yerí7 re-m re7 xpé7e, le Etwal, le Lonso le xqwelténs yem.
Those were the words of your late grandfathers, Edward and Lonso [Francis Ignace's nickname].

E-m-quqw7éles Yerí7 m tsk̓elél̓nemsten:
When they talked, I listened to them:

"Don't mark it on the ground."

E newt-ekwe yerí7 me7 súk̓wentem. Me7 llgúpes, e me7 llgupéles ucw tke7 st̓am̓alt, tke7 ntsé̓7sqéxe7.
They said if the wind blows, it gets blown away. And if it gets lost, you lose your goods, your cows, your horses.

Téke mé7e re sxexé7s re ol'-timers:
See how smart the old-timers were:

"Don't mark it on the ground."

Me7 ptínesemenc Ronnie, mé7e t̓ri7 e nek̓ú7es:
Think about that, Ronnie, it's the first principle:

"Don't mark it on the ground."

In Okanagan storyteller Harry Robinson's (2005, 64–85) long story "Coyote Makes a Deal with the King of England," Coyote intervenes with the king to persuade him to make a deal. But the king doesn't fully comply; rather, "they do some, just a little [perhaps a reference to the Royal Proclamation of 1763], and he [the king] leave it alone." Many monarchs later, the Crown brings over a book, the padlocked "Black and White." Although Robinson's story resembles a "yarn," it contains the connected dots of historical events. We interpret the "Black and White" to be the *Papers Connected with the Indian Land Question* (British Columbia 1875). At the same time, Robinson also adds symbolism, regarding the "Black" as the Indians. The "White," then, refers to the settlers. On written pages, the black ink contains the messages, or the information and knowledge, whereas the empty spaces are white. Thus the Indians are the source of knowledge and information, and the settlers are blank.

Last but not least, Harry Robinson's story leads to some Indians knowing about the "Black and White" book, which exists in four copies only. By hiding the book, the colonial powers keep Indians from successfully settling the land question. As research tells us (see chapter 13), this is precisely what happened when the federal and provincial representatives of the Special Joint Committee of the Senate and House of Commons established in 1927 to determine the land question refused the Allied Tribes access to the *Papers Connected with the Indian Land Question*, thus refusing them access to evidence respecting their land claims.

In summary, what may appear to be "mere stories" contain historical references and represent reflection on, and consciousness about, past events. In Peteség's case, the Secwépemc cultural heroes of the past get back at the colonizers. In Harry Robinson's case, Coyote is connected to the unfolding history of the land question. Finally, Sk̓elép makes a reappearance, reminding us of the limited uses of paper, as opposed to the detailed reading of nature, which can lead to arguably more accurate truths than writing on paper.[16]

14 Re Stsq̓ey̓s-kucw Wel Me7 Yews

Stories from the Past, Laws and Rights for the Future

Throughout these past thirteen chapters, we have delineated 10,000 years of Secwépemc history, as told through stories from multiple vantage points that have long connected people to the land and to one another, thus shaping the way that Secwépemc Indigenous law is written on the land in stories. For hundreds of generations of Secwépemc ancestors, these stories shaped our collective consciousness that the deeds, or actions, of the past generations of people who vanquished the "people eaters," transforming energy into matter in the process, gave us our *stsq̓ey̓* (laws) and our deeds, or rights, to the land. Weaving together past and present elders' memories about the deeds of the *tellqel̓múcw* (ancient ancestors) on the land and contextualizing them with knowledge from diverse disciplines like geology, paleoecology, archaeology, and historical linguistics, and more recently with the accounts of explorers and settlers, have enabled us to show the historic veracity of Secwépemc accounts from the past. To be sure, the genocide wrought by disease from the late 1700s to the late 1800s, and even well into the twentieth century, the colonization of Secwépemc peoples' livelihoods and souls, the parsimonious policies aimed at displacing the Secwépemc from Secwepemcúl̓ecw and preventing our possession and use of the land by privileging white settlers as the only ones who could acquire legal land title, the initiatives to take the "Indian out of the child," the muting of our language, and the splitting of the nation into small chunks of bands and reserves governed by the Indian Act – all of these experiences have left their mark. As the Truth and Reconciliation Commission of Canada (2015b, 1) has called it, and as Supreme Court Justice Beverly McLachlan (quoted in Fine 2015; see also McLachlan 2015) has voiced, the outcome was nothing but "cultural genocide."

Not only are Secwépemc people confined to reserves that comprise merely 1 per cent of Secwepemcúl̓ecw, but knowledge of the past and of the ways that the histories of Secwepemcúl̓ecw lay out Secwépemc law has also become a "broken cup." Like an elaborate basket, this knowledge has been rewoven here with Secwepemctsín, our language, as the fibre both to throw light on what happened and to show how historical events created a collective consciousness among our Secwépemc ancestors of a common interconnected history, of common practices, and of common laws emerging from them. In short, the consciousness of a common history is what shaped us as the Secwépemc into a nation.

Thus, in Secwépemc elders' consciousness, Secwépemc *stsq̓ey̓* (laws) emerged out of the deeds – in the double sense of "deeds" as both "actions" and "rights" – of Sk̓elép, Qweq̓wíle, and Tllí7sa and his brothers, as derived from the ways that people long ago interacted with powerful forces in nature, with outsiders who invaded the land, and with insiders who harmed their people. Our law was subsequently shaped over hundreds of generations by interactions among the Secwépemc, who kept reminding one another of the deeds of our ancestors, the consequences of the ancestors' actions, and the lessons learned from them. Throughout the past 4,500 years or so as further experiences shaped our ancestors' judgments, they refined our law regarding how to deal with things and continued advising, or *tk̓wenm7íple7* (counselling), one another. As we have seen throughout the chapters of this book, our *stsq̓ey̓* deal with land tenure and access as held by the collective of Secwépemc for the benefit of every member of the nation. From the early days when Sk̓elép (Coyote) met the outside transformers as he sat on a rock watching them enter the land, our laws have also dealt with reciprocity of access and with mutual help and assistance between and among peoples, cemented by alliances in kinship and marriage. They articulate the ways that all beings on the land, or "resources," must be managed responsibly through respectful, reciprocal, and accountable interactions with the land, all parts of which are sentient and alive. They address one's responsibility to train and practise in order not to be *yewy̓út* (a nuisance) to one's kin and community. And they entail reciprocal relations of helping one another out in tasks as well as during times of bereavement and hardship. Thus, historically, our *stsq̓ey̓* provided a social security network long before outside government agencies imposed their own network, to the detriment of the autonomy of the Secwépemc social security network ensured by the law of reciprocity. Today, our laws still speak to the consequences of *k̓estentsút* (irresponsible behaviour), which harms the life and reputation not only of the individual but also of the entire group. They address the responsibility of appointed leaders to put the well-being of our people first, to seek counsel and advice, and to put the interests of the community and nation ahead of their own interests.

During the nineteenth century and into the twentieth, despite the overwhelming forces of settlers' invasion and colonization, Secwépemc people continued to interact based on these norms, reminding one another of them in stories, some of which became stories of resistance that dreamed about and prophesized outsmarting the *séme7* (white people) with the powers of the ancestors.

This book's woven-together narrative of Secwépemc land and law ends with events and memories of the first decades of the twentieth century. As we write this chapter, more than ninety years have lapsed since the calculated imposition of a section of the Indian Act that aimed to silence our voices of resistance against the dispossession of our lands and against the curtailment of our decision making on our lands. Throughout these past ninety years, the full brunt of the Indian residential school policy took force, literally beating the Indigenous language out of three generations of children, thus muting our stories and much of our detailed knowledge and practices of, and on, the land. The final report of the Truth and Reconciliation Commission of Canada (2015a) has alerted the Canadian public to the brutal effects of Indian residential schools, which continue to linger in our communities, but we hope that there will be a willing path from the cultural genocide and the linguicide wrought on us to reconciliation.

In the decades since the late 1920s, ranching and agriculture, logging, mining, urban sprawl, shopping malls, and golf courses have dissected Secwepemcúl̓ecw, altering the landscape and stripping the land of its resources at the cost of Secwépemc people in more ways than one. As we stated at the outset of this chapter, the Secwépemc ancestors and past elders conceived of *stsq̓ey̓* as deriving from the old stories and their markings in rock and paint, which provided evidence of our ancestors' rights to land and their rights to political, cultural, and social autonomy. More than a century after the chiefs of the Interior, conscious of their ancestral *stsq̓ey̓*, addressed their grievances in their "Memorial to Sir Wilfrid Laurier" (Chiefs of the Shuswap, Okanagan, and Couteau Tribes 1910), in their "Memorial to the Hon. Frank Oliver" (Chiefs of the Shuswap, Couteau, and Thompson Tribes et al. 1911), and in their other petitions and declarations of the time, the recognition of Aboriginal title and rights remains to be solved.

The voices of Secwépemc people of the past also speak to fighting for the greater good of the collective – the nation and the larger network of kinship. Once again using a story to make a point, they expressed their struggle for the greater good in the story about Xus, the the people-eating Qwenímeqll (Mosquito). Stories are parables: in refracting the past, they allow us not only to see it but also to see it in a new light guided by the experience of the present. In addition, stories allow us to anticipate the future, as does the story of Xus.

Qwenímeqll | Story of Mosquito

told by Ida William, recorded by Marianne Ignace, 1987, translated and transcribed by Marianne Ignace and Mona Jules

Yem ell re Qwenímeqll.
And there was Mosquito.[1]

Qelmúcw-ekwe ri7 le q̓7éses.
She was a person long time ago.

Ri7 re Qwenímeqll. Tsukw ri7 re sxwistés es íllens re mítk̓ye.
That was Mosquito. All she liked to eat was blood.

Re qelmúcw tsyem nerí7. Sexqéĺqeltemc.
There were people camping there. It was summertime.

Tsyem te qelmúcw w7ec-enke k píxmes. Tshéqen-ke.
The people camped there must have been hunting. Perhaps.

Re Qwenímeqll wikt.s re qelmúcw ṫri7 tsyem, m-tsnes ne tsk̓émwel̓cén.
Mosquito saw the people camped there, she went there in a boat.

Estíĺ-ekwe ṫri7.
She stopped there, they say.

Néses nerí7 tsyem te qelmúcw.
She went to where the people were camping.

Re qelmúcw w7ec re k̓úlmes te sxúsem.
The people were getting soapberries.

Tsúntem-ekwe re Xus,
Xus was asked,

"*Xwistéc-en ke7 s7illen tek sxúsem?*"
"Would you like to eat some soapberries?"

"*Ta7 ṫri7 re stet̓ex7ém k stsetṡelóp̓st.s.*"
"No, older people are not supposed to get bitter in the buttocks."[2]

"*Íllentiye wellenwí7emp!*" *tsúntem-ekwe.*
"Eat it yourselves!" they were told.

"*Stém̓i cú7tsem ke7 s7íllen?*"
"What else do you have to eat?"

"*Tsukw ri7 re mítk̓ye.*"
"Nothing but blood" [they said].

Ṫhénes-enke k xíĺltses re mítk̓ye te smetés re Xus.
I don't know what they did to get the blood to feed Xus.

Tsútes re tutuwíwt nerí7,

Said the boys there,

"Cwuy̓, me7 metém, t̓hé7en re sxílltem re Qwenímeqll re sqwetsqwentém pyin."
"Let's feed her, any way we can, we are going to kill the Mosquito now."

"Yéwyut."
"She is a nuisance."

Tsut-ekwe re tuwíwt,
Said one of the boys,

"Cwuy̓, me7-néns-ken t̓lu7."
"Okay, I will go there."

"Me7 kwékwectnes te tsgetsúĺecw te cteq̓méw̓els."
"I will take her boat, which is tethered to the ground."

Qwetséts-ekwe t̓lu7, m-k̓wicwenses ye7éne t̓e stsgetsús, re spéts̓en.
He went there, he untied this knot, the string.

Qwetséts.t.s-ekwe re cteq̓méw̓els. Kúpens t̓úne.
He set out her boat. He pushed it out.

Qwetséts.st.s-ekwe re cteq̓méw̓els ne setétkwe.
He set out with her boat on the river.

M-tsúntem-ekwe re Xus,
[Another boy] said to Xus,

"Xus, le7 cteq̓méw̓el m-qwetséts, t̓e m-kwewt!"
"Xus, your boat has gone and floated away!"

Cwíselc-ekwe re Xus, estkíc.
Xus ran, she fell down.

Xetéqs m-tsut-ekwe,
First, she said,

"Tsxwénte, knúncwentselmiye, tskwékwctselmiye ten cteq̓méw̓el!"
"Come here, help me, get my boat for me!"

Ta7 ks k̓elél̓mentem te tutuwíwt.
The boys didn't listen to her.

"Re newí7 me7 tskwenc re7 cteq̓mew̓el!"
"Go and get the boat yourself!"

Estkíc-ekwe, m-tupéñk.
She fell and her stomach burst.

Re Xus qwtseq.
Xus died.

Ṫ7éne tsyem te qelmúcw m-tsut-ekwe,
The people that were camped there said,

"Me7 késtem?"
"What shall we do with her?"

M-tsúnses-ekwe re sec7ítemc,
They were told by elders,

"Cwítk̓entiye, me7 pekwmíntmes re tmicw."
"Cut her up, we will scatter her throughout the land."

Xillts-ekwe. Cwítk̓entem re Qwenírneqll.
They did it that way. The Mosquito was cut up.

Áxwentmes ṫ7éne te tmicw.
She was thrown away there, on the land.

"Telrí7 te7 sw7ec yéwyut-ucw, qelmúcw re sw7ec-wes."
[The elders said,] "There, you [Mosquito] will be a nuisance for them there, wherever there are people."

In the time of the ancient transformers, cannibal beings, or *tśecélemc* (people eaters), like Xus threatened the well-being of people and communities. As she was vanquished and scattered over the earth, Xus became the myriad tiny blood-sucking insects that the Secwépemc experience, a metaphor for the many small evils that afflict the people. Although, arguably, Secwépemc physical livelihood is not as threatened as it once was, the many interests pursued at the discretion of government by resource industries suck up the trees, fish, water, land, and even lives of people. Federal and provincial government agencies live off the plight of Secwépemc poverty.

We can also deploy this story as holding a mirror up to the way that the colonizing forces of the past and present have produced the nucleation of the Secwépemc nation, the latter having become fragmented into bands, diverse tribal councils, interest groups, and First Nations service agencies. Like the once mighty mosquito, whose potent sting became a mere nuisance when she was cut up and scattered, the power of the cut-up parts of the nation are a fragment of the collective force that unity holds.

Just as we can turn to the ways that our *stsptekwll* (ancient stories) refract the consequences of our colonial history, we can turn to them for wisdom about how to heal ourselves from being divided, broken into fragments, and colonized. We thus end this book with a little-known *stsptekwll* that shows us our ancestors' conception of how our people can overcome being divided internally by uniting and sharing advice and laws of good conduct. The story of Skú7pecen (Porcupine), which works on a number of levels and has many fine nuances, begins with two groups of people separated by a mountain who are at odds with each other. In their eagerness to outdo each other, they have become *qwenqwént* (pitiful) and are suffering. Secwépemc storyteller Sxwéẏlecken told this *stsptekwll* to James Teit in about 1900. Unfortunately, Teit's (1909, 658–9) rendition of the story, retold in his own prose, was the only telling of it we had until Marianne Ignace and members of the Skeetchestn elders' Secwépemc language group – Christine Simon, Amy Slater, Garlene Dodson, Daniel Calhoun, Leona Calhoun, Julie A. Antoine, and Doris Gage – produced a Secwepemctsín version in the fall of 2015, thus reclaiming our story for the benefit of present and future generations.

Skú7pecen | Story of Porcupine

from James Teit (1909, 658–9), retranscribed by Marianne Ignace and members of the Skeetchestn elders' Secwépemc language group, 2015

Cw7it te qelmúcw tsyem-ekwe ne nek̓úl̓ecw te tmicw.
A large number of people lived together in one place, so they say.

Re Speqmíc ri7 re kúkwpi7s-ekwe.
Swan was their chief, they say.

Ne kek̓éw te t̓ecwllúl̓ecw, te nek̓wésq̓t-ekwe me7 re scwesét-kt, te tkenú7s re skwelk̓wélt, tsyémes-ekwe te t̓ícwell te qelmúcw te sts7emét.stem Ts̓í7emc.
In another faraway place, one day's journey away and beyond the snowy mountains, lived another group of people. They were called the Deer People.

Ye7éne te tmescécen lu7 re ts̓i7, re teníye, re selcwéyecen, re sxwet̓éy, re yegelécken ell re s7i7llcw.
These people included deer, moose, caribou, mountain goat, mountain sheep, and some others.

Re Tcets̓-ekwe lu7 re kúkwpi7s.
They say that their chief was Elk.

Ye-ekwe yerí7 k scmentwécws te tsq̓wétsten te m-sq̓7es.
For a long time they had been enemies.

Kwemtús re sk̓elcmentwécws, ṫri7 yem wel re kwek̓wiyúsem re s7elk̓wstsíl̓lens.
They were interfering in each other's business all the time, which is why they had a hard time putting away food.

Tecṫícwell re stk̓wenm7íple7s ell re tsutsúwet.s.
They each had a different kind of government and different ways of doing things.

Nek̓úsem relrált re sw7ecs, k̓émell re ekúsem ta7 ṫri7 k sle7s, ṫri7 yem wel kwemtús re skwek̓wiyúsems.
What one group did well the other group did poorly, which is why all of them always suffered.

Re spipyúy7e tiṫéy̓pens re tmescécen ell re tmescécen tiṫéy̓pens re spipyúy7e ṫri7 wel qwenqwént xwexwéytes.
The birds were trying to act like four-legged animals, and the four-legged animals were trying to act like birds, which is why they were all pitiful.

Re Speqmíc qwenmíns es texwentés tkenhé7e re lele7stw7écwes, es ta7es cuy̓tsem re skelcmeńtwécws.
Swan wanted to fix how they could be good to each other so that they would not interfere in one another's affairs any more.

Re Speqmíc necwentés es pálpelt.s re tsqwétsten, ṫri7 yem wel w7ec re yewsentwécwes.
Swan believed that the people were stubborn, which is why they were troublesome and were being a nuisance to one another.

Nek̓u7 te sitq̓t te m-ístkmes, le gaṫṫes re swucwt ne skwelk̓wélt, m-melk̓wílcmens re k̓wséltktens re Speqmíc.
One day in winter when the snow was deep in the mountains, Swan gathered his people together.

Nerí7 m-lexéy̓ect.s steḿi re sptínesems, m-yews re sullţímt.s swéti7 me7 nes es tsxlitens re Tcetś, swéti7 ṫri7 re sxilems me7 éyentem cw7it te sxíxlem.
And he told them what he had thought, and then asked who would go to invite Elk to come, and whoever would do that would be paid lots of dentalium.

Tsúntem te Sk̓elép, "Re ntsétswe7 me7 néns-ken." M-yews re sllecwentés re s7ícenst.s te stemstíteḿt.s, tskerniy̓ te silltśu7úẃi, ell xwexwéyt re sxixlems ell re mémles.

Coyote said to him, "I will go." Then he put on his fancy clothes, his embroidered moccasins, all his dentalia, and his necklaces.

Le estk̓lúcwes m-qwetséts re Sk̓elép, k̓émell ta7 k sqwenénș es k̓uwéțems ne xgaṫt te swuçwt. Ṫri7 yem m-tentyénmens re c7ístkteń wel tskwtek̓ re skwék̓w7es le xqílltes re k̓wséltktens.
Coyote left at sundown, but he did not want to walk in the deep snow. That is why he kept circling the underground house until sunrise when his relatives woke up.

M-séwentem te Speqmíc, "Kénem mé7e ta7 ke7 sqwetséts ey?"
Swan asked him, "How come you have not left yet?"

M-éytsentem te Sk̓elép, "M-etsxmímen ṫucw ens cwíwselc, ṫri7 wel ta7 ey ken sqwetséts te sqeltús. E r7áles me7 qwetséts-wen."
Coyote answered, "I was practising running, that's why I haven't left for the mountains yet. I will leave tonight."

E m-r7áles tspíqwstem le qwetsétses te k̓wséltktens wel re m-legúp.
In the evening, the relatives watched him until he was out of sight.

Ta7 k sq̓7es m-xp̣qenwéńses k sgeṫt7uys re swucwt, cwelpílc m-tspelq̓ílcwes, m-stsílcwes ne k̓wellk̓émts re xnicw ne ck̓emqíns re c7ístkteń.
It was not long until he found the snow too deep, so he turned around and went back, and he lay down under the ladder on the roof of the underground house.

Le xqílltes re qelmúcw m-wíktem te xexé7 re s7itcs re Sk̓elép, m-xúq̓wleqses. M-séwentmes te Speqmíc, "Kénem mé7e ta7 ke7 sqwetséts ey?"
When the people woke up, they saw that Coyote was fast asleep and snoring. Swan asked him, "Why didn't you leave yet?"

M-tsúntem te Sk̓elép, "M-etsxmímen ens cwíwselc, ṫri7 yem wel cetsétsus-ken. E r7áleses me7 qwetséts-wen."
Coyote told him, "I was practising running, and that's why I got tired. I will leave tonight."

Re Speqmíc m-séwens re k̓wséltkens swéti7 me7 exték es qwetséts.ș. Xwexwéyt re stsetsút, "Yerí7 re Skú7pecen tikwemtús re skuk̓uwétems ne skwelk̓wélt, ne geṫt te swucwt, ṫri7 yem me7 exték es qwetséts.s."
Swan asked his relatives who would be the fittest one to go. They all said, "The Porcupine always walked in the snowy mountains in the deep snow, that is why he would be the fittest one."

Ṫri7 yem m-twinélesmentem re Skú7pecen es qwetséts.
Thus they depended on Porcupine to go.

Ṫqwentés re sillts̓u7úẇis ne sítest wel re m-cwéṅwen, m-yews re syexs te qwets.
He sewed his moccasins through the night until morning, and then he dressed warm.

Le-tsek̓úl̓ecwes re tmicw m-qwetsétses.
He left at the break of dawn.

M-wíktmes te Sk̓elép m-tul̓íl̓mentem, tsúntmes, “Yúmell re ntsétswe7 ta7 ks xenwéẇen ens qwetséts, tkenhé7e me7 xillt.s ye7éne te qwenqwént, te kenkínt, te ctsetsscécen te k̓wséltkten-kt es ṫ7eks ne get̓t te swucwt?”
When Coyote saw him, he laughed at him and said, “If even I could not make it, how can this pitiful, slow, and shortlegged relative of ours make it through the deep snow?”

E r7áleses m-kitsc re Skú7pecen ne Tcets̓ re tsitcws, xexé7 re stlel̓s, stsmuxwmúxw-ekwe te scúyent ell te swucwt.
In the evening, Porcupine arrived at Elk’s house. He was very exhausted and all covered in ice and snow.

Le qw7étses re Skú7pecen, m-kectés re Tcets̓ te stél̓tsnems re Speqmíc es tsxlítens re tcets̓ méte k̓wséltkens. M-yews re sulltímcwes te stíteṅc ell te ṫéq̇ceṅ es ṫqwentés re sillts̓u7úẇis.
After Porcupine had warmed himself, he gave Elk the message from Swan and asked for sinew and an awl to sew his moccasins.

Le-wí7es re stél̓tsnem̓s, m-tsúntem te Tcets̓, “Pexyéwt me7 tégwentp-kucw re ntsétswe7 méte n-k̓wséseltkten ne tmicw-emp.”
When he was finished, Elk told him, “Tomorrow I and my people will visit you in your country.”

M-pelq̇ílc re Skú7pecen ne tmicws, m-lexéẏect.ses re Speqmíc stém̓i7 lu7 re stél̓tsnem̓s re Tcets̓.
Porcupine returned to his country, and then he told Swan what Elk’s message was.

Le yigápes re Tcets̓ méte k̓wséltktens m-tsecwmíntem, m-yews re smetéms.
When Elk and his relatives arrived, they were greeted and then they were feasted.

Le wí7es re s7íllens m-xíṫelc well re Speqmíc méte k̓wséltktens ne sxetéqst.s re Tcets̓.

After they finished eating, Swan and his relatives knelt before Elk.

Re Speqmíc m-tslexemcít.s xwexwéyt re stem re stslexméms, ell m-lexéy̓ect.s tkenhé7e me7 tscentés re stsetśecwlementwécwes.
Swan shared his wisdom with them and told them how they could fix one another.

Ṫri7 yem m-kectéses re Tcetś xwexwéyt re texpqenwéllens ell re m-tk̓wenm7íplemeńses.
This is how he gave Elk all his knowledge and his advice.

M-yews re Tcetś méte k̓wséltktens m-xíṫeḷc ne sxetéqst.s re Speqmíc ell re Tcetś m-kectés xwexwéyt re sptínesems ell re tk̓wenm7ípe7s.
Then Elk and his relatives knelt before Swan, and Elk shared all his thoughts and his advice.

Yerí7 re sxepqenwellentwécws ell ṫqwews p̓7ecws re sle7s re sxenwéllens es tsetséts.s es yecwentwécws.
And this is how they learned from one another, and they were able to look after one another.

M-yews re sp̓7e7cws re sle7s re sw7ecs, m- le7stwécw wel me7 yews, m-ta7es cúy̓tsem re stśniqwentwécws.
Then they lived much better, they were good to one another from then on, and they stopped fighting.

Yerí7 re tk̓wenm7íplemeńtwecwes wel me7 tekwemíte7.
These are the laws [advice] they gave to one another.

Re Skú7pecen m-cwe7sqleẁ te sxixnem. M-yews re sk̓úcwsentem te Sk̓elép.
And Porcupine became rich with dentalia and was much envied by Coyote.

Yerí7 re stsecwtéps!
This is the end!

This *stsptekwll* tells us of two groups of people, the Swan People and the Deer People, each in disarray. Separated by a mountain, they try to outdo each other, they copy each other – their actions harkening back to the story "Coyote and His Hosts" (see chapter 2) – and they fight each other. As a result, they both become dysfunctional and pitiful. It takes the courage of one leader, Speqmíc (Swan), the peacemaker, to humble himself in order to set out a peacemaking process. It also takes the courage of quiet and tenacious Skú7pecen (Porcupine), as opposed to vain and self-serving Sk̓elép (Coyote), to make the trip through the deep snow of the mountain that separates the two groups. As a result of the combined heroic acts of Swan's humility and Porcupine's tenacity, the two groups transcend each other's differences and dysfunctions, instead sharing wisdom, knowledge, and advice that becomes their joint law and thus enables them to be what our chiefs in the Laurier memorial called "great and good" together. In its resolution of making peace, with those of one party showing initiative by taking the risk of humbling themselves while transcending their previous animosity, the story of Porcupine also echoes the events of the Fish Lake Accord (see chapter 8).

This *stsptekwll* thus gives us powerful food for thought about the ways our ancestors conceived of overcoming differences such as those that exist today between what have become nucleated communities in our nation, which are separated and divided by "mountains" and have been distracted by the "divide and conquer" tactics of the colonizers, who tried to divide our nation and people. The advice is about how humility and tenacity allow us to come together and about the empowering results of then being able to share knowledge and give advice to one another, which in turn leads to new laws based on that exchange. Whereas our sacred *stsq̓ey̓* (laws) come from the deeds and powers of our long ago ancestors, our *tk̓wenm7íple7* – or the advice we give one another based on those ancient deeds and everything we have learned that makes us wise – sets the path for our future interactions and common laws as Secwépemc.

Finally, we come full-circle to the beginning of our story. As noted in the Introduction, since the Supreme Court of Canada has recognized Aboriginal oral histories as valid evidence of Indigenous use and occupation of lands in a series of judgments, the onus is on us to weave together these histories in order to throw light both on our presence and on our particular ways of living on our land. For the Secwépemc, this undertaking means showing, in full detail, how we lived in Secwepemcúlecw, how we enacted its management and government at the time, and how our ways were disrupted when outsiders came into our land. Rather than privileging only the visible and material signs, or "evidence," of occupation left by Secwépemc people of the past, we have relied first and foremost on the stories of our ancestors and on the recollections of our elders as presenting the original rights and deeds to our land, while using the physical evidence that has been retrieved from the land to put those stories and recollections into perspective. The physical evidence gives us clues, but our *stsptekwll* (ancient stories) and our *stsq̓ey̓* (laws), as well as their embedded *tk̓wenm7íple7* (advice we give to one another that guides our conduct), give us knowledge for understanding the past, present, and future. They not only explain the past but also give us visions for the future. In this book, to make them accessible and to make them heard, we have turned the oral histories and stories of past generations of Secwépemc people into written words. However, we hope that this way of commemorating them will inspire present and future generations of Secwépemc to learn them, memorize them, and tell them to one another and the next generation in the spirit of the oral tellings of the past. For all others, we hope that the stories and knowledge we have presented, never complete, have provided more than a fleeting glimpse at the depth, meaning, and wisdom that they have entailed for generations of Secwépemc people.

Yerí7 re cwteps-kucw re slexéy̓ems wel me7 penhé7e. And here we finish our telling until another time.

Notes

ACKNOWLEDGMENTS

1 We share the concern of Sto:lo knowledge keeper and elder Naxaxalhts'i (Albert [Sonny] McHalsie) over missed opportunities when Sto:lo knowledge, as recorded by an outside linguist and amateur ethnographer, has been transmitted selectively and according to a specific discipline and inclination (Naxaxalhts'i 2007). This is not to say that we may not have missed opportunities to ask the "right" questions – those that would have invited the elders and knowledge keepers to further clarify words and to explain meanings, contexts, and connections regarding the stories they knew. Fortunately, we have had many opportunities to revisit stories and pieces of information with elders, thus continually mending the "broken cup" of knowledge.

CHAPTER ONE

The Secwepemctsín title of this chapter literally means "and here we start."

1 Stét̓emc is the Secwépemc way of saying St'at'imc, what the Fraser River Lillooet people call themselves. Unlike St'at'imcets, the Lillooet language, the Secwépemc language does not allow more than one glottalized consonant per word, so we simplify it to Stét̓emc.
2 Although the term *tś̓wen* is St'at'imc rather than Secwépemc, Tśwén̓emc ("dried fish people") is the term we Secwépemc use for the Syilx (Okanagan) people.
3 As we wrote this book, we adapted and rethought the terminologies we have in Canada for Indigenous peoples. The Canadian Constitution (sections 35.1 and 35.2) uses "Aboriginal" as a term for the "Indian, Inuit and Métis peoples of Canada." On the international scene, the term "Indigenous" has gained prominency, causing Indian and Northern Affairs Canada (INAC) to be renamed, while keeping the same acronym, Indigenous and Northern Affairs Canada. Throughout this book, we quote court decisions and legal documents according to the terms they employ, which, depending on time and context, are "Indian," "First Nation," or "Aboriginal," but we use both "Aboriginal" and "Indigenous" in our own writing.
4 For more than a decade starting in the mid-1900s, the Canadian Crown's position regarding the lack of evidentiary validity and reliability of Aboriginal oral narratives was advanced through the Crown's chief expert witness, Alexander von Gernet (1996, 2000). Bruce G. Miller (2011, xxxvi) provides an incisive critique of

what he calls "the Crown theory of oral narratives," based on a detailed analysis of von Gernet's methodology and detailed checking of von Gernet's mishandling of sources (ibid., ch. 4).

5 M. Ignace (1998), M. Ignace and R. Ignace (2013), and Hudson and M. Ignace (2013) provide analyses and overviews of Secwépemc and Plateau peoples' cultures, histories, and social organization.

6 For writings on James Teit's contribution to the ethnography of Plateau First Nations and his involvement in the Indian Rights Movement, see Wickwire (1988, 1998, 2001).

7 We think that this name derives from the Secwépemc word *sxwlécken* (buck, male deer). As is common in kinship terms and personal names, the term as a name involves a shift in stress to the first syllable and a glottalization of the vowel or resonant (here the *l̓*) that follows it.

8 In addition to some thirty narratives elicited from these storytellers, Kuipers (1989, 126ff) includes a set of short "Aesops Fables" about animals in Secwépemc country: the wolf, fox, coyote, crane, raven, grizzly bear, rabbit, and frog. Of these fables, he states that the versions in Eastern and Western Secwepemctsín were based on English-language texts prepared by Kuipers himself and then translated by Mary Palmantier and Cindy Belknap (ibid., 134–45). However, elder Nellie Taylor credited her telling of the Ant and Grasshopper story (see chapter 9) to her maternal great-grandmother, Agathe Llecwpusétkwe of Skeetchestn, who was born in the 1830s.

9 For an eloquent discussion of Indigenous experience, empiricism, spirituality, and story, see also Toelken (2003, ch. 6).

10 In this book, we use the terms "Aboriginal nations" and "Indigenous nations," as well as "Aboriginal peoples or people" and "Indigenous peoples or people," interchangeably (see note 3, above). The term "Aboriginal nations" is defined in the report of the Royal Commission on Aboriginal Peoples (1996a, iii) as a "sizeable body of Aboriginal People with a shared sense of national identity that constitutes the predominant population in a certain territory or collection of territories." This definition was subsequently picked up by the Supreme Court of Canada in the 1997 *Delgamuukw* judgment. "Aboriginal," of course, also has a continuing legal validity in section 35 of the Canadian Constitution, which speaks to the rights of the "Aboriginal peoples of Canada," defined as "Indian, Inuit and Métis." However, section 35 was legislated without the participation of Indigenous peoples, and thus, at least for some, the term "Aboriginal peoples" is laden with colonial impact. In contrast, with the growing weight that the *United Nations Declaration on the Rights of Indigenous Peoples* (2008) has had, especially since Canada adopted it in principle in 2011, the term "Indigenous" has gained weight. In addition, the term "Aboriginal peoples or people" appears to be losing ground to the term "Indigenous peoples or people." Each one bears the burden of history, misnomers, and government- or court-guided attempts to do better.

CHAPTER TWO

1 Teit (1909, 595) uses the term "cannibal" for what elder Ike Willard termed *tśecélemc* (people eater) (quoted in Bouchard and Kennedy 2002, 78n54). Some of them appeared to people in the shape of powerful animals that killed humans, and others could shapeshift.

2 For accounts of the paleoecology of the Southern Interior of British Columbia, see, for example, Hebda (1982, 1995), Mathewes (1985), Mathewes and King (1989), Mathewes and Pellatt (2000), and Walker and Pellatt (2001).

3 *T7íweltk* means "upriver" but also refers to "up the mountain" in altitude. It is the opposite of *wutémtk* (downstream or areas downriver) (see Kuipers 2002). *Wutémtk*, of course, is also the direction that the Salish immigrants, the Wutémtkemc ("downriver people"), came from. *T7íweltk* thus identifies the ancient country of the Coyote people. Table 7.2 provides a detailed listing of Secwépemc locational and directional terms.

4 For geological research on the glacial lake history of the Southern Interior, see Fulton (1969), Johnsen (2004), and Johnsen and Brennand (2004, 2006).

5 For information on Gore Creek Man, see Cybulski et al. (1981). Based on the principle that the isotopes of carbon ingested from marine (ocean) protein can be compared with those ingested from terrestrial (land) protein, the measurement of carbon isotopes in animal and human bones gives information about the portion of marine protein versus land protein that an animal or human ate during its lifetime. Since salmon would have been the single source of marine protein ingested by people on the Plateau during prehistoric times, this method is a useful way to find out about the percentage of protein that past Plateau people derived from salmon as opposed to other fish and land animals. Among other sources, Nancy Lovell and colleagues (1986) explain the methods and results of this kind of analysis. See also the boxed text "Salmon in the Prehistoric Diet" in chapter 5.

6 Recent analysis of the mitochondrial genomes of thirty-one unrelated Secwépemc individuals (Malhi et al. 2010) confirms "high nucleotide diversity" among these samples compared with Inuit and Alaskan Athapascan populations; in addition, among the thirty-one samples was one instance of a haplotype C4c shared with a haplotype sample from an Ijka individual of South America. Ripan Malhi and colleagues (ibid., 497) suggest, "The estimated coalescence date for the two mitochondrial genomes that belong to haplogroup C4c is 18,440 +/- 6,520 years before present (ybp). This date suggests an early split of the Shuswap and Ijka mitochondrial genomes and the early date combined with the large geographic distance between the Shuswap and Ijka confirms haplotype C4c as a founding haplotype in the Americas." They assign another sample to haplogroup C1d, suggesting a coalescence date of 15,210 years ago. Although this investigation needs more sampling and sequencing data, their data affirm the genetic diversity of the Secwépemc population, along with substantial time depth.

7 Glottochronology is a linguistic method of dating the time of split between two languages of the same stock based on the lexicostatistical measuring of the degree of divergence between basic word lists of the languages. Glottochronology cannot determine the exact time or earliest existence of a language family; it can determine only the sequence in which languages split from one another and estimate roughly how many years ago languages that are related on the basis of cognates split from one another. A problem is that, unlike the half-life of atoms, this rate of splitting or dispersal is by no means constant but is subject to social, political, environmental, and economic processes that cannot be predicted and do not occur at an even rate. A more integrated approach is to compare linguistic data with dated archaeological information, and even with other scientific information, like paleoecological data and timelines – an approach that we take in this chapter, with further focus on archaeological data presented in chapter 3.

8 M. Dale Kinkade and colleagues (1998, 68) note that they consider Swadesh's figures of 55 to 49 centuries ago for the Coast-Interior split and 45 centuries ago for the beginning of Interior Salish divergence as "a period that now seems too long." They do also note, however, that "these figures might give maximum possible dates for the beginning of the Interior Salish expansion" (ibid.). However, as we see, triangulated with other data, Swadesh's and Elmendorf's glottochronological estimates of the time of split or divergence of Coast and Interior Salish quite closely match the data about the nature and timeline of the Coast Salish influence on the Interior peoples that we now have from archaeology, paleoecology, and genetics, as well as from a rereading of Interior Salish oral traditions as history rather than myth. Thus, if triangulated with nonlinguistic data, glottochronological information can help us to verify dates and timelines in history, just as Kinkade's (1990, 1991) comparative studies of plant and animal terms have shed light on the location of the Salishan "homeland."

9 In his 1937 ethnography of the Flathead, Harry Holbert Turney-High mentioned peoples whom "the Kalispel and the Flathead claim to have inhabited the country before their arrival" (quoted in Kinkade et al. 1998, 68).

10 Fragments of Secwépemc and Nlaka'pamux oral traditions about the origin of the different languages in the Interior give few clues, perhaps for lack of ethnographers having asked the right questions. According to Secwépemc information, Old One, the "Chief of the ancient world," who had sent Coyote and had then come back to finish off some of his work, "led the different tribes into the countries which they now inhabit, and gave them the languages they were to speak" (Teit 1909, 596). Other short accounts about the "dispersion of tribes and origin of languages" recorded by Teit (1912a, 400–1) from Nlaka'pamux people transpose the dispersal of languages onto a plot that appears to be inspired in part by Old Testament stories and in part by nineteenth-century prophet narratives: people from the Lytton area get scattered over the land and develop different languages after failing to find the trail to the spirit world.

11 The Interior Salish languages, but not Coast Salish, all share cognates of the term for "Coyote." The Secwépemc call him Sk̓elép or alternately Sek̓lép, the Nlaka'pamux call him Snk'yep, the St'at'imc (Lillooet) call him Snk'yap, and the Syilx (Okanagan) call him Snk'lip (see chapter 4). Closely related to these terms are those used for "Coyote" in other Southern Interior Salish languages (see Kuipers 2002, 40). Aert Kuipers (ibid.) reconstructs "Sk̓lep" as the Proto-Salish form. Interestingly, Kuipers (ibid., 70) lists the Proto–Coast Salish word for "big canine or big feline" as *sṁγaw*, with the Proto-Salish "gamma" rather than the Secwepemctsín letter *g* standing for the throat or pharyngeal sound. In Interior Salish languages, including Secwepemctsín, the word transcribed as *semreẇ* means "lynx" and does not refer to big canines but to a particular feline. Okanagan storyteller Harry Robinson (1989, 55) says that Shimiyew (apparently a derivative of *semreẇ*) was the ancient name of Coyote before he received his powers from Old One, the Creator, and became Snk'lip.

12 These are the Nlaka'pamux near the mouth of the Nicola River area.

13 Jesus Garcia's ranch eventually became part of the town of Merritt.

14 The northern boundary of Secwepemcúlecw, when Europeans came into the country (see chapter 8), comprised the upper reaches of the Fraser River in the area from McBride to Teit Jaune Cache, the upper North Thompson River watershed, and the upper Columbia River watershed, which was accessed through trails

and canoe portages near Tum Tum Lake and which extended to Boat Encampment on the Columbia. In all likelihood, Teit's consultants described this passage from the upper Fraser and upper North Thompson watersheds into the Columbia. Teit did not visit this area while he conducted his research.

15 In Boas's (2002, 61) and Teit's (1909, 644) versions, Tllí7sa was the oldest of four brothers. However, Louisa Basil refers to three brothers and to the rock where they were frozen into stone as including three pillars (see below). The fourth "brother" is Q̓welálst, the brother or nephew who catches up to them near Hat Creek and who survives to tell about it. In all accounts, the brothers set out to vanquish powerful beings described in English as "cannibals" (Teit 1909, 595), or more aptly "people eaters," derived from the Secwépemc term *tśecélemc*, provided by elder Ike Willard (quoted in Bouchard and Kennedy 2002, 78n54). These "people eaters" were usually in animal shape and lived in prominent places throughout Secwépemc territory, there to kill or hurt humans. The brothers' mother or aunt alerts them to the people eaters' locations and advises them on how to vanquish the people eaters, also doctoring them with medicine. In Boas's (1895b, 2002) account, Tllí7sa himself is only partially doused with her medicine and becomes "transformed into a dog." However, it seems like the intent of the *stsptekwll* is to indicate that he becomes a *tellítśe7* (shapeshifter). Throughout the brothers' journey, he changes between dog shape and human shape as he leads the brothers in overcoming the dangerous powerful beings, although his brothers, rather than he himself, benefit from the rewards; indeed, most often they have consumed the meat of the animal that Tllí7sa has just vanquished by the time he is able to come to the scene. The Tsilhqot'in (Pesxíxlemc or Pesxíxnemc) story of Lhin Desch'osh includes many elements of the Secwépemc story of Tllí7sa but is uniquely centred in Tsilhqot'in territory, referring to its landmarks, geography, resources, and social relationships.

16 In Teit's (1909, 644–50) version, the person identified as "Kwelaa'llst" (Q̓welálst) was sent by the three brothers' mother or aunt to warn his brothers about Chipmunk, whom they would encounter near the end of their journey. Ike Willard pronounced his name as Q̓welálst ("biscuitroot rock," *Lomatium macrocarpum*) in the audio-recording that forms the basis of Bouchard and Kennedy (1979, 3). Teit (1909, 644n5) notes that in the North Thompson version, this character's name is "Iukema'llst or Iukemene'llst," likely his rendition of Gayeqenélst ("fernleaf biscuitroot rock," *Lomatium dissectum*). This difference in name is evidently connected to the fact that only *L. dissectum*, not *L. macrocarpum*, grows along the North Thompson River. Boas's (1895b, 2002) version identifies the nephew as Tq̓wemnélst ("rocks were thrown at him"), the latter also mentioned by Ike Willard and transcribed by Bouchard and Kennedy (1979, 3) as "T-qum-NALST," who is referred to as one of Tllí7sa's brothers. It is also possible that Q̓welálst took the name Tq̓wemnélst after Tllí7sa and his brothers threw rocks at him near the junction of Hat Creek and the Bonaparte River. Given the consistency in events and places between George M. Dawson's (1891) Q̓wele7ílt text and Teit's and Boas's Tllí7sa texts, it is also possible that the Q̓wele7ílt version of the text is telling of the same events as the Tllí7sa version but from the point of view of the nephew, who, after all, survived.

17 Skeetchestn elders reconstructed "Tllí7sa" as a shortening of the root *tell* for "change appearance" plus the lexical suffix *-sa*, a contraction (or possibly mistranscription) of *-ítśe7* (shortened to *-tśe7* given the stress on the first syllable)

for "skin, covering," the name thus meaning something like "shapeshifter." The same root, *t(e)ll*, also exists in the term *tellqelmúcw* ("long ago ancestors, transformers"), as in the title of this chapter. This term was attested by the late Mary Thomas to mean, "long ago ancestors."

18 The symbolism and meaning of the rattlesnake woman encounter and subsequent pregnancy are hauntingly portrayed in the "Seated Human Figure Bowl with Rattlesnakes" (Duff 1975, image 30). Although found in Victoria, this bowl was identified as having an Interior origin. Another seated human figure bowl from Tk̓emlúps (ibid., image 57), taken from an Indian burial ground, probably by Harlan Smith, is somewhat similar. Wilson Duff (ibid., 177) notes, "According to [Charles] Hill-Tout, this bowl was said by the Indians to have been used in women's puberty ceremonies. The sitting figure is said to represent a woman giving birth to a chid. The depression 'held the sacred water with which the shaman sprinkled the girl on her return from retirement in the woods.' A snake extends down the back." With these bowls dating back 2,000 years and more, it appears that there was a symbolic association between rattlesnakes and women's fertility.

19 The place called Pelltšegtín interestingly marks the eastern boundary of rattlesnake habitat in the area. Here, the bunchgrass and sagebrush terrain very rapidly transitions into moister grasslands interspersed with ponderosa pines and other vegetation.

20 Teit's (1909, 645n3) account places this episode "on the north side of Kamloops Lake," west of the confluence of the North and South Thompson Rivers, although Teit also notes that the Bonaparte Shuswap said the incident happened in the Arrowstone Hills above Cache Creek. Boas (1895b, 2) places it "above" Kamloops. Given the direction of the brothers' travel, it appears that their procurement of arrow stone from the grizzly bear sisters in the hills not far from the confluence references a place that is different from the well-known and documented basalt deposit in Arrowstone Hills near Cache Creek. Elder Clarence Jules Sr of Tk̓emlúps identified this place as being "near Barnhartvale," some 15 kilometres east of the confluence of the North and South Thompson Rivers.

21 Elder Chris Donald of Simpcw identified this place by its Secwépemc name and pointed to its location on the east side of the North Thompson River near Little Fort. He remembered that the place name commemorated a story involving two goat women.

22 One of the accounts of the Tllí7sa story at Cherry Creek says that Tllí7sa uses a shield of mica to defend himself. In the many thousands of years that they lived in the homeland, the Secwépemc ancestors obviously learned about minerals and their properties. Mica shows up as a shield in various transformer stories. The Western science of mica tells us that it indeed is a shield element that can keep different kinds of conductors apart.

23 The "tobacco tree" has been identified as the native species *Nicotiana attenuata* (Turner 1997, 176ff; Turner and Taylor 1972), which apparently grew in the Interior and was used by Aboriginal peoples (see also Teit 1909, 574), although to our knowledge no specimens were collected in the late 1800s. However, *Nicotiana attenuata* is a herbacious plant rather than a tree, so we think that the "tobacco tree," instead, is sumac, identified by Dog Creek elder Lilly Harry as *smenc* ("our real tobacco tree"). The four "hoodoos" on the east slope of Deadman's Creek

Valley near the base of Sk̓empél̓ecwqen, which in turn are the steep cliffs that mark the way to Pesmémenc, continue to bear witness to the brothers' presence in the valley. They represent four brothers. But the people in the Deadman's Creek Valley have largely forgotten the story and its connection to this landscape as reconstructed here.

24 According to Teit (1909), this incident occurred near "Doc English's ranch" in the Bonaparte Valley. The rock formation represents a bighorn ram with a dog barking at it, still visible about 500 metres south of the intersection of Highways 1 and 97 at Cache Creek.

25 The boulders at the bottom of the ridge are still visible just south of the junction of Highways 97 and 99, east of Hat Creek Ranch, although some of them were apparently removed when Highway 97 was widened some decades ago.

26 Kíkste7 of High Bar (Qʷiqwíyq̓wiyt) was a friend and contemporary of Louisa Basil.

27 Louisa Basil also had brief memories of additional episodes, including ones involving the brothers rolling rocks down on Q̓welálst, the Beaver at the Chasm, the Eagle at Marble Canyon, and the Rabbit.

28 This is probably Teit's attempt at writing "Senxwéxwlecwemc," from "Senxwéxwlecw," one of the terms for Coyote (see below).

29 According to the late Dr Mary Thomas and other elders, the term *tellqel̓múcw* (the root *tell* for "change appearance" plus *qel̓múcw* for "people who are able to do that") references ancient ancestors, more precisely the ancient "transformers" or "shapeshifters" who lived a long time ago. Teit (1909, 595) uses the term "spetakuł" (*stsptekwll? stsptekwle?*) to refer to "the people who inhabited the earth during [the mythological age and] partook of the characteristics of both men and animals," whereas Aert Kuipers's (1983) Secwépemc dictionary glosses *stsptekwll* as "myth, legend," "to tell a myth" – although the verb usually adds the intransitive suffix, producing the term *(ts)ptékwllem*. Since Secwépemc morphology in personal names suggests that the suffix *-(e)le* is a person suffix, often used in names that honour the deeds of a person, with *-ll* acting as a perpetual marker for nonhuman life forms, we use *stsptekwll* for "story" or "oral history" and *stsptékwle* for the "ancient storied beings," or the "transformers." In this and subsequent chapters, we use *tellqel̓múcw* and *stsptékwle* interchangeably to refer to the ancient people as "transformers" who developed the skills of visioning and shapeshifting through the *étsxem* (spirit guardian quest) and through being doctored by their own elders.

30 See http://legal-dictionary.thefreedictionary.com/nuisance.

31 The Secwépemc share many of these *stsptekwll* with the Nlaka'pamux (Egesdal, Thompson, and Jimmie 2011; Teit 1898, 1912a, 1937) and to a lesser degree with the Syilx (Okanagan) and St'at'imc (Lillooet) (Teit 1912b, 1917a, 1917b), suggesting, as we noted, their antiquity as preceeding the split between Secwepemctsín and Nlaka'pamuxcin, which was accompanied by continuing interactions, intermarriage, and knowledge exchange.

32 In a bit of word play, Andie Diane Palmer (personal communication, 2008), noting a typographical error in Ron Ignace's (2008) doctoral dissertation, also suggests that underlying the scatology was the eschatology that Sk̓elép re-embraced!

33 The names of the animal beings in this *stsptekwll* include the lexical suffix *-stemt*, *-stim̓t*, or *-stem̓t*, which still exists in reduplicated form in the Secwépemc word

stemstitemt (items of clothing). We believe it references that the animals in the stories are conceived of as human-like, sentient beings on the inside but dressed in the respective "clothing" of the characters they inhabit: Grizzly, Salmon, Beaver, and Kingfisher. The lexical suffix *-stemt*, *-stim̓t*, or *-stem̓t* also appears in personal names for people, where it implies the same connection between human sentience, animal characteristics, and appearance by way of the "clothing" or "dressing" that the name bearer has obtained, likely through spirit guardian questing (see chapter 11).

CHAPTER THREE

The Secwepemctsín title of this chapter literally means "the activities [or arguably, 'culture'] of our ancestors long time ago." The core part of this chapter was written by Mike K. Rousseau. Marianne Ignace wrote the introductory part about the history of Secwépemc archaeology and the conclusion, as well as co-editing the chapter with Rousseau.

1 For detailed articles on Indigenous peoples and archaeology, see also Murray (2011), Nicholas (2008), and Watkins (2005).
2 For a detailed assessment of the work of the Jesup North Pacific Expedition, see Krupnik and Fitzhugh (2001). For a discussion of Harlan Smith's work, see C. Carlson (2005) and Thom (2001).
3 This passage is quoted in Mathé and Miller (2001, 132), based on a Boas lecture given on 16 January 1897 to the British Association for the Advancement of Science. If the date is correct, it would have preceeded Boas's initial field season in the Interior in 1897. Since additionally there is no actual record of Boas having accompanied Smith to Kamloops in 1897, Boas's message to Chief Louis must have been communicated in a letter, likely translated by Father Le Jeune, whose role as intermediary Smith (1900) did not recognize in his publication on Thompson River archaeology.
4 The exhibit was "Drawing Shadows to Stone" (see Kendall, Mathé, and Miller 1997). The curator-researchers took time to visit the Secwepemc Museum and to consult the authors of this book, among others. On a separate note, the anthropometric data from the Jesup North Pacific Expedition show that measurements were by far most frequently obtained from the Shuswap, especially compared with measurements obtained from the Coast Salish, whose leaders and members saw no compelling cultural, let alone political, reason to participate.
5 As we noted in chapter 2, the remains of Gore Creek Man and a number of other human remains recovered during various archaeological projects that had been held in storage at the Royal British Columbia Museum were returned to Secwépemc communities in the late 1980s. Throughout Secwepemcúl̓ecw, there continue to be disputes over human remains found during construction and development projects.
6 The important Supreme Court of Canada decisions, some of which we referred to in the Introduction, include *Delgamuukw v. British Columbia* (1997), *Haida Nation v. British Columbia (Minister of Forests)* (2004), *Taku River Tlingit First Nation v. British Columbia (Project Assessment Director)* (2004), and *Tsilhqot'in v. British Columbia* (2014).

7 For a detailed discussion of the history of archaeology, specifically archaeology aimed at cultural resource management, during the past four decades, as well as a discussion of the emerging field of Indigenous heritage stewardship management in the Interior, see Klassen (2013).

8 Marianne Ignace was the academic coordinator of this program for twenty-three years and worked with the archaeology and anthropology departments in hiring Nicholas, who led a unique and successful archaeology field school for some fifteen years. Chief Ron Ignace functioned as its co-chair for more than fifteen years. Sadly, due to a perfect storm that included Thompson Rivers University in Kamloops wanting to be the "University of Choice for aboriginal students" (see http://www.tru.ca/aboriginaleducation.html), Simon Fraser University (SFU) declining to enforce its presence at Tk̓emlúps (Kamloops), and the Kamloops Band declining to commit a previously promised building to the SFU-Kamloops partnership, the program was shut down in late December 2010. This program graduated 450 mostly Indigenous students with degrees, certificates, and diplomas.

9 The archaeological "Coast Salish incursion model" was further developed by Arnoud Stryd and Mike K. Rousseau (1996) independently of the "historical linguistics model," which was initially presented by Wayne Suttles and William Elmendorf (1963) (see chapter 2) and was subsequently verified by M. Dale Kinkade (1991). The archaeological model at the time also did not consider oral history evidence, as does chapter 2 of this book. Interestingly, with the help of Harlan Smith's archaeological work, Franz Boas hoped to prove an Interior Salish to Coast Salish incursion model on the basis of skull types at the Eburne (Marpole) site on the Musqueam Reserve, which, however, he never achieved through data (see Thom 2001).

10 In his Nlaka'pamux ethnographies Teit (1900, 175; 1906) provided additional population data for the Interior Plateau, estimating the 1850 Nlaka'pamux population at 5,000 and the Lillooet (St'at'imc) population at 4,000.

11 For detailed information on Keatley Creek, see Hayden (1992, 1997, 2000a, 2000b). Teit (1909, 457–66), particularly in his footnotes, provides some information about population losses in many of the prehistoric Secwépemc villages, especially those of the Fraser Canyon division, caused by the 1862–63 smallpox epidemic.

12 For a brief description of the site, see Hall and Fladmark (1969).

13 Palmer (1975a, 204) provided an inaccurate estimate of the area of Secwepemcúlecw. Based on Teit's (1909) map, he estimated it at 70,000 square miles, or 180,000 square kilometres. Based on geographic information system (GIS) calculations, the area circumscribed by Teit's map is about 60,000 square miles, or 156,000 square kilometres. As chapter 8 shows, along with our map of Secwépemc territory (see fig. 1.1), there are also fairly large areas of overlapping use with neighbouring Indigenous nations.

CHAPTER FOUR

1 For linguistic works on the Secwépemc language, see Gardiner (1993), Gibson (1973), and Kuipers (1974, 1989), as well as the many technical papers on the structure of Secwepemctsín and neighbouring Plateau and Salish languages produced since 1967 by presenters at the annual International Conference on Salish and Neighbouring Languages, available at http://www.linguistics.ubc.ca/icsnl. The

history and structure of the Salish language family are explained in Czaykowska-Higgins and Kinkade (1998) and P.D. Kroeber (1999). On intellectual property and cultural heritage issues around Secwepemctsín and other First Nations languages, see M. Ignace and R. Ignace (2008).

2 The connection between language, thought/cognition, and culture has been poignantly stated and expressed by Indigenous peoples, including language advocates, elders, speakers, and linguists in Canada and British Columbia (e.g., Assembly of First Nations 1992; Canada, Department of Canadian Heritage 2005; Crystal 2000; Hinton and Hale 2001; and Romaine and Nettle 2000).

3 Based not only on intuition but also on many generations of experience and knowledge exchange, Indigenous-language speakers tend to be firmly on the side of perceiving their language(s) as deeply connected to their culture and as embedding knowledge and experience on the land shaped by the generations before them. The European discourse about the connection between language, culture, thought, and reality reaches back to the nineteenth century, and it was Franz Boas's and Edward Sapir's research with North American Indigenous languages that led to further stipulation about the connection between language and culture, culminating in the "Sapir-Whorf hypothesis," formulated by Sapir's student Benjamin Lee Whorf, which holds that the structure of a language affects the ways that its speakers conceptualize thought (linguistic relativism). Although it fell out of favour during the age of linguists that focused on the universal nature of human language (1960s–80s), the past twenty years have seen a resurgence of cognitive psychology and cognitive linguistics research in this field (e.g., Boroditsky 2011; Evans 2010; Gumperz and Levinson 1996; Levinson 2003; and Lucy 1992a, 1992b).

4 Although the terms look like they are not cognates, a detailed etymological and ethnoecological investigation of "Coyote" in northwestern languages might lead us to interesting results, perhaps in the end yielding unexpected cognates and historical relationships. Nancy J. Turner (2014) has provided interesting insights into plant terms for many dozens of languages throughout the Pacific Northwest. Such analysis can, and should certainly be, carried out for animal terms.

5 M. Dale Kinkade (1990, 1991) has suggested an Interior rather than coastal homeland, as well as an Interior migration route for Salish-speaking peoples into the Bella Coola Valley rather than a move directly up the central coast (see also Kinkade et al. 1998).

6 See Le Jeune and Poser (2011). The French manuscript, reviewed by us prior to William J. Poser's translation, is also in part cited in Dionne (1947).

7 The late Les William and Louis Matthew (personal communication, 1997) remembered accidentally stumbling upon an attic room at Kamloops Indian Residential School during their stay there in the late 1930s that held "stacks and stacks" of shorthand books and documents. They remembered that, subsequently, the priests must have burnt them because they never saw them again. Today, very few originals of Le Jeune's *Shushwap Manual, or Prayers, Hymns and Catechism, in Shushwap* (1906) remain in circulation and are rare collector items. In recent years, the University of Saskatchewan Library has digitized the *Kamloops Wawa*, thus making it accessible to present Indigenous and non-Indigenous scholars (see http://iportal.usask.ca).

8 When he was a doctoral student at the University of Victoria, David Robertson (2007) provided Marianne Ignace a manuscript transcription of Secwepemctsín shorthand writings from the *Kamloops Wawa*. Its analysis is forthcoming.

9 Some linguists may argue that reduplication involves grammaticalization, whereby consonant reduplication in conjunction with first-person singular affixation has lost its lexical function (i.e., diminuitive denotes humble speech). In describing consonant reduplication, Western Secwepemctsín speakers consistently connected it to socially correct, humble speech behaviour. Kuipers (1974, 38) reported an absence of first-person singular consonant reduplication among speakers in Skeetchestn and Tk̓emlúps, yet this absence is not noted among present elders/speakers, nor was it observed by them among their own ancestors' speech. Nonetheless, Kuipers's recordings of stories by Skeetchestn elders Charlie Draney and Seymour Pitel do show some instances where first-person consonant reduplication does not occur. It is possible that nonreduplicated first-person marking was a feature of narrative but not of conversation, the latter not recorded by Kuipers.

10 A preliminary analysis of evidential marking throughout handed-down narratives of the *stsptekwll* (ancient stories) and *slexéy̓em* (experienced stories) genres as presented throughout this book shows that not every sentence in such narratives is marked with the hearsay, or reportative, evidential suffix *-ekwe*. Instead, both kinds of narratives usually include an initial proposition marked with *-ekwe*, which identifies the narrative as handed-down, and then tend to reinsert the reportative evidential when new topics are introduced or when emphasizing the reported nature of events. The suffix *-enke* (knowledge according to physical evidence) is entirely predictable, for wherever there is mention of an event that has left a physical mark in the landscape, *-enke* is used. See, for example, Louisa Basil's narrative of Tllí7sa and his brothers in chapter 2.

11 For a detailed linguistic study of Salish lexical suffixes, see Hinkson (1999).

12 This chapter gives only a brief glimpse into Secwepemctsín grammatical and lexical categories, written from a nontechnical perspective. Linguist Laurence Thompson (1979, 1985) first proposed the existence of an "out of control" system in Salish, specifically Interior Salish, which not only exists in a variety of verbal roots but also exists in suffixes, through reduplication, and through other grammatical devices, including modality (see H. Davis, Matthewson, and Rullmann 2009; Demirdache 1997; and Jacobs 2011). At this time, it has been explored linguistically for St'at'imcets and Squamish but not for Secwepemctsín, although such categories exist in the language.

13 For accounts and testimony of how Indian residential schools, particularly in Kamloops and Williams Lake, brought about cultural and language loss, see Furniss (1992), Haig-Brown (1988), Jack (2006), Sellars (2013), and Sterling (1992).

14 Figures from the mid-1990s derive from a peer fluency assessment carried out by fluent speakers within seven southern communities (M. Ignace 1995b). An assessment of fluent speakers by Nathan Matthew (1999) expanded the data to some of the Northern Secwépemc communities, with similar results. The First Peoples' Cultural Council (2014, 6) reports 4.08 per cent of the Secwépemc population as fluent, 9.32 per cent as "semi-speakers," and 9.14 per cent as learners, although based on different measures. Based on our work in communities, we reckon that

the number of fully fluent first-language speakers is much lower than that, although it is encouraging that a small but important number of younger adults are attaining mid- to advanced-level fluency in the language at present.

CHAPTER FIVE

1 For a detailed ethnobiological analysis of Ida William's story "Coyote Juggles His Eyes," see M. Ignace, Turner, and R. Ignace (2017).
2 For further work on Plateau root plant use and root plant intensification, especially for the period after around 2,400 years ago, see M. Ignace, Turner, and Peacock (2017), Lepofsky and Peacock (2004), and Peacock (1998).
3 A fifth species of Pacific salmon, chum or dog salmon (*Onchoryncus keta*), runs in the tributaries of the lower Fraser River, well below the reaches of Secwépemc territory.
4 Reuben Ware (1983, 9) cites figures from "Report of the Chief Inspector, Major J.A. Motherwell … British Columbia for 1926," in Canada, Department of Marine and Fisheries, Fisheries Branch, *Annual Report*, 1926–1927 (Motherwell 1926). See also Canada, Department of Fisheries (1893, 131–2). The figures for Chinook salmon, or spring salmon, are even more remarkable when taking into account their much higher average weight. Steven Romanoff (1992, 228), based on interviews with Lillooet elder Sam Mitchell in the early 1970s, reports that earlier in the twentieth century, Chinook salmon were the main catch.
5 These figures are from J.A. Motherwell (1926).
6 Gary Palmer (1975a, 219) estimates that prior to the advent of railways and commercial fishing, sockeye runs in the Fraser River system, including the Thompson River tributaries, "may have approximated 6,500,000 in each of the low years of [their four-year] cycle, and 160,000,000 fish in the dominant year." Michael Kew (1992, 189, table 3) estimates that for runs between 1901 (dominant) and 1904 (subdominant), the Nlaka'pamux and Secwépemc who fished above the confluence of the Fraser and Thompson Rivers on the Main, North, and South Thompson Rivers had available between 121 million kilograms (1901) and 6.77 million kilograms (1904) of sockeye, Chinook, coho, and pink salmon. Even if adjusted in terms of loss of caloric value during the fish's upriver migration, this figure ranges from 50–60 million kilograms in the dominant year to 3 million kilograms in the subdominant year. These figures do not account for salmon runs in the mid-Fraser River system above Lytton available to the Fraser River Secwépemc people.
7 See British Columbia Archives, in Secwepemc Cultural Education Society Archives, Ba 109.
8 The mountain caribou that traverse the Quesnel, Monashee, and Central Selkirk Mountains are a subspecies of woodland caribou (*Rangifer tarandus caribou*). During the winter it relies on the tree lichen (e.g., *Bryoria fremontii*) of old growth coniferous forests. As Simpcw elders noticed, between the 1930s and 1950s the caribou populations in the Wells Gray area went into major decline. The most likely cause of this was logging of old growth coniferous forests throughout the montane parklands of the Interior, combined with habitat fragmentation (see Mountain Caribou Technical Advisory Committee 2002).
9 Teit (1900, 240, 242) presents illustrations of Interior Salish bows and arrows made from photographs taken by Harlan Smith (1899).

10 These colleagues included Harriet Kuhnlein of McGill University, George Nicholas of Simon Fraser University, and several then-graduate students who have now made their mark in their fields: Dawn Loewen, Ann Garibaldi, Stu Crawford, Sandra Peacock, Brenda Beckwith, Michele Wollstonecroft, Nancy Jules Bonneau, Celia Nord, and Nola Markey.

11 There is more to be learned about the origin of the potato (*Solanum tuberosum*) in Secwépemc territory. Testing has revealed that the genetic strain of *Solanum tuberosum* that existed on the Northwest Coast by the early 1800s is most closely related to the "Makah potato" of northwestern Washington and to "Mariah's potato," which were already grown by the Haida and Tlingit at the time when maritime traders encountered them. Both of these potatoes are close genetic neighbours to potato strains of Central and South America, which thus must have made their way to the Northwest Coast through prior existing Indigenous trade routes rather than through European introduction (Zhang et al. 2010). A further close genetical relative of the Northwest Coast potato is the "Chilcotin potato," grown by our close neighbours to the northwest (Nancy J. Turner, personal communication, 2015). In the 1980s, before the genetic origins of Northwest Coast potatoes became established, various Secwépemc elders, including Aimee August of Neskonlith, Mary Thomas of Enderby, and Leslie Jules of Tk̓emlúps (Kamloops), mentioned a different-looking small and elongated potato called *ctsetsíts. se7t* (short, narrow). Skeetchestn elder Christine Simon remembered an "ugly looking but great-tasting" elongated potato grown at Skeetchestn in her youth, which was called *yecyéyect* (really long ones). This type of potato is apparently what Simpcw elder Lizette Donald was describing when she talked of a tuber she remembered from her youth in the 1920s and 1930s called *yecyéỳce*. Elders Cecilia DeRose and Bridget Dan of Esk̓ét and Clara Camille of Dog Creek remembered a similar-looking variety of potato grown by their elders and still recently grown in some gardens in the area that was called *tyecyéỳcse* (oval-shaped really long ones). It was also referred to as *peteke7óỳ* ("real potato"). The potato in question appears to be the "Likely" variety of heritage potato (Richard Hebda, personal communication, 2016), whose genetic relationship to the "Makah" and "Mariah's" has not been determined.

12 For detailed descriptions and analyses of Indigenous resource management regimes in northwestern North America, see, among others, M.K. Anderson (2005), Berkes (2012), Blackburn and M.K. Anderson (1993), Deur and Turner (2005), Peacock, M. Ignace, and Turner (2017), Peacock and Turner (2000), and Turner (2005, 2014). On Indigenous burning techniques as important parts of resource management, see Boyd (1999b) and Lewis and M.K. Anderson (2002).

13 In this account, Lilly Harry focused on resource harvesting at higher elevations and on the west side of the Fraser River, not mentioning either salmon fishing in the Fraser or plant gathering and hunting near the river valleys of Dog Creek and Canoe Creek as well as near the Fraser itself, all of which have long been additional important aspects of the annual seasonal round.

14 Clara Camille (personal communication, 2016) remembered that there were only certain places near the mouths of Dog Creek and Canoe Creek where they could cross safely during late summer and winter. These places were in locations where the banks of the Fraser River were not steep and where the river flowed smoothly. During the earlier part of the twentieth century, people also swam their cattle

across to the west side during late summer, sending them out to pasture at Empire Valley.

15 Blackdome Mountain, known as Pesxwiyéy̓elst ("has sharp-edged rocks") to past and present Secwépemc people from the area, is not actually mentioned by name here. Pelltsq̓éy̓lecw ("has-markings place") is the Secwépemc name for Red Mountain, and in its vicinity is the boundary marker between the St'at'imc, Secwépemc, and Tsilhqot'in.

16 It should be stressed, however, that these female hunters were postmenopausal women. In Interior Plateau society, similar to other Indigenous hunting societies, menstruating women's powers interfered with and posed dangers to male powers of hunting, as well as polluting hunting weapons and hunting gear. Menstruating women also, in a very physical sense, attract predators like black bears and grizzly bears.

17 Only relatively recently have Western-trained cultural ecologists and ethnobiologists alerted us not only to the wisdom and sustainability inherent in Indigenous regimes of resource management but also to the ways that Indigenous peoples' resource management, as inherently anchored in spiritual beliefs, has been sustained by systems and practices shown to be more effective than the policies of Western resource management, which are ostensibly based on science and economy (see E. Anderson 1996; Berkes 2012; and Turner 2005, 2014).

18 For descriptions and analyses of Aboriginal resource management regimes in northwestern North America that deploy social institutions to transmit knowledge and sustain practices, see, among others, M. Ignace, R. Ignace, and Turner (2017), Peacock, M. Ignace, and Turner (2017), Turner (2005, 2014), Turner and Berkes (2006), and Turner, R. Smith, and Jones (2005).

CHAPTER SIX

The Secwepemctsín title of this chapter literally means "our travels long time ago."

1 Native copper is noted for its purity, often being greater than 99.9 per cent pure, with very small but important signatures of other minerals, notably silver (Ag), selenium (Se), and lead (Pb), as well as other trace elements. It is the extent of these impurities or trace elements that can provide clues to the specific local source of a copper deposit. Throughout North America, five major sources of precontact native copper have been noted in the following areas: (1) the Great Lakes, particularly Lake Huron, (2) the Copper River in south-central Alaska and theYukon Territory, (3) Nunavut, (4) the southern Northwest Coast, and (5) the Interior Plateau (Cooper 2007). According to Cooper (2007, 2011; Cooper et al. 2008), Alaska-Yukon native copper went through two phases of being worked: (1) cold hammering, which worked well with very pure copper deposits, and (2) heating the copper to usually 200 to 300 degrees Celsius, far below the melting point of copper, which is 1,085 degrees Celsius. No analyses to date have been conducted on native copper mined at Copper Creek. Brian Hayden (personal communication, 2016) adds that a further source of native copper may have been the Bridge River Valley.

2 This site, now destroyed, was close to the two Plateau pithouse village sites EeRb 3 and EeRb 10 depicted in figure 3.16.
3 In 2016 the Stk̓emlúpsemc te Secwépemc Nation, which comprises the Kamloops and Skeetchestn Bands as a division, commissioned a catalogue of copper artifacts associated with heritage sites on the Interior Plateau. It shows more than 400 occurences of copper artifacts at heritage sites on the Interior Plateau both within the confines of the Secwépemc nation as outlined on our map of Secwépemc territory (see fig. 1.1) and in closely adjacent areas (Ewing 2016).
4 See chapter 12 for details on the Fraser Canyon and Cariboo gold rushes, as well as others in Interior Salish country, which would have a far-reaching impact and were the beginning of the dispossession of our Secwépemc homeland.
5 See, for example, the grave concerns raised by the Northern Secwépemc in the aftermath of the Mount Polley tailing pond disaster in 2013, as well as the issues raised by the Stk̓emlúpsemc te Secwépemc Nation – the reconstituted division of the Stk̓emlúpsemc – during and after the hearings on this disaster.
6 For a detailed description and discussion of brigade and settler trails that originated in pre-existing Aboriginal trails, see Favrholdt (1997, 1999, 2009) and M. Ignace, R. Ignace, and Favrholdt (2010). Additional evidence of Aboriginal trails is provided in Alexander (1996, 1997).
7 For accounts of the arrival of horses on the Southern and Northern Plateau, see Teit (1930a) and Hunn and Selam (1990).

CHAPTER SEVEN

The Secwepemctsín title of this chapter literally means "knowing the land."

1 Here and elsewhere in the Sésq̓em story, Chris Donald repeats important lines of text to underscore their significance to the narrative, a common stylistic device in Secwépemc storytelling.
2 For many examples of important resource-producing areas throughout Secwepemcúl̓ecw impacted or threatened by forestry, mining, urban development, highway and railway construction, and other factors, see Thomas, Garibaldi, and Turner (2017). During a cultural heritage study around a proposed open-pit mine just on the outskirts of Kamloops, and firmly within Secwépemc territory (M. Ignace et al. 2014), we recovered Pípsell as the name of Jacko Lake, now a well-known sports-fishing lake restocked with all female triploid (sterile) fish. If mining development does go ahead enabled by the Canadian Environmental Assessment Review Agency, Pípsell will soon be surrounded by tailing ponds and a large open-pit mine 150 metres deep.
3 This song by Tk̓emlúps elder Nels Mitchell and his "Secwépemc Welcome Song" at the start of chapter 9 are part of a set of songs that have long been remembered and performed throughout communities in our nation. They were recorded with Nels Mitchell in the late 1960s or early 1970s, and this recording has enabled many current Secwépemc to hear and relearn these songs.
4 Curiously, the word for "drying fish" used in this place name is not *scwik̓*, the Secwépemc word normally used by the Símpcwemc, but *tśwen*, the St'at'imc (Lillooet) word, which intrigued Simpcw elders in the 1980s, although they knew of no story or oral tradition that explained it.

CHAPTER EIGHT

1 We are very aware that in the contemporary context of the litigation and negotiation of Aboriginal rights and title, the maps with demarcated boundaries of Indigenous nations, or even of exclusive First Nation (Indian band) territories, have taken on a new significance that has the potential to pit our communities against one another and to pit different Indigenous nations against one another. As provincial and federal governments assert their authority to adjudicate our "Aboriginal strength of claim" over lands that are subject to resource extraction and development projects, communities within our nation and those of neighbouring Indigenous nations have become pitted against one another as they assert their boundaries. In contrast with political assertions about extent of territory, the analysis we present here is based on gathering the best available evidence from sources.

2 Prehistoric settlement patterns apparently included larger winter villages occupied by hundreds of pithouses, along with small villages consisting of anywhere from two or three to a dozen homes. It is still unclear whether large village sites, as opposed to smaller ones, existed at certain periods in Secwépemc history, as Brian Hayden (1992) argues, with a later period dispersal of the Secwépemc population into small villages, or whether large and small villages existed simultaneously. During the early 1800s, it appears that large villages like Tk̓emlúps and Sk̓emqín, the latter of which was on the current town site of Savona on Kamloops Lake, existed along with smaller villages like K̓écse7ten and a multitude of locations along Kamloops Lake and the main Thompson River. Likewise, the South Thompson River between Tk̓emlúps and Chase was densely settled before the 1860s smallpox epidemic.

3 Teit (1909, 455) uses the reduplicated form "Stkamlu'lEpsEmux" (Stk̓emlúlepsemc) rather than Stk̓emlúpsemc. It appears that consonant reduplication, otherwise used to make a diminuitive and to designate humble and respectful speech in the first-person singular (see chapter 4), is used in geographic terms to show that the term does not refer to a general landform but is a proper name.

4 Teit (1909, 455) somewhat mistakenly names this division the "Sxeste'lln'mux" (Scstálenemc) rather than the Sexqéltkemc ("upstream people"). However, Cstálen is the name for the village at the northwest end of Little Shuswap Lake, the site of the current Adams Lake Reserve, whereas Sexqéltkemc is the term that contemporary elders use for this division, as we do here.

5 Clarence William of Seseléltkwe (Two Springs), close to Upper Hat Creek, noted that the meaning of St̓ells, which he identified as a Secwépemc term, is "something sticks to the ground," as did Daniel Calhoun of Skeetchestn. In his Nlaka'pamux ethnography, Teit (1900, 173) was "doubtful" about the meaning of "Stlaz" (St̓ells).

6 For a detailed assessment of Sheilagh Dehart's account of the Kinbasket migration, see Kennedy and Bouchard (2009, 31–9). Based on a slightly different account by Dehart (transcript at http://ourspace.uregina.ca/handle/10294/910) and her younger sister Tracie Williams (transcript at http://ourspace.uregina.ca/handle/10294/996) in a 1964 interview with CBC broadcaster Imbert Orchard, Dorothy Kennedy and Randy Bouchard estimate that the Kinbaskets' settlement in the Columbia Valley occurred around 1845–46. Dehart's narrative mentions

that her grandfather's grandfather, Yellheelna Kinbasket, on initially travelling from the Adams Lake or Little Shuswap (Squilax) area by way of Seymour Arm to the upper Columbia Valley, established friendly relations with the Ktunaxa living there. Dehart also mentions that her ancestors saw David Thompson in the Golden area. David Thompson's (1994) journals and narrative, as Kennedy and Bouchard (2009, 24) observe make no mention of him meeting Secwépemc.

7 Elsewhere, Teit (1909, 460) mentions the Styétemc hunting as far as Quesnel Lake, as did the Sṫemcúlecwemc (ibid., 453), who also frequented areas in the mountains west of Quesnel Lake where glacier lily roots were prolific. Several trails into the Quesnel Lake area, along with pithouse sites there, attest to Secwépemc use of the lakes and lands surrounding it.

8 Pierre Squinahan of Esk̓ét conveyed the same idea: "There was no real boundary. The different bands lived in different places [but] the land belonged to all the Shuswap" (quoted in J. Brow 1972, 46).

9 The term *tsqwatstn* (Eastern Secwepemctsín) or *tsqwétsten* (Western Secwepemctsín) is difficult to translate. It refers to groups of people who are friends, not enemies, but who are not actual close *k̓wséltkten* (relatives). It is used for people who are socially connected to one's own people and hence are the relatives of relatives.

10 This name derives from the root *kwel* (ammunition) (as in the word *tskwil* for "arrow") plus a reduplicated form of the lexical suffix *-le*, which commonly identifies personal names.

11 J. Michael Thoms (2002) provides a detailed description and analysis of how Pennask Lake, utilized by Secwépemc, Okanagan, and Nlaka'pamux people in the 1920s and highly prolific as a trout-fishing lake, was appropriated by white sports fishers starting in the 1920s.

12 K̓emqenétkwe is very similar to the Secwépemc name for Scheidam Flats, which is Ckemqenétkwe ("waters coming together at an angle at the top"), and it designates a similar geographic feature at the headwaters of the Nicola River. Herb Manuel of the upper Nicola mentioned "Qumqnatku" as a Secwepemc place name, although it is listed as being at Salmon Lake, which is much lower in elevation and does not have the geographic features attributed to K̓emqenétkwe.

13 The agreement between the Secwépemc, Ktunaxa, and Stony was made on 27 September 1895 at Windermere. It postdates British Columbia's entry into Confederation but precedes that of Alberta and was made in the presence of Indian agent Robert Leslie Thomas Galbraith. The speeches by the chiefs of the three nations are in the style of traditional oratory about relations between the three groups and about maintaining peaceful relations. Thus Chief Cheneka (Stony) said that "as long as he could remember, and he was now an old man, the best friendly relations had ever existed between the three tribes of Indians represented at the conference and his only wish was that nothing would occur to prevent their continuation in the future." The Indian agent emphasized the existence of British Columbia's game laws and noted the "various signs of progress in the art of civilization" made by these Indians, also commenting on the presence of an Indian Industrial School and of the Roman Catholic Church (quoted in Shuswap Nation Tribal Council 2015, 8–15).

14 For a short account titled "Two Shuswap Renegades, Wilpahan and His Brother," see D.S. Mitchell (1925). Although the particular two brothers in this *slexéy̓em*

(oral history), according to Ike Willard's account, were killed, as were their sons, the names Atahm and Wulpáxen lived on in the 1860s. The 1867–82 baptism records name Chief Adam (Atahm) and his son Adrian, as well as listing an adult "Wulpaxan" with several children. Given that Ike Willard's account probably took place in the 1780s (after the initial smallpox epidemic that affected the Interior), it is possible that the surviving wives of Atahm and Wulpáxen named their children or grandchildren to keep the ancestors' names alive.

15 Mosquito Flats is a flat described as located where people descended from Xwexwtéṫi ("mountain-goat place") (see chapter 2) on Boulder Mountain, where they used to camp. According to Chris Donald's story, this is *qelmecwúl̓ecw* ("Indian land"). The events described in the story took place before reserves were designated or allocated, but the wording implies that at Mosquito Flats the Simpcw were in territory close to home where they could expect to be safe from enemies, such as the Cree. It also indexes the existence of a habitual camping area there, thus a settlement of the kind we described using the Secwépemc terms *mut* and *tsyem* in chapter 5.

16 On the Secwépemc way that kinship terms are used, see chapter 9. The term "grandfather" does not necessarily apply to an actual father's father or mother's father but is also used to refer to the brothers of one's grandmother or grandfather, as well as to their cousins. Peter Moyís was the brother of Chris Donald's paternal grandfather. The church records list him as Peter Frezy, the son of Moise Frisé (born ca. 1832), who was baptized in 1872. Moise Frisé is the *ṫkwilc* (Indian doctor) "Pílsi" mentioned by both Chris Donald and Ida William in chapter 11. Like other medicine people, he was baptized but continued his own spiritual work.

17 Josephine Wenlock and Ida William described Tessie as the "sister" of their *kye7e7úẃi* ("real grandmother"), or the "auntie" of their mother, Mathilde – that is, the "sister" of their maternal grandmother Sudít (Judith). The Oblate baptism book for 1866–82 shows Tessie baptized as Anastasia, her Secwépemc name being recorded as "Sememolks" (Sne7emél̓qs, "spirit power robe"?), and she is listed as being twenty-five years old at the time of her baptism in 1867 (Oblate Missions of British Columbia 1866–82). Thus it appears that her capture and subsequent escape from a Blackfoot camp occurred between 1855 and 1860.

18 Tseqwtseqwél̓qw is the "old reserve" at Chu Chua (Simpcw), about 1.5 kilometres south of the current village where the band office, church, and school are located.

CHAPTER NINE

1 Angelo Anastasio (1972), writing about the Southern Plateau, provided a very detailed account of how, on the Plateau, the kinship and marriage system is connected to resource sharing and resource access among local groups and nations.

2 "Cognate" means that the term is similar to, and thus considered as deriving from, a term in a common ancestor language.

3 The late Dr Mary Thomas was a revered Secwépemc elder of Neskonlith (Salmon Arm). After raising her family, she devoted the last decades of her life to researching Secwépemc culture and traditions, in turn sharing her knowledge with us and with fellow elders, younger generations of Aboriginal people, and academic researchers, including Nancy J. Turner and several of the latter's students. She received numerous awards for her tireless work, including an environmentalist award and an honorary doctorate from Thompson Rivers University. She passed

away at nearly ninety years of age in 2008. The session where the story of Muskrat as well as the stories of Chickadee and of Salmon were recorded was a fortuitous interactive session with Mary Thomas, who spoke Eastern Secwepemctsín, and with Skeetchestn elders Nellie Taylor and Christine Simon, who spoke Western Secwepemctsín. They engaged us in dialogue and knowledge sharing during a five-hour trip home from the 1994 Society of Ethnobiology Conference in Victoria, to which they had accompanied us. With their permission, we recorded their extended discussion and sharing of stories across dialects.

4 Involved here are poetic parallel lines and a Secwépemc way of using alliteration of similar sounds between the line above "*stsqwatsítsimactsalp*" (you said pitiful things about me) and the name Q̓wetsetsútsu7 ("little fatty") as well as the reduplicated form Q̓wetsetsútsutsu7 ("little fatty all over and entirely"). Muskrat here mocks the words they called him and, by implication, mocks the way they used "pitiful" language with him.

5 The *wetscén* (lizard) is actually the long-toed salamander (*Ambystoma macrodactylum*).

6 "The Chipmunk and Owl Story" survived only in an English version, as recorded by Teit (1909, 654), until we collectively produced a telling in Secwepemctsín with Skeetchestn elders Christine Simon, Amy Slater, Daniel Calhoun, Leona Calhoun, Garlene Dodson, and Julie A. Antoine, figuring out the parallel lines "*tsqeq̓ipusél̓cken-k*" (your balls are wrinkled) and "*tsqeq̓ipúse7 re7 elk*" (your kinnikinnik berries are wrinkled).

7 The term *setsetatamámc* refers to younger siblings but seems to derive from *tsétse*, the root word for younger sister.

8 Teit (1930a, 232) notes, "The Indians pronounced it Nkwala'. He married 15 wives (according to other informants 17) from the Okanagan, Sanpoil, Colville, Spokan, Shuswap, Stuwi'x, Thompson, and perhaps others."

9 As explained in chapter 5, the term *petne7éws* derives from the English term "partner" plus the lexical suffix *-ews* for "to one another" or "mutual." Elders whose speech we heard and recorded in the 1980s used this term to refer to the mutual support and collaboration that should exist between husband and wife as they maintain different but complementary domestic and economic roles. The Secwépemc term *meméws* (couple) derives from the word for "wife" (Kuipers 2002, 174).

10 Obviously, this story is similar to Aesop's fable about Ant and Grasshopper, publicized in numerous versions in Europe. The plot of the story recounted here may be borrowed, but it may also have been conceived independently of the European fable. It is noteworthy that the source identified by Nellie Taylor is her great-grandmother. Agathe Llecwpusétkwe, who was born in the 1830s and lived until the 1920s. Thus such European tales *may* have circulated among the Secwépemc at the time. Regardless, Nellie Taylor thought of this story as a *stsptekwll* that represented a parable about Secwépemc values rather than as a borrowed text with a European theme. Both ants and grasshoppers are prominent native species in Secwepemcúlecw.

CHAPTER TEN

The Secwepemctsín title of this chapter literally means "our chiefs and their advisors [or councillors]."

1 Information about Chief Louis and his successors was provided by Jeannette Jules. Surprisingly, Teit's (1930a, 228) text asserts that Jean-Baptiste St Paul, an Iroquois Metis who worked for the Hudson's Bay Company and had married a Tk̓emlúps woman baptized as Marie, was chief of the band prior to the late 1850s, a claim vehemently denied by Kamloops elders (see M. Ignace 1995a).
2 This apparently is an honorific name, making reference to his being appointed as spokesperson of the Secwépemc and to his being one of a few chiefs who represented the Indian Rights Movement between his trip to London in 1906 and his participation, along with Peter Kelly, John Chilaheetza, and Andy Paull, in the submission to the Special Joint Committee of the Senate and House of Commons in 1927, which led to the Canadian government's refusal to recognize land rights in a coup of injustice enacted through section 141 of the Indian Act (Tennant 1990, 108; see also chapter 13). The late Basil Dick (Basil David) spent more than twenty-five years seeking to address Secwépemc title, as well as Aboriginal title altogether. He was the son of the *ṫkwilc* (Indian doctor) Sqéqxe, baptized Gaspard, and was born in 1855 with the name Getspúlecw ("the one who is tied to the land"), a prophetic name. Basil Dick himself, according to Louisa Basil and Rose Phillips, trained as a *ṫkwilc* in his youth. They recalled that his later name was Tṡelcwíẇelst ("the rock that came to be stood up"), in reference to his calm and persistent quest for justice (see chapter 13, note 9).
3 All three papers are London newspapers. The *Daily Graphic* mentions that it was Basil David who served in the war and lost an arm, whereas the report in the *Daily Herald* mentions that it was William Pierrish. Veterans' records for the First World War show that William Pierrish, indeed, served in that war, but no such record could be found for Basil David (see www.veterans.gc.ca/eng/search?q=service%20 records).
4 All of these instances of chiefly selection took place between the early 1800s and 1950. Until this time, chiefship continued to be determined "by appointment" of the community members and was usually granted "for life," although in the early 1900s Indian agents began to undermine this process. The instances of chiefly succession, however, throw light on selection criteria for chiefs that derive from, and show continuity with, political processes that existed before contact and colonization.
5 The term *tk̓wenm7íplem̓* or *tk̓wenm7íple7* means something like "giving advice or good counsel according to the *stsq̓ey̓* (laws) of the Secwépemc people." With the lexical suffix *-ten*, it refers to the people who do this. Although some people may translate *tk̓wenm7íple7* as the Secwépemc term for "law," we think that it more aptly describes the giving of advice about the course of action to follow based on *stsq̓ey̓*, or the laws laid down through the deeds of ancestors.
6 Haiqua shells, also known as dentalium shells, were obtained from a small mollusk (*Antilis pretiosa*). Bill Merilees (2013, 6) writes, "*A. pretiosa* is a sturdy attractive shell, an almost exact miniature of an elephant's tusk. During the period between 1750 and 1850 it was known as Haiqua and became the unit currency during the fur trade era. As such it was much sought after by First Nations people and fur traders alike. The Hudson['s] Bay Company quickly caught on to their trade value. The shells were strung and measured by the fathom (six feet), 40 shells making up a fathom. This would make the average length of each shell to be about 7 cm (1.8 inches) (Galois and Mackie, 1990, Mackie and Galois, 1990)."

7 We prefer the term "retribution" to the term "revenge" because the Secwépemc oral histories that detail how this sentencing process operated, along with the evidence from the fur trade era concerning relations between Europeans and Plateau people, point to the fact that Indigenous *stsq̓ey̓* (traditional laws) and *tk̓wenm7íple7* (judicial process) favoured restorative retribution over the nonrational and impulsive promotion of violent retribution that is usually associated with revenge or vengeance.

8 For a previous explanation of these Secwépemc criminal justice concepts and how they were upheld during the fur trade, see Thomson and M. Ignace (2005, 26ff). Our description of the Secwépemc system of criminal justice owes to our family's own experiences in the aftermath of our son's murder, where the convicted murderers were Secwépemc men from Tk̓emlúps.

9 For accounts of Samuel Black's murder and its causes, see Thomson and M. Ignace (2005) and Reid (1993). See also Belyk (1995) and Tod's own narrative account in Wolfenden (1954). There is a Secwépemc oral tradition about "Kiskowskin," noted as Black's murderer, who was the son or nephew of Chief Tranquille, and about what subsequently happened to him. According to a story told by Casimir Felix of Splatsín in 2011, "Kiskowskin" tried to escape after being surrendered by the Secwépemc and was captured and transported across Kamloops Lake by canoe. According to this account, instead of drowning in the lake, he transformed into a loon and became a *ṫkwilc* (Indian doctor)!

10 This particular statement pertains to Indians in Puget Sound. However, supported by data from numerous Oblate missions, Gabriel Dionne (1947, 91–101) maintains that the custom of "Kaltash bilalam," or "peniténces publiques," was practised throughout the coastal and mainland Pacific Northwest, amounting to an Indigenous legal institution that the Oblates were trying to mobilize in order to introduce the practice of confession – in vain, as Dionne shows.

11 There seems to be a widespread assumption among historians and some contemporary Secwépemc people that these "Indian courts" were introduced by the Oblates. Elders whose memories reached back to the early 1900s always talked of them as Indigenous institutions, although one could have assumed that they represented practices introduced by the Oblates and internalized by Secwépemc. However, the correspondence that Gabriel Dionne (1947) presents shows that the Oblates found Indian courts in existence and tried to rely on them to convey the idea of sin and penitence.

12 Ck̓écse7ten ("drying-meat place") was a village some 10 kilometres past Cyéyenwelc, the main village of Skeetchestn.

13 The elders in the 1980s remembered him as "Nigger Smith" – fondly, not disparagingly. For a detailed discussion of his Indian agent work, see T. Smith (1994).

CHAPTER ELEVEN

The Secwepemctsín title of this chapter literally means "our [not your] strength in our land."

1 Western science has long denied that plants are sentient beings. However, recent science research has shown the at times predatory and at times defensive nature of plants, as well as the communal nature of plant communities (see Buffie 2015).

"Sentient" in the sense of having senses, of course, does not apply, but instead the chemistry of scents and odours does some of the work, as do root systems, rizomes, and mycelia – the vast underground networks of the vegetative parts of mushrooms, which are in a symbiotic relationship with tree communities.

2 The term "sentient landscape" is used by Julie Cruikshank (2005, 142) in her ethnography of Yukon First Nations' connection to land, including glaciers.

3 The term *x7ensq̓t* derives from *x7en(s)* (warn someone) plus the lexical suffix *-(e)sq̓t* (day, sky, or air). In this era of human-made climate change, it seems appropriate to note that our ancestors not only regarded human agency as producing weather and climate changes but also maintained that we get warnings in the form of weather events.

4 It is not clear what biological species *tsecwyáńst* represents. It could be a mountain pine beetle or spruce budworm.

5 It should be pointed out that on the Interior Plateau, unlike on the Northwest Coast, the artistic representation of events and animals as possessing powers tended to be confined largely to private and secluded places or to involve symbolic representations that merely alluded to these powers rather than depicting their embodiment (see Teit 1898, 1930b), thus maintaining what Teit (1900, 1909) called their "mystery." This cultural context sheds different light on what has sometimes been perceived as the "lack" of artistic expression among peoples of the Interior Plateau. Because the signs and symbols of artistic expression are inextricably linked to the lingering power of *sk̓últen* (innate guardian spirits) and *seméc* (acquired guardian spirits), displaying them in public symbols is counterproductive in that it can misfire by exposing them to potential manipulation and thus to harm from others.

6 For an example of how this impediment manifests itself "on the ground" in contemporary *étsxem*, see M. Ignace (1999).

7 Having discussed the culturally private nature of *étsxem*, *sk̓últen*, and *seméc*, we are very aware that disclosing such sites or mapping such places is counterproductive and in contradiction to their meaning and function among our people. However, we have provided several examples of such spiritual sites being destroyed through actions as counterproductive as the invasion of sites by tourists or their defacement by spray paint. Making a case for Secwépemc historical, social, and spiritual connections to such places as an integral part of Secwépemc title and rights is one way of securing their protection while also telling their powerful story.

8 *Q̓éwens* (put a spell on someone) and *q̓éwentem* (be put under a spell) involve causing someone to act differently or impeding another person's own powers, thus enabling one to take control of the actions of that person. Although *ṫkwilc* harnessed such powers, often for good purposes but sometimes for dangerous and damaging purposes, we see in the Tllí7sa *stsptekwll* how, throughout his and his brothers' travels, he *q̓éwens* (harnesses) his powers to vanquish the power of the *ṫsecélemc* (people eaters).

9 *Twéxem* is also a way that we release power in order either to give life or to restore life. In stories, when a being or human is killed, a person endowed with powers can put his or her *seméc* to work by *twéxem* (jumping over) the one killed four times in order to bring that being or human back to life. Before submitting his doctoral thesis to Simon Fraser University, Ron Ignace *twéxwem* (jumped over) it four times in order to release its power by investing it with new life.

10 Additional versions of the story of Owl are in Teit (1909, 698), as told by Sxwéy̓lecken of Dog Creek, and in Bouchard and Kennedy (1979, 47–56), who have abridged and edited the version told by Charlie Draney of Skeetchestn.

11 The term *q̇ilye* can designate the practice of having a sweat or the institution of the sweat lodge, with the term *xq̇íl̓ye7ten* also being used for the sweat lodge itself.

12 Places and ways of burial have somewhat changed, although interment was the common way of dealing with the deceased in Secwépemc culture long before Europeans arrived (Teit 1909, 592). Long ago, the corpse was wrapped in a blanket and laid out for burial in either a supine or a fetus-like position. By the early part of the twentieth century, coffins were made locally to bury a person in the local graveyard. In recent decades, funeral homes have been providing coffins.

13 Louis Sisyésq̇t is also listed in the Hudson's Bay Company's 1863–64 account book, although it is unclear whether the latter is the brother or father of Hyacinth.

14 For literature on the historical development, structure, and impact of Indian residential schools in Canada see, for example, J.R. Miller (1996), Canada, Royal Commission on Aboriginal Peoples (1996a), Milloy (1999), and Regan (2010). For works on residential schools in Secwépemc territory (Kamloops and Williams Lake), see Haig-Brown (1988) and Furniss (1992), the anthology of narratives from Kamloops Indian Residential School in Jack (2006), and autobiographic accounts by Sterling (1992) and Sellars (2013). As we concluded writing this book, the Truth and Reconciliation Commission of Canada (2015a) published its final report on Indian residential schools.

15 In subsequent years, as written correspondence was increasingly carried out by Indian agents who had not learned our language, and who indeed were part of the efforts to oppress Indigenous languages, the first names given by the missionaries became the last names of these people's children. The Indigenous names eventually ceased being part of the public, written record. This explains the existence of names like Ignace, Jules, Pitel (from French Fidele), Simon, Abel, Manuel, Arnouse, William, Antoine, and the like in Secwépemc communities and in Interior Plateau communities in general that were missionized by French Oblates. For exmple, not all people named Jules are related, nor are all people named Ignace related, since the perpetuation of the name hinged on what we can call the "fluke of names" being given out in more than one community by the French-speaking missionaries with their own orientations around names like those mentioned above. Due to population loss and demographics, however, some families became big, whereas some declined. All of these names derive from the inventory of French baptismal names given out by the missionaries.

16 William Harold Gurney's (1943, 68) account shows Father Jean-Marie-Raphaël Le Jeune's travel itinerary over a period of three months from January to March 1893. It records that Le Jeune made return trips from Kamloops to Quilchena, Coldwater, and Spences Bridge, to Spuzzum and North Bend, to Lytton, to North Thompson, and to Savona (Deadman's Creek), before finally travelling to Shuswap Lake.

17 There seems to be a widespread assumption among historians and some contemporary Secwépemc people that these "Indian courts" were introduced by the Oblates. Elders whose memories reached back to the early 1900s always talked of them as Indigenous institutions, although one could have assumed that they represented practices introduced by the Oblates and internalized by Secwépemc.

However, the correspondence that Gabriel Dionne (1947) presents shows that the Oblates found Indian courts in existence and tried to rely on them to convey the idea of sin and penitence.

18 The salutations and short messages that Secwépemc people sent to one another after they had learned to write Secwepemctsín in Chinook shorthand are revealing given that they follow these protocols of speech. The priests, in fact, adopted this mode of speech in their own correspondence with each other. Father Edward Peytavin, who was active in Sto:lo country, wrote to Father Le Jeune in partially broken but partially accurate Secwepemctsín in 1893:

> Oh, re newí7 pere Le Jeune, Xetéqs k le7 stéṁi ke7 sqwlut? Le-en ke7 ṗúsmen? Stémes-enke, le7 ren tsutst-ken pyin. Me7 nes-ken ne Secwépemc pexyéwt méte Pere Lejacq. Q̇iyeṁ téke mé7e tikwemtús q̇iyéṁ téke mé7e: xwexwistén ṫe pipa: qwenqwént-ken. K̇wiyúsem-ken. Re ntsétswe7 Pere Peytavin.
>
> And you, Father Le Jeune, first, what good things do you have to say? Are you well? [lit. "Is your heart good?"] I don't know what it is, I am doing well. Tomorrow I will go to Shuswap [country] with Father Lejacq. See, they write, they always write: I like Chinook shorthand writing: I am poor. I suffer. I am Father Peytavin. (Robertson n.d., Secwepemctsín transliteration and translation by Marianne Ignace)

19 As we saw in chapter 4, Secwepemctsín has an inclusive "we" that includes the addressee and an exclusive "we" that excludes the addressee. "Our" in "Our Chief Above" is invariably inclusive.

20 We thank Dr Duane Thomson, formerly of Okanagan University College, for providing us with copies of Father Charles Grandidier's correspondence.

CHAPTER TWELVE

The Secwepemctsín title of this chapter literally means "this is how the white people stole our lands."

1 For an account of the arrival and availability of horses on the Plateau from south to north, see Hunn and Selam (1990).

2 For accounts of epidemics in the Pacific Northwest between the 1770s and late 1800s, see Boyd (1994, 1999a), Hunn and Selam (1990), and Galois (1996).

3 Partial accounts of Pelkamulox's death and N'Kwala's (Nicola's) revenge are reported in George M. Dawson's (1891, 26–8) report, in Teit's (1906) Lillooet monograph, and in Teit's (1930a) ethnography of the Okanagan and Southern Interior Salishan tribes. Numerous references to ongoing events around the death of N'Kwala's father, "Grand Picotte," are also reported in James McMillan and John McLeod's (1822) journal for the Thompson River post, as are the continuing war councils regarding the revenge of N'Kwala and his supporters against the Lillooet whom the Secwépemc, Nlakȧpamux, and Okanagan, remarkably, held at the fort throughout the winter. The subsequent raid into St'at'imc territory in the Seaton Lake and Anderson Lake area took place around 1823 (Teit 1906, 246).

4 This self-concealment resembles the Tlingit's behaviour when they first sighted Russians on ships coming into their territory. In that instance, they peeked out at

the Russians from behind Indian hellebore, known as a substance of power (see Dauenhauer and Dauenhauer 1987, 293–8).

5 This name must refer to Tséltšel, the father or grandfather of Charlie Tséltšel, whose name was Anglicized to Saul-John among some families and to Chelsea among others.

6 Upon review of all print sources of the name Tk̓emlúps, later Anglicized to Kamloops, Marianne Ignace and Kenneth Favrholdt are of the opinion that "Cumcloups" involves a typo or misreading by the publisher of Ross's handwritten manuscript source, which likely read "Cumeloups," a close approximation of Tk̓emlúps.

7 Partial records and journals from the Jasper House post survive, particularly the journals of trader Michael Klyne (1826–34).

8 It is not fully clear at this time whether the potatoes grown at Ck̓emqenétkwe and Neskonlith were indeed potatoes brought in by fur traders. As has been shown through genetic research on varieties of *Solanum tuberosum* grown by Makah, Tlingit, and Haida peoples (Zhang et al. 2010), these varieties are most closely related to Mexican and Chilean varieties rather than to varieties of *Solanum tuberosum* introduced to Europe and then brought to North America by traders and settlers since the 1700s. It appears that the Tsilhqot'in, aside from harvesting "wild potatoes" (*Claytonia lanceolata*) in great quantities at Potato Mountain, grew a variety of this Indigenous *Solanum tuberosum* garden potato (Nancy J. Turner, personal communication, 2015). Secwépemc elder Mary Thomas grew a variety that she called *petak7úw̓i* ("real garden potato"), and it is possible that this potato was another such variety. Skeetchestn elder Christine Simon remembered a small, longish, "ugly-looking," but delicious variety that her own elders grew in gardens and baked in the oven, which they called *yecyéyect* (many long things). Simpcw elder Lizette Donald had a similar name, *yecyéy̓ce* (root like a potato), for a variety that was grown in Chu Chua when she grew up and "came to her senses" (early 1920s), which Nancy J. Turner and Marianne Ignace have not been able to identify as any of the Indigenous "wild" roots and bulbs used by the Símpcwemc. For more information on Indigenous growing of potatoes on the Northwest Coast, see Suttles (1987a), Moss (2005), and J. McDonald (2005).

9 Teit (1912a, 410) reports on this event as an "Account of the Lytton Chiefs," mentioning war parties from Kamloops, Bonaparte, and Savona. Interestingly, the Lytton chiefs' account (ibid., 412) mentions Governor James Douglas as being present during the treaty making at Lytton; however, as Marshall (2000) and Harris (1997) show, there is no record of Douglas being in the area in August 1858, when the treaties were made.

10 The Fraser Canyon War, its implications, and the fact that it was all but wiped from the narrative of British Columbia colonial history are detailed in the 2009 documentary *Canyon War: The Untold Story*, written by Don Hauka and directed by Eva Wunderman. For written accounts of the Canyon War, see Hauka (2003), Marshall (2000), and a brief account by Harris (1997).

11 Douglas set acreage limits for reserves in his instructions to the commissioner of lands and works, Richard Clement Moody, and to other colonial officials. In a January 1864 address to the colonial Legislative Council, he referred to reserves that were not to exceed 10 acres per family, yet ten years later, he clarified that

he had no specific number of acres in mind (Canada, Indian Claims Commission 2008, 21).

12 Despite the documentary evidence of Cox's instructions to Chief Nesqénell, Moberly's map, and other documentation submitted by the bands, including oral history evidence from elders, the federal government (Canada, Indian Claims Commission 2008, 45) rejected the specific claim by the Neskonlith, Adams Lake, and Little Shuswap Bands to their Douglas Reserve: "We find that the Crown did not intend to create a reserve at Shuswap in 1862." Although the Indian Claims Commission agreed that Governor Douglas could legally create reserves in the colony and intended to achieve that objective by means of a defined process, it determined that Cox, as his assistant commissioner of lands and works, was not in a position to legally create reserves and, at the same time, was at fault for not having followed up on his initial communications with Nesqénell. The Kamloops Indian Band's specific claim to its Douglas Reserve was also dismissed by the Indian Claims Commission in 2008. However, the band and the federal government began a negotiating process in 2012, which remained unconcluded at the time of this book's completion in early 2017.

13 Robert Boyd (1994, 1999a) suggests that the earliest epidemic struck in the 1770s, with a second one in 1801. Sarah Campbell (1990) makes a case that earlier smallpox epidemics struck throughout North America as early as the 1500s.

14 Furniss (1995, 238) quoting Father Morice's *The History of the Northern Interior of British Columbia* (1904), reports that smallpox arrived among the Northern Secwépemc through traders' blankets "that the Shuswap had acquired from the Thompson River area." However, Morice (ibid., 317), citing information from Alfred Waddington published in a letter in the *Victoria Daily Colonist* on 13 June 1864, writes that smallpox arrived among the Tsilhqot'in's main settlement at Nakuntlun, brought in by infected blankets: "Two white men, Angus McLeod and a certain Taylor went and stealthily gathered the blankets of the dead which had been thrown away in the bush, and were therefore infested with smallpox, which they sold out again to the Indians without revealing their origin, thus causing a second visitation of the plague, which carried off the second third of the native population." These events, and the threats they imposed on the Tsilhqot'in, are considered to be a contributing factor to the Chilcotin War of 1864, which, as acknowledged in *Tsilhqot'in Nation v. British Columbia* (2007, 2014) figured importantly in the historical memory and consciousness of the Tsilhqot'in in defending title and rights to their land as settlers encroached.

15 In addition, the Secwépemc people who inhabited the valley at Kelly Creek, west of Clinton, were exterminated at some point, although this may have happened before the 1862–63 smallpox epidemic.

16 This location must be the large pithouse village at North Thompson River Park, a few kilometres south of Clearwater (see Hall and Fladmark 1969).

17 According to medical studies on smallpox contagion, the virus can stay alive for about one and a half years in blankets and fabrics. Diseased blankets that were either purposefully passed on to Indians or left behind by settlers affected by the disease are thus a plausible source of the epidemic (see also A.D. Palmer 2005, 37ff).

18 Although Robin Fisher (1992) has been rightfully credited with exposing the racist land policies pursued by Joseph Trutch, Tom MacInnes, who wrote a legal opinion

on the Indian land question in British Columbia for Prime Minister Wilfrid Laurier, seized on Trutch's role in the oppression of land rights and inadequate reserve allocation in British Columbia nearly seventy years earlier (Foster 1999).

19 As the federal government acknowledges (Canada, Indian Claims Commission 2001), it appears that preceding British Columbia's entry into Confederation in 1871, the Dominion government remained largely ignorant of the colony's modus operandi in dealing with, or rather refusing to deal with, the Indigenous title issue (see also Fisher 1992; Foster 2007; and Tennant 1990). During Governor General Lord Dufferin's visit to British Columbia in 1876, however, Dufferin himself raised the issue.

20 Although on various occasions Grandidier wrote letters on behalf of Interior Aboriginal people in order to advocate for adequate reserves and access to resources, he also acted as an informer for provincial and federal government sources. Throughout the 1870s, he employed two "half-breeds" from the Adams Lake area to provide him with "intelligence" about the political intentions and actions of the chiefs in the Secwépemc nation (see Oblate Missions of British Columbia 1866–74).

21 The church's efforts to undermine chiefly authority and impose its form of social control during this period were followed and accompanied by the Indian agents' attempts to manipulate leadership and chiefly office (see Carstens 1991; and Furniss 1995). Kamloops Indian Agency records from the early 1900s show numerous other instances and examples (see K.D. Smith 2009, 58; and T. Smith 1994, ch. 7).

22 The Joint Reserve Commission of 1876–78 included three commissioners: Gilbert Malcolm Sproat, Alexander Caulfield Anderson, and George McKinley. Sproat, who had lived for some years among Indigenous peoples on Vancouver Island, was jointly appointed by the federal and provincial governments. Anderson, who had served for many years as a Hudson's Bay Company officer engaged with Interior Indigenous peoples (see chapter 5), was the federal appointee. And McKinley, a settler, was the provincial appointee. Within two years (i.e., 1876–78), the commission disbanded, following Sproat's and Anderson's resignations due to the provincial government's refusal to acknowledge the needs and interests of Indigenous peoples who had already been displaced from lands and who were now feeling the encroachment of settlers since the latter were able to pre-empt their lands even as Indigenous peoples were being refused both the right to pre-emption and fee-simple title and the right to citizenship. Sproat then continued to make some reserve allocations until 1878. From 1880 to 1889, reserve allocations were continued by Joseph Trutch's brother-in-law Peter O'Reilly, who also downplayed Indigenous peoples' interests and their need for land.

23 This figure can be verified by the number of crosses from the epidemic that mark where the dead were buried in one section of the Chu Chua graveyard. There are fifty crosses. Given that some days more than one person died, with those who died the same day being buried together, fifty-nine seems a very accurate figure. Such sections in the graveyards of other Secwépemc communities indicate similar losses of about one-third of the population during the 1918–19 influenza epidemic.

24 This is only a short summary of some of the disturbing issues around the BC government's denial of our water rights during this time and around the fact that, in the end, the federal government was negligent in its responsibility to ensure

our water rights. For detailed information, see Matsui (2005) and several of the sources he cites.

CHAPTER THIRTEEN

1 Chilaheetza is also variously spelled Chilihitza, Chilheetsa, and TsElaxitsa.

2 Of the petition itself, Keith Carlson (2005, 12) notes, "it was explicitly an attempt to alert the monarch to breaches of the promises made in his mother Queen Victoria's name many years earlier. As such, it was both an appeal to the Crown's honour and an effort to reaffirm the intimate familial relationship that they had come to consider existed between themselves (as disenfranchised residents of the Canadian Dominion) and the Royal family. If, however, this proved inadequate to move the king to action, other rationales were also provided."

3 In terms of the particular course of action to follow, Laurier, who "seemed sympathetic to their cause" (Tennant 1990, 88), advised the Indians to take their grievance to the Judicial Committee of the British Privy Council in London, whose authority at this time superseded that of the Supreme Court of Canada. He also commissioned Tom McInnis to write a legal opinion on the issue of what we would call in today's terms "Aboriginal title."

4 Teit himself was not present at the meeting but, at Edward Sapir's request, had left for the Northern Interior to begin ethnological work among the Kaska and Tahltan.

5 According to Hamar Foster (1999, 195), McBride had initially been in favour of a reference case involving the Indigenous peoples on the Skeena River, namely the Gitksan. However, "at the eleventh hour Premier McBride, who only two years earlier had approved an attempt to refer Indian land issues to the Full Court in British Columbia, refused to consent. One cannot know, but perhaps by then he had realized that the case for Indian title was legally much stronger than he had previously thought."

6 Paul Tennant (1990, 96–113) provides a detailed account and analysis of the Allied Tribes and their submission to the Special Joint Committee of the Senate and House of Commons, where submissions were made by Peter Kelly on behalf of the Haida, by Andrew Paull on behalf of the Squamish, and by John Chilaheetza and Basil David (Basil Dick) on behalf of the Interior Tribes. On the basis of the minutes of the hearings of the joint committee, Tennant also shows how evidence, particularly the not widely available *Papers Connected with the Indian Land Question* (British Columbia 1875), was withheld from the Allied Tribes. This action flew in the face of the principle of the "honour of the Crown."

7 The notations of Teit as interpreter on these occasions throw some light on his linguistic skills in Salish languages. He interpreted for John Chilaheetza, who spoke Okanagan but likely also spoke Nlaka'pamuxcin (Thompson). Teit also interpreted for Nlaka'pamux chief John Tetlenitsa and for Shuswap chief Basil David (Basil Dick), who would have spoken Secwepemctsín, although he may have known Nlaka'pamuxcin. St'at'imc chief James Raitasket of Lillooet, however, was interpreted by Chief Thomas Adolph of Fountain, whose speech, either Secwepemctsín or Nlaka'pamuxcin, was in turn interpreted by Teit.

8 As perhaps a footnote to history, it appears that Edward Sapir, who employed Teit through the National Museum in Ottawa at the time, recruited the members of

the chiefs' delegations to serve as linguistic and ethnographic informants. They also posed for photographs as physical anthropology "specimens," as arranged by Sapir and Teit (see chapter 3), and likely helped to finance their trips to London and Ottawa through their ethnographic and linguistic consultancy.

9 "Ratskola," which is apparently an Anglicization of Getspúlecw ("the one who is tied to the land"), was the name that, according to his baptism record, Basil David already had in his youth. It was a prophetic one, given his life-long involvement in addressing the land question. Louisa Basil and Rose Phillips recalled that, later on, Basil David acquired a second name, Ts̓elcwíw̓elst ("the rock that came to be stood up"), a fitting description of his calm and persistent quest for justice in the face of the indignities the chiefs endured as they met with governments and bureaucrats in Ottawa, London, and elsewhere.

10 Teit (1909, 569ff) notes that Secwépemc and Plateau chiefship in general often involved patrilineal succession, although he notes that the person best suited for office was invariably selected Instances of chiefly succession in the Secwépemc nation during the nineteenth and early twentieth centuries reveal the prominence of the latter.

11 It is not clear whether Peteség was an imagined character, deployed here and elsewhere to get back at the Crown. Nels Mitchell (ca. 1970) thought that he was "real" but that he was not from Tk̓emlúps. Regardless, we think that the Peteség stories are "true stories" in the sense that Secwépemc storytellers use the term given that the Peteség stories throw light on human experiences and their consequences.

12 The pinto tomcat is a play on pinto horses as powerful Secwépemc guardian spirits (Teit 1909, 606), on the one hand, and European upper-class women's fondness for pet cats, on the other hand, which must have been exotic to Secwépemc people of the late nineteenth century. By inhabiting the cat with guardian spirit power, Butcetsā´ is able to control White-Chief's (i.e., the king's) wife and steal her away from him.

13 Nels Mitchell (n.d.) tells another story of Peteség, similar to the one transcribed by Teit.

14 We interpret "tektsiqw re qmuts" (his hat is red on top), translated as "Red-Cap" by Kuipers (1974, 110), as referring to the red velvet fabric on the crown of the British king, thus indicating that Red-Cap represents the king of England.

15 The Indian Rights Association's 1912 delegation to Ottawa consisted of Chiefs Basil David (Basil Dick), John Chilaheetza (Douglas Lake), John Tetlenitsa (Nlakápamux), and James Raitasket (St'at'imc). The written transcript of the "Deputation from the Indian Rights Association of British Columbia upon the Prime Minister of Canada," dated 8 January 1912, together with the text of the Laurier and Oliver memorials, as well as various other petitions and treaties, has been reprinted in Shuswap Nation Tribal Council (2015).

16 Keith Carlson (2011) has also written about "the 'black and white' of Salish history" – a bit differently from how we present it here but in the same spirit.

CHAPTER FOURTEEN

The Secwepemctsín title of this chapter literally means "our laws [writings, rights] forever and in the future."

1 As noted in chapter 4, Secwepemctsín is gender-neutral in the third person, and there is nothing in the Xus story that suggests a male or female gender. However, only female mosquitos are bloodsuckers, so "she" is more appropriate than "he" or "it."

2 The phrase "bitter in the buttocks" is a reference to the bitter taste of soapberries being in the mosquito's digestive system. Metaphorically, *tsetśelóps* (here in the grammatical construction *stsetśelópst.s*) means "have a tantrum," which implies the social norm of not causing one's elders to be upset. Xus thus puts herself in the position of being an elder who can refuse the bitter soapberries because of her preference for the blood she is seeking.

Bibliography

Ackerman, Lillian A. 1994. "Nonunilinear Descent Groups in the Plateau Culture Area." *American Ethnologist* 21, no. 2: 286–309.

– 1998. "Kinship, Family and Gender Roles." In *Handbook of North American Indians*, vol. 12, *The Plateau*, ed. Deward Walker Jr, 515–24. Washington, DC: Smithsonian Institution Press.

Alexander, Diana. 1992. "A Reconstruction of Prehistoric Land Use in the Mid-Fraser River Area Based on Ethnographic Data." In *A Complex Culture of the British Columbia Plateau: Traditional Stl'atl'imx Resource Use*, ed. Brian Hayden, 99–176. Vancouver: UBC Press.

– 1996. *A Cultural Heritage Overview of the Western Half of the Williams Lake Forest District.* Williams Lake, BC: Ministry of Forests.

– 1997. *A Cultural Heritage Overview of the Cariboo Forest Region.* Williams Lake, BC: Ministry of Forests.

– 2000. "Pithouses on the Interior Plateau of British Columbia: Ethnographic Evidence and Interpretation of the Keatley Creek Site." In *The Ancient Past of Keatley Creek*, vol. 2, *Socioeconomy*, ed. Brian Hayden, 29–56. Burnaby, BC: Archaeology Press, Department of Archaeology, Simon Fraser University.

Allied Indian Tribes of British Columbia. 1919. "Statement of the Allied Indian Tribes of British Columbia for the Government of British Columbia." Vancouver: Cowan and Brookhouse Printers.

Ames, Kenneth M. 1988. "Early Holocene Forager Mobility Strategies on the Southern Columbia Plateau." In *Early Human Occupation in Far Western North America: The Clovis-Archaic Interface*, ed. Judith A. Willig, C. Melvin Aikens, and John L. Fagan, 325–60. Carson City: Nevada State Museum.

Anastasio, Angelo. 1972. "The Southern Plateau: An Ecological Analysis of Intergroup Relations." *Northwest Anthropological Research Notes* 6, no. 2: 109–229.

Anderson, Alexander Caulfield. 1877. "Commissioner's Journal," 16 July. Library and Archives Canada, RG 10, vol. 11028, file 9500.

Anderson, Eugene. 1996. *Ecologies of the Heart: Emotion, Belief and the Environment.* London and New York: Oxford University Press.

Anderson, M. Kat. 2005. *Tending the Wild: Native American Knowledge and Management of California's Natural Resources.* Berkeley: University of California Press.

Armstrong, Jeannette C. 2009. "Constructing Indigeneity: Syilx Okanagan Oraliture and Tmixwcentrism." PhD diss., University of Greifswald, Germany.

Assembly of First Nations. 1992. *Towards Rebirth of First Nations Languages.* Ottawa: AFN Languages and Literacy Secretariat.

Balf, Mary. 1980. *Savona's Ferry*. Kamloops, BC: Kamloops Museum and Archives.
Balf, Ruth. 1975. *Kamloops 1914–1945*. Kamloops, BC: History Committee, Kamloops Museum and Archives.
Belyk, Robert C. 1995. *John Tod: A Rebel in the Ranks.* Victoria, BC: Horsdal and Schubert.
Berkes, Fikret. 2012. *Sacred Ecology*. 3rd ed. New York and London: Routledge.
Berkhofer, Robert F. 1965. *Salvation and the Savage: An Analysis of Protestant Missions and American Indian Response*, 1787–1862. Lexington: University of Kentucky Press.
Black, Samuel. 1836. "Hudson's Bay Company Journal." Hudson's Bay Company Archives. Typescript on file at Kamloops Museum and Archives, Kamloops, BC.
Blackburn, T.C., and M. Kat Anderson. 1993. *Before the Wilderness: Environmental Management by Native Californians*. Menlo Park, CA: Ballena.
Blackstock, Michael, and Rhonda McAllister. 2004. "First Nations Perspectives on the Grasslands of the Interior of British Columbia." *Journal of Ecological Anthropology* 8, no. 1: 24–46.
Blake, Lynn. 1998. "Oblate Missionaries and the 'Indian Land Question.'" *BC Studies*, no. 119: 27–44.
Boas, Franz. 1890. "The Shuswap." In British Association for the Advancement of Science, *Sixth Report on the North-Western Tribes of Canada*, 80–163. London: British Association for the Advancement of Science.
– 1895a. "Report on the Indians of British Columbia: Physical Characteristics of the Tribes of the North Pacific Coast, the Tinneh Tribe of the Nicola Valley, the Ts'ets'a'ut, the Nisk'a, Linguistics of Nisk'a and Ts'ets'a'ut, and Vocabulary of the Tinneh Tribes of Canada." In British Association for the Advancement of Science, *Annual Meeting Report, 1895*, 523–92. London: John Murray.
– 1895b. *Indianische Sagen von der Nord-Pacifischen Küste Amerikas*. Berlin: A. Asher.
– ed. 1917. *Folk-Tales of Salishan and Sahaptin Tribes*. Collected by James A. Teit, Marian K. Gould, Livingston Farrand, and Herbert J. Spinden. New York: American Folklore Society.
– 2002. *Indian Myths and Legends from the North Pacific Coast of America: A Translation of Franz Boas' 1895 Edition of Indianische Sagen von der Nord-Pacifischen Küste Amerikas*. Ed. Randy Bouchard and Dorothy Kennedy. Vancouver: Talon Books.
Boelscher [Ignace], Marianne. 1990. "Passive and Agency in Shuswap Narrative Discourse." In *Papers for the 25th International Conference on Salish and Neighbouring Languages*, 61–70. Vancouver: University of British Columbia.
Boroditsky, Lera. 2011. "How Language Shapes Thought: The Languages We Speak Affect Our Perceptions of the World." *Scientific American*, 1 February, 62–5.
Borrows, John. 1998. "Wampum at Niagara: Canadian Legal History, Self-Government, and the Royal Proclamation." In *Aboriginal and Treaty Rights in Canada*, ed. Michael Asch, 155–72. Vancouver: UBC Press.
– 2001. "Listening for a Change: The Courts and Oral Tradition." *Osgoode Hall Law Journal* 39, no. 1: 1–38.
– 2010a. *Canada's Indigenous Constitution*. Toronto: University of Toronto Press.
– 2010b. *Drawing Out Law: A Spirit's Guide*. Toronto: University of Toronto Press.
Bouchard, Randy, and Dorothy Kennedy. 1975. "Utilization of Fish by the Chase Shuswap Indians." Library and Archives Canada, MG 55/28, vol. 13.
– 1979. *Shuswap Stories*. Vancouver: CommCept.
– 1985. "Lakes Indian Ethnography and History." Report prepared for the BC Heritage Conservation Branch, Victoria, British Columbia.

– 1986. "Appendix 1." In Arcas Associates, *Highway 1: Four Laning Project, Cambie to Revelstoke, B.C.*, 73–94. Report prepared for the BC Heritage Conservation Branch, Victoria, British Columbia.
– 1991. "Appendix 2: Indian Place Names." In I.R. Wilson, *Archaeological Overview, Highway 1 Corridor Study, Kamloops to Canoe*, 40–6. Victoria, BC: Archaeology Branch, BC Ministry of Small Business, Tourism and Culture.
– 1992. "Stl'atl'imx (Fraser River Lillooet) Fishing." In *A Complex Culture of the British Columbia Plateau: Traditional Stl'atl'imx Resource Use*, ed. Brian Hayden, 266–354. Vancouver: UBC Press.
Boyd, Robert. 1994. "Smallpox in the Pacific Northwest: The First Epidemics." *BC Studies*, no. 101: 5–40.
– 1999a. *The Coming of the Spirit of Pestilence: Introduced Infectious Diseases and Population Decline among Northwest Coast Indians, 1774–1874*. Seattle: University of Washington Press.
– ed. 1999b. *Indians, Fire and the Land in the Pacific Northwest*. Corvallis: Oregon State University Press.
British Columbia. 1875. *Papers Connected with the Indian Land Question*. Victoria, BC: Richard Wolfenden, Government Printer.
Brow, Catherine Judith. 1967. "A Socio-cultural History of the Alkali Lake Shuswap, 1882–1966." MA thesis, University of Washington, Seattle.
Brow, James. 1972. *Shuswap of Canada: A Cross-cultural Study of Ethnocentrism*. New Haven, CT: Human Relations Area Files.
Buffie, Erna, dir. 2015. "Smarty Plants: Uncovering the Secret World of Plant Behaviour." Episode 17 of *The Nature of Things with David Suzuki*, CBC Television, 25 April. http://www.cbc.ca/natureofthings/episodes/smarty-plants-uncovering-the-secret-world-of-plant-behaviour.
Burley, David V. 1980. *Marpole: Anthropological Reconstructions of a Prehistoric Northwest Coast Culture Type*. Burnaby, BC: Department of Archaeology, Simon Fraser University.
Campbell, Peter. 1994. "'Not as a White Man, Not as a Sojourner': James Teit and the Fight for Native Rights in British Columbia, 1884–1922." *Left History* 2, no. 2: 37–57.
Campbell, Sarah. 1990. *Postcolumbian Culture History in the Northern Columbia Plateau, A.D. 1500–1900*. New York: Garland.
Canada, Department of Fisheries. 1893. *British Columbia Fishery Commission Report 1892*. Ottawa: S.E. Dawson.
Canada, Department of Indian Affairs. 1864–1990. *Indian Affairs Annual Reports, 1864–1990*. Library and Archives Canada, http://www.bac-lac.gc.ca/eng/discover/aboriginal-heritage/first-nations/indian-affairs-annual-reports/Pages/introduction.aspx.
– 1878. Library and Archives Canada, Indian Affairs RG 10, vol. 3612, file 1279.
– 1884. *Annual Report of the Department of Indian Affairs for the Year Ended 31st December 1883*. Ottawa: MacLean, Roger and Company, Wellington Street.
– 1885. *Official Report of the Debates of the House of Commons of the Dominion of Canada, Third Session – Fifth Parliament, 48-49 Victoriae, 1885, Vol. XVIII, Comprising the Period from the Twenty-Seventh Day of March to the Eighth Day of May, 1885*. Ottawa: MacLean, Roger and Company, Wellington Street.
– 1889. *Annual Report of the Department of Indian Affairs for the Year Ended 31st December 1888*. Ottawa: MacLean, Roger and Company, Wellington Street.

– 1892. *Annual Report of the Department of Indian Affairs for the Year Ended 31st December 1891.* Ottawa: MacLean, Roger and Company, Wellington Street.
– 1902. *Annual Report of the Department of Indian Affairs for the Year Ended June 30, 1902.* Ottawa: S.E. Dawson.
– 1914. Library and Archives Canada, Indian Affairs RG 10, vol. 7472, file 19154-5.
– 1923. "Annual Report of the Department of Indian Affairs." In Canada, Department of Indian Affairs, *Sessional Papers, 1923*. Ottawa: Department of Indian Affairs.
Canada, Department of the Interior. 1876. "Correspondence on the Subject of the Indian Land Question in British Columbia." In *Annual Report of the Department of the Interior for the Year Ended 30th June 1875*. Ottawa: MacLean, Roger and Company, Wellington Street.
Canada, Indian Claims Commission. 2001. *Esketemc First Nation Inquiry: IR 15, 17, and 18 Claim*. http://publications.gc.ca/collections/Collection/RC31-10-2001E.pdf.
– 2006. *Williams Lake Indian Band: Village Site Inquiry*. http://publications.gc.ca/Collection/RC31-35-2006E.pdf.
– 2008. *Neskonlith, Adams Lake, and Little Shuswap Indian Bands: Neskonlith Douglas Reserve Inquiry*. http://publications.gc.ca/collections/collection_2009/indianclaims/RC31-80-2008E.pdf.
Canada, Joint Reserve Commission. 1877. "Correspondence." British Columbia Archives, RG 10, file 8497.
Canada, Royal Commission on Aboriginal Peoples. 1996a. *Report of the Royal Commission on Aboriginal Peoples.* Vol. 1, *Looking Forward, Looking Back.* Ottawa: Minister of Supply and Services.
– 1996b. *Report of the Royal Commission on Aboriginal Peoples.* Vol. 2, *Restructuring the Relationship.* Ottawa: Minister of Supply and Services.
Canada, Royal Commission on Indian Affairs for the Province of British Columbia (McKenna-McBride Commission). 1913–16. "Transcripts of Evidence." British Columbia Archives, GR-1995, fol. 1.4 and 2.1 (Kamloops Agency), fol. 4.2 (Okanagan Agency), and fol. 5.3 (Williams Lake Agency).
Carlson, Catherine. 2005. "Letters from the Field: Reflections on the Nineteenth-Century Archaeology of Harlan I. Smith in the Southern Interior of British Columbia, Canada." In *Indigenous Archaeologies: Decolonizing Theory and Practice*, ed. Claire Smith and Hans Martin Wobst, 134–69. London: Routledge.
– 2006. "Indigenous Historic Archaeology of the 19th-Century Secwepemc Village at Thompson's River Post, Kamloops, British Columbia." *Canadian Journal of Archaeology* 30, no. 2: 193–250.
Carlson, Catherine, and Kenneth Klein. 1996. "Late Pleistocene Salmon of Kamloops Lake." In *Life in Stone: A Natural History of British Columbia's Fossils*, ed. Rolf Ludvigsen, 274–80. Vancouver: UBC Press.
Carlson, Keith Thor. 2005. "Rethinking Dialogue and History: The King's Promise and the 1906 Aboriginal Delegation to London." *Native Studies Review* 16, no. 2: 1–38.
– 2007. "Reflections on Indigenous History and Memory: Reconstructing and Reconsidering Contact." In *Myth and Memory: Stories of Indigenous-European Contact*, ed. John Lutz, 46–68. Vancouver: UBC Press.
– 2011. "Orality about Literacy: The 'Black and White' of Salish History." In *Orality and Literacy: Reflections across Disciplines*, ed. Keith Thor Carlson, Kristina Fagan, and Natalia Khanenko-Friesen, 43–69. Toronto: University of Toronto Press.

Carlson, Roy L., and Luke Dalla Bona, eds. 1996. *Early Human Occupation in British Columbia*. Vancouver: UBC Press.

Carlson, Roy L., and Martin P.R. Magne, eds. 2008. *Projectile Point Sequences in Northwestern North America*. Burnaby, BC: Archaeology Press, Department of Archaeology, Simon Fraser University.

Carstens, Peter. 1991. *The Queen's People: A Study of Hegemony, Coercion, and Accommodation among the Okanagan of Canada*. Toronto: University of Toronto Press.

Carter, Sarah. 1990. *Lost Harvests: Prairie Indian Reserve Farmers and Government Policy*. Montreal and Kingston: McGill-Queen's University Press.

Chiefs of the Shuswap, Couteau, and Thompson Tribes et al. 1911. "Memorial to the Hon. Frank Oliver, Minister of the Interior." Library and Archives Canada, RG 10, vol. 7780, file 27150-3-1.

Chiefs of the Shuswap, Okanagan, and Couteau Tribes. 1910. "Memorial to Sir Wilfrid Laurier, Premier of the Dominion of Canada, from the Chiefs of the Shuswap, Okanagan, and Couteau Tribes of British Columbia, Kamloops, 25 August 1910." Library and Archives Canada, Laurier Papers, Series A Correspondence, 22 July to 30 August 1910, MG 26-G, vol. 641, files 174,070 to 174,077.

Chisholm, Brian S. 1986. "Reconstruction of Prehistoric Diet in British Columbia Using Stable-Carbon Isotope Analysis." PhD diss., Simon Fraser University.

Chisholm, Brian S., and D. Erle Nelson. 1983. "An Early Human Skeleton from South-Central British Columbia: Dietary Inference from Carbon Isotopic Evidence." *Canadian Journal of Archaeology* 7, no. 1: 85–6.

Choquette, Wayne. 1981. "The Role of Lithic Raw Material Studies in Kootenay Archaeology." In *Fragments of the Past: British Columbia Archaeology in the 1970s*, ed. Knut R. Fladmark, special issue of *BC Studies*, no. 48: 21–36.

– 1996. "Early Post-glacial Habitation of the Upper Columbia Region." In *Early Human Occupation in British Columbia*, ed. Roy L. Carlson and Luke Dalla Bona, 45–50. Vancouver: UBC Press.

Cole, Jean M. 1981. *Exile in the Wilderness: The Biography of Chief Factor Archibald McDonald, 1790–1853*. Seattle: University of Washington Press.

Cooper, H. Kory. 2007. "The Anthropology of Native Copper Technology and Social Complexity in Alaska and the Yukon Territory: An Analysis Using Archaeology, Archaeometry, and Ethnohistory." PhD diss., University of Alberta.

– 2011. "The Life (Lives) and Times of Native Copper in Northwest North America." *World Archaeology* 43, no. 2: 252–70.

Cooper, H. Kory, M.J. Duke, A. Simonetti, and Guang Cheng Chen. 2008. "Trace Element and Pb Isotope Provenance Analyses of Native Copper in Northwestern North America: Results of a Recent Pilot Study Using INAA, ICP-MS and LA-MC-ICP-MS." *Journal of Archaeological Science* 35, no. 6: 1732–47.

Crawford, Stuart. 2017. "The Ethnolichenology of Wila (*Bryoria fremontii*): An Important Edible Lichen of Secwepemc Country and Neighboring Territories." In *Secwepemc People and Plants: Research Papers in Shuswap Ethnobotany*, ed. Marianne Ignace, Nancy J. Turner, and Sandra Peacock, 279–316. Tacoma, WA: Society of Ethnobiology, Department of Sociology and Anthropology, University of Puget Sound.

Crellin, David. 1994. "Is There a Dog in the House? The Cultural Significance of Prehistoric Domesticated Dogs in the Mid-Fraser River Region of British Columbia." MA thesis, Simon Fraser University.

Crellin, David, and Ty Heffner. 2000. "The Dogs of Keatley Creek." In *The Ancient Past of Keatley Creek*, vol. 2, *Socioeconomy*, ed. Brian Hayden, 151–66. Burnaby, BC: Archaeology Press, Department of Archaeology, Simon Fraser University.
Cruikshank, Julie. 1991. *Life Lived Like a Story*. Lincoln: University of Nebraska Press.
– 1998. *The Social Life of Stories*. Lincoln: University of Nebraska Press.
– 2005. *Do Glaciers Listen? Local Knowledge, Colonial Encounters and Social Imagination*. Vancouver: UBC Press.
Crystal, David. 2000. *Language Death*. Cambridge, UK: Cambridge University Press.
Cybulski, Jerome S., Donald E. Howes, James C. Haggarty, and Morley Eldridge. 1981. "An Early Human Skeleton from South-Central British Columbia: Dating and Bioarchaeological Inference." *Canadian Journal of Archaeology* 5: 49–59.
Cybulski, Jerome S., Alan D. McMillan, Ripan S. Malhi, Brian M. Kemp, Harold Harry, and Scott Cousins. 2007. "The Big Bar Lake Burial: Middle Period Human Remains from the Canadian Plateau." *Canadian Journal of Archaeology* 31, no. 1: 55–78.
Czaykowska-Higgins, Ewa, and Dale M. Kinkade, eds. 1998. *Salish Languages and Linguistics*. Berlin and New York: Mouton deGruyter.
Daily Chronicle (London). 1926. "Red-Indian Chiefs in London, 5,000 Miles with Grievance to See the King." 27 June.
Daily Graphic (London). 1926. "Red Indian Chiefs in England." 24 June.
Daily Herald (London). 1926. "Red Indian Chiefs Visit – Second Attempt to Interview the King." 27 June.
Darwent, John. 1998. *The Prehistoric Use of Nephrite on the British Columbia Plateau*. Burnaby, BC: Archaeology Press, Department of Archaeology, Simon Fraser University.
Dauenhauer, Nora Marks, and Richard Dauenhauer. 1987. *Haa Shuka – Our Ancestors: Tlingit Oral Narratives*. Seattle and London: University of Washington Press.
– 1990. *Haa Tuwunáangu Yís, for Healing Our Spirit: Tlingit Oratory*. Seattle and London: University of Washington Press.
Davis, Henry, Lisa Matthewson, and Hotze Rullmann. 2009. "'Out of Control' Marking as Circumstantial Modality in St'át'imcets." In *Cross-linguistic Semantics of Tense, Aspect, and Modality*, ed. Lotte Hogeweg, Helen de Hoop, and Andrej Malchukov, 205–44. Amsterdam and Philadelphia: John Benjamins.
Davis, Loren G., and Charles E. Schweger. 2004. "Geoarchaeological Context of Late Pleistocene and Early Holocene Occupation at the Cooper's Ferry Site, Western Idaho, USA." In *Geoarchaeology* 19, no. 7: 685–704.
Davis, Wade. 2007. "Dreams from Endangered Cultures." Interview. https://www.ted.com/talks/wade_davis_on_endangered_cultures/transcript?...en.
Dawson, George Mercer. 1891. "Notes on the Shuswap People of British Columbia." *Transactions of the Royal Society of Canada*, 1st ser., 9, no. 2: 3–44.
– 1896. *Geological Survey of Canada – Annual Report (New Series)*. Vol. 7. Ottawa: Queen's Printer.
Deloria, Vine, Jr. 1995. *Red Earth, White Lies: Native Americans and the Myth of Scientific Fact*. New York: Scribner.
Demirdache, Hamida. 1997. "Out of Control in St'át'imcets Salish and Event (De)composition." In *Theoretical Issues in the Morphology-Syntax Interface*, ed. Amaya Mendikoetxea and Myriam Uribe-Etxebarria, 97–143. San Sebastian: ASJU.
De Smet, Pierre-Jean. 1847. *De Smet's Oregon Missions and Travels over the Rocky Mountains, 1845–1846*. New York: Edward Dunigan.

Delgamuukw v. British Columbia [1997] 3 SCR 1010.
Dixon, E. James. 1999. *Bones, Boats, and Bison: Archaeology and the First Colonization of Western North America*. Albuquerque: University of New Mexico Press.
Deur, Douglas, and Nancy J. Turner, eds. 2005. *Keeping It Living: Traditions of Plant Use and Cultivation on the Northwest Coast of North America*. Seattle: University of Washington Press; Vancouver: UBC Press.
Dickason, Olive Patricia, with David McNab. 2009. *Canada's First Nations: A History of Founding Peoples from Earliest Times*. 4th ed. Don Mills, ON: Oxford University Press.
Dionne, Gabriel. 1947. "Histoire des méthodes missionaires utilisées par les Oblats de Marie Immaculée dans l'évangelisation des Indiens du 'Versant Pacifique' au dix-neuvième siècle." MA thesis, University of Ottawa.
Dixon, May, Mary Palmantier, and Aert Kuipers. 1982. *A Western Shuswap Reader*. Leiden: University of Leiden.
Dobyns, Henry. 1966. "Estimating Aboriginal American Population, 1: An Appraisal of Techniques with a New Hemispheric Estimate." *Current Anthropology* 7, no. 4: 395–416.
Douglas, James. 1857a. Letter to Henry Labouchere, Secretary of State for the Colonies, 15 July. Hudson's Bay Company Archives, A11/76, fol. 655.
– 1857b. Letter to George Simpson, 17 July. In "Fort Victoria, Western Department Letterbook, 1855–57." Hudson's Bay Company Archives, A-11/74.
Duff, Wilson. 1975. *Images, Stone, B.C.: Thirty Centuries of Northwest Coast Indian Sculpture*. Seattle: University of Washington Press.
Dyck, Noel. 1991. *What Is the Indian "Problem": Tutelage and Resistance in Canadian Indian Administration*. St John's, NL: Institute of Social and Economic Research, Memorial University of Newfoundland.
Egesdal, Stephen M. 1992. *Stylized Characters' Speech in Thompson Salish Narrative*. Missoula: Linguistics Laboratory, University of Montana.
Egesdal, Stephen M., M. Terry Thompson, and Mandy N. Jimmie. 2011. *Nłeʔkèpmxcín: Thompson River Salish Speech*. Bellingham, WA: Whatcom Museum Publications.
Elmendorf, William W. 1961. "System Change in Salish Kinship Terminologies." *Southwestern Journal of Anthropology* 17, no. 4: 365–82.
– 1965. "Linguistic and Geographic Relations in the Northern Plateau Area." *Southwestern Journal of Anthropology* 21, no. 1: 1–16.
Elsey, Christine. 2013. *The Poetics of Land and Identity among British Columbia Indigenous Peoples*. Halifax, NS: Fernwood.
Elwyn, Thomas. 1862. Letter to Colonial Secretary, 17 December. British Columbia Archives, Colonial Correspondence, GR-1372, fol. 525, reel B-1327.
– 1863. Letter to Colonial Secretary, 27 January. British Columbia Archives, Colonial Correspondence, GR-1372, fol. 526, reel B-1327.
Evans, Nicholas. 2010. *Dying Words: Endangered Languages and What They Have to Tell Us*. Malden, MA: Wiley-Blackwell.
Ewing, Robyn G. 2016. *Documentation of the Use and Occurrence of Copper on the Plateau*. Skeetchestn, BC: Skeetchestn Natural Resource Corporation.
Favrholdt, Kenneth. 1997. "The Cordilleran Communication: The Brigade System of the Far Western Fur Trade." MA thesis, University of British Columbia.
– 1999. "Report on Aboriginal Claims on the South Side of Kamloops Lake with Particular Reference to the Six Mile Ranch and Cherry Creek Areas." Prepared for Skeetchestn Indian Band.

– 2009. "Report on Trails of Aboriginal Interest to Sexqéltkemc (Lakes Division) within the BC Hydro Mica 5–6 Project Area." Prepared for Adams Lake Indian Band.

Feltes, Emma. 2011. "We will help each other to be great and good": The Memorial to Sir Wilfrid Laurier and Resolving Indigenous-State Relations in Canada." MA Thesis, Dalhousie University.

Fine, Sean. 2015. "Chief Justice Says Canada Attempted 'Cultural Genocide' on Aboriginals." *Globe and Mail*, 28 May. http://www.theglobeandmail.com/news/national/chief-justice-says-canada-attempted-cultural-genocide-on-aboriginals/article24688854.

First Peoples' Cultural Council. 2014. *Report on the Status of B.C. First Nations Languages*. 2nd ed. Brentwood Bay, BC: First Peoples' Cultural Council. http://www.fpcc.ca/language/status-report.

Fisher, Robin. 1992. *Contact and Conflict: Indian-European Relations in British Columbia, 1774–1890*. 2nd ed. Vancouver: UBC Press.

Foster, Hamar. 1999. "A Romance of the Lost: The Role of Tom MacInnes in the History of the British Columbia Indian Land Question." In *Essays in the History of Canadian Law: In Honour of R.C.B. Risk*, vol. 8, ed. G. Blaine Baker and Jim Phillips, 171–212. Toronto: University of Toronto Press.

– 2007. "We Are Not O'Meara's Children: Law, Lawyers and the First Campaign for Aboriginal Title in British Columbia, 1909–1928." In *Let Right Be Done: Aboriginal Title, the Calder Case, and the Future of Indigenous Rights*, ed. Hamar Foster, Heather Raven, and Jeremy Webber, 61–84. Vancouver: UBC Press.

Fraser, Simon. 1960. *Simon Fraser: Letters and Journals, 1806–1808*. Ed. W. Kaye Lamb. Toronto: Macmillan.

Fulton, Robert J. 1969. "Glacial Lake History, Southern Interior Plateau, British Columbia." Geological Survey of Canada Paper 69–37. Ottawa: Department of Energy, Mines and Resources.

Furniss, Elizabeth. 1992. *Victims of Benevolence: Discipline and Death at the Williams Lake Indian Residential School, 1891–1920*. Williams Lake, BC: Cariboo Tribal Council.

– 1995. "Resistance, Coercion, and Revitalization: The Shuswap Encounter with Roman Catholic Missionaries, 1860–1900." *Ethnohistory* 42, no. 2: 231–63.

– 2004. "Cycles of History in Plateau Sociopolitical Organization: Reflections on the Nature of Indigenous Band Societies." *Ethnohistory* 51, no. 1: 137–70.

Galois, Robert M. 1992. "The Indian Rights Association, Native Protest Activity and the 'Land Question' in British Columbia, 1903–1916." *Native Studies Review* 8, no. 2: 1–34.

– 1996. "Measles, 1847–1850: The First Modern Epidemic in British Columbia." *BC Studies*, no. 109: 31–46.

Galois, Robert M., and Richard Mackie. 1990. "A Curious Currency, Part 1: Haiqua Shells on the Northwest Coast in the 19th Century." *The Midden* 22, no. 4: 1–3.

Gardiner, Dwight. 1993. "Structural Assymmetries and Preverbal Positions in Shuswap." PhD diss., Simon Fraser University.

Gerdts, Donna B., and Lisa Matthewson. 2004. *Studies in Salish Linguistics in Honor of M. Dale Kinkade*. Missoula: University of Montanta.

Gibson, James A. 1973. *Shuswap Grammatical Structure*. Honolulu: Department of Linguistics, University of Hawaii.

Gilbert, Rick. n.d. "The Sugar Cane Hereditary Chief Custom." http://www.rickgilbert.ca/hereditarychiefsystem.htm.

Grant, George M. 1873. *Ocean to Ocean: Sanford Fleming's Expedition through Canada in 1872*. 1st ed. Toronto: James Campbell and Son.
Grek-Martin, Jason William. 2009 "Making Settler Space: George Dawson, the Geological Survey of Canada and the Colonization of the Canadian West in the Late 19th Century." PhD diss., Queen's University.
Gumperz, John J., and Stephen C. Levinson, eds. 1996. *Rethinking Linguistic Relativity*. Cambridge, UK: Cambridge University Press.
Gurney, William Harold. 1948. "The Work of Reverend Father J.M.R. Le Jeune, O.M.I." MA thesis, University of British Columbia.
Haida Nation v. British Columbia (Minister of Forests) [2004] 3 SCR 511.
Haig-Brown, Celia. 1988. *Resistance and Renewal: Surviving the Indian Residential School*. Vancouver: Tillacum Library.
Hall, John, and Knut R. Fladmark. 1969. "Report on Excavation at Clearwater River Park (EiRal)." Prepared for the BC Heritage Conservation Branch, Victoria, British Columbia.
Halpern, Marjorie, and Margaret Seguin Anderson. 2000. *Potlatch at Gitsegukla: William Beynon's 1945 Field Notebooks*. Vancouver: UBC Press.
Hanna, Darwin, and Mamie Henry. 1995. *Our Tellings: Interior Salish Stories of the Nlha7kapmx People*. Vancouver: UBC Press.
Hanson, Gordon W. 1973. "The Katz Site: A Prehistoric Pithouse Settlement in the Fraser Valley, British Columbia." MA thesis, University of British Columbia.
Harris, Cole. 1997. *The Resettlement of British Columbia*. Vancouver: UBC Press.
Hauka, Don. 2003. *McGowan's War*. Vancouver: New Star Books.
Hayden, Brian, ed. 1992. *A Complex Culture of the British Columbia Plateau: Traditional Stl'atl'imx Resource Use*. Vancouver: UBC Press.
– 1997. *The Pithouses of Keatley Creek*. Fort Worth, TX: Harcourt Brace.
– ed. 2000a. *The Ancient Past of Keatley Creek*. Vol. 1, *Taphonomy*. Burnaby, BC: Archaeology Press, Department of Archaeology, Simon Fraser University.
– ed. 2000b. *The Ancient Past of Keatley Creek*. Vol. 2, *Socioeconomy*. Burnaby, BC: Archaeology Press, Department of Archaeology, Simon Fraser University.
Hayden, Brian, and Rick Schulting. 1997. "The Plateau Interaction Sphere and Late Prehistoric Cultural Complexity." *American Antiquity* 62, no. 1: 51–85.
Hayden, Brian, and Jim Spafford. 1993. "Keatley Creek Site and Corporate Group Archaeology." *BC Studies*, no. 99: 106–39.
Hebda, Richard J. 1982. "Postglacial History of Grasslands of Southern British Columbia and Adjacent Regions." In *Grassland Ecology and Classification, Symposium Proceedings, June 1982*, ed. A.C. Nicholson, A. McLean, and T.E. Baker, 157–94. Victoria, BC: Ministry of Forests.
– 1995. "British Columbia Vegetation and Climate History with Focus on 6 KA BP." *Géographie physique et quaternaire* 49, no. 1: 55–79.
– 2007. "Biodiversity: Geological History in British Columbia." Paper prepared for the Biodiversity BC Technical Subcommittee, 7 September. http://www.biodiversitybc.org/assets/Default/BBC%20Biodiversity%20and%20Geological%20History.pdf#search="Biodiversity Geological History in British Columbia".
Hill-Tout, Charles. 1978. *The Salish Peoples*. 4 vols. Ed. Ralph Maud. Vancouver: Talonbooks.

Hinkson, Mercedes. 1999. "Salishan Lexical Suffixes: A Study in the Conceptualization of Space." PhD diss., Simon Fraser University.

Hinton, Leanne, and Kenneth Hale. 2001. *The Green Book of Language Revitalization in Practice.* New York: Academic Press.

Hudson, Douglas, and Marianne Ignace. 2013. "Overview for Part VII: The Plateau." In *Native Peoples: The Canadian Experience*, 4th ed., ed. C.R. Wilson and Christopher Fletcher, 380–91. Don Mills, ON: Oxford University Press.

Hudson's Bay Company. 1863–64. "Thompson's River Post Accounts and Wages." Kamloops Museum and Archives, Kamloops, BC.

Hunn, Eugene, with James Selam and Family. 1990. *Nch'i-Wána, "The Big River": Mid-Columbia Indians and Their Land.* Seattle: University of Washington Press.

Ignace, Marianne. 1992. *Preliminary Report on the Aboriginal Territories of the Shuswap Nation.* Kamloops, BC: Shuswap Nation Tribal Council.

– 1995a. "Anthropological Expert Witness Report, Jules v. Harper." Prepared for Rush, Crane and Guenther, Barristers and Solicitors, and Kamloops Indian Band.

– 1995b. "Shuswap Language Framework Assessment." Prepared for Secwepemc Cultural Education Society and BC School District 73.

– 1998. "Shuswap." In *Handbook of North American Indians*, vol. 12, *Plateau*, ed. Deward Walker Jr, 203–19. Washington, DC: Smithsonian Institution Press.

– 1999. "Guardian Spirit Questing in the Nineties: A Mother's Thoughts." In *Coyote U: Stories and Teachings from the Secwepemc Education Institute*, ed. Peter John Murphy, George P. Nicholas, and Marianne Ignace, 184–8. Penticton, BC: Theytus.

Ignace, Marianne, and Ronald E. Ignace. 2008. "Canadian Aboriginal Languages and the Protection of Cultural Heritage." In *First Nations Cultural Heritage and Law: Case Studies, Voices, and Perspectives*, ed. Catherine Bell and Val Napoleon, 417–41.Vancouver: UBC Press.

– 2013. "The Secwepemc: Traditional Resource Use and Rights to Land." In *Native Peoples: The Canadian Experience*, 4th ed., ed. C.R. Wilson and Christopher Fletcher, 418–43. Don Mills, ON: Oxford University Press.

Ignace, Marianne, Ronald E. Ignace, and Kenneth Favrholdt. 2010. "Report on Secwepemc Land Use and Occupancy in the Seymour Arm Watershed of Shuswap Lake." Prepared for Sexqeltkemc Division of the Secwepemc Nation.

Ignace, Marianne, Ronald E. Ignace, and Nancy J. Turner. 2017. "Re tmicw te skukwstéls es tuwitentels: Secwepemc Traditional Ecological Knowledge and Wisdom Now and in the Future." In *Secwepemc People and Plants: Research Papers in Shuswap Ethnobotany*, ed. Marianne Ignace, Nancy J. Turner, and Sandra Peacock, 407–40. Tacoma, WA: Society of Ethnobiology, Department of Sociology and Anthropology, University of Puget Sound.

Ignace, Marianne, Dan Marshall, Mike Anderson, and Celia Nord. 2014. *SSN Cultural Heritage Study – Final Report: Ajax-KGHM Mine Proposal.* Kamloops and Skeetchestn: Stk̓emlupsemc te Secwépemc Nation.

Ignace, Marianne, Nancy J. Turner, and Ronald E. Ignace. 2017. "Coyote, Grouse and Trees: Secwepemc Lessons about Ethnobiological Knowledge." In *Secwepemc People and Plants: Research Papers in Shuswap Ethnobotany*, ed. Marianne Ignace, Nancy J. Turner, and Sandra Peacock, 379–406. Tacoma, WA: Society of Ethnobiology, Department of Sociology and Anthropology, University of Puget Sound.

Ignace, Marianne, Nancy J. Turner, and Sandra Peacock, eds. 2017. *Secwepemc People and Plants: Research Papers in Shuswap Ethnobotany.* Tacoma, WA: Society of

Ethnobiology, Department of Sociology and Anthropology, University of Puget Sound.

Ignace, Ronald E. 2008. "Our Oral Histories Are Our Iron Posts: Secwepemc Stories and Historical Consciousness." PhD diss., Simon Fraser University.

Ignace, Ronald E., and Marianne Ignace. 1999. "Commentary on 'The Priest and the Altarboy.'" In *Coyote U: Stories and Teachings from the Secwepemc Education Institute*, ed. Peter John Murphy, George P. Nicholas, and Marianne Ignace, 53–7. Penticton, BC: Theytus.

Indian Rights Association of British Columbia. 1912. "Deputation from the Indian Rights Association of British Columbia upon the Prime Minister of Canada." 8 January. In Shuswap Nation Tribal Council, *Fight for Our Rights: Aboriginal Title and Rights Appeals for Justice*, 2nd ed., 37–9. Kamloops, BC: Shuswap Nation Tribal Council, 2015.

Jack, Agnes, ed. 2006. *Behind Closed Doors: Stories from the Kamloops Indian Residential School*. Penticton, BC: Theytus.

Jacobs, Peter W. 2011. "Control in Skwxu7mesh." PhD diss., University of British Columbia.

James, Malcolm A. 1994. "Spahomin Archaeological Inventory Project: Phase One." Report prepared for BC Heritage Conservation Branch, Victoria, British Columbia.

Johnsen, Timothy F. 2004. "Late Glacial Lakes of the Thompson Basin, Southern Interior of British Columbia: Paleogeography and Paleoenvironment." MSc thesis, Simon Fraser University.

Johnsen, Timothy F., and Tracy A. Brennand. 2004. "Late Glacial Lakes in the Thompson Basin, British Columbia: Paleogeography and Evolution." *Canadian Journal of Earth Sciences* 41, no. 11: 1367–83.

– 2006. "The Environment in and around Ice-Dammed Lakes in the Moderately High Relief Setting of the Southern Canadian Cordillera." *Boreas* 35, no. 1: 106–25.

Kendall, Laurel, Barbara Mathé, and Thomas Ross Miller, eds. 1997. *Drawing Shadows to Stone: The Photography of the Jesup North Pacific Expedition, 1897–1902*. New York: American Museum of Natural History; Seattle: University of Washington Press.

Kennedy, Dorothy, and Randy Bouchard. 2009. "A Review of First Nations Rights and Title Interests, Columbia Valley Transmission Project Area." Prepared by Bouchard and Kennedy Research Consultants.

Kew, Michael. 1992. "Salmon Availability, Technology and Cultural Adaptation in the Fraser River Watershed." In *A Complex Culture of the British Columbia Plateau: Traditional Stl'atl'imx Resource Use*, ed. Brian Hayden, 177–221. Vancouver: UBC Press.

Kinkade, M. Dale. 1990. "Prehistory of Salishan Languages." In *Papers for the 25th International Conference on Salish and Neighbouring Languages*, 197–206. Vancouver: University of British Columbia.

– 1991. "Prehistory of the Native Languages of the Northwest Coast." In *Proceedings of the Great Ocean Conferences*, vol. 1, *The North Pacific to 1600*, 137–58. Portland: Oregon Historical Society Press.

Kinkade, M. Dale, William W. Elmendorf, Bruce Rigsby, and Haruo Aoki. 1998. "Languages." In *Handbook of North American Indians*, vol. 12, *The Plateau*, ed. Deward Walker Jr, 49–72. Washington, DC: Smithsonian Institution Press.

Klassen, Michael A. 2013. "Indigenous Heritage Stewardship and the Formation of Archaeological Practice: Two Studies from the Mid-Fraser Region of British Columbia." PhD diss., Simon Fraser University.

Klyne, Michael. 1826–34. "Jasper House Post Journals." Hudson's Bay Company Archives, B94/a/1.

Knight, Rolf. 1978. *Indians at Work: An Informal History of Native Indian Labour in British Columbia, 1858–1930*. Vancouver: New Star Books.

Kroeber, Alfred. 1939. *Cultural and Natural Areas of Native North America*. Berkeley: University of California Press.

Kroeber, Paul D. 1999. *The Salish Language Family: Reconstructing Syntax*. Lincoln: University of Nebraska Press.

Krupnik, Igor, and William W. Fitzhugh, eds. 2001. *Gateways: Exploring the Legacy of the Jesup North Pacific Expedition, 1897–1902*. Washington, DC: Arctic Studies Center, National Museum of Natural History, Smithsonian Institution.

Kuipers, Aert. 1974. *The Shuswap Language*. The Hague: Mouton.

– 1983. *Shuswap-English Dictionary*. Leuven: Peeters.

– 1989. *A Report on Shuswap*. Paris: Peeters/Selaf.

– 2002. *Salish Etymological Dictionary*. Missoula: Linguistics Laboratory, University of Montana.

Kuzmin, V. Yaroslav, Susan G. Keates, and Chen Shen, eds. 2007. *Origin and Spread of Microblade Technology in Northern Asia and North America*. Burnaby, BC: Archaeology Press, Department of Archaeology, Simon Fraser University.

Lawhead, Stephen, and Arnoud H. Stryd. 1985. "Excavations at the Rattlesnake Hill Site (EeRh 61)." Report on file at the Department of Archaeological Planning and Assessment, Victoria, British Columbia.

Leacock, Stephen. 1941. *Canada, the Foundations of Its Future*. Montreal: n.p.

Le Jeune, Jean-Marie-Raphaël. 1892. Letter to Louis-Joseph d'Herbomez, 1 April. Archives of Oblates of Mary Immaculate, Vancouver.

– 1896. *The Wawa Shorthand Instructor, or The Duployan Stenography Adapted to English*. Kamloops, BC: n.p. https://babel.hathitrust.org/cgi/pt?id=aeu.ark:/13960/t9q24f63h;view=1up;seq=5.

– 1906. *Shushwap Manual, or Prayers, Hymns and Catechism, in Shushwap*. Kamloops, BC: A. Dontenwill. https://archive.org/details/cihm_78315.

– 1925. *Studies on Shuswap*. Kamloops, BC: n.p.

Le Jeune, Jean-Marie-Raphaël, and William J. Poser. 2011. "How the Shorthand Was Introduced among the Indians." *Northwest Journal of Linguistics* 5, no. 3: 1–10. http://www.sfu.ca/nwjl/Articles/V005_N03/LejeunePoserWawa.html.

Lepofsky, Dana, and Sandra Peacock. 2004. "A Question of Intensity: Exploring the Role of Plant Foods in Northern Plateau Prehistory." In *Complex Hunters-Gatherers: Evolution and Organization of Prehistoric Communities on the Plateau of Northwestern North America*, ed. William Prentiss and Ian Kuijt, 114–39. Salt Lake City: University of Utah Press.

Levinson, Stephen C. 2003. *Space in Language and Cognition: Explorations in Cognitive Diversity*. Cambridge, UK: Cambridge University Press.

Lewis, Henry T., and M. Kat Anderson, eds. 2002. *Forgotten Fires: Native Americans and the Transient Wilderness*. Norman: University of Oklahoma Press.

Lewis, Meriwether, and William Clark. 2003. *The Journals of Lewis and Clark*. Ed. Frank Bergon. London and New York: Penguin.

Lillard, Charles, ed. 1987. *The Nootka: Scenes and Studies of Savage Life*. Vancouver: Sono Nis.

Loewen, Dawn. 1998. "The Chemistry of Pit-Cooking." PhD diss., University of Victoria.

Loewen, Dawn, Nancy J. Turner, and Mary Thomas. 2017. "Yellow Glacier Lily (*Erythronium grandiflorum*): An Important Root Vegetable for the Secwepemc and Neighbouring Peoples of the Northwest Interior Plateau." In *Secwepemc People and Plants: Research Papers in Shuswap Ethnobotany*, ed. Marianne Ignace, Nancy J. Turner, and Sandra Peacock, 219–78. Tacoma, WA: Society of Ethnobiology, Department of Sociology and Anthropology, University of Puget Sound.

Lovell, Nancy C., Brian S. Chisholm, D. Erle Nelson, and Henry P. Schwarcz. 1986. "Prehistoric Salmon Consumption in Interior British Columbia." *Canadian Journal of Archaeology* 10: 99–106.

Lucy, John A. 1992a. *Grammatical Categories and Cognition: A Case Study of the Linguistic Relativity Hypothesis*. Cambridge, UK: Cambridge University Press.

– 1992b. *Language Diversity and Thought: A Reformulation of the Linguistic Relativity Hypothesis*. Cambridge, UK: Cambridge University Press.

Mackenzie, Alexander. 1970. *The Journals and Letters of Sir Alexander Mackenzie*. Ed. W. Kaye Lamb. Cambridge, UK: Cambridge University Press.

Mackie, Richard, and Robert M. Galois. 1990. "A Curious Currency, Part 2: The Hudson's Bay Company's Trade in Haiqua Shells." *The Midden* 22, no. 5: 6–9.

Malhi, Ripan S., Jerome S. Cybulski, Raul Y. Tito, Jesse Johnson, Harold Harry, and Carrie Dan. 2010. "Brief Communication: Mitochondrial Haplotype C4c Confirmed as a Founding Genome in the Americas." *American Journal of Physical Anthropology* 141, no. 3: 494–7.

Manson, William. 1860–62. "Kamloops Journal, Thompson's River Post, Hudson's Bay Company." Typescript on file at Kamloops Museum and Archives, Kamloops, BC.

Manuel, George, and Michael Posluns. 1974. *The Fourth World: An Indian Reality*. Don Mills, ON: Collier McMillan.

Marshall, Daniel P. 2000. "Claiming the Land: Indians, Goldseekers, and the Rush to British Columbia." PhD diss., University of British Columbia.

Martindale, Andrew. 2006. "Methodological Issues in the Use of Tsimshian Oral Traditions (Adawx) in Archaeology." *Canadian Journal of Archaeology* 30, no. 2: 159–93.

Martindale, Andrew, and Susan Marsden. 2003. "Defining the Middle Period (3500 BP to 1500 BP) in Tsimshian History through a Comparison of Archaeological and Oral Records." *BC Studies*, no. 138: 13–50.

Mathé, Barbara, and Thomas Ross Miller. 2001. "Kwazi'nik's Eyes: Vision and Symbol in Boasian Representation." In *Gateways: Exploring the Legacy of the Jesup North Pacific Expedition, 1897–1902*, ed. Igor Krupnik and William W. Fitzhugh, 107–38. Washington, DC: Arctic Studies Center, National Museum of Natural History, Smithsonian Institution.

Mathewes, Rolf W. 1985. "Paleobotanical Evidence for Climatic Change in Southern British Columbia during Late-Glacial and Holocene Time." In *Climatic Change in Canada 5: Critical Periods in the Quaternary Climatic History of Northern North America*, ed. C.R. Harrington, 397–422. Ottawa: Canadian Museum of Natural Sciences.

Mathewes, Rolf W., and Miriam King. 1989. "Holocene Vegetation, Climate, and Lake-Level Changes in the Interior Douglas-Fir Biogeoclimatic Zone, British Columbia." *Canadian Journal of Earth Sciences* 26, no. 9: 1811–25.

Mathewes, Rolf W., and Marlow G. Pellatt. 2000. "Holocene Climate in the South Central Interior of British Columbia." In *The Ancient Past of Keatley Creek*, vol. 1, *Taphonomy*, ed. Brian Hayden, 59–64. Burnaby, BC: Archaeology Press, Department of Archaeology, Simon Fraser University.

Matthew, Nathan. 1999. "Secwepemc Language Immersion Project." Report prepared for the Secwepemc Cultural Education Society under the direction of the Critical Language Working Group, Kamloops, British Columbia.

Matson, R.G., and Gary Coupland. 1995. *The Prehistory of the Northwest Coast*. New York: Academic Press.

Matsui, Kenichi. 2005. "'White Man Has No Right to Take Any of It': Secwepemc Water-Rights Struggles in British Columbia." *Wicazo Sa Review* 20, no. 2: 75–101.

– 2009. *Native Peoples and Water Rights: Irrigation, Dams, and the Law in Western Canada*. Montreal and Kingston: McGill-Queen's University Press.

Mayne, Richard Charles. 1859. "Report on a Journey in British Columbia in the Districts Bordering on the Thompson, Fraser, and Harrison Rivers." http://hdl.handle.net/2027/aeu.ark:/13960/t43r1dw3v.

McDonald, Archibald. 1826–27. "Journal of Occurences at Thompson's River (Fort Kamloops)." Hudson's Bay Company Archives, B97/a/2.

– 1827. "Thompson River District Report." In George Simpson, *Part of a Dispatch from George Simpson*, ed. E.E. Rich, 224–33. Toronto: Champlain Society, 1947.

– 2001. *This Blessed Wilderness: Archibald McDonald's Letters from the Columbia, 1822–44*. Ed. Jean M. Cole. Vancouver: UBC Press.

McDonald, James. 2005. "Cultivating in the Northwest: Early Accounts of Tsimshian Horticulture." In *Keeping It Living: Traditions of Plant Use and Cultivation on the Northwest Coast of North America*, ed. Douglas Deur and Nancy J. Turner, 240–73. Seattle: University of Washington Press; Vancouver: UBC Press.

McGuckin, J.M. 1878. Letter to Superintendent of Indian Affairs James Lenihan, 15 April. Library and Archives Canada, RG 10, vol. 3663, file 9803.

McLachlin, Beverley. 2015. "Unity, Diversity and Cultural Genocide: Justice McLachlin's Complete Speech." *Globe and Mail*, 29 May.

McLeod, John. 1822–23. "Spokane House Report." Hudson's Bay Company Archives, B202/e/1.

McMillan, James, and John McLeod. 1822. "Thompson's River Journal, 1822–1823." Hudson's Bay Company Archives, B97/a/1.

Merilees, Bill. 2013. "Dentalium Encounters." *The Dredgings* 53, no. 3: 6. http://www.bily.com/pnwsc/web-content/Articles/Dentalium%20Encounters.pdf.

Michel, Joe Stanley. 2005. Testimony during Neskonlith Douglas Reserve Claim, Specific Claims Commission Hearings, file no. 2109-32-01, 6 July.

Miller, Bruce G. 2011. *Oral History on Trial: Recognizing Aboriginal Narratives in the Courts*. Vancouver: UBC Press.

Miller, John R. 1996. *Shingwauk's Vision: A History of Native Residential Schools*. Toronto: University of Toronto Press.

Milloy, John S. 1999. *A National Crime: The Canadian Government and the Residential School System*. Winnipeg: University of Manitoba Press.

Milton, William Fitzwilliam, and Walter Butler Cheadle. 1865. *The Northwest Passage by Land: Being the Narrative of an Expedition from the Atlantic to the Pacific*. London: Cassell, Petter, and Galpin.

Mitchell, D.S. 1925. *A Story of the Fraser River's Great Sockeye Runs and Their Loss: Being Part of a Local History Written for My Neighbors of the Shuswaps*. http://shuswapwatershed.ca/pdf/DS_Mitchell.pdf.

Mitchell, Nels. n.d. Unidentified tape. Oral History Collection, Secwepemc Cultural Education Society.

– ca. 1970. Audio recording. Secwepemc Archives.

Mitchell v. MNR [2001] 1 SCR 911.

Mooney, James. 1928. *The Aboriginal Population of America North of Mexico*. Ed. John R. Swanton. Washington, DC: Smithsonian Institution Press.

Morice, Adrien-Gabriel. 1904. *The History of the Northern Interior of British Columbia (formerly New Caledonia), 1660 to 1880*. Reprint, Smithers, BC: Interior Stationary, 1978.

Moss, Madonna. 2005. "Tlingit Horticulture: An Indigenous or Introduced Development?" In *Keeping It Living: Traditions of Plant Use and Cultivation on the Northwest Coast of North America*, ed. Douglas Deur and Nancy J. Turner, 274–95. Seattle: University of Washington Press; Vancouver: UBC Press.

Motherwell, J.A. 1926. "Report of the Chief Inspector, Major J.A. Motherwell, British Columbia, for 1926." In Canada Department of Marine and Fisheries, *Annual Report, 1926–1927*. Ottawa: Department of Marine and Fisheries, 1926–27.

Mountain Caribou Technical Advisory Committee. 2002. *A Strategy for the Recovery of Mountain Caribou in British Columbia*. Victoria, BC: British Columbia Ministry of Water, Land and Air Protection. http://www.env.gov.bc.ca/wld/documents/mtcaribou_rcvrystrat02.pdf.

Murray, Tim. 2011. "Archaeologists and Indigenous People: A Maturing Relationship?" *Annual Review of Anthropology* 40, no. 1: 363–81.

Naxaxalhts'i (Albert [Sonny] McHalsie). 2007. "We have to take Care of Everything That Belongs to Us." In *Be of Good Mind: Essays on the Coast Salish*, ed. Bruce Granville Miller, 82–130. Vancouver: UBC Press.

Napoleon, Val. 2007. "Thinking about Indigenous Legal Orders." Research Paper prepared for the National Centre for Indigenous Governance, Australian National University.

Nelson, Richard. 1983. *Make Prayers to the Raven: A Koyukon View of the Northern Forest*. Chicago, IL: University of Chicago Press.

Newman, Dwight. 2005. "*Tsilhqot'in Nation v. British Columbia* and Civil Justice: Analyzing the Procedural Interaction of Evidentiary Principles and Aboriginal Oral History." *Alberta Law Review* 43: 433–9.

Nicholas, George P. n.d. "Archaeology as a Transformative Practice in Secwepemc Territory." http://www.academia.edu/3501688/Archaeology_as_a_Transformative_Practice_in_Secwepemc_Territory.

– 2002. *Preliminary Report on the Kamloops Fish Weir Project, Kamloops, British Columbia*. Burnaby, BC: Archaeology Press, Department of Archaeology, Simon Fraser University; Kamloops, BC: Secwepemc Cultural Education Society.

– 2008. "Native Peoples and Archaeology." In *Encyclopedia of Archaeology*, vol. 3, ed. D. Pearsall, 1660–9. New York: Academic Press.

Nicholas, George P., Nancy Jules Bonneau, and Leisl Westfall. 2017. "Archaeological Approaches to Long-Term Secwepemc Plant Use in the Interior Plateau, British Columbia." In *Secwepemc People and Plants: Research Papers in Shuswap Ethnobotany*, ed. Marianne Ignace, Nancy J. Turner, and Sandra Peacock, 63–118. Tacoma, WA: Society of Ethnobiology, Department of Sociology and Anthropology, University of Puget Sound.

Oblate Missions of British Columbia. 1859–60. "Baptismal Records, Okanagan Mission." Diocese of Nelson, Kelowna, British Columbia.

– 1866–74. "Grandidier Letters and Papers." Oblate Historical Archives, St Peter's Province, Holy Rosary Scholastie, Ottawa, M707, reel 3.

– 1866–82. “Register of Baptisms.” Saint Joseph’s Mission, Williams Lake, British Columbia.
– 1867–82. “Kamloops and District Baptisms 1867–1882, Marriages 1873–1874.” Kamloops Museum and Archives, Kamloops, BC.
– 1882–90. “Baptism Records.” Roman Catholic Diocese of Kamloops, British Columbia.
– 1882–1900. “Marriage Records.” Roman Catholic Diocese of Kamloops, British Columbia.
Palmer, Andie Diane. 2005. *Maps of Experience: The Anchoring of Land to Story in Secwepemc Discourse*. Toronto: University of Toronto Press.
Palmer, Gary. 1975a. “Cultural Ecology in the Canadian Plateau: Pre-contact to the Early Contact Period in the Territory of the Southern Shuswap Indians of British Columbia.” *Northwest Anthropological Research Notes* 9, no. 2: 199–245.
– 1975b. “Shuswap Ethnobotany.” *Syesis* 8: 29–81.
Peacock, Sandra. 1998. “‘Putting Down Roots’: The Emergence of Wild Plant Food Production on the Canadian Plateau.” PhD diss., University of Victoria.
Peacock, Sandra, and Nancy J. Turner. 2000. “‘Just Like a Garden’: Traditional Plant Resource Management and Biodiversity Conservation on the British Columbia Plateau.” In *Biodiversity and Native North America*, ed. Paul E. Minnis and Wayne J. Elisens, 133–79. Norman: University of Oklahoma Press.
Peacock, Sandra, Marianne Ignace, and Nancy J. Turner. 2017. “Re Secwepemc re Syecwmenúlecwems: Secwepemc Stewardship of Land and Resources.” In *Secwepemc People and Plants: Research Papers in Shuswap Ethnobotany*, ed. Marianne Ignace, Nancy J. Turner, and Sandra Peacock, 167–206. Tacoma, WA: Society of Ethnobiology, Department of Sociology and Anthropology, University of Puget Sound.
Peers, Laura. 1996. “‘The Guardian of All’: Jesuit Missionary and Salish Perceptions of the Virgin Mary.” In *Reading beyond Words: Contexts for Native History*, ed. Jennifer S.H. Brown and Elizabeth Vibert, 284–303. Peterborough, ON: Broadview.
Pemberton, A.G. 1866. Letter to Joseph Trutch, 26 July. In British Columbia, *Papers Connected with the Indian Land Question*, 37. Victoria, BC: Richard Wolfenden, Government Printer, 1875.
Pokotylo, David L., Marian E. Binkley, and A. Joanne Curtin. 1987. *The Cache Creek Burial Site (EeRh 1), British Columbia.* Victoria, BC: Royal British Columbia Museum.
Pokotylo, David L., and Patricia D. Froese. 1983. “Archaeological Evidence for Prehistoric Root Gathering on the Southern Interior Plateau of British Columbia: A Case Study from Upper Hat Creek Valley.” *Canadian Journal of Archaeology* 7, no. 2: 127–57.
Pokotylo, David, and Donald Mitchell. 1998. “Prehistory of the Northern Plateau.” In *Handbook of North American Indians*, vol. 12, *The Plateau*, ed. Deward Walker Jr, 81–102. Washington, DC: Smithsonian Institution Press.
Prentiss, Anna Marie, and Ian Kuijt. 2012. *People of the Middle Fraser Canyon: An Archaeological History*. Vancouver: UBC Press.
Prentiss, William, and Ian Kuijt, eds. 2004. *Complex Hunter-Gatherers: Evolution and Organization of Prehistoric Communities on the Plateau of Northwestern North America.* Salt Lake City: University of Utah Press.
Preston, Chris. 2005. “A Past of Tragic Stories: The (Non-)Treatment of Native Peoples’ Oral Histories in Canada.” *Undercurrents* 2, no. 1: 54–64.

Pryce, Paula. 1999. *"Keeping the Lakes' Way": Reburial and Re-creation of a Moral World among an Invisible People*. Toronto: University of Toronto Press.

R. v. Marshall [1999] 3 SCR 456.

R. v. Marshall [1999] 3 SCR 533.

Ray, Verne F. 1939. *Cultural Relations in the Plateau of Western America.* Los Angeles, CA: Southwest Museum.

Regan, Paulette. 2010. *Unsettling the Settler Within: Indian Residential Schools, Truth Telling, and Reconciliation in Canada.* Vancouver: UBC Press.

Reid, J.P. 1993. "Principles of Vengeance: Fur Trappers, Indians and Retaliation for Homicide in the Transboundary North American West." *Western Historical Quarterly* 24, no. 1: 21–43.

Richards, Thomas H., and Mike K. Rousseau. 1987. *Late Prehistoric Cultural Horizons on the Canadian Plateau.* Burnaby, BC: Archaeology Press, Department of Archaeology, Simon Fraser University.

Ridington, Robin. 1990a. "Cultures in Conflict: The Problem of Discourse." *Canadian Literature* 124–25: 273–89.

– 1990b. *Little Bit Know Something: Stories in a Language of Anthropology.* Iowa City: University of Iowa Press.

Ridington, Robin, and Jillian Ridington. 2006. *When You Sing It Now, Just Like New: First Nations Poetics, Voices, and Representations.* Lincoln: University of Nebraska Press.

Robertson, David. n.d. *Kamloops Wawa Index.* Special Collections Holdings, University of Saskatchewan Library.

– 2007. "Secwepemctsín Shorthand Interlinearized Texts." Unpublished manuscript.

Robinson, Harry. 1989. *Write It on Your Heart: The Epic World of an Okanagan Storyteller.* Compiled and edited by Wendy Wickwire. Vancouver: Talonbooks/Theytus.

– 2005. *Living by Stories: A Journey of Landscape and Memory.* Compiled and edited by Wendy Wickwire. Vancouver: Talonbooks.

Romaine, Suzanne, and Daniel Nettle. 2000. *Vanishing Voices: The Extinction of the World's Languages.* New York and Oxford: Oxford University Press.

Romanoff, Steven. 1992. "Fraser Lillooet Salmon Fishing." In *A Complex Culture of the British Columbia Plateau: Traditional Stl'atl'imx Resource Use*, ed. Brian Hayden, 222–65. Vancouver: UBC Press.

Rosaldo, Renato. 1980a. "Doing Oral History." *Social Analysis*, no. 4: 89–99.

– 1980b. *Ilongot Headhunting, 1883-1974: A Study in Society and History.* Stanford, CA: Stanford University Press.

Ross, Alexander. 1849. *Adventures of the First Settlers on the Oregon or Columbia River.* Corvallis: Oregon State University Press.

– 1855. *The Fur Hunters of the Far West: A Narrative of Adventures in the Oregon and Rocky Mountains.* 2 vols. Ed. Kenneth A. Spaulding. Norman: University of Oklahoma Press, 1956.

Rousseau, Eunice, and Mike K. Rousseau. 1978. "Burials from Site EiRn15, Canoe Creek, B.C." Report prepared for the Archaeology Division, BC Heritage Conservation Branch, Victoria, British Columbia.

Rousseau, Mike K. 1993. "Early Prehistoric Occupation of South-Central British Columbia: A Review of the Evidence and Recommendations for Future Research." *BC Studies*, no. 99: 140–83.

– 2004. "A Culture Historic Synthesis and Changes in Human Mobility, Sedentism, Subsistence, Settlement, and Population on the Canadian Plateau, 7000–200 BP." In

Complex Hunter-Gatherers: Evolution and Organization of Prehistoric Communities on the Plateau of Northwestern North America, ed. William C. Prentiss and Ian Kuijt, 3–22. Salt Lake City: University of Utah Press.
– 2008. "Chipped Stone Bifaces as Cultural, Behavioural, and Temporal Indices on the Central Canadian Plateau." In *Projectile Point Sequences in Northwestern North America*, ed. Roy L. Carlson and Martin P.R. Magne, 221–50. Burnaby, BC: Archaeology Press, Department of Archaeology, Simon Fraser University.
– 2015. "Primary Toolstone Sources and Pre-contact Period Quarrying Behaviour in the Thompson River Drainage of South-Central British Columbia." In *Toolstone Geography of the Pacific Northwest*, ed. Terry L. Ozbun and Ron L. Adams. Burnaby, BC: Archaeology Press, Department of Archaeology, Simon Fraser University.
Rousseau, Mike K., and Thomas H. Richards. 1985. "A Culture-Historical Sequence for the South Thompson River–Western Shuswap Lakes Region of British Columbia: The Last 4000 Years." *Northwest Anthropological Research Notes* 19, 1: 1–32.
Roy, Patricia. 2012. *Boundless Optimism: Richard McBride's British Columbia*. Vancouver: UBC Press.
Sanger, David. 1967. "Prehistory of the Pacific Northwest as Seen from the Interior of British Columbia." *American Antiquity* 32, no. 2: 186–97.
– 1968a. "The Chase Burial Site in British Columbia." *National Museum of Canada Bulletin* 224: 86–185.
– 1968b. "Prepared Core and Blade Traditions in the Pacific Northwest." *Arctic Anthropology* 5, no. 1: 92–120.
– 1968c. *The Texas Creek Burial Site Assemblage, British Columbia*. Ottawa: National Museum of Canada.
– 1969. "Cultural Traditions in the Interior of British Columbia." *Syesis* 2: 189–200.
– 1970. "The Archaeology of the Lochnore-Nesikep Locality, British Columbia." *Syesis* 3, suppl. 1: 1–129.
Secwepemc Fisheries Commission. 2003. *Spallumcheen (Splatsin) Traditional Use Study: Columbia River*. Prepared for BC Hydro. 24 July.
Secwepemc News. 2013. "Secwepemc History – Chief William." May-June.
Seguin Anderson, Margaret. 1985. *Interpretive Contexts for Traditional and Current Coast Tsimshian Feasts*. Ottawa: National Museum of Canada.
Sellars, Beverley. 2013. *They Called Me Number One: Secrets and Survival at an Indian Residential School*. Vancouver: Talonbooks.
Shuswap Indian Band. 2008. *Re Tsqwatstens-kucw ne Csaliken: Our People between the Two Mountain Ranges*. Calgary, AB: Fish Creek Press.
Shuswap Nation Tribal Council. 2015. *Fight for Our Rights: Aboriginal Title and Rights Appeals for Justice*. 2nd ed. Kamloops, BC: Shuswap Nation Tribal Council.
Smith, Harlan I. 1897. Letter to Franz Boas, 18 July. American Museum of Natural History, Anthropology Division, accession no. 1897–27.
– 1898. "The Jesup Expedition Collection." *American Antiquarian and Oriental Journal* 20: 101–4.
– 1899. "Archaeology of Lytton, British Columbia." *Memoirs of the American Museum of Natural History* 1, part 3.
– 1900. "Archaeology of the Thompson River Region." *Memoirs of the American Museum of Natural History* 2, part 6.
Smith, Keith Douglas. 2009. *Liberalism, Surveillance, and Resistance: Indigenous Communities in Western Canada, 1877–1927*. Edmonton, AB: Athapasca University Press.

Smith, Trefor. 1994. "'A Very Respectable Man': John Freemont Smith and the Kamloops Agency, 1912–23." MA thesis, Simon Fraser University.

Speare, Jean, ed. 1973. *The Days of Augusta*. Vancouver: J. Douglas.

Sproat, Gilbert Malcolm. 1877. "Joint Reserve Commission Census: Kamloops-Okanagan." Library and Archives Canada, RG 10, vol. 10011.

– 1878. "Report." Royal British Columbia Museum, RG 10, Black Papers, 1879.

Sproat, Gilbert Malcolm, and Alexander Caulfield Anderson. 1877. Letter to Minister of the Interior David Laird, 27 August. British Columbia Archives, Colonial Correspondence, GR-0494.34, fol. 94-8225.

Sterling, Shirley. 1992. *My Name Is Seepeetza*. Vancouver and Toronto: Douglas and McIntyre.

Stryd, Arnoud H. 1972. "Housepit Archaeology at Lillooet, British Columbia: The 1970 Field Season." *BC Studies*, no. 14: 17–46.

Stryd, Arnoud, and J. Baker. 1968. "Salvage Excavations at Lillooet, B.C." *Syesis* 1: 47–56.

Stryd, Arnoud, and Mike K. Rousseau. 1996. "The Early Prehistory of the Mid Fraser–Thompson River Area." In *Early Human Occupation in British Columbia*, ed. Roy L. Carlson and Luke Dalla Bona, 177–204. Vancouver: UBC Press.

Suttles, Wayne. 1987a. "The Early Diffusion of the Potato among the Coast Salish." In *Coast Salish Essays*, ed. Wayne Suttles, 137–51. Vancouver: Talonbooks; Seattle: University of Washington Press.

– 1987b. "Northwest Coast Linguistic History: A View from the Coast." In *Coast Salish Essays*, ed. Wayne Suttles, 265–81. Vancouver: Talonbooks; Seattle: University of Washington Press.

Suttles, Wayne, and William W. Elmendorf. 1963. "Linguistic Evidence for Salish Prehistory." In *Symposium on Language and Culture: Proceedings of the 1962 Annual Spring Meeting of the American Ethnological Society*, ed. Viola E. Garfield and Wallace L. Chafe, 42–52. Seattle: University of Washington Press.

Swadesh, Morris. 1950. "Salish Internal Relationships." *International Journal of American Linguistics* 16, no. 4: 157–67.

Taku River Tlingit First Nation v. British Columbia (Project Assessment Director) [2004] 3 SCR 550.

Teit, James Alexander. 1896. "A Rock Painting of the Thompson River Indians, British Columbia." *American Museum of Natural History* 8, part 12.

– 1898. "Traditions of the Thompson River Indians of British Columbia." *Memoirs of the American Folk-Lore Society* 6, no. 1: 1–137.

– 1898–1910. "Salish Ethnographic Materials." Original manuscripts held by the American Philosophical Society Library, Philadelphia. Copy obtained from the British Columbia Archives, Victoria, and held at the Simon Fraser University Resource Library, Kamloops, British Columbia.

– 1900. "The Thompson Indians of British Columbia." Ed. Franz Boas. *Memoirs of the American Museum of Natural History* 2, part 4.

– 1906. "The Lillooet Indians." Ed. Franz Boas. *Memoirs of the American Museum of Natural History* 4, part 5.

– 1907. Letter to Franz Boas, 22 May. American Philosophical Society, Boas Collection, reel A-239.

– 1909. "The Shuswap." Ed. Franz Boas. *Memoirs of the American Museum of Natural History* 4, part 7.

– 1912a. "Mythology of the Thompson Indians." Ed. Franz Boas. *Memoirs of the American Museum of Natural History* 8, part 2.
– 1912b. "Traditions of the Lillooet Indians of British Columbia." *Journal of American Folk-Lore* 25, no. 98: 287–371.
– 1915–21. "Fieldnotes on Interior Salish Groups." Manuscripts held by the Ethnology Division, Canadian Museum of History, Ottawa. Copies held at the Simon Fraser University Resource Library, Kamloops, British Columbia.
– 1917a. "Okanagon Tales." In *Folk-Tales of Salishan and Sahaptin Tribes*, ed. Franz Boas, 65–97. Lancaster, PA: American Folklore Society.
– 1917b. "Tales from the Lower Fraser River." In *Folk-Tales of Salishan and Sahaptin Tribes*, ed. Franz Boas, 129–34. Lancaster, PA: American Folklore Society.
– 1917c. "Thompson Tales." In *Folk-Tales of Salishan and Sahaptin Tribes*, ed. Franz Boas, 1–64. Lancaster, PA: American Folklore Society.
– 1930a. "The Salishan Tribes of the Western Plateaus." In *Forty-Fifth Annual Report of the Bureau of American Ethnology to the Secretary of the Smithsonian Institution, 1927–1928*, ed. Franz Boas, 23–396. Reprint, Seattle, WA: Shorey Book Store, 1973.
– 1930b. "Tattooing and Face and Body Painting of the Thompson Indians, British Columbia." In *Forty-Fifth Annual Report of the Bureau of American Ethnology to the Secretary of the Smithsonian Institution, 1927–1928*, ed. Franz Boas, 397–439. Reprint, Seattle, WA: Shorey Book Store, 1973.
– 1937. "More Thompson Indian Tales." *Journal of American Folklore* 50, no. 196: 173–90.
Tennant, Paul. 1990. *Aboriginal Peoples and Politics: The Land Question in British Columbia, 1849–1989*. Vancouver: UBC Press.
Thom, Brian. 2001. "Harlan Smith's Jesup Fieldwork on the Northwest Coast." In *Gateways: Exploring the Legacy of the Jesup North Pacific Expedition, 1897–1902*, ed. Igor Krupnik and William W. Fitzhugh, 139–80. Washington, DC: Arctic Studies Center, National Museum of Natural History, Smithsonian Institution.
Thomas, Mary. 2001. *The Wisdom of Dr. Mary Thomas*. Ed. Nancy J. Turner, Robin June Hood, Jennifer Infanti, and Diane Peacock. Victoria, BC: School of Environmental Studies, University of Victoria.
Thomas, Mary, Ann Garibaldi, and Nancy J. Turner. 2017. "'Everything Is Deteriorating': Environmental and Cultural Loss in Secwepemc Territory." In *Secwepemc People and Plants: Research Papers in Shuswap Ethnobotany*, ed. Marianne Ignace, Nancy J. Turner, and Sandra Peacock, 345–78. Tacoma, WA: Society of Ethnobiology, Department of Sociology and Anthropology, University of Puget Sound.
Thompson, David. 1994. *Columbia Journals*. Ed. Barbara Belyea. Montreal and Kingston: McGill-Queen's University Press.
Thompson, Laurence C. 1979. "Salishan and the Northwest." In *The Languages of Native America: Historical and Comparative Assessment*, ed. Lyle Campbell and Marianne Mithun, 692–765. Austin: University of Texas Press.
– 1985. "Control in Salish Grammar." In *Relational Typology*, ed. Frans Plank, 391–428. The Hague and Berlin: Mouton.
Thoms, J. Michael. 2002. "A Place Called Pennask: Fly-Fishing and Colonialism at a British Columbia Lake." *BC Studies*, no. 133: 69–98.
Thomson, Duane, and Marianne Ignace. 2005. "They Made Themselves Our Guests: Power Relationships in the Interior Plateau Region of the Cordillera in the Fur Trade Era." *BC Studies*, no. 146: 3–35.

Tod, John, and Donald Manson. 1841, 1842, 1843. "Thompson's River Post Journal, Hudson's Bay Company." Typescript on file at Kamloops Museum and Archives, Kamloops, BC.

Toelken, Barre. 2003. *The Anguish of Snails: Native American Folklore in the West*. Logan: Utah State University Press.

Tonkin, Elizabeth. 1992. *Narrating Our Pasts: The Social Construction of Oral History*. Cambridge, UK: Cambridge University Press.

Truth and Reconciliation Commission of Canada. 2015a. *Final Report of Truth and Reconciliation Commission of Canada*. http://www.trc.ca/websites/trcinstitution/index.php?p=890.

– 2015b. *Honouring the Truth, Reconciling for the Future: Summary of the Final Report of Truth and Reconciliation Commission of Canada*. http://www.trc.ca/websites/trcinstitution/index.php?p=890.

Tsilhqot'in Nation v. British Columbia, 2007 BCSC 1700.

Tsilhqot'in Nation v. British Columbia, 2014 SCC 44.

Turner, Nancy J. 1997. *Food Plants of Interior First Peoples*. Vancouver: UBC Press.

– 1999. "'Time to Burn': Traditional Use of Fire to Enhance Resource Production by Aboriginal Peoples in British Columbia." In *Indians, Fire and the Land in the Pacific Northwest*, ed. Robert Boyd, 185–218. Corvallis: Oregon State University Press.

– 2005. *The Earth's Blanket: Traditional Teachings for Sustainable Living*. Vancouver: Douglas and McIntyre; Seattle: University of Washington Press.

– 2014. *Ancient Pathways, Ancestral Knowledge: Ethnobotany and Ecological Wisdom of Indigenous Peoples of Northwestern North America*. 2 vols. Montreal and Kingston: McGill-Queen's University Press.

Turner, Nancy J., and Fikret Berkes. 2006. "Coming to Understanding: Developing Conservation through Incremental Learning in the Pacific Northwest." *Human Ecology* 34, no. 4: 495–513.

Turner, Nancy J., Marianne Ignace, and Dawn Loewen. n.d. "Secwépemc Ethnobotany." Unpublished manuscript.

Turner, Nancy J., Marianne Ignace, and Ronald E. Ignace. 2000. "Traditional Ecological Knowledge and Wisdom of Aboriginal Peoples of Northwestern North America." In *Ecological Applications* 10, no. 5: 1275–87.

Turner, Nancy J., and Dawn Loewen. 1998. "The Original 'Free Trade': Exchange of Botanical Products and Associated Plant Knowledge in Northwestern North America." *Anthropologica* 40, no. 1: 49–70.

Turner, Nancy J., and Sandra Peacock. 2005. "Solving the Perennial Paradox: Ethnobotanical Evidence for Plant Resource Management on the Northwest Coast." In *Keeping It Living: Traditions of Plant Use and Cultivation on the Northwest Coast of North America*, ed. Douglas Deur and Nancy J. Turner, 101–50. Seattle: University of Washington Press; Vancouver: UBC Press.

Turner, Nancy J., Robin Smith, and James T. Jones. 2005. "'A Fine Line between Two Nations': Ownership Patterns for Plant Resources among Northwest Coast Indigenous Peoples." In *Keeping It Living: Traditions of Plant Use and Cultivation on the Northwest Coast of North America*, ed. Douglas Deur and Nancy J. Turner, 151–80. Seattle: University of Washington Press; Vancouver: UBC Press.

Turner, Nancy J., and R.L. Taylor. 1972. "A Review of the Northwest Coast Tobacco Mystery." *Syesis* 5: 249–57.

United Nations. 2008. *United Nations Declaration on the Rights of Indigenous Peoples.* http://www.un.org/esa/socdev/unpfii/documents/DRIPS_en.pdf.

Vansina, Jan. 1985. *Oral Tradition as History*. Madison: University of Wisconsin Press.

von Gernet, Alexander. 1996. *Oral Narratives and Aboriginal Pasts: An Interdisciplinary Review of the Literature on Oral Traditions and Oral Histories.* Ottawa: Indian and Northern Affairs, 1996.

– 2000. "What My Elders Taught Me: Oral Traditions as Evidence in Aboriginal Litigation." In *Beyond the Nass Valley: National Implications of the Supreme Court's* Delgamuukw *Decision*, ed. Owen Lippert, 103–29. Vancouver: Fraser Institute.

Wade, M.S. 1981. *The Overlanders of '62*. Surrey, BC: Heritage House.

Walkem, Ardyth. 2005. "Bringing Water to the Land: Re-cognize-ing Indigenous Oral Traditions and the Laws Embodied within Them." ML thesis, University of British Columbia.

– 2009. "An Unfulfilled Promise: Still Fighting to Make Space for Indigenous Legal Traditions." In *Aboriginal Law Since Delgamuukw*, ed. Maria Morellato, 393–423. Aurora, ON: Canada Lawbooks.

Walker, Ian R., and Marlow G. Pellatt. 2001. *Climate Change and Impacts in Southern British Columbia: A Palaeoenvironmental Perspective.* Vancouver: Western Canada Service Centre, Parks Canada.

– 2008. "Climate Change and Ecosystem Response in the Northern Columbia River Basin: A Paleoenvironmental Perspective." *Environmental Reviews* 16, no. 1: 113–40.

Ware, Reuben. 1983. *Five Issues, Five Battlegrounds: An Introduction to the History of Indian Fishing in British Columbia, 1850–1930*. Sardis, BC: Coqualeetza Education Centre.

Watkins, Joe. 2005. "Through Wary Eyes: Indigenous Perspectives on Archaeology." *Annual Review of Anthropology* 34, no. 1: 429–49.

Whitehead, Margaret. 1981. *The Cariboo Mission: A History of the Oblates*. Victoria, BC: Sono Nis.

– ed. 1988. *They Call Me Father: Memoirs of Father Nicolas Coccola*. Vancouver: UBC Press.

Wickwire, Wendy. 1994. "To See Ourselves as the Others' Other: Nlakapamux Contact Narratives." *Canadian Historical Review* 75, no. 1: 1–20.

– 1998. "We Shall Drink from the Stream and So Shall You: James A. Teit and Native Resistance in British Columbia, 1908–22." *Canadian Historical Review* 79, no. 2: 199–236.

– 2001. "The Grizzly Gave Them the Song: James Teit and Franz Boas Interpret Twin Ritual in Aboriginal British Columbia, 1897–1920." *American Indian Quarterly* 25, no. 3: 431–52.

– 2005. "Introduction." In Harry Robinson, *Living by Stories: A Journey of Landscape and Memory*, compiled and edited by Wendy Wickwire, 7–33. Vancouver: Talonbooks.

Wilson, Ian R., B. Smart, N. Heap, J. Warner, T. Ryals, S. Woods, and S. MacNab. 1992. "Excavations at the Baker Site, EdQx 43, Monte Creek." Report on file at the Department of Archaeological Planning and Assessment, Victoria, British Columbia.

Wilson, Ian R., Kevin Twohig, and Bruce Dahlstrom. 1998. "Archaeological Overview Assessment, Northern Secwepemc Traditional Territory." Prepared for the First Nations of Canim Lake, Canoe Creek, Soda Creek, and Williams Lake and for the Ministry of Forests, Cariboo Forest Region, Williams Lake.

Wilson, Robert L., and Catherine Carlson. 1980. *The Archaeology of Kamloops*. Burnaby, BC: Department of Archaeology, Simon Fraser University.

Wolfenden, Madge, ed. 1954. "Career of a Scotch Boy Who Became Hon. John Tod: An Unfashionable True Story." *British Columbia Historical Quarterly* 18, nos 3–4: 133–238. http://www.library.ubc.ca/archives/pdfs/bchf/bchq_1954_2.pdf.

Yellowhorn, Eldon. 2006. "The Awakening of Internalist Archaeology in the Aboriginal World." In *Archaeology of Bruce Trigger: Theoretical Empiricism*, ed. Ronald Williamson and Michael S. Bisson, 194–209. Montreal and Kingston: McGill-Queen's University Press.

Zhang, Linhai, Charles R. Brown, David Culley, Barbara Baker, Elizabeth Kunibe, Hazel Denney, Cassandra Smith, Neuee Ward, Tia Beavert, Julie Coburn, J.J. Pavek, Nora Dauenhauer, and Richard Dauenhauer. 2010. "Inferred Origin of Several Native American Potatoes from the Pacific Northwest and Southeast Alaska Using SSR Markers." *Euphytica* 174, no. 1: 15–29.

Index